Citizenship, Borders,
and Human Needs

DEMOCRACY, CITIZENSHIP,
AND CONSTITUTIONALISM

Rogers M. Smith, Series Editor

A complete list of books in the series
is available from the publisher.

CITIZENSHIP, BORDERS, AND HUMAN NEEDS

Edited by

Rogers M. Smith

PENN

UNIVERSITY OF PENNSYLVANIA PRESS

PHILADELPHIA

Published by
University of Pennsylvania Press
Philadelphia, Pennsylvania 19104-4112
www.upenn.edu/pennpress

Printed in the United States of America
on acid-free paper

10 9 8 7 6 5 4 3 2 1

Library of Congress Cataloging-in-Publication Data

Citizenship, borders, and human needs / edited by Rogers M. Smith.—1st ed.
    p. cm.— (Democracy, citizenship, and constitutionalism)
    Includes bibliographical references and index.
    ISBN 978-0-8122-4283-6 (hardcover : alk. paper)
    1. Emigration and immigration—Economic aspects.   2. Emigration and
immigration—Government policy.   3. Immigrants—Economic
conditions.   4. Citizenship.
I. Smith, Rogers M.
    JV6217.C58   2011
    304.8—dc22

                                                                  2010028884

Contents

Introduction

Rogers M. Smith

As Demetrios Papademetriou points out in the overview of modern migration trends with which this volume begins, as a percentage of the world's population, there are not actually more immigrants today than there were at the start of any decade since 1960. And even though the countries of North America and Europe are host to some 110 million immigrants and receive several million more each year, it is Asia—for economic, demographic, social, and other reasons—that is likely to be the largest receiver of immigrants in the decades to come. In light of those facts, perhaps we should expect that economic, political, and cultural issues concerning the national borders that stand as partial barriers to immigration would not be any more acute today than in most of the modern past, especially in North America and Europe.

But such expectations would be wrong. Disputes over immigration-related issues in both North America and Europe have proliferated and intensified in recent years, especially in the United States and the European Union. For most of the EU nations, as Papademetriou observes, large-scale immigration is a relatively recent phenomenon; and much of the immigration originates from predominately Arab or Muslim countries to societies that either have long histories of conflict with culturally distant populations or relatively little past contact. A considerable portion of the immigrants are also seen as nonwhite, in societies that historically gave birth to doctrines of European, Christian, and also white racial superiority that have since been repudiated, but that still have legacies. All this has contributed to Europe's difficulties in accepting the new immigrants. In the United States, the 1965 Immigration Act generated an influx of legal Hispanic and Asian immigrants that most of the act's proponents did not anticipate. The 1970s also saw rising numbers of unauthorized, primarily Mexican and Central Amer-

ican immigrants, and efforts to assert greater control of the southern border
in the 1980s and 90s failed abjectly. Both these developments again provided conditions conducive to immigration controversies.[1] As the second
decade of the twenty-first century approached, those conditions were com-
pounded by a global economic crisis, and in North America by cross-border
violence spurred by drug trafficking. Hence disputes over immigration in
North America and Europe show no signs of going away, or of being resolved to virtually anyone's satisfaction. The issues are economic, cultural,
and political; they are deeply interrelated; and they involve great empirical
complexities as well as difficult normative questions.

    This volume draws together scholarship from a number of disciplines
and countries to provide an array of the most informed and thoughtful
current academic thinking on this great range of empirical and normative
controversies. Contributors were encouraged to consider one of four questions. First, whose and what economic needs are helped and harmed by
current patterns of immigration flows and immigration regulations? Second, what should we make of the much-discussed cultural dimensions of
current immigration issues, in regard to the cultures of members of sending
countries, receiving countries, and the immigrants themselves, in all their
diversity? Third, what are the political choices in terms of institutions and
policies faced by both immigration-receiving and immigration-sending nations? And fourth, what, in the end, are the normative precepts that should
guide policy making on immigration in the twenty-first century around the
globe?

    There is little doubt that the answers to each question are bound up
with the answers to the others, but the connections are much disputed.
Some see the economic needs of immigrants and members of receiving
societies, and to a lesser degree those of sending countries, as driving virtually all immigration issues. Others, however, believe that, especially, the
cultural concerns of receiving societies cannot be reduced to their economic
interests and in fact often operate contrary to them, posing obstacles to the
addition of economically valuable newcomers. Most scholars agree that the
politics of immigration are shaped by unusual combinations of economic
and cultural concerns involving a wide range of advocacy groups and more
diffuse but constraining public sentiments—so that both economic and
cultural needs must be taken into account by policy makers. But there are
major normative disagreements on what sort of weight receiving countries
should give to the economic, cultural, and political needs of immigrants

and of sending countries, in relation to what the receiving countries perceive to be their own needs, as well as over what obligations immigrants and sending countries have to give weight to the needs of others.

The resulting essays do not address, much less answer, every one of the empirical and normative questions that could be considered under these broad categories of topics. The importance and complexity of the issues raised by modern systems of borders are so great that no one volume could ever do so. Written largely though not entirely by scholars residing in immigrant-receiving areas of the world, the essays give more attention to economic, cultural, and political issues in receiving nations than in sending ones. Even so, these essays provide illuminating discussions of many of the most significant of the questions raised by immigration today—displaying some important points of empirical and normative agreement but also equally important disagreements.

In Part I, "Citizenship, Borders, and Economic Needs," Mexican economist Antonio Yúnez-Naude provides a balanced assessment of what scholarship in his and the cognate social sciences tells us about who benefits and who is harmed economically in both Mexico and the United States by the continuing flow of immigrants north across their shared border—a flow that has become the source of one of the most passionately divisive domestic policy disputes in America today. Yúnez-Naude's analyses are not likely to provide full comfort to either side in those clashes. He recognizes, with immigration restrictionists, that there is some evidence that immigrants lower wages and add public service costs in the geographic and economic sectors where they gain employment in the United States, and that their remittances home may actually work against economic self-development in Mexico. At the same time, there is also evidence that both national economies benefit from such labor migration, as many traditional economic models would predict. And there are many empirical issues that are unresolved—a message that may suggest that, at least in relation to economic needs, both pro- and anti-immigration forces might be wise to place more emphasis on obtaining light and less on emitting heat.

The sociologist Saskia Sassen's essay calls attention to further complexities of economic needs that again do not neatly reinforce either pro- or anti-immigration positions. She calls attention to how modern migration flows include two sorts of immigrants: highly skilled and highly paid professionals and executives, who often move between what she has previously termed "global cities," and low-skilled, low-paid workers, both authorized and unauthorized. The latter often do the domestic and service sector labor of child care, home and restaurant cooking and cleaning, laundering, lawn work, automobile maintenance, cosmetics care, and much more that the (often literally) high-flying lifestyles of the professional immigrants require. So these two immigration flows are, in Sassen's analysis, profoundly symbiotic, making it hard to favor one without the other. Whether they can be structured to be beneficial and just to both classes of immigrants and to the different populations in their sending and receiving countries is obviously unclear, but Sassen makes these issues impossible to ignore.

Howard Chang, whose writings on immigration law and policy draw not only on his expertise as a law professor but also his doctoral training in economics, focuses here on Sassen's second category, less skilled immigrant workers. It is these workers who are, rightly or wrongly, the objects of (and to a much lesser degree participants in) the roiling debates over immigration today in the United States, the main locus of Chang's analysis. He does not shirk from placing both the legal and economic considerations raised by these alien workers in the philosophic context of distributive justice. He argues concretely that when moral issues of global justice are seen in light of the legal, economic, and political realities that prevail in the United States, and in related forms in many other advanced industrialized societies, the most promising policy route to pursue may be to establish guest worker programs for less skilled aliens, so long as they include robust protections for their rights and an ultimate route to citizenship for those who stay long. In so contending, Chang proposes a path for addressing the issues of inequity raised by Sassen's account of the interconnections between the more and less affluent streams of immigrants, as well as between many in the native populations of more affluent receiving and less affluent sending states. But such guest worker proposals represent an intensely controversial policy path in the United States and many other countries, both sending and receiving. They often fail to satisfy many nationalists, who think they give too much to noncitizens, and many cosmopolitans, who do not think they share enough.

Some of the reasons for those dissatisfactions are further illuminated in the anthropologist Karolina Szmagalska-Follis's ethnographically based analysis of economic migration issues on the eastern border of the European Union, in her native Poland. These issues are in some ways parallel to those arising along the U.S.-Mexican border, though in other ways they are not. Szmagalska-Follis shows how even the category of "economic migrant" is a politically charged one, since in Europe as in the United States, "economic migrants" are more easily refused entry or later deported than those who are deemed asylum-seeking "refugees." Her work suggests that the European Union has chosen to delegate much of the actual decision making over how those who seek entry from the east should be categorized to Polish border police and officials. The Polish authorities have often been receptive to permitting the legal or even illegal entry of culturally similar Ukrainian workers, who are seen as making economic contributions and as causing few problems when present, and who can and do easily return home. But the Poles are often far less receptive to Chechens, Pakistanis, and Afghanis, many of whom can legitimately claim political persecution but who are seen as culturally, politically, and economically "undesirable aliens," and who are therefore treated not as refugees but as unwanted economic migrants. We might speculate that when Mexican workers act more like comparatively congenial Ukrainians and less like resettling Pakistanis, they are also more acceptable in the United States. Whether or not that is so, the analyses of all four scholars of the economic issues involved in immigration suggest that economic analysis alone, though valuable, does not provide clear policy answers—and that there are daunting political challenges facing any policy that might be proposed, however desirable it may appear in the abstract.

The essays in Part II of the volume, "Citizenship, Borders, and Cultural Needs," further complicate but also clarify those political challenges by highlighting both the cultural conflicts and the cultural consequences that are bound up with various immigration policy regimes. They provide strong support for claims that these cultural factors are intertwined with but cannot be reduced to the economic needs of the individuals, communities, and governments involved. Immigration historian Mae Ngai opens this section with a revealing study of a Chinese American family, the Tapes, whose members played a role often necessitated by enforced borders, by policies of immigration restriction. Some in several generations of Tapes were what Ngai terms "immigrant brokers." They used their knowledge of the languages, cultures, policies, and interests of both the Chinese and the Americans to assist Chinese immigrants in gaining access to the United States, but on terms acceptable to the native American populace and governments. Playing the variety of roles necessary to broker such entry led to real economic benefits for all concerned, immigrants, Americans, and brokers alike. There were, however, also costs—including, often, the development of habitual practices of corruption, since bribery and deception were frequently required to complete the transactions involved, or at least to conduct them profitably. And so Ngai's "micro-history" requires us to reflect broadly on how far high barriers to entry, often defended as means to preserve the distinctive cultural character of different communities, may in fact involve degradation as well as preservation of such cultural mores.

Reflecting primarily on European experience, political sociologist Christian Joppke perceives a different cultural and also moral and political paradox or tension engendered by modern efforts at immigration restriction. He notes that European polities today seek to structure their citizenship laws and to define their broader civic identities in universalistic terms, as embodiments of enlightened principles of human rights, human dignity, and democracy. At the same time, they are concerned that immigrants come to share the distinctive national political cultures that are presented as embodying such commitments. Newcomers should integrate if not assimilate into the ways of life most commonly pursued in the societies that permit them to join. Joppke argues that the tensions between these aspirations to universalistic citizenship and to culturally integrated civic communities creates pressures for modern immigrant-receiving societies to embrace forms of liberalism which insist that all must adhere to substantive values of individual autonomy, rather than liberalisms that are genuinely tolerant of a broader range of moral commitments and cultural identities. The immigration restrictions that many think appropriate to preserve distinct yet still liberal national states may, in Joppke's analysis, contribute to those states having less liberal political cultures, or at least political cultures far less receptive to cultural differences than many believe they should be. And they may do so even if the immigrant newcomers are contributing or are capable of contributing greatly to meeting the economic needs of those national states. Wherever they are perceived instead as economic burdens, receptivity is even less likely.

Legal scholar Leti Volpp explores a closely related phenomenon. She sees in the discourses addressing immigration in advanced industrial Western societies tendencies to depict the cultures of immigrant communities as dangerously illiberal, particularly in their treatment of women. But she believes that these characterizations are often at best one-sided, at worst fundamentally inaccurate, and that they support among the citizens of the West flattering self-portraits of their relatively egalitarian gender statuses that are often unjustified. What are presented as egalitarian liberal concerns can, in her view, often work (and often can be politically deployed) to promote broad acceptance of misleading and biased cultural stereotypes that can indeed undermine toleration and understanding, as Joppke indicates, and again serve as barriers to reform efforts and to what might be mutually economically beneficial inclusive arrangements. At the same time, Volpp does not deny that cultural traditions of gender roles really do vary in important ways—but argues that these variations need to be understood as shaped by political, social, and economic forces.

As a result, immigrant-receiving societies inescapably face the challenge of deciding which variations should be tolerated, respected, and perhaps even emulated, and which, if any, should not be. Political theorist Sarah Song seeks to clarify the political and cultural choices these circumstances present to us by delineating three models of civic solidarity, three understandings of how particular liberal democratic political communities can foster allegiance and cooperation among their members without violating their other normative commitments. The models she explores are, first, "constitutional patriotism," loyalty to principles of popular sovereignty and human rights as defined and institutionalized within the political traditions and institutions of particular countries; second, "liberal nationalism," which more strongly embraces distinctive national cultures in order to ensure the senses of fellow feeling needed to support redistributive social programs and democratic engagement; and third, "deep diversity," in which citizens agree broadly on common political institutions and practices, but for reasons that vary widely, both in their philosophic or religious grounding and in their ultimate goals. By examining what each model implies for the treatment of immigrants who wish to become members of their adopted countries, Song's analysis shows that the political cultures envisioned in these three distinct models are indeed sharply contrasting. Constitutional patriotism requires professing allegiance to shared values, and liberal nationalism demands assimilation into a thick national culture. Yet constitutional patriotism is not easily separable from nationalism, and liberal nationalism does not adequately recognize the ethnic core of nations. Song argues that deep diversity is the most inclusive of the three. It recognizes not only diverse ways of life but also diverse ways of belonging to a polity.

Although no writer in Part III, "Citizenship, Borders, and Political Needs," seeks to address all of the economic and cultural concerns raised in the preceding sections, each does make arguments for desirable political institutions and policies that respond to many of those issues and that can usefully be evaluated in light of them. In the first essay, international relations scholar Christopher Rudolph extends his analyses of a topic that the preceding essays only touch upon, though it underlies many of the concerns about intolerant nationalism visible in several of them. That topic is the vital one of the relationship of national security concerns to immigration policy. Rudolph recognizes that, particularly after the September 11, 2001, attacks on the World Trade Center and the Pentagon, there have been overwhelming political pressures in the United States to find better ways to identify and curb immigrants who pose threats to national security. Similar pressures have also mounted in other countries subjected to radical Islamist terrorist attacks, such as Britain and Spain, even when the perpetrators were in fact homegrown. One might well expect these political dynamics to issue in harsh and intolerant treatment of immigrants, and many perceive just such conduct in the special initiatives to question, register, detain, and often deport immigrants that the U.S. government undertook after 9/11.[2]

But Rudolph stresses that, in historical perspective, the recent U.S. restrictions imposed on immigrants in the name of national security have been comparatively mild, falling far short of, for example, Japanese American internments during World War II. He also sees no strong national security case for heightened immigration regulations and restrictions. After the election of Barack Obama, many anticipated that the United States might further decouple immigration policies from security concerns; but many observers are finding significant continuities in American policies concerning the legal rights of noncitizens and the desirability of heightened immigration law enforcement.[3] It remains to be seen whether the United States over time, and other governments of wealthy non-Islamic states, will continue to believe that national security interests, including the health of the national economy, require even stronger actions against immigrants perceived as threats.

In his essay for this volume as well as in his other scholarship, Kamal Sadiq, a student of comparative politics, turns attention to the parts of the world where the numbers of immigrants are in fact greatest, South and East Asia. Here his focus is on India, which combines a remarkably efficient electronic voting system with considerable state *incapacity* to track or document migrants accurately. The result is that there is in India a small percentage of the electorate—but in India this still means literally millions of people—who vote and sometimes even hold elective offices without actually being Indian citizens. Related patterns in other states of South and East Asia mean that there are growing numbers of persons who are acquiring various forms of government documentation, without genuinely acquiring legal citizenship. Many of these persons may then be issued governmental passports and approval to immigrate to other parts of the world, including many Western states.

Thus the patterns Sadiq describes can raise concerns about the legitimacy of democratic institutions and of civic membership in the countries where "illegal immigrant voters" reside, and they can also provoke national security concerns in some countries to which the immigrants may eventually go. But as Sadiq notes, these same phenomena can be seen as economically, culturally, and politically desirable forms of transnational, plural, or cosmopolitan citizenship. So whether these newly prevalent illegal immigrant voters should be seen as failures of political institutions and policies in ways that demand reforms, or whether they should be tolerated or even celebrated, is less obvious on reflection than it may appear at first glance.

Yet complex as all the issues reviewed so far are, the final two contributors to this section do not hesitate to argue that some political institutions and policies regulating immigration and immigrants are more workable and desirable in important respects than others. Sociologist Irene Bloemraad contrasts the more "multicultural" immigrant-receiving governmental structures in countries such as Canada and to a lesser degree Australia, which provide various forms of assistance permitting immigrant groups to remain partly distinct cultural groups, with their more demandingly "assimilationist" counterparts in nations like France and particularly the United States, who stress the need for immigrants to absorb the dominant culture on the path to gaining their individual citizenships. Bloemraad finds that multiculturalist institutions and policies actually promote naturalization and many forms of political participation more effectively than assimilationist ones—though political integration sometimes runs much further ahead of socioeconomic integration in the multicultural nations. The persistence of economic problems among immigrant communities might well give both policy makers and normative analysts pause. Still, most readers are likely to read the bulk of Bloemraad's evidence as favorable to at least certain sorts of multicultural approaches to immigration.

The Dutch social and political theorist Veit Bader analyzes a still-broader range of institutional and policy models and reaches what appear to be somewhat different conclusions. He, too, discusses "cultural assimila-

tion" approaches characteristic of France and the United States and "corporatist multiculturalist" approaches characteristic of Canada, Switzerland,
and Belgium. He also analyzes aspirations to inclusive yet individualistic
policies, as in goals for a "postethnic" or "color-blind" America, models of
overtly illiberal and undemocratic exclusion, like apartheid and colonial
regimes, and more moderate models of "differential exclusion," such as
systems that rely heavily on temporary immigrants and guest workers. But
Bader's preferred approach is what he terms "associative democracy," a
form of institutional pluralism more flexible and democratic than he thinks
existing multiculturalist societies attain. He is concerned about unduly reifying existing groups and acquiescing in their internal undemocratic and
illiberal practices, yet he also wishes to avoid the dangers of assimilationist
repression that concern many of the authors here. How far his prescriptions
for "associative democracy" actually depart from Bloemraad's depictions
of Canadian-style multiculturalism may be debated, but his essay is remarkable both in addressing an impressive number of concrete economic, cultural, and social policies and for recognizing that, even under his preferred
approach, many difficult problems remain.

In Part IV, "Toward Normative Principles," three political theorists take
up as their central task the development of compelling normative arguments for how those problems should be constructively addressed. Stephen
Macedo makes the case for what Song might term "liberal nationalism,"
contending that to fulfill their obligations to all their citizens and especially
their most economically disadvantaged ones, liberal democracies may be
not just permitted but required to restrict immigration under some circumstances. There may be times when only by doing so can the society muster
adequate support to pursue social justice for all within its boundaries. At
any rate, Macedo insists firmly that immigration cannot be discussed without regard for its implications for domestic justice.

Chandran Kukathas begins with a stronger normative presumption in
favor of open borders that is partly rooted in the general desirability of
economic freedoms. But he similarly insists that this presumption must be
tested by examining the tradeoffs it involves; and if immigration burdens
domestic economic productivity or undermines social control, as well as
undermining the political will for policies that treat all members in socially
just ways, then the presumption in favor of open borders may well be overcome. Openness to immigration remains his default position, but Kukathas

does not anticipate that there will be many real-world situations where it will prove to be the unqualified right answer.

Building on his extensive earlier writings on these topics, Rainer Bauböck provides perhaps the most detailed account of how far and under what circumstances states should uphold free movement rights, permitting people to cross borders relatively unimpeded. He, too, does see a variety of reasons why states valuing democracy and human rights might rightly impose immigration controls, but he also elaborates a number of reasons why they might find it both just and in their interests to form regional unions and to accept multiple citizenships, permitting at least some persons free movement across at least some borders. Such policies require the development of appropriate transnational agreements and institutions, and so they represent an overcoming of at least some borders in the name of greater contributions to the fulfillment of human needs.

But it remains hard to see how a whole range of human needs can be met without some sort of bordered communities; and as the experiences of the European Union and North America after the North American Free Trade Agreement both show, the opening up of borders to some forms of mobility does not in any way mean that controversies over other forms will be lessened. Both the problems of the European Union's eastern border detailed by Szmagalska-Follis and the problems of the U.S.-Mexican border detailed by Yúnez-Naude demonstrate that contentious efforts to fence out economic and cultural undesirables even as others are welcomed persist in transnational arrangements.

It is fair to say that the views expressed in the concluding normative essays and in many of the preceding ones are, like much academic thought, more receptive to immigration in principle and less attracted to the fortification of existing boundaries than the bulk of political opinion in many existing societies. It is all the more noteworthy, then, that none of these analysts believes that borders can rightly be seen simply as unjust obstacles to human freedom. All argue that the maintenance of national borders is under many circumstances a precondition for meeting many forms of human needs. Immigration does appear to impose economic, cultural, and political burdens on at least some groups, communities, and governments within both receiving and sending societies and often on immigrants themselves, even when these burdens appear to immigrants as improvements on their previous circumstances and even when immigrants are making economic contributions both to their new countries and, via remittances, to their old ones.

Yet the essays in this volume leave no room to doubt that the enforcement of existing borders works at the same time against the fulfillment of some of the needs of very large numbers of people. Restrictive immigration policies prevent both employers and job-seeking immigrants from forming profitable economic relationships; if restrictions are less than fully enforced, they can generate large populations living in a nation's legal shadows, in ways that may erode solidarity and trust; and so such policies may perpetuate or strengthen tendencies in receiving countries toward cultural insularity at best, xenophobic intolerance at worst, sometimes culminating in violence and repression. The tensions generated by these grim realities do not mean that policy makers and analysts have no hope of discovering better ways to meet the needs of more people than we do now. Most of the essays can be read to support relative optimism that appropriately structured policies for welcoming, assisting, and utilizing immigrants in ways that help both receiving and sending nations can in principle be found, even if they are politically hard to achieve in practice. It does seem clear, however, that addressing these tensions constructively will require the efforts, expertise, and good will of an exceptionally broad and diverse array of scholars, as well as leaders and citizens, for as far into the future as we can see. This volume provides an example of the contributions such wide-ranging scholarly discussions can provide.

Chapter 1

International Migration:
Global Trends and Issues

Demetrios G. Papademetriou

For nearly two decades now, capital and the market for goods, services, and workers of many types have woven an ever more intricate web of global economic and, increasingly, social interdependence.[1] In the past few years, however, globalization seems to be on the defensive as governments and publics alike across the globe have begun to reexamine some of the phenomenon's tenets and to look more carefully at its effects.

No component of this introspection has fared more poorly than the labor market effects of deeper interdependence—effects that had long been posited to be strongly positive across the board. Evidence is mounting that substantial segments of the population of rich and poor countries alike are indeed affected adversely—at least in the short-to-medium term—and that governments along the development continuum have been caught unprepared to assist them adjust to the new competitive environment. Concerns that openness could also be facilitating the financing of the activities and movement of terrorists have added to the sense of skepticism about further openness along the lines promoted by the World Trade Organization (WTO), which has itself become a lightning rod for antiglobalization animus. As a result, and rather suddenly and in many ways unexpectedly, the road to deeper global interdependence has developed enough bumps, diversions, and detours to make predictions about the timing and direction of the next big "breakthrough" in internationalization uncertain.

Few by-products of globalization are pricklier for the publics of the advanced industrial societies than the movement of people. Such movement, of course, also preoccupies the less developed countries, albeit from different perspectives. For them, movement is an essential lifeline both to their citizens and to their economies. (In the most obvious example, the World Bank reports that formally recorded financial remittances to developing countries are now more than $327 billion per year.[2] Informal transactions bring that amount even higher.)

The less developed countries are preoccupied with more than the movement of people, however. They are deeply concerned about three additional issues. The first of these is that some of the behavior of the authorities and the populace in the countries in which their citizens live and work borders on a gross disregard for their human, labor, and other basic rights. The second is that the trafficking industry that has grown around the unauthorized movement of their nationals systematically exploits them and endangers their lives, while undermining the legitimacy of their public institutions and complicating their relationships with the governments in transit and destination countries. The third concern is that increasingly selective immigration policies by the advanced industrial societies may be tapping too deeply into their human capital pool, whose education has been paid for by public funds (the "brain drain" issue).

At the root of these sets of contradictory interests and reactions to international migration is the plain fact that the phenomenon's reach is nearly universal. Migration now touches the lives of more people and looms larger in the politics and economics of more states than at any other time in the modern era. With the United Nations estimating that the stock of persons living outside their country of birth will reach 214 million in 2010,[3] almost no country is untouched by international migration or is immune to its effects. This reality alone guarantees that migration will remain a top item in national, regional, and "global" conversations for the foreseeable future.

Few social phenomena in recorded human history are as civilizationally consequential as migration. History is in fact dotted with "ages of migration"—from the establishment of the Greek colonies and the Roman conquests, through the Byzantine, Arabic, Ottoman, and various Asian empires, and from the European colonizations to the great migrations of the nineteenth and early and late twentieth centuries. Furthermore, few other large social phenomena are as intertwined with human progress or have been as deeply implicated in the rise and decline of organized political entities as migration. Remarkably, however, such long-standing human experience with migration does not seem to have translated into models of good management practices that can be readily adapted to and then applied effectively in different settings.

A large part of the explanation for this anomaly lies in the fact that large-scale migration, by challenging the receiving society's sense of identity and exposing the weaknesses of its social and economic models of governance—as well as its capacity to enforce its laws—quickly leads to political contentiousness. Deeply fractured politics, in turn, interfere with the ability of governments to pursue domestic and foreign policies that deal with the phenomenon thoughtfully and, more important, *to the systematic advantage of most of those involved in or affected by migration.*

Furthermore, when support for immigration collapses (something that occurs with pendulum-like regularity), the duration and depth of a society's engagement with the process does not seem to inoculate it against excessive reactions to it. This is as close to a "law" of migration as any one might posit. And as with most laws, it seems to hold independently of such factors as the size of organized immigration's imprint on a society's evolution and economic progress or the benefits and experience that a society has gained from immigration.

This essay focuses mostly on the advanced industrial world.[4] As a result, it at times moves too quickly over issues that are best discussed in the context of specific migration relationships or seemingly papers over (by overgeneralizing about) the circumstances and perspective of the less developed world, whose nationals are migration's protagonists. This choice results in a regrettable loss in the precision that comes from focusing on a single case or the comprehensiveness that comes from a truly global perspective.

The essay aims to draw out the benefits of immigration in a better and more systematic way for all principals in the process while controlling for its most negative and perverse consequences. Managing international migration to collective advantage, I argue, can be done best through laws and regulations grounded in a realistic policy vision, a sensitivity to domestic requirements (itself a balancing act of the first order), and clarity about international obligations and objectives. The ambitiousness of these requirements suggests that managing uncertainty and learning to deal with imperfection may be absolute requirements, and the only realistic policy goals, in a policy domain as complex as international migration.

The International Migration System: An Overview

The international migration system binds together sending, receiving, and transit countries in increasingly complex wholes. Altogether, more than half of all the world's states "play" in this system in significant ways, and increasingly, more countries play multiple roles simultaneously in it—as places from which immigrants come, through which they pass, and in which they settle or, increasingly, just work for a period of time. Also increasingly, one notes an almost symbiotic coincidence of interests on migration. In addition to those of the immigrants, these interests include employers, consumers of all goods and services, families, transnational networks of all types (including criminal syndicates), and a variety of national domestic, foreign, and economic policies.

Migration Stock

The stock of international migrants is approaching 214 million persons. However, this figure of 214 million includes about twenty-six million persons (most of them ethnic Russians) who were internal migrants until the early 1990s. These persons were reclassified as international migrants when the Soviet Union collapsed around them and broke up into a large number of independent states. It is thus important to attempt to disaggregate these "global" estimates and to look at their component parts. The reason goes beyond the obvious one of due diligence—there is a caveat emptor component to using all statistics—and has to do with the fact that careless and/or misleading statistics are often the tools of the trade of the many prophets of doom on this and other divisive issues.

Table 1.1 shows the ten largest immigrant-receiving countries in the world in 2005 and projections for 2010. These ten countries are home to more than half of all migrants in the world.

Migration Flow

Migration flows, both permanent and temporary, are much harder to estimate than the stock. A best guess may be that the permanent flows from the developing to the developed world number 2.5 million, while temporary flows, *tourists aside*, from the South to the North include approxi-

Table 1.1 Ten Largest Immigrant-Receiving Countries in 2005 and 2010 (projected)

Country	Number of immigrants in millions (2005)	As a percentage of total (%)	Projected number of immigrants in millions (2010)	As a percentage of total (%)
World	195.2	100.0%	213.9	100.0%
United States of America	39.3	20.1%	42.8	20.0%
Russian Federation	12.1	6.2%	12.3	5.7%
Germany	10.6	5.4%	10.8	5.0%
France	6.5	3.3%	6.7	3.1%
Saudi Arabia	6.3	3.2%	7.3	3.4%
Canada	6.3	3.2%	7.2	3.4%
India	5.9	3.0%	5.4	2.5%
United Kingdom	5.8	3.0%	6.5	3.0%
Ukraine	5.4	2.8%	5.3	2.5%
Spain	4.6	2.4%	6.4	3.0%

Source: United Nations, Department of Economic and Social Affairs, Population Division (2009), *Trends in International Migrant Stock: The 2008 Revision* (United Nations database, POP/DB/MIG/Stock/Rev.2008).

mately two million international students, 2.5 million temporary workers, and 280,000 asylum seekers.[5] Of the approximately ten million nontourist migrants who gain access to the advanced industrial societies each year, about 90 percent do so legally. The United States and Canada together take a strong plurality of them—with the United States accounting for the entry of around four million temporary short-term residents.[6] The other advanced industrial societies combined probably take another 20 to 25 percent.[7] Among them, a significant and, in recent years, increasing number enter through the asylum application route.[8] Vibrant economies in the top quintile of the developing world absorb most of the rest. It is hard even to speculate about South-to-South movements beyond the broad strokes employed here.

The remaining migrants either continue their quest to reach their desired destinations or otherwise become stranded for more or less extended periods of time in intermediate locations. Few are thought to return *and remain* in their home countries for long.

Table 1.2 Female Migrants as a Percentage of the International Migrant Stock in 2000, 2005, and 2010 (Projected)

Major geographic area	2000 (%)	2005 (%)	2010 (%)
World	49.4	49.2	49.0
More developed regions	51.8	51.6	51.5
Less developed regions	46.1	45.6	45.3
Africa	46.7	46.7	46.8
Asia	45.7	45.0	44.6
Europe	52.8	52.5	52.3
Latin America and the caribbean	50.0	50.1	50.1
Northern America	50.5	50.4	50.1
Oceania	50.2	50.7	51.2

Source: United Nations, Department of Economic and Social Affairs, Population Division (2009), *Trends in International Migrant Stock: The 2008 Revision* (United Nations database, POP/DB/MIG/Stock/Rev.2008).

Migration Composition

In terms of gender composition, the immigrant stock is probably more or less equally divided between men and women. According to the United Nations, women make up about 52 percent of migrants to the developed world and 46 percent of migrants to the developing world (Table 1.2).[9]

Some international organizations, such as the International Labor Office (ILO), suggest that women now exceed men in the overall immigrant stock, in large part on the basis of some Asian flows that are now dominated by women and the observation that several classes of movers (see immediately below) now consist mostly of women. The fastest-rising immigrant cohorts, however, both in terms of the stock and particularly in terms of the flow, are those of children, followed by women. (The number of children is still small, but the development is a troubling one nonetheless.)

Immigrant Entry Classes

In terms of immigrant entry classes, the largest category has been and continues to be that of families. Family (re)unification remains the basic unit and building block, the key multiplier, of virtually all organized immigration systems. In fact, even in the most highly selective immigration systems, such as that of Canada with its highly emulated "points"-based immigrant selection system, families remain the formula's principal pillar. That is because the skills-based part of the Canadian point system, which accounts for a little more than half of the country's total permanent immigrant admissions ("landings") tests only the principal applicant for skills. This means that less than a quarter of all foreigners admitted to Canada for permanent residence at any given year are skills tested. In the United States, family-based permanent immigration accounted for 65 percent of all individuals who became lawful permanent residents in fiscal year 2008.[10]

The rest of the class-of-entry sequence stands as follows. Family immigrants are followed in overall size by those entering with *work visas*, whether temporary or permanent. This is also the fastest-rising entry class, with the exception of unauthorized entries (see immediately below). Many in that group enter with their immediate family, while others are able to (re)unite with their families some time after entry. (The administrative definition of "immediate family" varies from place to place.)

Asylum seekers and refugees are the third basic entry "stream" and represent a small proportion of the overall stock. The Office of the U.N. High Commissioner for Refugees (UNHCR) estimates that at the end of 2008 there were forty-two million forcibly displaced people worldwide, including 15.2 million refugees, 827,000 asylum seekers, and twenty-six million *internally* displaced persons. Overall, less than 10 percent of the total stock of immigrants are thought to be asylum seekers or refugees at most times.

Finally, one last category is increasingly of note: *unauthorized or irregular migration*. As noted, this form of migration has been by far the fastest-rising single form of migration during the past fifteen years.

Forms and Definitions of Illegal Immigration

Illegal immigration takes several forms, four of which are the most common.

Undocumented/unauthorized entrants. These are nationals of one state who enter another state clandestinely. Most such entrants cross land borders, but sea routes are also employed regularly, and, wherever inspection regimes are permeable, so are air routes. In all instances, the entrant manages to avoid detection, and hence inspection. (In the United States, where persons who use this type of entry account for somewhat more than 50 percent of all illegally resident immigrants,[11] the category is called "entry without inspection," or EWI.) Increasing proportions of such clandestine immigrants are smuggled or trafficked.

Individuals who are inspected upon entry into another state but gain admission by using fraudulent documents. The fraud in question may involve the person's identity and/or documentation in support of admission. In recent years, border agencies have witnessed widespread use of genuine or altered travel documents provided by human smugglers, who are increasingly important in enabling otherwise unauthorized individuals to cross borders "legally." A variant of this class of entry involves the making of fraudulent asylum claims, in which issues of identity and the documentation and the narrative in support of the asylum claim may be falsified.

Violators of the duration of a visa. These are individuals who enter another state properly but "willfully" (see below) overstay their period of legal stay, thus lapsing into illegal status. In the United States, 39 percent to 50 percent of unauthorized immigrants are illegal because they overstayed the duration of their visa.[12]

Violators of the terms and conditions of a visa. These are nationals of one state who enter another state with the proper documents and procedures but at some point violate the terms of their visa. The most frequent such violation is the acceptance of employment. In a nearly institutionalized variant of this violation, language schools in some countries, such as Japan, have become notorious for admitting students whose course of study becomes the nominal activity while (often full-time) employment, a commonly allowed ancillary activity to studying, is in fact the principal activity. Another variant of this class of violation is when persons with special visa privileges—such as holders of "border crosser visas" that allow border residents from an adjacent country to reside and be employed in the other country within strictly prescribed time and geographic parameters—abuse these parameters.

While these four classes of illegal entries and stays capture the overwhelming majority of all immigration violations, it is important to note that many foreigners may also find themselves in brief temporary violation of the host nation's immigration laws in what are otherwise legal entries and fundamentally legal stays. For instance:

- A tourist may exceed his or her duration of stay pending a decision on the application for an extension of that term.
- A business visitor may engage in a business activity that may require a different visa classification.

- A student may work for short intervals of time in violation of the terms of his or her visa, either by working more than the maximum time allowed while attending school or working in an unapproved occupation during the practical training part of his or her education.
- Workers on temporary work visas may change employers (or even employment sectors) without obtaining the proper authorization from the immigration authorities.

While these sorts of violations of immigration laws happen with some frequency, and some are important, most are relatively "innocent," that is, they are not systematic and are of short duration. In fact, most statistical systems either ignore these infractions or are otherwise incapable of capturing and counting them. Furthermore, in administrative and regulatory terms, many of these violations are typically the result of inflexible rules and understaffed (and thus overworked) immigration bureaucracies that do not have the resources to adjudicate immigration petitions in a timely fashion.

For instance, more than six million immigration petitions—many of them requests for a change in immigration status—were pending in the United States in 2004. (More recent data are difficult to reconcile with this figure because the U.S. Department of Homeland Security [DHS] has since changed the way it reports these data.) Some of these petitioners will typically lapse into illegality during lengthy adjudication delays.

Distribution of the Immigrant Stock

The distribution of the immigrant stock stands roughly as follows. The political space occupied by the North American Free Trade Agreement (NAFTA), that is, the United States, Canada, and Mexico, accommodates approximately forty-five million of the world's immigrant stock and close to three million of the annual immigrant flow. The twenty-seven nations of the European Union plus the members of the European Economic Area (EEA) probably include a roughly similar proportion of the total immigrant stock in a population base that is about 12 percent larger than NAFTA's.[13] This makes Europe, broadly defined, a remarkably significant (if "newer") destination area for immigrants. In fact, according to the latest U.N. estimates, Europe has the highest absolute number and share of immigrants in the world.[14] Table 1.3 provides a breakdown of immigrants by major geographic area.

Asia, however, which has the second-highest number and proportion of migrants in the world, is the most likely locus of large-scale migration activities in the decades ahead as the largest continent (by far) and the space with the two largest (and still growing) multistate and multiethnic countries experiencing an economic takeoff: China and India. Continuing instability in South Asia, the Middle East, and the Persian Gulf only adds to this region's volatility—and hence, to its potential for large-scale migration flows.

Immigrant Density

Finally (here I use the broadest and most politically neutral measurement for "immigrants"—the *foreign born*), as regards per capita immigrant density, the leading advanced industrial countries in terms of the foreign born as a proportion of those born in the country of immigrant destination are listed in Table 1.4 (which highlights immigrant densities in selected countries). Other than the Gulf states, seven of which (the United Arab Emirates, Qatar, Jordan, Kuwait, the Occupied Palestinian Territory, Israel, and Bahrain) have foreign-born densities of approximately 40 percent or higher, the top tier is composed of Singapore, Liechtenstein, and Luxembourg (with a rate of about 35 percent), Australia (with approximately 25 percent), and Switzerland and New Zealand (with a bit less than 25 percent).[15] The second tier is led by Canada, at about 20 percent, followed by Ireland, at 15 percent, and Germany and the United States, each at about 13 percent. These two sets of countries are followed by a third tier of countries, with foreign-born immigrant density levels of between 8 and 12 percent. Among them, one finds Sweden, France, the Netherlands, Belgium, Spain, and Greece.

Nonetheless, measurement anomalies abound. The United States, for instance, includes in its estimates approximately twelve million of its unauthorized immigrants and between 1.5 and two million of its longer-term temporary residents. It is almost unique in the advanced industrial world in doing so.

Summary

By way of summary, two observations may be worth reiterating here. First, if one removes from the total stock of immigrants the twenty-six or so

Table 1.3 Number and Proportion of Immigrants in the World in 1990, 2005, and 2010 (projected) by Major Region

Major region	1990		2005		2010	
	Number (in millions)	Share of Total (%)	Number (in millions)	Share of Total (%)	Number (in millions)	Share of Total (%)
Africa	16.0	10.3%	17.7	9.1%	19.3	9.0%
Asia	50.9	32.7%	55.1	28.2%	61.3	28.7%
Europe	49.4	31.8%	64.4	33.0%	69.8	32.6%
Latin America and the Caribbean	7.1	4.6%	6.9	3.5%	7.4	3.5%
Northern America	27.8	17.9%	45.6	23.4%	50.0	23.4%
Oceania	4.4	2.8%	5.5	2.8%	6.0	2.8%

Source: United Nations, Department of Economic and Social Affairs, Population Division (2009), Trends in International Migrant Stock: The 2008 Revision (United Nations database, POP/DB/MIG/Stock/Rev.2008).

Table 1.4 Immigrant "Density" (Foreign-Born Per Capita) in 2005 and 2010 (Projected)

Tiers	Country	2005 (%)	2010 (%)
More than 1 in 2	Qatar	80.5	86.5
	United Arab Emirates	70.0	70.0
	Kuwait	69.2	68.8
About 2 in 5	Jordan	42.1	45.9
	Israel	39.8	40.4
	Hong Kong	39.5	38.8
About 1 in 3	Singapore	35.0	40.7
	Liechtenstein	34.2	34.6
	Luxembourg	33.7	35.2
About 1 in 4	Saudi Arabia	26.8	27.8
	Oman	25.5	28.4
	Switzerland	22.3	23.2
	Australia[a]	21.3	21.9
About 1 in 5	New Zealand	20.9	22.4
	Canada	19.5	21.3
	Ireland	14.8	19.6
About 1 in 8	United States	13.0	13.5
	Germany	12.9	13.1
About 1 in 10	Spain	10.7	14.1
	Netherlands	10.6	10.5
	France	10.6	10.7
	United Kingdom	9.7	10.4

Source: United Nations, Department of Economic and Social Affairs, Population Division (2009), *Trends in International Migrant Stock: The 2008 Revision* (United Nations database, POP/DB/MIG/Stock/Rev.2008).
[a]There are discrepancies between data provided by national statistical agencies and the United Nations. This table purely draws from U.N. data.

million, mostly Russians, who became international migrants under rather "technical" circumstances (it was state borders that actually moved, not the migrants), the immigrant stock today stands at a bit more than 2.6 percent of the earth's population. This is a proportion that is only marginally higher (by between 10 and 20 percent) than the estimates for 1960, 1970, 1980, and 1990.[16] It is only by the second half of the 1990s that migration seems to have spiraled higher, led by increasingly organized flows of unauthorized entries.

Second, although there are a number of trends in international migration that are valid, to a larger or smaller degree, for most advanced industrial societies, there is only one that is truly global in character. Much of the growth in and maintenance of high levels of international migration is almost as much the result of market realities in advanced industrial societies as of migrants somehow crashing the West's gates and "imposing" themselves on it. This point goes to the root of an analytical perspective that, perhaps provocatively, incorporates fully the receiving countries' "complicity" in providing conditions and circumstances in which immigration *of all forms* survives and thrives—a perspective that is often missing or, more frequently, underemphasized in many analyses.

Changing Contexts

There is no denying that migration today is sufficiently large to be fueling rapid, profound, and highly visible social and cultural change. In fact, among the defining features of today's flows is that strong majorities of those who move—and most of those who move outside legal channels—come from countries of vast social, cultural, and often racial "distances" from the countries they seek to enter. And there is more. In the world of the September 11, 2001, attacks on the United States and subsequent attacks or attempted attacks in Madrid, London, and elsewhere, religious distance (specifically, Islam) seems to be taking pride of place among these differences. These realities increase the visibility and "otherness" of many newcomers, which in turn fuel the discomfort of host populations.

Public and private sector institutions in host societies are struggling to respond to the challenges of present-day migration, but none seems to find it more difficult to adapt than those in member states of the European Union. Their efforts are complicated by the weight of earlier policy choices with regard to immigration and integration. Some European governments and societies, most notably Germany, chose to deny for far too long the permanence of immigration and its embeddedness in the life of the host society—thus delaying essential efforts to have immigrants become true members of the German polity and society. Remarkably, alternative policy choices, whether officially "welcoming" (the Dutch and Nordic models) or ones of "splendid neglect" (the French model), seem to have had similar outcomes. In most cases, immigrants and their offspring are well behind natives in educational achievement, in economic benchmarks (employment rates, earnings, quality of housing, and so on), in access to opportunity, and in social and political engagement. These cumulative disadvantages translate into varying degrees of economic, social, and political marginalization. Marginalization, in turn, breeds mutual wariness: many immigrant communities see themselves as aggrieved, while many natives view immigrants and their children with impatience, if not mistrust and suspicion.

The size, rate of growth, and characteristics of today's, and even more so tomorrow's, international migration are thus challenging nations to manage much better the transformation the process entails. Success promises political and economic gains through migration's dynamism and potential for contributing to the host country's growth and prosperity, especially at a time when demographics will make such contributions nothing short of essential. Failure risks social unrest and political instability. It also forgoes the opportunity to improve dramatically the circumstances of the migrant and his or her family.

With the benefits from success and the costs of failure both so high and hanging in the balance, managing the international migration process through thoughtful regulation and other policy interventions at the local, national, regional, and, gradually and carefully, international levels becomes paramount. The case for doing so is strengthened further when the development potential of well-regulated migration for the countries of origin is also taken into account.

Triggers, Drivers, and Facilitators of International Migration

Wars and large-scale disasters, whether natural or of human causes, are obvious migration triggers as people flee for their lives. Beyond them, the triggers of international migration can be found in the quest to protect oneself and one's family from sustained jeopardy and to escape dramatic and persistent declines in economic opportunities. This cause of migration is qualitatively different from the search for economic improvement, which is one of the migration constants.

Two elements within those broad causes are likely to remain important migration drivers in the next two decades. The first is political, social, and cultural intolerance or, at the extreme, group-based, gross violations of human rights. The second is the systematic failure (some would say willful indifference) of governments to redress issues of *cumulative disadvantage*— that is, the various forms of economic exclusion and ethnoracial, religious, or linguistic discrimination that systematically disadvantage certain segments of a population.

Both of these migration drivers are always more or less in evidence. In most instances, however, they are not sufficient either to start a large new migration flow or to *suddenly expand substantially* an existing one. For that to happen, a number of preconditions ("facilitators") must be in place. The following are among the most notable such facilitators.

A Tradition of Migration

The preexistence of a long-term political, social, and economic relationship between a sending society and a destination society that includes a tradition of migration is a most potent facilitator of migration. When such a tradition exists, it simply leads to more migration until either a significant new variable enters the picture or the value of one of the existing variables changes decisively. An example of the former would be a dramatic and regimewide change in attitudes toward some or all immigrants at the receiving-society end. Terrorism concerns that prove real and sustained may in fact act in such a way, as might ethnic or religious violence that is thought to be exacerbated by migration. In this regard, it will be worth watching in the years ahead how (or whether) the industrial West will accept immigrants and other entrants from predominantly Muslim and Arab countries. An example of the latter would be the persistent reduction in the economic, *but especially the opportunity,* differential between countries. The story of the dramatic decline in West European immigration to the United States and the rest of the traditional countries of immigration that began in the 1960s or the stabilization of intra-E.U. migration since the 1980s are instances of this phenomenon. (The massive emigration from the post-2004 E.U. member states[17] to the pre-2004 ones is an example of the obverse phenomenon.)

Economic and Internationalist Elites

When receiving-society elites are convinced of the economic benefits of legally authorized and orderly migration (and, within certain parameters, even of unauthorized migration), they can typically organize themselves to open the immigration valve further. (Their recent failure in the United States requires its own analysis that goes well beyond the scope of this general essay.) In this scenario, migration's benefits will have to be thought of as being substantial enough—and government policies inadequate enough to meet perceived needs—to motivate economic and international-ist (what Kant referred to as "cosmopolitan") elites and their political allies to support significant openings to immigration flows. Canada's sustained interest in immigration is an example of such elite-driven legal opening, as are recent openings to migration in the United Kingdom and elsewhere in the European Union. The United States' glaring tolerance of unauthorized immigration until recently is an example of how far some pro-immigration elites may go when adequate legal openings to immigration are politically unachievable.

The twin forces most responsible for the growth in illegal migration can be found in two actions. The first is the developed world's extreme governmental bias *against* low-skilled migration in the face of market forces that strongly value it (and broad classes of people who need it). The second is what broad segments of the developed world's nongovernmental sector view as extreme niggardliness regarding various forms of social and human-itarian immigration.

Governmental bias against low-skilled migrants is most obvious when a variety of personal and low-value-added service jobs go begging. Among these jobs are assistants and caregivers for children and the elderly, jobs in the hospitality industry, jobs in much of the retail sector, and so forth, as well as seasonal and other types of difficult and low-wage jobs—work which first-worlders no longer aspire to or wish to accept.

Communities of Coethnics

Mature and influential anchor ethnic communities in the country of desti-nation can and do mobilize to become enablers of substantial migration flows when faced with a sharp deterioration in the circumstances of their coethnics or coreligionists in another country. This enabling function often includes offering to assist with the initial integration of the newcomers. Much of post-1970 Jewish emigration to the United States and elsewhere in the West fits this model well.

Enablers, however, do not stop there. If the receiving society is unre-sponsive to their advocacy, they will often provide the essential lubricants for the unauthorized migration of their brethren. These may include the commitment of the necessary capital for their travel and entry and the provision of an incubating social and economic environment within their own community upon the newcomers' arrival. Examples of such network behavior abound throughout the advanced industrial world, although the role of the Mexican and Mexican American communities in the United States may be classified as archetypical—and is now widely replicated throughout the world.

Civil Society

When key civil society institutions in the prospective destination country, such as religious and human rights ones, stand in strong philosophical opposition to the circumstances migrants are attempting to escape—and are willing to use their political capital in support of migration as a solution to the problem—they can be at least partially successful. The resettlement of many Southeast Asians in the 1970s and 1980s throughout much of the West and the admission of those who managed to leave such places as Iran and much of the Middle East in the past two decades are good examples of such "success."

Civil society institutions typically pursue their pro-"protection" and, secondarily, pro-immigration work in alliance and through coalitions with ethnic, ideology-driven, and economic interests. In doing so, they and their allies quickly become key stakeholders in the effort to sustain and widen an opening to migration to the point where it becomes a permanent feature of a society. Once such coalitions mature, unilateral efforts by state bureaucracies to change the migration status quo have low probabilities of success—particularly when other important societal actors, such as certain progressive trade unions, join in. The support of much organized labor in the United States for offering illegally resident immigrants legal permanent status, and its countenance of most forms of immigration, are examples of alliances that cross interests in ways that have made them seem strange bedfellows.

Trends to Watch for in International Migration

At the dawn of the twenty-first century, and looking ahead to the next two decades, three types of situations require separate mention because they have recently gained in both virulence and importance for migration.

- The first type is outright ethnoracial and/or religious conflict in which forcing a targeted group to abandon the contested area is a major policy objective (so-called ethnic cleansing). A variety of recent examples from Rwanda, the Caucasus region, the former Yugoslavia, the Sudan, and Iraq makes this point all too obvious.
- The second type of situation involves the deterioration of ecosystems to the point where life is unsustainable—with limited access to water and extensive degradation in water quality, the contamination of basic foodstuffs, and the consequences of both rising sea levels and desertification being prime concerns in this regard. The long conflict in the Sudan and elsewhere in North Africa may be classic examples of this migration cause, while the Middle East and South Asia may become even more of a cauldron of instability because of it.
- The third type of situation concerns flight from various forms of natural and man-made disasters. (This situation is often related to the one immediately above, in that climate change and deterioration of ecosystems can affect both the frequency *and the catastrophic potential* of natural disasters.) A series of recent disasters in Central America have brought that topic home to U.S. policy makers, while concerns about the safety of nuclear power plants in the western parts of the former Soviet Union are (or should be) of intense interest to Europe.

These three types of situations are not the only forces that analysts and policy makers must bear in mind on an ongoing basis. A number of additional trends also have an impact on the size, direction, *and type* of international migration, if on smaller scales. Among them one finds the following:

- The first, and perhaps most troubling, trend is the refusal to adjust immigration policies to reflect market realities better. In this refusal, governments surrender ever-larger proportions of their immigration decisions to smuggling syndicates and their human cargo.
- The second trend has two dimensions and focuses on the emerging competition for immigrants of many different types and skill levels. Competition for the most skilled immigrants is now well-established and entails students, engineers, persons with advanced

technical, technological, and communications skills, as well as medical professionals of all types. Such competition stems in large part from the widespread recognition that individual initiative, education, and talent are both valuable and scarce resources. Guaranteeing those who have these attributes nearly unimpeded access to a country has become a priority across much of the world—but where these individuals choose to go is at the heart of that sense of competition. Less appreciated (and more politically controversial) is a trend that is only slowly coming to the surface and is still struggling to gain political acceptance. This trend focuses on the temporary (and also, but much less, on the permanent) entry of immigrants who are willing to play by the rules and work hard in jobs that many of the citizens of the developed world find increasingly unappealing. This is the form of migration that is expected to grow most robustly in the next two decades. It is also the one that is likely to be most contested.

• The third trend presents the world community with a governance and ethical challenge of the first order: the growth in migration involving false promises and indentured servitude. These two phenomena, often linked, go far beyond the sex trade that has become such a fashionable topic of conversation in some advanced industrial countries; they include the large segments of migrants who are now systematically trafficked by increasingly sophisticated (and well-financed) smugglers and profiteers.

Looking Ahead to the Next Two Decades

Projecting how international migration is likely to evolve in the next twenty years is both easier and more difficult than it may appear at first. It is easier because we understand the behavior of migrants well enough now both from what might be called the supply side and, increasingly, from the demand side. We now also understand the triggers, drivers, and facilitators of migration much better. It is more difficult because of three factors whose effect is akin to that of wild cards in a game of chance: security (terrorism), the massive destruction of jobs in the recession that seems to have ended in the second half of 2009, and the sociocultural reaction to migration. Both of these factors have been discussed already.

For the next twenty years, the supply—the so-called migration pipe-line—will remain robust. There is nothing on this rather near horizon that will change dramatically *for the better* to affect the major developing coun-try suppliers of immigrants in ways that will lead to a pronounced drop in the interest to emigrate. If anything, a number of still relatively small migra-tion players are likely to grow in importance, while China and the Indian subcontinent could well become massive players in certain components of the international migration system with relatively little notice.

While the supply is thus expected to remain, in practical terms, nearly infinite, the demand for immigrants will also grow substantially, though arithmetically. Three factors will account for the lion's share of that growth. First, demography—especially the one-two punch of the low birth rate and the growth in the proportion of the old and the very old in the North's population. Second, increasing shortages of skilled and more general labor (including skill and geographic demand and supply mismatches). Third, the sheer momentum of the process itself, whereby pro-immigration coali-tions form in support of immigration while formulaic, legal, and rights-based openings to migration—such as family (re)unification, refugee reset-tlement, and asylum grants—continue to build stronger immigration streams.

Of course, the terrorist issue may yet play a bigger role than it has to date in reshaping the environment in which international migration has thrived in recent decades. In that regard, terrorism and the "war" against it have introduced a degree of uncertainty into the calculus that underlies this essay. That uncertainty raises the possibility, if not yet the likelihood, of extreme state reactions to most migration. If, however, we are on the brink of a new era of nihilistic conflict rooted in resurgent nationalism (centered not only in the developing world), politically expressed religious fundamentalism, and various other nearly forgotten "-isms," and if the casualties on both sides grow at rates commensurate with the capabilities of our era's instruments of destruction, the scenario outlined here may indeed be nullified. And if such a scenario of conflict and chaos comes to pass, the only reasonable projection is that national security will trump all other policy priorities with regard to migration for an indeterminate period—and that most forms of international migration to the developed world will be cut dramatically.

Otherwise, migration's reach during the next two decades will expand and go beyond the advanced industrial West—to Japan and the "Asian

Tigers," as well as to emerging market societies everywhere. The seeds for such an expansion are sown everyday. Initially, the government-led or -assisted part of this expansion will most likely take the form primarily of regulated temporary entry by needed high-skilled *and* low-skilled foreign workers. But it will not stop there. Front gate provisions for converting valued temporary legal immigrants into permanent ones will also proliferate; that is, governments will increasingly turn temporary admission streams into filtration and transition systems for selecting permanent immigrants. In addition, opportunities for admitting better-skilled foreigners outright as permanent immigrants will also increase, particularly as the world economy rebounds and global competition for talented foreigners intensifies.

At the same time, pressure from unauthorized migration is also likely to remain robust, and managing it will continue to be a major preoccupation of governments. Changing the status quo, however, will require moving beyond the tried and failed paradigms of simply applying always greater resources to border and interior controls and adding to them interventions that are as multifaceted as the phenomenon itself. It will also require unaccustomed discipline, unusual degrees of coordination across policy competencies, and new models of cooperation between countries of origin and destination.

Summary and Conclusions

Given the significant economic, political, human rights, and demographic differentials that continue to divide the world, the realistic response to migration cannot be denial. Advanced industrial societies cannot exhort people to stay at home without a serious commitment to a long-term and costly endeavor to improve conditions there. Open and democratic societies must also understand that investing substantially in attacking the root causes of flight, a worthy and necessary effort, has a far horizon that will exact substantial domestic political costs before it yields measurable long-term benefits.

In the interim, advanced industrial societies must resist the temptation to retreat in the face of immigration's challenge and retrench behind increasingly restrictive, and ultimately undemocratic, controls. As has become apparent, unilateral actions and fortress mentalities misread the complexities of the migration system while denying receiving societies an essential ingredient for their own economic success and social enrichment. Policies designed within such naïve frameworks are destined to fall short of even relative long-term success.

A more insightful set of policies would take into account the variety of experiences of advanced industrial societies and their different levels of success—while appreciating that "success" is overwhelmingly a function of effort, resources, commitment, flexibility, and consonance with a state's culture and history. This is true both for the control of illegal flows and for the broader management of legal flows. Greater success in solving the immigration puzzle also requires confidence, sure-footedness, leadership, and vision in the public arena. These are certainly precious—and hence scarce—commodities, but they are well within the realm of realistic possibility in the advanced democratic world.

The facts are not in dispute. Migration ties sending, transit, and receiving countries—as well as immigrants, their families, and their employers—into often reinforcing and always intricate systems of complex interdependence. It takes the cooperation of virtually all these actors—as well as smart policy decisions, thoughtful regulation, and sustained enforcement—to make real progress in limiting the effects of migration's challenges sufficiently to draw out even more of its benefits.

Whether or not the age of mobility is already upon us or just over the horizon, the only projection one can make is that mobility in all its forms will only increase. There are four choices: we can hide our heads in the sand about it; we can resist it; we can ratify it; or we can shape it so that we can gain most from it. The thrust of this essay is that there is, really, *only* one choice: shaping it.

For the purposes of this essay, then, the reality is as follows. There will be more global firms seeking to move their management and technical personnel with complete predictability and minimum disruption across borders. More industries will seek (and win) the right to access the global labor pool subject to rules of variable rigor but also greater clarity. More workers at all skill levels will seek to migrate for work in other countries; and some of them will stay there. And more people—tourists, business persons, students, family members, performers, seasonal workers, border-crossing workers, and adventurers and troublemakers of all types—will be on the move.

The advent of the age of mobility does not mean that the age of migration is over. For longer than many may wish, people will continue to seek to move and settle elsewhere for reasons that are as old as civilization itself: economic and physical survival (security); improvement of circumstances for themselves and their families; freedom from real and imagined threats; opportunity, however one chooses to define it; and sheer frustration or just a spirit of adventure. For many of these people, the channels that the new mobility age opens up will continue to be channels for starting all over in a new place. Over time, however, with the systems that are imagined in this essay in place, fewer and fewer movers will do so "forever."

Hence the imperative to shape the mobility system well and to manage it better. Both of these actions require far greater across the board cooperation than is now the case (or even possible)—across relevant governmental agencies within a single state, across relevant competencies across states, and between the governmental and nongovernmental sectors within and across state actors.

Remarkably, few states seem to be acting decisively on the knowledge that managing migration/mobility effectively and to sustained advantage requires the active engagement of a large number of government agencies—a "whole-of-government" approach. And certainly no government is even beginning to create the necessary organic alliances with its civil society that is one of the prerequisites of much better outcomes.

The future is unclear indeed, especially in the European Union. Will such key E.U. member states as Germany and France continue to dither about greater openings to managed immigration when they know how successful economies and labor markets will operate in an increasingly interdependent world? If they do continue on this course, what are the steps they are prepared to take in order to remain internationally competitive? And if they change course and do open themselves up to greater, much greater, immigration of all types, what are the steps they propose to take, what investments are they prepared to make, in order to deal effectively with the diversity that more immigration implies and thus safeguard the cohesion of their communities and societies? Finally, if they enter the immigration game with their eyes open and their self-interest sharply in focus, what decisions about immigration and the many issues it intersects with—education policy, workforce training policy, housing and internal mobility policy, antidiscrimination policy, and so forth—are they prepared to make?

In closing, this essay has attempted to think through today's immigration policies and regimes and imagine the answer to a set of questions that will come to preoccupy the international system: What will the international mobility system look like and who will shape it, in whose image, and to whose advantage?

There is no easy answer to this set of questions. There is, however, clear agreement that reform is long overdue. Whether such reform will be the product of a judicious effort to address all of a nation's interests, as well as balance those interests with international obligations, or be little more than the by now typical knee-jerk yank on the control levers, cannot be known at this time.

PART I

Citizenship, Borders,
and Economic Needs

Chapter 2

Rural Migration and Economic Development with Reference to Mexico and the United States

Antonio Yúnez-Naude

In the age of globalization, migration movements across national borders are increasing the flows of people to more and more distant places. International labor migration arises when people look for better living conditions. It is a structural phenomenon resulting from economic asymmetries, networks, and the growing interdependence among countries.

According to the International Organization for Migration, the number of international migrants (i.e., people residing in a country other than their country of origin) increased from an estimated seventy-six million in 1965 to 188 million in 2005. Female international migration has grown in recent years to the point where about half of all migrants are women. The United States of America attracts the highest proportion of international migrants (around 20 percent).[1]

The flow of international migrant remittances has increased more rapidly than the number of international migrants themselves, from an estimated US$2 billion in 1970 to $216 billion in 2004.[2] Most contemporary international remittances are from migrants in developed countries (DCs) to their places of origin in less developed countries (LDCs). During the first years of the twenty-first century, nearly 70 percent of total remittances went to LDCs.[3] In 1990 three European countries (Italy, Germany, and Portugal) shared first place as the destinations of the world's migrant remittances, receiving an average of $4.8 billion (Mexico was in eighth place, with $3.1

billion). By 2003, the composition of remittances had changed radically. Three countries among the LDCs were the main recipients of remittance flows: India with $17.4 billion, Mexico with $14.6 billion, and the Philippines with $7.9 billion. In 2002, Mexico was the world's largest country of emigration, with two million people living abroad (most of them in the United States).[4]

International labor migration is a complex phenomenon, involving, among other things, factors of attraction in DCs and expulsion in LDCs; the role of networks in labor-importing countries; the short-, medium-, and long-term effects of remittances and labor migration in migrant-sending countries; migration policies; the influence of economic growth on labor demand in receiving and sending countries and regions within these countries; and the impact of migration and remittances on economic livelihoods and development in both receiving and sending countries.

In DCs, perceptions differ as to whether international labor immigration promotes growth, reduces employment for nationals in receiving regions, and/or represents a continuous burden to public finances. The effect of emigration on development in LDCs is also a controversial subject, since out-migration creates both losses and gains in these countries. LDCs lose millions of skilled and unskilled workers but gain as a result of the remittances received. Both positive and negative effects have to be considered in any attempt to evaluate the impact of migration on development. Taylor formulates the dilemma in the following terms: "If migration and underdevelopment go hand in hand, it might be because the loss of people to migration retards development. Or it might be that people migrate away from underdeveloped areas, which have little to offer them if they stay. Both may be true; the question is which dominates, and it is difficult to separate cause from effect."[5] A similar dilemma applies to the effects of immigration in receiving countries.

This essay summarizes the main contemporary economic models of the determinants of labor migration and the main findings from empirical economic research on the effects of migration on welfare and development in both sending and receiving countries.[6] The focus is primarily on rural-to-rural international migration for various reasons. They include the complexity of studying migration processes and impacts in general terms, the fact that the satisfaction of basic needs is most urgent in LDC rural areas, and the disproportionate reliance on immigrant labor in agricultural production areas of DCs. The case of migration from rural Mexico to rural

California is used to draw lessons, conclusions, and policy implications with regard to economic development in sending and receiving areas.[7]

The second part of the essay presents the two major contemporary strands of thought about the economic determinants of labor migration and the empirical evidence to support them. The third part discusses the effects of migration in both receiving and sending countries. It first examines the major channels through which labor migration affects the economy of receiving and sending countries. It then presents evidence from the case of migration from the Mexican rural sector to rural California. The fourth part discusses immigration policies and the effects of immigration in the United States. It then proposes policies to enhance the effects of migration on rural development in Mexico and provide alternatives to unauthorized migration for rural households. The fifth part offers conclusions.

Determinants of Migration

Most formal migration models focus on economic determinants: opportunities and constraints on income at migrant origins; labor and income opportunities at migrant destinations; and migration costs (travel, networks of contacts at migrant destinations, border policies). Not all context variables are exogenous to migration; some may be influenced by migration decisions (e.g., when migration creates labor scarcity in migrant-sending areas).

Main Streams of Thought on Migration Determinants

Economic research presents two major formal approaches to model the migration phenomenon.

One theoretical model of migration is that of Todaro.[8] Todaro proposed a modification of the neoclassical migration model in which each potential rural-to-urban migrant decides whether to move according to an *expected-income* maximization objective, and not only according to *wage differentials* between the urban and rural sectors, as is proposed in the neoclassical model. The power of Todaro model is that it can explain the continuation and increase in rural-to-urban migration in the face of high and rising urban unemployment. As opposed to perfect-markets neoclassical models, Todaro's model does not assume the existence of full employment; hence, wages or income higher in the urban sector than in the rural sector is not a sufficient condition for migration.

The Todaro model has been applied to international labor migration. However, a limitation of this model (shared by neoclassical migration models) is that it can explain neither temporary migration nor the substantial flow of income remittances from migrants to their places of origin.

The so-called new economics of labor migration (NELM) is able to include these phenomena. In the NELM approach, migration decisions are viewed as taking place within a context larger than the individual: the household. The NELM argument is that household members—especially in rural areas of LDCs—act collectively not only to maximize incomes but also to minimize risks and to loosen constraints created by a variety of market failures, including missing or incomplete capital, insurance, and labor markets.

Stark[9] and Bloom and Stark[10] argue that an implicit contractual arrangement exists between migrant and household. A farm household in a LDC wishing, for example, to make the transition from subsistence to commercial production lacks access to both credit and income insurance. By placing a family member in a migrant labor market, such a household can create a new financial intermediary in the form of the migrant. Rural households absorb the initial costs of supporting migrants. Once migrants become established in their destination labor market, they provide liquidity (in the form of remittances) and insurance (because of a low correlation between incomes in migrant labor markets and farm production) to their households. Mutual altruism reinforces this implicit contract, as do inheritance motivations (e.g., nonremitting migrants stand to lose their land inheritance), and migrants' own aversion to risk encourages them to uphold their end of the contract in order to be supported by the rural household should they experience hardship in the future, such as unemployment.

Human capital theory has been incorporated into the NELM, which recognizes that skill-related attributes of individual family members influence the costs and benefits of migration for households and individuals. In addition, the household in the NELM perspective implies interactions between individual and household characteristics, such as assets and the human capital of household members other than the migrants.

Market imperfections in rural areas—not (or in addition to) the distortions in labor markets emphasized by Todaro—are hypothesized to be a primary motivation for migration. And, from a migration policy point of view, the NELM shifts the focus of migration policy from intervention in the rural or urban labor markets to intervention in other markets (most notably, rural capital and risk), in which an underlying motivation for migration is found.[11]

Evidence

Notwithstanding data limitations to test Todaro's model against other approaches—in particular those emphasizing the role of uncertainty in shaping migration decisions[12]—there is evidence that supports Todaro's expected-income migration theory. In relation to migration from LDCs to DCs, aggregate studies find that the effects of employment-related variables generally equal or exceed those of the wage-related variables. For example, Maldonado found that differentials in both unemployment and wages significantly explained the volume of migration from Puerto Rico to the United States, but the effect of the unemployment variable dominated that of the wage variable.[13] Massey et al. reestimated the Maldonado model, replacing the wage ratio with the ratio of expected wages (wages times employment probabilities).[14] They found that unemployment rates still dominated the expected wage ratio in predicting out-migration to the mainland.[15]

Empirical research in the beginning of the 1980s supports the NELM view that migration decisions take place within a family or household context and that they are influenced by the family's efforts to overcome poorly functioning or missing risk and credit markets.

Taylor's econometric findings for a sample of households in rural Michoacan, one of the largest source regions of Mexico-to-United States migration, are consistent with both the Todaro expected-income model and the NELM model.[16] Taylor's results show that increases in expected income contributions from migration by individual family members significantly and positively explained the attraction of migration for these individuals. However, controlling for this gain in expected income, several individual and household variables significantly explained migration, through their effect on migration costs or other NELM considerations. Taylor also found that family members with the highest expected contributions to rural Mexican households as nonmigrants were significantly less likely to migrate to the United States. Also, in accordance with the NELM models, econometric research by several authors provides evidence suggesting that families participate in migration in an effort to overcome liquidity constraints on local production.

In the empirical literature family migration networks or contacts in prospective migrant destinations have consistently been found to be among the most important variables driving migration.[17]

Quantitative studies on the determinants of migration also show that migrants are selected according to crucial characteristics, including their expected earning potential as migrants versus as nonmigrants. Individual human capital and household variables, in turn, affect individuals' and households' incomes with and without migration. As a result, there is a "derived" selectivity of migration according to specific individual and household characteristics through the differential effects of these characteristics in migrant and nonmigrant labor markets. Household variables that influence individuals' income creation as migrants and/or nonmigrants (e.g., family migration networks or landholdings) are also often found to significantly affect migration. The effects of some human capital variables differ sharply across migrant destinations. For example, education promotes rural out-migration, but not to all potential migrant destinations. Individuals significantly take their education to labor markets where they will obtain the highest economic return on their education.

Characteristics of migrants, their households, and their areas of origin can shape migrants' success in their areas of destination as well as their impact at home. They determine which households and communities bear the costs of human capital lost to migration, as well as the distribution of migration's potential benefits through remittances and the income multipliers they may create.

Few surveys provide the data required to implement selectivity-correction techniques in order to study empirically migration decisions by individuals or households. An exception is the 2003 Mexico National Rural Household Survey (Encuesta Nacional a Hogares Rurales de México, or ENHRUM). Using ENHRUM data, Mora and Taylor employ limited-dependent variable methods to model the selectivity of internal and international migration to farm and nonfarm jobs.[18]

The econometric results of Mora and Taylor confirm that migration from rural Mexico is highly selective as regards individuals, families, and communities, and that this selectivity differs significantly by migrant destination and sector of employment (farm versus nonfarm jobs).[19]

These results are relevant to this discussion in several ways. Individuals' schooling has a significant positive effect only on internal migration to non-farm jobs. The finding that schooling has no significant effect on international migration to farm jobs could be a result of undocumented entry and work in low-skill labor markets where the returns on schooling obtained in Mexico are likely to be small (see the discussion below on immigration to rural California). Family contacts in the United States importantly affect international migration to both farm and nonfarm jobs. Work experience has a substantial positive effect on internal migration only for nonfarm migration. Household landholdings have positive effects on international migration to farm jobs, and wealth has also a positive impact on international migration to both sectors.

Mora and Taylor's results suggest that only a few variables have relatively uniform effects across migration-sector regimes. Schooling of household heads appears to raise the opportunity cost of migration by other household members. Males are more likely to migrate to any destination/sector combination than females, and insecurity of market access during weather shocks uniformly stimulates migration.[20] The authors also find that migrant networks are significant in shaping migration. This result supports the conclusion of several past studies that networks with existing contacts at migrant destinations are a basic determinant of the magnitude of migration and sector of employment for future migrants.[21]

Individual and family characteristics are not the only variables affecting rural out- migration; community characteristics are also significant. Mora and Taylor show that access to markets at the community level—and exposure to marketing risks—may influence migration and sector of employment. Integration with outside markets, ceteris paribus, could make it easier to migrate, and exposure to market risks may create migration incentives.[22]

With respect to the dynamics underlying female and male migration from rural Mexico to the United States, there is evidence that there are significant differences according to the migrant's gender. Using ENHRUM data, Richter, Taylor, and Yúnez-Naude find that the effects of changes in Mexico's gross domestic product (GDP) are significant only for female migration, while changes in U.S. GDP are significant only for male migration.[23] These findings may suggest that female migration is more sensitive to liquidity constraints that can be loosened by income growth in Mexico, and that male migration, on the other hand, is sensitive to U.S. economic growth. This study also found that while own-gender migration networks are significant and large, cross-gender network effects are small (i.e., estimates of a gender's participation in labor migration do not improve appreciably when the other gender's migration network is included in our estimation). Past research has suggested that female migrants follow males, for example, for purposes of family reunification. However, we find that past labor migration by male villagers has a very small though significant effect on female labor migration. That is, controlling for community effects and long-run migration dynamics, labor migration networks seem to be largely gender specific. The gender asymmetries we found in our study show the importance of including gender in the studies of migration determinants and effects, an area of economic research that has been overlooked.[24]

Effects of International Migration with Reference to Mexico and the United States

Migration can have both positive and negative impacts in receiving and sending countries, and no agreement can be found among researchers on the final outcome of these two processes.[25] As I mentioned in the opening portion of this essay, basic reasons explaining these discrepancies are related to the impossibility of distinguishing causes from effects, due to the fact that international migration is a dynamic phenomenon that changes through time.

Effects in the Receiving Countries

The impact of international migration in DCs discussed in the economic literature is based on the externalities immigration unleashes in DC labor and capital markets, on demographic variables, and on the distributive and pecuniary effects in migrant-labor-receiving countries.

In relation to *labor*, a controversy prevails as to whether immigrants substitute for or complement local workers. Inspired by neoclassical trade theory, some researchers argue that immigrants take over local jobs, competing with at least some groups of local native workers. In turn, native workers are likely to respond to the arrival of immigrants by moving to labor markets less affected by immigrants, shifting the labor-supply curve inward and dissipating the impact of immigration through internal migration.[26]

The argument that migrant labor replaces local labor could be fallacious, as it assumes a fixed number of jobs in the immigrant-receiving country. As DeVoretz shows theoretically, in a dynamic setting it is possible that immigrants may be a complement to and not a substitute for destination labor. Even when unskilled workers (authorized or nonauthorized) enter the DC labor market and work for a lower wage, it is possible that native-born workers are not displaced and yet a sector can eventually become dominated by low-cost foreign labor.[27]

Empirical research shows that most recent immigrants to DCs are concentrated in distinct labor-market segments. That is, the jobs that immigrants take tend to be low skilled and generally low paying; they often involve hard or unpleasant working conditions and considerable insecurity; and they seldom offer chances of advancement toward better-paying, more attractive job opportunities.[28] Because of this, migrants and native workers tend to be complements, not substitutes, in production (for evidence for rural California, see below).

One more possible effect of migration is that migrants can augment the supply of *capital* (human and financial) in the receiving country. As I observed in the previous section, migrants from rural Mexico to the rural United States embody relatively little human capital. However, the same may not be the case for financial capital. Hinojosa argues that positive effects of rural Mexican to rural U.S. migration on financial capital exist and can be enhanced by appropriate binational policies, through the mobilization of migrants' resources in both countries (see below).[29]

The *demographic* impact of immigration includes the smoothing of age-specific labor force shortfalls owing to a collapse in crude birth rates. Immigrants could lower the dependency ratio and could provide semiskilled labor to care for an aging population. However, and according to DeVoretz, the effectiveness of using immigration to prevent a decline in the dependency ratio has not been established.[30]

A *pecuniary externality* of immigration is related to redistributive effects on relative factors and good prices from the presence of immigrant labor. Under static conditions the price of labor-intensive goods (e.g., agricultural products and services) will decline in immigrant-intensive sectors. This latter effect will raise the consumer surplus of these immigrant-intensive goods or services. However, recent research has also noted that immigrants may have diverse demand or taste patterns and may adversely affect the domestic price of nontradables, such as housing in immigrant-receiving urban centers. Unless an applied general equilibrium approach is used, it is difficult to estimate the changes in consumer surplus derived from immigration, since the prices of some nontradable goods will increase while the prices of labor-intensive services may decline.[31]

Immigration may or may not make a positive and growing *public finance* contribution in receiving countries. Three key findings were obtained by a panel of experts to assess the demographic and economic ramifications of immigration in the United States assembled in 1995 by the U.S. National Research Council. First, at the state and local levels immigrants impose a net fiscal burden in both the short run and the long run, particularly in states, like California and New Jersey, that are major immigrant destinations. The fiscal impacts vary by immigrants' age on arrival in the United States and over time. Immigrants, like natives, are costly in childhood and in old age, but they are net payers of taxes during their working years. Second, the fiscal impacts of immigrants are different at different levels of government. In the long run, although negative at the state and local levels, they are large and positive at the federal level. The fiscal benefits at the federal level are shared evenly across the nation, but the fiscal costs are concentrated in a few states and localities that attract most of the nation's immigrants. Third, fiscal impacts of immigration are different for different immigrant groups, closely tied to the skills and incomes of immigrants.[32] Details on the fiscal burden for rural California are given below.

These results indicate that the degree of economic integration of immigrants is related to the fiscal effects of immigration in receiving countries. There are two basic questions in this regard: how long it takes immigrants to catch up to the income level of the native born, and why there should be a period of earnings catch-up, especially if immigrants have been screened for human capital. The economic answer to the second question may be that immigrants must equip themselves after arrival with country-specific human capital, and must learn networking techniques to achieve labor market mobility. Concerning the first question and the United States, DeVoretz finds that among two types of migrants, Ukrainians and the rest of the foreign-born population, the former are overachievers in the United States, as they do not experience an earnings penalty upon arrival.[33] This contrasts with the catch-up point of the remaining immigrants, which occurs at the end of their working life.[34]

Evidence: Migration from Rural Mexico to Rural California

In econometric research based on census data and case studies of rural California communities, Taylor, Martin, and Fix reach the following general conclusions: (1) Immigration, principally from rural Mexico, is fueling an unprecedented growth in population and poverty in rural California communities; (2) upward mobility of immigrant farmworkers in rural California is the exception rather than the rule; (3) public resources available to integrate newcomers are declining even though the number of immigrants is increasing; (4) federal assistance programs originally created for other purposes have become de facto immigrant assistance programs (however, the authors find no evidence that poor immigrants are more likely to receive welfare income than poor nonimmigrants in rural California); (5) there is no evidence that the poverty impact of immigration spills over into adjacent communities; and (6) the resulting mixture of positive income linkages for some groups and competition for low-wage, seasonal farm jobs among low-skilled immigrants creates a socioeconomic geography of contrast: while California's twelve major agricultural counties had farm sales of more than $12 billion in 1993, more than any of the U.S. states except California itself, an average of 26 percent of all residents of farm towns in these twelve counties lived below the poverty line in 1990.[35]

In a more recent article, Taylor and Martin consider that these findings are consistent with those of others who documented a positive relationship between out-migration and rural incomes in earlier periods. "Just as rural out-migration appears to have resolved the poverty associated with 'too many farmers' between 1940 and 1970, immigration, stimulated by the expansion of low-skill farm jobs, appears to be creating a poverty associated with 'too many workers' in the 1980s and 1990s. If history repeats itself, this new rural poverty will stimulate rural-to-urban migration. However, given an elastic supply of low-skilled workers from abroad, it is not clear whether future rural out-migration will alleviate poverty in rural communities."[36]

The findings of Taylor and Martin are in line with some of the negative consequences of migration in DCs that were discussed in the previous section, in particular, that recent immigration depresses wages in migrant-receiving regions, pushing locals to migrate to other places, and that increasing immigration constitutes a burden to public finances at the state and local levels. However, the links between immigration and development are dynamic, and more research is needed to understand the immigration-employment-poverty relationship in rural areas.[37]

Effects in the Sending Countries

A major problem for researchers trying to test whether or not migration affects development in LDCs is that development is complex, and under-development also drives emigration. Research has been conducted on the effects of migration on two measures of welfare in migrant-sending areas: income inequality and poverty.

Studies show conflicting findings about the way international migrant remittances affect income distributions in migrant-sending areas. Some have found that inequality goes up when remittances flow in, and others find the opposite—that is, that remittances are income equalizers.[38] An explanation for this disagreement may be the following: Based on evidence from rural Mexico, "pioneer" migrants tend to belong to households that can afford the costs and risks of international migration, and they send remittances primarily to households at the upper-middle level of the income distribution. This increases income inequality directly, and it has little effect on poverty reduction. However, over time, as more and more households (including poorer ones) gain access to international migration networks, the effect of remittances becomes less unequal and may even become income equalizing and poverty reducing in migrant-sending areas.[39]

Using ENHRUM data for rural Mexico during 2002 (see footnote 18), econometric research provides evidence that remittances from rural migrants to the United States slightly increase rural income inequalities in Mexico. However, remittances have an equalizing effect on incomes in high-migration areas of rural Mexico (the west-central region). This suggests that the expansion of migration has an initially unequalizing effect on rural income distribution, but the diffusion of access to migration eventually makes the effect of remittances on rural incomes more equitable (or at least, less inequitable). In addition, this research shows that international migrant remittances reduce rural poverty in Mexico, and this ameliorative effect increases as rural economies become more integrated with migrant labor markets.[40]

As discussed above, it has been hypothesized that one of the motives of migration is to loosen liquidity constraints caused by restrictions in rural credit markets in migrant-sending regions. A way to test this hypothesis is to study empirically whether differences exist in expenditure demand patterns between migrant and nonmigrant households. Results of an econometric study using ENHRUM data reveal that as total expenditures in households with migrants increase, the share of income used for investments also increases, while the share spent on consumption falls, relative to otherwise similar households without migrants.[41]

A different approach to evaluating the effects of migration in sending countries and rural areas has been advanced using multisector general equilibrium models.[42] Direct and indirect influences of migration are estimated, as well as the net impact of the two opposite effects associated with migration: labor loss and remittances. This approach calculates the impact of *exogenous* shocks, such as a sudden increase in remittances due, for example, to the devaluation of the currency of migrant-sending countries.[43] For Mexico's rural sector, results of simulating an exogenous rise in international remittances using multisector models conclude that this shock depresses local production (especially that of labor-intensive agricultural products). This result is attributed, along with other general equilibrium effects, to the fact that more remittances promote migration, to the detriment of labor-intensive production. At the same time, more remittances raise rural household income.[44] However, as discussed earlier, remittances may also promote investment in rural areas; thus, the negative effect of increasing remittances on local production may become positive after the first round of general equilibrium effects has unfolded.[45]

Policies

Immigration Policies in Receiving Countries:
The Case of the United States

Immigration policies in DCs, whose purpose is to reduce undocumented international immigration flows, have in general proven to be unsuccessful.

The 1986 Immigration Reform and Control Act (IRCA) aimed to restrict the flow of undocumented migrants to the United States. Using ENHRUM data on Mexico's rural migration to the United States from 1980 to 2002, one of the few econometric studies on the impacts of IRCA (and of the North American Free Trade Agreement, or NAFTA) concludes that there is no evidence that these policies curtailed the supply of rural Mexican labor to U.S. farms.[46] One possible explanation for the failure of IRCA to reduce immigration is that this policy strengthened migration networks, which accelerate the movement of populations out of rural Mexico.[47]

The association between trade liberalization and migration is complex. For example, the U.S. Commission for the Study of International Migration and Cooperative Economic Development concluded that expanded trade between the sending countries and the United States is the most important remedy for "unwanted" migration. However, it also warned that the economic development process itself tends in the short-to-medium run to stimulate migration. U.S. farm jobs represent an employment alternative for low-skilled workers in rural Mexico, who have confronted particular challenges in making the transition from agricultural work to employment in Mexico's dynamic sectors during the adjustment to NAFTA and other policy reforms in Mexico.

The huge expenditure increases on Mexican-U.S. border enforcement that the U.S. government has implemented since the 1980s appear to have had no considerable effect on farm labor migration from Mexico. This insignificant impact could be explained as follows: stricter border enforcement increases the risk of apprehension on any crossing attempt and raises the cost of entry into the United States for undocumented migrants, but most migrants eventually succeed in crossing the border, and once they do, they now appear to stay longer in the United States.

More recently, the United States has been attempting to reverse the treasury burden caused by immigrants, as discussed above. A series of U.S. state laws were initially passed to prohibit immigrants and their children from securing a series of state-sponsored health and education benefits. With the overhaul of the U.S. welfare laws, immigrants were excluded from all federally financed benefits until they gained citizenship.[48] However, at least in California, these policies have not reduced the number of immigrants in the rural sector.[49]

These findings reflect the difficulty of designing and implementing policies in migrant-receiving countries to break the rural out-migration dynamic, and they suggest that, in the short run, policy reforms may have accelerated the movement of populations out of rural Mexico.

Policies in Migrant-Sending Countries: The Case of Rural Mexico

Until recently, the Mexican government had no policies related to migration, either to limit "brain drain" or to discourage undocumented international migration from Mexico.

An ideal government intervention to increase the benefits of Mexican-U.S. migration—applicable also to other labor-sending and -receiving countries—is policy reforms designed to improve remittance intermediation for investment in both migrant-sending and migrant-receiving areas.[50] Transnational community networks and resources can be mobilized in both countries to do this, by transnational policy coordination in the North American context.

However, to date, policy reforms involving both the Mexican and U.S. governments have not been popular politically in the United States.[51] If immigration to rural areas of DCs causes a vicious circle of poverty, if rural international out-migration is explained by underdevelopment in rural areas of LDCs, and if this emigration, through remittances, could promote development in rural sending regions, there may be room for policies to raise welfare in both countries by promoting the attainment of basic needs in the migrant-sending country. This has to be done by the government of the migrant-sending country. The validity of this proposal remains even if a guest worker program is established by the U.S. government, since it is likely to be specific to the sector of employment (i.e., agriculture) and will not by itself reduce the incentives for Mexicans to migrate. Thus, a guest worker program is a second-best option that could partially reduce non-documented migration in the short and medium runs. Even though policies designed to attain sustainable development in Mexico are of the medium and long term, they need to be implemented right now.[52]

A basic and more concrete principle of rural development policies related to international migration is that the governments of migrant-sending countries have to act to enhance the positive effects of migration, by reducing remittance transaction costs, by promoting the leveraging of remittances, and by increasing the use of remittances for investment.

High transaction costs in financial markets limit the amount of remittances that can be sent to rural migrant-sending households. Few remittance recipients have bank accounts in rural areas. Improving remittance-receiving households' access to banks is a way toward reducing high transaction costs of international migrant remittances. Another is to facilitate relationships between banks at home and in migrant destinations abroad.

An additional area of policy intervention is leveraging remittances to stimulate investments in migration source areas. This type of policy means seeking ways to multiply the amount of funds available to invest. This can be done by making it possible for individuals to obtain credit for production using remittances as collateral. If nonmigrant households also have bank accounts, the local credit markets can be used as a means to make savings by migrant households available to other households that may be in a better position to invest these savings productively. In addition, groups of individuals can organize and seek remittance matches for larger development projects. This has been the case with the Home Town Associations and Clubs that have been formed by migrants from Mexico (and other countries) in the United States. These immigrant organizations have gathered resources for investment in various public services in the immigrants' villages and towns of origin. More recently these grassroots initiatives have been extended in rural Mexico through the program *tres por uno* that the Fox administration (2001–2006) began to implement. Under this program, for every dollar that the migrant association in the United States provides for specific projects, the federal, state, and municipal governments in Mexico each supply an additional dollar. This triples the funding made available by remittances for local development and civic projects. There is yet another way that the investment potential of remittances can be multiplied: through government collateralizing remittance flows, for example, government debt can be collateralized with future receipts, not just existing assets.

The biggest challenge for public policy is to create an environment in which the income multipliers of remittances can increase. Multipliers in rural areas will not be large if the remittances do not promote the purchase of inputs, the application of new technology, or productive investments, whether in migrant or in nonmigrant households. There must be incentives and reduced constraints, and public programs should aim to create a favorable investment atmosphere via micro credit, infrastructure development (roads, communications), marketing, education, technology, and extension programs.[53]

As I have already indicated, when international migration accelerates, it is very difficult to reduce it. If local opportunities (in the rural or in the urban sector) are to be an alternative to international migration to satisfy the basic needs of people in countries with high undocumented emigration, development policies must encompass rural areas where international migration has not begun to open up.[54]

Concluding Remarks

Migration is a complex phenomenon, and it is difficult to separate the causes and effects of migration in the receiving and sending countries. It is thus not surprising that there is controversy in the literature about the overall effects of migration at migrant origins and destinations.[55] More focused studies address specific emigration and immigration areas, particular economic sectors of expulsion and reception, gender-related differences in determinants and impacts, and selected impacts of migration. They provide more rigorous and reliable findings about the economic effects of international migration. A research challenge is to link these micro, sector-specific, and regional studies of the impacts of migration and remittances with national and multinational, economy-wide economic models, and in a more dynamic manner.

Migration policies in receiving countries such as the United States aimed at curtailing undocumented international immigration have generally been unsuccessful. A sensible option for accomplishing this objective might be to design and put into practice policies in labor-sending LDCs, with the objective of promoting market development, increasing the investment of remittances in productive activities, and creating remunerative employment, especially in rural areas and regions of LDCs where international migration has not yet accelerated. For this, coordination between governments in sending and receiving countries would be ideal. Unfortunately, at least in the case of migration from Mexico to the United States, such coordination has proven not to be politically viable. It appears that the Mexican state, pressured by its civil society, will have to reduce emigration by designing and implementing more solid development policies at home.

Chapter 3

Global Migrations and Economic Need

Saskia Sassen

Across the centuries, the international division of labor has included a variety of translocal circuits for the mobility of labor and capital.[1] These circuits have varied considerably across time and space, shaped at least partly by the specific constitution of labor and capital. Many older circuits continue to exist today. But there are often new dynamics that feed them. And there are new types of circuits as well. One outcome is the emergence of novel global geographies that cut across the old North-South divide. They are constituted through a variety of familiar processes: the increasingly globalized operations of firms and markets, through the multiplication of firms' affiliates and partnerships. These new geographies are also constituted by far less familiar dynamics, such as new types of mobility through digitization and virtual outsourcing[2] and, perhaps at the other end, global peddling.[3]

Migrations of workers are one key feature in these global geographies. These migrations include not only those of low-wage workers. They also include those of high-level professional and executive workers whom we do not usually examine through the lens of migration. One way of finding a conceptual shape and institutional anchor for these diverse migrations is to posit that a good share of these migrations are leading to the incipient formation of two global labor circuits, respectively at the top and at the bottom of the economic system.[4] One of these global labor circuits is that of the transnational managerial and professional workforce that comprises a variety of economic sectors, from finance to highly specialized engineering, and is characterized by a growing set of public and private regulations.[5]

The other global labor circuit consists of an amalgamation of mostly informal flows (including both authorized and unauthorized workers), with perhaps the most visible circuits those of the "global care chains."[6]

These two global labor circuits are constituted through multiple specialized or particular migrations and are far from clearly legible as two distinct global labor circuits. Thus the aggregation implied by the notion of a global labor circuit is an analytic step. This analytic step facilitates a measure of abstraction from a data field that is enormously detailed and comprises hundreds of specific flows, some having little to do with work. At the same time, the analytics of a labor circuit allows one to narrow down the questions for study. Further, taking the analytic leap to posit that these are incipient global labor circuits pushes us to recover the multiple sites constituting the circuit, not only the end point of jobs in the destination site. This matters because most of the analysis of these workforces is in terms of the local labor markets in the destination site; the tendency is to overlook the fact that some of these local labor markets might be one site in global labor market circuits. Finally, this type of analytics also allows us to posit, by default, that the middle sectors of firms and of the workforce in developed countries are more likely to remain overwhelmingly centered in nationally/locally scaled labor markets—they are far less likely to be incipient global formations than the top and the bottom of the system.

There are sites where these two incipient global labor circuits intersect. This essay focuses on two such sites, one in the global South and one in the global North. Given space limitations and the concerns of this volume, I confine myself largely to the lower labor circuit. Within this circuit I focus particularly on migrations where women are a key labor supply, partly because the migrant female workforce at this point actually illuminates more sharply current processes of economic restructuring. One site for such intersections is the global city, specifically the forty-plus global cities that today constitute a kind of organizational platform for the global economy. The other site is a set of global South countries, or subnational regions within them, subject to the international debt-financing regime, which put governments, firms, and households under enormous constraints to survive. Becoming part of global labor migrations increasingly emerges as one survival strategy for people in these countries; this in turn produces synergies both with governments' growing dependence on migrants' remittances and with trafficking as one entrepreneurial option. Focusing on women is particularly illuminating in the current phase; they emerge as actors situated at the intersection of major dynamics, ranging from hyperindebtedness among governments of poor countries to the mix of labor markets that secure the necessary functions in global cities.

Mapping a Multisited Conceptual Landscape

The growing immiseration of governments and whole economies in the global South has promoted and enabled the proliferation of survival and profit-making activities that involve the migration and trafficking of people. To some extent these are older processes, which used to be national or regional and today can operate on global scales. The same infrastructure that facilitates cross-border flows of capital, information, and trade is also making possible a whole range of cross-border flows not intended by the framers and designers of the current corporate globalization of economies. Growing numbers of traffickers and smugglers are making money off the backs of men, women, and children, and many governments are increasingly dependent on their remittances. A key aspect here is that through their work and remittances, migrants enhance the government revenue of deeply indebted countries. The need for traffickers to help in the migration effort also offers new profit-making possibilities to "entrepreneurs" who have seen other opportunities vanish as global firms and markets enter their countries, and to longtime criminals who can now operate their illegal trade globally. These survival circuits are often complex, involving multiple locations and types of actors, and constituting increasingly global chains of traders, traffickers, and workers.

Globalization has also produced sites that concentrate a growing demand of particular types of labor supplies. Strategic among these are global cities, with their sharp demand for top-level transnational professionals and for low-wage workers, often women from the global South. These are places that concentrate some of the key functions and resources for the management and coordination of global economic processes. The growth of these activities has in turn produced a sharp growth in the demand for highly paid professionals. Both the firms and the lifestyles of their professionals generate a demand for low-paid service workers. Thus global cities are also sites for the incorporation of large numbers of lowly paid immigrants into strategic economic sectors. This incorporation happens directly through the demand for mostly lowly paid clerical and blue-collar service workers, such as janitors and repair workers. And it happens indirectly through the consumption practices of high-income professionals both at work and in their households, practices that generate a demand for low-wage workers in expensive restaurants and shops as well as for maids and nannies at home. In this way low-wage workers get incorporated into the leading sectors, but they do so under conditions that render them invisible, undermining what had historically functioned as a source of workers' empowerment—being employed in growth sectors.

This mix of circuits for labor supply and demand is deeply imbricated with other dynamics of globalization: the formation of global markets, the intensifying of transnational and translocal networks, and the geographic redeployment of a growing range of economic and financial operations. The strengthening, and in some of these cases the formation, of new global labor circuits is embedded in the global economic system and its associated development of various institutional supports for cross-border markets and money flows. These circuits are dynamic and changing in their locational features. Some of these circuits are part of the shadow economy, but they use some of the institutional infrastructure of the regular economy. Most of these circuits are part of the formal economy, and they service leading economic sectors and places worldwide. This mix of labor supply circuits and labor demand circuits is dynamic and multilocational.

All of this has happened at a time when developing economies have had to implement a bundle of new policies to accommodate the conditions associated with globalization: the often forced adoption of structural adjustment programs (SAPs), including prominently the opening up of developing economies to foreign firms;[7] the elimination of multiple state subsidies to vulnerable or development-linked sectors, from public health to road construction;[8] and—almost inevitably—financial crises and the prevailing types of programmatic solutions put forth by the International Monetary Fund (IMF).[9] In most of the countries involved—whether Mexico or Thailand or Kenya—these conditions have created enormous costs for certain sectors of the economy and for most of the people, but have not fundamentally reduced government debt. Among these costs are the growth in unemployment, the closure of a large number of firms in traditional sectors oriented toward the local or national market, the promotion of export-oriented cash crops that have increasingly replaced subsistence agriculture and food production for local or national markets, and, finally, an ongoing and mostly heavy burden of government debt in most of these economies.

One question running through this essay is whether there are systemic links between, on the one hand, the growing presence of women from developing economies in a variety of global migration and trafficking circuits, and, on the other, the rise in unemployment and debt in those same economies. There is a large body of data on each of these two major processes, but it does not necessarily address and develop the connection between them.[10] More substantively, we can posit that the following conditions in poor countries have all contributed to raise the importance of alternative ways of making a living, making a profit, and securing government revenue: (a) the shrinking opportunities for male employment, (b) the shrinking opportunities for more traditional forms of profit making as these countries increasingly accept foreign firms in a widening range of economic sectors and are pressured to develop export industries, and (c) the fall in government revenues, partly linked to the first two conditions and to the burden of debt servicing.

The evidence for any of these conditions is incomplete and partial, yet there is a growing consensus among experts about their importance in the expansion of alternative survival strategies for households, enterprises, and governments. I will go further and argue that these three conditions are contributing to an alternative political economy, one arising partly from global North interventions in poor countries and extending eventually back into those same global North countries but through circuits (notably trafficking of women) different from those of the earlier interventions. Women from developing or struggling economies play an increasingly important role in the constituting of this alternative political economy, even when their role is often not self-evident or visible. This lack of visibility has long marked much of the difficulty in understanding the role of women in development generally, and it continues today,[11] a subject I return to in the next section. In many ways, the three conditions listed above are not new. What is different today is their rapid internationalization and considerable institutionalization.

At the other end of the politico-economic spectrum, major changes in the organization of economic activity since the 1980s are contributing to a growth of low-wage jobs in today's most developed and strategic economic centers in both the global North and the global South. Such trends, in turn, contribute to general economic insecurity and new forms of employment-centered poverty among workers, even when employed.[12] This is a broad subject, which includes, importantly, the fact that such strategic economic centers are emerging fast in the global South as well, though not in the poorest economies. Questions of racism, colonialism, and resistance all are at work in some of these configurations in both the South and the North.[13]

There are at least three processes in these strategic economic centers that constitute new forms of inequality within which we can situate the growing demand for low-wage workers, including a large share of foreign-born women. While these processes are not necessarily mutually exclusive, it is helpful to distinguish them analytically. They are: (a) the growing inequality in the profit-making capacities of different economic sectors and in the earnings capacities of different types of workers and households; (b) socioeconomic polarization tendencies resulting from the organization of service industries and from the casualization of the employment relation; and (c) the production of urban marginality, particularly as a result of new structural processes of economic growth rather than those producing marginality through decline and abandonment.

What I have described above is partly a conceptual landscape. The available evidence is inadequate to prove the argument in full detail. There are, however, partial bodies of data to document some of these developments. Further, it is possible to juxtapose diverse data sets, even when gathered autonomously, to document some of the interconnections presented above.

Strategic Gendering in the Global Division of Labor

There is by now a fairly long-standing research and theorization effort engaged in uncovering the role of women in international economic processes. The central effort in the earlier research literature was to balance the almost exclusive and mostly implicit focus on men in international economic development research. In the mainstream development literature, these processes have often, perhaps unwittingly, been represented as neutral when it comes to gender. We can identify at least two phases in the study of gendering in the recent history of economic internationalization—all processes that continue today.

A first phase focused especially on the implantation, typically by foreign firms, of cash crops and wage labor generally. The critical analytical variable introduced by feminist scholars was the partial dependence of commercial agriculture on women subsidizing the wage labor of men through their household production and subsistence farming. Boserup, Deere, and many others produced an enormously rich and nuanced literature showing the variants of this dynamic.[14] Far from being unconnected, the subsistence sector and the modern capitalist enterprise were shown to be articulated through a gender dynamic; this gender dynamic, in turn, veiled this articulation. It was the "invisible" work of women producing food and other necessities in the subsistence economy that helped to maintain extremely low wages on commercial plantations and mines producing for export. Women in the so-called subsistence sector thereby contributed to the financing of the "modernized" sector through their largely unmonetized subsistence production. This contrasted sharply with the standard development literature, which represented the subsistence sector as a drain on the modern sector and as an indicator of backwardness. It was not measured in standard economic analyses.

A second phase was the scholarship on the internationalization of manufacturing production that took of in the 1970s and the feminization of the proletariat in the developing countries that came with it.[15] The key analytic element in this scholarship was that off-shoring manufacturing jobs from developed economies under pressure of low-cost imports generated a disproportionately female workforce in the poorer countries where those jobs moved. These women had hitherto largely remained outside the industrial economy. In this regard it is an analysis that also intersected with national issues, such as why women predominate in certain industries, notably garment and electronics assembly, no matter what the level of development of a country.[16] From the perspective of the world economy, the formation of a feminized offshore proletariat helped firms in the developed countries in their efforts to weaken what had become increasingly strong unions, and it helped firms secure competitive prices for the reimported goods assembled offshore.

Thus the strategic sites where the international division of labor can be studied from a feminist perspective in these earlier literatures varied across different components of the economy. In the case of export-oriented agriculture, this strategic site is the nexus between subsistence economies and capitalist enterprise—where the former actually subsidize and partly enable the latter. In the case of the internationalization of manufacturing production, it is the nexus between, on the one hand, the dismantling of an established, largely male "labor aristocracy" in major industries whose gains spread to a large share of the workforce in developed economies and, on the other, the formation of a low-wage offshore, largely female proletariat in new and old growth sectors. Offshoring and feminizing this proletariat has kept it from becoming an empowered workforce, including actual union power, and prevented existing, largely male unionized workforces from becoming stronger. Introducing a gendered understanding of economic processes lays bare these connections—the existence of a gender nexus as an operational reality and an analytic category.

But what about the strategic sites for gendering in today's leading processes of globalization? In part at least, the long-standing role of gendering remains a critical variable insofar as both the expansion of commercial export-oriented agriculture and the offshoring of jobs to low-wage countries continue today. They do so often with new contents and through new economic geographies. Examples are the proliferation of outsourcing activities and China's massive expansion of offshore manufacturing regions since the 1990s. In many, though not all, ways these developments are predicated on dynamics identified and theorized in that earlier literature.

But continuity, albeit with different contents and a broader range of economic sectors and geographies, is only half the story.

Strategic Gendering in Today's Global Economy

Each phase in this long history of international divisions of labor has generated specific forms of strategic gendering. So has today's global phase. We can identify a mix of literatures that amount to a third phase in the feminist analysis of economic development, even though they often contain an elaboration of the categories and findings of the previous two phases discussed above.

One type of scholarship that uncovers the specifics of the current global phase focuses on transformations in women's subjectivities and in women's notions of community of membership. As did the older development literature, today's literature on economic globalization tends to assume gender neutrality. And it tends to proceed as if questions of subjectivity somehow were not part of the diverse workforces involved. Among other publications, the special issue on globalization and feminism of the *Indiana Journal of Global Legal Studies* addresses the impacts of economic globalization on the partial unbundling of sovereignty and what this means for the emergence of cross-border feminist agendas, the place of women and of feminist consciousness in the new Asian mode of implementing advanced global capitalism, and the global spread of a set of core human rights and its power to alter how women themselves understand their position in various potential communities of membership.[17] Among the richest literatures, and most pertinent to the issues discussed in this article, is a feminist scholarship specifically focused on women immigrants, including research on how international migration alters gender patterns and how the formation of transnational households can empower women.[18]

Far more specific is the question of strategic gendering in the leading global economic sectors. Research on the particular instances where gendering is actually strategic to such sectors is still rare.[19] The cross-border circuits examined in this essay are instances in which the role of women, especially the condition of being a migrant woman, emerge as crucial to the formation of novel economic arrangements—notably, particular components of global cities and of the alternative political economies posited in the preceding section.

Strategic gendering in the global city occurs both through the sphere of production and that of social reproduction.[20] The critical background variable is that these cities are a crucial infrastructure for the specialized servicing, financing, and management of global economic processes. It means that all key components of this infrastructure need to function like clockwork. One such key component is the professional workforce. Gendering becomes strategic in a specific function of globalizing firms: cultural brokering. Professional women are emerging as a key type of worker insofar as they are considered good at building trust across sharp cultural boundaries and differences.[21] The globalizing of a firm's or a market's operations entails opening up domains (sectors, countries, the world of consumers) to new kinds of businesses, practices, and norms. This kind of cultural brokering is critical, especially given the mistrust and the resistances that had to be overcome to implement economic globalization.

Gendering also becomes strategic in the global city for the social reproduction of the high-level professional workforce. There are two reasons for this. One is the growing demand for women professionals, and the other the strong preference among both male and female professionals for living in the city, given long work hours and very demanding responsibilities at work. The result is a proliferation in cities of what I like to refer to as "the professional household without a 'wife.'" What matters here is that the absent "wife" is a factor precisely at a time when professional households are crucial to the infrastructure for globalized sectors and need to function like clockwork. The demands placed on the top-level professional and managerial workforce in global cities are such that the usual modes of handling household tasks and lifestyle are inadequate. As a consequence we are seeing the return of the so-called serving classes in all the global cities around the world, made up largely of immigrant and migrant women.[22]

Most of the research on this subject has focused on the poor working conditions, exploitation, and multiple vulnerabilities of these household workers. This is a fact. But analytically what matters here is the strategic importance of well-functioning professional households for the leading globalized sectors in these cities, and hence the importance of this new type of serving class. For a variety of reasons, developed elsewhere, immigrant and minoritized women are a favored source for this type of work.[23] Theirs is a mode of economic incorporation that makes their crucial role invisible; being immigrant or minoritized citizens facilitates breaking the nexus between being workers with an important function in the global information economy, that is to say, in leading industries, and the opportunity to become an empowered workforce—as has historically been the case in industrialized economies. In this sense the category "immigrant women" in global cities emerges as the systemic equivalent of the offshore proletariat.

IMF Programs and the Need for Alternative Survival Circuits

The second site I consider in this essay is the alternative political economies emerging out of a mix of major global trends that become concrete in many of the struggling underdeveloped economies. One of these concrete forms is the formation of alternative survival circuits for individuals, firms, and governments. While many of these circuits do not generally get coded as having anything to do with the global economy, I argue that they are to some extent localizations of that global economy, which in their aggregate then constitute alternative political economies. In the next section I give a first empirical specification of some of these localizations. Because the data are inadequate, this is a partial specification. Yet it should serve to illustrate some of the key dimensions.

Debt and debt servicing problems have become a systemic feature of the developing world since the 1980s. They are also a systemic feature inducing the formation of the new global circuits that concern me here. The impact on women and on the feminization of survival is mediated through the particular features of this debt rather than the fact of debt per se. Among these particular features are cuts in specific government programs and the tendency for households to have to absorb the costs of male unemployment. It is with this logic in mind that this section examines various features of government debt in developing economies.

Much research on poor countries documents the link between hyperindebted governments and cuts in programs for women and children, notably education and health care, both clearly investments necessary to ensure a better future.[24] There is by now a large literature in many different languages; it also includes a vast number of limited-circulation items produced by various activist and support organizations. An older literature on women and debt during a first generation of SAPs (structural adjustment programs) in the 1980s in several developing countries in response to growing government debt also documents the disproportionate burden these programs put on women.[25] Unemployment, of women themselves but also more generally of the men in their households, has added to the pressure on women to find ways to ensure household survival.[26] Subsistence food production, informal work, emigration, and prostitution have all become survival options for women and by extension often for their households.[27]

Heavy government debt and high unemployment have brought with them the need to search for survival alternatives not only by people but also by governments and enterprises. And a shrinking regular economy in a growing number of poor countries has brought with it a widened use of illegal profit making by enterprises and organizations. Thus we can say that through their contribution to heavy debt burdens, SAPs have played an important role in the formation of countergeographies of survival, of profit making, and of government revenue enhancement.[28] Further, economic globalization has provided an institutional infrastructure for cross-border flows and global markets, thereby facilitating the operation of these countergeographies at a global scale. Once there is an institutional infrastructure for globalization, processes that have basically operated at the national or regional level can scale up to the global level even when this is not necessary for their operation. This would contrast with processes that are by their very nature global, such as the network of financial centers underlying the formation of a global capital market.

Even before the economic crises of the mid-1990s, the debt of poor countries in the South had grown from US$ 507 billion in 1980 to US$ 1.4 trillion in 1992. Debt service payments alone had increased to $1.6 trillion, more than the actual debt. According to some estimates, from 1982 to 1998 indebted countries paid four times their original debts, and at the same time their debt stocks went up fourfold.[29] These countries had to use a significant share of their total revenues to service these debts. Thirty-three of the forty-one highly indebted poor countries (HIPCs) paid three dollars in debt service payments to the North for every one dollar in development assistance. Many of these countries pay more than 50 percent of their government revenues toward debt service, or 20 to 25 percent of their export earnings.[30] Today, before the debt cancellations of early 2006 (see n. 10), as a proportion of GDP, these debt-servicing levels remain high for most of these countries. As of 2006, the poorest 49 countries (i.e. low income countries' with less than $935 per capita annual income) had debts of $375 billion. If to these 49 poor countries we add the "developing countries," we have a total of 144 countries with a debt of over $2.9 trillion and $573 billion paid to service debts in 2006.[31]

The debt burden inevitably has large repercussions on state spending composition. This is well illustrated in the case of Zambia, Ghana, and Uganda, three countries that have been seen as cooperative and responsible by the World Bank as well as effective in implementing SAPs. In Zambia, for example, the government paid $1.3 billion in debt but only $37 million for primary education; Ghana's social expenses, at $75 million, represented 20 percent of its debt service; and Uganda paid $9 per capita on its debt and only one dollar for health care.[32] In 1994 alone these three countries remitted $2.7 billion to bankers in the North. After a decade of the new generation of adjustment programs, Africa's payments reached $5 billion in 1998, which means that for every one dollar in aid, African countries paid $1.4 in debt service in 1998. In many of the HIPCs debt service ratios to GNP exceed sustainable limits; many are far more extreme than what were considered unmanageable levels in the Latin American debt crisis of the 1980s.[33] Sticking with 1998, debt to GNP ratios were especially high in Africa, where they stood at 123 percent, compared with 42 percent in Latin America and 28 percent in Asia. Generally, the IMF asks HIPCs to pay 20 to 25 percent of their export earnings toward debt service. By contrast, in 1953 the Allies cancelled 80 percent of Germany's war debt and only insisted on 3 to 5 percent of export earnings debt service. Similar conditions were applied to Central European countries in the 1990s. By 2003 (Table 3.1) debt service as a share of exports only (not overall government revenue use) ranged from extremely high levels for Zambia (29.6 percent) and

Table 3.1 Highly Indebted Poor Countries: Exports, Foreign Investment, and Debt Service as Share of GDP, 1995–2006

	Trade Export of Goods and Services (% of GDP)				Foreign Direct Investment (% of GDP)			Debt Service Total (% of GDP)			
	1995	2003–2004	2005	2006	1995	2003	2006	1995	2003	2005	2006
1. Benin	20.2	13.7	13	/	0.4	1.4	0.5	6.8	6.9	7.4	—
2. Bolivia	/	/	36	42	/	/	−3	/	/	14.3	8.5
3. Burkina Faso	12.4	8.6	10	11	0.4	0.3	0.4	12.2	11.2		—
4. Ethiopia	13.6	16.9	16	16	0.2	0.9	2.4	18.4	6.8	4.1	6.8
5. Ghana	/	/	36	39	/	/	1	/	/	7	4.9
6. Guyana	/	/	88	/	9.8	/	/	88	—		—
7. Honduras	24.1	28.4	/	—	/	/	5.6	14.9[a]	—	3.8	3.4
8. Madagascar	21.2	26.4	27	30	0.3	0.2	0.6	13.4	6.1	5.7	—
9. Mali	49.1	40.2	27	30	4.5	3	3	22.9	5.8	5.7	—
10. Mauritania	15.2	22.8	36	55	0.7	18.1	6.2	34.5	27.7[b]		1.9
11. Mozambique	/	/	33	41	1.9	7.8	1.6		6.9	3.8	4.1
12. Nicaragua	/	/	29	31	/	/	4.9	16.7	/	6.7	
13. Niger	17.2	15.5	15	—	0.4	1.1	0.4	20.4	/	5.9	9.6
14. Rwanda	5.2	8.6	11	12	0.2	0.3	0.4	16.8	14.6	8.1	
15. Senegal	34.5	27.8	27	26	0.7	1.2	0.7	/	8.7		3.4
16. Tanzania	/	/	24	24	/	/	3.9	19.8	/	4.3	4.8
17. Uganda	—	—	13	15	2.1	3.1	2.9	/	7.1	9.3	
18. Zambia	36	20.9	34	38	2.8	2.3	3.6	47.0[c]	29.6	10.9	3.6

Sources: United Nations Development Programme Annual Report 2005, "A Time For Bold Ambition: Together We Can Cut Poverty in Half"; United Nations Development Programme, "Human Development Report 2007–2008"; World Bank, "Global Economic Prospects 2005: Trade, Regionalism and Development" (Washington, D.C.: World Bank, 2005); World Bank, "Increasing Aid and Its Effectiveness," in Global Monitoring Report: Millennium Development Goals: From Consensus to Momentum, 151–87 (Washington, D.C.: World Bank, 2005); http://siteresources.worldbank.org/intglobalmonitoring/Resources/ch5_GMR2005.pdf. http://hdrstats.undp.org/indicators/174.html.

Notes: An additional twenty countries are eligible for classification as HIPC program but have not yet met the necessary conditions.

[a] 1995–97; [b] 1998; [c] 1997.

/ = Countries eligible for HIPC, but not listed by World Bank and UNDP as Less Developed Countries (LDCs).

Mauritania (27.7 percent), to significantly lowered levels compared with the 1990s for Uganda (down from 19.8 percent in 1995 to 7.1 percent in 2003) and Mozambique (down from 34.5 percent in 1995 to 6.9 percent in 2003).

These features of the current situation suggest that many of these countries cannot get out of their indebtedness through such strategies as SAPs. Generally, using IMF policies to manage the crisis can be shown to have worsened the situation for the unemployed and poor.[34] The 1997 financial crisis in the rich and dynamic countries of Southeast Asia shows us that accepting the types of loans offered, and indeed pushed, by private lenders can create unmanageable debt levels even among rich and high-growth economies—bringing bankruptcies and mass layoffs to a broad range of enterprises and sectors. Even a powerful economy such as South Korea found itself forced into structural adjustment programs, with attendant growth in unemployment and poverty due to widespread bankruptcies of small and medium-sized firms catering to both national and export markets.[35]

It is in this context that alternative survival circuits emerge. The context can be specified as a systemic condition comprising a set of particular interactions among high unemployment, poverty, widespread bankruptcies, and shrinking state resources (or allocation of resources) to meet social needs. The key implication is that the feminization of survival extends to firms and governments besides households. There are new profit-making and government-revenue-making possibilities built on the backs of migrants, women migrants in particular. I shall now briefly examine the question of immigrant remittances as one lens into the broader subject of the formation of alternative political economies and how these unsettle older notions of an international division of labor.

Labor Exports and Remittances:
One Alternative Survival Source

Immigrants enter the macro level of development strategies through the remittances they send back home. These represent a major source of foreign exchange reserves for the government in a good number of countries. While the flows of remittances may be minor compared to the massive daily capital flows in global financial markets, they can matter enormously to developing or struggling economies. The World Bank estimates remittances worldwide reached $230 billion, up from $70 billion in 1998; of this total amount, $168 billion went to developing countries, up 73 percent over 2001.[36] Immigration country firms can also benefit. Thus the Inter-American Development Bank (IADB) estimates that in 2003, immigrant remittances generated $2 billion in handling fees for the financial and banking sector on the $35 billion sent back home by Hispanics living in the United States.[37] The Bank also found that for Latin America and the Caribbean as a whole, in 2003 these remittance flows exceeded the combined flows of all foreign direct investment and net official development assistance.[38]

To understand their significance, these figures should be related to the GDP and foreign currency reserves in the specific countries involved, rather than compared to the global flow of capital. For instance, in the Philippines, a key sender of migrants generally, particularly of women for care industries and sex-work , remittances have been the third-largest source of foreign exchange over the past several years. In Bangladesh, another country with significant numbers of its workers in the Middle East, Japan, and several European countries, remittances represent about a third of foreign exchange. In Mexico, remittances are the second source of foreign currency, just below oil and ahead of tourism, and are larger than foreign direct investment.[39] The financial crisis of 2007–2008 has reduced the levels of remittances, but they still remain a significant factor in these economies.

Table 3.2 provides an overall distribution of remittance flows by economic development level and by region. Overall, it becomes clear that remittances are not a particularly significant factor for most countries. This once again underlines the specificity of the geographies of migration, which is a critical factor in my own research because of its political implications: most people do not want to move to another country. As an aggregate for all countries in each category, we can see that remittances are between 0.2 percent in high-income Organisation for Economic Co-operation and Development (OECD) countries to 3.7 percent for middle-income countries and 4.1 percent in the Middle East and North Africa. The figures change dramatically when we rank countries by remittances as a share of GDP (Table 3.3). Remittances are more than a fourth of GDP in several poor or struggling countries: Tonga (31.1 percent), Moldova (27.1 percent), Lesotho (25.8 percent), Haiti (24.8 percent), Bosnia and Herzogovina (22.5 percent), and Jordan (20.5 percent). However, if we rank countries by total

Table 3.2 Remittance Inflows by Level of Development and Region, 2002–2005 (US$ Million)

	2002	2003	2004 (estimate)	2005 (estimate)	Remittances as a share of GDP, 2004
All developing countries	113,416	142,106	160,366	166,898	2.0%
Low-income countries	33,126	41,789	43,890	45,064	3.7%
Middle-income	80,290	100,317	116,476	121,834	1.7%
Lower MICs	57,305	75,520	83,475	88,021	2.2%
Upper MICs	22,985	27,797	33,001	33,813	1.1%
High-income OECD	52,076	57,262	64,260	64,260	0.2%
East Asia and Pacific	27,168	35,797	40,858	43,138	1.7%
Europe and Central Asia	13,276	15,122	19,371	19,892	1.1%
Latin America and Caribbean	28,107	34,764	40,749	42,419	2.0%
Middle East and North Africa	15,551	18,552	20,296	21,263	4.1%
South Asia	24,155	31,109	31,396	32,040	3.6%
Sub-Saharan Africa	5,159	6,762	7,696	8,145	1.5%
World	**166,217**	**200,216**	**225,810**	**232,342**	**0.6%**

Source: World Bank, *Global Economic Prospects 2006: Economic Implications of Remittances and Migration*

Table 3.3 Countries with Highest Remittance Inflows as Share of GDP, 2002–2005 (US$ million)

Country	2002	2003	2004 (estimate)	2005 (estimate)	Remittances as a share of GDP, 2004
1. Tonga	66	66	66	66	31.1%
2. Moldova	323	486	703	703	27.1%
3. Lesotho	194	288	355	355	25.8%
4. Haiti	676	811	876	919	24.8%
5. Bosnia/Herzegovina	1,526	1,745	1,824	1,824	22.5%
6. Jordan	2,135	2,201	2,287	2,287	20.4%
7. Jamaica	1,260	1,398	1,398	1,398	17.4%
8. Serbia/Montenegro	2,089	2,661	4,129	4,650	17.2%
9. El Salvador	1,954	2,122	2,564	2,564	16.2%
10. Honduras	718	867	1,142	1,142	15.5%
11. Philippines	7,381	10,767	11,634	13,379	13.5%
12. Dominican Republic	2,194	2,325	2,471	2,493	13.2%
13. Lebanon	2,500	2,700	2,700	2,700	12.4%
14. Somoa	45	45	45	45	12.4%
15. Tajikistan	79	146	252	252	12.1%
16. Nicaragua	377	439	519	519	11.9%
17. Albania	734	889	889	889	11.7%
18. Nepal	678	785	785	785	11.7%
19. Kiribati	7	7	7	7	11.3%
20. Yemen, Rep.	1,294	1,270	1,283	1,315	10.0%

Source: World Bank, Global Economic Prospects 2006: Economic Implications of Remittances and Migration.

Table 3.4 Top Twenty Remittance-Recipient Countries, 2004 (US$ billions)

Country	Billions of dollars
India	21.7
China	21.3
Mexico	18.1
France	12.7
Philippines	11.6
Spain	6.9
Belgium	6.8
Germany	6.5
United Kingdom	6.4
Morocco	4.2
Serbia	4.1
Pakistan	3.9
Brazil	3.6
Bangladesh	3.4
Egypt, Arab Rep.	3.3
Portugal	3.2
Vietnam	3.2
Colombia	3.2
United States	3
Nigeria	2.8

Source: International Monetary Fund, *Balance of Payments Statistics Yearbook, 2004.* World Bank, *Global Economic Prospects 2006: Economic Implications of Remittances and Migration.*

value, the picture again changes sharply (Table 3.4). The top remittance recipient countries in 2004 include rich countries such as France, Spain, Germany, and the United Kingdom, indicating that transnational professionals also send remittances home; this is a fact often overlooked in discussions of remittances, a term which has become almost synonymous with the migrations of poor people. Overall, in 2004 the top recipients are India ($21.7 bn), China ($21.3 bn), Mexico ($18.1 bn), France ($12.7 bn), and the Philippines ($11.6 bn).

Governments often see exporting workers and receiving their remittances as means of coping with unemployment and foreign debt. While the second might be a fact, the first is not; further, emigration may be contributing to slow down development as the most entrepreneurial and often well-educated leave. Some countries have developed formal labor export programs. Systemically this fits into the reorganizing of the world economy that began in the 1970s and took off in the 1980s. Probably the strongest examples are South Korea and the Philippines.[40] In the 1970s, South Korea developed extensive programs to promote the export of workers as an integral part of its growing overseas construction industry, initially to the Middle Eastern members of the Organization of Petroleum Exporting Countries (OPEC) and then worldwide. As South Korea entered its own economic boom, exporting workers became a less necessary and less attractive option. In contrast, the Philippine government, if anything, expanded and diversified the concept of exporting its citizens as a way of dealing with unemployment and securing needed foreign exchange reserves through their remittances. After the 1997–8 financial crises, several countries launched new or renewed efforts to export their workers. Thailand started a campaign in 1998 to stimulate migration for work and to promote recruitment by firms overseas of Thai workers. The government sought to export workers to the Middle East, the United States, the United Kingdom, Germany, Australia, and Greece. Sri Lanka's government tried to export another 200,000 workers in addition to the one million it already had overseas; Sri Lankan women remitted $880 million in 1998, mostly from their earnings as maids in the Middle East and Far East. Bangladesh was already organizing extensive labor export programs to member of OPEC in the Middle East in the 1970s, and these efforts continued and expanded after the crisis, along with individual migrations to the United States and the United Kingdom. At the time, migration became, and continues to be, a significant source of foreign exchange, as workers annually remitted an estimated $1.4 billion in the second half of the 1990s.[41]

The Philippines is the country with the most developed labor export program.[42] The Filipino government has played an important role in the emigration of Filipina women to the United States, the Middle East, and Japan, through the Philippines Overseas Employment Administration (POEA). Established in 1982, it organized and oversaw the export of nurses and maids to high demand areas in the world. High foreign debt and high unemployment combined to make this an attractive policy. In the last few years, Filipino overseas workers sent home almost $1 billion on average a year. The various labor importing countries welcomed this policy for their own specific reasons. The OPEC members in the Middle East saw the demand for domestic workers grow sharply after the 1973 oil boom. Confronted with a shortage of nurses, a profession that demanded years of training yet garnered rather low wages and little prestige or recognition, the United States passed the Immigration Nursing Relief Act of 1989, which allowed for the import of nurses; about 80 percent of the nurses brought in under the new act were from the Philippines.[43] The Philippines government also passed regulations that permitted mail-order-bride agencies to recruit young Filipinas to marry foreign men as a matter of contractual agreement.[44] The rapid increase in this trade was due to the organized effort by the government.[45] Among the major clients were the United States and Japan. Japan's agricultural communities were a key destination for these brides, given enormous shortages of people and especially young women in the Japanese countryside when the economy was booming and demand for labor in the large metropolitan areas was extremely high. Municipal governments made it a policy to accept Filipina brides.

The largest number of Filipinas going through these channels work overseas as maids, particularly in other Asian countries.[46] The second-largest group and the fastest growing is entertainers, who go largely to Japan.[47] In the 1980s Japan passed legislation that permitted the entry of "entertainment workers" into its booming economy marked by rising expendable incomes and strong labor shortages. The rapid increase in the numbers of migrants going as entertainers is largely due to the more than five hundred "entertainment brokers" in the Philippines operating outside the state umbrella—-even though the government still benefits from the remittances of these workers. These brokers work to provide women for the sex industry in Japan, which is basically supported or controlled by organized gangs, rather than going through the government-controlled program for the entry of entertainers. These women are recruited for singing and entertaining, but frequently—perhaps mostly—they are forced into prostitution.

Inequality in Profit Making and Earnings Capacities

Inequality in the profit-making capacities of different sectors of the economy and in the earnings capacities of different types of workers has long been a feature of advanced economies. But what we see happening today takes place on an order of magnitude that distinguishes current developments from those of the postwar decades. The extent of inequality and the systems in which it is embedded and through which these outcomes are produced are engendering massive distortions in the operations of various markets, from investment to housing and labor.

Two of the major processes lying behind the possibility of the increased inequality in profit-making and earnings capacities are an integral part of the advanced information economy. One is the ascendance and transformation of finance, particularly through securitization, globalization, and the development of new telecommunications and computer network technologies. The other is the growing service intensity in the organization of the economy generally, which has vastly raised the demand for services by firms and households.[48] Insofar as there is a strong tendency toward polarization in the technical levels and prices of services as well as in the wages and salaries of workers in the service sector, the growth in the demand for services contributes to polarization and, via cumulative causation, to reproduce these inequalities.

The superprofit-making capacity of many of the leading service industries is embedded in a complex combination of new trends: technologies that make possible the hypermobility of capital at a global scale; market deregulation that maximizes the implementation of that hypermobility; financial inventions such as securitization that liquefy hitherto unliquid or relatively unliquid capital and allow it to circulate faster and hence make additional profits; the growing demand for services in all industries along with the increasing complexity and specialization of many of these inputs that has contributed to their valorization and often overvalorization, as illustrated in the unusually high salary increases beginning in the 1980s for top-level professionals.[49] At the heart of these major trends lies a sharp increase in the demand for professional workers who can handle increasingly complex functions, with the consequent sharp increase in pay, enabled by the sharply increased profits of these firm-to-firm sectors which produce increasingly strategic material and immaterial goods.[50] Globalization further adds to the complexity of these services, their strategic character, their glamour, and so to their overvalorization.

The ascendance of finance and specialized services, particularly concentrated in large cities, creates a critical mass of firms with extremely high profit-making capabilities. These firms contribute to bid up the prices of commercial space, industrial services, and other business needs, and thereby make survival for firms with moderate profit-making capabilities increasingly precarious. Among the latter, informalization of all or some of a firm's operations can emerge as one of the more extreme responses, further contributing to polarization in the urban economy. More generally, we see segmentation between firms making high profits and firms making relatively modest profits.

One of the key outcomes of this transformation has been the ascendance of expertise and specialization in the organization of the economy. This ascendance of expertise in economic organization in turn has contributed to the overvalorization of specialized services and professional workers. And it has contributed to marking many of the "other" types of economic activities and workers as unnecessary or irrelevant to an advanced economy. As I have sought to show at length elsewhere, many of these other jobs are in fact an integral part of internationalized economic sectors but not represented as such or valued (i.e., compensated) as such. This contributes to creating a vast number of both low-income households and very-high-income households.[51]

The growing service intensity in the organization of the economy generally that has vastly raised the demand for services by firms in all economic sectors has contributed to the enormous expansion of an intermediate economy of firm-to-firm sales and acquisitions. For instance, taking a high-growth period, the gross output of FIRE (finance, insurance, and real estate) overall (including for firms and for consumers) grew by 7.6 percent from 1999 to 2003 in the United States, almost double the 4.1 percent overall growth rate for those years. But if we only measure what was sold to other firms and markets in FIRE, the growth rate jumps to 11.8 percent; and if we break it down even further and measure only securities and linked trading, we reach 34 percent. Similar, though less dramatic, wholesale trade as an intermediate input grew by 9.4 percent from 1999 to 2003, versus 4.4 percent as gross output. Overall, private services production as an intermediate input grew by 9 percent versus 6.2 percent gross output growth. But also sectors such as construction are doing better as an intermediate sector (7.2 percent average growth rate from 1998 to 2003) than as a final consumer sector (4.3 percent).[52] This intermediate economy of services for firms, both specialized corporate and industrial services, has been a key dynamic in the growth of the demand for professionals that has been key to the new type of economy we see in cities. At the top level of the urban system, especially in global cities, we see the mix of outcomes discussed in this essay. In cities at lower levels of the urban system, catering to more standardized and national rather than global firms, we see a parallel development, though the earnings and profits are not as dramatic as in global cities.

Among the major systemic tendencies in the organization of the service sector contributing to polarization is the disproportionate grouping of service industries at either end of the technology spectrum. Service industries that can be described as information and knowledge intensive have generated a significant share of all new jobs created over the past fifteen years in developed economies, while most of the other jobs created in the service sector fall at the other extreme. For instance, the two broad occupational categories projected by the U.S. Bureau of Labor Statistics to increase are professional specialty occupations and service occupations. The bureau's data and projections show that the incomes in these two occupations in the 1990s and into the twenty-first century are on opposite ends of the earnings spectrum, with earnings for service workers about 40 percent below the average for all occupational groups. In contrast public sector low-wage jobs, which are better paid and have more fringe benefits, saw a fall in their share of all new jobs and are not expected to reverse this trend.

Key issues are the types of jobs being created and the systemic tendencies organizing the service sector as this sector sets the terms of employment for today and tomorrow. Jobs and organization are, clearly, overlapping and mutually shaping factors. However, they do not overlap completely: the labor markets associated with a given set of technologies can, in principle, vary considerably and contain distinct mobility paths for workers. But today sector organization, types of jobs, and labor market organization are all strengthening the tendencies toward polarization.

This mix of trends and conditions has produced an overall outcome of growing inequalities of all sorts, as Figure 3.1 and Table 3.5 illustrate.

Producing a Demand for Low-Wage Service Workers in Growth Sectors

Cities are a nexus where many of the new organizational tendencies come together. They are also the sites for a disproportionate concentration of both the top level and the bottom level of the occupational distribution. The new employment regimes that have emerged in major cities of highly developed countries since the 1980s have reconfigured the job supply and employment relations. Much analysis of postindustrial society and advanced economies generally posits a massive growth in the need for highly educated workers. This suggests sharply reduced employment opportunities

Figure 3.1 Top Decile Income Share, 1917–2005

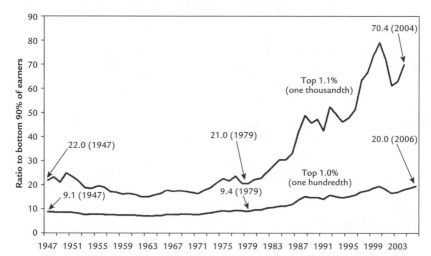

Source: Lawrence Mishel, "Unfettered Markets, Income Inequality, and Religious Values," *Viewpoints,* May 19, 2004. Economic Policy Institute, www.epi.org/content.cfm/webfeatures_ viewpoints_moral_market s_presentation.

for workers with low educational levels generally and for immigrants in particular. Yet detailed empirical studies of major cities in highly developed countries show ongoing demand for low-wage workers and a significant supply of old and new jobs requiring little education and paying low wages.

One critical distinction for the concerns in this essay is whether this job supply (a) is merely or largely a residual partly inflated by the large supply of low-wage workers, or (b) is mostly part of the reconfiguration of the job supply and employment relations that are in fact a feature of advanced service economies, that is to say, a systemic development that is an integral part of such economies. There are no precise measures, and a focus on the jobs by themselves will hardly illuminate the issue. We know generally what they are: low-wage, requiring little education, undesirable, with no advancement opportunities, and, often, few if any fringe benefits. We need to go beyond the characteristics of these jobs and workers and get at the growth dynamics in advanced service economies, especially systemic outcomes in terms of labor demand. What looks backward may well be part of today's advanced economies.

In the day-to-day work of the leading sectors in global cities, a large

Table 3.5 Economic Inequality in Major U.S. Cities by Race, 2006

	White Median Income	Black Median Income	Latino Median Income	Asian Median Income	White Poverty Rate (%)	Black Poverty Rate (%)	Latino Poverty Rate (%)
Atlanta	$77,236	$25,674	$37,673	$44,102	7.2	32.8	—
Boston	60,521	31,915	28,276	37,044	12.9	26.8	27.0
Chicago	60,166	28,607	39,526	51,677	9.7	32.0	21.6
Dallas	60,191	28,200	31,466	46,779	7.6	28.2	29.0
Houston	61,124	29,772	32,367	42,455	8.9	29.9	25.5
Los Angeles	62,634	31,051	35,496	49,920	10.0	26.3	24.9
Miami	63,723	18,710	25,673	36,541	14.7	41.0	24.8
New York	62,931	36,589	32,791	48,951	11.1	22.7	27.9
Philadelphia	43,580	26,728	23,469	36,221	13.8	31.6	39.2
San Francisco	82,177	31,080	49,561	55,072	9.1	31.1	15.2
Wash., D.C.	91,631	34,484	43,547	67,137	8.1	26.8	18.4
Average	65,992	29,346	34,531	46,900	10.3	29.9	25.2

Source: Based on Brookings Institute, "Living Cities Census Series" [data file], at http://www.brookings.edu/projects/Living-Cities.aspx.

share of the jobs involved are lowly paid and manual, many held by immigrant women. Even the most advanced professionals will require clerical, cleaning, and repair workers for their state-of-the art offices, and they will require truckers to bring the software but also the toilet paper. Although these types of workers and jobs are never represented as part of the global economy, they are in fact part of the infrastructure of jobs involved in running and implementing the global economy, including such an advanced form of it as is international finance. The specific trends discussed below are part of a larger reconfiguring of employment in global cities of the North, and increasingly also in those of the South.[53]

High-level corporate services, from accounting to decision-making expertise, are not usually analyzed in terms of their work process. Such services are usually seen as a type of output, that is, high-level technical knowledge. Thus insufficient attention has gone to the actual array of jobs, from high-paying to low-paying, involved in the production of these services. A focus on the work process brings to the fore the labor question. Information outputs need to be produced, and buildings to hold the workers need to be built and cleaned. The rapid growth of the financial industry and of highly specialized services generates not only high-level technical and administrative jobs but also low-wage unskilled jobs. In my research on New York and other cities I have found that between 30 percent and 50 percent of the workers in the leading sectors are actually low-wage workers.[54] These trends are part of a larger reconfiguring of employment in global cities of the North, and increasingly also in those of the global south.[55]

Further, the similarly state-of-the-art lifestyles of the professionals in these sectors have created a whole new demand for a range of household workers, particularly maids and nannies. The presence of a highly dynamic sector with a polarized income distribution has its own impact on the creation of low-wage jobs through the sphere of consumption (or, more generally, social reproduction). The rapid growth of industries with strong concentration of high-and low-income jobs has assumed distinct forms in the consumption structure, which in turn has a feedback effect on the organization of work and the types of jobs being created. The expansion of the high-income workforce in conjunction with the emergence of new lifestyles has led to a process of high-income gentrification that rests, in the last analysis, on the availability of a vast supply of low-wage workers.[56] High-price restaurants, luxury housing, luxury hotels, gourmet shops, boutiques, hand laundries, and special cleaning services are all more labor intensive than their lower-price equivalents. This has reintroduced—to an extent not seen in a very long time—the whole notion of the "serving classes" in contemporary high-income households.[57] The immigrant woman serving the white middle-class professional woman has replaced the traditional image of the black female servant serving the white master. All these trends give these cities an increasingly sharp tendency toward social polarization.

We are beginning to see the formation of global labor markets at the top and at the bottom of the economic system. At the bottom much of the staffing occurs through the efforts of individuals, largely immigrants, though we see an expanding network of organizations getting involved. Outsourcing of low-level manual, clerical, and service jobs happens largely through firms. Recruitment or more generally satisfying the demand for household work happens through the migration process but also increasingly through agencies. Finally, a growth sector is global staffing companies, which provide firms with a rather broad range of types of workers for mostly standardized jobs. Some of these companies have expanded into dealing with household work to help the transnational professional workforce. For instance, Kelly Services, a Fortune 500 services company in global staffing, which operates offices in twenty-five countries, now has added a home care division, which provides a full range of workers. It is particularly geared to people who need assistance with daily living activities but also for those who lack the time to take care of the household, which in the past would have been taken care of by the mother/wife figure in the household.[58] More directly pertinent to the professional households under discussion here are a growing range of global staffing organizations whose advertised services cover various aspects of day care, including dropping off and picking up, as well as in-house tasks, from child minding to cleaning and cooking.[59] One international agency for nannies and au pairs (EF Au Pair Corporate Program) advertises directly to corporations, urging them to make the service part of their employment offers to potential employees to help them address household and child care needs. Increasingly, the emergent pattern is that the transnational professional class can access these services in the expanding network of global cities among which they are likely to circulate.[60]

At the top of the system, several major Fortune 500 global staffing companies provide firms with experts and talent for high-level professional and technical jobs. In 2001, the largest of these was the Swiss multinational

Adecco, with offices in fifty-eight countries; in 2000 it provided firms worldwide with three million workers. Manpower, with offices in fifty-nine different countries, provided two million workers. Kelly Services, mentioned above, provided 750,000 employees in 2000. More important, there is an emergent system that protects the rights of the new transnational professional and managerial workforce. This system is embedded both in today's major free trade agreements and in a series of new types of visas issued by governments.[61]

It is, thus, both at the top and at the bottom of the occupational distribution that labor market internationalization is beginning to happen. Mid-level occupations, even though also increasingly handled through temporary employment agencies, have been less likely to internationalize their supply. These mid-level occupations include a broad range of professional and supervisory jobs, many subject to automation but many sufficiently specific to a country's larger culture and politico-economic organization to be unlikely candidates for outsourcing. They also include a range of mid- and high-level government jobs, notably in the civil service.[62] The types of occupations involved both at the top and at the bottom are, in very different yet parallel ways, sensitive to global dynamics. Firms need reliable and somewhat talented professionals, and they need them specialized but standardized so they can use them globally. And professionals want the same in the workers they employ in their homes. The move of staffing organizations into the provision of domestic services signals both the emergence of a global labor market and efforts to standardize the service delivered by maids and nannies and home care nurses across the globe.

The top end of the corporate economy—the highly paid professionals and the corporate towers that project engineering expertise, precision, "techie"—is far easier to recognize as necessary for an advanced economic system than are truckers and other industrial service workers or maids and nannies, even though all of them are a necessary ingredient. Firms, sectors, and workers that may appear as though they have little connection to an urban economy dominated by finance and specialized services can in fact be an integral part of that economy. They operate, however, under conditions of sharp social, earnings, and, often, sex and racial/ethnic segmentation. They become part of an increasingly dynamic and multifaceted lower circuit of global capital that partly parallels the upper circuit of professionals and leading corporate service firms—the lawyers, accountants, and telecommunications experts who service global capital.

New Employment Regimes in Global Cities

There are three processes of economic and spatial organization I see as central to address the question of new employment regimes in global cities. One is the expansion of the producer services and corporate headquarters sector, and their consolidation into the economic core of major cities. While this sector may not account for the majority of jobs, it establishes a new regime of economic activity and the associated spatial and social transformations evident in major cities.

A second process is the downgrading of the manufacturing sector, a notion I use to describe a mode of political and technical reorganization of manufacturing that is to be distinguished from the decline and obsolescence of manufacturing activities. The downgraded manufacturing sector represents a mode of incorporation into the "postindustrial" economy rather than a form of obsolescence. Downgrading is an adaptation to a situation where a growing number of manufacturing firms need to compete with cheap imports, and, second, the profit-making capacities of manufacturing overall are modest compared with those of leading sectors such as telecommunications or finance and its companion industries.

A third process is the informalization of a growing array of economic activities, which encompasses certain components of the downgraded manufacturing sector. Like the downgraded manufacturing sector, informalization is a mode of reorganizing the production and distribution of goods and services under conditions where a significant number of firms have an effective local demand for their goods and services but cannot compete with cheap imports or cannot compete for space and other business needs with the new high-profit firms engendered by the advanced corporate service economy. Escaping the regulatory apparatus of the formal economy, even if partially, enhances the economic opportunities of such firms.

Whether articulation and feedback effects exist among these different sectors matters to the question in this essay. If there is articulation among the different economies and labor markets embedded in them, it could be argued that we need to rethink some of the basic propositions about the postindustrial economy, that is, the notion that it needs largely highly educated workers and advanced firms, and the notion that informalization and downgrading are just a third world import or an anachronistic remnant of an earlier era. The argument here is that we are seeing new employment regimes in these urban economies dominated by advanced services, which create low-wage jobs and do not require particularly high levels of education. Politically and theoretically this points to low-wage jobs and low-profit firms as a systemic development of the advanced urban economy.

The expansion of low-wage jobs as a function of growth trends implies a reorganization of the employment relation. To see this we have to distinguish the characteristics of jobs from their sectoral location.[63] That is to say, highly dynamic, technologically advanced growth sectors may well contain low-wage dead-end jobs. Furthermore, the distinction between sectoral characteristics and sectoral growth patterns is crucial: backward sectors such as downgraded manufacturing or low-wage service occupations can be part of major growth trends in a highly developed economy. It is often assumed that backward sectors express decline trends. Similarly, there is a tendency to assume that advanced industries, such as finance, have mostly good white-collar jobs. In fact they contain a good number of low-paying jobs, from cleaners to stock clerks.[64]

The Casualization of the Employment Relation

In terms of the organization of labor markets, we are seeing the formation of new types of labor market segmentation, which began emerging in the 1980s and sharpening from the 1990s onward. Two characteristics stand out. One is a shift of some labor market functions and costs to households and communities. The second is the weaker role of the firm in structuring the employment relation. More is now left to the market.

The shift of labor market functions to the household or community is particularly evident in the immigrant community. But it is possibly part of a more generalized pattern that deserves further research: there is a large body of evidence showing that once one or a few immigrant workers are hired in a given workplace, they will tend to bring in other members from their communities as job openings arise. There is also evidence showing great willingness on the part of immigrant workers to help those they bring in with some training on the job, teaching them the language, and just generally socializing them into the job and workplace. This amounts to a displacement of traditional labor market functions such as recruitment, screening, and training from the labor market and the firm to the community or household. The displacement of labor market functions to the community or household raises the responsibility and the costs of participating in the labor force for workers, even if these costs are often not monetized.[65]

These are all subjects that require new research given the transitions that we are living through.

As for the weaker role of the firm in organizing the employment relation, it takes many different forms. One is the declining weight of internal labor markets in structuring employment. This corresponds both to the shrinking weight of vertically integrated firms and the restructuring of labor demand in many firms toward bipolarity—a demand for highly specialized and educated workers alongside a demand for basically unskilled workers, whether for clerical work, services, industrial services, or production jobs, as discussed in the preceding section. The shrinking demand for intermediate levels of skill and training has in turn reduced the need and advantages for firms of having internal labor markets with long promotion lines that function as training-on-the-job mechanisms. The decentralization of the large, vertically integrated manufacturing firms, including the offshoring of parts of the production process, has contributed to the decline in the share of unionized shops, the deterioration of wages, and the expansion of sweatshops and industrial homework. This process includes the downgrading of jobs within existing industries and the job supply patterns of some of the new industries, notably electronics assembly. Further, part-time and temporary employment is growing at a faster rate than full-time employment. In the United States, growing shares of service workers are in part-time jobs, and they are so twice as often as average workers; involuntary part-time employment has grown significantly over the past decade. Yet another empirical referent for the casualization of the employment relations is the rapid rise of employment agencies that take over the supplying of a growing range of skills under highly flexible conditions. The terms of employment have been changing rapidly over the past fifteen years for a growing share of workers.

In my reading, the overall tendency is toward a casualization of the employment relation that affects not only the types of jobs traditionally marked as casual jobs but also high-level professional jobs that in many respects are not casual.[66] It might be useful to differentiate a casualized employment relation from casual jobs in that the latter connotes such added dimensions as the powerlessness of the workers, a condition that might not hold for some of the highly specialized professional part-time or temporary workers. This is a subject that requires more research.[67]

One of the most extreme forms of the casualization of the employment relation and of the changes in economic organization generally is the informalization of a growing array of activities. This is a development evident in cities as diverse as New York, Paris, London, Amsterdam, and so on.[68]

The Increased Informalization of Work

Theorization about the informal economy has until recently been grounded in the incapacities of less developed economies: the inability to attain full modernization of the economy, stop excess migration to the cities, and implement universal education and literacy programs. Rather than assume that global South migration to the global North is causing informalization, what we need is a critical examination of the role it might or might not play in this process. Immigrants, in so far as they tend to form communities, may be in a favorable position to seize the opportunities represented by informalization. But immigrants do not necessarily create the opportunities. They are a structured outcome of current trends in advanced economies.

A central hypothesis organizing much of my research on the informal economy is that the processes of economic restructuring that have contributed to the decline of the manufacturing-dominated industrial complex of the postwar era and the rise of the new, service-dominated economic complex provide the general context within which we need to place informalization if we are to go beyond a mere description of instances of informal work. The specific set of mediating processes I have found promoting informalization of work are (a) increased earnings inequality and the associated restructuring of consumption in high-income strata and in very-low-income strata, and (b) the inability among the providers of many of the goods and services that are part of the new consumption to compete for the necessary resources in urban contexts where leading sectors have sharply bid up the prices of commercial space, labor, auxiliary services, and other basic business inputs.[69]

One major trend is that the decline of the middle class, the growth of a high-income professional class, and the expansion of the low-income population have all had a pronounced impact on the structure of consumption, which has in turn had an impact on the organization of work to meet the new consumption demand. Part of the demand for goods and services feeding the expansion of the informal economy comes from the mainstream economy and the fragmentation of what were once mostly homogeneous middle-class markets. And another part of this demand comes from the internal needs of low-income communities increasingly incapable of buying goods and services in the mainstream economy.

The recomposition in household consumption patterns particularly evident in large cities contributes to an organization of work different from that prevalent in large, standardized establishments. This difference in the organization of work is evident both in the retail and in the production phase. High-income gentrification generates a demand for goods and services that are frequently not mass produced or sold through mass outlets. Customized production, small runs, specialty items, fine food dishes are generally produced through labor-intensive methods and sold through small, full-service outlets. Subcontracting part of this production to low-cost operations, and also sweatshops or households, is common. The overall outcome for the job supply and the range of firms involved in this production and delivery is rather different from that characterizing the large department stores and supermarkets, where standardized products and services are prevalent and hence acquisition from large, standardized factories located outside the city or the region is the norm. Proximity to stores is of far greater importance with customized producers. Further, unlike customized production and delivery, mass production and mass distribution outlets facilitate unionizing.[70]

The expansion in the low-income population has also contributed to the proliferation of small operations and the move away from large-scale standardized factories and large chain stores for low-price goods. In good part the consumption needs of the low-income population are met by manufacturing and retail establishments, which are small, rely on family labor, and often fall below minimum safety and health standards. Cheap, locally produced sweatshop garments, for example, can compete with low-cost Asian imports, and the small immigrant-owned grocery shop can replace the large, standardized, and typically unionized supermarket. A growing range of products and services, from low-cost furniture made in basements to "gypsy cabs" and family day care is available to meet the demand for the growing low-income population.

In any large city, there also tends to be a proliferation of small, low-cost service operations made possible by the massive concentration of people in such cities and the daily inflow of commuters and of tourists. This will tend to create intense inducements to open up such operations as well as intense competition and very marginal returns. Under such conditions the cost of labor is crucial and contributes to the likelihood of a high concentration of low-wage jobs.

This would suggest that a good share of the informal economy is not a result of immigrant survival strategies but rather an outcome of structural patterns of transformation in the larger advanced urban economy. Immigrants have known how to seize the "opportunities" contained in this combination of conditions,[71] but they cannot be said to cause the informal economy. Informalization emerges as a set of flexibility-maximizing strategies by individuals and firms, consumers and producers, in a context of growing inequality in earnings and in profit-making capabilities discussed earlier.

It is, then, the combination of growing inequality in earnings and growing inequality in the profit-making capabilities of different sectors in the urban economy that has promoted the informalization of a growing array of economic activities. These are integral conditions in the current phase of advanced capitalism as it materializes in major cities dominated by the new advanced services complex typically geared to world markets and characterized by extremely high profit-making capabilities. These are not conditions imported from the third world.

Conclusion

Socioeconomic and political conditions typically conceptualized in micro-level terms actually have complex interactions with particular macro-level economic restructuring processes. Thus labor migrations are not simply about the survival strategies of migrants and their households. They are also micro-level enactments of larger processes of economic restructuring in sending and receiving countries. These include IMF and World Bank programs that have devastated traditional economies in the global South and forced states to shift growing shares of revenue into debt servicing. And they include the growing demand for a wide range of very low-wage jobs in some of the most advanced, rather than declining or backward, economic sectors in highly developed countries.

Gendering becomes strategic for the emergence and for the functioning of these restructuring processes and the partial economies they give rise to. Thus trafficking in women is not only about traffickers and their victims. It has multiple insertions, from micro to macro levels, in key components of these restructured economies. Trafficking in women for the sex industry feeds into the larger political economy by generating entrepreneurial opportunities for small and large traffickers, and from there a whole range of components of the larger tourism industry and various consumer services. And such trafficking feeds government revenues, especially significant when IMF and World Bank adjustment programs force much government revenue into interest payments to the international system. More generally, immigrants' remittances are a significant source of foreign exchange for several poor countries. Also here the essay lays bare the specificity and particularity of these processes rather than general and diffuse effects.

I posit that this mix of conditions and trends amounts to an alternative political economy emerging out of major global trends that become concrete in many of the struggling underdeveloped economies. One of these concrete forms is the formation of alternative survival circuits for individuals, firms, and governments on the backs of mostly poor and undervalued women.

Strategic gendering in the global city is evident both in the sphere of production and in that of social reproduction in the advanced sectors of the urban economy. The macro-level context is the fact that these cities are a crucial infrastructure for the specialized servicing, financing, and management of global economic processes. Everything in this infrastructure needs to function well, including the professional workforce. Gendering becomes strategic in the production sphere because women excel at cultural brokering, at building trust across sharp cultural boundaries and differences. Cultural brokering has emerged as critical because globalizing firms and markets continuously enter new environments at home and abroad, each with its own specificities.

As for the sphere of social reproduction, gendering becomes strategic for the high-level professional workforce in the global city for two reasons. One is the disappearing subject that is the "wife" in the urbanized professional household given long work hours and very demanding responsibilities at work. The result is a proliferation in global cities of what we might think of as "the professional household without a 'wife,'" precisely at a time and in a context where these households need to ensure not simply survival but state-of-the-art survival. I posit that these households should be reconceptualized as part of the strategic "infrastructure" of global cities and that the low-wage domestic workers are in fact strategic infrastructure-maintenance workers. I argue that the social systems represented by these households cannot be fully understood simply in terms of patriarchy, though that is clearly one dynamic—where the professionals, whether men or women, function as a male subject. Nor can this household be explained simply in terms of the return of the serving classes: there is a more specific maintenance function when this domestic work takes place in high-level professional households. Finally, we cannot limit the analysis to the poor working conditions, exploitation, and multiple vulnerabilities of these household workers. All three of these lenses get at critical facts about these households. But, analytically, they do not help in capturing the strategic importance of well-functioning professional households for the leading globalized sectors in global cities; hence my positing that they are actually maintaining a strategic infrastructure—their workplace is the global corporate economy—and should be valued correspondingly.

Immigrant and minoritized women are a favored labor supply for this type of household work, marking a key intersection point between conditions in global South countries and in global cities of the North. Further, being immigrant or minoritized women facilitates breaking the nexus between being workers with an important function in the global corporate economy, and the opportunity to become an empowered workforce, as has historically been the case in industrialized economies. In this sense, the category "immigrant women" emerges as the systemic equivalent of the offshore female proletariat.

Chapter 4

The Immigration Paradox:
Alien Workers and Distributive Justice

Howard F. Chang

With the number of unauthorized immigrants living in the United States estimated to be about twelve million, accounting for 4 percent of our total population, and growing at a rate of more than half a million per year,[1] it seems apparent that we need immigration reform. The country, however, is bitterly divided over what we must do. For those who advocate comprehensive immigration reform, the changes in our immigration laws must include expanded opportunities for relatively unskilled alien workers to gain legal access to our labor markets.

President George W. Bush proposed a large-scale guest worker program that would not only allow unauthorized immigrants to legalize their status as guest workers but also attempt to satisfy the large and persistent demand for relatively unskilled labor in the United States that attracts so many unauthorized immigrants. The Senate passed a comprehensive immigration reform bill in 2006 that would establish such a guest worker program and also expand opportunities for legal immigration and permanent residence. After the failure of the House of Representatives to pass that bill, the Senate considered another comprehensive immigration reform bill in 2007 that would have created such a guest worker program. Thus, recent reform proposals debated in Congress would have brought large numbers of relatively unskilled alien workers into the United States on nonimmigrant visas rather than on immigrant visas.

I argue in this essay that the immigration of relatively unskilled workers poses a fundamental problem for liberals. While from the perspective of the economic welfare of natives the optimal policy would be to admit these aliens as guest workers, as I explain in the first part of this essay, this policy would also violate liberal ideals. These ideals would treat these workers as equals, entitled to access to citizenship and to the full set of public benefits provided to citizens. If the welfare of incumbent residents determines admissions policies, however, and we anticipate the fiscal burden that the immigration of the poor would impose, then our welfare criterion would preclude the admission of relatively unskilled workers in the first place. Thus, our commitment to treat these workers as equals once admitted would cut against their admission and make them worse off than they would be if we agreed never to treat them as equals.

In the second part of this essay, I outline how a liberal can avoid this "immigration paradox" by adopting a cosmopolitan perspective that extends equal concern to all individuals, including prospective immigrants and other aliens. This cosmopolitan perspective suggests liberal immigration policies for relatively unskilled workers. I argue that the liberal ideals espoused by countries like the United States require a global view of distributive justice, and I respond to some of the alternative conceptions advanced by critics of this cosmopolitan perspective. Finally, in the third part of this essay, I conclude with normative implications for immigration reforms in liberal states given the constraints of political feasibility.

The Problem of the Relatively Unskilled Alien Worker

First, I suggest that if we concern ourselves only with the economic welfare of natives, then the optimal policy with respect to relatively unskilled alien workers would be to admit them as guest workers only. Furthermore, if we seek not only to maximize real income for natives but also to seek an equitable income distribution among natives, then we have an even greater interest in denying these workers access to public benefits and to citizenship. Second, however, I note that once we introduce considerations of justice, the exclusion of these aliens from the benefits of full membership in our society becomes troubling, in light of the claims that aliens could make under liberal theories of justice. Third, I argue that if such a theory of distributive justice fails to give the welfare of aliens the same consideration in the formulation of admissions policies, then this notion of justice proves to be hollow, because it implies that it would be best to exclude relatively unskilled aliens from our territory. This result would be perverse from the perspective of the alien excluded, the supposed beneficiary of the proposed obligations of distributive justice.

The Welfare of Natives

From the perspective of the economic interests of natives, guest worker programs may be an optimal response to concerns regarding the impact of relatively unskilled alien workers on the public treasury. Natives of a host country, taken together, will gain from the entry of alien workers into the labor market.[2] In the case of relatively unskilled alien workers, however, the cost that they impose on the public treasury may outweigh the economic benefits that natives derive from these workers in the labor market. Empirical evidence suggests that relatively unskilled immigrants on average have a net negative fiscal impact on natives in the United States. The National Research Council, for example, found in 1996 that the average immigrant with less than a high school education imposed a net fiscal cost of $13,000, even after taking into account the fiscal benefits that the immigrant's descendants would confer in the future.[3]

Through guest worker programs, natives can enjoy the gains from trade with these workers in the labor market without bearing the fiscal burden of providing the full set of public benefits that these workers would receive if they had access to permanent residence and, ultimately, citizenship. In the United States, we generally exclude not only unauthorized immigrants but also nonimmigrants, including temporary workers, from a broad range of public benefits. With only narrow exceptions, these aliens are ineligible for "any Federal public benefit."[4] Although immigrants can gain full access to public benefits upon naturalization, only aliens "admitted for permanent residence" may naturalize as U.S. citizens.[5] Aliens admitted on nonimmigrant visas only, including temporary guest workers, are not admitted as permanent residents and are thus not eligible for most public entitlements and not eligible to naturalize.

The exclusion of alien workers from these programs leaves the host country free to use these programs to transfer income among natives without also shifting wealth to aliens in the process. This freedom may be especially important if host countries rely on such programs to address any adverse effects that the entry of alien workers may have on the distribution of income among natives. In particular, some economists claim that immigration has had a significant adverse impact on the least skilled native workers.[6] Estimates of the impact of immigration on native workers in the United States, however, indicate that only the least skilled native workers suffer adverse effects and that these effects are small.[7] In any event, even if present levels of immigration have little effect on the wages of the least skilled natives, a more liberal immigration policy might produce more significant effects, especially if relatively unskilled workers were to make up an increasingly large fraction of the flow of immigrants. Thus, the exclusion of alien workers from transfer programs permits a host country to adopt more liberal admissions policies without an adverse effect on either the public treasury or the distribution of income among natives. If instead the host country could not exclude these aliens from these programs, then the fiscal burden of liberal admissions policies would jeopardize the political support either for liberal admissions polices or for the amount of redistribution effected by those transfer programs.[8] Because guest worker programs can give relatively unskilled aliens access to our labor markets without necessarily providing full access to the benefits provided to citizens, these programs may allow the most liberal admissions policies possible for these aliens.[9]

Justice and Social Cooperation

Critics of guest worker programs commonly object that these programs violate principles of justice. The communitarian political theorist Michael Walzer, for example, argues that the disenfranchisement of guest workers violates the "principle of political justice" in a "democratic state."[10] "Political justice is a bar to permanent alienage" for guest workers, according to Walzer, "either for particular individuals or for a class of changing individuals."[11] Walzer claims that a society that relies on guest workers to meet its labor needs is "a little tyranny,"[12] in which guest workers "are ruled . . . by a band of citizen-tyrants."[13]

We might derive a similar conclusion from the liberal theory of justice developed by John Rawls, who asks what principles individuals would choose behind a "veil of ignorance."[14] In this "original position," individuals know nothing about their own personal circumstances or traits, and thus "they do not know how the various alternatives will affect their own particular case and they are obliged to evaluate principles solely on the basis of general considerations."[15] This condition ensures that the parties are "fairly situated and treated equally as moral persons," because "a knowl-edge of particulars" would produce an "outcome . . . biased by arbitrary contingencies."[16] Rawls includes all persons within a single "society," which he describes as "a cooperative venture for mutual advantage," as partici-pants in the original position.[17] Rawls concludes that principles of distribu-tive justice would require members of this society to maximize the welfare of those who are least advantaged.[18]

A liberal might conclude that our obligations of distributive justice ex-tend to all workers who participate in a scheme of social cooperation with us. From this perspective, we cannot limit these obligations to natives alone. This perspective suggests that if we admit workers to our labor market, we must extend the benefits of full membership to them as well. From this perspective, by admitting relatively unskilled alien workers we make them objects of our concern and thus worthy recipients of the full set of public benefits that we provide to natives. We would then take a broader view of national economic welfare: our welfare objectives would include the welfare of not only natives but also guest workers. From this perspective, we must treat guest workers as equals, providing them the access to citizenship that those admitted as immigrants would enjoy.

By the same token, however, by excluding aliens from our labor market and our society, we can avoid the obligations that we would incur by admit-ting them. Rawls assumes that the "boundaries" of his principles of justice "are given by the notion of a self-contained national community."[19] In fact, both Rawls and Walzer defend the right of a nation to exclude prospective immigrants free of the obligations of justice that would apply among mem-bers of the national community.[20]

The Immigration Paradox

This view of justice, however, produces an anomaly. If our admission poli-cies are based on the welfare of natives and immigrants already here, then we would refuse to admit poor immigrants because we would anticipate the public benefits that they would consume and the fiscal burden that they would impose on incumbent residents.[21] Thus, our commitment to treat them as equals once admitted would cut against their admission and make them worse off than they would be if we rejected such a commitment. That is, by agreeing to obligations of distributive justice toward them if admitted, we harm them. Our promise of justice and equality for these aliens proves to be hollow. These aliens would be better off if we agreed never to care about their welfare and never to treat them as equals.

If concern for the welfare of poor immigrants motivates generous fiscal policies toward them, then it seems perverse to cite these policies as a reason to exclude the very immigrants whose welfare we would seek to improve through these policies. This moral stance is unsatisfactory from the standpoint of human welfare. The liberal who prevents a poor alien from escaping poverty while citing principles of justice and equality for that alien seems vulnerable to the charge of "superstitious 'rule worship,'" that is, "the charge of heartlessness, in his apparently preferring abstract conformity to a rule to the prevention of avoidable human suffering."[22] If we pursue such a perverse notion of justice, without serving the welfare of those on whose behalf we would invoke its principles, then our concern for equality among the inhabitants of our country looks more like a fetish than the product of a coherent theory of justice.

It seems incoherent public policy to turn away the poor immigrant, citing a negative effect on the welfare of current residents, given that we always have the option of admitting the poor immigrant subject to restrictions on access to public benefits and to citizenship. This option would improve the welfare of both the poor immigrant and the welfare of current residents. This admission would also transform the poor immigrant into a resident, however, and if our social welfare criterion includes the welfare of all residents, then the same distributive concerns that justified generous policies for other poor residents would apply to the poor immigrant as well. In short, no measure of social welfare that counts an individual's welfare if and only if the individual is a resident can provide a coherent criterion for immigration policies, because these policies determine the identity of the population of residents.

This moral stance harms the very individuals whose welfare we would invoke as the basis for their access to citizenship and public benefits. This paradox lies at the heart of immigration policy. A commitment to treat the immigrant as an equal can backfire against the alien seeking to immigrate, because the immigrant's access to equal status does not arise unless we admit the immigrant. If the act of admission triggers obligations of justice, then we can avoid these obligations by choosing to exclude. Indeed, if admission polices are determined by the welfare of incumbent residents, then we would be obliged to exclude relatively unskilled alien workers. This stance begs the question of whether we can legitimately base admission policies on the interests of incumbent residents alone.

Unless the admission decision itself also respects the alien as an equal, the result is perverse. Thus, the source of the immigration paradox is the contingent nature of the obligation to treat the alien as an equal. That is, this problem is inherent in making obligations of justice contingent on voluntary acts of cooperation. If we refuse to admit alien workers, then we owe them no explanation within the framework that Rawls proposes for deriving principles of distributive justice. This approach reconciles the exclusion of aliens with egalitarian principles of social justice only by fiat: it assumes the result rather than deriving it.

We cannot begin our normative analysis by *assuming* that we do not admit the aliens in question. As the example of immigration policy demonstrates, the question of which individuals we choose as partners in cooperation is itself an open question of public policy that we may want to answer using our principles of justice. If we make obligations of justice contingent on whether we admit them in the first place, then this normative framework becomes a function of our admissions policies and cannot work as an independent standard that we can use to evaluate these policies.

That is, if admission to our labor market implies status as a constituent and as a member of our society, then the set of individuals whose welfare we seek to promote becomes endogenous. By choosing our members, we also choose our moral obligations and our welfare objectives. If our obligations depend on our admission policies, however, then our analysis becomes circular: we are justified in discriminating against aliens in employment precisely because our refusal to hire them relieves us of the obligations of justice that we would owe equals. Such a theory begs the question of whether our choice of partners is itself justifiable.

This immigration paradox is quite general: the problem arises regardless of what act of admission we deem sufficient to trigger the alien's claim to justice. For example, if admission to our labor market triggers this claim, then we have a reason to exclude relatively unskilled aliens from our labor market, even if they seek to work only temporarily as guest workers. This approach allows us to avoid obligations of justice by refusing to employ these aliens, even if they would be better off as guest workers with no claim to distributive justice.

If instead it is admission to permanent residence that triggers the alien's claim to justice, then we have a reason to prevent poor aliens from residing permanently within our borders. We might admit guest workers on a strictly temporary basis, for example, and invest significant resources in efforts to ensure that these workers depart at the end of their authorized stay. Again, we avoid the burdens that obligations of distributive justice would impose on us, but only by expelling aliens who may be better off if allowed to enjoy access to our labor market for a more extended period of time, even without access to public benefits or citizenship.

The immigration paradox arises even if de facto permanent residence is sufficient to trigger claims of justice. If unauthorized immigrants have claims to justice based on long-term residence, for example, then these claims do not derive from formal admission as a legal immigrant. Nevertheless, such claims would generate a reason for host countries to exclude, to hunt down, and to deport unauthorized immigrants before they can acquire the rights of a long-term resident. Thus, even unauthorized immigrants may be better off if we rejected notions of justice granting their claims to legal permanent residence or to public benefits, because we might then tolerate their presence more readily and invest fewer scarce resources in draconian efforts to drive them out.

Global Distributive Justice and Its Critics

To avoid the immigration paradox, we need a normative criterion that is independent of our immigration policies and thus avoids the circularity that underlies the immigration paradox. A cosmopolitan theory of distributive justice that extends equal concern to all individuals, including aliens, regardless of their immigration status, could provide such a solution by granting all persons the same claim to distributive justice. Some cosmopolitan theorists argue that a world in which nations engage in international trade in goods, services, capital, and labor is a "cooperative venture for mutual advantage" sufficient to trigger Rawlsian obligations of distributive justice worldwide. In light of this international cooperation, Charles Beitz and others have argued that the entire world is a "society" in which all individuals would be parties to the original position.[23] Beitz suggests that "we should not view national boundaries as having fundamental moral significance" and that "principles of justice" should "therefore apply globally."[24]

Others, however, dispute the claim that the world is a "cooperative venture for mutual advantage" within the meaning of the theory of justice developed by Rawls.[25] For critics of the cosmopolitan perspective, the obligations of distributive justice among residents of one nation are more extensive than those that apply across national borders. Thus, for those who stress cooperation as the basis for obligations of distributive justice, "the salience of global justice is increasing in the density of interactions across borders."[26] Andrea Sangiovanni calls such a claim "relational," because it asserts that "the content and scope of distributive equality" depends on "the current extent and degree of interaction."[27]

Any theory of justice that makes obligations of distributive justice contingent on the actual degree of cooperation between parties, however, creates a problem analogous to the immigration paradox. If voluntary acts of cooperation trigger obligations of distributive justice, then wealthy societies have a reason to avoid cooperating with poor societies. The wealthy would seek to avoid the burdens that such obligations impose by shunning interactions with the poor, to the detriment of the very individuals whose welfare we would seek to improve through those obligations. This "cooperation paradox" is simply a more general version of the immigration paradox.

We can avoid the cooperation paradox only if we instead adopt a normative criterion that is independent of all of our policy choices. For example, we could include a prospective party in the Rawlsian original position in any case where cooperation with that party is feasible, regardless of whether we are actually engaged in such cooperation. Sangiovanni would call such a theory of justice "nonrelational," because its obligations do not depend on the degree of current interaction.[28] Under this approach, the mere feasibility of cooperation should be sufficient to trigger obligations of distributive justice.

Another nonrelational alternative would be to base the claim to distributive justice simply on an individual's status as a human being. After all, place of birth would appear to be a circumstance that Rawls should deem "arbitrary from a moral point of view."[29] Thomas Pogge notes that nationality based on such a circumstance "is just one further deep contingency (like genetic endowment, race, gender, and social class), one more potential basis of institutional inequalities that are . . . present from birth."[30] "Within Rawls's conception," Pogge suggests, "there is no reason to treat this case differently from the others."[31] Thus, Pogge and others argue in favor of globalizing Rawls's principles of justice.[32]

Citing Beitz and others, Joseph Carens addresses the issue of immigration restrictions in particular as a question of social justice using a global interpretation of Rawls's original position.[33] In seeking a justification for the exclusion of aliens, he suggests, "we don't want to be biased by self-interested or partisan considerations" and instead "can take it as a basic presupposition that we should treat all human beings, not just members of our own society, as free and equal moral persons."[34] Carens identifies this premise as a basic feature of all liberal political theories, concluding that we should "take a global, not a national view of the original position."[35]

If we begin with equal concern for all persons, then immigration barriers are morally suspect and demand justification. All immigration restrictions discriminate against individuals based on their alienage. Most aliens are born aliens because our nationality laws deem them to be aliens based on immutable characteristics, including the geographic location of their birth (that is, national origin) and the citizenship of their parents at the time of their birth.[36] This discrimination based explicitly on circumstances of birth is at odds with liberal ideals. Carens concludes that we cannot justify restrictions "on the grounds that those born in a given territory or born of parents who were citizens were more entitled to the benefits of citizenship than those born elsewhere or of alien parents."[37] Similarly, in a utilitarian calculation of global welfare, "current citizens would enjoy no privileged position."[38] Carens concludes from these liberal premises that "we have an obligation to open our borders much more fully than we do now."[39] Carens condemns our immigration restrictions: "Like feudal barriers to mobility, they protect unjust privilege."[40] Thus, from a cosmopolitan perspective, principles of justice require us not only to grant immigrant workers liberal access to public benefits and to citizenship but also to grant aliens liberal access to our labor market and to permanent residence in our territory.

Nevertheless, some liberals defend immigration restrictions and reject the extension of our principles of distributive justice to prospective immigrants. Critics of cosmopolitan liberalism propose various alternative theories that limit obligations of distributive justice to members of the same national community. I shall now review the reasons advanced by these critics for more limited theories of distributive justice and argue that these theories do not offer a satisfactory alternative to cosmopolitan liberalism. I suggest instead that the liberal ideals expressed in our declaration that "all men are created equal"[41] require a cosmopolitan perspective.

State Coercion

Although Michael Blake concedes that liberalism is "committed to moral equality, so that the simple fact of humanity is sufficient to motivate a demand for equal concern and respect,"[42] he defends "distinct principles of distributive justice applicable only within the national context."[43] In particular, he argues that "a concern for specifically economic egalitarianism is only morally required within the context of a domestic legal system,"[44] where "distinct burdens of justification" apply "between individuals who share liability to the coercive power of the state."[45] He claims that it is only in the "search for the justification of state coercion" that "egalitarian distributive justice becomes relevant."[46]

Although Blake seeks to distinguish the domestic context from the international context based on the presence of state coercion, his suggestion that we focus on state coercion does not distinguish the prospective immigrant coerced by our immigration laws from incumbent residents. After all, we exclude prospective immigrants through the use or threat of force applied by the state. In this sense, all aliens are subject to exclusion under the immigration laws enforced by our state, and they may demand that we justify this coercive exclusion within a framework of equal concern and respect for all.

Blake recognizes this problem, but he asserts that "each distinct form of coercion requires a distinct form of justification."[47] Without elaborating, he claims that the justification that we owe to a prospective immigrant "would be significantly different from that offered to a present member for the web of legal coercion within which she currently lives" and that only inequality among "current" members of our society "gives rise to a legitimate concern for relative deprivation."[48] This limit on the justification owed the prospective immigrant seems at odds with Blake's broad claim that "Rawls's . . . theory of justice might profitably be viewed as a theory by which the coercive force of the state might be justified to free and equal persons who have a prima facie moral entitlement to be free from *all* coercion."[49] Blake does not qualify this claim based on the nature or the scope of the coercion to be justified. His treatment of immigration begs the question: Why should the prospective immigrant accept a justification for our immigration laws that does not offer the alien the equal concern embodied in the Rawlsian original position, including a concern for relative deprivation?

It is unclear why we should limit our concern for relative deprivation to those currently living within our "web of legal coercion." If the claim is that prospective immigrants are burdened in only a minor way by our immigration laws, which therefore require little justification, then this empirical claim is questionable, given the significant harm suffered by those excluded from our labor market. Although prospective immigrants do not currently live under all our laws, this fact does not diminish the coercion they suffer and the costs they bear under our immigration laws. This fact may change the law in question that requires justification, but it should not change what counts as a justification. That is, a defense of our immigration laws must give the aliens coerced by our state the same equal concern extended to citizens coerced by our state, including a concern for relative deprivation.

Even if we grant Blake's claim that one must live within our web of coercive laws to be entitled to a concern for relative deprivation, we must extend such concern to the unauthorized immigrant who also lives within this web. If we seek to deport the unauthorized immigrant as a means of enforcing our immigration laws, for example, then the immigrant may demand that we justify those laws in terms that reflect concern for the relative deprivation that we impose through those laws. This right to distributive justice may well block deportation in the case of an immigrant excludable at the border in the absence of such a right.

Yet it seems perverse and unfair to give the unauthorized immigrant a right to distributive justice that we do not extend to the prospective immigrant who obediently complies with our immigration laws. Such a stance invites prospective immigrants to enter illegally so that they may obtain the right to distributive justice that we grant to immigration lawbreakers. On the other hand, if we cite the unauthorized immigrant's violation of our immigration laws as the reason to deny that immigrant a right to distributive justice, then how are we to respond to that immigrant's demand that we justify those immigration laws first? After all, we owe even criminals a justification for the laws we invoke to punish them, and Blake agrees that "a concern for relative deprivation" is relevant in such a demand for justification.[50]

Collective Self-Governance

If we deny the unauthorized immigrant a right to distributive justice in the justification of our immigration laws, then we must be requiring something more than simply living under our web of coercive laws to generate such a right. One response to this problem might be to distinguish both prospective and unauthorized immigrants from citizens by pointing to some other feature of citizens. Thomas Nagel, for example, suggests that "the objection to arbitrary inequalities" arises only among "fellow participants in a collective enterprise of coercively imposed legal and political institutions that generates such arbitrary inequalities."[51] He claims that "it is only from such a system, and from our fellow members through its institutions, that we can claim a right to democracy, equal citizenship, nondiscrimination, equality of opportunity, and the amelioration through public policy of unfairness in the distribution of social and economic goods."[52] Similarly, Stephen Macedo asserts that we should confine "the extensive obligation of distributive justice to self-governing and self-responsible political communities: peoples who share a common political life and who exercise extensive authority over one another."[53]

Like Blake, Nagel notes that a regime's "requirements claim our active cooperation, and this cannot be legitimately done without justification."[54] By participation in such a collective enterprise, however, Nagel means more than mere cooperation through obedience. The law-abiding prospective immigrant, after all, cooperates with us by complying with our immigration laws. Nagel stresses that "we are both putative joint authors of the coercively imposed system, and subject to its norms, i.e., expected to accept their authority."[55] Prospective and unauthorized immigrants are not putative joint authors of our immigration laws. Furthermore, Nagel claims, "the laws are not imposed in their name, nor are they asked to accept and uphold those laws."[56]

It is obscure, however, in what sense prospective immigrants are not "asked to accept and uphold those laws," given that we threaten criminal penalties for aliens who enter illegally.[57] Nagel's claim would come as a surprise to the unauthorized immigrant sentenced to imprisonment for violating our immigration laws. If we do not ask immigrants to "accept and uphold" these laws, then why do we punish violators? It is certainly difficult to perceive any respect in which we do not ask aliens to "accept and uphold" our immigration policies, given the way that we treat violators under our laws and in our public discourse, which seems to regard unauthorized immigrants simply as lawbreakers deserving of punishment.

Furthermore, Nagel's observation that our immigration laws "are not imposed in their name" merely begs the question of whether we *should* instead impose immigration laws that we can justify in the name of *all* those affected. His observation provides no persuasive defense for immigration laws that are too restrictive to be justified in such terms. If Nagel intends to cite our failure to give equal consideration to the interests of prospective immigrants as a defense for immigration laws that fail to give their interests equal consideration, then his reasoning would seem to prove too much.

Consider a society that permits slavery. Suppose it seeks to defend its laws by noting that the slaves do not participate in that society's collective enterprise of self-governance and are thus not "putative joint authors of the coercively imposed system," adding that "the laws are not imposed in their name." We would not find this proposed justification persuasive, precisely because the very fact that the laws exclude them from participation and are *not* imposed in their name is a reason to deem them unjust. Thus, a person's participation in the collective enterprise of self-governance as a putative joint author of the "coercively imposed system" cannot be a necessary condition for that person's right to distributive justice in that system. Therefore, it would not be an adequate defense of guest worker programs, for example, to declare that guest workers are not putative joint authors of the "coercively imposed system."

If we reject the proposed defense of slavery on the ground that the exclusion of slaves from political participation and from the sphere of equal concern is unjust and a violation of human rights, then we beg the question of whether restrictive immigration laws are also unjust because they exclude both prospective and unauthorized immigrants from full participation in our society. Before we cite participation in self-governance as a basis for the right to distributive justice, we must first demonstrate that the restrictions we impose on this participation, including immigration restrictions, are themselves justified. The implicit assumption is that we are justified in discounting the welfare of prospective immigrants when we formulate our immigration laws.[58] This proposed justification for our immigration laws would suffer from circular reasoning if it ultimately relies on an assumption that these laws are just.

Reciprocity

In an effort to avoid such objections to Nagel's theory, Sangiovanni attempts to defend obligations of distributive justice that are limited to residents of the same state without requiring "the 'state' (or for that matter any of its officials) taking a certain kind of attitude toward us."[59] For Sangiovanni, what matters instead is "reciprocity among those who support and maintain the state's capacity to provide the basic collective goods necessary to protect us from physical attack and to maintain . . . a stable system of property rights."[60] This reciprocity applies among "citizens and residents" of a state, who "maintain the state through taxation, through participation in . . . political activity, and through simple compliance" with the state's laws.[61]

This theory of reciprocity, however, does not provide much of a defense of restrictive immigration laws. Like Blake's theory based on coercion, a theory based on reciprocity does not distinguish the unauthorized immigrant from the slave, as both would be residents entitled to distributive justice. After all, laws can exclude both residents from the electorate and thus from voting, one form of political participation. The unauthorized immigrant may pay taxes and generally obey most laws, as other residents do. Most residents, after all, will violate some laws, such as speed limits. Furthermore, even the law-abiding prospective immigrant supports the state through compliance with the state's immigration laws. Do these forms of support for the state allow unauthorized or prospective immigrants to raise objections to the relative deprivation imposed on them by the state's immigration laws? If not, then why not?

Ultimately, Sangiovanni does not offer a persuasive reason to limit the requirements imposed by "equality as a demand of justice" to "fellow citizens or residents."[62] He asserts that the parties behind the Rawlsian "veil of ignorance should be citizens and residents," because "those who have submitted themselves to a system of laws and social rules in ways necessary to sustain our life as citizens, producers, and biological beings are owed a fair return for what those who have benefitted from their submission have received."[63] If this logic is the rationale for inclusion in the Rawlsian original position, however, then why not include the aliens abroad who sustain the status quo through their compliance with our immigration laws? Those aliens would be making as much of a contribution as citizens who "are able but unwilling to work," who Sangiovanni says are "contributing to the maintenance of the state" as long as "they continue to comply with the laws" and "continue to pay taxes, *assuming they have any to pay*."[64] One could say the same of aliens abroad who comply with our immigration laws and owe us no taxes.

Indeed, if the basis for the egalitarian claim to distributive justice is the way in which anyone's enjoyment of "social advantages" inevitably "depends on the contributions of others,"[65] as Sangiovanni suggests, then why not include everyone who participates in the world economy and thereby contributes to our affluence? Why privilege those who happen to contribute to our affluence by supporting our state? Sangiovanni asserts that this type of contribution is "more fundamental than mutual contribution to economic production,"[66] but his assertion begs the question: Why should the form of the contribution rather than the magnitude of the contribution matter? After all, an alien abroad who supplies a resource essential to our standard of living (like oil, for example) may make a greater contribution to our affluence than a relatively unskilled citizen who pays little in taxes. Why should the citizen who contributes less have a greater claim to distributive justice than the alien abroad who contributes more?

Involuntary Residence

We might distinguish all immigrants from natives on the ground that they seek to associate with us voluntarily whereas natives are born into our society and have no choice. Nagel, for example, stresses "the contingency of involuntary rather than voluntary association," claiming that "an institution that one has no choice about joining must offer terms of membership that meet a higher standard" than voluntary associations.[67] Similarly, Joseph Heath notes that "being born into society is a *circumstance*, while moving into one is a *choice*,"[68] arguing that "involuntarily incurred obligations must meet a much higher standard in order to be considered binding."[69] In particular, Heath claims that "the conditions under which immigrants secure admittance . . . are not involuntary," and therefore, "the strict criterion of equality . . . need not apply."[70]

This distinction would allow us to justify not only laws discriminating against unauthorized or prospective immigrants but also nativist laws that fail to extend equal concern to *legal* immigrants *after* admission. This nativist theory of distributive justice favors the interests of natives and discounts the interests of immigrants. Like the cosmopolitan theory of distributive justice, this nativist theory can provide a normative criterion that is independent of our admission policies and thus avoids the circularity that underlies the immigration paradox. As we saw, this nativist perspective suggests guest worker programs as the optimal immigration policies for relatively unskilled aliens.

The welfare objective that is consistent with liberal ideals, however, is cosmopolitan rather than nativist. The nativist theory turns liberalism on its head insofar as it entitles natives in rich countries to advantages based on immutable circumstances of birth. "We do not deserve to have been born into a particular society any more than we deserve to have been born into a particular family," Nagel concedes, yet he maintains that only natives enjoy a presumption against arbitrary inequality, "so an arbitrary distinction is responsible for the scope of the presumption against arbitrariness."[71] This suggestion seems to fly in the face of reality when those born in rich countries cite the circumstances of their birth as if it were some sort of disadvantage justifying privileges not extended to those born in poor countries who seek to move "voluntarily" into those rich countries. After all, those born into poor countries involuntarily incur poverty and the legal obligation to comply with the immigration laws of rich countries. Given those realities, why not impose the same standard of distributive justice to bind prospective immigrants under our immigration laws as we apply to natives under other laws? A view more sensitive to social, legal, and economic realities would recognize the claims of prospective immigrants based on all the burdens they have involuntarily incurred.

The claims advanced by Nagel and Heath assume that natives are not free to emigrate and therefore reside involuntarily in their country of origin. They may base their assumption on a realistic evaluation of the feasibility of emigration under current conditions. Insofar as they base this assumption on the immigration barriers raised by other countries, however, they make our right to distributive justice curiously contingent on the immigration policies of other countries. If another country opens its borders to some, most, or all prospective migrants from our country, do those who are free to emigrate thereby become voluntary residents who are therefore not entitled to distributive justice?

Nagel and Heath may invoke not only legal barriers to migration but also those barriers raised in practice by the social or economic costs of migration for the individual migrant. Heath, for example, suggests that "the costs associated with emigration are so high that nationality is *de facto* involuntary," conceding that "the distinction between voluntary and involuntary is determined by some notion of which options an individual could *reasonably* be expected to exercise."[72] Often, however, these costs are quite low, as when a native of the United States contemplates migration to Canada, or when a native of Australia contemplates migration to New Zealand. If such emigration is quite easy for the native, then does this option undermine that native's claim to distributive justice? Furthermore, once we recognize that the difference between "involuntary" residence and "voluntary" migration is not only a matter of degree but also a question of what options we should deem "reasonable," then the claims advanced by Nagel and Heath beg the question: Should we regard residence in a poor country to be so costly as to make it unreasonable for us to expect the prospective migrant to refrain from migration to a rich country?

The Absence of a Cosmopolitan State

Macedo rejects claims of cosmopolitan distributive justice, finding it "hard to understand the reasonableness of making people responsible for the welfare of others without also making them responsible for their governance."[73] "Cosmopolitan distributive justice," he concludes, "makes no sense absent a cosmopolitan state."[74] The absence of a cosmopolitan state, however, merely restricts the set of instruments at our disposal with which to further the cause of global distributive justice. That absence hardly justifies our failure to consider global distributive justice when we *do* have control over matters, such as our own immigration policies, that affect the distribution of opportunities for people all over the world.

Thus, even if we assume that the absence of a cosmopolitan state implies some limits on our obligations of distributive justice, this absence would not justify immigration restrictions that neglect principles of global distributive justice.[75] After all, the admission of any given set of immigrants *would* make us "responsible for their governance" as well as responsible for their welfare. Upon joining our society, the immigrant could agree to the same terms of the social contract as the native born into our society. Why should our inability to govern them prior to admission justify our failure to consider global distributive justice in the admission decision, as long as we can govern them after admission?

Perhaps the concern is that immigrants may not have paid their fair share of tax revenues and could thereby unfairly exploit the public treasury in the country of immigration. Heath, for example, worries that "if states lifted immigration controls in the current global context, they would open themselves up to a variety of forms of harmful predation."[76] "No welfare state could survive," he notes, "if people chose to spend their childhood and retirement in a welfare state, yet their working lives in a low-taxation state with minimal public services."[77] These concerns, however, only justify policy responses tailored to those specific concerns, not general restrictions on immigration. We might address such concerns, for example, with fiscal policies that impose appropriate conditions on immigration. To ensure that immigrants do not unfairly drain the public treasury, we might restrict the access that immigrants enjoy to the particular public entitlements raising such concerns, for example, or impose special taxes on immigrants as a form of admission fee in appropriate cases. These policies would be less restrictive than immigration restrictions that exclude the prospective immigrant from our country entirely and thereby needlessly destroy gains from trade in the labor market. More important, any such concern would seem to raise questions only regarding the particular policies that could be justified within a framework of equal concern. Fiscal concerns would not seem to provide much of a reason to question the basic premise that any law is morally justified only if its rationale extends equal concern to all those affected, including a concern for relative deprivation.

We might say the same regarding suggestions that liberal immigration policies would pose various other problems. For example, Heath worries about the possibility that liberal immigration would undermine the incentives for "the provision of public goods for future generations, by such measures as encouraging a high rate of savings, controlling public debt, preventing long-term environmental degradation, [and] implementing population control measures."[78] Rawls expresses similar concerns, worrying that people may be tempted to "make up for their irresponsibility in caring for their land and its natural resources . . . by migrating into other people's territory."[79] If Heath and Rawls are worried about the incentives to invest in local public goods in countries of emigration, then two considerations suggest that their concerns provide little support for immigration restrictions.

First, we should recognize that it is entirely appropriate for a country of emigration to take future emigration into account in deciding how much to invest in local public goods. Insofar as emigration implies a smaller population in the future than would otherwise exist, the benefits derived from a local public good will be smaller, and a reduced investment in such a good would be socially optimal. A legitimate concern arises only if the prospect of future emigration leads some residents in the country of emigration to withdraw support for even this optimal level of investment because they anticipate their own future emigration.

Second, even if the prospect of emigration distorts investment below the optimal level, there are probably better policy responses available to the country of immigration than immigration restrictions. If the country of immigration is actually concerned about local public goods in countries of emigration, then the country of immigration can always use its jurisdiction over immigrants to collect tax revenue from them to finance subsidies for investments in public goods in countries of emigration. Such subsidies would be better than the exclusion of prospective immigrants insofar as a policy of exclusion needlessly destroys gains from trade in the labor market.

Heath may also be worried about incentives to invest in public goods in the country of *immigration*. Immigrants may congest local public goods and thereby reduce the return that natives enjoy on their investment in these public goods. Again, these concerns arise even within a framework of distributive justice for all, and we could address these concerns through measures more narrowly tailored than general immigration restrictions. We could, for example, charge immigrants an appropriate fee for access to any public good subject to congestion without imposing other immigration restrictions. Such fees can internalize negative externalities from immigration, deter inefficient immigration, and compensate natives for any congestion of local public goods arising from immigration. We can weigh all of these concerns against the claims of the immigrant in deciding what policy responses are appropriate.

After all, similar concerns also arise within a society in the absence of any international migration. We may worry that redistribution from the rich to the poor, for example, undermines the incentives of poor families to save or to have fewer children. I do not deny that analogous problems may arise with liberal immigration policies. My only claim is that our policy response to these concerns in the immigration context should extend equal concern to all those affected, just as our policy response to similar concerns in the domestic context should be based on equal concern. If we understand in the domestic context that it is unfair for a native born into a large and poor family to suffer as a result of circumstances beyond that person's control, for example, then we should also understand in the immigration context that it is unfair for an alien born into a poor and populous country to suffer as a result of similar circumstances. I have suggested that the attempts by some liberal theorists and philosophers to distinguish immigration policies from laws in the domestic context in this regard are all ultimately question-begging.

Political Feasibility and the Second Best

I have suggested that liberal ideals require a global view of distributive justice, and I have outlined critiques of some of the alternative conceptions of justice advanced by critics of this cosmopolitan perspective. I conclude that considerations of global justice militate in favor of liberalized migration. Considerations of justice suggest that liberal states should seek to liberalize their immigration policies, thereby reducing global inequalities in economic opportunity. It is incumbent upon liberal states to pursue such liberalizing reforms if they are to remain faithful to the egalitarian ideals that they espouse.

Given the failure of most citizens to adopt this cosmopolitan perspective, however, cosmopolitan liberals face a constraint of political feasibility that prevents realization of all their ideals. As a matter of political reality, the interests of citizens have in fact played a dominant role in the public debate over immigration policies. Any national government, including that of the United States, will likely continue to deem the promotion of the interests of its own citizens to be the paramount objective of its immigration policies. This feature of the real world may impose a constraint on the set of policy alternatives open to us as a practical matter.

The cosmopolitan liberal would prefer that aliens have access to our labor market and ready access to public benefits and to citizenship. As a matter of political reality, however, incumbent citizens are unlikely to admit relatively unskilled aliens under those generous conditions in the numbers that cosmopolitan ideals would require, given the fiscal burden that those liberal policies would entail. As long as citizens are limited in their willingness to bear this burden, they are likely to restrict alien access to immigrant visas.

The self-interest of citizens will inevitably impose constraints of political feasibility on the availability of immigrant visas. These constraints are likely to exclude many relatively unskilled aliens from labor markets in wealthy countries unless these aliens are willing to immigrate illegally or have access to guest worker visas. Given these constraints, cosmopolitan liberals face a tradeoff: significantly liberalized access to our labor markets for relatively unskilled alien workers will likely require some restrictions on access to public benefits and citizenship to have a realistic chance of enactment.[80] Under these circumstances, guest worker programs may represent the only alternative to exclusion for many aliens.

If so, then cosmopolitan liberals must settle for second-best policies that fall short of their ideals. For many relatively unskilled alien workers, guest worker programs may be the best one can achieve under current circumstances. These programs may be incompatible with liberal ideals, but as Carens and others have argued, the exclusion of aliens is also incompatible with these ideals. If political realities require us to choose between these two departures from our liberal ideals, then how can we justify the choice that inflicts the greater harm on the alien as well as on natives? Exclusion is the more costly response for both natives and aliens, because it excludes aliens not only from our public benefits but also from our labor market and thereby sacrifices the gains that we and they would otherwise derive from trade in that market.

James Woodward notes that if we act against a "background of non-ideal institutions and behaviour" in a world "in which large numbers of people and institutions fail to do what justice requires," we may "acquire obligations which are different from those [we] would acquire under more perfectly just institutional arrangements."[81] In Woodward's formulation of the theory of the second best, "It is not in general a defensible moral principle that if it is obligatory (or even a good thing) to do P under ideal, utopian circumstances, then it is also obligatory (or even a good thing) to do P under the actual circumstances, no matter how far they may differ from the ideal."[82] Woodward advances this claim in defense of immigration restrictions, but as we have seen, they could more plausibly justify restrictions on alien access to public benefits and to citizenship. Indeed, Woodward himself notes that "it is far from obvious that it would be wrong . . . to limit eligibility for social welfare programmes to citizens or long-term residents, if failure to do so would jeopardize the continued existence of such programmes."[83] We might say the same about restrictions on alien access to public benefits and citizenship if these restrictions are necessary to make politically feasible the alien's access to our labor market and the alien's admission in the first place.

These second-best arguments require us to rank two nonideal alternatives, both of which fall short of our moral ideals. If we seek to maximize an appropriate measure of global economic welfare, taking not only global wealth but also its distribution into account, then a guest worker program represents the lesser of two evils when compared with the alternative of exclusion. Exclusion not only decreases global wealth but also worsens its distribution, whereas a guest worker program would improve social welfare on both counts by increasing labor mobility.[84]

In this sense, from a consequentialist perspective that extends equal concern to aliens and natives, expanded guest worker programs represent an improvement over the status quo alternative of exclusion.[85] Therefore, I suggest, cosmopolitan liberals should support liberalizing reforms that include guest worker programs, even while seeking the broadest rights possible for aliens within the constraints of political feasibility. For example, although past guest worker programs tied each guest worker to a specific employer, there is no need for such programs to limit the worker's mobility in this way in the future. Freedom to leave an employer and to take employment elsewhere would give workers greater power to assert their rights against employers and thus prevent abuses, without either destroying the economic gains that natives enjoy from employing alien workers or generating a fiscal burden. Indeed, cosmopolitan liberals should seek to give the guest worker full mobility, including the ability to move freely among various sectors of the economy.[86] While it would be a mistake to pretend that any guest worker program is ideal from a liberal perspective, it would also be a mistake to sacrifice worthwhile reforms because they fall short of the ideal.

Chapter 5

What Is an Economic Migrant? Europe's New Borders and the Politics of Classification

Karolina Szmagalska-Follis

In Contradiction: Economics, Security, and Human Rights

After the United States–Mexico border, the second longest border between a poor and an affluent region is the eastern external boundary of the European Union.[1] This essay discusses the selective permeability of this border, drawing on a larger study of the emergence of a new border regime between Poland and Ukraine following the 2004 expansion of the European Union. In 2005–2006 I conducted twelve months months of field research in Poland and Ukraine, among border guards and immigration officials as well as in migrant communities and civil society organizations. As a participant-observer of cross-border human traffic, I gathered vernacular accounts of crossing, policing, and subverting the border. I relied on historical sources, legal acts, policy handbooks, official statements, and independent reports to situate the accounts I collected within the larger context of "building Europe" east of the former Iron Curtain.[2]

It merits emphasizing that the sheer fact of Poland's entry into the European Union did not result in any sharp increase in the numbers of migrants coming into the country. Since 2000 it has oscillated between three hundred thousand and five hundred thousand, depending on who is counting and how.[3] But what did change is how migrants entering Poland are classified, assigned legal status, and represented in the public discourse. Drawing on fieldwork among Polish immigration officials whose job of rejecting and admitting foreigners into Poland has become intensely complex in the aftermath of E.U. expansion, I ask what is the place, in these fraught politics of classification, of the capacious category "economic migrant."

Who are economic migrants in the "new" Europe? Which economic opportunities can they take advantage of? Which are foreclosed, and for whom? These questions are made particularly urgent by the fact that the once sharp categorical distinction between economic migrants and refugees is growing increasingly blurred. For most of postwar European history, and especially in the aftermath of the 1951 Geneva Convention Relating to the Status of Refugees, persons fleeing political crises and seeking protection abroad were defined as refugees, while those migrating voluntarily in pursuit of better earnings were characterized as economic migrants.[4] Today, besides wars, among the most formidable hardships that trigger refugee flows are poverty, natural and man-made disasters, and prolonged low-intensity conflict. The experience of persons displaced under such conditions increasingly defies the distinction between economic migration and migration to seek political refuge. Their legal status is also ambiguous. But the restrictive asylum reforms of the past decade that seek to reduce to a minimum the numbers of refugees admitted to E.U. territory have led to the practical narrowing of the definition of the refugee and to the dismissal of the majority of asylum seekers precisely as "economic migrants," in practice persons at the mercy of the state, ineligible for international protection.[5]

If "third-country nationals" arriving from conflict-ridden and impoverished regions like the Caucasus and parts of Central Asia are increasingly unlikely to be legally recognized as refugees, can they take advantage of any alternative paths? Or will they be permanently sorted out and barred from access to European territories and resources, as the European Union as a whole and member states individually develop selective immigration policies that privilege some sending countries over others? As Sandra Lavenex observed, "At the national level, the claims for restrictive asylum reforms and internal security are linked through a fear of welfare losses and a spread of racism and xenophobia. Within the European Union, the need to cooperate in asylum matters has been presented from the outset as a necessary compensation for the abolition of internal border controls in the single market with its associated 'dangers' for internal security."[6]

Thus claims of internal and international security converge on the figures of the immigrant and refugee, and they lend legitimacy to the classificatory system that distributes categories of migrant legality.[7] These claims proved to be immensely versatile, responding to the fears of European constituencies over international crime, terrorism, drug trafficking, and job and welfare losses in the aftermath of the opening of internal borders.

It was in this context that asylum reform became an issue of border control, not of human rights. With the imperative to "fix" the system of admitting foreigners by, among other efforts, curtailing the "abuse of asylum" that was decried in Europe in the 1990s, the issue of refugees receded as a humanitarian concern and resurfaced as a matter of national and E.U. security. This new, security-driven approach to asylum not only obfuscates complex and ambiguous realities of human mobility, where persecution, victimhood, suffering, and voluntary versus forced departure are all relative and contested matters.[8] It is also a harbinger of a new politics of access and exclusion, especially in places like Poland, where state authorities are attempting to develop an immigration policy for the first time in the history of a nation that for centuries experienced mostly emigration. This policy must at once conform to E.U. security standards, respect the state's human rights commitments, and respond to national economic needs (affected, among other factors, by massive departures of Poles seeking employment elsewhere in the European Union). Driven by these conflicting imperatives, the emerging approach to foreigners in Poland tends toward the lowest common denominator, that is, the connected assumptions that (a) asylum seekers are a suspect group of whom the majority are seeking to exploit the system while only the slim minority are the "truly" suffering deserving of political recognition extended via the granting of asylum; and (b) economic migrants are needed on the local market but they ought not to present security or integration challenges or drain the scarce resources of the state.

These assumptions are reinforced on the one hand by anti-Muslim sentiments radiating via the media from countries of the "old" European Union and on the other by the contemporary and historical representations of Poles abroad as "the good immigrants," self-reliant, hard-working, often victimized, but minimally burdensome to their hosts. According to some policy makers and media, there is a lesson to be learned from "old" Europe's immigration woes, or from what one Polish Interior Ministry official responsible for immigration policy described as the "French mistakes with the Arabs and the German mistakes with the Turks."[9] Judging from this official's rather typical comments on the Muslim's "inability to assimilate,"

that lesson seems to be "don't admit too many, avoid the 'culturally different' and make sure that in the end they leave."

Against this background, the bureaucracy of legal status and the funnel-
ing of people into respective legal and administrative pipelines emerge not
as neutral efforts to order human flows but as inherently political interventions that actively shape the contested landscape of immigration in Europe.
Zygmunt Bauman notes that the sole existential mode of the ubiquitous
boundaries that divide our world into the included and the rejected is the
"incessant *activity* of separation."[10] In this vein, I am concerned here with
the practices and tools for the sorting out of migrant persons, and with the
precarious condition of people who are "classified out."

The sorting unfolds in institutional contexts that form the interconnected nodes of the border regime. One such node is the Warsaw Aliens
Bureau, the governmental authority coordinating the legalization of foreign
citizens in Poland and representing the first instance in asylum procedures.[11] When I met with the head of the bureau in the fall of 2005, he
defended the high rate of asylum claim rejections on the grounds that "we
cannot accept every economic migrant who just wants a better life and just
waits for the opportunity to go farther west, to Germany or elsewhere in
Europe." He said further:

> Poland recognizes as many refugees, as many persons, in the course
> of the administrative procedure we conduct, convince us that they
> fulfill the requirements stemming from the Geneva Convention.
> That they are individually persecuted because of race, religion, na-
> tionality, or political views. This is the first thing. The second thing
> is that indeed we receive many, compared to other European Union
> countries, Russian-speaking candidates for refugees, but in great
> majority these people are *classic economic migrants* [klasyczni mi-
> granci ekonomiczni]. This means that they left their own country
> primarily because of the economic situation in that part, where they
> . . . [hesitation] for example in the Russian Federation from where
> they originate.

This official's use of the notion of "classic economic migrants" deserves
a closer look. In applying it to persons who have been denied recognition
as victims of persecution, he symbolically displaces them from the community of refugees and characterizes their journey across borders as an act of

choice rather than necessity. He delegitimizes them as potential beneficiaries of the asylum system, which in theory is animated primarily by human rights concerns.[12] Instead the "Russian-speaking candidates for refugees" (and, indeed, non-Russian-speaking candidates as well) are recast as voluntary migrants, and as such subject to the policies and politics of border security and economic immigration. Rhetoric corresponds to practice—failed asylum seekers lose the right to accommodation in refugee centers, and in some circumstances can be detained and deported even while their appeals are pending.[13] No longer assumed to be victims in need of protection, these third-country nationals instantly become undesirable and thus deportable. Even if what pushed them to leave home were indeed primarily economic and not safety needs, they are not the people who would be given the chance to meet the sizable demand for immigrant labor in Poland. For them, the asylum pipeline is the only chance to be legally admitted into Polish/E.U. territory, but when it fails, it is supposed to shoot them right back out (a perverse effect indeed when we note that one role of the sorting machinery is to guard against the abuse of human rights provisions). Meanwhile economic migrants from Ukraine (and to a lesser extent Belarus) are in the ideal structural position to meet the labor market's demand for immigrant workers.

The creation of the common "area of freedom, security, and justice," first declared as the European Union's goal in the Treaty of Amsterdam (1997), accelerated the abolition of checks on internal borders between member states and the reinforcement of external E.U. borders that had been planned as part of the Schengen Accords since the 1980s.[14] The opening of internal borders to flows of goods, people, and capital went hand in hand with what Peter Andreas called the European Union–wide "pooling of sovereignty"[15] in matters of internal security. New modes of policing were introduced (for example, enhanced policing of the interior, increased border guard powers at external borders, international police cooperation) that were to compensate for the opening of borders.[16] Asylum and immigration were key areas affected by this rebordering. The freedom of movement within Europe had been designed for Europeans. But with internal borders open, third-country nationals admitted to one E.U. country could travel to another just as easily as citizens. This caused a great deal of anxiety in Western Europe on the eve of expanding the Union eastward. Politicians, the media, and especially representatives of immigration-weary constituencies were asking if the new members were fit to defend and protect the external boundaries of Europe.[17] Or would they be the weak link, allowing an uncontrolled influx of criminal and illegal immigrants into E.U. territory? Such fears, grounded as they were in xenophobia and a wider anti-enlargement sentiment, were not entirely baseless. In Poland the eastern borders after 1989 became an easy gateway chiefly for citizens of the former Soviet Union wishing to take advantage (primarily as petty traders and seasonal workers) of the opportunities of Poland's emerging capitalist economy, or to attempt an unauthorized westward crossing via Poland into Germany.[18] This generally unobstructed traffic where small and large contraband was shuttled daily across the border between Poland and Ukraine, Belarus, Lithuania, and Russia's Kaliningrad District was a radical change after decades of maintaining a near-impermeable boundary between the Soviet Union and its western neighbors. For the impoverished inhabitants of eastern Poland and Western Ukraine, where I did fieldwork, this largely illicit but anemically policed traffic provided a source of livelihood, vital especially in the first decade of the postsocialist economic transition. But within the hegemonic discourse of systemic transition such flows were framed as a manifestation of disorder rife with corruption and lawlessness. They had to be curbed, if not entirely eliminated, if Poland was to become an E.U. member. During the period of preparing for accession the securing of borders emerged as a complex problem, requiring an ever-expanding body of professional expertise and involving the adjustment of laws, imposition of visa requirements, investment in high-tech border surveillance and the retraining of border guards for new tasks and responsibilities.[19] Ensuring that foreigners entering Poland—be they short-term visitors, immigrants, exchange students, or asylum seekers—do so in an orderly and controlled manner was a critical and contested part of the rebordering endeavor. Critical, because tight borders were a condition of E.U. entry; contested, because the idea of raising a new wall between Poland and Ukraine undermined mutually beneficial cross-border contacts and thus triggered protests on both sides.

At its core, the European Union's "area of freedom, security, and justice" is an entire system of laws and regulations intended to demarcate political entities, police inclusion and exclusion, sense of belonging, and citizenship itself. It is a border regime of greater complexity than for example the Cold War division between East and West Germany. But like the *Grenzregime* in John Borneman's analysis of life in bisected Berlin, it organizes human experience in ways both mundane and profound.[20] The laws, regulations, and bureaucratic arrangements of the new European "area of freedom, security, and justice" are designed to order and regulate heterogeneous forms of human and other traffic across international boundaries. Ostensibly animated by the ethos of open borders, E.U. national agents compensate for internal openness by constructing an intensely policed external borderline.[21]

To understand the new European border from an ethnographic vantage point is to abandon the certitude of territorial borders as clearly locatable political artifacts, markers of sovereignty, and privileged locations for the articulation of difference. The new borders are rather, as Chandran Kukathas argues in this volume, "complex systems of machinery" where the degrees of openness and the extent of permeability are determined along multiple axes. "Policy can . . . make borders more open and yet, at the same time, more closed. This is because policy can change the terms of entry in a number of different respects. It can vary the terms by specifying (i) what kinds of people may enter and what status they may hold on entering; (ii) how long they may stay; (iii) what qualifications or characteristics they must possess to enter; and (iv) what procedures they must follow to remain within a territory. Policy can also specify (v) the number of people admitted in various categories."[22]

If this selective and variable permeability is a key feature of contemporary borders, then this insight must also guide ethnography. Therefore borders ought to be conceptualized as key sites in a tentative, mutable, and situated regime, which proliferates the categories and regulations for the sorting out of people, things, and territory in Europe today. To account for rebordering is to attend to the specific places, agents, and practices whereby sorting is performed on a day-to-day basis. Third-country nationals arriving at the external gates of the European Union are assigned different types of legal status with or without the right to work, such as temporary visas, residence, subsidiary protection ("tolerated status"), or refugee status. For others, the border regime stipulates no legal status, and therefore no sanctioned way to be present within E.U. borders.

The Sorting Machine

Jarek's looks were far from the stereotype of a square bureaucrat. On a spring day in 2005, when he greeted me at the guarded entrance of the

Aliens Bureau, he was sporting a ponytail, jeans, and a T-shirt, and only the ID card with a magnetic stripe that he was wearing around his neck served as a reminder of the fact that he was actually working there, employed by the Polish state to facilitate the sorting of "true refugees" from those who, well, apparently only pretended to be ones.

Jarek agreed to meet with me in order to explain how the Aliens Bureau, or more precisely its Asylum Department, protects itself from bogus asylum claims and how it sorts truth from lies in the testimonies of asylum seekers who explain to the bureau's caseworkers the specific conditions that had forced them to flee their home countries in the Caucasus, Central and Southeast Asia, the Middle East, and Africa. Since 1991 Poland is a signatory to the Geneva Convention on the status of refugees, and in the course of its accession to the European Union (finally completed in 2004) it also embraced the Common Asylum System that harmonizes administering refugee status in the European Union. That policy affirms the Union's commitment to the Geneva Convention, but it also introduces measures designed to (a) reduce the overall numbers of asylum seekers in Europe and (b) to ensure that the burden of admitting them is distributed among all member states, including the new ones.[23]

The Geneva Convention defines a refugee as someone who, "owing to well-founded fear of being persecuted for reasons of race, religion, nationality, membership of a particular social group or political opinion, is outside the country of his nationality and is unable or, owing to such fear, is unwilling to avail himself of the protection of that country; or who, not having a nationality and being outside the country of his former habitual residence as a result of such events, is unable or, owing to such fear, is unwilling to return to it."[24] Of the approximately eight thousand people every year who file their asylum claims with the Warsaw Aliens Bureau, only about 5 percent are found to meet the Geneva criteria. Of the remaining applicants, approximately 40 percent receive (often as a result of an appeal) so-called tolerated status, that is, a form of subsidiary protection that protects them from deportation but grants no social benefits and no right to travel in the European Union.[25] The remaining applicants become "failed asylum seekers" whom the officials describe as "economic migrants" who are "simply searching for a better life." Having no access to legalization, they are either detained and deported to their countries of origin or—if they succeed in avoiding apprehension—disappear from the official radar and sink into a life of legal nonexistence in Poland or elsewhere in the European Union.

After greeting me at the door, Jarek took me upstairs to the smallish office where he and his team of five equally casually dressed colleagues (three men and two women) conduct their daily research on the situation in the non-European countries that generate refugees. They utilize vast resources of international Internet-based information services to answer detailed queries from caseworkers who interview asylum seekers whose applications are pending with the bureau. Everyone in the office holds an advanced university degree. There are three M.A.s in linguistics, one in ethnology, one in political science, and one in theology. All of the employees are well traveled and seem passionate about the countries they research. Languages spoken in the office include Russian, English, Ukrainian, Arabic, Spanish, French, and Georgian. At the time of my research the bureau's main object of interest was the situation in Chechnya, as approximately 90 percent of all persons seeking asylum in Poland came from there.[26] From their desks at the office the team members could compile detailed and up-to-date information on places and events in Grozny and vicinity, as well as in other places in Central Asia, the Caucasus, the Middle East, and Africa.[27] Their work yielded responses, as Jarek said, "that are precise down to the smallest detail, including local sports clubs, neighborhood stores and what one could buy there, restaurants, radio stations, neighbors, circumstances of particular raids, who was the chief of the village and what is the name of the street a person claims they lived on."

These data are then used in order to verify such details of asylum seeker testimonies as geographical locations, timelines of particular conflicts, armed attacks, kidnappings, and relations between different political factions or kinship groups. Ultimately, the data serve the cause of sifting what the officials regard as credible cases of individual persecution from those that will be dismissed as unfounded. "We know from experience," said Jarek, "that very many testimonies are simply made up." He explained that if applicants claim to be fleeing persecution, they should be able to provide verifiable information concerning who, and when and under what circumstances, has been a threat to them. Fleeing a situation that is not life threatening but merely difficult, whether on the account of war, political instability, or poverty, does not, he said, warrant international protection under the Geneva Convention. Moreover, echoing many of my other informants, Jarek added that Poland is not a wealthy country and does not have the resources to support refugees other than those who truly *had to*, not just *wanted to*, leave. ("There are five million Polish citizens who live in poverty," another official at the bureau said to me, "they are the ones deserving the state's care and interest before we extend it to foreigners.")[28]

The work of Jarek's office and the rationales behind it are emblematic of the larger conceptual basis that underpins contemporary approaches to third-country nationals in the expanded European Union. The discourses and practices of regulating immigration at the outer edges of Europe today are not about blind exclusion. Instead they depend on the construction, maintenance, and legitimation of a sharp distinction between voluntary and forced migration. Economic migrations are assumed to be voluntary, driven by a desire for a better life; only those migrants who were directly forced to leave their home countries can benefit from the privilege of asylum and the associated financial assistance that eases their entry into the new society.

The stakes of maintaining this distinction are high: Poland and other new member states located at the European Union's eastern edges must square their declared commitment to the protection of human rights with the imperative to guard the borders of the entire community against an "uncontrolled" influx of immigrants. To use Didier Fassin's terms, they must reconcile institutional compassion for the few recognized as legitimate victims of persecution with repression of the many assumed to be "merely" seeking an improved material standing.[29] National authorities do so in ways that are specific to local economic, social, and political contexts. But notwithstanding such particularities, they are all involved in policing the boundary between "genuine refugees," who will be offered the opportunity of legal inclusion, and presumably voluntary "economic migrants," who will not. Maintaining this boundary requires the production and sophisticated application of specialized knowledge, the task with which Jarek's team is charged. It is no accident that his unit is the youngest and best-educated one in the entire Aliens Bureau. As one of one of Jarek's bosses told me, "The foreigners don't like them. But they are in the avant-garde of the modern and truly European state administration."

Selective Permeability

As the case of Poland's eastern borders amply demonstrates, the refashioning of the national border into a supranational boundary does not happen seamlessly. Rather, it produces puzzling contradictions and dilemmas for those in charge of protecting and enforcing borders. The new external boundary of the European Union is administered by the Polish government and patrolled by Polish border guards who (as I document elsewhere), conceive of themselves first and foremost as keepers of the national territory.[30] Yet the new policing protocols that govern their work emphasize impermeability and firm restrictions on the entry of non-E.U. citizens. These protocols are grounded primarily in E.U. internal security concerns, especially in the imperative to curb and prevent illegal immigration. The need to embrace the larger E.U. border agenda created an awkward dilemma for Polish authorities: how to fulfill Polish commitment to maintaining a tight boundary without stifling the ongoing traffic between Poland and Ukraine that since the early 1990s has been all but the lifeblood of the border region, and that in recent years has been bringing into Poland the urgently needed migrants eager to work in agriculture and construction and to fill the growing demand in domestic jobs as maids, nannies, and caregivers.[31]

This dilemma pushed Polish authorities to simultaneously embrace and resist the rigid border agenda. As E.U. border administrators and enforcers, the government bureaucrats and rank-and-file border personnel must show efficacy in maintaining strict control over human traffic and preventing the influx of "undesirable aliens." They rely on cutting-edge surveillance technology (digital X-ray machines and thermal cameras for detecting illegal immigrants, fingerprint scanners and microscopes for detecting document forgeries) and on new legal categories (such as E.U. and non-E.U. citizen, asylum seeker, Schengen visa holder, and so on) in the relentless practice of watching, sorting, admitting, and disposing of foreigners. In so doing, they convey and perform their civilizational aptitude and competence in "European standards."

However, notwithstanding their role as protectors of shared E.U. territory, the guards are simultaneously in charge of administering and enforcing the national border. With this task, the priorities change. While the invincibility of external boundaries serves the political demands of integration and is an essential element of the sense of supranational cohesion carefully crafted by agents of integration in Warsaw and Brussels, it can be politically problematic and economically impractical on the ground. In Poland, the need for good relations with Ukraine is a long-standing dogma of foreign policy, based on the premise that drawing former Soviet republics closer to "Europe" is beneficial in that it weakens Russia's imperial claims. Closing off the border does not serve this end.

More important, overall economic growth and the exodus of two million Polish workers to Western Europe—after E.U. borders and labor markets were opened—increased the demand for cheap labor that has been emerging with post-1989 economic growth and that was not matched by local supply. Opening the European Union to migrant workers from outside the Union would have required a political decision that no one was eager to make. Politicians on the left and on the right (whatever those imprecise terms mean in Poland) worried that creating favorable conditions for the legal employment of foreigners would be both politically risky and technically challenging.[32] It would involve sanctioning the presence of third-country nationals and convincing the rest of the European community that these workers would not subsequently move farther west.

In the face of these challenges, the quotidian policing of boundaries, as I observed it during my fieldwork, entails keeping at bay immigrants and asylum seekers presumably headed for Western Europe, while cautiously admitting a steady flow of persons apparently seeking to enter the local labor market. Until December 2007, the document allowing most Ukrainian workers to enter Poland was a tourist visa.[33] Everybody—the guards, the consular officers, the Interior Ministry officials—knew that the Ukrainians presenting those visas were not tourists. Yet the unofficial policy has been, as the spokesman for one of the border guard units told me off the record, to "not make life difficult for them." Thus the purportedly tight border was undermined by its own agents, so that the precarious and unregulated labor market at a postsocialist frontier could stay alive. In this sense, the E.U. external border has been no "fortress Europe" or new Iron Curtain. Instead it has developed into a flexible tool operating based on political rationales that are calibrated behind the scenes by administrators at various levels and that determine the openings and foreclosures experienced by the people who cross it.

Conclusion: Desirable and Undesirable Economic Migrants

Access to low-paid jobs without the right to legal residence or social protections is the opening available in Poland to economic migrants from neighboring countries, especially Ukraine. The migrants participate in a highly structured migration circuit, following well-traveled routes and tapping into existing immigrant networks to find employment on farms, in construction, and as participants in what Saskia Sassen calls in this volume "the return of the serving class." These Ukrainian nannies, housekeepers, cooks, maids, and caregivers make it possible for Polish middle-class women to step away from their traditional duties of household maintenance and to engage instead in lifestyles revolving around professional activities.[34] The presence of these workers is well known, accepted, and even desired, even though their work has not been legalized and therefore their rights as laborers are not subject to state protection.[35] Poland's E.U. accession increased the demand for their work, and its December 2007 admission into the Schengen zone without checks on internal borders forced the first serious attempts to regulate this segment of the labor force.

These same jobs remain unavailable to economic migrants from farther away, notably to those who attempt to enter the European Union as asylum seekers and fail. Based on the assumption that they will not stay in Poland but will migrate farther west, thus undermining Poland's reputation as a capable protector of the E.U, border, the asylum seekers are prevented from crossing the border in the first place. Chechens, Afghanis, Pakistanis, and others are excluded from legal means of entry. Unlike the Ukrainians, they face often insurmountable expenses and intense scrutiny in their visa applications, and even if they manage to obtain a visa, they are often returned from the border on the grounds that they lack the means to finance their stay. The asylum process is their only opportunity to enter, save for an illegal crossing of the green border. Yet due to the extra surveillance and tremendous resources devoted to sorting "true refugees" from "economic migrants," few are allowed to stay. As far as those who clandestinely sneak across the border, as with all illegal crossings, it is impossible to say how many people actually pursue this option, given that—as Peter Andreas has shown in his analysis of the use of statistics by the U.S. Border Patrol—the official statistics capture only those who attempted to cross and failed.[36] Currently in Poland this number oscillates around fifteen hundred people annually and does not include those immigrants who were apprehended by the Ukrainian patrols.[37] Either way, failed asylum seekers and failed clandestine crossers meet in the same detention centers maintained by border authorities in Poland and Ukraine, where they await deportation or the results of their appeals.

As Verena Stolcke noted in her prescient analysis of the rhetoric of inclusion and exclusion that has risen in Europe since the 1970s, it is not quite accurate to describe anti-immigrant constituencies as racist. Rather, their contribution to the shameful history of prejudice and discrimination is a cultural essentialism that postulates "a propensity in human nature to reject strangers."[38] Stolcke shows that the construction of a radical opposition between nationals and foreign migrants relies on "a reified notion of bounded and distinct localized national-cultural identity and heritage that is employed to rationalize the call for restrictive immigration policies."[39] In postaccession Poland curious things are happening to this form of essentialism. An adherence to it is reflected for example in the remark by the head of the Aliens Bureau who expressed to me the view that "that there are things in the culture and psyche of the Chechen nation that just make it impossible for them to adapt to life in European society." But at the same time, the collective Polish experience of emigration to more affluent countries of Europe (and to the United States), with its ethos of hard work and pathos of underdog endurance, makes wholesale anti-immigrant arguments generally unpalatable and unpopular. Nonetheless, the stringent asylum policy and maintenance of a tight border trigger no protests and appear as wholly reasonable. Representing them as security devices partially accounts for their appeal. But equally important is the fact the border regime was implemented in ways that by and large didn't block traffic between Poland and Ukraine. This made it possible to view it not as directed against all migrants in general but rather as a tool for defending Europe from specifically those foreigners considered irredeemably other, possibly troublesome, and therefore undesirable. It is a particularly pernicious effect of the European Union's new border that those who are most energetically kept from entering are the ones whose human rights are often in the most dire need of protection.

As for the fact that economic migrants are needed west of the border, it appears that in the ongoing battle of contradictory imperatives that the immigration conundrum presents, one way out has been to agree that some foreigners are less foreign than others. "Those who easily adapt and whose culture is similar to ours will always be welcome," according to the same Interior Ministry official whose warnings against the French and German mistakes I cited at the start of this essay.[40] Ukrainians are the ones who fit the bill as white, Christian, and unthreatening non-E.U. Europeans. Chechens, Afghanis, Pakistanis, and others from beyond the continental boundaries don't meet the criterion of cultural proximity and therefore, unless they must be admitted under international law as human rights subjects and legalized as refugees, they will be excluded as a residual and disposable category, economic migrants beyond demand.

Epilogue: Some Human Consequences

The contradictions of the border regime created a system that is now in flux. As a result, economic migration is highly structured yet largely unregulated. In Poland, as elsewhere, abstaining from creating possibilities for legal employment while tolerating a vast so-called gray zone of unauthorized employment exacerbates the anxiety and determination in communities of actual and potential economic migrants.[41] This vulnerability is exploited by outlaw entrepreneurs and their abettors recruited among the locals and in the ranks of state functionaries. On the Polish-Ukrainian border, a vast scope of illicit cross-border transactions—from the trade in cheap tobacco to the buying and selling of women—relies on tacit complicity and active collusion between various groups that participate in the borderland economy.

Ira, a Ukrainian woman in her thirties who has been coming to Poland since 2000 and recently legalized her stay through marriage to a Polish citizen, offered the following account of illicit dealings on the border:

> *I:* When you come from Ukraine, there is a line. Sometimes you have to wait for three days. So, if you want to get in faster, you must pay.
>
> *K.:* Who do you pay?
>
> *I:* To the *mafiozy* [mobsters] who sit there and rip the money. They rip off everyone. They make this artificial line, the longer it gets, the more they can rip. Usually ten to fifteen dollars per person. So think about how much money this is, from so many people. From everyone in a *marshrutka* [minibus], eight people in each one.
>
> *K.:* What about the police?
>
> *I:* What do you think. The police are there the whole time. After you pay they take you to the gate and you cross. This [payment] is called *pod budke*, "to the booth."

The observation that foreigners without papers are vulnerable to abuse might seem so obvious as to appear banal. Indeed, it is not lost on E.U.

legislators who devise the large-scale frameworks for keeping immigrants at bay. Investigating and prosecuting such crimes is a large part of the Border Guard's mandate, and one of the key elements in the European Union's commitment to cooperation in the realm of internal security. The policing of such infringements as the smuggling and trafficking in people, drugs, and other goods is motivated as much by the rhetoric of the rule of law as it is by the political urgency of meeting the oft-cited "E.U. standards." In Poland in the early 2000s, showing efficacy in investigating and prosecuting organized infringements on the border was part of demonstrating preparedness for "joining Europe." The numbers of prosecutions and convictions in smuggling and trafficking cases have risen.[42] But even though statistics were showing an improved effectiveness of policing, the murky territory in the shadows of legality remained a fertile ground for maltreatment and exploitation. Persons I spoke to—especially young women traveling to Poland for work and young Ukrainian men working in Poland in construction—offered accounts of violence and shady dealings (for example, employers locking up workers, or mafia associates extorting a percentage of earnings from migrant workers).

Zina, a forty-three-year-old woman from a village near Ternopil, told me of being robbed at a bus terminal after she refused to voluntarily hand over three hundred zloty to the men who "protect" her cross-border bus route. She lost everything that she had earned during a three-month stint as a cleaning lady at multiple households in Poland. She returned with nothing to her husband and two teenage sons who had stayed back home.

Olena, twenty-five, told me about the time she got a job relabeling pickled vegetables that were past expiration date. She and a friend had to detach old labels and replace them with ones that carried a later date. They got locked up in the small factory for the night. They forfeited whatever income they might have earned while doing the job, and escaped through a window. Later, they avoided nonurban jobs, reasoning, rather naively, that getting enslaved and isolated is more likely in a scarcely populated rural area than in a town or city.

Zhenia, in his late twenties, who is from L'viv but lives in Poland without papers and alternates between renovation jobs and unloading produce at supermarkets, offered a story of a protracted argument with a private employer over pay. The employer, a well-heeled businessman with a large villa in a relatively wealthy Warsaw suburb, had hired Zhenia to rip out old tiles from his kitchen and bathroom. Zhenia was never told that the owner apparently intended to reuse the tiles and that they were supposed to be taken out intact. ("It's impossible, anyway," he said of the idea that all the tiles be unbroken). After seeing the outcome of the job, the businessman concluded that Zhenia had to pay, with his own wages, for the broken tiles. "He even started counting them," Zhenia said. The argument between the two men lasted for a few days, when Zhenia would show up, alone and with a friend, and demand pay. Finally, desperate, he contacted other friends, to whom he referred as friends with "position." For a cut of the recovered earnings, they threatened the employer with a beating, thus persuading him to pay. The man was reluctant to report them to the police; there are fines for employing illegal migrants. For Zhenia's friends it was a standard service they provide to their oft-cheated compatriots.

As long as Zina, Olena, Zhenia, and hundreds of thousands of others have at most a tourist visa legitimating their stay in Poland, the moves and transactions that they engage in must stay invisible to the gaze of the state. This means that if abuse and other problems ensue, they are rectified (or not) independently of the state's control. This underside of the new E.U. border regime is only beginning to be addressed. As of 2007, the Polish government was taking steps to legalize the status quo. It is now easier than at the time of my fieldwork to register citizens of Ukraine and Belarus for seasonal employment in Poland. They are allowed to enter the country on a visa and work legally for 180 days of the year. If they exceed their stay, they fall right back into legal limbo. Alternatively, at six-month intervals they can shuttle between work and home. Thus they never settle down and never need to be integrated—yet another characteristic of a desirable economic migrant.

PART II

Citizenship, Borders,
and Cultural Needs

Chapter 6

Brokering Inclusion: Education, Language, and the Immigrant Middle Class

Mae M. Ngai

Immigration poses challenges for several normative principles of democratic society. Liberalism's assumptions of universal equality and inclusion are qualified by the question of community definition, the drawing and maintaining of boundaries that simultaneously include and exclude.[1] Within the modern nation-state the liberal, rights-bearing subject is the citizen; as Earl Warren famously wrote, "Citizenship *is* man's [*sic*] basic right, because it is nothing less than the right to have rights."[2] Thus even within the territorial boundaries of inclusion there exist persons—aliens—whose claims to political inclusion are limited, deferred, or altogether denied.[3] Decisions to exclude immigrants or to diminish their standing and opportunities are often made democratically by elected bodies or by referenda but arguably undermine basic democratic values, and also may serve as legal openings for restricting the rights of citizens.[4]

In the case of the United States the exclusion of resident aliens from full rights is mitigated by the assumption that immigrants become citizens. Theoretically their liabilities are temporary and conditional.[5] Naturalization is relatively easy, affords the same rights as birthright citizenship (save for holding the office of president), and is nearly impossible to revoke.[6] Naturalization, however, is available only to legally resident aliens; undocumented immigrants remain forever outside the polity and as such constitute a degraded-caste group. Moreover, until 1952 access to naturalization was racially qualified.[7] However, these liabilities are again tempered by the citizenship principle of jus soli, enshrined in the Fourteenth Amendment, by which the U.S.-born children of immigrants (whether legal or illegal) are citizens.[8]

The path from immigration to citizenship comprises settlement and assimilation—the assumption that immigrants are readied for citizenship by their incorporation into the host society and by their embrace of its values and norms.[9] The telos of immigration, settlement, assimilation, and citizenship is an enduring narrative of U.S. history, the central content of America's identity as an "immigrant nation." We know of course that it has not always been the reality of migrants' desires or their experiences and interactions with American society and state. In addition to obstacles posed by native prejudice, legal liabilities, and segmented labor markets, recent scholarship has underscored obstacles to immigrant incorporation posed by transnational migrant practices and identities. Especially at the turn of the twenty-first century, it is widely argued, transportation, communication, and information technologies enable people to live simultaneously in two national cultures, undermining older paradigms of assimilation.[10] Social scientists are also questioning older models that viewed as normative a generational path of Americanization, socioeconomic mobility, and political inclusion. Segmented labor markets and transnational cultures, among other influences, have retarded or prevented the full incorporation of the second generation and even beyond. At stake in this line of inquiry are the limits of democratic political culture in the incorporation of immigrants.[11]

This essay builds on recent scholarship on immigrant and generational incorporation by arguing that exclusion and inclusion are not necessarily successive phases in a linear process but, rather, may be dynamically entwined and contingent. It uses a micro-historical study of one Chinese American family, the Tapes (*Jeu* in Cantonese, *Zhao* in Mandarin), to examine closely the complexities of these processes. The Tapes interest me because they were *immigrant brokers:* members of two generations of the Tape family were transportation agents, immigration-bonds brokers, labor contractors, and language interpreters. They were exemplars of a "brokering class" that emerged in the last quarter of the nineteenth century as the legal status of Chinese in America was being adjudicated in the courts.

The work of the agents, brokers, and interpreters may be distinguished from that of elite-culture brokers. The latter were intellectuals and writers whose work was discursive and political as they advocated for cross-cultural understanding and civil rights before Euro-American audiences.[12] While their endeavors obviously were important to the Chinese community's struggles against exclusion, this essay is more interested in the brokers who facilitated transactions of everyday immigrant life and survival—gaining admission into the country, securing employment, importing merchandise, answering to the police. An examination of these quotidian brokers' social location, activities, and self-fashioning reveals a complex web of ideas and practices embracing both immigrant inclusion and immigrant exclusion.

To summarize the argument: the brokers were both liminal and powerful figures. Their bilingualism and biculturalism were unusual among both Chinese and Euro-Americans; they were needed by both and mistrusted by both. The brokers promoted the incorporation of immigrants and simultaneously were invested in the immigrants' exclusion (especially their social isolation and lack of proficiency in the English language), which was the condition of their dependency on the brokers. Although the condition of legal exclusion makes the Chinese American historical example unique, the dynamics of brokering, I argue, are broadly applicable to American immigrant and ethnic experience. All immigrant ethnic groups have their brokers, who promote their co-ethnics' interests while exploiting their disadvantage.

Further, I argue that Chinese American and other ethnic brokers were constitutive figures of the ethnic middle class. Not only was brokering indispensable for the settlement and protection of the immigrant laboring classes, it was a means for achieving wealth and social status for the brokers themselves. Because the brokers' work was rooted in their contact with and insinuation within mainstream institutions (especially transportation companies government offices) they were among the first of their co-ethnics to acculturate to mainstream social and political norms. They achieved citizenship by dint of their aggressive pursuit of opportunities found in the interstices of two social worlds, which involved advocacy of civil rights and democratic inclusion but which also, at times, included illicit, undemocratic, and exploitative practices.

To illustrate these social processes, this essay turns its attention to the Tape family's role in two realms of social life, education and language, which have been long regarded as important, even principal, levers for immigrant incorporation into civil society. I focus on the 1885 civil rights case *Tape v. Hurley*, in which the California Supreme Court ruled that Chinese children could not be excluded from public schools.[13] I argue that *Tape v. Hurley* marked a turning point both in the status of Chinese in California and in the careers of members of the Tape family as Chinese-language interpreters. These two trajectories converged in a process of ethnic middle-class formation and, in particular, the brokering class.

Tape v. Hurley and the Peculiarity of Chinese American Civil Rights Jurisprudence

In *Tape v. Hurley*, the California Supreme Court ruled that public schools in California could not exclude Chinese children on account of race. The holding in the case, a straightforward reading of the statute, is unremarkable, which is perhaps why the case has not received the same attention as the landmark constitutional cases decided by the U.S. Supreme Court in the same decade, notably the Chinese exclusion cases (*Chae Chan Ping* and *Fong Yue Ting*) and *Yick Wo v. Hopkins*.[14]

Tape v. Hurley is typically described as a kind of forerunner to the landmark civil rights ruling of 1954, *Brown v. Board of Education*. In fact, Tape is both temporally and substantively more proximate to *Plessy v. Ferguson*, in which the Supreme Court justified the "separate but equal" doctrine, than it is to *Brown*. For when the court ruled that Chinese could not be excluded from public schools, San Francisco immediately established a segregated Chinese school. *Tape v. Hurley*, then, was a kind of Pyrrhic victory.[15]

But *Tape* is also not exactly like *Plessy*. In the latter case, the Court established for African Americans a second-class citizenship but affirmed the exclusion of Chinese in America from citizenship. The distinction was clear to Supreme Court Justice John Marshall Harlan. In his famous "colorblind" dissent in *Plessy*, Justice Harlan compared the Negro citizen with the Chinese foreigner. Whereas the former had shed his blood for the nation and deserved the full rights of citizenship, argued Harlan, the Chinese were "*a race so different from our own* that we do not permit those belonging to it to become citizens of the United States. Persons belonging to it are, with few exceptions, absolutely excluded from our country."[16]

The problem of Chinese segregation thus must be understood in the context of a complex negotiation of the status of the Chinese that was being worked out in the federal courts in the late nineteenth century, a status that came under competing pressures of exclusion and inclusion. Put another way, the Chinese Exclusion Act of 1882 aimed to stop Chinese immigration and denied the Chinese the right of naturalization, but—Justice Harlan's dissent notwithstanding—the exclusion law could not altogether eliminate the presence of the Chinese in the United States. These included laborers already lawfully domiciled, merchants and others exempt from the exclusion laws, and those born on U.S. soil. What rights, if any, these Chinese possessed remained a contested issue throughout the late nineteenth century.

California's first laws on common-branch schooling provided for segregated schools for "Negroes, Indians, and Mongolians," but the Chinese found even segregated schools hard to come by.[17] The first school for the Chinese in San Francisco, started in 1853, was not a public school but was funded by Chinese merchant leaders and white Christian missionaries. Contemporaries understood the link between language acquisition and assimilation, and English classes for some twenty Chinese boys and men were held in a small room on Sacramento Street.[18]

For the missionaries, English-language instruction was, of course, linked to the goal of conversion and to the missionaries' hopes of recruiting native (Chinese) Christians for missionary work in China. The Presbyterian minister William Speer, who spent four years in China before opening the first Chinese mission in San Francisco in 1853, wrote, "I have considered it an important branch of my missionary work to impart a knowledge of the English language, literature and science . . . and such things as would best illustrate our later advancement and tend to disabuse their minds of idolatrous fears and superstitions."[19]

Nearly all the Protestant mission–sponsored schools and classes were for adults and were held during evenings and on Sunday. Only in San Francisco, where there was a relatively larger and more settled community, did the missionaries operate day schools for children. Speer, who was dedicated both to religious conversion and to opposing race discrimination against the Chinese community, directly appealed to the school board to provide instruction for the Chinese, arguing that "as taxpayers, they have a civil right to school privileges."[20]

With Speer's prodding, the San Francisco school board in 1857 unanimously agreed that "Asiatics, and particularly the Chinese youths, should have every opportunity to acquire a knowledge of the English language." But the board voted not to admit Chinese to the evening school, on grounds that their presence would excite white students.[21] Instead, the school system provided limited resources for a separate Chinese school. Beginning in 1859, the board paid for a teacher for a single class for Chinese pupils, which was held in the "gloomy basement" of Speer's Presbyterian mission in Chinatown. Bible reading was the principal form of instruction. The superintendent of schools, James Denman, was pessimistic about the project. "The prejudices of caste and religious idolatry are so indelibly stamped upon their character and existence," he said, that teaching them was "almost hopeless."[22]

Yet the teacher, Mr. Lanctot, soon proudly reported that the "little Celestials were very apt at learning. The younger ones knew nothing whatever of the English language on entering, but they picked it up with marvelous facility. Writing they learned with even greater ease than Yankees."[23]

Over the years, the board frequently closed the school, citing low attendance or lack of funds, only to reopen weeks or months later, under pressure from the community. At times, the board authorized only evening classes, which catered to adult learners.[24] The sporadic nature of public schooling was consistent with the indeterminate general status of the Chinese in the pre-exclusion years. There was racism against the Chinese, but it was not yet ubiquitous or codified. Many white San Franciscans found the Chinese a curious but a benign, even necessary, presence, for the manufacturing and commercial class depended on Chinese labor and on Chinese connections for trade to China.[25]

But racial animosity toward the Chinese grew in the 1870s. The opening of the transcontinental railroad brought to San Francisco growing numbers of Euro-American migrants from the East Coast; Chinese laborers, who had formerly been employed in the construction of the railroad; and a national market, which introduced new pressures on local manufacturing and wages. The economic recessions of the 1870s exacerbated the growing sense of competition between Chinese and Euro-American laborers. By the late 1870s, there was a full flowering of anti-Chinese racism in San Francisco. That racism fueled mob violence, the expulsion of Chinese workers from many manufacturing jobs, and a hardening of residential segregation.[26]

The anti-Chinese movement, which vociferously agitated for exclusion, just as adamantly opposed granting rights to resident Chinese. After all, its rallying cry was "the Chinese must go"—its aims were exclusion and expulsion, not segregation, which was the policy for African Americans and American Indians. Racist thinking blamed the Chinese for being unassimilable, yet that same thinking opposed education precisely because it threatened to incorporate, even assimilate, and, hence, permanently establish the Chinese population. The exclusionists believed that the practice of keeping out new immigrants would be for naught if a permanent settlement were allowed to establish and accrete by natural increase. The *Call* summed up the danger of public schooling: "The [Chinese] race is striving to take root in the soil. They desire or profess to desire, to mingle their youth with ours, with a view, doubtless, to more thorough assimilation in the body politic."[27]

Public education was thus one of the first casualties of the anti-Chinese movement. In 1871, the San Francisco school board terminated support for the Chinatown school, upon the recommendation of school superintendent James Denman. Denman found sanction in California's 1870 school law, which required districts to operate separate schools for "African and Indian children" but omitted any mention of the Chinese or "Mongolians." There is no record explaining the change in the law; it may well have reflected the growing animosity toward the Chinese in California. In any event, Denman concluded that San Francisco had "no obligation to continue support" for the schooling of the Chinese.[28]

The closing came at a time when there was a growing population of school-age Chinese children in California. By the 1870s and early 1880s, there were three thousand Chinese children in the state, two-thirds of whom lived in San Francisco. Education was no longer the concern only of young adults in mercantile and other businesses. Yet only a few hundred Chinese children attended the missionary schools each year.[29]

Throughout the 1870s, the school board ignored or dismissed numerous individual and collective petitions from the Chinese for admission to public schools. In 1878, the state legislature similarly disregarded a petition from thirteen hundred Chinese residents of San Francisco, Sacramento, and other towns, on behalf of three thousand Chinese children residing in California. "Chinese merchants and laborers," the petitioners averred, "being under the protection of your Constitution and laws, are entitled to the same rights and privileges accorded to foreigners generally." Excluding the Chinese from the benefit of public education when they paid more than $40,000 a year in taxes to the state, the petitioners added, "we hold to be unjust."[30]

Then, in October 1884, Joseph and Mary Tape, an "Americanized Chinese" couple, tried to enroll their eight-year-old daughter, Mamie, in Spring Valley Primary School on Union Street in San Francisco. Joseph Tape was a drayman and expressman who was raising his family not in the Chinese quarter but in the Cow Hollow, a white middling neighborhood between Russian Hill and the Presidio.[31] The principal, Miss Jennie Hurley, refused to admit Mamie because the school board had explicitly instructed all school principals to deny entry to children of Chinese descent, under pain of dismissal.[32]

After Jennie Hurley barred Mamie from Spring Valley School, Joseph Tape went to the Chinese consul's office in San Francisco and asked for assistance. The vice-consul, Frederick A. Bee—a white attorney who represented the Chinese Six Companies in the 1870s—lodged a protest with the school board and retained a lawyer to sue on Mamie's behalf. The lawyer, William Gibson, was the son of the Reverend Otis Gibson, a Methodist missionary who was a prominent defender of the Chinese in California.[33] Bee and William Gibson argued that the exclusion of Mamie Tape violated both state law and the Fourteenth Amendment, "especially so in this case as the child is native-born."[34]

California had amended its state education law in 1880 to provide public schooling for all children in the state. The law specified that "schools must be open for the admission of all children" and that only "children of filthy or vicious habits, or children suffering from contagious or infectious diseases" could be excluded.[35] Coming in the period following the Civil War, the reform was aimed chiefly at eliminating California's "colored schools." It resulted from many years of lobbying on the part of the state's small but persistent black population, as well as from a move by elites, who considered the funding of the colored schools a tax burden during economically difficult times.[36]

San Francisco's school superintendent Andrew Jackson Moulder did not believe that the 1880 law applied to the Chinese. State superintendent of public instruction William Welcher agreed that the law was "meant to apply only to the African race." Excluding the Chinese from the schools, Welcher emphasized, was consistent with the California constitution's declaration that the Chinese were "dangerous to the well-being of the state."[37]

The school board concurred. If the Chinese were admitted to public schools, it asked, "will assimilation begin and race mixture follow?" It proclaimed: "Guard well the doors of the public schools that they do not enter. For however stern it might sound, it is but the enforcement of the law of self-preservation . . . by which we hope presently to prove that we justly and practically defend ourselves from this invasion of Mongolian barbarism."[38]

However, confronted with the plain wording of the statute, the court ruled against the school board's exclusion of Mamie Tape. The judge was not unsympathetic to the board's concerns. According to the Sacramento *Union*, Judge Maguire stated that "if evil resulted followed this decision it was not the fault of the judiciary. The Legislature possessed the power to provide separate schools for distinct races." The board appealed to the state supreme court but, in the meantime, rushed to Sacramento and secured a law authorizing the creation of separate schools for "Mongolian" children. The state supreme court upheld the lower court's ruling in favor of Mamie Tape. The San Francisco school board immediately announced that it would open a separate Chinese primary school in Chinatown.[39]

Tape v. Hurley signaled an important shift in the status of the Chinese, for it had in effect recognized their presence and elevated them to the status of African Americans and American Indians. This may seem a dubious promotion, but it was an important concession that distinguished between exclusion as a policy goal and presence as a social fact. Indeed, *Tape v. Hurley* was decided during the same time that the status of the Chinese was being adjudicated in the federal courts. These Chinese cases followed two tracks. On one track, a series of immigration and deportation cases upheld Chinese exclusion and pronounced the doctrine of Congress's plenary, or absolute, power over matters of immigration.[40] However, along a second track, the courts ruled that the equal protection clause of the Fourteenth Amendment applied to resident Chinese and that the citizenship clause applied to Chinese born on U.S. soil. Thus were two policies, exclusion and inclusion, born and entwined, creating a fundamental tension in the status of Chinese in America.

Today, we take the universality of principles like equal protection and birthright citizenship as self-evident meanings of the Fourteenth Amendment. But in the late nineteenth century, this was not certain. After the Civil War, when Congress amended the naturalization law to include in its scope "persons of African nativity and descent," in addition to "white persons," it chose its words deliberately in order to exclude the Chinese from the privilege of naturalization. Once Chinese exclusion was enacted, it became commonly argued that "imposing" citizenship on Chinese born "accidentally" on U.S. soil contradicted the will of Congress to exclude the Chinese.[41]

The federal justices who decided the Chinese cases made no effort to hide their racial animus toward the Chinese. The civil rights cases might be best understood in terms of Derrick Bell's theory of interest convergence. In other words, the courts were willing to concede certain rights to the Chinese because it suited other agendas. In *Wong Kim Ark*, for example, the U.S. Supreme Court narrowly upheld birthright citizenship of Chinese

Americans because to deny them citizenship would have jeopardized the "citizenship of thousands of persons of English, Scotch, Irish, German or other European parentage, who have always been considered and treated as citizens."[42]

Just as important, federal judges found in the Chinese civil rights cases occasion to extend the application of the Fourteenth Amendment to economic rights. Before *Yick Wo*, the Supreme Court had limited the Fourteenth Amendment to protecting the civil rights of former slaves, which was also an effort to limit the scope of federal powers after the Civil War.[43] *Yick Wo*, which concerned the city's regulation of laundries, widened the scope of the equal protection clause to include the right of individuals to pursue "ordinary trades" free from state interference. To achieve this aim, *Yick Wo* applied the equal protection clause to all "persons," not just citizens. The move held profound implications for the application of equal rights and due process for both aliens and legal economic actors (i.e., corporations).[44]

The Chinese immigration and civil rights cases established the basic doctrine that continues to apply to all immigrants in the United States—in matters of admission aliens are not protected by the Constitution, and in matters of expulsion they have only very limited procedural rights. However, when aliens are territorially present, they have rights of equal protection and of substantive due process. The two principles exist in constant tension, each qualifying the meaning of the other.[45] But whereas in the case of European immigrants the presumption of assimilation and eventual citizenship has generally tended to privilege their inclusion, the Chinese were until the mid-twentieth century defined principally in terms of their exclusion.[46]

The Tape Family: Roads Taken and Not Taken

Let us turn now to the plaintiffs in *Tape v. Hurley*. Public statements made by the Tapes purposefully project an image of a highly assimilated family. Joseph Tape's affidavit to the court explained that he and his wife had been married in a Christian church and in conformity with state law; that he had been engaged continuously for the past ten years in the business of draying and expressing; and that his family had lived continuously in the same place of residence for the past seven years. In other words, he was a stable, working, and moral family man, not a sojourner or a "coolie." Moreover, he wrote, "Fifteen years ago I discarded my queue, and have never since worn one. My wife and I are now, and for fifteen years past, have been clothed in the American costume. The said Mamie Tape is now and always has been dressed in the American costume, in the manner common and usual for a child of her years."[47]

A family photograph taken during the school dispute supported the image of assimilation. The family presents itself in Western-style clothing; the parents' garments in particular are typical of contemporary Victorian fashion, although it is impossible to know whether these were their own clothes or costumes provided by the studio. Perhaps more telling as to the purpose of the photograph is Mamie, who is positioned strategically at the center. Instead of the neutral gaze favored in family portraiture, her look is proud, almost defiant. She holds her brother's hand, giving unity to the family's image while also possibly steadying her nerves (Figure 6.1).

In these words and images, the Tapes presented themselves as a heteronormative bourgeois family, far removed from the stereotype of sojourning coolies and prostitutes. In fact, this was a typical strategy used by all ethnoracial groups in civil rights cases, in which plaintiffs create a social distance between themselves and the unassimilated lower classes. Aimed at minimizing racial bias by minimizing racial difference, the legal strategy was akin to the racial "uplift" ideology that was widespread among African American and other nonwhite minorities in the late nineteenth and early twentieth centuries.[48]

Mary Tape's letter to the school board again reinforced the image of the Tapes as a bourgeois family. That letter was written as an angry protest when, after Mamie Tape won her case at trial, the school board announced that it would create a segregated school for the Chinese. Mrs. Tape wrote: "Dear sirs: Will you please to tell me! Is it a disgrace to be Born a Chinese? Didn't God make us all!!! . . . Do you call that a Christian act to compel my little children to go so far to a school that is made in purpose for them." She continued: "My children don't dress like the other Chinese. They look just as phunny amongst them as the Chinese dress in Chinese look amongst you Caucasians. . . . Her playmates is all Caucasians ever since she could toddle around. If she is good enough to play with them! Then is she not good enough to be in the same room and studie with them? You had better come and see for yourselves. See if the Tape's is not same as other Caucasians, except in features. It seems no matter how a Chinese may live and

Figure 6.1 The Tape family, 1885. From left: Joseph, Emily, Mamie, Frank, Mary. (Jack Kim collection.)

dress so long as you know they Chinese. Then they are hated as one. There is not any right or justice for them." Finally, Mary Tape swore: "Mamie Tape will never attend any of the Chinese schools of your making! Never!!! I will let the world see Sir What justice there is When it is govern by the Race prejudice men!"[49]

These documents make the Tapes appear proud and heroic as they refuse to submit to discriminatory policies and practices. Indeed, the image of resistance to racial oppression is favored in academic and lay narratives about *Tape v. Hurley*, and undoubtedly it has much appeal.[50] Yet the Tapes' resistance seems to be grounded in their claim that they are the "same as other Caucasians." That is, they make a claim to whiteness, not a claim that they, as Chinese, should be treated the same as whites. The Tapes seem to be ambivalent about, if not outright rejecting, an identity as Chinese, "except in features."

A number of questions arise. What accounts for the Tapes' apparent assimilation and their view that they are the "same as Caucasians"? What explains their agency? Moreover, if we read *Tape v. Hurley* not as an unalloyed civil rights victory but as part of a trend that established both segregation and exclusion, we will also want to know how that trend influenced the Tape family. To answer these questions, we need to consider the broader context of the family's development over time.

The Tapes had come to the United States in the 1860s, before exclusion, when things were still fluid for Chinese immigrants. They came separately, each at a young age and without parents, and they each lived among white people. He was fourteen or younger when he arrived;[51] his Chinese name was Zhao Qia, or Jeu Dip in Cantonese. He worked for a Scots dairy farmer on Van Ness Avenue, first as a servant boy and then driving the milk wagon, laying the basis for his future career as a teamster and expressman.[52] She was only eleven when she came; although the circumstances of her arrival are vague, evidence suggests that she was brought as a servant girl, possibly intended for prostitution, and that she was one of the first Chinese girls to find refuge among Christian missionaries. We do know that she was raised in the home of the Ladies Protection and Relief Society, a residence for abandoned children. She was the only Chinese child at the home. She did not have a Chinese name that she ever acknowledged and was called Mary McGladery after the assistant matron in the home who raised her. Miss McGladery taught the girl to read and write English, to play the piano, and to draw.[53]

At the time, nearly all Chinese in San Francisco were first-generation immigrants. The few merchant families with American-born children lived in the Chinese quarter and were not acculturated to American ways. We might think of Chew Dip and Mary McGladery as proto-Chinese Americans, whose knowledge of English and adoption of American manners and customs evinced an unusual degree of acculturation for the time. They were liminal subjects, the only Chinese in their respective worlds and marked by a double difference—different from the white people around them, different from other Chinese.

After they married in 1875, they took the name Tape, most likely because "Joe Tape" sounded a little like "Jeu Dip," and built a little house with a stable in the back on Green Street in a neighborhood called the Cow Hollow (now Pacific Heights). At the time, there were few people living in the area and almost no other Chinese—just a few domestic servants living in the homes of whites and, a bit farther out near the Presidio, Chinese farmers who held vegetable plots and a peach orchard.[54]

Jeu Dip was not able to build a business in general drayage, probably because by the mid-1870s there was already too much prejudice against the Chinese. But he did find a niche working for Chinese merchants, hauling their imported goods up from the docks to Chinatown, and then expressing baggage for the Chinese immigrants arriving on Pacific Mail steamships. The young couple may have chosen to live in the Cow Hollow because Mary was not comfortable in Chinatown, perhaps because she associated it with her childhood traumas. Also, unlike her husband, who was from Xinning (Taishan), she did not speak Cantonese and did not have Chinese friends. Mary's inability to speak Cantonese also meant that she and Joseph spoke English, not Chinese, to each other.[55]

Mary Tape's domestic and social activities suggest a woman who was highly acculturated to conventional middle-class, Euro-American social norms. She gave birth to her children at home, attended by a Euro-American doctor. Unlike most Chinese merchants' wives in America, who were confined to the home, Mary participated in civil society. She exhibited her paintings at the Mechanics Institute's juried art shows, and as she became interested in photography, she joined the California Camera Club, an amateur society. By the 1890s, she had established a small reputation in San Francisco as a maker of lantern slides.[56]

Still, the Tapes sustained contacts with other Chinese, mainly through Joseph's business dealings. The vegetable men from the Presidio routinely left bok choy and gailan (*baicai* and *jiecai*, Chinese cabbage and mustard greens) on the Tapes' doorstep, as they passed through the neighborhood. Joseph also hired a Chinese nanny (*ah-ma*) to take care of his wife when she was ill.[57] Although details are sparse, the Tape household appears to have been a culturally hybrid space, where English was the dominant (but not the only) language spoken, Chinese food was consumed, and company was mixed. Although highly acculturated to American ways, the Tapes apparently were more bicultural than asserted in Mary Tape's letter, that they were "same as Caucasians, except in features."

The Tapes could not have been unaffected by the anti-Chinese movement that gripped San Francisco politics in the late 1870s and 1880s. Joseph Tape must have experienced the violence of the anticoolie movement first hand; in the late 1870s hooligans regularly stoned wagons carrying new arrivals from China along the route from the docks to Chinatown, and in 1877 a mob tried to burn down the Pacific Mail wharf. Yet still the Tapes tried to enroll Mamie in Spring Valley School, perhaps because they yet harbored the hope that the girl, who spoke English and who could already read and write, would not be treated like ordinary Chinese. Years later Mamie Tape recalled that her father was "determined to have us educated and [fought] like heck" to get her admitted to school.[58] The elder Tapes' commitment reflected their desire for assimilation. Both were literate in English, if not formally schooled, and they knew that their children had to be educated in order to participate in and be accepted by white society. Moreover, Mary's unusual upbringing by the English matron McGladery ensured that the Tapes' commitment applied to their daughters as well as their son.

The creation of the segregated Chinese Primary School, however, suggested that assimilation, which had been a tenuous proposition at best, was now impossible. Indeed, notwithstanding their mother's vow that her children would "never!!!" attend the Chinese school, Mamie and her younger brother Frank were the first students to arrive when the Chinese Primary School opened, just five days after Mrs. Tape wrote her letter. For the Tapes, the decision to go to the Chinese school represented their determination to educate their children, but it also must have meant that they realized that the path to full acceptance by white society was closed. It is this recognition of their inability to assimilate that accounts for the deep anger in Mary Tape's letter.

According to a news story in the *Evening Bulletin*, a certain irony pervaded the first day of school. The Tape children were "dressed neatly in clothes like those worn of American children," but having never been to school before, they were "restless," unaccustomed to schoolroom discipline. The other four children who came to school, ten- and twelve-year-old boys wearing "queues and distinctive style of [Chinese] clothing," had all been to mission schools. The reporter observed that they all could read and write English, were proficient in arithmetic, and complied with the teacher's method of instruction.[59]

For several years, the Tape children commuted to Chinatown, riding to school each morning in their father's horse-drawn wagon. But things on Green Street were changing. By 1890, the block had become completely built up with a row of vernacular housing, and the neighborhood was filled with Euro-Americans of the middling class. Frank fought with the Irish boys in the neighborhood.[60] The Tapes also worried that their children's marriage prospects would be dim unless they met other Chinese. Interracial unions were not uncommon in the Northeast, but in California both law and social custom precluded such marriages. Mamie Tape recalled, "The folks moved downtown [to Chinatown], because there was too much *fan-yun* [fanren, or "barbarians," i.e., white people] they thought, [so they wanted us] to get acquainted with some Chinese boys and girls." In 1891, the Tapes moved to Chinatown.[61]

By now the Chinese Primary School had some seventy students. There were just two girls, including Mamie. Mamie and Frank probably did look "phunny" next to the other children in Chinese attire and likely took some abuse for their acculturation and privilege (they brought roller skates to school). Mary Tape did her best to maintain a household organized around Euro-American norms, with Western-style furnishings and music lessons for the children. But the Tape children were also becoming Sinicized. Most important, they learned to speak Cantonese. They had already learned some Chinese at home, from their mother's amah, but now they needed it to survive the Chinatown school yard.[62]

Mamie and Frank went to the Chinese school through the eighth grade. By then, enrollment had grown and the school had run out of space. The board came up with a plan to move the Chinese school into the basement of Commercial High School, on Powell Street between Clay and Sacramento. The fact that the high school had been closed and condemned as unsafe did not seem to worry the board, which calculated that the new site would save $1,000 a year. The Chinese Primary School was already run on a meager budget; by one account, the expense of the existing school was $2,800 a year, far less than the $8,000 it received from the state to educate Chinese students.[63]

But the plan faced heated opposition from white property owners on Powell Street, which was one block outside the territory that had come to be defined as the Chinese quarter. The up-and-coming residents of Powell Street now associated themselves with the elites on adjacent Nob Hill. They deployed incendiary language to police the racial boundary, claiming that the Chinese had an offensive smell and warning that that the value of their property would drop by 25 percent if Chinese began "strutting" along Powell Street. School board members offered plans to require the Chinese students to enter and leave the school by way of a side alley or a back staircase, which the board proposed to build "up over the forty-five foot hill from Clay Street," but these failed to appease the Powell Street residents. The board found an alternate site for the school on Clay Street.[64]

Perhaps it was this ugly incident that prompted the Tapes to leave Chinatown. Or maybe it was just the accumulation of racist incidents, large and small, that continued to dog the Chinese of San Francisco. True, the elder Tapes maneuvered around the strictures of segregation—Joseph worked for the Pacific Mail, and Mary was known as "the Americanized Chinese lady" among the city's artists and photographers.[65] But it was another matter that their children were growing up in Chinatown. Here, they were being socialized under conditions of racial isolation and the stigma of segregation. So, in 1895 Joseph bought a house on Russell Street in Berkeley, in a newly subdivided area in the south part of town, just a block from the Southern Pacific's rail line on Shattuck, and the family moved across the bay.[66]

Although the Tape family lived in Chinatown for only about five years, their stay there was terribly important. Joseph Tape's business success, of course, depended on a Chinese clientele, and his office would always be in Chinatown. Living in Chinatown was, perhaps, even more important for the Tape children. Attending the public school there not only gave them formal schooling but, more important, also made them part of a social cohort of Chinese Americans. The Tape girls would all marry Chinatown boys. In 1897, Mamie married Herman Lowe, who was born in Chinatown and educated in the Baptist mission school there, and the couple settled in Chinatown. In 1901, Emily Tape married Robert Leon Park, the son of a

Chinatown teamster. In 1913, Gertrude, the youngest Tape child, married Herbert Chan, the son of a Chinatown merchant.[67]

The men who married into the Tape family were themselves second-generation Chinese Americans who also became interpreters and brokers. In 1905, Frank Tape, Herman Lowe, and Robert Park's brother Edward were among the first Chinese to get jobs as interpreters for the Immigration Bureau. Robert Park worked as the official Chinese interpreter for the San Francisco Hall of Justice (the city's criminal court). The most highly educated member of the extended Tape family, Park graduated from high school in San Francisco and attended the University of California. He was a founding member of the Native Sons of the Golden State, the forerunner of the Chinese American Citizens Alliance, as well as a president of the powerful Sam Yup (*Sanyi*) Association.[68]

Joseph Tape himself became quite wealthy from the baggage monopoly he held for the Pacific Mail and the Southern Pacific Railroad and from myriad other kinds of brokering work, all related to the business of immigration. He became the Chinese passenger agent for Pacific Mail and Southern Pacific as well as a bonds broker, who guaranteed the departure of Chinese arriving in San Francisco on transit tickets for Mexico and Cuba and of Chinese ship crewmen desiring shore leave while in port.[69] A journalist described Tape's office in Chinatown as a quintessential immigrant brokerage and clearinghouse, a "link between Orient and the Occident" that served as an "informal information bureau where [immigrants'] problems are solved and questions are answered."[70]

Joseph and Mary Tape's effort to distance themselves and their children from other Chinese was not, in the end, a strategy that would lead the family to economic or social achievement. The better strategy, as they discovered, the strategy that turned their liminality to greatest advantage, would be to play the broker and the interpreter.

The Rise of the Brokering Class

The broker is an interstitial subject, who translates and facilitates transactions between two cultures. Guides, envoys, translators, notaries, negotiators, and labor contractors are common figures in histories of conquest, colonialism, and immigration. Some possess iconic status in nation-founding myths, like La Malinche, Cortés's translator-mistress, and

Squanto, the Wampanoag at Plymouth. Every immigrant group in American history has had its brokers—the Italian *padrone*, the Irish ward boss, the Mexican *coyote*. Bilingual and bicultural, the brokers were able to navigate the institutions of the host society on behalf of its newcomers.[71]

The Chinese immigration brokers and language interpreters were arguably the first "hyphenated" Chinese Americans. Contemporaries commonly called people like the Tapes "Americanized Chinese" well before sociologists theorized and circulated the concept of "assimilation."[72] In contemporary journalistic accounts, "Americanized Chinese" were defined by conversion to Christianity, acquisition of the English language, and adoption of Western-style clothing and customs. Writing in the early 1960s, sociologist Milton Gordon would consider these to be evidence of acculturation, a step toward assimilation. But Gordon also considered language and "exterior" matters like dress to be superficial adaptations to the "cultural patterns" of the host society. He believed that the "adoption of core values and life goals" indexed more durable acculturation, although he did not specify those values and goals. But even though Gordon believed that acculturation was a prerequisite for assimilation, he did not believe that the former inevitably led to the latter.[73]

According to Gordon's concept, it is difficult to say just how acculturated the Tapes were. They were associated with the Presbyterian Church, but there is no evidence that they were baptized or that they were devout. They seem to have been like many other Americanized Chinese, who learned from the mission schools and churches Western social mores and conventions but not a deep sense of religiosity.[74] The Tapes' entrepreneurialism might be considered an American "core value," but it was also quintessentially Chinese. In any event, we can say that during Chinese exclusion, acculturation, even if extensive, did not lead to structural assimilation.

The brokers' knowledge and practice of American ways held a special premium in the segregated and marginalized community of Chinese immigrants. Their position as middlemen gave them an unusual measure of power. The brokers found their markets in the legal and social world of Chinese immigration, and brokering became particularly lucrative under the regime of legal exclusion. Although many immigration brokers engaged in legitimate businesses—in Joseph Tape's case, in expressing, bonding, and ticketing—exclusion also created an underground economy that supported illegal immigration. Indeed, exclusion generated a robust market for selling fake certificates of identity and coaching books, for arranging surreptitious border crossings and for jumping ship, and for bribing immigration inspectors. Chinese secret societies ("tongs") controlled much of the smuggling business, but they invariably involved persons in the employ of transportation companies and the government. Corruption was not limited to the Chinese but involved Euro-Americans as well, including ship's officers, immigration officials, and attorneys.[75]

Joseph Tape was implicated several times in illegal smuggling schemes, although he was never arrested. Twice he was suspected of having a role in alleged plots to land stowaways and in "substitution" schemes, whereby Chinese seamen, employed on transpacific steamships and bonded (by Tape) for shore leave while docked at San Francisco, remained in the United States and Chinese wishing to return to China took their places on the return voyage.[76]

If Joseph Tape eluded arrest, his son Frank was not as fortunate. The younger Tape's career as a Chinese interpreter for the Immigration Bureau was marked by notoriety and scandal. In the 1910s, Tape, who was assigned to the Seattle immigration office, came under suspicion for alleged extortion of Chinese immigrants seeking admission into the country.

Complex dynamics constituted Frank Tape's notoriety. There was the question of his racial identity and what relation it bore to his alleged corruption. Although Tape was a native English speaker he had only an eighth-grade education and spoke Cantonese poorly; he could not read or write Chinese at all.[77] In fact, Tape was highly Americanized. His acculturation unsettled conventional ideas about what "Chinamen" were supposed to be like. Tape's racial identity was the matter of some uncertainty and speculation.[78]

Some of Tape's associates perceived him as a crass American. He led an extravagant lifestyle; he wore a diamond ring, owned a beautiful home, drove a Kissel touring car, and "always [had] gold in his pocket." Some of Tape's colleagues believed he had the kind of personality that craved status and attention, implying that he was harmless, even if he was obnoxious. Others saw in his behavior Chinese, not American, cultural practices. In this view, Tape played a conventional role in Chinese communities, "the man with the big pull with [government] officials," with whom it was ordinary practice to broker the "purchase of official favors,"[79] a vulgarization of *guanxi*, the culture of obligation in social networks.

Also damaging to Tape were rumors that he was cohabitating with a white divorcee from Pennsylvania named Lena Sutherland, who was herself rumored to be a blackmailer. Tape referred to Sutherland as his wife, but authorities did not believe they were married; in either case he would have violated state laws against either miscegenation or cohabitation.

These racial suspicions and jealousies inflected the charges that Tape was corrupt. In 1914 he was tried on criminal charges of conspiracy to smuggle aliens and of extorting immigrants seeking entry into the United States. He was acquitted of criminal charges of conspiracy to smuggle aliens after a sensational trial that involved the murder of a witness in Seattle's Chinatown. [80]

Tape lost his job with the bureau and returned to San Francisco, where he went to work at his father's bonding business. Within a few years, he had reinvented himself as a respectable middle-class citizen, marrying a Chinese American socialite and becoming, in 1923, the first Chinese American to serve on a jury in San Francisco. The *Chronicle* lauded him as a "real American." [81]

Of course, not all Chinese interpreters were corrupt. More important, perhaps, not all corrupt employees of the Immigration Bureau were Chinese. Exclusion had created a large market for enabling illegal immigration, including the sale of documents, testimonies, and government employees, high and low. During the 1910s the Department of Labor conducted several internal investigations into corrupt practices at the Angel Island station in San Francisco, which resulted in sensational findings that implicated white inspectors, interpreters, watchmen, clerks, and other employees at the station in landing stowaways, stealing documents, bribery, and extortion. The Chinese interpreters were but part of a large-scale scheme, in which the greatest sums of money were made by white inspectors, attorneys, and brokers. [82]

Conclusion

As gatekeepers and facilitators, brokers and interpreters like the Tapes operated along opposite vectors of immigrant experience: inclusion and civil rights, on the one hand, and exclusion and illegal immigration, on the other. The brokers both protested and profited from the discrimination against their coethnics; they both enabled and subverted legal exclusion. They were esteemed and mistrusted by Chinese immigrants and Euro-Americans alike. The very structure of brokering involved pleasing or serving two sides, so the broker's loyalties were necessarily divided. The broker had to know how to navigate that divided terrain through negotiation, manipulation, and accommodation; ultimately, the broker's loyalty was to his own survival and advancement. The Tapes' involvement in illegal immigration was thus not necessarily inconsistent with their advocacy for civil rights; each trend derived from their interstitial location and from their pursuit of self-interest.

Among Euro-American ethnic groups, the power of brokers diminished with the social mobility of the second generation, which cut into the brokers' monopoly of access to resources. The Chinese exclusion laws, however, meant that the Chinese American brokers had greater power over a longer period of time. But it also meant that they occupied a more prolonged liminal status. They were prototypes of another sociological figure, the "marginal man," the racial or cultural hybrid who lived with a foot in each culture but belonged fully to neither. Sociologists imagined the marginal man as a figure of alienation and conflict but they also saw him as a pioneer at the vanguard of group assimilation.[83]

The Chinese American brokers, however, did not pave the way for immigrant assimilation or racial amalgamation. Indeed, their existence, their fortunes as well as their woes, derived from the persistence of exclusion and segregation. But the brokers were pioneers of another sort. The history of the Tape family is a story about how immigration and exclusion created a site for the accumulation of wealth and social status among the first Chinese Americans as well as a site for the production of a Chinese American ethnic identity, an identity that valorized acculturation, education, and material success. In this version of Chinese American history, exclusion and inclusion were not successive phases of immigrant incorporation but were dynamically entwined, the result of a legal status that combined exclusion from immigration and naturalization with limited inclusion for residents and birthright citizens.

Chapter 7

Immigration, Citizenship,
and the Need for Integration

Christian Joppke

One of the political needs created by immigration is that for integration. A classic mechanism of integration in the modern state is citizenship, understood as shared beliefs and identities that tie the members of society into a collectivity. This essay investigates what kind of citizenship identities European states display and further in their recent citizenship and integration campaigns concerning immigrants and ethnic minorities. I argue that citizenship identities are increasingly universalistic, which is paradoxical because what states have in common cannot possibly lend distinctness to them and bind immigrants to a particular state and not just any state.

The question of whose political needs are helped or harmed by immigration and by the policies that enable such immigration can be answered in many ways. A source of variation in this respect is the underlying definition of "political." A modern understanding of politics, in which politics deals with domestic interest conflict ("who gets what, when, and how," to quote Lasswell's famous definition), will yield an answer that focuses on how immigration benefits or harms the many groups and sectors that make up a complex society, and especially how immigration may divide and realign the political parties as the main interest mediators and aggregators in society.

By contrast, a classic understanding of politics, according to which politics deals with the definition and implementation of the common good, will yield an answer that looks at society as a totality, and how its overall stability and integrity are affected by immigration. This is the variant of political need that I wish to explore in this essay.

From the point of view of society as a totality, immigration raises the problem of integration. What integrates society, and why there is order and not chaos, has been one of the main questions of political theory since Hobbes, and of social theory since Durkheim. It is interesting that contemporary discussions of integration are oblivious to this legacy of the integration concept, which was initially developed along the very different European experiences of seventeenth-century intrasocietal religious strife (Hobbes) and nineteenth-century industrialization (Durkheim).[1] Today, the concept of integration takes for granted that domestic integration exists, but that it is put to the test, from the outside, by the arrival of newcomers. This is, in many ways, a skewed and alarmist perspective, because— sociologically speaking—a nonintegrated immigrant, short of being stranded like Robinson Crusoe, is impossible. The perspective that is taken in today's immigrant-related integration discourse is that of the political system, or rather of the nation-state, which integrates people not functionally and role-specifically but as entire persons who are members either of this or of that nation-state, but not of two or more simultaneously. In Niklas Luhmann's terminology, the world's nation-states are differentiated according to segment (that is, divided into mutually exclusive units that are alike, subsuming individuals in their entirety), while most other sectors in society are differentiated according to function (that is, divided into mutually dependent units that are not alike, subsuming individuals only under a specific aspect, and who are therefore participating in multiple systems at the same time). From this anomaly stems much of the specificity of the integration discourse surrounding immigrants. It also reveals that integration, all liberal elite rhetoric notwithstanding, at heart means assimilation, in the sense of neutralizing a perceived fundamental threat to the stability and integrity of society that is presumed to exist before the immigrant sets foot in it.

A cursory look at political debates across immigrant-receiving states will confirm that perhaps the main political need (in the classic sense defined above) generated by immigration is a need for integration. How it is responded to, however, varies widely. The United States, qua state, decided not to respond, and to leave the process of integration to the fabled absorptive and time-tested self-regulatory powers of society—above all, underregulated labor markets and mass culture. Its northern neighbor, Canada, perpetually ignored down south, by contrast, makes integration a matter of state policy, in terms of official multiculturalism. European states, which are the focus of this essay, share the Canadian penchant for making immigrant integration a matter of explicit state policy, though increasingly in other than multicultural terms.

A central mechanism in states' integration policies is citizenship—in this residual sense even the United States has an integration policy, as it has a policy and programs framing the acquisition of citizenship by newcomers (though one that is much less successful than the Canadian one, as Irene Bloemraad has observed).[2] The centrality of citizenship for integration is not by accident, because among the many things that "citizenship" may mean, including formal state membership and the rights attached to such membership, has always been a reference to the unity and identity of a national society.[3]

In recent years, European states in particular have sought to reinvigorate centrist citizenship identities as an antidote to centrifugal immigrant societies. These citizenship and integration campaigns are the subject of this essay. But less than in their effects, I am interested in the contents of these campaigns, in particular what kinds of unity and identity are projected in them. I argue that citizenship and integration campaigns become caught in the paradox of universalism: they aim at integrating immigrants into a particular society that is different here from there, but they can do so only in a universalistic rhetoric that dodges the particularism they aim at. The reason for this is the exhaustion of nation and nationalism in Western Europe, at least as a state project, and an increasing recourse to liberal self-definitions. However, liberal identities may still be exclusive, as certain policies surrounding Muslim immigrants and ethnics in Europe show.

In the first part of this essay, I suggest that "political liberalism," more than being a philosophical stance, adequately delineates the constraints for contemporary European states' citizenship and integration campaigns concerning immigrants. These campaigns are discussed in the second part of the essay. I conclude with reflections on liberalism as identity, which is projected by these campaigns, and which—like any "identity"—has exclusive possibilities.

Political Liberalism

At a theoretical level, the problem of unity and integration in a liberal society has been neatly formulated in John Rawls's idea of political liberalism. If one stipulates that in a liberal society the individual is free to choose the ends of her actions, the state has to remain neutral about competing conceptions of the good life ("comprehensive doctrines," in Rawls's terminology) that inform these choices. Social unity, then, cannot derive from a consensus on some conception of the good; in any society there will be a multiplicity of conflicting and incommensurable conceptions of the good. Instead, social unity and stability can only derive from an "overlapping consensus" on principles of justice, the first and foremost of which is that "each person has an equal right to a fully adequate scheme of equal basic rights and liberties."[4] Such an "overlapping consensus," Rawls claims, can in turn be derived from the substantive moral or religious doctrines that people may adhere to, as long as these doctrines (or the people that hold them)[5] are "reasonable." There is an evolution within Rawls's thinking about the nature of liberalism undergirding this theory, ethical and grounded in a metaphysical conception of the person (as "autonomous" or "individualistic,"[6] or political and independent of any substantive conception of the person.[7] And communitarian critics have pointed to the difficulties of the political version of liberalism, which forces the individual to abstract from her moral and religious views for the purposes of public life, in which she is supposed to embrace the ethereal "ideal of public reason" (Rawls).[8]

But one may respond to this that some form of public reason or "transcendence"[9] is precisely the abstraction that modern citizenship, as the space where "strangers can become associates" (Ulrich Preuss), is based on. Political as against ethical liberalism simply exacerbates this abstraction, it does not create it. And, importantly, the neutrality mandate of the state applies to both versions of liberalism. If one takes the neutrality mandate seriously, one has to abandon the view that nation or nationalism could integrate a liberal society: "The hope of political community must indeed be abandoned, if by such a community we mean a political society united in affirming a general and comprehensive doctrine. This possibility is excluded by the fact of pluralism together with the rejection of the oppressive use of state power to overcome it."[10] This is another way of saying that social unity in a liberal society cannot derive from the "good" of nation and nationalism; it can come only from a consensus on the "rights" that should accrue to each individual.

Jürgen Habermas has formulated the same idea as "constitutional patriotism."[11] He shares the Rawlsian divorce between culture and politics, arguing that the social bond in a liberal-democratic state should be "juridicial, moral and political, rather than cultural, geographical and historical."[12] "Constitutional patriotism" holds that the ultimate motives for attachment to a political community are universalistic, not particularistic: in the last instance, one sticks to it because its values, goals, and outlook are rationally justifiable, not because they are contingently what they are.

Whether you call it "overlapping consensus in a political conception of justice" (Rawls) or "constitutional patriotism" (Habermas), the idea is that in a liberal society the ties that bind can only be thin and procedural, not thick and substantive. Otherwise individuals could not be free. A critic of the "unencumbered self" stipulated by the procedural liberalism of Rawls has crisply articulated the necessary link between state neutrality and individual freedom: "It is precisely because we are free and independent selves, capable of choosing our own ends, that we need a framework of rights that is neutral among ends."[13]

However, this is frustrating advice for the attempts of contemporary states to foster integration and unity in diverse societies. The shortcoming of procedural liberalism has been neatly identified by a variety of "civic nationalists," who point to its incapacity to motivate a preference for "this" over "that" collectivity.[14] For instance, Will Kymlicka, advocate of the most concise and influential theory of minority rights, admits that "social unity" in a multiethnic state is a "valid concern."[15] But to achieve it "shared political values" are not enough. Kymlicka points to the arresting example of Quebec. At the very moment that political values converged across Canada around a consensus for liberal democracy, Quebec, defined by the French Fact, came to insist ever more stridently on its independence, close to the point of seceding from Anglophone Canada. Kymlicka rightly concludes that social unity must consist of more than "shared political values"; it requires a "shared identity," a "communality of history, language, and maybe religion," that is, "the things exactly not shared in a multination state."[16] Rogers Smith's argument that the bonds of societies ultimately rest on "stories of peoplehood" expresses the same objection to procedural liberalism.[17]

Identity is what does not happen twice in the world. Shmuel Eisenstadt and Bernhard Giesen depicted it as "the center, the present, the subject," that what is exactly "in between" the dichotomous distinctions of "left and right," "past and present," "God and the world," by means of which human beings construct their worlds. From this point of view, the notion of collective identity has to be categorically distinguished from that of rule of law, and it is wrong to fuse them, as "political liberalism" and "constitutional patriotism" do.[18] Identity sets the boundaries within which the law can be effective.[19]

Kymlicka's case against procedural liberalism's claim that universalism can provide social unity is compelling. There are indeed strong empirical reasons to believe that there is "the need for a national culture . . . that supplies the integrative forces that binds modern societies together," and it is "disingenuous," as Krishan Kumar put it, to disguise the fact that "national culture" is always "the achievement of particular groups of people acting over determinate periods of time," and that it is thus inherently particularistic.[20] However, as the following discussion of states' integration and unity campaigns concerning immigrants demonstrates, the possibilities of states to enact such particularism are tightly limited, essentially by rules of nondiscrimination and a positive evaluation of diversity. In essence, identity cannot be legislated. Accordingly, the actual content of the citizenship identities fostered by the state resembles much more closely the precepts of "constitutional patriotism" or "political liberalism" than those of a particular Dutch or British or German national culture.

Citizenship and Integration Campaigns

There are two different kinds of citizenship campaign in contemporary states. One is the neoliberal campaign to devolve responsibility for welfare and subsistence from the state to the individual and to her voluntary engagements in civil society. In Britain, for instance, "active citizenship" was discovered at the very moment Margaret Thatcher pronounced that there "is no such thing as society"—by which she meant national society, and this before "globalization" made it an obvious fact. Accordingly, the 1990 report of the House of Commons Commission on Citizenship, *Encouraging Citizenship*, envisioned citizenship as "voluntary contributions by individual citizens to the common good."[21] Such citizenship is unrelated to its bounded nature—it does not demarcate "us" from "them." Instead, it seeks an internal rebalancing of citizenship from rights to duties, and a devolving of responsibilities from the welfare state to the individual. Once globalization set in, this neoliberal citizenship could easily be married with cosmopolitan themes. Katheryne Mitchell, for instance, identified the emergence of neoliberal-cum-cosmopolitan citizenship in revamped public school curricula in three major Anglo-Saxon countries, where there has been a change of emphasis from the production of community-minded "national" or "multicultural" citizens toward "strategic cosmopolitans," whose technical skills are essential for mastering the exigencies of global competition.[22] Under the logo "Nation at Risk," in terms of having "neglected educational quality in the name of equality,"[23] the United States began the change in the early 1980s, with a reorientation of the public school curriculum from social studies toward math, science, and reading. A similar reorientation of public education and turn toward individual "choice," "excellence," and "accountability" occurred in Canada and Britain in the late 1980s.

Since the late 1990s, and with a rather opposite thrust, a second type of citizenship campaign moved to the fore, one that focuses on citizenship as a force of social unity and integration in an ethnically diverse society. While the neoliberal theme of unburdening the state of its costly welfare provisions and of an internal rebalancing from the rights to the duties of citizenship is still present, the focus of integrationist citizenship campaigns is more on citizenship's bounded nature. If you will, neoliberal citizenship looks at society as a society of natives; integrationist citizenship looks at society as one that includes immigrants and ethnic minorities, and who are to be made part of "us."

This invites reflection on who the "us" is, and such reflection is inevitably colored by historically varying understandings of citizenship. In Britain, for example, integrationist citizenship campaigns are conducted against the backdrop of a historically thin sense of citizenship. As the 1990 Commission on Citizenship put it already, "An immediate difficulty facing us is that in our society the term 'citizenship' is an unfamiliar notion."[24] Accordingly, in Britain "citizenship" always figures as something that does not yet exist. A case in point is the 1998 Crick Commission, which was charged with developing a citizenship curriculum for government schools. "Worrying levels of apathy, ignorance and cynicism about public life" were to be countered by the "teaching of democracy in schools," and the instilling of "social and moral responsibility" (a common theme already in the 1990s' *Encouraging Citizenship*), "community involvement," and "political literacy."[25] In a second, typically British theme, this attempt to "restore a sense of common citizenship" is tightly limited by respecting "the plurality of nations, cultures, ethnic identities and religions long found in the United Kingdom."[26]

A comparison of new programs for teaching citizenship in schools, which were simultaneously introduced in France and Britain in the late 1990s, found that in the British Crick Commission's report there was "no reference to national symbols such as the Queen, the national flag and the national anthem," and that it was accordingly not "prescriptive of a national identity."[27] By contrast, in France there was a "clear sense of national identity associated with the Republic,"[28] along with an unabashed imposition of national symbols to be known by students, such as the Phrygian hat, Marianne, the flag, the national motto, and the national anthem. However, such particularism was framed in universalistic terms, as these symbols were all symbols of human rights. As Emmanuel Todd inimitably put it, French Republican particularism is enabled by the happy circumstance that "our particularism is universalism."[29] We shall see that this is the red thread of all contemporary citizenship campaigns, only that outside France, the land of the modern democratic revolution, this stance has distinctly less nationalist credentials.

In Britain, the theme of citizenship as tool of integration moved into high gear only after the Northern England race unrests of 2001, which revealed an alarming degree of ethnic separatism that had been allowed to accumulate under the cloak of multiculturalism. Only now, "citizenship" and "cohesion" became the buzzwords of the day. It is perhaps misleading to brand this as a "retreat of multiculturalism" (though this diagnosis remains true for the European continent).[30] In Britain, at least, the new focus on citizenship is more one of strengthening the centrist elements in the continued project of "multiculturalism-in-one-nation."[31]

This is evident in the 2003 report of the second Crick Commission, "Life in the United Kingdom," which was to advise the government on including an English-language and civics test in a more demanding naturalization procedure. To be British is defined there as "respect(ing) the laws, the elected parliamentary and democratic political structures, traditional values of mutual tolerance, respect for equal rights and mutual concern; and that we give our allegiance to the state (as commonly symbolized in the Crown) in return for its protection."[32] This way of being British contains only one particularism: "the Crown," which appositely appears only in parentheses, subsumed under an anonymous, exchangeable "state." Further, while there is greater attention than before on knowing English as a prerequisite for British citizenship, this is still no matter of identity. As the Crick Commission recommended, the language test was "not to be unduly onerous," especially for those "who will be contributing to the needs of the economy through unskilled employment."[33] And when stipulating the contents of the civics part of the new naturalization test, the commission frowned upon "a memorized history curriculum," putting the emphasis instead on "practical knowledge."[34] Concretely, the civics course preparing for the naturalization test was to include six components, in "descending order" of importance: first, and thus of highest priority, "British National Institutions," which is an overview of British government structures; second, "Britain as a multicultural society" (e.g., knowing "the old and new ethnic and religious communities and their different cultures"); third, "knowing the law" (e.g., "what the police can and cannot do"); fourth, "employment" (e.g., "understanding how to get a job"); fifth, "sources of help and information"; and, finally, "everyday needs" (e.g., "ways of paying bills"). If the Cantle Report, reflecting on the causes and implications of the 2001 race unrests, had called for "reinforce[d] feelings of citizenship and shared elements of nationhood," the one policy that had a lever on this was a reformed naturalization policy. But it boiled down to being a primer in British government, closely followed to being a reaffirmation of multi-culturalism, with the bulk of the policy consisting of disseminating practical knowledge that helps newcomers to get by.

The British state is caught in the paradox of universalism: it perceives the need to make immigrants and ethnic minorities part of *this* and not of *that* society, but it cannot name and enforce any particulars that distinguish the "here" from the "there." This paradox is visible in the government pronunciations of what it takes to be British, of which there have been many in the past few years. Take, for instance, the Home Office's recent "Strategy to Increase Race Equality and Community Cohesion."[35] It stresses, again, that a "greater sense of inclusive British citizenship" does not imply "assimilation of cultural difference"; in fact, "no one set of cul-tural values," including that of the majority, is to be "privileged more than another."[36] And the "essential values of Britishness," which—in contrast to all other values—are not up for negotiation, are nationally anonymous. In fact, these values are applied political liberalism: "(the) values of respect for others and the rule of law, including tolerance and mutual obligation be-tween citizens."[37] Surely this goes along with stepped-up efforts to strengthen the ceremonial aspects of citizenship, such as introducing (in

October 2005) a Citizenship Day, in addition to public citizenship cere-monies (which have existed since February 2004). But, as if to apologize for the pomp, it is held to be government's "first priority" to "keep people safe"—by means of more rigorous persecution of racially motivated of-fenses.[38]

The paradox of universalism also permeates departing Prime Minister Tony Blair's legacy statement on race relations, which is appositely a reflec-tion on the meaning of integration, particularly with respect to Muslims.[39] In a reiteration of political liberalism, it renounces the idea that to be Brit-ish is a matter of "culture or lifestyle." In fact, the very notion of identity is reserved to religion: "Christians, Jews, Muslims, Hindus, Sikhs" are en-dowed with a "perfect right" to their "identity". Conversely, to be British is presented as a matter of "essential values," which—again—are mostly universalistic: "belief in democracy, the rule of law, tolerance, equal treat-ment for all, respect for this country and its shared heritage." Of course, smuggled into this invitation to "continue celebrating (multicultural Brit-ain)," which was not by accident delivered to one of British multicultur-alism's intellectual bastions, the Runnymede Trust, were themes less germane to the etiquette of multiculturalism—that there is a "duty" to integrate, that "forced marriage" was no good thing, that "religious law" had no place in the United Kingdom, that "unacceptable actions" would lead to expulsion, that a language test would henceforth be a requirement for permanent residency (and not only for naturalization), and that the full-body veil was a barrier to the ability to "communicate directly with people." But these qualifications of the "right to be different" were not in the name of a British particularism but of the universalism of liberal democracy.

If, as Blair concluded, "being British" is a combination of "the right to be different" and "the duty to integrate," this also suggests that the compo-nent of integration is experienced more as a constraint, a duty than as affective loyalty, an identity. Instead, one's identity continues to rest on one's membership in one of the religious or ethnic communities that, in their combination, are conceived of as constituting "Britain."

While meant to be a qualification of multiculturalism, Blair's legacy statement really demonstrates the unfettered reign of unreconstructed multiculturalism in Britain. This is visible in the final report of the Com-mission on Integration and Cohesion, which was set up by the British gov-ernment in 2006, one year after the bombings of the London Underground, to find remedies to the alarmingly domestic sources of Islamic terrorism. "Groups" are presented here, in classic multicultural fashion, as the building blocks of society, with "cohesion" as the envisioned state where "different groups . . . get on well together."[40]

However, there is a noteworthy new source for "cohesion" and "integration" identified by the Commission on Integration and Cohesion: the future. Indeed, if the past, in classic multicultural diction, is what makes people different, and if the present is by definition paltry (otherwise there would be no need for a corrective policy), the only temporal source of unity left is—the future. Accordingly, the commission report, programmatically entitled *Our Shared Future*, stipulates: "The concept of a shared future will be what binds local communities together whatever their histories."[41] While the idea is compelling, one is astounded to learn what this "shared future" might be. Candidates for "a chance to deepen a sense of our shared futures" (appositely in the plural) are the European Year of Intercultural Education (in 2008) and the Olympic Games in London (2012). These are not only rather thin and spotty "futures," they are also devoid of a genuinely national dimension. In fact, these motley "shared futures" suggest that the future, if anything, is likely to hold even more national unbounding in store.

In a globalizing age, the future must be discounted as source of integration and cohesion. As a perceptive Israeli sociologist suggested, it may be the very mark of postmodernity, where time is "open" and does not allow for "closure," that the future can no longer "anchor" a collectivity—*mit uns zieht die neue Zeit*, the slogan of the nineteenth-century German working-class movement, has become anachronistic.[42]

Are there any alternatives to ground a collective identity? Two often invoked alternatives are language and religion. But a closer look finds both of them wanting, language being intrinsically weak as identity marker, and religion being in violation of constitutional rights.

Without doubt, language is perhaps the strongest (or only) particularism that can be found in tightened naturalization rules and in the new civic integration policies for immigrants across Europe. But only in specific contexts, most notably in multinational states like Canada and Belgium, is language a marker of identity (and then only on the part of the minority national group, not the majority). In most other countries, obliging immigrants or citizenship applicants to learn the domestic language is a matter of practical exigency, not of identity. To be German cannot be a matter of

German-language competence if Austria and parts of Switzerland too speak German. Nevertheless, the German civic integration policy for newcomers, as well as the German naturalization rules, make the relatively demanding, intermediate B1 language standard (according to the Common European Reference Framework for Languages) a condition for passing the required tests. By contrast, France, which is far more insistent on the domestic purity and international recognition of French language, is rather lax about its formal integration requirements, asking only for oral competence in the context of naturalization and for the even more elementary A1.1 level within the Contrats d'Acceuil et d'Intégration (CAI) for newcomers.[43] If identity concerns were driving the emphasis on language competence for civic integration, one would expect the exact opposite outcome, with France setting the hurdle high and Germany setting it low. In reality, the main worry is societal adjustment, especially labor market integration. This is less of a concern in France, where most immigrants arrive from franco-phone Africa, and more of a concern in Germany, where most immi-grants—even those arriving with German-descent credentials—speak no German at all at the point of arrival. Overall, in the context of civic integra-tion, language is conceived of less in terms of identity than of the functional capacity of the newcomer to adjust and get by without the help of the state.

Religion is a more serious candidate for being a marker of identity. This is because one cannot adhere to two religions at one time, in contrast to language, the adoption of which is additional and capacity-enhancing, not substitutive.[44] However, if language falters for its intrinsic weakness as a marker of identity, religion falters for constitutional reasons. To make a particular religion obligatory for the acquisition of citizenship, and to prop-agate religious citizenship identities, would contradict elementary individ-ual rights. Consequently no contemporary Western state would dare advocate such stance. In fact, liberalism itself was born in the very differen-tiation between state and religion in early modern Europe, which remains valid today.

But still, there are religious temptations, especially in the confrontation with Muslims and Islam. In Denmark, for instance, populist right-wing forces around the small Danish People's Party (DPP) insist that Christianity is a defining element of Danish national culture, which newcomers have to adopt or adjust to: "We live in a Christian country, and when you come here you must conform to Danish norms, laws and habits," declared a DPP member of Parliament.[45] As Per Mouritsen stresses, this reference to

Christianity is sheer particularism, devoid of the missionary zeal of historical Christianity. There is no claim to moral superiority in it; instead, it
blends with a right of place ("we were here first") and with a view of "Danish cultural heritage" as "indefinable," as "all the 1000 little things" and
"the air that we breathe" (DPP leader Kjaersgaards).[46] To say that such
a stance, if turned into a policy, would contradict the precepts of liberal
constitutionalism is perhaps not even the relevant objection; how can
something that is deemed "undefinable" become a matter of policy in the
first place?

A reference to Christianity is also, next to one to the German language,
the only particularism that one can find in the German concept of *Leitkultur*, which was proposed by circles within the conservative Christian
Democratic Party (CDU) early in the millennium. This was a delicate matter, indicated by the fact that Christianity did *not* appear in the original
formulation of a "liberal German Leitkultur" by the CDU leader in parliament, Friedrich Merz. Only the CDU Immigration Commission (2000) included it.[47] But this was Christianity with a universalistic touch, in terms
of the "value system of our Christian-Occidental culture" that had to be
"accepted" by immigrants. The compound "Christian-Occidental" is programmatic, because the values to be inculcated in immigrants were to be
not religious but secular—most notably, "freedom, solidarity, and justice,"
which could be "deduced" from the "Christian understanding of the
person."[48]

The notion of Leitkultur had to be quickly withdrawn, because it was
suspected to be too close to an assimilationist stance. However, something
akin to it has informed the Islamic headscarf laws passed by several German
Land (state) governments in 2004 and 2005.[49] In Baden-Württemberg and
Bavaria, for example, these laws prohibit the wearing of the Islamic headscarf by public school teachers, while explicitly endorsing a Catholic ward-
robe. The crypto-nationalist argument is that the German state is not just
any state but a state shaped by the Christian-Occidental tradition, which
the state had not only the license but also the mandate to be partial about
and to help reproduce across the generations. The selective exclusion of
Islam and endorsement of Christianity rests on a subtle distinction between
religion as faith and religion as culture. Of course, the neutral state could
not inculcate a faith; doing so would revoke the Westphalian Peace formula
that had ended the intra-Christian bloodletting in early modern Europe.
But the state could see itself as guardian of the secular culture derived from

this faith and be partial in the sense that only "this" religion and not "that" religion has made "us" who we are today.

However secularized, Christian particularism is still problematic. Concretely, it requires the contorted legal construct that veiled Catholic nun teachers are not expressing a faith but "performing a tradition."[50] More important, the selective ban on the wearing of the Islamic headscarf by public school teachers violates the constitutional equality principle. In its *Ludin* decision of September 2003, which had kicked off the flood of *Land* legislations in the ensuing years, the German Federal Constitutional Court had argued that the state was free to exclude religious symbolism from the public sphere. But if it decided to do so, in deviation from the German tradition of "open" neutrality and in approximation of the French tradition of "laicist" neutrality, *all* religious symbolisms had to be excluded— Christian ones included. Evidently, in the German headscarf conflict legislatures and courts espoused contradictory understandings of the German state: Christian-particularistic versus universalistic.

Overall, the grounding of collective identity in religion runs up against constitutional obstacles, because the liberal state is obliged to be agnostic or at least impartial about religion.

The typical solution to the problem of collective identity across Europe today is the one pioneered by Republican France, according to which to be national is defined in the light of the universalistic precepts of human rights and democracy. In an interesting discussion of the Danish case, Per Mouritsen found that a "Nordic version of the French-Jacobin short circuit" dominated over its main rival, "secularized-Christianity-as-culture."[51] Accordingly, the program of the Social Democratic Party, traditionally Denmark's strongest political force, defines "Danish values," which are challenged by globalization, in terms of the French Republican triplet "freedom, equality, and solidarity."[52] Prime Minister Rasmussen expressed the Danish "particular universalism" as follows: "Danish society has been built on some fundamental values, which must be accepted, if you are to live here. In Denmark, politics and religion are separated. In Denmark, there is inviolable respect for human life. In Denmark . . . women are equal to men."[53] Or, as in the case of the so-called Danish cartoon affair, to be Danish is to advocate free speech. Again, this way of being Danish is no different from being French or British or German or Dutch.

The national particularisms immigrants and ethnic minorities are asked to accept across European states are local versions of the universalistic idiom of liberal democracy. But why this reluctance to ask for more? The answer is that more would amount to a regress from "integration" to "assimilation," the imposition of a particular culture or way of life that contemporary liberal constitutional states are set to avoid. Of course, assimilation may still be the desired goal of immigrant absorption, and there may even be no reasonable alternative to it.[54] But in a liberal setting, such assimilation can only be "intransitive," not "transitive," the result of voluntarism on the part of migrants, not of forced imposition by the state.[55]

However, this is not to say that universalism cannot be exclusive. In fact, especially with respect to Muslims, universalism is the main form in which Western states practice exclusion today. The examples reach from the French antiheadscarf law of 2004 to the invocation of "Dutch norms and values" in the Dutch civic integration policy for immigrants. Let us look more closely at the Dutch case. Many have seen the Netherlands regressing from integration to assimilation, but in the transitive way theoretically ruled out by Brubaker.[56] Has it? If it has, then only in the specific sense that liberalism has thickened from procedural framework for toleration into substantive way of life, which the members of the majority consider "their" way of life and which is expected to be shared by immigrants and ethnic minorities. Jan Willem Duyvendak et al. have interestingly argued that the Netherlands was never as proverbially multicultural as the stereotype would have it.[57] Instead, not unlike the small Nordic countries, the Netherlands is marked by a "progressive monoculture," in which, say, men and women are equal, homosexuality is widely accepted, and religion is marginal and strictly private.[58] The "Dutch norms and values" that immigrants are expected to adopt are not a preference for wooden clogs, Gouda, and windows without curtains. Instead, these norms and values are the progressive outlook shared by the majority. If the Dutch information DVD, disseminated in the context of the new policy of "integration from abroad," contains pictures of nude women on Dutch beaches and of kissing homosexuals, the message is, "This is Holland," a country of progressive people, and whoever takes issue with this should stay away.

The exclusive and thus identity-forging dimension of universalism can be formulated as the notion that the liberal state is only for liberal people. This is, of course, a profoundly illiberal idea, because it casts people into a standard mould and robs them of the possibility to decide for themselves who they want to be. Ever since Kant, it has been a key precept of liberalism that law and public policy can regulate only the external behavior of people, not their inner convictions. Accordingly, the German Constitutional Court stipulated that citizens are "not legally required to personally share the values of the Constitution."[59] All that, say, can be expected of religious believers is to respect in their behavior the priority of the secular legal order, and not to harm the constitutional rights of third parties. Accordingly, an exacting loyalty requirement, which aims at "an inner disposition, a mindset [*Gesinnung*], not external behavior," has been deemed contrary to the constitution by the German Constitutional Court.

Citizenship tests that ask for factual knowledge about a country's history and institutions are unproblematic in this respect, because such matter is merely cognitive: it can be learned and mechanically reproduced. Even a signed loyalty declaration or an oath to the constitution does not raise eyebrows, because it consists of an external behavior that only actualizes the contractual underpinnings of liberal citizenship. However, a citizenship test that scrutinizes a candidate's "inner disposition" does raise eyebrows, precisely for transgressing the thin line that separates the regulation of behavior from the control of beliefs. This line has been infamously transgressed in the so-called Naturalization Guidelines, which were issued by the *Land* government of Baden-Württemberg in September 2005. Their professed purpose was to check whether a citizenship applicant's written "declaration of loyalty" (*Bekenntnis*) to the constitution, which has been a component of the German naturalization procedure since 2000, also corresponded to the applicant's actual beliefs or "inner disposition."[60] A legal evaluation of the guidelines found them in violation of national and international law, in two respects.[61] First, in being applied only to citizenship applicants from member states of the Islamic League, the guidelines "discriminated" against Muslim applicants for citizenship. In fact, the guidelines, which consisted of thirty questions about applicants' views on parental authority, religion, homosexuality, gender equality, terrorism, and other issues, construed the "liberal democratic order primarily as one that is contrary to the presumed values of a specific group," Muslims.[62] Second, and more important for our purposes, by intruding in the intimate sphere of the person, the guidelines violated the liberty rights of the constitution, especially the freedom of negative opinion and conscience. As Rüdiger Wolfrum and Volker Röben explicate the constitutional status quo, "the mere holding of an opinion is no threat to the liberal democratic order, if it is not expressed in concrete action that is directed against this order."[63] Appropriately condemned for being a discriminatory, inquisitive morality test, the guidelines had to be quickly shelved. But they epitomize the illiberal potential of a liberalism that transmutes into an identity, an ethical way of life that everyone is expected to be conformant with, and that is brought forward with an unabashedly exclusionary intention against liberalism's presumed Other: Islam and Muslims.

Liberalism as Identity

If modern citizenship had always combined "internal inclusion" with "external exclusion,"[64] its externally exclusive dimension has notably weakened in the past half century. The weakening of the particularistic, identity-lending dimension of citizenship is tantamount to the retreat of nationalism, at least in the West. Habermas's brief synopsis of nationalism's decline is as good as any.[65] First, especially in Europe, the long peace after 1945, which coincided with the building of a European polity, has blunted the edges between nation-state societies. Second, if the camp, with denationalized inmates stripped to the condition of bare life, was the enigmatic experience of the twentieth century, it is one that has pushed for the universalization of rights, beyond the confines of citizenship. Third, to the degree that academic history once provided the cognitive coordinates for nationalist thought, the internationalization and professionalization of academic history has removed them. One sees the imprints of this change in history curricula in public schools that are less geared toward inculcating nationalist loyalty than toward disseminating reflexive knowledge.[66] Finally, with the rise of mass communication, mass travel, and international migration, as a result of which multiple ways of life clamor for coexistence and equal treatment, "all alternatives to a universalistic broadening of moral consciousness are being decimated."[67] To these concrete historical changes Habermas adds the evolutionary advance of "post-conventional" identities, at the individual and the collective level alike, which are marked by reflexivity and a capacity to step back from one's contingent views and identifications in the light of universal ethical principles. Now any blind identification with a quasi-sacred object, such as the nation, becomes anathema. From this admittedly Habermasian angle, democratic citizenship does not require a national identity, but only a shared political culture, which is more procedural than substantive, captured in Habermas's famous notion of "constitutional patriotism."

However one judges the viability of constitutional patriotism to forge unity and integration in plural societies, the decoupling of citizenship from nationhood is the incontrovertible exit position for contemporary state campaigns for unity and integration, especially with respect to immigrants. Talcott Parsons, writing decades before globalization would undermine the comprehensively national organization of society, saw modern societies marked by a trend toward increasing "value generalization," which makes for values that are unspecific to any one society.[68] In fact, what Parsons attributed and limited to the "new lead society," the United States, has come to mark all Western societies: citizenship "dissociated from ethnic membership," and nation-states "emancipated from specific religious and ethnic control."[69] With Eric Kaufmann, one can depict the underlying process as a "decline of dominant ethnicity," that is, a decline of the notion of the state as the property and instrument of self-realization of a particular group.[70]

Apart from the heights of social theory and macro history, one can detect the decoupling of citizenship from nationhood in the changing micro rules of access to citizenship, which have generally become nondiscriminatory, in the sense of shunning group-level exclusions on the basis of ethnicity or race, and which do not require a particular cultural identity as a prerequisite for citizenship. Overall, the same centrifugal tendencies that have *raised* the issue of unity and integration in contemporary state societies also *limit* the state's possibilities to bring about such unity, most notably the negative norm of nondiscrimination and its positive flip side, the celebration of diversity.

Arash Abizadeh persuasively denied that there is a "conceptual or metaphysical necessity" for collective identities to be particularistic and thus intrinsically in need of an excluded Other.[71] Further, he argued that the "particularist thesis" reifies on the theoretical plane the contingent, Westphalian "ideology of indivisible sovereignty."[72] But this advocate of cosmopolitanism conceded that lesser identities might still be the empirically more potent, especially at the level of the state. A state is like an individual in that it does not happen twice in the world. This locks both, the individual and the state, into being a singular unit. Accordingly, when the German interior minister Wolfgang Schäuble called on "Muslims in Germany" to become "German Muslims," he also found that a generic "constitution" was not sufficient for "successful integration": "Constitutional patriotism, as a matter of reason (and not of emotion), is not sufficient. . . . If we want to feel part of a collectivity, then there must be something that connects us at a deeper, human level, at the level of religion and culture, values and identity."[73] The problem is that such identity would exactly separate "Germans" from "Muslims" and thus forfeit the very attempt at integration. The German state could not impose it without being openly discriminatory, because a state of "Christian origins and traditions" is one of which Muslims could not be an equal part.

Cornered by the dilemma of a particularistic identity that is deemed necessary for integration yet cannot be supplied by a law or policy that must remain formally nondiscriminatory, contemporary states are inclined to call a certain idea of liberalism to the rescue. Liberalism has always had two different sides, one that prescribes autonomy and reason over heteronomy and faith, and thus prescribes an ideal way of life, and a second that limits itself to procedural toleration and noninterference in a society marked by an intrinsic multiplicity of ways of life.[74] Of course, both sides of liberalism require one another, as either a single-minded toleration of the intolerant or the intolerant's ruthless suppression would be destructive of liberalism. But it still makes sense to conceive of both sides of liberalism as variables that may be differently developed in different times and places.

In retrospect, the flowering of multiculturalism across Western societies in the past few decades was premised on a prevalence of the toleration mode over the autonomy mode of liberalism. This does not mean that other core values of liberalism, such as autonomy and reason, were extinct in this period. On the contrary, there was no need to assert them, because nobody questioned them. As Kymlicka showed in a revealing discussion, "liberal multiculturalism" in Canada is enabled by the fact that European ethnics have been its propelling force, acting and reasoning within a liberal-democratic framework.[75] Conversely, with a comparative eye on the rougher quarters of contemporary Europe, where multiculturalism has been largely discredited by "illiberal" Muslim practices, Kymlicka speculates that "the debate in Canada might have been very different if, as in Europe, ninety percent of our immigrants were Muslim."[76]

In fact, in the wake of Islamic terrorism, toleration liberalism has receded behind a less procedural, more substantive variant of liberalism that prescribes a shared way of life in which, say, men and women are equal and the secular trumps the religious. Such liberalism is potentially an identity, separating liberal from illiberal people. It had its first lease of life in the context of colonialism, where it allowed the hierarchical demarcation between European and non-European ways of life, with the Europeans figuring as "superior people."[77] Though devoid of such hierarchical pretensions, liberalism as identity is currently having a second lease on life in the confrontation with politicized Islam. For good or bad, it is the stuff out of which the universalistic citizenship identities propagated by contemporary states are made. If not moderated by liberalism-as-toleration, liberalism may be more at risk from a one-sided version of itself than from its belligerent Other, the illiberals of Muslim and other stripes.

Chapter 8

Engendering Culture: Citizenship, Identity, and Belonging

Leti Volpp

Academics writing about immigration, citizenship, and integration have in recent years been much preoccupied with the following question: How should Western liberal democracies respond to the cultural difference of immigrants, manifested through practices that stand in tension with liberal values, especially gender equality? A debate then ensues, which weighs the relative merits of the competing values of feminism and multiculturalism, group rights and individual rights, or universalism and relativism.[1] Especially in the post–September 11 world, popular discourse has sharply turned away from dallying over the weighing of these relative merits, in favor of the stark demand that immigrants abandon problematic gendered practices, and assimilate.[2]

Whether academic or popular, both approaches rely on problematic baseline assumptions, variously phrased as "we have values, you have culture"[3] and "our culture is superior to yours." Rather than engage in a debate that relies upon these problematic assumptions, in this essay I seek instead to briefly outline why they exist, and then demonstrate some of their consequences, in particular for reform efforts that seek to remediate the lives of immigrant women.

The values/culture dichotomy and belief in a superior culture is rooted in what we could call cultural racism, whereby cultures are essentialized and posited to be either inferior to or incompatible with the values of the dominant community.[4] Cultural racism shapes how we process and understand individual cases of gendered subordination, and it also motivates and molds particular reform efforts. Host societies are believed to be liberal, to uphold the value of gender equality, and to be free of practices of gender subordination. Immigrants are believed to be directed not by values but by tradition-bound and premodern culture, and to routinely engage in practices of gender subordination. But these beliefs are more the product of discursive effect than empirically accurate.

Two major and interlocking strands weave together to create this effect. One strand is the metanarrative of self and other that defines the host society of the West as progressive, democratic, civilized, and feminist, against immigrants—and in Europe and in the United States after 9/11, most especially Muslim immigrants—as backward, barbaric, primitive, and misogynist. The other strand is the way in which specific incidents of gendered subordination are understood differently depending upon the identity of the perpetrator. We selectively blame culture for bad behavior.[5] When a bad act is done by one of "us," it is usually explained as the act of an individual deviant, and accounted for through the language of psychology. In contrast, when a bad act is done by an immigrant, the act is explained as the product of culture. In the words of the geographer Alan Pred, "Through the metonymical magic of cultural racism, through its invisible logic, through the working of its common-sense discourses, individual transgression becomes collective guilt, becomes a confirmation of what the Other does *and what we do not do*, of who all of Them are *and who We are not*."[6]

An example may help illustrate the explanatory power of cultural racism. On New Year's Day of 2008, seventeen-year-old Sarah and eighteen-year-old Amina Said were shot to death by their father, Yaser Said, an Egyptian-born Muslim, in a suburb of Dallas, Texas. Just before the murders, the sisters and their mother had moved to Oklahoma to escape Said and his violence. He had been accused of sexual abuse by both girls when they were eight and nine years old in 1998 (charges were dismissed after they recanted the accusations the following year).[7] Friends and relatives reported years of physical and emotional abuse perpetrated by Said against his children. Their maternal aunt reported that she had told one of the girls when they returned from Oklahoma to Dallas on New Year's Eve that they needed to get a restraining order.

The motive of Yaser Said, who is still at large, in killing his daughters remains unclear. In interviews, Sarah and Amina Said's mother angrily rejected the idea that her husband's religion or culture had anything to do with the murders, as did their brother. The deaths of Sarah and Amina Said could be understood through the rubric of family violence, as the product of violence against women, endemic in the United States, or as an act of individual pathology—all explanations that would narrate their murder in a way that would not exaggerate the difference of Yaser Said from "us." Nonetheless, former Dutch member of Parliament and current American Enterprise Institute fellow Ayaan Hirsi Ali took the opportunity in February 2008 to tell a crowd of five hundred in Dallas that the sisters were the victims of an "honor killing." "I want to tell you why their father killed them," she said. She asserted that the daughters were known to date non-Muslim men and dress in Western clothing, and that, in her estimation, the perceived loss of honor motivated Yaser Said to take his children's lives. "The essence of a woman in this culture is reduced to the value of their hymen. In countries ruled by Islam, women are treated as slaves or pets," she said.[8]

Certain narratives have traction because of already existing scripts about gender, culture, immigration, and Islam.[9] Across the blogosphere, the "honor killing in Texas" has been used to buttress claims that Islam is evil, and that the worst fate imaginable is to be born female into a Muslim family.[10] According to these commentators, Muslims engage in honor kill-ings, illustrating their barbaric essential nature; in contrast, "we" do not.[11] Thus, how individual cases are categorized both reflects and further fuels already existing perceptions about "illiberal minorities" and "liberal us."[12] As Pred writes:

> If one young Turk viciously stabs his sister outside a Stockholm discotheque, if one Lebanese beats his twenty-one-year-old former wife to death in Malmø, if a fifteen-year-old girl of Iraqi background is murdered in Umeå by her brother and cousin, it confirms that all Muslim men are guided by their female-oppressing scriptures of Islam, that they will not permit "their" women the freedoms of Swedish women, that they will mete out violent punishment if fam-ily "honor" is blemished by sisters, daughters, or wives who dress or behave in a sexually "provocative" manner. Always have done so and always will do so. Uniform and unchanging. It's in Their culture—but not Ours.[13]

These scripts are very powerful, and have the capacity not only to shape how stories about individual cases are told but also to motivate legal re-

form. Across Europe, legislation has been enacted in the past several years
that seeks to address practices of forced and arranged marriage, honor-
based violence, female genital mutilation/cutting, and the wearing of a hijab
or headscarf.[14] The concern about "traditional" practices of Muslim
women, in particular, has intensified against a backdrop of concern about
global terrorism. As part of the effort to combat terrorism, Western governments seek to transform Islam with, for example, the U.S. State Department's program "Muslim World Outreach," which attempts to disseminate
"American values" of "democracy, women's rights and tolerance," using
teams specialized in military psychological operations, covert CIA operatives, think tanks, and U.S.-funded media. As purportedly the most abject
victims of Islam, women are seen as the entry point in the project to "bring
democracy" to Islam.[15]

The intensification of concern about Muslim women has coincided with
the turning away from multiculturalism in Western liberal democracies,
most of which are now calling not for integration but for assimilation.[16]
Irene Bloemraad describes a transition toward stronger policies of cultural
and civic assimilation, visible, for example, in the new citizenship tests of
the United Kingdom and the Netherlands, in the French ban on the headscarf in public elementary and secondary schools, and in the traction in the
United States of Samuel Huntington's recent screed.[17] In Sherene Razack's
words, in Canada there has been a shift in discourse from "we are multicultural and the U.S. is not," to "we have to get over the phase when we were
nice—we have accommodated them too much."[18]

I will look more closely at these dynamics by focusing on particular
reform efforts that target arranged marriage and the wearing of the headscarf—and in doing so, make two different theoretical points. The specific
cases I examine are historically and geographically diverse. With the example of arranged marriages I seek to show that, despite frequent claims that
the intent of reform efforts is to help women, reform efforts are often part
of a generalized tightening of immigration restrictions, or a reduction in
the rights of citizenship. We can see this in contexts where a population in
general is targeted as the subject of uplift and where specific gendered practices are among many practices listed for reform, as well as in contexts
where gendered uplift is the single ostensible rationale for reform. We could
call this the "proxy effect," whereby assistance to the imperiled immigrant
woman actually functions as a proxy for restrictions imposed against an
immigrant community in general. With the headscarf example I demon-

strate how the obsession with culture masks the role of other issues at work in the lives of immigrant women or immigrant communities in general, and inevitably results in "reforms" that are less productive than regressive. We could call this "depoliticization through culture," for the intense focus on culture diverts attention away from political origins of and political solutions to gendered subordination, violence, and general disenfranchisement.[19]

Arranged Marriage

At the outset, we should understand arranged marriage as a method of entering into marriage, which functions as a counterpart to what some call "love marriage." There is an enormous range of practices that could constitute how one enters into an arranged marriage, from situations where bride and groom can exercise no consent, to situations where a third party introduces the bride and groom, who decide if they want to get married. Thus, while this is not the conventional categorization, we could think of many marriages (or romantic partnerships) as "arranged," in cases where we begin relationships because we are introduced to another person by a third party we know in common—rather than relationships that begin with random strangers. While many fuse the idea of "arranged marriages" with "forced marriages" and violent outcomes, there is no reason why one should assume that a "love marriage" will not have a violent outcome,[20] and no reason why one should link the idea of "arranged," given the broad continuum of practices that constitute "arranged," with "forced."[21]

Nonetheless, the idea of arranged marriages is conjoined with assumptions about traditional pasts, about coercion, and about strong communal ties that link families through marriage for reasons of property, connection, or wealth, in contrast to the idea of romantic marriage, which is associated with the concepts of choice, love, freedom, and modernity.[22]

To begin to unpack these assumptions, we could look at the 2003 Fox Television show *Married by America*—which bizarrely provided arranged marriages, courtesy of the viewing audience. The show's Web site asks:

Are you ready to be "MARRIED BY AMERICA"? In America, people usually find love and marriage in the traditional way. You meet, fall in love and tie the knot. But the failure rate is pretty high.

What if there's a better way?

MARRIED BY AMERICA is a groundbreaking reality-based show that invites the viewing audience to be your personal matchmaker.

With the help of relationship experts, potential mates will be hand picked, especially for you.

Then, your closest friends and family will have the chance to meet these singles, and winnow them down to two.

All the while the home audience will be getting to know you and what you're looking for in love, so they can weigh in and make the final decision—which of these partners is right for you.

We're looking for singles, men and women who've never been married, who are interested in being setup in an arranged marriage and willing to get engaged to someone they've never met. You should be between the ages of 21–39, with no children.[23]

Thus, the "home audience"—providing comfort in its invocation of "home," as opposed to "public," or "complete strangers"—has the final decision as to whom participants marry. Obviously, one television show does not represent an enormous cultural shift in American marital practices. However, I think it worthwhile to contrast the rhetoric used to describe arranged marriage on the Web site with popular conceptions of the practice. In the literature on multiculturalism, arranged marriage functions not, as suggested on the Married by America Web site, as a salutary remedy to failed romantic marriages, or as a practice engaged in by participants turning from the "traditional way" to a "groundbreaking" show, but as a sign of difference practiced only by immigrants stuck in traditional ways that the liberal state chooses either to accept or not tolerate. Of course, arranged marriages without romance and love were the norm in the West for most of its history. And one could argue that many contemporary marriages in the West occur for reasons other than romance and love (say, for reasons of financial security, or childbearing). But arranged marriage today stands in for what the immigrant other should escape, in order to move on to enlightened liberalism, defined through the citizen's ability to engage in freedom.[24]

Arranged marriages feature prominently in the multiculturalism literature—as Bhikhu Parekh writes, "Many liberals would like to ban or at least discourage the practice on the grounds that it offends against the values of personal autonomy and choice, as universal values, especially in such crucial matters as marriage."[25] Ayelet Shachar, in her otherwise careful work *Multicultural Jurisdictions: Cultural Differences and Women's Rights*, presumes that "the practice of arranged marriages" may cause "intangible damage," even if the parties are permitted to divorce.[26] Her focus here is on duress and coercion that may shape the decision to engage in an arranged marriage.[27] Again, there is no reason for one to assume that "arranged marriages" are more difficult to exit from than "love marriage," when we have now in Louisiana, Arkansas, and Arizona the practice of "covenant marriage."[28] Furthermore, I would argue that duress and coercion are better understood as involved in the entry into a "forced marriage" than into the generic "arranged marriage."

But because arranged marriage is conflated with negative cultural tradition, those who practice arranged marriage are considered undesirable citizens. Let me first share an example that is historical, where the practice of arranged marriage was considered only one shortcoming among many. The War Relocation Authority (WRA), during the internment of Japanese Americans during World War II, grappled with the question of integrating internees into the general U.S. population. The WRA used cultural assimilation to both measure and produce Japanese Americans' loyalty, seeking to eradicate traditions not considered conducive to liberal citizenship.[29]

As part of the process of integration, all draft-age Nisei men, and eventually all adults, were required to answer a loyalty questionnaire. This questionnaire has been notorious for two particular questions, numbers 27 and 28, which asked, "Are you willing to serve in the armed forces of the United States on combat duty, wherever ordered?" and "Will you swear unqualified allegiance to the United States of America and faithfully defend the United States from any or all attack by foreign or domestic forces, and forswear any allegiance or obedience to the Japanese emperor, or any other foreign government, power, or organization?"[30] Answering no to both questions produced what have been called "No No Boys," who were then shipped for special incarceration for the noncompliant in the Tule Lake internment camp.[31]

Less studied by scholars of the internment are other questions on the Leave Clearance Questionnaire, which suggest some new ruminations about the culture one is to shed in order to become assimilated into citizenship.[32] These questions include the following: "Will you try to develop such American habits which will cause you to be accepted readily into American social groups?" and "Will you conform to the customs and dress of your new home?"[33] As Caroline Chung Simpson and Orin Starn have demonstrated, Japanese culture was the subject of serious study in the camps. The WRA established an anthropological study of Japanese Americans in the camps, for the explicit purpose of developing theories of Japanese behavior that would be useful after the war when the United States occupied Japan.[34] What the anthropologists theorized was a tense duality between Japan and America, played out as intergenerational conflict between Issei (traditional) and Nissei (modern), which suggested that Japanese Americans had to be freed from the values of filial piety in order to embrace a modern existence in America. Within the camps, Japanese Americans were aggressively reeducated to abandon traditional family practices, including arranged marriage, thought to inhibit the "natural" development of character that would allow one to progress.[35] The political disenfranchisement of Japanese Americans, thrust from citizenship into the category of "enemy alien," was in part justified through a purported cultural difference;[36] this cultural difference was to be shed in the internment camps to enable successful incorporation into the American way of life.

Ansel Adams gave one of his photographs of teenage Japanese girls in the Manzanar camp this caption: "Manzanar is only a detour on the road to American citizenship."[37] The young girls in the photograph were presumably American citizens as a matter of birthright, a citizenship whose associated rights, as interned citizens, they could not enjoy. We could read Adams's label as suggesting that Manzanar was a necessary detour to allow Japanese Americans to better learn to be American citizens before they could realize their rights as American citizens—a detour that was perhaps more accurately described as a necessary reeducation process before American citizenship. With this historical example, we see arranged marriage as one practice among many that had to be eradicated before assimilation into citizenship.

A contemporary example shows arranged marriage as featuring more directly in immigration controls. In the United Kingdom, in 2002, Tony Blair's administration issued a White Paper on immigration and citizenship entitled *Secure Borders, Safe Haven: Integration with Diversity in Modern Britain*.[38] Among new policies on border controls, asylum seekers, and illegal immigrants, the document included a chapter that addressed "arranged marriages."[39] (This was chapter 7, which lumped together as its chapter title "Marriage/Family Visits and War criminals.")[40] In its introductory paragraph, the chapter states: "As time goes on, we expect the number of ar-

ranged marriages between UK children and those living abroad to decline. Instead, parents will seek to choose a suitable partner for their children from among their own communities in this country."[41] At the press conference where the White Paper was launched, Home Secretary David Blunkett explained that British Asians should confine arranged marriages to partners already living in the United Kingdom rather than flying in spouses from South Asia. He said that the government was not going to "ban arranged marriages" but that he believed young women in Britain from Asian families wanted to marry someone who also spoke English, and held similar educational and social backgrounds and attitudes.[42]

We can see here the slippage between concern about a specific practice, "arranged marriage," and its immigration consequences. Clearly, if the British government were concerned about the practice, per se, it would not espouse parents continuing to choose a "suitable partner" for their children, only now one already residing within Britain. As Ratna Kapur notes, the White Paper caused a furor in Britain by singling out South Asian marriages for suspicion and for appearing to use arranged marriages as a proxy for cutting back on legal immigration by specific communities.[43] More recently the Home Office, under the rubric of tackling forced marriage, raised the minimum age at which a person can sponsor a marriage partner from overseas from eighteen to twenty,[44] but was careful to state that it was "not expressing any concern about arranged marriages, which we know to be a part of many cultural traditions, and which involve the consent of both parties."[45]

The White Paper represents a shift from an earlier era in British history, when South Asian women seeking admission to Britain in the 1970s as spouses in arranged marriages were subjected to virginity tests at Heathrow Airport. This was to ensure that the women were "bona fide" immigrants; in other words, if they were not virgins, they would not be true brides and would be attempting to enter the country under false pretenses.[46] In the United Kingdom, we see a change from the government's unquestioning endorsement of arranged marriage in the virginity tests to its attempt to limit the practice in the name of protecting young Asian women in the White Paper of today. Even with the change from lack of concern to stated concern, both policies rely on arranged marriage in order to engage in, or threaten to enact, immigration restrictions.[47] As lawful admission into a country is a prerequisite to citizenship through naturalization, a policy limiting immigration constitutes a policy limiting citizenship; thus, the

British government has relied upon arranged marriage to patrol British citizenship.

Arranged marriage functions as a particular trope for immigrant culture: restricting arranged marriage has worked to restrict minority communities from gaining citizenship. We see this both in the context of citizenship as formal legal status in terms of threatening to bar entry into the nation in the British context, and in the context of citizenship in the form of identity, in terms of the mandate to Japanese Americans to cast off the practice in the name of progress from enemy alien to American citizen. Because arranged marriage is equated with gender subordination, governments have successfully deployed policies addressing the practice to target minority communities in the name of gender or community uplift.[48]

The Headscarf Debate

Let me now turn to the headscarf debate in France to make my second theoretical point. The typical sealed chamber of discussion as to how the liberal state is to address the cultural difference of immigrants relies upon the presumption that the gendered culture of immigrants is the problem. This presumption evacuates all forces other than culture from the discussion, and results in "reforms" that fail to address how racism, the state, histories, and geopolitics have already shaped and will continue to shape the lives of the communities at issue.

In February 2004, the French legislature passed an amendment to the French Code of Education that banned students from wearing "conspicuous religious symbols" in French public primary and secondary schools. President Jacques Chirac had convened a commission in July 2003, known as the Stasi Commission, to examine how the principle of laïcité, or secularity, should apply in practice. The Stasi Commission recommended prohibiting the wearing of headscarves by Muslim girls, yarmulkes by Jewish boys, and large Christian crosses. Small crosses, and discreet pendants, such as a Star of David or hand of Fatima, were ruled to be acceptable.

The idea behind the ban, implemented in September 2004, reflected a strict separation between church and state that is believed to foster French republicanism. France's long history of religious conflict and persecution led both to the idea that secularism was the only guarantor of national peace and to the official separation of church and state in 1905. In address-

ing the French nation about the ban of conspicuous religious symbols, President Chirac explained that what was at stake was "the principle of secularism," one of "the pillars of our Republic."[49] The school, he urged, "must remain a privileged place for the transmission of republican principles and a melting pot for equal opportunity."[50]

But it would not be accurate to think that the law emerged from a concern about the boundary between religion and state in general. In the same statement, President Chirac contended that the ban "protects our schools from breaking down along ethnic lines." Thus, we see in his words a glimmer of what else is at work, as evidenced by the use of the word "ethnic," not "religious." For Muslims in France, the state perspective on their religious practice conjoins with concerns about ethnic, not religious, difference. Culture and religion become fused. I would argue that this fusing of culture and religion also occurs in the United States. When white religious minorities engage in particular practices that diverge from the norm, those practices tend to be discussed under the rubric of religious difference; when minorities are racial as well as religious, their practices tend to be discussed under the rubric of ethnic as well as religious difference. This is linked to what some have described in the post-9/11 era as the racialization of Muslims, where to be Muslim becomes linked with purported racial attributes, such as the notion of "looking Muslim."[51] I am therefore arguing that for French Muslims, religious difference is conflated with a racialized cultural difference.

The impetus for the law clearly emerged from controversy about Muslim girls wearing headscarves to school.[52] President Chirac admitted there had never been a problem with Catholic students wearing crosses "obviously of an excessive dimension," and most Jewish students who wear skullcaps attend private Jewish schools.[53] Thus, the formally "neutral" breadth of the law with its focus on the conspicuousness of any religious symbol masked the particular concern underlying the law. The headscarf, in comparison to the cross and the yarmulke, clearly raised issues in France beyond the mere principle of laïcité. In December 2003, sixty prominent French women had signed a letter in the magazine Elle, demanding the ban of the veil, a "visible symbol of the submission of women."[54] We could consider the furor about the headscarf a moral panic, whereby the headscarf literally demonstrates the failure of Muslims to assimilate, a failure that is believed to be the result of the sexism of Islam. A veritable firestorm of controversy ensued, with most commentators presuming that women who sought to wear the hijab were imperiled by Islam and either were being pressured by their family or communities or were victims of false consciousness.

Evicted from the conversation were questions of what the headscarf represents to which person in which context. As we can see, to many French feminists the headscarf symbolizes the submission of women. Wearing a headscarf can connote just what it purports to connote: religious piety.[55] Some girls may wear the headscarf because of parental or community coercion.[56] Some may wear the headscarf as a shaming device to ward off sexual harassment. At this point, some may wear the headscarf to signal their position on this controversy, as a political statement against a government that has banned the practice.[57]

A petition initiated by French sociologist Christine Delphy and the Feminists for Equality collective makes apparent one factor that generally disappeared in the debate.[58] The petition directs our attention to the question of race.[59] Pointing out the slippage whereby certain citizens, born and educated in France, are turned into "eternal migrants," the authors of the petition assert that because the French cannot send them "back home," they are treated as "second-class citizens," as an "inferior caste."[60] This, the authors say, is the issue that the debates on the headscarf attempt to "veil"; this is the "crux of the only true problem of, and for, the Republic."[61] The petition both calls for an abandonment of France's de facto system of national preference for the "true French" and for research on how racism is institutionalized and can be redressed. The petition also warns that so long as France denies the existence of this discrimination and refuses to provide equality to the descendents of people colonized by the French, the country will only develop greater problems.[62] This discrimination has profound material consequences in the workplace, the neighborhood, the school. The petition states: "Not a single act of daily life in France is free of racism against those who through all our colonialist history were perceived as inferior human beings."[63] The petition also importantly points to the manner in which broader geopolitical issues shape race, in its desire to rebut the claim that girls and women who wear the "Islamic scarf" constitute a "fifth column of a foreign power."[64] French Muslims are racialized as putative terrorists. The headscarf is now considered a "provocation": it represents global Islamic terrorism.[65]

The petition by Delphy et al. suggests that the condition of French Muslims cannot be addressed solely through that topic of obsession, the headscarf. In fact, the Stasi Commission had actually recommended twenty-five measures in addition to the ban on conspicuous religious symbols, which the commission's report stated were essential for the French government to implement. These measures included the destruction of urban ghettos and the replanning of the cities, the addition of Yom Kippur and Eid as national holidays, the creation of an antidiscrimination authority, instruction about slavery, immigration, colonization, and decolonization in public schools, and policies against racism in schools.[66] But the French legislature chose only to implement the ban on religious symbols.

The opposition that is posed—for or against the religious ban, gender equality versus minority community rights—creates an impoverished analysis by removing these other questions from the conversation. We thus have the absurd result of all the tremendous weight of concerns circulating about French Muslim communities—public racism, fear of rising fundamentalism and global terrorist networks, unemployment rates as high as 60 percent in the *banlieues*, and enormous social isolation—literally placed on the heads of girls.[67] When culture is the sole filter through which we understand issues, when the gendered culture of immigrant communities is presumed to be the key problem facing liberal democracies in forestalling assimilation or integration, realms that otherwise have explanatory power—the political, the social, the economic, the affective—all disappear.[68] Noncultural causes of disenfranchisement and subordination drop out of the picture.[69]

While it might have seemed that France had "solved" the issue of the headscarf and could move on to address other issues,[70] the recent denial of French citizenship to Faiza Silmi suggests this is hardly the case. In June 2008, France's highest administrative court upheld a decision to deny citizenship on the ground that Silmi's "radical practice" of Islam, in the form of her wearing a niqab, was "incompatible with essential values of the French community, particularly the principle of equality of the sexes." As reported in the *New York Times*, in a sign of the nature of some of the criteria used to evaluate Silmi's fitness to become French, the government commissioner "approvingly noted in her report that she was treated by a male gynecologist during her pregnancies."[71] The idea that the exposure of Faiza Silmi's genitalia to a man other than her husband could constitute a reason to grant someone French citizenship can only be explained by historian Joan Scott's observation that in France sexual difference has been elevated to a distinct cultural character trait with great emphasis on the public display of women's bodies, so that the concealment of such is considered antithetical to French mores.[72] The political culture that is expected to be recognized by all citizens, regardless of background, is inseparable from the cultural mores of the majority—which are invisible to the majority as particular cultural mores.[73]

Conclusion

The raid on April 3, 2008, of a polygamist sect in Texas, which led to the removal of 555 women and children from the Yearning for Zion Ranch after a phone call to a domestic violence hotline from a reportedly pregnant sixteen-year-old girl who said she was beaten and raped by her fifty-year-old husband,[74] provides us with the opportunity to consider how gendered cultural difference engaged in by white, nonimmigrant communities does not raise the specter of a multiculturalism threatening liberal values.

This is not to say that there is no perception of difference. Historically, Mormons were subjected to a campaign against polygamy couched in terms of national morality, a campaign that linked the Mormon practice of polygamy with polygamy practiced in nonwhite communities.[75] And the failed campaign of Mitt Romney for the Republican presidential nomination in 2008 raised the question whether a Mormon would be considered sufficiently Christian to be elected president of the United States.[76] But the difference purportedly practiced on the Yearning for Zion Ranch is not so far from collective historical national memory—including frontier dress, Western mores of self-sufficiency and isolation from government, and whiteness.[77]

Perhaps as a result, we saw editorializing that since April is child abuse awareness month, the raid on the ranch reminds us of dangers to "our children."[78] We also saw the state taking considerable pains to attend to the specific needs of the women and children who were removed from the ranch, including the provision of a unique diet (all natural, since "they shun all things processed"), specially tailored clothes, and counseling of the relocated women and children, all costing the state upward of $25,000 per day.[79]

As I argued above, given the reflexive equation of cultural difference with racialized bodies, practices engaged in by white religious minorities tend to be seen as the product of religion, not culture. When difference is coded as religious and not cultural, it ordinarily leads to accommodation, as opposed to a demand for assimilation. Of course, the allegation of harm to children provided a limiting principle on the accommodation in which the state is willing to engage—Texas initially sought to strip parents of custody and place the children in foster care or put them up for adoption, we saw the painful separation of mothers from children over five years of age, and, twelve sect members were charged with crimes that included failure to report child abuse, bigamy, and sexual assault.[80] At the same time, we witnessed some accommodation in other ways: accommodation of dress and diet of those removed from the sect.

Let us engage in a thought experiment and imagine that there was a secretive compound in Texas of hundreds of Muslim immigrants, where there were allegations of child abuse, forced sex, and girls as young as fourteen made to enter polygamous marriages with much older men. It seems impossible to imagine any kind of accommodation by the state. And demands for assimilation can only be made to those considered assimilable. We can imagine that, in a case like this, cultural difference would be considered so threatening to the body politic that the only answer would be casting out, in the form of deportations for those who were removable and imprisonment for the rest.[81] One thing we know for sure:—there would be a veritable firestorm about the barbaric cultural practices perpetrated by Islam.

Chapter 9

Three Models of Civic Solidarity

Sarah Song

The question of how to forge solidarity across diversity is a familiar one, but it is being pursued with renewed urgency in contemporary liberal democratic societies grappling with the challenges raised by large-scale immigration. There has been a retreat from multiculturalism policies in Britain and the Netherlands toward an emphasis on social cohesion in approaching the integration of ethnic and religious minorities. In the United States many have called for stricter immigration controls, in part on the grounds that immigration, especially immigration from Mexico, threatens to undermine the American way of life. The renewed emphasis on social unity reflects a desire to preserve what many take to be the core of a country's values and identity in the face of the incredible diversity generated by large-scale immigration. This leads us to ask what sort of civic solidarity, if any, might be desirable.

Answering this question requires consideration of what civic solidarity is for, what purposes it is supposed to serve in a liberal democratic society. There are at least three important roles attributed to civic solidarity. First, it is said to be integral to the pursuit of distributive justice. The institutions of the welfare state serve as redistributive mechanisms that can offset the inequalities of life chances that a capitalist economy creates and raise the position of the worst-off members of society to a level where they are able to participate as equal citizens. While self-interest alone may motivate people to support social insurance schemes that protect them against unpredictable circumstances, a sense of civic solidarity helps foster support redistribution from the rich to aid the poor, including housing subsidies, income supplements, and long-term unemployment benefits.[1] The underlying idea is that people are more likely to support redistributive schemes when they trust one another, and they are more likely to trust one another when they regard others as like themselves in some meaningful sense.

Second, civic solidarity is also said to support democracy. In his account of freedom in a democratic state, Rousseau suggests that to legislate for one another in a way that is not dominating, democratic citizens must share a form of solidarity sufficient to motivate them to take one another's interests into account. If we view democratic activity as involving not just voting but also deliberation, then people must make an effort to listen to and understand one another. Moreover, they must be willing to moderate their claims in the hope of finding common ground on which to base political decisions. Such democratic activity cannot be realized by individuals solely pursuing their own interests; it requires some concern for the common good. A sense of solidarity can help foster certain desirable civic virtues and attitudes, including mutual sympathy and respect, which in turn support citizens' orientation toward the common good.

Third, civic solidarity offers more inclusive alternatives to chauvinist models that often prevail in political life around the world. For example, the alternative to the Nehru-Gandhi secular definition of Indian national identity is the Hindu chauvinism of the Bharatiya Janata Party, not a cosmopolitan model of belonging. "And what in the end can defeat this chauvinism," asks Charles Taylor, "but some reinvention of India as a secular republic with which people can identify?"[2] It is not enough to articulate accounts of solidarity and belonging only at the subnational or transnational levels while ignoring senses of belonging to the political community. One might believe that people have a deep human need for belonging in communities, perhaps grounded in even deeper needs for recognition and freedom, but even those skeptical of such claims might recognize the importance of articulating more inclusive models of political community as an alternative to the racial, ethnic, or religious narratives that have permeated political life.

Social scientists offer some empirical evidence for these roles of civic solidarity. For instance, Robert Putnam has shown that communities with higher levels of racial and ethnic diversity exhibit lower levels of trust. As Putnam puts it, "Inter-racial trust is relatively high in homogeneous South Dakota and relatively low in heterogeneous San Francisco or Los Angeles. The more ethnically diverse the people we live around, the less we trust them." It is not only out-group trust but also in-group trust that is lower in more diverse settings. In ethnically diverse neighborhoods, residents of all groups tend to "hunker down" or pull in like turtles.[3] Other studies have found negative correlations between ethnic diversity and levels of redistributive expenditures at the local and state level in the United States.[4] We need to be careful in the conclusions we draw from such studies, since the causal mechanisms between ethnic diversity and social trust, as well as between ethnic diversity and redistribution, are not obvious. Saying that ethnic diversity and distrust are strongly correlated is not to say that diversity *causes* distrust. And there are places with high ethnic diversity and low social trust that exhibit higher levels of support for redistributive policies (San Francisco) than places with lower levels of ethnic diversity and higher levels of social trust (South Dakota). If one accepts that solidarity and trust are important for the reasons stated above, then a clear and deeply troubling implication of these studies is that a solidaristic political community may come at the price of cultural homogeneity.[5] Taylor also suggests that the drive toward homogeneity and exclusion may be an ineluctable aspect of democracy. There is a "standing temptation to exclusion" in democracy, which "arises from the fact that democracies work well when people know each other, trust each other, and feel a sense of commitment toward each other."[6]

The challenge, then, is to develop a model of civic solidarity that is "thick" enough to motivate support for social justice and democracy while also "thin" enough to accommodate racial, ethnic, and religious diversity. In this essay, I explore three different models of civic solidarity. What sorts of ties or attachments unite members of a political community? Can the model deliver the goods that civic solidarity is said to deliver? And what is its response to diversity? To flesh out the different models of civic solidarity, I consider what each implies for newcomers who wish to become members, as set forth in the naturalization policies of various countries.

Constitutional Patriotism

We might look first to Habermas's idea of constitutional patriotism (*Verfassungspatriotismus*). The idea emerged from a particular national history, to denote attachment to the liberal democratic institutions of the postwar Federal Republic of Germany, but Habermas and others have taken it to be a generalizable vision for liberal democratic societies, as well as for supranational communities such as the European Union. On this view, what binds citizens together is their common allegiance to the ideals embodied in a shared political culture and expressed in the constitution. For constitutional patriots, constitutions are more than a set of regulative ideals constraining government power; they are also national symbols that foster civic unity and inspire allegiance. It is shared constitutional principles, not a shared ethnocultural identity, that unite citizens. As Habermas put its, the only "common denominator for a *constitutional* patriotism" is that "every citizen be socialized into a common political culture."[7]

Constitutional patriotism is a crucial supplement to the republican ideal of citizenship, which views citizens as free and equal legislators of the basic terms under which they live. Modern republican citizenship emerged out of the French Revolution in alliance with modern nationalism. Modern nationalism has relied on ethnocultural notions of identity to foster citizens' "social-psychological" attachment to the role of republican citizenship, which demands a high degree of personal sacrifice.[8] Yet, republicanism is not conceptually tied to ethnic nationalism; it must learn, argues Habermas, "to stand on its own feet" because the fantasy of an ethnoculturally homogenous nation can only be pursued at the cost of intolerance and ethnic cleansing. Citizens' attachment must be redirected toward a set of political principles and procedures.

Constitutional patriotism is deeply attractive for the same reasons that Kantian deontological theories are attractive. It retreats from the terrain of argument about the good life and focuses instead on achieving agreement on a thin set of principles. This agnosticism about particular moral and religious outlooks and particular identities is said to respect people's freedom to choose and pursue their own way of life. It also promises a fair way of deciding issues we face in common without having to favor the outlooks of some against others. Constitutional patriotism also offers an answer to the problem of motivation in democratic societies. As Habermas and other republican theorists have emphasized, political freedom cannot be realized by individuals privately pursuing their own interests; it can be realized only by all citizens together in "intersubjectively shared practice." Modern coercive law cannot extend all the way down to the motives and basic attitudes of citizens to compel civic practices without violating basic liberties. Constitutional patriotism offers a source of motivation for citizens, inspiring them to "cooperative efforts of civic practice."[9]

Yet, constitutional patriotism may be too thin a basis for uniting citizens. In the words of one critic, "Patriotism is not enough."[10] Habermas himself acknowledges this concern in discussing the tendency for liberal democracies to "lurch into nationalism." To unite and motivate citizens, liberal democratic regimes have historically appealed to ethnocultural myths of common descent, which appeal "more strongly to their hearts and minds than the dry ideas of popular sovereignty and human rights." Habermas suggests two reasons for the lurch into nationalism. First, the artificiality of national myths makes nationalism susceptible to misuse by political elites in mobilizing citizens toward some common goal, whether in support of war or in diversion from class conflicts. Second, one cannot explain in purely normative terms how the political community should be composed. The boundaries marking off one political community from another are contingent, not voluntarily chosen by its members. Nationalism provides a solution to this problem of boundaries that has proved seductive in practice: nations are presented as organic developments that need no justification beyond their sheer existence.[11] The recurring lurch into nationalism suggests that attachment to constitutional norms may only be possible via "supplements of particularity."[12]

Habermas points to the United States as a leading example of a multicultural society where constitutional principles have taken root in a political culture without depending on "all citizens' sharing the same language or the same ethnic and cultural origins."[13] The historian Philip Gleason outlines this popular narrative of American identity: "To be or to become an American, a person did not have to be any particular national, linguistic, religious, or ethnic background. All he had to do was to commit himself to the political ideology centered on the abstract ideals of liberty, equality, and republicanism. Thus the universalist ideological character of American nationality meant that it was open to anyone who willed to become an American."[14] To take the motto of the Great Seal of the United States, *E pluribus unum*—"From many, one"—in this context suggests not that manyness should be melted down into one, as in Israel Zangwill's image of the melting pot, but that, as the Great Seal's sheaf of arrows suggests, there should be a coexistence of many-in-one under a unified citizenship based on shared ideals.

Of course, the story is not so simple, as Gleason himself went on to note. However much the United States has come to stand for certain political principles, it also comes "loaded with inherited cultural baggage" that is contingent upon its particular history.[15] America's history of racial and ethnic exclusions has undercut the universalist stance; for being an American has also meant sharing a national culture, one defined in racial, ethnic, religious, and gendered terms. As Rogers Smith puts it, the United States has been "not only the cradle of democracy and personal liberties, profound as these features are. It has also been a patriarchal land, an overwhelmingly Christian land, and perhaps most of all, the land of some of the world's most epic struggles over slavery and white supremacy."[16] The seductive power of such ascriptive doctrines lies in their ability to demarcate and sustain particular community memberships more effectively than appeals to political principles or economic interests alone.

What does constitutional patriotism suggest for the sort of reception immigrants should receive? There has been a general shift in Western Europe and North America in the standards governing access to citizenship from cultural markers to values, and this is a development that constitutional patriots would applaud. In the United States those seeking to become citizens must demonstrate basic knowledge of U.S. government and history, and promise to "support and defend the Constitution" and "to bear true faith and allegiance to the same."[17] A newly revised U.S. citizenship test was instituted in October 2008 with the hope that it will serve, in the words of the chief of the Office of Citizenship, Alfonso Aguilar, as "an instrument to promote civic learning and patriotism."[18] The revised test attempts to move away from civics trivia to emphasize political ideas and concepts. (There is still a fair amount of trivia: "How many amendments does the Constitution have?" "What is the capital of your state?") New questions ask more open-ended questions about government powers and political concepts: "What does the judicial branch do?" "What stops one branch of government from becoming too powerful?" "What is freedom of religion?" "What is the 'rule of law'?"[19]

Constitutional patriots would endorse this focus on values and principles. In Habermas's view, legal principles are anchored in the "political culture," which he suggests is separable from "ethical-cultural" forms of life. Acknowledging that in many countries the ethical-cultural form of life of the majority is "fused" with the political culture, he argues that the "level of the shared political culture must be uncoupled from the level of subcultures and their pre-political identities."[20] All that should be expected of immigrants is that they embrace the constitutional principles as interpreted by the political culture, not that they necessarily embrace the majority's ethical-cultural forms.

Yet language is a key aspect of ethical-cultural forms of life, shaping people's worldviews and experiences. It is through language that individuals become who they are. Since a political community must conduct its affairs in at least one language, the ethical-cultural and political cannot be completely "uncoupled." As theorists of multiculturalism have stressed, complete separation of state and particularistic identities is impossible; government decisions about the language of public institutions, public holidays, and state symbols unavoidably involve recognizing and supporting particular ethnic and religious groups over others.[21] In the United States, English-language ability has been a statutory qualification for naturalization since 1906, originally as a requirement of oral ability and later as a requirement of English literacy. Indeed, support for the principles of the Constitution has been interpreted as requiring English literacy.[22] The language requirement might be justified as a practical matter (we need some language to be the common language of schools, government, and the workplace, so why not the language of the majority?), but the language requirement is also a key marker of national identity.

Given the continuing centrality of language in naturalization policy, it is simply false to conclude that constitutional patriotism would not mandate immigrant integration policies "contaminated with culture and ethnicity."[23] Christian Joppke contends that the language requirement is "a matter of practical exigency, not of identity. To be German cannot be a matter of German language competence if Austria and parts of Switzerland speak it, too."[24] While the rules of access to citizenship have been liberalized with a shift toward official emphasis on values over cultural markers, I think Joppke overstates the extent of decoupling of citizenship and national culture. Just because German is spoken outside Germany or English outside the United States does not mean that these languages are not viewed by many citizens to be a crucial marker of national identity.

Another misconception about constitutional patriotism is that it is necessarily more inclusive of newcomers than are cultural nationalist models of solidarity. Its inclusiveness, however, depends on which principles are held up as the polity's shared principles, and its normative substance depends on and must be evaluated in light of a background theory of justice, freedom, or democracy; it does not by itself provide such a theory. Consider ideological requirements for naturalization in U.S. history. The first naturalization law of 1790 required nothing more than an oath to support the U.S. Constitution. The second naturalization act added two ideological elements: the renunciation of titles or orders of nobility and the requirement that one be found to have "behaved as a man . . . attached to the principles of the constitution of the United States."[25] This attachment requirement was revised in 1940 from a behavioral qualification to a personal attribute, but this did not help clarify what attachment to constitutional principles requires.[26] Not surprisingly, the "attachment to constitutional principles" requirement has been interpreted as requiring a belief in representative government, federalism, separation of powers, and constitutionally guaranteed individual rights. It has also been interpreted as disqualifying anarchists, polygamists, and conscientious objectors for citizenship.[27] In 1950, support for communism was added to the list of grounds for disqualification from naturalization—as well as grounds for exclusion and deportation.[28] The 1990 Immigration Act retained the McCarthy-era ideological qualifications for naturalization; current law disqualifies those who advocate or affiliate with an organization that advocates communism or opposition to all organized government.[29] Patriotism, like nationalism, is capable of excess and pathology, as evidenced by loyalty oaths and campaigns against "un-American" activities.

The exclusionary potential of a values-based, as opposed to ethnocultural identity-based, solidarity is also reflected in the Dutch government's new policy of "integration from abroad." Since 2006, the Dutch government has distributed a Dutch information video for would-be migrants in which two gay men are kissing and a topless woman is walking on a beach. The film sends the message that respect for the rights of gays and lesbians, as well as toleration of nude beaches, are at the core of Dutch culture. The film seems to have been made with Muslim immigrants in mind. About one-third of the three million *allochtonen* (immigrants and their children who were born in the Netherlands) are Muslim, most of them Moroccans and Turks. The demand for acceptance of particular liberal values may not be as thin as constitutional patriots suggest; it will depend on the values and how they are interpreted. From the point of view of many Muslim minorities, the acceptance of certain liberal principles, such as gender equality and separation of religion and state, may be more demanding than accepting the language requirement.

Constitutional patriotism, then, is at once both too thin and too thick. Too thin to deliver the desiderata of civic solidarity as evidenced by the perennial lurch into nationalism, and too thick from the perspective of some newcomers in terms of the values they are asked to embrace. A values-based solidarity in liberal democratic societies is not necessarily any less demanding than a culture-based solidarity from the point of view of non-liberal religious minorities.[30]

Liberal Nationalism

In contrast to constitutional patriots, liberal nationalists acknowledge that states cannot be culturally neutral even if they tried. States cannot avoid coercing citizens into preserving a national culture of some kind, because state institutions and laws define a political culture, which in turn shapes the range of customs and practices of daily life that constitute a national culture. David Miller, a leading theorist of liberal nationalism, defines national identity according to the following elements: a shared belief among a group of individuals that they belong together, historical continuity stretching across generations, connection to a particular territory, and a shared set of characteristics constituting a national culture.[31] It is not enough to share a common identity rooted in a shared history or a shared territory; a shared national *culture* is a necessary feature of national identity. I share a national culture with someone, even if we never meet, if each of us has been initiated into the traditions and customs of a national culture.

What sort of content makes up a national culture? Miller says more about what a national culture does not entail. It need not be based on biological descent. Even if nationalist doctrines have historically been based on notions of biological descent and race, Miller emphasizes that sharing a national culture is, in principle, compatible with people belonging to a diversity of racial and ethnic groups. In addition, every member need not have been born in the homeland. Thus, "immigration need not pose problems, provided only that the immigrants come to share a common national identity, to which they may contribute their own distinctive ingredients."[32]

Liberal nationalists focus on the idea of culture, as opposed to ethnicity or descent, in order to reconcile nationalism with liberalism. Thicker than constitutional patriotism, liberal nationalism, Miller maintains, is thinner than ethnic models of belonging. Both nationality and ethnicity have cultural components, but what is said to distinguish "civic" nations from "ethnic" nations is that the latter are exclusionary and closed on grounds of biological descent; the former are, in principle, open to anyone willing to adopt the national culture.[33]

Yet the civic-ethnic distinction is not so clear-cut in practice. Every nation has an "ethnic core." As Anthony Smith observes: "Modern 'civic' nations have not in practice really transcended ethnicity or ethnic sentiments. This is a Western mirage, reality-as-wish; closer examination always reveals the ethnic core of civic nations, in practice, even in immigrant societies with their early pioneering and dominant (English and Spanish) culture in America, Australia, or Argentina, a culture that provided the myths and language of the would-be nation."[34] Once liberal nationalists acknowledge that all national cultures have ethnic cores, they need an answer to why those outside this core should embrace the national culture. There are at least two strategies of argument one could adopt. One might take the democratic line that says ethnic minorities should embrace the national culture because they have opportunities to contribute to it through processes of collective dialogue and decision making. Alternatively, one might take a liberal contractualist line based on actual or hypothetical consent.

Miller takes the democratic line. He acknowledges that national cultures have typically been formed around the ethnic group that is dominant in a particular territory and therefore bear "the hallmarks of that group: language, religion, cultural identity." Muslim identity in contemporary Britain becomes politicized when British national identity is conceived as containing "an Anglo-Saxon bias which discriminates against Muslims (and other ethnic minorities)." But he maintains that his idea of nationality can be made "democratic in so far as it insists that everyone should take part in this debate [about what constitutes the national identity] on an equal footing, and sees the formal arenas of politics as the main (though not the only) place where the debate occurs."[35]

The major difficulty here is that national cultures are not typically the product of collective deliberation in which all have the opportunity to participate. Miller's redescription of "national character" as the capacious-sounding "common public culture" sidesteps the violent history of modern nation building. This is not to suggest that national cultures are solely the legacy of the conquest and domination of particular racial and ethnic groups over others. Surely the truth is somewhere in between the latter and the claim that nations are the legacy of relations of mutual respect and agreement among different groups. The challenge is to ensure that historically marginalized groups, as well as new groups of immigrants, have genuine opportunities to contribute "on an equal footing" to shaping the national culture. Special group-based accommodations, which Miller argues are inconsistent with his vision of liberal nationalism, may be necessary to establish a more equal footing for marginalized groups.[36]

The liberal contractualist approach also runs into the demand for special accommodations for those outside the ethnic core of nations. Neither ethnic minorities nor members of the dominant culture actually consent to the national culture. The hypothetical contract approach asks if it would be reasonable for ethnic minorities to accept the national culture of the host society. The reasonableness of the demand for integration into the national culture depends in part on the content of the national culture and the nature of the interests that would be burdened when ethnic minorities are asked to assimilate into national cultures with ethnic cores that are not their own. If the ethnic core includes religious beliefs and practices, then the religious liberty of those who adhere to minority religions will be burdened. But religious liberty is a fundamental liberty, and if all members of society are equally entitled to this liberty, as liberals typically maintain, then such burdens will not be justifiable. It would be reasonable for religious minorities to resist the demand for assimilation into "Anglo-Protestant culture."

Regarding language, liberals may view the burdens imposed by the requirement to learn the dominant language as less weighty than burdens on religious liberty. Yet the relationship between language and dignity needs to be considered in the historical context in which language rights claims appear. In the course of liberalization, Western nation-states relinquished the notion that a common religion was integral for national integration, but the opposite occurred with respect to language, which moved to the fore as the single most important element in the construction of national identity.[37] A common means of communication was seen as crucial to nation building. The consolidation of a single national language was driven not only by a desire for ease of communication or to foster a common national culture but also by racism and xenophobia. That forging a common language has historically involved the domination and suppression of minority languages and identities is most apparent in the case of Native American languages. Multicultural theorists have argued that groups whose languages were made vulnerable by historical injustices perpetrated by the state, as in the case of indigenous groups, are owed special accommodations to protect or revive their languages.[38] Special accommodations may also be owed to immigrants who are outside the linguistic mainstream not only to ensure their access to the labor market but also to offer fair terms of integration. Otherwise, it would be reasonable for them to resist integration into the national culture.

Without such accommodations and opportunities to participate "on an equal footing" in the making of the national culture, liberal nationalism collapses into conservative nationalism of the kind defended by Samuel Huntington. He calls for immigrants to assimilate into America's "Anglo-Protestant culture." Like Miller, Huntington views ideology as "a weak glue to hold together people otherwise lacking in racial, ethnic, or cultural sources of community," and he rejects race and ethnicity as constituent elements of national identity.[39] Instead, he calls on Americans of all races and ethnicities to "reinvigorate their core culture." Yet his "cultural" vision of America is pervaded by ethnic and religious elements: it is not only of a country "committed to the principles of the Creed" but also of "a deeply religious and primarily Christian country, encompassing several religious minorities, adhering to Anglo-Protestant values, speaking English, maintaining its European cultural heritage."[40] That the cultural core of the United States is the culture of its historically dominant groups is a point that Huntington unabashedly accepts.

Cultural nationalist visions of solidarity would lend support to immigration and immigrant policies that give weight to linguistic and ethnic preferences and impose special requirements on individuals from groups deemed to be outside the nation's "core culture." One example is the practice in postwar Germany of giving priority in immigration and naturalization policy to ethnic Germans; they were the only foreign nationals who were accepted as permanent residents set on the path toward citizenship. They were treated not as immigrants but "resettlers" (*Aussiedler*) who acted on their constitutional right to return to their country of origin. In contrast, nonethnically German guest workers (*Gastarbeiter*) were designated as "aliens" (*Ausländer*) under the 1965 German Alien Law and excluded from German citizenship.[41] Another example is the Japanese naturalization policy that, until the late 1980s, required naturalized citizens to adopt a Japanese family name. The language requirement in contemporary naturalization policies in the West is the leading remaining example of a cultural nationalist integration policy; it reflects not only a concern with the economic and political integration of immigrants but also a nationalist concern with preserving a distinctive national culture.

Deep Diversity

Constitutional patriotism and liberal nationalism are accounts of civic solidarity that deal with what one might call first-level diversity. Individuals have different group identities and hold divergent moral and religious outlooks, yet they are expected to share the same idea of what it means to belong to a country: either patriots committed to the same set of ideals or co-nationals sharing the relevant cultural attributes. Charles Taylor suggests an alternative approach, the idea of "deep diversity." Rather than trying to set some minimal content as the basis of solidarity, Taylor acknowledges not only the fact of a diversity of group identities and outlooks (first-level diversity) but also the fact of a diversity of ways of belonging to the political community (second-level or deep diversity).

Taylor introduces the idea of deep diversity in the context of discussing what it means to be Canadian: "Someone of, say, Italian extraction in Toronto or Ukrainian extraction in Edmonton might indeed feel Canadian as a bearer of individual rights in a multicultural mosaic. . . . But this person might nevertheless accept that a Québécois or a Cree or a Déné might belong in a very different way, that these persons were Canadian through being members of their national communities. Reciprocally, the Québécois, Cree, or Déné would accept the perfect legitimacy of the 'mosaic' identity."[42] Civic solidarity or political identity is not "defined according to a concrete content"; rather, it is defined "by the fact that everybody is attached to that identity in his or her own fashion, that everybody wants to continue that history and proposes to make that community progress."[43] What leads people to support deep or second-level diversity is both the desire to be a member of the political community and the recognition of disagreement about what it means to be a member. In our world, membership in a political community provides goods we cannot do without; this, above all, may be the source of our desire for political community.

The clear appeal of this model of solidarity is its potentially greater inclusiveness. It gives more room to diversity than the other two models I have considered. Taylor emphasizes that deep diversity is the only formula on which a united federal Canada can be rebuilt. Many other countries resemble Canada in having diversity generated not only by voluntary migration but also by conquest and coercion. Even though Taylor contrasts Canada with the United States, accepting the myth of America as a nation of immigrants, the United States also has a need for acknowledgment of diverse modes of belonging based on the distinctive histories of different groups. Native Americans, African Americans, Irish Americans, Vietnamese Americans, and Mexican Americans: across these communities of people, we can find not only distinctive group identities but also distinctive ways of belonging to the political community.

Deep diversity is not a recapitulation of the idea of cultural pluralism first developed in the United States by Horace Kallen, who argued for assimilation "in matters economic and political" and preservation of differences "in cultural consciousness."[44] In Kallen's view, hyphenated Americans lived their spiritual lives in private, on the left side of the hyphen, while being culturally anonymous on the right side of the hyphen. The ethnic-political distinction maps onto a private-public dichotomy; the two spheres are to be kept separate, such that Irish Americans, for example, are culturally Irish and politically American. In contrast, the idea of deep diversity recognizes that Irish Americans are culturally Irish American and politically Irish American. As Michael Walzer put it in his discussion of American identity almost twenty years ago, the culture of hyphenated Americans has been shaped by American culture, and their politics is significantly ethnic in style and substance.[45] The idea of deep or second-level diversity is not just about immigrant ethnics, who are the focus of both Kallen's and Walzer's analyses, but also about racial minorities, who, based on their distinctive experiences of exclusion and struggles toward inclusion, have distinctive ways of belonging to America.

While attractive for its inclusiveness, the deep-diversity model may be too thin a basis for civic solidarity in a democratic society. Can there be civic solidarity without citizens already sharing a set of values or a culture in the first place? As Kymlicka puts it, deep diversity is "the product of mutual solidarity, not a possible basis for it."[46] In writing elsewhere about how different groups within democracy might "share identity space," Taylor himself suggests that the "basic principles of republican constitutions—democracy itself and human rights, among them"—constitute a "nonnegotiable" minimum. Yet, what distinguishes Taylor's deep-diversity model of solidarity from Habermas's constitutional patriotism is the recognition that "historic identities cannot be just abstracted from." The minimal commonality of shared principles is "accompanied by a recognition that these principles can be realized in a number of different ways, and can never be applied neutrally without some confronting of the substantive religious ethnic-cultural differences in societies."[47] And in contrast to liberal nationalism, deep diversity does not aim at specifying a common national culture that must be shared by all. What matters is not so much the content of solidarity but the ethos generated by making the effort at mutual understanding and respect.

Canada's approach to the integration of immigrants may be the closest thing there is to deep diversity. Canadian naturalization policy is not so different from that of the United States: a short required residency period, relatively low application fees, a test of history and civics knowledge, and a language exam.[48] Where the United States and Canada diverge is in their public commitment to diversity. Through its official multiculturalism policies, Canada expresses a commitment to the value of diversity among immigrant communities through funding for ethnic associations and supporting heritage language schools.[49] Constitutional patriots and liberal nationalists say that immigrant integration should be a two-way process, that immigrants should shape the host society's dominant culture just as they are shaped by it. Multicultural accommodations actually provide the conditions under which immigrant integration might genuinely become a two-way process. Such policies send a strong message that immigrants are a welcome part of the political community and should play an active role in shaping its future evolution.

Conclusion

The question of solidarity may not be the most urgent task facing citizens of liberal democracies today; war and economic crisis loom larger. But the question of solidarity remains important in the face of ongoing large-scale immigration and its effects on intergroup relations, which in turn affect our ability to deal with issues of economic inequality and democracy.

In examining three leading ideals of solidarity, I hope to have demonstrated the appeal and limits of each. Habermas's constitutional patriotism is seductive for its thinness in contrast to nationalism, but in practice it is both too thin and too thick. Too thin to forge solidarity without lurching back into nationalist appeals, and too thick from the perspective of religious minorities who view a model of solidarity based on liberal values as very demanding and potentially exclusionary. In contrast, Miller's liberal nationalism admirably acknowledges the role that ethnocultural particularity has played in forging civic solidarity, but by making the national culture a central object of attachment while also disavowing multiculturalism, it falls short of including those who stand outside the cultural core. Of the three, I believe deep diversity is the most attractive ideal, for its potentially greater inclusiveness. By attempting to accommodate both first- and second-level diversity, it opens up the possibility for citizens to make their own connections between particularistic beliefs and identities and the overarching values and identities upon which civic solidarity might be based.

What is now formally required of immigrants seeking to become members of liberal democracies most clearly reflects the first two models of solidarity: professed allegiance to the principles of a constitution (constitutional patriotism) and the beginnings of a shared culture in the form of demonstrating the ability to read, write, and speak the dominant language of the country (liberal nationalism). In the United States, the revised citizenship test makes gestures toward respect for first-level diversity and inclusion of historically marginalized groups with such questions as "Who lived in America before the Europeans arrived?" "What group of people was taken to America and sold as slaves?" "What did Susan B. Anthony do?" "What did Martin Luther King Jr. do?" The election of the first African American president of the United States is a significant step forward.

A more inclusive model of civic solidarity requires even more—acknowledging that a polity is constituted not only by a diverse people but also by diverse ways of belonging to the polity. Whether the deep-diversity approach can achieve the desired balance between fostering solidarity thick enough to support social justice and democracy while also thin enough to accommodate diversity will ultimately depend on citizens and the sorts of attachments they forge through democratic politics.

PART III

Citizenship, Borders,
and Political Needs

Chapter 10

Immigration and Security in the United States

Christopher Rudolph

The terrorist attacks on New York and Washington, D.C., in 2001 had a profound effect on how American national security is conceived and the ways that immigration may impact it. The 9/11 Commission Report outlined the ways that terrorists were able to take advantage of the American system of immigration and border control in order to carry out their mission.[1] All nineteen hijackers had visas to enter the United States. However, eight had passports that showed evidence of fraudulent manipulations, and another five had "suspicious indicators." Some were known Al Qaeda operatives, yet somehow were either not included on government watch lists or managed to avoid apprehension if they were listed. More broadly, studies have shown that terrorists have not only exploited loopholes in the U.S. immigration and border control system, but have been able to use all available channels of entry in order to infiltrate the country.[2] Without a doubt, international migration has been increasingly recognized as a potential vector for the spread of global terrorism, and control over the entry of persons across the border represents the front line of defense in terms of homeland security interests.

Prior to 2001, placing international migration in the context of national security was largely considered a discourse strategy of xenophobes seeking to use fear to press the government for more restrictive policies. Now, however, it is widely accepted that international migration has significant implications for security.[3] What is less often recognized is that migration has long had security implications and that immigration and border policies since 1945 have been strongly influenced by security interests.[4] In this essay

I offer a brief account of how security interests have shaped American responses to immigration.[5] Moreover, I argue that the same logic that drove
policies pre-9/11 still applies today, though these events have reshaped the
way we think about security. I begin by outlining a theory of immigration
policy making driven by security interests, followed by a brief overview of
the empirical evidence drawn from the period 1945 to 2001. I then explain
how the post-9/11 security environment has altered key dynamics that
shape policy, followed by an outline of the U.S. policy response. Though
this discussion emphasizes these dynamics from the U.S. perspective, these
same issues and challenges are faced by all major immigrant- and refugee-
receiving countries.

Explaining Policy: The National Security Model

Although the events of 9/11 may have put the issue of migration more
squarely on the "security map," particularly in the United States, the security environment had had a significant influence on the timing and characteristics of immigration and border policies long before 2001.[6] When
considering security, it is important to recognize that this involves much
more than traditional notions of geopolitics and military defense.[7] It includes thinking about security in both external and internal terms, as well
as considering economic and societal dimensions.[8]

If we consider the external/internal logic first, it is reasonable to assume,
as realists do, that geopolitical security (i.e., military defense) has held a
dominant position in the policy hierarchy.[9] From this point of view, material power is the necessary condition to support defense, and thus maintain
security. This subsequently raises the question of how best to maximize
material power. In the premodern era of empires, military prowess was a
tool not only of defense but also of power acquisition. For numerous reasons, modern statecraft increasingly has turned to nonmilitary means of
acquiring power, particularly among advanced industrial countries, and
"trading states" have increasingly replaced garrison states.[10] What that
means in terms of policy is that rational states are likely to respond to
external (geopolitical) threats with policy that not only considers military
mobilization but also promotes alliance building, and/or maximization of
economic production.[11]

How would this affect immigration and border policy making, given that such policies may be instrumental to the process of alliance building and the accumulation of material wealth? In terms of alliances, restricting the immigration of nationals from current or potential allies conveys a strongly negative symbolic message to the allies. Conversely, making the country more welcoming to nationals of allies affirms positive relations and extends goodwill. Conforming policy to aggregate national economic interests is less clear, as it is influenced by the dominant economic ideas of the time. In other words, ideas about what types of policies produce higher gains relative to other options shifts across time. Among the Western advanced industrial countries after World War II, the emergent conventional wisdom was based on the reemergence of the classical economic models of Adam Smith and David Ricardo that emphasize openness to trade and mobile factors of production. Thus, during the post–World War II period, we might expect policies in general to be more open and more responsive to macroeconomic demand for labor.

What about times when external threats are low (or nonexistent)? In times when there is no external enemy, it stands to reason that there will be a higher likelihood that insecurities will generally be internal. One way to think about security's internal dimension is in terms of social cohesion. "National identity" is one way to reflect the basis by which national societies find commonality and a sense of belonging within the polity. It also identifies, through the institution of citizenship, whose interests the government is entrusted to promote—the fundamental basis of the Westphalian system that Stephen Krasner referred to as "domestic sovereignty."[12] Ole Wæver introduced the concept of "societal security" to capture social apprehensions about changes to national identity while allowing for the possibility that societies may find some levels of change to be perfectly natural and/or desirable.[13] He defines societal security as "the sustainability, *within acceptable conditions for evolution,* of traditional patterns of language, culture, association, and religious and national identity and custom."[14] Given this definition, we could surmise that internal security is not necessarily threatened when national identity undergoes change due to changing demographics, culture, or ideology. Rather, it is when (1) such changes take place faster than society is able to comfortably adjust to them, (2) change occurs to higher degrees than society is able to comfortably adjust to it, and/or (3) both of the above. In other words, societal insecurities may be manifest as racism or xenophobia, but may also manifest themselves by a discourse of a "loss of control"—in other words, when notions of sovereignty lie at the core of the debate.[15]

Internal (societal) security dynamics are more likely to exert influence on political outcomes when external (i.e., geopolitical) threats decline. The rationale behind this is simple and draws on the work of sociologists like Lewis Coser: external threats create common interests and can contribute to a shared sense of common identity, bolstering domestic societal cohesion and reducing societal insecurities.[16] Samuel Huntington has drawn on these same insights to argue that the loss of the Soviet Union as an external enemy increased domestic sensitivity to cultural difference in the United States after the Cold War and heightened anxiety about the demographic effects of immigration.[17] Conversely, given this logic, the presence of a strong external threat or enemy would be likely to produce little pressure for cultural restrictivism in terms of immigration and border policy, since commonality of interest is reinforced and societal security as a state priority declines relative to geopolitical interests.[18] What do these insights suggest in terms of policy outcomes? In times of lower relative external threats, we might have a higher probability of seeing societal insecurities becoming more significant, especially if migration flows are large and less culturally proximate than the receiving society. We can also anticipate that migration policy will likely become more closed and increasingly restrictive—attempting to slow the degree and pace of social demographic change in accordance with societal security interests.[19]

When we examine post–World War II U.S. immigration and border control policies prior to 9/11 within this framework, it would seem that outcomes largely conform to those predicted by the security model (Table 10.1). For the early Cold War period, the severe external threat would lead us to expect policy that becomes relatively more open, supports macroeconomic needs, and supports foreign policy interests. At the same time, we should see declining emphasis on ethnic or cultural preference criteria. Policy outcomes largely conform to these predictions. Migration played a key role in foreign policy, especially in light of the Truman Doctrine. Ad hoc admission of refugee flows fleeing communism after World War II, was an active policy tool that sought to (1) weaken the Soviet Union by draining skilled manpower resources and (2) weaken the legitimacy of communism by showing that it was incapable of containing its own citizenry. In contrast, by showing its openness, the U.S. was able to convey evidence of its position as the defender of freedom. Though this was not manifest in official policy, National Security

Table 10.1 Policy Development in Three Security Environments, 1945–2001

	External Threat Level	Major Policy
Early Cold War	Severe	Bracero Program (1947) McCarran-Walter Act (1952) Ad hoc refugee admissions 1965 INA
Détente	High	Per-country limits (1976) Interagency Task Force (1977) SCIRP (1978) IRCA (1986)
Post–Cold War (1990–2001)	Low	IMMACT (1990) Gatekeeper (1993–1998) IIRAIRA (1996) American Competitiveness in the 21st Century Act (2000)

Council documents in the early 1950s specifically mentioned both aspects of refugee admissions as important elements of Cold War containment.[20] Moreover, the executive branch was granted considerable latitude to conform refugee admissions to foreign policy interests. The 1952 McCarran-Walter Act gave the attorney general "parole power" to grant admissions if it was considered in the national interest. Regularization of these flows through acts of Congress followed ex post facto. The McCarran-Walter Act bridged migration policy with foreign policy in other ways as well. Specifically, the act reversed the existing ban on immigration from Asian countries—the so-called Asiatic-barred zone—because this blatant racial discrimination strained key alliance relationships throughout the Asia-Pacific region. Though levels afforded by the act were less than president Truman wanted, the establishment of these quota allocations was extremely significant given the national origins system that had prevailed since 1924.[21] In an important sense, it was the first break in the wall of a racialized preference system for immigration. The move away from ethnic preferences was more substantial in the 1960s. The 1965 Immigration and Nationality Act officially reversed the national origins quota system and instead instigated a preference system based on family unification, economic needs, and foreign policy considerations. This landmark change in policy was the result of a combination of two factors: foreign policy interests and the civil rights movement.[22] Foreign policy interests made racial discrimination a barrier to alliance building, while ethnic preferences were anathema to the civil rights movement's core principle of racial equality.

In terms of liberalization based on economic needs, there is overlap with some of the actions discussed above. First, as reflected in U.N. Security Council memoranda, refugee admissions were in part considered a means of acquiring skilled manpower. In addition, the McCarran-Walter Act provided increased leverage for business to make use of foreign labor by providing exemption from prosecution for hiring undocumented workers —what was referred to as the "Texas proviso."[23] Moreover, the Bracero program opened the door to 4.6 million temporary workers from Mexico to work in key economic sectors, including agriculture, construction, and industry.[24] This also enabled domestic labor to shift toward the growing manufacturing sector. Lastly, an economic preference quota for highly skilled labor was established in the 1965 Immigration and Nationality Act. In general, what we see is a relative liberalization occurring in the period, emphasizing economic and foreign policy aims and deemphasizing societal security interests.

As we shift to the détente period—loosely defined—the model predicts that societal security interests will gain in relative salience as external threats decline, and security priorities will turn increasingly inward. Given that the previous period liberalized policy, we might also expect that the effects such policies had on migration patterns will tend to exacerbate these societal security interests. Again, the empirical evidence from the period seems consistent with this prediction. In the wake of declining public support for immigration, both the executive and legislative branches established committees to discuss immigration—particularly illegal immigration. These included the Interagency Task Force in 1977 and the Select Commission on Immigration and Refugee Policy in 1978. We also see more restrictive policy, focused largely on curbing migration from Mexico, which had increased markedly since 1965. Restrictions were directed at both "legal" and "illegal" flows, but the focus was on Mexican migration. First, the application of universal per country limits that were established in 1976 had the greatest impact on Mexican migration, even though it did not specify an overt intent to focus on this flow. However, because Mexico was subject only to the hemispheric limit of 120,000 migrants prior to 1976 and generally consumed a large majority of this quota, subjecting Mexico to the 20,000 cap represented an acute restriction. Moreover, the Immigration Reform and Control Act enacted in 1986 continued this trend toward restricting Mexican migration. Though the act provided an avenue for undocumented workers living in the country to regularize their status (and some three million took advantage of this opportunity), IRCA was a primarily a comprehensive attempt to crack down on illegal immigration from Mexico. In addition to their conforming largely to expected policy outcomes, it's important to recognize a gradual change in ideas regarding migration during this time. Specifically, the "problem" of immigration was defined largely in terms of Mexican migration and the southern border.

After the Cold War, a decrease in external threats continued to be associated with rising societal insecurity in the 1990s. Given this, we should expect increasing degrees of closure and restrictionism, and a growing emphasis on ethnocultural selection criteria. Overall, we find that policy in the 1990s is consistent with the outcomes predicted by the security model. First, the 1990 Immigration Act established a new set of "diversity visas" intended to "correct" unintended effects of the 1965 act. In addition, we see a dramatic increase in efforts to control illegal immigration—beginning with Border Patrol programs like Operation Hold-the-Line in El Paso and Operation Gatekeeper in San Diego. Congressional action followed in 1996 with the Illegal Immigration Reform and Immigrant Responsibility Act. The act restricted access to public entitlements to illegal immigrants and provided a dramatic increase for funding Border Patrol operations.

Although policy is largely consistent with the hypotheses during the post–Cold War (but pre-9/11) period, there are some unexpected outcomes as well. In addition to setting up diversity visas, the 1990 act provided additional skills-based visas. It doubled employment-based immigration and included an annual quota of 65,000 H1-B visas for highly skilled workers. These levels were increased even more dramatically in subsequent legislation in 1998 and 2000, when the number is H1-Bs was temporarily raised to 195,000. Why would a country that expresses increased societal insecurities and politicization of immigration support policies of openness? The answer, I believe, lies in changing ideas reflected in policy-maker discourse. Over time it seems that policy makers became increasingly aware that the societal security aspects of migration were a purely political phenomenon—one driven by perceptions. Rightly or wrongly, the societal "problem" of migration was increasingly localized on one flow—Mexican migration. In *National Security and Immigration*, I describe policy in the 1990s as policy makers attempt to "finesse" societal security concerns by establishing largely symbolic policy—in the form of border control measures to the south.[25] Visibility seems to play a key role in how severe societal insecurities are felt—and can vary depending on things like: (a) cultural proximity; (b) concentration (short time or in one place, like the border); (c) settlement patterns; and (d) assimilation patterns.[26] Visibility also seems to play a key role in curbing insecurities. Even though the border control programs initiated in the 1990s did little to stop the flow of illegal immigration, it did serve to allay societal pressures for closure and reduce opposition to economic liberalization. So what we have in terms of a grand strategy in the 1990s is: (1) a heightened politicization that focused on societal security concerns; (2) an aggressive response by the state to the "source" of these insecurities—the porous southern border; and (3) a steady though much less publicized liberalization for highly skilled immigration to maintain the tremendous economic growth of the period. In terms of societal insecurities, policies can be explained largely by the predominance of an emerging attitude among policy makers of "out of sight, out of mind."

The National Security Model and Policy After 9/11

It has been said that "9/11 changed everything." Although security interests seemed to play an important role in the design and timing of immigration and border policies during and after the Cold War (see Table 10.1), does this framework still provide a useful means of understanding policy outcomes in the post-9/11 environment? The argument thus far predicts that when external threats are high, policy will become relatively more open, responsive to interests for increases in aggregate wealth and power; be increasingly used as a tool of foreign policy statecraft; and reduce emphases on ethnic selection preferences. At first blush, it would seem that policy doesn't conform to the predicted outcomes of either hypothesis. Since 9/11, some of the most conspicuous policy developments have been largely restrictive. How do we explain this divergence from expected outcomes?

I argue that the national security model does, in fact, largely fit the empirical evidence post-9/11. The key here is to understand that the ideational variable(s) in play in the model are not static but change according to circumstances and political learning. Ideas shape the type of policy preferences that inform particular outcomes given changes in the security environment. In the early Cold War period, a (perhaps *the*) dominant idea shaping American grand strategy was that neoclassical economics were the

Table 10.2 Security Logics and Their Migration Policy Preferences

Security dimension	Preference (before 9/11/2001)	Preference (after 9/11)
Military/Geopolitical	Open	Closed
Economic	Open	Open
Societal	Closed	Closed

best way to increase material (and subsequently, military) power in the face of a growing geopolitical threat. This aligned the policy preferences of the geopolitical and economic dimensions of security (Table 10.2). Combined with the relative deemphasis on societal dimensions of security in a period of acute external threats, grand strategy was largely skewed toward more open policy until the emergence of the détente era in the 1970s. Since 9/11, however, a fundamental transformation has taken place in the way that security in America is considered. Homeland security emerged as the central issue of defense, and the global "war on terror" largely supplanted geopolitical realpolitik as the primary security challenge facing the United States.

In terms of migration and border policy, the clear policy preference to respond to threats to homeland security is one of closure and restriction. Since human mobility serves as a vector for the spread of global terrorism and the proliferation of terrorist agents, the "safe" strategy is one that eliminates (or at least mitigates) such movement. In other words, states should be less willing to "risk migration." What this does is link homeland security preferences with societal security preferences, both of which prefer increased closure (for different reasons), and offset economic interests for openness and labor market elasticity. Given this new security logic, movement toward a relatively more restrictive policy would conform to the security paradigm and be consistent with its predicted outcomes.

Numerous measures have been taken to respond to the terrorist threat to homeland security interests, including government restructuring, increasingly restrictive policy, and a slew of new programs and initiatives. Certainly the most dramatic response has been the complete reorganization of the federal government and the creation of the Department of Homeland Security (DHS) with a cabinet-level secretary. In this process of restructuring, the Immigration and Naturalization Service (INS) was separated into two new agencies, the U.S. Citizenship and Immigration Services and the

Bureau of Immigration and Customs Enforcement. In addition, jurisdiction and oversight for these agencies was transferred from the Justice Department to the DHS. In essence, the dawn of the Bush administration's "global war on terror" placed migration and border control squarely in the security realm—one that now emphasized the homeland security dimension over more traditional geopolitical concerns.[27]

Initial policy developments with applications to migration and border control were primarily restrictive in nature. Primary legislation passed to address homeland security concerns includes the USA Patriot Act and the Enhanced Border Security and Visa Entry Reform Act (EBSVERA). The primary goals of these new laws and the new programs associated with them in terms of immigration and border control are (1) to facilitate screening of those seeking entry into the country, (2) to track their status once admitted, and (3) to verify their departure.

Among its provisions, the USA Patriot Act provides tools for law enforcement to facilitate intelligence gathering necessary to better screen visa applicants and others seeking entry into the country.[28] The Patriot Act dismantled the statutory "wall" between foreign intelligence and law enforcement agencies by amending the Foreign Intelligence Surveillance Act (FISA), a move that was intended to facilitate interagency cooperation. Subsequently, the Foreign Intelligence Surveillance Court of Review endorsed the Justice Department's new Intelligence Sharing Procedures on November 18, 2002. In addition, procedures allow the attorney general to approve emergency FISA surveillance and search warrants at his or her discretion. Between September 11, 2001, and March, 2003, more than 170 emergency FISA warrants were authorized by the Office of the Attorney General, three times the number authorized over the previous twenty-three years.[29] The Patriot Act also expanded the definition of "terrorist activity" to include material support for terrorists and/or terrorist organizations as well as harboring known or suspected terrorists. This expanded definition of "terrorist activity" has directly affected immigration policy. This more expansive definition is now used as grounds for inadmissibility for entry into the country.

Much of the new intelligence gathered has been added to existing antiterrorism databases used to screen immigrants and visitors. For example, in the first year following 9/11 more than seven million names from FBI records were added to the Consular Lookout Support System (CLASS), which is used by the State Department and DHS. This brought the number of name records included in the CLASS database to some fifteen million. Unfortunately, fifteen different antiterrorism and law enforcement databases were in use at the time, managed by several agencies dealing with homeland security at different levels. In order to integrate the wealth of new intelligence information being gathered by intelligence and law enforcement agencies, a multiagency Terrorist Threat Integration Center was established in 2003 to coordinate incoming intelligence information. Subsequently, a Terrorist Screening Center was established to consolidate existing security databases and to provide 24/7 operational support for security screening by authorized agencies. This has now been subsumed within the more expansive National Counterterrorism Center in Washington, D.C.

More stringent screening procedures for visa applicants have been applied that rely on these intelligence systems. Visa Mantis screening protocols have been in place since 1996, originally designed to stem the proliferation of expertise in knowledge relating to the creation of weapons of mass destruction, delivery systems, chemical and/or biological agents, and sensitive industries. Mantis procedures come in two forms: those that can be handled entirely by the consular office ("Eagle Mantis") and those that can issue a visa only after clearance by the State Department ("Donkey Mantis"). Procedures have been tightened since 9/11, requiring a Donkey Mantis clearance for applicants having passports or who are employed by states designated by the U.S. government as "sponsors of terrorism."[30] In addition, a new Visa Condor protocol has been established that requires that all applicants from certain nationalities (known as "List of Twenty-six" countries) be checked against CIA and FBI databases of known and suspected terrorists (including, but not limited to, the list of "state sponsors of terrorism").[31] In accordance with the protocol, men in these groups between the ages of sixteen and forty-five have to wait up to thirty days for the Condor check before a visa can be issued. Critics of the new security measures suggest that the emphasis on counterterrorism has instigated a "just say no" mentality among bureaucrats who issue visas. This view would seem corroborated by the statements of those directing policy and procedures in the area of visa issuance. Janice Jacobs, deputy assistant secretary of state for visa services, remarked, "In the post-9/11 environment, we do not believe that the issues at stake allow us the luxury of erring on the side of expeditious processing."[32] However, though the more stringent application of security cables certainly must be seen as a rise in the level of restriction, approval rates do not suggest that these have necessarily closed

Figure 10.1 Student Visas Issued, FY 1998–2005

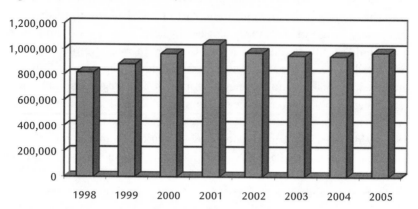

Source: U.S. Department of Homeland Security, Office of Immigration Statistics.

the door to migrants and travelers. The approval rate for visa applications in 2004 remained about the same as it was prior to 2001—75 percent.[33] The overall number of visas issued has declined, but this is attributed to a 35 percent drop in applications rather than increasingly restrictive security checks.[34]

Several new programs have been established to track visitors to the United States in compliance with the directives set forth in the Patriot Act and EBSVERA. The use of American flight schools as a key component of the 9/11 plot brought the issue of monitoring foreign students to the fore. To address this situation, a new Student and Exchange Visitor Information System was established in January 2003 that requires schools to provide completed electronic files to immigration offices and the State Department for all students studying at their institution. This, in addition to the Mantis and Condor security protocols, served to restrict student entry which had previously increased annually. Security checks complicated and significantly slowed down the visa process for students, acting as a disincentive to studying in the United States. Figure 10.1 shows the initial decline in the number of student visas issued following the events of 2001. Enrollment of students in U.S. institutions dropped 28 percent in 2004, the first such decline in thirty years.[35] Moreover, the number of educational institutions permitted to host foreign students declined sharply. Prior to 9/11, there were approximately 77,000 schools permitted to host foreign nationals. By 2004, this number declined to some seven thousand schools.[36]

In addition to tracking students, two systems have been developed to track nonstudent visitors to the country. The National Security Entry-Exit Registration System (NSEERS), established in 2002, required male foreign visitors from "politically sensitive areas" (primarily Muslim and/or Arab states) over the age of sixteen to register with the INS. More than a hundred thousand complied with the directive.[37] In January 2004, a new visitor tracking system was implemented that is intended to eventually replace NSEERS. Under the new US-VISIT system, nonimmigrant visitors to the United States must submit fingerprints and a digital photo upon entry into the country and receive security clearance prior to admission.[38] US-VISIT represents a significant expansion of NSEERS, in that it does not limit its scope to travelers from specific places of origin. US-VISIT has been implemented in stages, a process as yet incomplete. Beginning at U.S. airports in early 2004, it was later expanded to include the fifty busiest land border entry points in December of 2004. Though initially exempt, nationals of visa waiver program countries were also required to submit fingerprints under the US-VISIT program in April 2004.

Although measures to screen and track migrants and visitors can be seen as a step toward increased restriction over movement, much of the emphasis has been placed on border security. Initially, increased border security responded to concerns along the northern border, which was largely unguarded. The fact that known terrorists, such as Ahmed Ressam, have sought to enter the United States across the northern border made such moves rational from the standpoint of homeland security.[39] In accordance with provisions contained in both the Patriot Act and EBSVERA, Border Patrol deployment along the U.S.-Canadian border was tripled from 2001 to 2004, increasing from about 350 to about one thousand agents. In addition, a comprehensive Integrated Surveillance Intelligence System was deployed at fifty-five sites along the northern border that includes seismic, magnetic, and infrared ground sensors and high-resolution infrared video cameras. This has also been complemented by increased cooperation between U.S. and Canadian personnel, including the creation of Integrated Border Enforcement Teams and the Smart Borders Agreement.[40] More generally, increased funds have been appropriated for the Border Patrol, funding a sharp increase in the number of border agents. The budget for the Border Patrol increased from $400 million in FY1994 to $1.2 billion in FY2004, an increase of 300 percent. The total number of Border Patrol agents increased from 4,200 in 1994 to 11,200 in 2004.[41]

The emphasis on border control escalated in 2005 when then-secretary of homeland security, Michael Chertoff, announced the Secure Border Initiative (SBI). The SBI outlined a series of objectives to secure the borders and better regulate migration. It calls for more agents to patrol the borders, secure ports of entry, and enforce immigration laws. The Homeland Security Appropriations bill was signed by the president, providing for an 11 percent increase in funding for U.S. Customs and Border Protection and a 9 percent increase for Immigration and Customs Enforcement. These funds were earmarked to add eleven hundred new Border Patrol agents. The SBI also called for expanded detention and removal capabilities. New detention centers have been added, bringing the number of immigrants detained in such centers up from 19,718 a day in 2005 to 26,500 a day in 2006.[42] The new detention facilities are intended to end the practice of "catch and release," whereby undocumented immigrants (other than those of Mexican origin) were processed and released pending the judicial review of their case. The SBI also called for increased investment in infrastructure improvements at the border and greatly increased interior enforcement. Lastly, the SBI provided for a comprehensive and systemic upgrading of the technology used in controlling the border, including increased use of manned aerial assets, unmanned aerial vehicles, and next-generation detection technology. Part of this effort came in the form of SBInet, a high-tech "virtual fence" intended to supplement physical barriers along the border. In 2006, Boeing was awarded a three-year, $2.5 billion contract to install eighteen hundred sensor towers to detect illegal entry into the United States, beginning with a pilot program deployed on a twenty-eight-mile section of the border near Tucson, Arizona. Taken together, these programs of the SBI were intended to achieve "operational control" of both the northern and the southern border within five years.

The SBI highlights the centrality of migration and border control to the issue of homeland security. Though homeland security interests did not necessarily dominate social and political discourse in the United States as time passed, it did seem to dominate policy outcomes. As the shock of 9/11 became less acute over time, social and political discourse entertained the notion of comprehensive immigration reform. Indeed, this had long been a priority for the Bush administration, which originally sought to establish a migration accord with Mexico prior to 9/11. On January 7, 2004, the president once again put the issue on the agenda, proposing "Fair and Secure Immigration Reform" that would better match "willing foreign

Figure 10.2 Department of Homeland Security Budget, FY 2002–2008

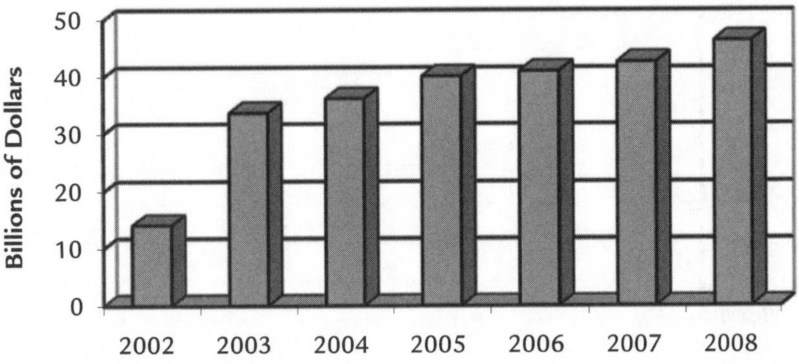

Source: U.S. Department of Homeland Security.

workers with willing U.S. employers when no American can be found to fill those jobs."[43] New immigration reform packages that included guest worker programs and amnesty (or "earned legalization") for undocumented immigrants were offered in both the House and the Senate in 2005 and debated in 2006. At the same time, hundreds of thousands of immigrant advocates took to the streets in huge public demonstrations in major U.S. cities. The stage seemed set for comprehensive change that would integrate homeland security interests while also promoting economic and liberal social interests.

However, in the process of deliberation, only increased border enforcement found consensus in Congress. In 2005, the Real ID Act was passed that increased restrictionism by (1) providing approval for the construction of fencing along a fourteen-mile section of the southern border that was deemed environmentally sensitive; (2) prohibiting federal agencies from accepting drivers' licenses as identification from states that issue them to undocumented immigrants; and (3) tightening asylum processing by giving more latitude to judges to deny asylum applications. This was followed in 2006 by the Secure Fence Act, which called for the construction of an additional seven hundred miles of fifteen-foot-high double-layered fencing along the U.S.-Mexican border. The act appropriated $1.2 billion to complete the fence.

The cost of supporting such homeland security–oriented programs clearly puts homeland security policy preferences at odds with the eco-

Figure 10.3 Immigrants Receiving Permanent Resident Status, FY 1999–2005

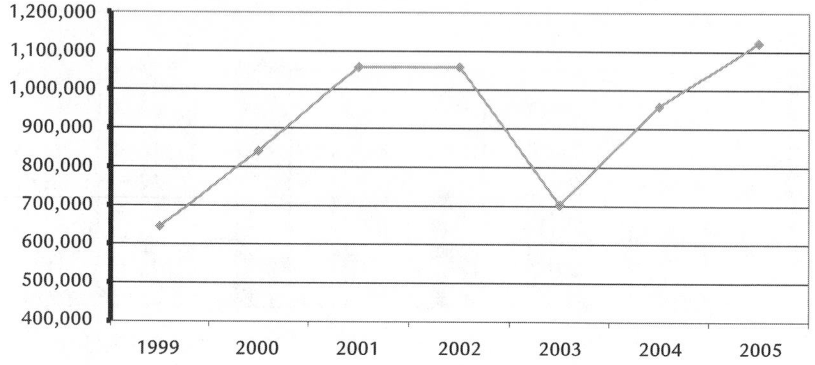

Source: U.S. Department of Homeland Security, Office of Immigration Statistics.

nomic security interests necessary to fund such policies. Figure 10.2 shows the consistent rise in the operating budget for the Department of Homeland Security since its inception, rising from $14.1 billion in fiscal year 2002 to $46.4 billion in fiscal year 2008. When you add in the cost of its foreign policy components, including U.S. military interventions in Iraq and Afghanistan, this global war on terror comes with a considerable price tag. In the pre-9/11 era, geopolitical pressures for economic wealth to support defense skewed policy preferences toward more openness. A similar pressure has been exerted in the post-9/11 period. What's different now is that policy preferences are no longer congruent between defense (homeland security) and economic security. How is this tension reconciled politically? The answer lies in recognizing that migration policy is far more nuanced than the terms "open" and "closed" allow. Traditionally, immigration policy has been thought of largely in these terms—of state regulation using policy as a sort of valve that either lets in more immigrants or reduces their number. Because responding to homeland security interests with this type of absolute closure is contrary to national economic interests, policies of restrictionism are based more on adding levels of screening and selection rather than altering overall volume.[44] The types of policies outlined above promote two primary agendas: they (1) redirect undocumented flows through proper channels, and they (2) increase screening and tracking capabilities to reduce the risk of terrorist infiltration.

Levels of permanent immigration have actually increased since 9/11.

Figure 10.3 shows that levels of immigrants receiving permanent residence status remained stable in the year following 9/11. The number declined in 2003, but that was a largely the result of the economic downturn rather than changes in policy. As the economy rebounded in 2004–2005, levels of permanent immigration again rose sharply and surpassed the pre-9/11 levels in 2005. There have also been increases in the number of business-oriented, skills-based migrants permitted to enter the country. Though a sunset provision of the American Competitiveness in the Twenty-first Century Act of 2000 returned H1-B visa quotas to their previous limit of 65,000 in October 2003, subsequent Congressional actions have moved to increase limits. In 2004, the Visa Reform Act exempted up to 20,000 foreign workers holding master's degrees or higher from the 65,000 cap. Moreover, skilled workers employed at institutions of higher education, nonprofit research organizations, and government research organizations were also exempt from the quota limits. In addition, in 2004 a new H1-B1 visa became available to nationals from Chile (1,400) and Singapore (5,400) who held a B.A. degree (or more) as part of trade agreements with those countries.[45] L-1 visas for management and other highly skilled workers of multinational corporations have remained free of specific quota limitations, allowing economic labor market forces to direct levels of inflows.

At the same time policies were in place to ensure business had access to needed supplies of labor, the immigration bureaucracy contributed to the business-friendly environment. Amid the tightening restrictions outlined above, immigration control agencies refrained from unnecessarily "harassing" domestic employers of immigrant workers. Employer sanctions laws, on the books since the 1986 Immigration Reform and Control Act, have a long history of benign neglect.[46] This practice of noninterference seems to have become even more pronounced after 9/11, even though political discourse projected a new "get tough" stance. The number of employers fined for hiring undocumented immigrants declined from 944 to 124 from 1993 to 2003. In addition, the number of workers apprehended by immigration authorities at work places fell from 7,630 to 445 during the same period.[47] Yet, increasing work site enforcement is one of the stated goals of the Secure Border Initiative. Again, however, we see security practices crafted to reduce negative impact on business. Rather than an across-the-board crackdown on employers of undocumented workers, Immigration and Customs Enforcement agents have focused on checking employment records at critical infrastructure workplaces. These include airports, nuclear facilities, refineries, and seaports.[48]

What we see in terms of policy in the United States is an effort to bridge economic and homeland security interests by increasing regulatory control over flows—not just stemming flows generally. It represents unprecedented expectations of the immigration control bureaucracy. While the empirical evidence since 9/11 does lend some support for the security paradigm, the new conditions are clearly more complex than conditions before 2001. Increased levels of threat have pressed the state to act on its defense (now defined as homeland security) and economic security interests. Because the policy preferences of these facets present contradicting logics (one pressing for more openness, the other for closure), the state is left with two choices: (1) prefer one over the other or (2) attempt to bridge the gap by increasing screening and tracking abilities while maintaining a generally liberal posture vis-à-vis migration. Clearly, the U.S. government has attempted to build grand strategy along the latter lines.

Conclusion

The increasingly complex politics of immigration and border policy raise additional questions. Though the evidence seems largely supportive of the expectation of receptivity to many kinds of immigration in times of external threat, it is less clear that there is support for the notion that such a structural environment is conducive to a societal "rally effect" that makes societies more accepting of such flows. The mobilization of mass pro-immigrant demonstrations in spring 2006 might be some evidence of a push for openness in times of external threat. However, poll data are much less conclusive. A *Washington Post* poll taken in January 2005 found that 61 percent of respondents supported access to legalization for undocumented workers now living in the United States, suggesting some receptiveness to liberalization of what has long been a politically contentious issue. However, a *Wall Street Journal*–NBC poll taken in December 2005 found that 57 percent of respondents felt that the United States was "too open" to immigration. Hence, there is no clear empirical support that a rally effect will make society more accepting of open policies.

If public opinion seems somewhat mixed concerning immigration in general, it is much more homogeneous in terms of attitudes toward illegal immigration. The post-9/11 threat environment clearly had a negative impact on people's concerns about illegal immigration. A Fox News poll from May 2005 found that 91 percent of respondents considered illegal immigration to be a "serious" problem.[49] Likewise, a California Field poll found that 73 percent of respondents were "concerned" about illegal immigration, including 43 percent who responded that they were "very concerned."[50] The emphasis on illegal immigration in public opinion raises one of the more puzzling questions of policy development since 9/11: If illegal immigration is a potential conduit for terrorist aliens and border security is necessary to thwart this threat, why has U.S. policy focused disproportionately on the southern border? This question is even more perplexing given the fact that the only publicly known foreign terrorists that used clandestine border crossing as a means of entry into the United States came from the north, not the south.[51]

There are a few possible explanations. The first is that the government knows something that the rest of us don't. In testimony before Congress on February 16, 2005, top government officials suggested that there was evidence that Al Qaeda was considering using the southern border to gain entry into the United States. Admiral James Loy, deputy secretary for homeland security, testified that new intelligence "strongly suggests" that terrorists are considering this mode of entry and that "several Al Qaeda leaders believe operatives can pay their way into the country through Mexico and also believe illegal entry is more advantageous than legal entry for operational security reasons."[52] Since this testimony, however, there have been no reports of Al Qaeda operatives apprehended while attempting to cross the U.S.-Mexican border, nor have there been further reports of intelligence corroborating such concerns.

A second possibility is that U.S. policy makers are reluctant to establish a more stringent border regime with Canada because they are reluctant to initiate policy that may hamper U.S.-Canadian relations. In the same way that national-origins quota restrictions and the Asiatic barred zone strained U.S. alliance relationships in Asia following World War II, reinforcing the northern border would likely cause irreparable damage to U.S.-Canadian relations. One might add that, as Mexico is its second-largest trading partner, the United States should hold equal restraint in its dealings with Mexico. However, the two situations are fundamentally different, as border enforcement is nothing new to the south. To the north, however, increased fortification would be a definitive foreign policy transition for the United States—one that would have significant implications for U.S. alliances.

A third possibility involves the way we think about threats post-9/11. Perhaps similar to the "red scare" of the 1950s, the current threat of global terrorism presents us with a shadowlike nemesis—one not easily identified. Potential terrorists can be anyone and have no predetermined source of origin or physical appearance. The case of the American-turned-Muslim radical John Walker Lindh, who was captured fighting with the Taliban in Afghanistan, suggests that terrorist organizations can recruit anyone from anywhere to join their cause. Because the source of the threat is imprecise, it is likely that public opinion turns to "old enemies" to give shape to the new threat. If clandestine border crossing represents the potential means of terrorist infiltration, then perhaps the general public and policy makers alike have turned to prior conceptions of the source of this threat—border crossers from Mexico. Indeed, there is reason for such long-held views, as Mexicans represent 50 percent of the undocumented migrants apprehended by U.S. border authorities. Thus, the preoccupation with the southern border can be likened to a roundup of the "usual suspects" in the initial stages of a criminal investigation. Certainly, public opinion polls seem to support this view. In the December 2005 *Wall Street Journal*–NBC poll that showed 57 percent of respondents felt the United States was "too open" to immigration, 78 percent of those polled said that they favored "tightening" the border with Mexico. Two-thirds of respondents in the May 2005 Fox News poll supported putting U.S. troops on the southern border.

Lastly, the preoccupation with illegal immigration from Mexico may also reflect a fundamental transformation in the way security is considered post-9/11—at least in terms of homeland security. Global terrorism is fundamentally different than the traditional security threat—another state. Instead, it blurs the line between "security" and "policing," and subsequently, notions of lawbreaking may be emerging in the homeland security discourse. Certainly, negative public attitudes about illegal immigration find common ground between political Right and Left when the issue of "legal channels" is raised. In congressional debates about immigration reform in 2005–2006, a common theme that linked conservatives and liberals was that migration must be orderly, be secure, and respect the law and sovereignty of the receiving country. In this sense, this new preoccupation with lawbreaking may work together with the "usual suspects" rationale outlined above—as Mexico and the southern border represents the public stereotype of the "illegal immigrant." This is nothing new. Even before 9/11, policy discourse in the 1990s emphasized the need to control flows across the border, even though it was widely known that some 40 percent to 50 percent of illegal immigrants did not cross the southern border clandestinely. Nor were they all of Mexican origin. Instead, these "out of status" migrants (a.k.a. "visa overstayers") simply entered through regular channels and then violated the terms of their visa.

The events of September 11, 2001, complicated our notions of security. Moreover, they have had a profound effect on the complexity of crafting policy that is able to respond to security's various facets without creating new vulnerabilities. To achieve this end, U.S. policy makers have put the burden on the border control bureaucracy to establish a level of control to date unprecedented. At this point, this process remains very much a work in progress.

Chapter 11

Citizenship's New Subject:
The Illegal Immigrant Voter

Kamal Sadiq

Citizenship has a new subject: the illegal immigrant. Citizenship has traditionally covered a political space that included among its subjects the native-born citizen and the naturalized citizen. This political space has recently been extended to the dual citizen and the transnational citizen. Since modern citizenship denotes a legal relationship between the individual and the state, a bond sanctified by law, it creates subjects based on legal coverage.[1] At the very top of the citizenship stratum is the full citizen. Such a member of the political community has all the rights and protections of the state as well as attendant duties and obligations (such as the right to vote, the duty to pay taxes, the obligation of military service). Along a gradient of legalized relationships with the state stand a range of subjects, ranging from dual and transnational citizens to global and cosmopolitan citizens, each connected to the state(s) through a legalized regime of rights and duties. The extension of each right brings into the legal fold a new state-authorized member.

For example, in this schema, further away from the full citizen is the denizen—a member of the political community who is *extended* certain rights but not all, namely, voting in national elections or eligibility for public office.[2] Outside this legalized citizenship structure is the illegal immigrant, residing without state authorization, deprived of the rights and protections of an official status, ineligible for *full* political participation, and excluded from a path to citizenship. A wall separates the illegal immigrant from a bounded polity of state-authorized members. The illegal immigrant is the paradigmatic outsider—excluded, marked for expulsion, officially nonexistent. But what if the illegal immigrant was able to enter a polity and gain access to all the rights of full citizenship without state recognition? Citizenship would then have to contend with a new subject—the illegal immigrant.

When a range of citizenships arise from an individual's legal relationship to the state, recognition becomes critical. After all, citizenship "in a state is an institutionalized form of solidarity" that "constitutes an expression of full and formal membership."[3] Institutionalizing the networks of solidarity requires identification. State identification and recognition of a subject creates a formal relationship marked by transparency and accountability. The relationship between a subject and the state is only possible once each actor is identified and mutually recognized. Legal principles such as *jus sanguinis* (blood-based citizenship) and *jus soli* (birth-based citizenship), sometimes tracing the origin of an individual to cultural principles such as ethnic descent, are meant to define a polity.[4] With a clear community bound by the state—the contours of a "national identity" or "political community" become visible. Knowing the subject of citizenship is a political undertaking. A transparent political community (i.e., an easily identifiable polity) is imperative for the political needs of the state—such as welfare or security in a post-9/11 world. To mark this political community, state documentation is dispersed to help verify eligible members and their identity. This documentation assists the state in determining who is a citizen and who is not. Only once you define and identify a polity can you effectively contend with the political needs of the state, such as maintaining order, the sanctity of state services, and immigration control or integration.

A state's political needs are not the same everywhere in the world. In the West, the cultural and political integration of immigrants is the main concern of states.[5] The integration of immigrants, Arabs in Western Europe and Mexicans in the United States, is a critical political need of the Western state. In contrast, developing countries such as India struggle to identify and exclude well-integrated illegal immigrants exercising national franchise. In an inversion of Western experience and theory, easily absorbed illegal immigrants are generating a political need among developing states to distinguish and restrict the already integrated.

Illegal immigrants in India, Malaysia, and Pakistan are exercising the entire range of citizenship rights—civil, social, and political, including national suffrage. Behaving and living like many poor native citizens, they are indistinguishable from locals. Increasingly, the presence of illegal immigrants on national electoral rolls is raising concerns about the character of citizenship and democratic politics in developing countries. Voting by illegal immigrants is not confined to India. Elsewhere, I have recorded the common occurrence of "documentary citizenship"—that is, illegal immigrants behaving as citizens by acquiring varieties of citizenship-identifying documents in India, Malaysia, and Pakistan.[6] The need to identify a citizenry is present in every democracy, as only totalitarian or single-party authoritarian regimes can wholly mark and document every member of society (through restrictive and repressive state policies).[7] Democracies in the developing world are hard pressed to achieve such full legibility and transparency in their population. Concomitantly, illegal immigrants in every part of the world continue to assault the authority of the state by integrating (some more successfully than others) as full citizens. Traditionally, the state is the only apparatus that bestows citizenship status and therefore grants the right to vote in national elections. In India, however, illegal immigrants are able to bypass the state, sustain full community membership, and exercise all the rights of citizenship (including national-level voting). Therefore, I will argue that being a subject of citizenship in developing countries entails the exercise of rights, with or without the status of "citizen" from the state. Citizenship status loses its meaning if all the rights of citizenship can be accessed without it.[8] Illegal immigrant voters in developing countries have decoupled citizenship status from rights and duties; consequently, citizenship is evolving, producing newer forms of membership in developing countries.

How does the state define the subjects of citizenship, and what are the benefits of such legal status? Importantly, where does the illegal immigrant stand in relation to the state? What other relationships are emerging between the state (the guarantor of citizenship status), the citizen, and the illegal immigrant (the recipients of citizenship rights)? How do these relations influence our understanding of citizenship in India and other states in the developing world? What follows is an attempt to look beyond the traditional, often Western, accounts of citizenship and its many subjects.

The Subject

Who are citizenship's subjects? This evokes two responses, a "nationally particularist" response, in which members are bound to a specific state, and a "universalist" one, in which everyone is a subject of some form of citizenship.[9] The state is central to both these approaches, both in allocating membership to actors and in dispensing rights. Accordingly, two types of citizen emerge—one bound to a single state, and the other shared by multiple states.

Single State Citizenship

Single state citizenship is the institutional embodiment of a "social contract"[10] based on mutual recognition and acceptance among citizens. As the legal manifestation of this agreement, the state is able to regulate access to citizenship based on principles established by the political community—*jus sanguinis, jus soli,* and so on. The distinctions between the differing principles of citizenship are beginning to blur. States combine both *jus sanguinis* and *jus soli* to accommodate and extend membership and rights to immigrants. A common thread among these principles is they are practiced most often by "liberal-democratic nation-states as welfare states, characterized by high degrees of regulation and redistribution which require institutionalized solidarity."[11] The trajectory of this accommodation is to produce authorized legal subjects (i.e., citizens, denizens, authorized immigrants), each identified separately, each possessing a separate set of rights and duties—and all bound by a common legal framework arising from the state. These legal subjects are privileged, and formal recognition of them from the state signifies their investment in the political outcomes of the community. In contrast, the illegal immigrant is not equally placed with others eligible for accommodation under these legal regimes and remains outside the web of authorizations that precede the path to citizenship. The illegal immigrant is criminalized for violating the territorial sanctity of the community and is seen as an outsider, even though he or she may reside in the same territory.

Transnational Citizenship

A trend toward transnational citizenship is emerging as states absorb the effects of greater global integration and interaction. The emergence of dual, multiple, or transnational citizenship is due to the expansion of a transnational social space, which is "combinations of ties, positions in networks and organizations, and networks of organizations that reach across the borders of multiple states."[12] Significantly, there exists a transnational space, unauthorized and often undetected by the state, which is multisited in scope (a flow that traverses multiple state borders), involves the use of various forms of capital (human, goods, services), and generates integrative linkages (economic, social, cultural). This unregulated transnational space—that of illegal immigrants, traffickers, and smugglers—blurs the territorial and political sovereignty of states, just as regulated transnational social space does.[13]

Recognized political communities overlie states that maintain separate territorial space and authority, thus producing transnational citizenship. Diasporas (Armenian, Indian, Jewish) and immigrant communities (Bangladeshis, Indians, Filipinos) all occupy a transnational social space by maintaining economic and social linkages across territorial borders. These linkages create multiple identities, test national loyalties, and challenge singular political membership. When "a triangular" relationship exists between "individuals and two or more independent states in which these individuals are simultaneously assigned membership status and membership-based rights or obligations," we are presented with a thick web of authorizations shared by multiple states.[14]

How does transnational citizenship define its subjects? For Bauböck there are three categories of transnational subjects, the first being "multiple nationals who are formally recognized as citizens by two or more independent countries."[15] Dual citizens are an example. The second subject of transnational citizenship is the "denizen," who is (often) a long-term resident foreigner.[16] Eligible for most civil, social, and economic rights, a denizen is on the path to citizenship. Yet, national voting and public service are withheld from a denizen until his or her full legal confirmation as a citizen. Denizenship is partial citizenship, for denizens continue to be viewed as "foreign" nationals to whom another state extends its status, rights, and protection.[17] The last subjects of transnational citizenship are those eligible for citizenship rights on the basis of actual or perceived common ethnic descent, even though they are "neither citizens nor residents" of the state extending these privileges.[18] States in Eastern Europe as well as Japan, Spain, and Germany grant legal naturalization to individuals with shared ethnic descent and ancestry.[19] This blood-based citizenship becomes transnational when extended to a real or mythical diaspora. Too often transnational citizenship appears to be an extension of the legal regime that forms single state citizenship. Transnational citizenship may challenge the maintenance of a singular national identity and territorial sovereignty, but it never escapes legality. The extension and retraction of a legal web of authorizations, accommodating and excluding individuals, produces a range of citizenships. Such legal transnationality always excludes illegal immigrants. The legal regime has no space for those violating its domestic and interstate authority. Only with legal authorizations do the unwanted possess the "right to have rights."[20]

Status and the State

To have full citizenship status is to have state authorization for the *permanent* physical presence of an individual within its territorial jurisdiction. This authorization entails verification of an individual's identity, civic values, and indivisible loyalty to the state before making him or her eligible to receive the full bundle of rights offered by the state. Anything less (refugee status, guest worker status, resident alien status, and so on) puts the individual *on a path to* citizenship with rights increasing incrementally as one gets closer to full citizenship status, commonly known as the naturalization process. The naturalization process is particularly important for meeting the political needs of the state. It is through this legal regime that the state exercises its power to deny or revoke citizenship status and rights. Importantly, illegal immigrants are not eligible for naturalization—the path to citizenship. They do not have state-recognized status; these individuals are "legally defined as lacking in full national membership, and are subject to certain disabilities, including lack of political rights and potential deportation as a result."[21] Citizenship status matters because it is a way of prioritizing claims on the state in the distribution of welfare and the allocation of rights based on legal standing. Full citizenship status comes with full citizenship rights, guest worker status comes with fewer rights, and so on. Consequently, illegal immigrants are without status.

The legal regime of the state attempts to record and therefore identify all its members and foreigners. Each individual is knowable or can be made visible through records and local affirmations. Such a legal regime works more or less efficiently in Westphalian states. Hence, every foreigner enters and stays at the discretion of the state. The regime of law embraces the political community fully, while extending partial coverage to foreigners within the territory. What happens if the legal regime is weak in its coverage of the territorial community? The state will be unable to determine and distribute differential access to the political community through the graded system of membership—citizenship, quasi-citizenship, authorized immigrant, and so on. Without an expansive legal regime the state will not be able to distinguish between the eligible and the noneligible—a foreigner, a migrant worker, or a citizen.

When the legal regime of the state has limited authority over society, it also lacks the power to reach and organize individual members according to legal norms. Individual members in society will practice their rights and obligations according to local customs and culture. If the state has no power to impose legality over individual members, it often accommodates cultural practices by recognizing customary law or adopting such practices into common law. In such societies, citizenship is practiced without the presence of a legal regime. Lack of a legal regime allows anyone to walk in and practice rights as long as he or she does not contradict local norms and cultural mores. If local and immigrant cultures overlap, acceptance is immediate. Local acceptance and practice of rights bring with them an acknowledgment of membership in the local and the national community. Such an extension of membership occurs without the state's recognition or verification. The state is absent in all these local practices of community membership. In such circumstances, states lack the legal ability to identify and exclude foreigners, who over time become full members without official status.

India and Other Developing Countries

The ability to effectively meet a political need of the state—to identify and separate citizens from noncitizens—is complicated in developing countries. The aspiration toward a watertight Westphalian model with a well-defined citizenship regime is undermined by the interpenetration of diverse cultural, religious, and regional forms of membership present in large parts of Africa, Asia, and Latin America. For example, the world's largest democracy, India, finds itself in a precarious situation when attempting to successfully identify and define all citizens.

The legal citizenship regime is based on constitutional provisions dealing with citizenship located in Articles 5 to 12 in Part II of the Constitution of India.[22] Given the variation in the social (i.e., caste, tribal, religious, linguistic) and economic (i.e., rural communities, urban middle class, the landless poor, and the rich) profiles of the population, India finds itself stretched to the limit to meet the demands of all of its citizens, such as the need to distribute welfare and harmonize common democratic practices. Like its Westphalian counterparts, India attempts to produce a verifiable membership bound in a web of legality to the Indian state. Therefore, each social grouping and economic activity produces a document of authorization from a plethora of Indian institutions. This is how Indian citizenship is recorded, identified, and circumscribed. The birth of a child at a hospital results in a birth registration, which can lead to a birth certificate if one is applied for. If the child is born at home or is lacking a birth certificate, then education provides another occasion for acquiring a citizenship-identifying document. The state uses the educational system to identify its members through student identity cards or high school graduation certificates. If one belongs to a marginalized caste and is eligible for affirmative action or preferential hiring, the legal regime distributes caste certificates. If one is disabled, the state has institutions confirming an individual's identity and disability. Firearm licenses, drivers' licenses, income tax identity cards, farmers' banking pass books, railway identity cards, ration cards (for state-subsidized grains), and even proof of having participated in the anticolonial movement results in a Freedom Fighter card. Across time and space a web of legal authorizations through paperwork signal Indian citizenship.

In keeping with the range of documents used to verify individual identity and citizenship status in India, there is also a document for democratic politics—the electoral roll. Participation in Indian national elections is one of many secure rights of Indian citizenship. Therefore, presence on the national electoral rolls signals membership and full citizenship in the political community. The electoral roll is the wall demarcating a full Indian "citizen" from an "illegal immigrant." Importantly, it is the symbol of a responsible citizenry representing a dynamic democratic polity. The electoral roll embodies the democratic process, eligible members of a political community determining who will govern them via a legal regime in which they are easily identifiable. Accordingly, democratic practice defines the boundaries of the eligible citizenry. In India the electoral roll is sure proof of citizenship.

How does an Indian citizen acquire a place on the electoral rolls? All Indian citizens above the age of eighteen years are eligible to be on the electoral rolls of the constituency in which they commonly reside by filling

out Form 6 of the Election Commission in the presence of the local electoral registration officer.[23] Since 1993, the process of verification and authorization has also generated a voter identification card, which can be
substituted by approximately fifteen to twenty authorized identity cards,
depending on the region. For example, in the Indian state of West Bengal
fourteen alternate documents can be presented, ranging from school certificates to railways passes.[24] Each document identifies a potential national
voter, drawing yet another boundary around the political community. Such
a wide range of identity documents is necessary to accommodate the social,
economic, and geographical spread of the Indian citizenry. India relaxes the
criterion for electoral participation to satisfy another democratic goal—
increased "accessibility."[25]

Regardless of the Indian government's attempts to identify citizens
through flexible criteria, a segment of the population remains left out of
civic and political participation. Lack of documentation to prove individual
identity arising from extreme and chronic poverty, religious and ethnic
prejudice, gender bias in patriarchic societies, and isolation of indigenous
communities undermines the practice of citizenship by native residents.
Marginalized communities, low and backward castes, sex workers, and social outcasts such as abandoned elderly and widows face immense social
discrimination, inhibiting their ability to exercise citizenship rights. They
also face hurdles in authenticating and documenting their identity. If democratic politics hinges on one vote per eligible citizen, identifying every
individual with multiple identity documents is vital in reaching out to marginalized groups. Since multiple documents embody individual identity and
citizenship, the consequences of not having a document are immense. Iron-
ically, the reverse is also true: a fraudulent acquisition of a legal identity
document brings forth full citizen rights.

The Illegal Immigrant Voter

Voting in national elections is viewed as a key performance of citizenship.
It is a right that can only be bestowed by the state on a subject—the bundle
of rights is granted *by* the state. However, when illegal immigrants are able
to participate in an act of citizenship, such as voting in national elections,
based on their community membership, these rights are no longer fully
regulated by the state but are exercised *in spite* of the state. In India, *citizen-*

ship from below, from civil society, is widespread. Here society-based citizenship trumps citizenship from the state. Illegal immigrant voting exemplifies such membership. Concomitantly, how do illegal immigrants acquire electoral rights in India?

Immigration from what is now Bangladesh (formerly East Pakistan) to adjacent parts of what is now India has a long history. Under the British colonial government this entire region was one sovereign territory, so what is now international migration was internal migration between two regions of the British Empire. The geographic region stretching across West Bengal (in India) and into Bangladesh is one linguistic and cultural belt. The Indian state of Assam borders this area. The inhabitants of the region live on the banks of the Brahmaputra River, speak the same language, have the same phenotypic features, and adopt similar cultural dress and food habits. The flow of illegal immigrants from Bangladesh to India was complicated by a civil war between East and West Pakistan in 1971. What was initially a case of immigrants fleeing from the devastation of war transformed into a major illegal immigration flow to India. In the past thirty-nine years varying estimates of the number of Bangladeshi illegal immigrants in India have been given. In 2003 the former Indian defense minister George Fernandes gave a figure of twenty million illegal Bangladeshis across India, though the actual number could be anywhere between fifteen and twenty million.[26] What further complicates the data is that the Bangladeshi government refuses to acknowledge these illegal immigrants as Bangladeshi citizens. The states of Assam and West Bengal have been the major receivers of illegal immigrants in India. In 2004 the Union Minister of State for Home, Prakash Jaiswal, stated in Parliament that there were over 5 million Bangladeshis in the state of Assam alone—one-fourth of the entire Bangladeshi illegal immigrant population of India.[27] Resentment over large numbers of illegal immigrants exercising franchise as citizens in Assam came to the fore in 1979. A parliamentary by-election for the Mangaldoi constituency in March 1979 began with the discovery of about forty-five thousand Bengali illegal immigrants on electoral rolls. By voting and behaving as full citizens, these illegal immigrants had clearly breached the conceptual wall separating immigrants and citizens. Further, because they had obtained the "proper" documentation no one questioned their claims to citizenship, and thus these "documentary citizens" were able to access the national franchise.[28] Without naturalization and authentication from the state, illegal Bangladeshi immigrants had gained Indian citizenship.

Presence on the electoral rolls, with or without a voter identification card (voter ID), has become a marker of citizenship status. Recall that in order to include an individual's name on an electoral roll, a voter ID or any of twenty other substitutable documents can be presented to a local electoral commission. Obtaining these documents for the purpose of including a name on the electoral rolls is tantamount to gaining citizenship in India, as it is difficult to question one's citizenship after one has already exercised citizenship's most secure right. Consequently, government-distributed documents are highly sought after and remain easy to obtain. For example, "18 year old Deb Kumar Biswas crossed over from Bangladesh to Garapota village in 2003. He obtained admission to a local school in Class IX and left it months later and obtained a certificate from the school attesting he was a student there. The certificate doubled as proof of his age and he [later] applied for a ration card."[29] A ration card indicates a citizen is eligible for government-subsidized grains and other welfare; it is also a proof of identity and can be used to vote in elections. In cases such as this, we see how an *illegal immigrant* exercising the rights of citizenship accumulates proof of citizenship. Alternatively, one can purchase a fraudulent voter ID and bypass the state completely; "it takes only about Rs. 5 to make a fake card, which sells for as much as Rs. 1000."[30]

The pervasiveness of illegal immigrant voting in India has caused the Election Commission of India to officially create a subcategory for individuals on electoral rolls with "doubtful" citizenship. These "doubtful" voters are placed in a special "D" category on the voters' list and are unable to cast ballots until their citizenship can be confirmed. Citizenship is verified through documentation, such as birth certificates or land deeds—which are plentiful and easy to obtain. In 1997, the Electoral Commission detected 370,000 "D" voters in the state of Assam, of whom only 3,686 could not prove citizenship.[31] Individuals who are placed in the "D" subsection, more often than not, find a way to prove citizenship. In Assam, the number of "D" voters remains extensive (Table 11.1).

Bordering Assam is the Indian state of West Bengal, which also receives large numbers of Bangladeshi illegal immigrants. The district of Nadia in Calcutta, West Bengal, is notorious for the proliferation of fake voter-identification and ration cards—both used as proof of identity and citizenship. Prior to recent municipal elections, the opposition Trinamool Congress Party alleged that several thousand Bangladeshis vote for the Communist Party Marxist (CPM) in every election in West Bengal. A mem-

Table 11.1 Assam "D" Voters by District

Assam constituency	"D" voters
Barchalla	7,983
Majbat	5,856
Dhekiajuli	5,787
Udalguri	3,086
Paneri	4,936
Golakganj	4,756
Dhubri	3,912
Gauripur	4,069
Total	181,619

Source: Rajeev Bhattacharyya, "Assam 'D' Voters in Vanishing Act," Telegraph (Calcutta), July 16, 2005.

ber of the Congress Party went so far as to say "that he could prove at least 7000 Bangladeshis vote for the CPM every election."[32] Furthermore, there were 100,000 fake ration cards in circulation in addition to the 10,000 fake voter IDs confiscated by the police.[33]

It is interesting to note that the official figures are more than four times higher. Observers for the Election Commission of India in the district of Nadia discovered "about 30,000 Bangladeshis on voter lists."[34] An official stated,"if such a huge number of Bangladeshis can find their way into the voter list, there must be a larger number of them who are actually residing in Nadia illegally."[35] In another district of West Bengal, Chandan Bhowmik, district Trinamool secretary of Jalpaiguri, proclaimed, "We apprehend that over one lakh [100,000] Bangladeshi voters are there in Jalpaiguri."[36] If citizenship is about exercising social and economic rights and performing civic duties such as national voting, then Bangladeshi illegal immigrants have become de facto citizens. They practice national-level franchise and affirm civic duties in their host state. This both gives them citizenship and strengthens their citizenship claim.

In light of these developments the Election Commission has introduced a photo-electoral roll in parts of India. These voter lists will now include a photograph along with the name and address of genuine Indian citizens. Since proof of citizenship can be established with a range of documents, however, a mere photograph is unlikely to control access to Indian citizenship. Already, in the northeastern state of Tripura, the state Youth Congress questions the legitimacy of the photo electoral roll. For example, Pradeep

Das, a Bangladeshi illegal immigrant, is "a lecturer of a college in Cummilla district of Bangladesh [who] has been enrolled as a voter of Pratapgarh Assembly constituency [in India]."[37] In addition, the Election Commission engages in elaborate "electoral revision" exercises, in which commission officers and observers attempt to verify the identities of individuals on electoral rolls. In India, the challenge is not how to integrate illegal immigrants—it is the reverse; their easy incorporation and practice of citizenship is raising political challenges for various Indian institutions such as the Election Commission.

Illegal immigrants move from smaller districts and towns to larger cities such as Mumbai and Delhi, just like the majority of Indian citizens who live in rural regions. According to the Hindu nationalist Bharatiya Janata Party (BJP) spokesman Madhav Bhandari, in August 2007 the electoral revision drive in Mumbai counted 84 lakh (8.4 million) voters, by October 25th of the same year the figure had increased to 88.31 lakh (8.8 million). Bhandari asserts, "the country, on an average, recorded a rise of 0.3 % in the number of voters per year on the basis of the natural population rise of 2 % per annum. But the number of voters in Mumbai constituencies has risen by 4.92 % in just two months."[38] His judgment was that fake proofs of identity such as voter IDs were being issued to "bogus voters"—an obvious reference to illegal immigrant voters. Similarly, "35,000 names of fake voters [had] been deleted from the electoral rolls of Delhi by the State Election Commission which [was] carrying out a revision of rolls to check bogus voting."[39] Not all illegal immigrants who are on voter rolls are detected by authorities. It is important to note that while 35,000 names may have been deleted in India's capital, the actual number of illegal immigrants on electoral rolls may be higher. If "civic virtues" are a marker of citizenship, then "active citizenship" exists among illegal immigrants who vigorously participate in the electoral process.

With millions of illegal immigrants as potential voters, political parties are scrambling to vie for their support. In Karimganj, Assam, a tribunal governed by the Foreigners Act sent mass "quit [India] notices" that required suspect individuals to appear before the tribunal with valid documents to prove Indian citizenship. The BJP threatened political agitation "if the notices were not revoked."[40] Biswarup Bhattacharjee, an outraged member of the BJP district committee, argued that "all the recipients of these notices were 'very much Indian citizens.' "[41] Similarly, in neighboring West Bengal, Anil Biswas, state secretary of the ruling party—the CPM—

criticized the Election Commission for "carrying out a survey to weed out names of Bangladeshis from electoral rolls."[42] At a party rally eighty kilometers outside Calcutta, he reassured those affected, "We share your concern and will not allow anybody to uproot you. We consider you Indians."[43]

With illegal immigrants confirming their citizenship by voting, and political parties actively recruiting them as potential voters, citizenship has acquired a new subject—the illegal immigrant. Already integrated illegal immigrants practicing citizenship rights, behaving as citizens, further dilutes the significance of official citizenship status. Citizenship no longer exists as a legal incarnation of the state; unable to distinguish "legitimate" from "illegitimate" citizens, it is diminishing in value as a sign of privilege and a marker of state-verified membership.

Importantly, there is no sure way to prove that suspect individuals are in fact illegal immigrants. With natives and indigenous communities lacking proper citizenship documents, and illegal immigrants with various proofs of citizenship, the political need of the state to define and identify its citizenry is complicated. If illegal immigrants all have the same documents as citizens and are accepted as members of the community, at both practical and conceptual levels the individual is in effect a citizen. For example, in the town of Krishnaganj, West Bengal, a thousand warrants for villagers suspected of being Bangladeshis were delivered through local police, but most individuals who received warrants had documentation to prove citizenship. Krishnapada Dutta was among them; he "runs a phone booth and gift item shop, has a photo-I-card (No.WB/11/074/534698) and claims his late father, Satyacharan, had migrated to India in 1948. His ration card proves that, he says."[44] In addition, he notes that he has been voting in elections since 1991; how can the government prove he is *not* an Indian?

Contrary to traditional assumptions about citizenship, which define a citizen by "biographical circumstances"—place of birth, location of residence, or native ancestry (citizen parent)[45]—the developing world identifies citizens based on the rights they can exercise. An individual's exercise of political and civic rights (whether they can vote in national elections, are able to send children to local schools, or participate in government subsidy programs) defines citizenship, not status. For many in developing countries, citizenship exists without status. Yet citizenship continues to be thought of as a status bringing with it an attached bundle of rights. But the relationship is reversed in the developing world; citizenship is defined by the practice of rights in which status loses meaning. In such circumstances, national voting by illegal immigrants and citizens alike is a confirmation of citizenship.

(Un)doing Democracy?

Is democracy being undermined by the illegal immigrant voter? The Indian state's central concern is accessibility to society, and therefore it has to contend with the varying economic and social background of its subjects. Accessibility can function top down, with the government accessing society for census, taxation, recruitment, local development, and planning. Here recognition—the ability of the state to effectively verify individual identity—becomes a top priority. Without effectively assessing the needs of the population, resource distribution is complicated to say the least. On the other hand, accessibility can operate bottom up, with the population gaining access to government programs (health care, education, subsidies) and democratic elections through grassroots social movements and struggles. In order to effectively manage accessibility, the state employs an expansive document scheme designed to incorporate all of India's citizens—with limited success. Illegal immigrants seep onto the electoral rolls to exercise the franchise and affirm their claim to Indian citizenship. In contrast, developed states have greater resources and stronger institutions to implement rigorous authentication procedures. Developing countries like India, though democratic, cannot restrict electoral participation—all residents, citizens and illegal immigrants alike—are able to exercise the franchise. Is this a violation of democratic integrity?

Democratic integrity is dependent on the "authenticity, secrecy, security, and reliability" of the electoral process.[46] Illegal immigrant voting diminishes democratic integrity in India. The vote should be authentic in the sense that it reflects the "preference" of the voter, but in our case the entire vote is based on false identifications (the individuals are not who they say they are), and the voters' list no longer reflects the sanctity of juridical Indian citizenship. In addition, the vote cast should be secret, so that no one can coerce or pressure the voter. However, since illegal immigrants often get onto electoral rolls through the assistance of corrupt political officials or administrators, they vote as a bloc in a particular way (for parties that protect illegal immigrants). Because they are constantly under pressure, their vote is not a secret. Finally, the electoral roll should be secure, protecting the integrity of the democratic process by ensuring that only eligible voters are able to exercise suffrage. As illegal immigrants manage to bypass electoral regulations, enter electoral rolls, and vote as native citizens, some would argue that elections are no longer secure (despite voter IDs, photo electoral rolls, and the like). After all, the electoral participation of illegal immigrant voters violates the territorial and political sovereignty of the state and breaches the wall around citizenship. It thus undermines the security of the electoral process, and by extension the integrity of Indian democracy.

The illegal immigrant voter also violates another principle of democratic politics—the right of citizens to recognize one another as fellow citizens and to set policies regulating how others can be so recognized. This is a basic contractarian trait of liberal democracy: the right that members of a political community have to constitute themselves *as* a political community and decide on the conditions of membership and immigration. It is not simply an artifact of social contract theory; it allows citizens to determine the character of their shared culture, religion, and ethnic and linguistic identity, allowing them to establish legal and political systems appropriate to their common customs, values, and expectations. In short, these forms of mutual recognition and self-determination lie at the heart of democratic sovereignty. When illegal immigrants incorporate themselves into the political order as citizens, they short-circuit such forms of collective self-determination and adopt a status that citizens can only confer on one another by recognizing each other as fellow citizens.

A contrarian view would see Indian citizenship and the current electoral process as inclusionary, in the sense that they privilege accessibility to the democratic process over stringent verification schemes. To the extent that illegal immigrants are de facto (if not de jure) recognized by fellow citizens (legal as well as illegal) as participants in the process, their citizenship practices necessarily entail the kind of mutual recognition that collective will formation requires. If such illegal processes are an organic form of community building, state control of such practices appear arbitrary and theoretically problematic. The election process is "free and fair" in India precisely because accessibility to democratic participation is high. All long-term residents, including illegal immigrants, participate in the democratic process and have equal access to it. In addition, because illegal immigrants are long-term residents of the local community, they can be viewed as "stakeholders"[47] in electoral politics. Illegal immigrants have a genuine investment in who gets elected to represent them. They need certain political parties in power to protect them. As they are directly impacted by development projects in the community, they have a direct interest in the running of community affairs. Having a stake in the future vitality of the polity, whether through direct or through indirect residence, has been recognized as crucial to citizenship. Hence, a trend toward external political participation and the granting of voting rights to expatriate candidates who have naturalized abroad.[48] When political boundaries radiate outward and overlap in an inclusionary fashion with multiple stakeholders in multiple residences (as in the European Union), democratic participation expands exponentially. Illegal immigrants too can be included in such an expansion of the democratic process.

Concomitantly, the emergence of cosmopolitan norms also challenges the contradictions within citizenship. Cosmopolitan norms, those which prioritize universal human rights, are increasingly confronting the desire of states to maintain territorial and popular sovereignty.[49] The adoption of international human rights standards[50] privileges the exercise of rights embedded in the "personhood" of each individual—these are natural rights that inhere in every human being. Opposing the nation-state's desire to privilege national membership, rights reach across territorial boundaries to protect an individual's need for survival, security, and representation. While many may view universal human rights as above the state, in reality they are practiced within the state. Cosmopolitan regimes such as nongovernmental organizations, independently funded health clinics and social workers, and international human rights treaties in effect grant human rights (education, health care, housing, and so forth) to everyone at the local level. Since all rights, including national rights, are exercised within the local community, thus confirming membership, legal authorizations may sound hollow. If citizenship is a practice of citizenship rights, as is the case in developing countries, illegal immigrants will continue to exercise them as a matter of individual personhood while concomitantly integrating as citizens. In such a situation, status fails to echo the authority of a state over membership.

The subject of citizenship is no longer preset by the state. Those residing beyond the state's reach can no longer be seen as ubiquitous "outsiders." Citizens, noncitizens eligible for naturalization, and illegal immigrants are all filtering into the state—each an agent with stakes in the political community. Illegal immigrant voting in India exposes the growing subjects of citizenship, altering the relationship between status and rights, and transforming democratic practice.

In sum, the practice of Indian democracy poses fundamental challenges to our thinking about citizenship and democracy in a globalizing age. From one perspective it can be seen as a dysfunctional, poorly worked-out version of liberal democracy, with its porous borders, documentary chaos, and easy access to full citizenship status. From another perspective, however, this regime could represent something like the cosmopolitan future called for by Benhabib and others. Rather than a poorly functioning Westphalian state, we could see India as a new articulation of democracy and citizenship—not one in which contractarian dreams of exclusive, carefully controlled sovereignty are realized, but one in which self-government takes new and creative forms. Here the new subject of citizenship—the illegal immigrant—is not an anomaly so much as an expression of the ways that stakeholders can be incorporated into political regimes precisely because they have a stake in what goes on there. Borders, nationality, and thorough control give way to a more porous, postnational form of democratic enfranchisement. While this new subject of citizenship is certainly unsettling to many, it arguably represents elements of a future that seems increasingly present among us.

Chapter 12

"We the People" in an Age of Migration: Multiculturalism and Immigrants' Political Integration in Comparative Perspective

Irene Bloemraad

The past decade has seen the retreat, if not demise, of multiculturalism in numerous Western liberal democracies.[1] Among its flaws, critics especially attack multiculturalism's apparent failure to integrate immigrants into host societies.[2] Some worry about socioeconomic exclusions. Multiculturalism is believed to encourage immigrants' self-segregation and, in doing so, impedes their integration into mainstream social and economic structures. Others complain about civic and political integration. Immigrants' cultures, values, and insular behaviors are perceived as antithetical to the liberal democratic creed that unites citizens in Western countries; foreign cultures should not be encouraged with multicultural recognition. Across the Western world, observers of immigration politics note a shift to government and media discourses favoring cultural and civic assimilation.[3]

The backlash against multiculturalism and the new emphasis on national cohesion can be seen in many immigrant-receiving countries. Politicians in the Netherlands, a country that previously embraced the rhetoric of multiculturalism, no longer use this language. Legislators passed the 2003 Law on Dutch Citizenship, which requires immigrants to demonstrate oral and written knowledge of the Dutch language as well as Dutch politics and society. Some Dutch politicians have even suggested an outright ban on wearing the full-length *burka* in public, a debate echoed in France's 2004 legislation forbidding Muslim headscarves (or any "ostentatious" religious symbol) in public schools. The United Kingdom's Nationality, Immigration, and Asylum Act of 2002 introduced a citizenship ceremony to mark the importance of and foster pride in British citizenship. In Canada, the province of Quebec established a special "Consultation Commission on Accommodation Practices Related to Cultural Differences," which heard repeated claims that immigrants in Quebec remain apart from the French-speaking majority and demand too many cultural and religious accommodations. Even in the United States, where the dominant axes of the immigration debate revolve around security concerns, undocumented migration, and economics, sociocultural worries capture public and scholarly attention, as seen in the controversy over Samuel Huntington's fear that Hispanic migration will dilute the "core values" of the United States and claims that multiculturalism fosters the "disuniting" of America.[4] Such complaints are echoed across the Western world.

These debates illuminate a hole in social scientists' theories of (variously) immigrant assimilation, integration, and incorporation. Sociologists have long focused on socioeconomic integration (e.g., education, income, employment), residential dispersion, acculturation (including self-identities), language shift, and intermarriage to measure assimilation. They have been remarkably silent on political or civic integration.[5] Political scientists have also directed limited attention to immigrant civic and political engagement.[6] Instead, particularly in the United States, they have grouped immigrant and native-born participation under the rubric of minority politics, and they have directed virtually no attention to the intersection of political and socioeconomic integration.

In this chapter, I consider how prominent social science models of assimilation make sense of political and civic integration, or fail to do so. I extrapolate from existing scholarship to identify two models of political integration: an individual-driven political assimilation model, and a group-based political incorporation model. I contend that the group-based approach offers greater chances for political integration, and I argue that multiculturalism facilitates this precisely because it supports "groupedness." Thus, contrary to conventional wisdom, multicultural policies beget democratic inclusion. In making this argument, I provide a brief overview of the political theory of multiculturalism as well as the concerns of its critics. I emphasize that assertions of multiculturalism's socioeconomic failures misread its goals: it is, above all, a theory of political inclusion and citizenship. As such, there is good evidence for its success, and I offer some empirical evidence, drawn from a variety of countries, to support this claim. I conclude by speculating about the relationship between multiculturalism and economic inequality.

Sociological Models of Immigrant Assimilation and the Absence of Politics

Most theories of immigrants' social, cultural, and economic integration stem from the American experience with immigration during the twentieth century. From the early 1900s into the 1960s, classic models of assimilation viewed immigrant adaptation as a linear process, with integration occurring through a progression of steps.[7] Scholars debated whether the process was one of Anglo-conformity or amalgamation in a melting pot, and they disagreed over whether some types of assimilation, such as acculturation, inevitably led to others.[8] They generally agreed, however, that with time and generational succession, immigrants would give up their distinctive languages, norms, identities, and practices to become part of an American mainstream.

Beginning in the 1960s and continuing to the present, models of resurgent or reactive ethnicity and segmented assimilation have challenged the idea of a single sequential assimilatory path.[9] Segmented assimilation, in particular, claims that integration experiences are stratified by class and race. Depending upon race, human capital, and residential location, the second generation will follow one of three trajectories: straight-line assimilation into the white middle class; downward assimilation into an urban minority underclass; or upward socioeconomic assimilation through the retention of ethnic culture and the mobilization of ethnic social capital.[10] The segmented assimilation approach breaks sharply with prior theorizing by presenting multiple trajectories for the descendents of late twentieth and early twenty-first century migrants, and in claiming that the retention of ethnic culture and ethnic solidarity helps integration, rather than hinders it. Segmented assimilation also places strong emphasis on the structural constraints imposed by racial hierarchies and economic restructuring, which limit immigrants' ability to achieve socioeconomic success.

More recently, Richard Alba and Victor Nee have offered a "new" assimilation model, one that tries to avoid the ethnocentrism and determinism of old assimilation models, while retaining the key notion that, over generations, immigrants' children and grandchildren integrate into a cultural, social, and economic American mainstream.[11] According to them, assimilation occurs when individual immigrants and families make purposive decisions to get ahead. Because opportunities are greater within mainstream institutions, most immigrants will rationally choose to assimilate by learning English and being part of the dominant American socioeconomic structure. This process is facilitated by civil rights legislation and the contemporary acceptance of diversity, which make discrimination illegal or illegitimate.

Strikingly, these predominant sociological models treat immigrants' civic and political integration as a secondary concern. There is little consideration of politics, either as a measure of integration or as a solution to problems. Cultural assimilation, social integration, and economic mobility receive primary attention.

Through the lens of segmented assimilation, global and local economic restructuring, rather than political decisions, limit immigrants' economic mobility. The origins of racial hierarchy and discrimination are only loosely linked to politics, since racism is portrayed as a largely permanent part of American society. Alejandro Portes and Min Zhou[12] suggest that immigrants' residential concentration within cities brings their children into contact with poor, native-born minorities, with negative consequences, but they are silent on the politics of public services and schooling in the urban core, even though some research supporting segmented assimilation documents the detrimental impact of poor inner-city schools.[13] While scholars advancing a segmented assimilation framework suggest that government policy provides a more receptive integration context to political refugees than other immigrants,[14] the politics of entry are less prominent in later accounts of Vietnamese immigrants' educational success.[15] More generally, it is unclear how or whether politics affects segmented assimilation because "the typology is largely based on the different *class* resources that immigrants bring with them, while . . . ethnicity regularly trumps class as a motive for collective mobilization."[16] From the perspective of segmented assimilation, ethnic community, solidarity, and culture facilitate economic mobility because they insulate immigrant children from the negative influence of native-born minority peers, not because they act as a resource to affect political change.[17]

Contemporary "new assimilation" models provide little additional guidance. Alba and Nee's formulation rests on a microeconomic view of new institutionalism; they present no empirical data on political or civic integration.[18] State action is important in their model, but the dynamics of politics are largely left outside it. Their (guardedly) optimistic view that assimilation will occur, despite racial and economic hierarchies, hinges on the presence of civil rights laws that provide immigrants with a reasonable chance of fair treatment within the mainstream. In discussing the historical record, Alba and Nee point to the importance of social policies such as the G.I. Bill and federal mortgage efforts that helped the children of European immigrants achieve socioeconomic mobility. They explicitly say, however, that understanding the evolution of those laws and policies is outside the scope of their project, as is a consideration of the organizational infrastructure located between individual actions and macro-level institutions. These very organizations—unions, religious institutions, political clubs, and the like—are, I argue, central to understanding immigrants' political integration.

Theorizing Immigrants' Political Integration: Assimilation or Incorporation

We can identify two models of immigrants' political integration embedded within the existing scholarship on immigrant adaptation in sociology and political science. These models differ based on whether scholars perceive American society as basically open to integrating diverse immigrants (by taste or legal necessity) or whether racism, economic inequality, or a reluctance to share power keeps newcomers outside the mainstream.

One model, which I call *political assimilation*, delineates political integration as a micro-level process by which individual immigrants (or their descendents) assimilate into an established political and civic system such that those of immigrant origins become indistinguishable from native-born Americans in their political attitudes, partisanship, and behaviors. A classical example is Robert Dahl's 1961[19] study of pluralist politics in New Haven, Connecticut. Dahl suggests that democratic decision making in New Haven was issue-based and dependent on a changing coalition of actors, some of whom responded to or represented immigrant concerns. Importantly, Dahl argues that many "immigrant issues" stem from immigrants' working-class backgrounds rather than their cultural or ethnic differences. He contends that as immigrants and their descendents achieve upward mobility and social assimilation, ethnic groups pass through three stages of political assimilation that eventually render persons of immigrant descent indistinguishable from others in their civic and political activities.[20] In this view, political assimilation either follows or occurs simultaneously with other forms of assimilation.

A second model, which I call *political incorporation*, presumes that immigrants' integration into political systems occurs as a process of conflict and contestation because those in power are reluctant to share decision making with newcomers. Faced with political closure, immigrant communities are theorized as potential or actual political groups that work to have collective influence on politics, akin to advocacy or interest groups. Political incorporation is group-based because discrimination and blocked mobility stem from group membership, motivating collective responses. Collective grievances also spur resurgent or reactive ethnicity, which becomes a collective identity resource to generate solidarity and mobilize resources. In some versions of the political incorporation model, a degree of socioeconomic mobility facilitates group-based political incorporation: with economic mobility, group members have more resources to sustain ethnic organizations, greater confidence in the group's ability to organize, and concrete grievances as they face prejudice despite socioeconomic gains. Across such accounts, ethnicity and immigrant origins help define common interests, generate collective identity and solidarity, aid with mobilization, and provide material resources for collective action to redress inequalities and discrimination through the political system.[21]

Individual-level political assimilation and group-based political incorporation are two different paths to political integration: in both models immigrants and their children become part of the political system. A third situation, in which immigrants are absent from domestic politics, by choice or through exclusion, indicates a lack of political integration. This might happen when groups faced with prejudice or blocked mobility do not have the ability or resources to engage in group-based politics, or when migrants see themselves as temporary sojourners and keep their attention and energies focused on the homeland.

With the benefit of hindsight, we can ask whether the political integration of European immigrants and their children was characterized by individual-level assimilation or group-based incorporation. At first blush, the second path seems to have led to greater political success than the former, though we need more empirical research on this question. Indeed, it is possible, in line with the presumption of reactive ethnicity, that group-based politics facilitated socioeconomic integration. Space constraints prevent an extended discussion why this might be so, but I will offer one example.

Milton Gordon's 1964[22] refinement of linear assimilation is considered a canonical account within the sociology of immigration. According to Gordon, assimilation consists of seven components, with cultural assimilation, or acculturation, as the first step.[23] Gordon contends that while most groups acculturate quickly, the other components of assimilation do not automatically follow. The lynchpin is structural assimilation, "large-scale entrance into cliques, clubs, and institutions of the society."[24] Once immigrants enter into personal relations with those in the "core society," intermarriage will occur, a sense of common peoplehood will develop, prejudice and discrimination will die away, and political assimilation will follow.[25]

Yet Gordon's own empirical analysis contradicts his theoretical account. In comparing four different ethnoracial groups, Gordon notes—in keeping with his argument—that three of the four exhibit substantial acculturation, but none demonstrates assimilation across the other elements.[26] Gordon remains curiously silent, however, about the fact that *all four* of his groups show partial, substantial, or even complete political integration, the only dimension on which all groups can be considered significantly assimilated. Gordon's own data consequently imply that political integration is *not* dependent on cultural, structural, or social assimilation into the "core group" of the receiving society. Instead, "structural" difference (akin to contemporary discussions of bonding social capital and civic associationalism) might promote political integration through group-based incorporation.

Thus, while groupedness is considered by traditional linear assimilation models as a marker of failed social assimilation, it might well be a prerequisite for political incorporation. In the case of contemporary integration models, both segmented assimilation and new assimilation approaches make passing reference to European immigrants' use of ethnic politics, implying that immigrant groups might have political and economic interests in "groupedness." The underlying impression, never fully theorized, is that group-based political incorporation can precede or complement individual socioeconomic advancement. Indeed, political incorporation might be central to socioeconomic integration if immigrants and their children can change institutional barriers through political voice.

The Multicultural Debates and Groupedness

Groupedness and the importance of cultural community are central to multicultural theory, but not because of any presumed link with socioeconomic outcomes. The normative end behind arguments for multiculturalism lies in broad notions of justice and fairness. Since democracy is based on government by the majority, minorities face inherent disadvantages in the public sphere. The standard liberal response is to erect a system of rights, such as freedom of speech and religion, but multicultural theorists claim that cultural inequality remains pervasive. Multiculturalism consequently requires immigrant-receiving countries to recognize cultural diversity and make accommodations for the needs of cultural minorities.[27] Further, since humans are inherently social beings—not atomized individuals as assumed under many liberal accounts—their identities, desires, and political preferences are closely linked to the communities within which they are born and live.[28] Group recognition is consequently not just empty symbolism but provides dignity and legitimacy, presumably helping immigrant communities become part of civic and political life. Group accommodations promote equality by preventing domination by the majority and helping to dismantle barriers to full participation. According to multicultural theorists, facilitating the survival and vitality of cultural communities is a matter of fairness, justice, and equality.

Critiques of Multiculturalism: Immigrant Integration Failures

As noted at the beginning of this chapter, the multicultural view is under attack in many Western immigrant-receiving countries. Such attacks take at least three forms. The first rests on a fear of political fragmentation: if we all celebrate the distinctions that make us different from each other, we weaken the bonds that hold a country together. Thus Samuel Huntington calls for a return to the roots of the American creed that are based on "the English language; Christianity; religious commitment; English conceptions of the rule of law . . . and dissenting Protestant values of individualism, the work ethic and the belief that humans have the ability and duty to try to create a heaven on earth."[29] Without a clear message that tells immigrants about a country's core values, immigrants supposedly live in their own communities and enclaves, emboldened by multiculturalism to live a life apart. The response is a call for strong assimilatory citizenship.

A second concern also highlights the putative loss of shared community, not so much for itself, but because it could undermine public support for redistribution. According to this argument, specific collective endeavors such as the establishment of the welfare state rely on sentiments of shared fate with fellow citizens. When multiculturalism valorizes particularistic memberships, support for universal social policies can wither. Given economic inequalities—which seem to be growing in countries like the United States—some suggest that multiculturalism creates false boundaries between similarly situated socioeconomic groups, diverting political energies away from economic redistribution.[30]

A final critique suggests that multiculturalism creates or reifies invidious distinctions that can relegate some to "second class" citizenship despite their individual desires.[31] Multiculturalism's emphasis on identity and recognition increases the salience of immigrant background and ethnicity, thereby reifying the very categories that served as the basis for unequal rights in the past, and it forces hyphens or labels on people who might not want them. The genius of individual liberalism, in this formulation, is its refusal to consider particularities and instead to treat people as equals irrespective of background or ethnicity.

Immigrants' Political and Civic Integration: The Importance of Groups

The question of whether multiculturalism reifies differences in a negative way is one of the most difficult questions in immigrant integration. Members of the majority group criticize ethnic differentiation as a sign of immigrants' rejection of mainstream society, while immigrants and their children charge that ethnic labels provide those in the majority with a convenient way to marginalize, stigmatize, and exclude them. Any analysis of reification requires a nuanced accounting of the costs and benefits of publicly acknowledging ethnic, racial, religious, and cultural differences. In particular, it requires a consideration of the alternatives. If difference is not recognized and acknowledged, how do we manage immigrant-generated diversity? I suggest that despite reification problems, the advantages of facilitating group-based action among immigrants outweigh the costs.

Many of those against multicultural recognition advocate a universal, republican citizenship à la française. Citizens have equality before the state and enjoy direct relations to government as individuals rather than members of any particular group. Indeed, to facilitate a neutral and liberal public space, government must bypass intermediate collectives based on religion, ethnicity, or culture, or relegate them to the private sphere.[32] Proponents of this position are found on the political left and right, in Europe and in North America.

Making ethnicity an illegitimate basis for identification and political action carries significant dangers, however, especially when it is a basis for unequal treatment. Blindness to ethnic categories runs the risk of making inequality invisible and leaving minorities out of the political process altogether. State-sanctioned categories of ethnicity (or race, or religion, or national origin) clearly reinforce the salience of those categories for the individuals who check off the boxes and who analyze the statistics, but absent such information, it is impossible to know whether discrimination or institutional barriers generate inequality between groups on the basis of ascriptive characteristics.[33]

Ignoring ethnicity also likely hurts immigrants' political integration, increasing rather than decreasing civic and political divides between the mainstream and immigrant groups. Although the theory of liberal democracy focuses on the individual—as a voter and as a possessor of rights—politics demands action by groups of like-minded people. In the French republican model, the individual citizen is the primary political actor. In the reality of French politics, groups of people—brought together in political parties, unions, or some other collective—work together to influence outcomes.

The foundations of groupedness are not equally compelling. While immigrants might have various affiliations—to other homebuyers, to other parents, to other soccer enthusiasts—ties based on ethnicity are surely among the strongest and most deeply felt. Some immigrants might chose not to privilege such ties, but for many people shared origins, similar migration experiences, common language, similar cultural habits, dress, and food all create a sense of common identity and even interests, despite intraethnic differences based on accent, class, region, or even religion. Even immigrants who come with strong desires to assimilate and blend into their new home face numerous obstacles to learning about the new society and negotiating their participation within it. Language is an especially strong barrier, but so too is the fact that immigrants' prior civic and political socialization occurred in a different society. Field research shows that immigrants' political integration is grounded in informal ethnic networks, local immigrant community organizations, and the mobilization of coethnic leaders.[34] To ignore the ethnic community blinds us to a key mechanism facilitating immigrants' inclusion in the political system.

Of course, other vehicles for collective voice exist. Civic associations, unions, and political parties can integrate, and have integrated, immigrants into the civic and political life of the receiving country, but these organized collectives entail some practical problems. Civic associations, identified as a key vehicle for civic engagement and political mobilization in the United States, appear to make limited overtures to immigrant residents, and local organizing appears stratified such that immigrant groups command relatively little visibility or weight among government decision makers.[35] Outside northern Europe, union membership is in relatively sharp decline;[36] only a small minority of immigrants might be mobilized through labor organizing. Political parties appear to engage in limited outreach to immigrants in the United States[37] and in Europe.[38] On a practical level, then, ethnicity or national origin is a particularly effective way to organize for group ends. Critics who worry that multiculturalism ghettoizes immigrants overlook the fact that the alternative to coethnic communities and mobilization might be no participation at all.[39]

Evaluating Multiculturalism as a Path to Political Integration

The discussion thus far has been largely theoretical. As Noah Pinkus notes, abstract analysis provides conceptual and normative clarity, but it is often detached from practical realities.[40] Empirically, does multiculturalism hinder the integration of diverse peoples into a common citizenry?

Multiculturalism and Immigrants' Political Integration: Some Comparative Evidence

I evaluate this question by comparing immigrants' political integration in countries with different degrees of multiculturalism. To do so, I build on Banting, Johnston, Kymlicka, and Soroka's[41] categorization of countries as strong, moderate, or weak multicultural states, which is based on an enumeration of eight types of multiculturalism policy: formal affirmation of multiculturalism; multicultural school curricula; insertion of ethnic representation/sensitivity in public media or licensing; exemption codes for ethno-religious minorities (of dress, Sunday store closing, and so on); dual citizenship; state funding for minority cultural activities; funding of bilingual or mother tongue language instruction; and affirmative action for disadvantaged immigrant groups.[42] By these measures, Canada and Australia rank as the only two "strong" multicultural states, the United States ranks as a "moderate" multicultural state along with countries such as the Netherlands, Sweden, and the United Kingdom, and France sits among "weak" multicultural states, alongside Germany, Japan, Norway, and a number of others.[43]

To evaluate political integration, I use two indices: the proportion of the foreign-born population that have become citizens of their country of residence, and the proportion of foreign-born legislators in national office. These two measures arguably reflect two ends on a spectrum of formal political integration. At the one end, citizenship is seen as a mark of full political and legal status in many countries, it is available to most immigrants, and it is usually a requirement for electoral participation, though some countries allow local or even regional voting rights.[44] At the other end of the spectrum, running for—and winning—national office not only measures high-level, elite engagement in a country's political system but also symbolizes a degree of integration and acceptance of the immigrant community by the majority population.[45]

Considering citizenship, the available evidence suggests that strong multiculturalism, as measured by government policies, is correlated with *higher* levels of citizenship acquisition, not detachment and disengagement from the host state. As seen in Table 12.1, the two countries categorized as "strong" multicultural states, Canada and Australia, report the highest naturalization levels of any in the table, 72.6 percent and 68.4 percent, respectively. We find more variability among the "moderate" and "weak" multicultural states, with some of the moderate states, the Netherlands and Sweden, closer to the citizenship levels of Canada and Australia, while others are more similar to countries with weaker multiculturalism. Nevertheless, across the three levels of multiculturalism, the strong multicultural states average a citizenship level of 70.5 percent, the moderate multicultural ones average 52.4 percent, and the weak multicultural ones report, on average, that only 45.4 percent of the foreign-born have acquired citizenship.[46]

The data are suggestive: immigrants in multicultural states are not so "apart" from mainstream society that they do not bother to take up citizenship in their country of residence. The figures cannot tell us whether multi-

Table 12.1 Multiculturalism and Immigrant Political Integration, Foreign-Born Residents

Country	Number of foreign-born	% Foreign-born in population[a]	% Foreign-born with citizenship	Representation index (national legislature)[b]
Strong multiculturalism				
Australia	4,003,000	23.0	68.4	.45
Canada	5,717,000	19.0	72.6	.78
Moderate multiculturalism				
Belgium	1,098,000	9.3	40.8	
Netherlands	1,615,000	10.1	65.0	.72
Sweden	1,078,000	12.0	62.5	
United Kingdom	4,897,000	8.3	47.2	.60
United States	34,635,000	11.1	46.4	.17
Weak multiculturalism				
Austria	1,002,000	12.5	40.7	
Denmark	361,000	6.8	40.3	
France	5,868,000	7.4	53.1	.59 (<.10)
Ireland	396,000	10.4	45.2	
Norway	334,000	6.7	47.6	

[a] Where possible, these figures exclude natural citizens born abroad (e.g., children of diplomats or military personnel).

[b] The index measures the proportion of foreign-born elected representatives in the popularly elected national legislature divided by the proportion of foreign-born residents in the general population. An index of "1" indicates similar proportions in the legislature and population. A value less than 1 suggests foreign-born underrepresentation. Data for Canadian House of Commons, Dutch Second Chamber and U.S. House of Representatives is from 2000–2002; data for the Australia House of Representatives, U.K. House of Commons, and French National Assembly are from 2006.

Sources: Multiculturalism categorization from Keith Banting, Richard Johnston, Will Kymlicka, and Stuart Soroka, "Do Multiculturalism Policies Erode the Welfare State? An Empirical Analysis," in *Multiculturalism and the Welfare State: Recognition and Redistribution in Contemporary Democracies*, ed. Keith Banting and Will Kymlicka (Oxford: Oxford University Press, 2006), 49–90; foreign-born and citizenship data from Organisation for Economic Co-Operation and Development, *Trends in International Migration: Annual Report, 2004 Edition* (Paris: OECD Publications, 2005), 142–43, 284, and Migration Policy Institute Data Hub; elected representation data for Canada/United States from Irene Bloemraad, *Becoming a Citizen: Incorporating Immigrants and Refugees in the United States and Canada* (Berkeley: University of California Press, 2006), 60–61, for the Netherlands from Han Entzinger, "The Rise and Fall of Multiculturalism: The Case of the Netherlands," in *Toward Assimilation and Citizenship: Immigrants in Liberal Nation-States*, ed. Christian Joppke and Ewa Morawska (New York: Palgrave Macmillan, 2003), 66, for Australia, the United Kingdom, and France from Michael Adams, *Unlikely Utopia* (Toronto: Viking Canada, 2007), 75.

culturalism policies produce higher levels of citizenship acquisition or whether other factors drive both policy adoption and immigrants' naturalization, but they imply that multiculturalism policies encourage common bonds of community rather than undermine them.

The picture for elite political representation is more mixed. The last column of Table 12.1 presents an "index of representation," calculated by dividing the percentage of foreign-born legislators in the national popularly-elected legislature by the proportion of foreign-born people in the total population. This is far from a perfect measure: some might prefer that the denominator be the percentage of foreign-born individuals among the electorate, while others might want to include the adult native-born children of immigrants in the calculation. Perhaps surprisingly, assembling cross-national representation data creates formidable challenges, making a foreign-born index one of the few straightforward comparative indicators. For this reason, I use it to provide a rough sense of elite political integration.[47]

With data from only six countries, no clear pattern emerges. Canada, with an index of representation at .78, has the highest degree of foreign-born representation of the six, and it is also one of the most multicultural. In 2002, forty-five foreign-born members of Parliament sat in a 301-person House.[48] While the slight majority of these MPs hailed from Europe or the United States, three were born in India, two in China, two in the Middle East (Lebanon and Syria), five in the Caribbean or Latin America, four in Africa, and one in the Philippines.[49] Overall, the proportion of foreign-born MPs does not reach parity with the percentage in the general population— and people from East Asia are especially underrepresented—but the Canadian House exhibits a relatively high degree of immigrant diversity. Significantly, each of the major federal parties, including the separatist Bloc Québécois, has at least one foreign-born member.

In contrast, representation in Australia's legislature is only about half of what we would expect given the percentage of immigrants in the general population. In 2006, foreign-born politicians should have occupied thirty-three seats in Canberra, but only fifteen members were born outside Australia, eleven of whom hailed from Europe.[50] The resulting index of representation, at .45, is substantially less than in the Netherlands, at .72, or in the United Kingdom, at .60. Yet Australia is arguably more multicultural in policy than the latter two countries.

Many factors complicate a simple analysis of foreign-born legislators.

Electoral systems, irrespective of multiculturalism policy, probably matter. Proportional representation electoral systems—as used in the Netherlands—are usually considered beneficial to minority representation, provided that the parties make a commitment to put minorities on party lists. The Dutch PR system may consequently facilitate high level foreign-born representation, though it bears noting that the first-past-the-post system, traditionally thought to be a barrier to geographically dispersed minority representation, does not appear an insurmountable obstacle in Canada or the United Kingdom. There, as in the PR system, the key likely lies in parties' active recruitment and nomination of immigrant candidates, which might be affected by ideological multiculturalism.[51]

Indices of representation are also very sensitive to who, exactly, is counted as foreign-born. In the reported data, a nationally elected politician counts as foreign-born if his or her birthplace lies outside the country of residence. This rough cut is necessary because who's who guides to legislators do not include information about representatives' citizenship status at birth. The foreign-born count thus includes the foreign-born children of citizens living abroad (as in the case of former Canadian prime minister John Turner, born in the United Kingdom), who acquire their country's citizenship at birth from their parents, and it includes those born in the former colonies to parents from the metropole (as in the case of 2007 French presidential candidate Ségolène Royale, born in Senegal).

The inclusion of those born in former colonies skews, in particular, the data for France. Whereas thirty-six members of the 2006 National Assembly were not born in continental France or the DOM-TOM (French overseas territories),[52] many appear to be the children of metropole-born bureaucrats and administrators who were living in former French colonies in Africa. Indeed, in 2007, not a single National Assembly representative was of Maghrébin origin, although Muslim and Berber North Africans make up about 5 percent of the national population,[53] and a significantly higher percentage in some cities and suburbs. If we broaden the count to "visible minority" (nonwhite) representatives, we find only three such politicians among the 555 in the National Assembly: Henri Jibrayel, born in France of Lebanese background, George Pau-Langevin, born in Guadeloupe, and Elie Aboud, born in Lebanon.[54] The representation index for visible minorities in France is consequently less than .10, a paltry figure in line with the hypothesis that universal republican citizenship does not facilitate, but rather hinders, political integration.

It is nonetheless worth noting that even with this adjustment, the index of representation in France, a country renowned for its official color-blind universalism, is not far off the .17 index of foreign-born representation in the United States, a country of greater multiculturalism. Indeed, at .17, the American index of representation is the lowest of the six countries considered, a meager eight foreign-born representatives out of 435 seats. However, the United States probably has a very high proportion of unauthorized migrants among its total foreign-born population; these people cannot become citizens and cannot vote for fellow immigrants. If we recalculate the U.S. representation index using the proportion of foreign-born citizens as the denominator, the representation index increases to .41, still a relatively low level of integration into the highest offices of the United States.[55]

The upshot of the representation data is ambiguous. Considering visible minorities, rather than the foreign-born, in France, and adjusting the American figure to take into account the significant undocumented population, the representation pattern among strong, moderate, and weak multicultural countries looks a bit more like the citizenship pattern, but the correlation is much weaker. The conservative conclusion is that there is no clear pattern linking multiculturalism policies to immigrants' success accessing the highest political offices of their adopted countries.

That said, we also find no evidence that countries with more robust multicultural policies are *less* likely to have immigrants devote their time and energies to domestic politics. One criticism of multiculturalism charges that recognition and celebration of differences make immigrants less committed to their adopted country and more likely to orient political activities to their country of origin. The evidence in Table 12.1 does not support such fears. This conclusion finds an echo in the analysis of Koopmans and colleagues,[56] who demonstrate that claims making around homeland concerns was much more prevalent in Germany and Switzerland, countries with historically ethnic rather than civic orientations to national belonging, while minorities in more multicultural countries such as the Netherlands and the United Kingdom engaged primarily in domestic claims making.

The Mechanisms of Immigrant Political Integration

A truism in statistics is that correlation does not demonstrate causation. We must thus ask, What *mechanisms* would link multicultural policies to immigrants' political integration? To explicate possible mechanisms, I draw on my comparative research on the United States and Canada.[57]

Comparing the two countries, we find a significant gap in immigrants' political integration over the past thirty years. In 1970, 64 percent of the foreign born in the United States held a U.S. passport, while in Canada the figure was 60 percent.[58] By 2001, only 40 percent of the foreign born in the United States were citizens, but in Canada it was 72 percent.[59] Taking into account the much larger unauthorized and temporary immigrant population in the United States—a group legally barred from citizenship—the gap attenuates, to 49 percent naturalized in the United States compared with 75 percent in Canada, but the difference remains striking and historically unprecedented.[60] It also persists after controlling for immigrants' place of birth and length of residence.[61] Most surprisingly, it runs counter to a simple cost-benefit calculation of the relative advantages of citizenship: the benefits of citizenship, especially for family reunification and access to certain social programs, are more substantial in the United States than in Canada. In part due to higher levels of citizenship in Canada, but also reflecting immigrants' greater penetration into Canadian politics, we find substantial differences in the number and proportion of foreign-born legislators, as reported above. Clearly, first-generation immigrants have made much further inroads into politics in Canada than in the United States.

The reasons for these differences are complex, but Canada's more extensive and more developed policies of multiculturalism and immigrant settlement play a critical role. Immigrants' political integration can be conceived of as a nested process of structured mobilization. Many immigrants, especially those with few individual resources, use informal networks and institutions within the immigrant community to learn about, access, and participate in civic and political life. These networks and community institutions are in turn influenced by government policies directed to immigrants and minorities. Governments provide material resources through grant or contract funding, programmatic access to bureaucrats and policy makers, and technical support in leadership training, acquiring nonprofit status for community organizations, and so forth. These policies also provide symbolic resources and influence immigrants' understanding of their place and legitimacy in the civic and political sphere. With official recognition through multiculturalism, ordinary immigrants and ethnic leaders feel more empowered to participate and make claims within the system.

As a nested process, political integration relies heavily on the activities and vitality of community-based organizations. The budgets of such community organizations in an immigrant city like Toronto show that many stay afloat on small grants from various levels of government, allowing such organizations not only to provide a range of services but also to act as vehicles for political learning and engagement.[62] We can consequently trace a direct line from governmental policy, to immigrant communities, to individual behaviors such as citizenship acquisition.

In Canada, funding for such groups grew rapidly with the development of multiculturalism and settlement policies. In the 1966–67 fiscal year, the Citizenship Branch of the Department of the Secretary of State gave $88,150 to twelve groups concerned with immigrant settlement and participatory citizenship, but by 1974–75, the branch gave $2.65 million in grants to 648 groups, an amount that grew to more than $20 million in 1987–88 and almost $60 million in 1996–97.[63] In the mid-1990s moneys for immigrant settlement totaled about $166 million, an amount that remained relatively steady for about a decade.[64] In 2004, the Canadian federal government spent about $1,500 per new immigrant.[65] And federal government funding is often supplemented by provincial and municipal programs.

Nonprofit organizations and civic associations play a similar political integration role in the United States.[66] However, with much less public support, especially directed to immigrant issues such as naturalization and language training, migrant communities in the United States face more barriers in building strong organizational infrastructures.

The case of refugee resettlement in the United States provides additional support for the perspective that active state intervention can facilitate civic and political integration. Refugees, especially those "allied aliens" fleeing communist regimes, face a more receptive government environment than other migrants.[67] The U.S. government provides social benefits to individuals and families, as well as community grants to mutual assistance associations. Over the past twenty years, the annual budget of the federal Office of Refugee Resettlement has fluctuated between about $350 million and $450 million, while numbers of official refugees run between 65,000 and 80,000. This represents, at a minimum, an investment of at least $4,375 for each refugee.

Such public outlays produce material and interpretative effects. For example, government funding has had a clear effect on the ability of Vietnamese communities to build a robust organizational infrastructure.[68] Despite fears of welfare stigma, government-funded health care benefits appear to

make medical professionals and administrators treat Cubans as more deserving and more able to make claims than Mexicans, regardless of legal
status.[69] Although refugees have clear political reasons to naturalize and
participate in U.S. politics, the public support given to them probably plays
an important role in explaining Cuban Americans' substantial political incorporation, as well as refugees' greater propensity to naturalize than eligible nonrefugee migrants with similar socioeconomic and demographic
characteristics.[70]

Attention to multiculturalism and settlement policies helps explain the
timing of the divergence in U.S. and Canadian political integration. Canada's policy of official multiculturalism was first announced in the House of
Commons in 1971. Language urging judges to consider the multicultural
heritage of Canada was included in the Canadian Charter of Rights and
Freedoms in 1982, and Parliament passed the Canadian Multiculturalism
Act in 1988. Settlement programs, especially around language training but
also for labor force insertion, experienced growth through the 1970s and
into the 1980s. This was precisely the period that the divergence between
the United States and Canada began. The available empirical evidence,
often lost in the heat of political rhetoric, consequently suggests that multicultural policies and public programs targeted specifically to immigrants—
acknowledging and accommodating differences in background and
situation—facilitate political integration.

Beyond Multiculturalism: Welfare States
and State-Society Relations

I have argued that multiculturalism promotes immigrants' civic and political integration. It provides immigrant groups with recognition that legiti-
mizes their place in their adopted country and policy support that facilitates
participation. The discussion has not, however, addressed another important critique of multiculturalism, namely, that multicultural policies impede socioeconomic mobility, creating silos of underclass minorities. In the
Netherlands, perceived failures of social and economic integration are central to attacks against multiculturalism.[71]

If founded, the danger of socioeconomic segregation is a genuine threat
to national cohesion, political stability, and overall immigrant integration.
Immigrants who cannot break into the economic mainstream might take

their frustrations into the streets or channel their energies to violent ends, while majority taxpayers—who come to associate ethnic minorities with welfare use and marginality—might draw increasingly rigid distinctions between an "us" of many generations and a "them" of immigrant origins.

This final section speculates about the relationship between political and civic integration and other forms of integration. Such an exercise is critical because *the political theory behind multiculturalism has little to say about socioeconomic integration.* Implicitly, multiculturalism suggests that with recognition and accommodation, immigrants gain psychological resources and a more even playing field within which they can achieve socioeconomic mobility. Explicitly, however, key theorists in this tradition underscore that the cultural concerns of multiculturalism are intellectually distinct from concerns over class inequalities and social mobility.[72] There is no multicultural theory of socioeconomic integration.

The preceding discussion of immigrant integration models suggests two hypotheses about the relationship between socioeconomic integration and multiculturalism. First, all things equal, immigrant communities with greater political incorporation and mobilization around national origins or ethnicity should, with time, experience more rapid socioeconomic integration. This hypothesis is based on the assumption that participation in democratic politics can and will create positive policy change that helps remove barriers to social and economic integration, or that allows groups to capture certain state resources. For example, within the United States, we would expect different socioeconomic outcomes between more and less politically organized groups. Or, comparing countries, we might expect quicker socioeconomic integration for the children of immigrants in Canada and the Netherlands, given high levels of citizenship and political participation, compared to the United States and Germany.

It is possible, however, that immigrants might face an integration trade-off. Political mobilization might create an anti-immigrant or antiethnic backlash by those in the majority. Research on white political attitudes in the United States suggests a "group threat" model where majority whites react against the presence and mobilization of blacks and American Indians.[73] In this case, immigrants might face an uncomfortable choice between pursuing individual socioeconomic projects, but remaining politically silent, or engaging in democratic mobilization, but stirring up animosity that hurts social integration and economic mobility.

If group threat is a possibility, multicultural theory suggests that official multiculturalism, encompassing formal recognition and active support for cultural groups, should mitigate rather than exacerbate political conflicts. It could do so by influencing majority members' perception that minorities have legitimate standing in society, and by improving minorities' ability to organize with dignity rather than as a form of protective and potentially explosive reactive ethnicity. A second hypothesis then suggests that multicultural policies will promote socioeconomic integration more rapidly than absent such policies, because these policies facilitate a positive political dialogue and process of accommodation between immigrants and established majority residents.

We possess, to the best of my knowledge, no empirical evidence on the relationship between multicultural policies and immigrants' socioeconomic outcomes. Increasingly, however, academics echo public concerns regarding the impact of ethnoracial diversity on states' willingness to adopt redistributive policies. Economists Alesina, Glaeser, and Sacredote speculate that with increased diversity residents feel less reciprocal altruism toward others, and are thus less likely to support the welfare state.[74] Robert Putnam claims that social capital in the United States—a factor facilitating democratic engagement and the social trust needed for redistribution—diminishes in places of greater ethnoracial diversity.[75] Such findings lend credence to claims that countries must respect a certain *seuil de tolérance* when it comes to immigration: too much, too fast, the argument goes, leads to a backlash.

Indeed, a recent study by Banting and colleagues finds that significant changes in the proportion of immigrants in a country—but not the absolute number—might slow down growth in social spending.[76] However, they also find that multiculturalism policies appear to attenuate, rather than exacerbate, such spending slowdowns. Countries with strong multiculturalism policies saw the largest rise in social spending and the greatest strengthening of their redistributive effort. In a similar manner, an analysis across nineteen highly industrialized countries finds that multiculturalism policies and economic inequality mediate the effect of immigrant-generated diversity on social trust, civic engagement, and political participation.[77] Significantly, in countries that are more multicultural and more economically equal, negative effects of increasing immigration are mitigated and even reversed: in these societies, civic and political engagement can *rise* with immigration. Echoing other studies, economic inequality appears to play a particularly decisive role in driving down social capital indicators.[78] These studies suggest that rather than thinking about how diversity undermines redistribution, we should ask how greater redistribution and more equal societies deal better with diversity.

Conclusion: Engagement over Values

Public debates over multiculturalism have been hobbled by an unrealistic understanding of what multiculturalism seeks to address, especially among policy makers and the general public. It is primarily a political theory about equality and inclusive citizenship centered on culture; it does not formally tackle immigrants' socioeconomic integration. At the same time, those who have most clearly theorized immigrants' social and economic integration have often neglected political integration, especially as it intersects with other assimilation or incorporation processes. Future scholarship needs to bring these different forms and processes of immigrant integration together.

We especially need more empirical research on immigrants' civic and political integration, to balance the rich theoretical and philosophical debates of the past two decades. Understanding such processes is not only important from the perspective of immigrants but central to contemporary Western nation-states' attempts to recraft self-understandings in an era of global migration, international trade, and reduced sovereignty. Global migration, in particular, raises concerns due to the ethnic, religious, racial, and cultural diversity that migration brings. Accommodating diversity often forces countries to develop more "civic" conceptions of national unity, but many worry that such nationalism becomes unduly thin, lacking cohesive glue. The tension between thinner and thicker national understandings has led many governments in the Western world recently to encourage, through voluntary or coercive means, integration rather than multiculturalism. Integration, in this view, usually means that immigrants need to change and adopt the common civic values of the majority.

Unfortunately, debates over integration quickly become reduced to a question of whether immigrants are adopting the "right" values, rather than one about participation and engagement. The discussion here is animated by the belief that participation and engagement are more fruitful ways to reinforce the ideals of civic citizenship than imposing or "teaching" them in a unidirectional way, where those of the majority are presumed to have civic virtue while those of foreign birth are presumed to lack it. The chapter argues that promoting immigrants' group-based action, such as through policies of multiculturalism, encourages political integration and could have positive effects on socioeconomic incorporation, though this remains an open, empirical question. If true, the contemporary turn away from multiculturalism is misguided.

This is not to say that all multiculturalism is the same: policies promoting it need to be embedded in an understanding of immigrants as future members of society, rather than as temporary guest workers. When applied to those not considered future citizens, multiculturalism can exacerbate segregation and exclusion. In these cases, multiculturalism becomes a thinly disguised attempt by receiving states to keep foreign workers apart from mainstream society. Conversely, however, ignoring particularities by adopting a republican universalism does not seem helpful: a color-blind approach appears to have led to the absence of color among French representatives in the National Assembly, not equality. The failure to integrate immigrants into politics may help explain the fall 2005 riots in the suburbs of Paris.

Immigrant integration is frequently described as a two-way street. Yet contemporary discussions in the media and public sphere usually imply that immigrants should take a fast-lane highway toward the majority, with only a narrow, rutted country road for native-born citizens to meet immigrants on their trip. A renewed focus on multiculturalism and accommodation policies would serve to widen the path majority residents take toward immigrants, and in the process could lead to greater integration for everyone.

Chapter 13

Associational Governance of Ethno-Religious Diversity in Europe: The Dutch Case

Veit Bader

The focus on ethno-religious needs and claims in this chapter is clearly one-sided. It presents the danger of reproducing the increasingly predominant myth that the cultural dimension is the most important dimension in explaining and addressing so-called integration problems, rather than socioeconomic, legal, and political incorporation processes of immigrant majorities and the respective, often quite counterproductive, policies of incorporation. Readers should not misunderstand my excluding here the economic incorporation of immigrants as workers or employers (and the presence or absence of targeted policies to increase their chances as workers and/or entrepreneurs), along with my exclusion of housing and neighborhood problems and policies, of educational problems and policies, of problems surrounding the insecurity of their legal status, and of the serious limitations of political incorporation. All these problems are clearly more important in explaining the overall success or failure of incorporation of immigrants, and all policy initiatives to address these issues are more important than cultural integration policies. But cultural incorporation and incorporation policies are important in their own right.[1] Moreover, they can only analytically be separated from, and are theoretically and empirically very much intertwined with, the other dimensions of incorporation.

Some of these conceptual and analytical distinctions and interpenetrations are only briefly summarized in the first section, because I have dealt with them elsewhere. The second section reviews typologies of institutional incorporation and of policy—types also discussed elsewhere. The mixes and shifts of these types are then sketched for some European states in comparative perspective. The third section leads us beyond abstract types, appealed to in political rhetoric in order to legitimize existing policies and their declared changes, toward what happens on the ground in the case of the Netherlands in actual practice and in actual policies, particularly at the municipal level. I hope to show that we find practices of accommodation of cultural/religious needs and claims at odds with predominant politics of symbolic action. My normative claim, finally, is that associational governance is a morally more promising and at the same time more feasible alternative compared with assimilation, with corporatist multiculturalism, and with increasingly fashionable "diversity" policies.

Cultural Practices and Ethno-Religious Needs and Claims

Most immigrants come as temporary or permanent, legal or irregular workers, small-scale employers, refugees, asylum applicants, or for purposes of family reunification. They may be categorized by others and also may see themselves as workers, as political refugees, as women or men, as first or second generation (youngsters), or as racialized groups. All this has nothing to do with their presumed culture, ethnicity, or religion. Yet they usually also speak foreign languages, except in cases of migrants from former colonies, and they practice (or are perceived to practice) ethno-religious cultures that to a greater or lesser extent diverge widely and deeply from the predominant cultures in the receiving-state societies.

Cultural Practices, Categorizations, and Self-Definitions

For many reasons, it seems appropriate to use an anthropological concept of culture, broadly defined as ways of doing, seeing, and organizing things, that focuses on actual practices: what practitioners actually do even without necessarily having to be aware of this fact. These practices may be specific to some groups or categories of practitioners in some fields or they may encompass more and more, even nearly all, fields of life: cultures of work and organization; of consumption in the broadest sense (including cooking, fashion, and so on); of housing and building; of family, kinship, and friendship; of health; of leisure and feasts; of arts and Arts; of religion; of raising and educating; of sciences; of politics and policies; of law; of warfare. These material cultures are intrinsically interrelated with symbolic cultures, with languages, cognitive, normative, and expressive frames and pictures of the world, society and self (the symbolic aspects of cultures are drastically reduced to so-called norms and values, nowadays so fashionable in assimilationist politics in Europe). These practices are not invented from scratch (there are "traditions" of practices), and they are at least to a certain degree habitual and shared with other practitioners. In the assimilationist policies in Europe, not only is culture reduced to its symbolic aspects, expression of those aspects is sometimes curtailed.

It is self-evident that cultural practices are not primordial, not smoothly integrated into all fields of life, not ultrastable or unchanging essences. They emerge and develop in contact and in opposition to or conflict with other practices; they are heterogeneous, dynamic. Yet this does not dissolve cultural practices into pure processes or performances without any structure or causal capacities, into discourses or into identities, as radical anti-essentialist constructivists try to make us believe.[2] Cultural practices are relational in a double sense: they are shared with other practitioners (hence cultures are not private isolated individual things), and they are distinct from practices of other (groups of) practitioners. Practitioners form groups to the degree that they are aware of the fact that they do things more or less the same, and differently from other practitioners. If this is not the case, they can only be seen and categorized by (scientific) observers.

All these distinctions are relevant for the theoretical and empirical study of processes of categorization and the formation of groups, associations, and organizations. The basic distinction is between categorization by others and self-definition. Categorizations of people by others can use a whole range of criteria, among them ascriptive criteria that are more or less completely unconnected to actual characteristics of people, actual cultural practices among them. Socially defined, real or presumed "natural" characteristics such as kinship and descent, sex, age, and skin color, are used in practices of discrimination, oppression, and exclusion legitimized by biological legends. Sociohistorical characteristics, real or presumed, such as community of territorial space, history, language, gender, ethnonational habits, customs, or lifestyles, religion or church membership, social class, and political culture serve the same aims and are legitimized by ethnocentric legends; (forced) membership of states or (political) organizations is commonly legitimized by more or less civic legends.[3]

It cannot be stressed enough that both categorizations of people by others and self-definitions are highly contextual, occurring in situations of comparative rivalry and conflict.[4] They are subject to sometimes astonishing changes that are often completely unconnected to actual changes in ethnonational or religious practices. As we know, Muslim immigrants from former colonies in Britain have been made into "Asians" or "Pakis"; Berbers have been made into Moroccans and both, together with Turks, into "Muslims" in the Netherlands; increasingly all over Europe, immigrant workers from so-called Muslim-majority countries are made into "Muslims" regardless of linguistic or ethnic diversity, or whether they believe and practice different varieties of Islam or not.

All these differences in and changes of categorizations of people by others depend on the predominant regimes of governance of ethnic and religious diversity and on changes in the predominant public discourse in the respective receiving countries. Immigrants also react to these categorizations in their different, changing self-definitions whether they are aware of it or not, whether they like it or not. Second-generation immigrants from Muslim countries may either become radically aggressive secularists or may reactively ethnicize or religionize, partly through interaction with different strands of political Islamism in Muslim-majority countries and in receiving countries in Europe, and with the emerging global Internet.[5] For the formation of an ethno-religious group as traditionally understood, it is not sufficient that people are seen as different by others or that they objectively share certain practices. They also have to be minimally aware of this (e.g., by speaking the same language, sharing some religious beliefs or practices). This "we" feeling or, more broadly, this group identity is the precondition of, and vice versa massively stimulated by, ethno-religious networks, associations, organizations, and leaders, mobilization and conflict.[6]

Yet, the link between cultures or cultural practices and collective identities is not as simple as is often assumed, even by authors who do not conflate culture with identity. We should carefully distinguish the perspectives of cultures and identities for two reasons. First, cultural practices may be relatively stable, whereas definitions of individual and collective identities may change rapidly, or vice versa.[7] Second, cultural practices may serve as one of the possible bases of identity definitions but this need not be so, as three cases show clearly: (1) cases in which collective identity definitions are limited almost exclusively to the strategic pursuit of economic interests without any reference to culture at all (e.g., "we" as "immigrant workers" or just "workers"); (2) cases in which collective identity definitions appeal to purely imagined cultural distinctions or invented histories; and (3) cases in which movements and organizations of people that are exploited, dominated, discriminated against, excluded, or marginalized on the basis of purely ascribed criteria protest against these practices without developing a common cultural identity or a new common culture ("we" the "foreigners," the so-called *allochtonen*, and the like). A purely negative collective identity may be enough to induce them to organize, mobilize, and fight; it may also be not as weak as is so often assumed.[8] Yet for raising cultural claims, a certain minimum of shared cultural practices and a certain positive collective identity is required, though the rejection of the predominantly negative evaluation of these stereotyped practices by majorities need not go as far as to reverse completely the dominant hierarchies of prestige (claiming the superiority of the own, stylized and purified cultural practices, as of "Islam").

Immigrants' Cultural "Needs" and "Interests" and Claims-Making

Cultural practices, generally speaking, are so important for making sense of the world, of social life, and of the self, that they may be even seen as basic needs (along with basic security, subsistence, and so forth). They are also increasingly articulated as individual and collective rights, such as the right to speak one's own language[9] or to practice one's own religion.[10] As in all other cases, "needs" are articulated as "interests" when not fulfilled but contested or denied; this is no different in the case of immigrants' cultural needs/interests.[11] Immigrant minority practices of language, working and organizing, cooking, dressing, housing, friendship, mating and marrying, raising and educating children, leisure and feasts, burying, health (-care), the arts and Art, politics, law, and conflict resolution may differ significantly to a greater or lesser extent from majority practices and from other minority practices in the receiving society. The most common simplification is to categorize these practices as ethnolinguistic and religious practices, though in many cases ethnic and religious practices are so intertwined, particularly in cases of fairly ritualistic, practice-centered religions such as Judaism or Hinduism, that it is hard to categorize them separately.[12] In other cases, however, especially when it comes to predominant anti-Islam prejudices, such a distinction may be crucial: female genital mutilation and honor killing, for example, are ethnic practices proscribed by Islam.

My central theoretical and empirical thesis is that immigrants, if their cultural interests are smoothly accommodated, would have no reason to, and actually would not, raise cultural claims. That they do so almost everywhere is a first indication of the fact that states do not accommodate these interests easily, for example, claims by new religious communities to be registered as religions, to exemptions from taxes and military conscription, or other exemptions from rules and regulations that hinder or forbid living according to religiously prescribed codes of diet, dress, prayer, holy days, burial, and the like, and to fair or evenhanded financing of faith-based organizations (FBOs) in education, health care, social services, and welfare in all countries in which majority FBOs or other providers receive public funding.

Before discussing the respective normative problems, I will present a brief summary of my theoretical analysis of the "demandingness" of typical claims by ethno-religious minorities and the expected resistance they meet. Claims to accommodate private religious beliefs/practices of minorities that do not also claim public recognition and or financing can be most easily met. Claims to receive public money can expect more resistance but can be more easily accommodated if other ethno-religious minorities and majorities receive public funding (equal treatment claims). Following Koenig, I distinguish four overlapping types of increasingly demanding claims for public recognition.[13] First, there are the claims that challenge the legitimacy of political symbols of national identity and request freedom of public articulation of different identities, such as toleration of religious dress in public. Second, there are minorities' claims for autonomy in some organized societal sphere, such as private religious schools or some free spaces in public education. Both are claims to mere toleration (exemptions and some autonomy) that do not challenge predominant practices and symbols. Third, we find more demanding claims to what may be termed "respect tolerance," aimed at a recombination of the central symbols of national identity, like new religious holidays or inclusive blasphemy laws, and at pluralizing public education or cultural practices in other public organizations. Fourth, there are claims for equal chances in the political center to participate in defining and fashioning society and politics in ways that do not exclude minorities' religious interests, identities, and convictions. The latter claims demand changes in public culture, political institutions, collective political identity definitions, and national symbols, and can be expected to meet the fiercest resistance.[14] Theoretically we can expect, and empirically it has been widely demonstrated, that forms, types, and intensity of claims-making are highly influenced, though not determined, by the political opportunity structure (POS) in different countries, in particular by their regimes of religious government (church-state relations) and governance.[15]

Cultural Differences, Cultural Inequalities, Relational State Neutrality and Fairness as Evenhandedness

Public recognition claims by ethnonational religious minorities raise complex conceptual, theoretical, empirical, and normative questions. It is crucial, in my view, to distinguish cultural diversity and the existence of more or less widely diverging cultural practices under conditions of rough socioeconomic, legal, political, and cultural equality from cultural inequalities. The latter come in two distinct varieties. First, structural (socioeconomic, prestige, legal, political) inequalities are tied to ascribed, imagined, or real cultural differences (the appropriate moral principle in these cases should be justice-as-hands-off).[16] Second, inequalities between cultural majorities and minorities continue to exist even after serious socioeconomic, legal, and political inequalities have been overcome.[17] The appropriate principle of justice in this case of cultural inequality that should guide minority protection and liberal accommodation cannot be fairness-as-hands-off, because it neglects the inevitable partiality of all cultures, public cultures of liberal-democratic polities included. In the end, strict neutrality and fairness-as-hands-off would literally strip people of their histories, languages, public holidays based on religion, public monuments, rituals and symbols of national identity, public dress codes, history and literature canons in public education, and so forth.[18] Hence, the more appropriate principle of justice in cultural matters is fairness-as-evenhandedness.

Empirically, liberal-democratic polities cannot be strictly culturally neutral, for four interrelated reasons.[19] First, the laws of any country have been deeply molded by cultural practices of the predominant (male, ethnonational, religious) majorities, and this bias is very difficult to surmount, particularly if one focuses not only on constitutional rights and legal rules but also on unspecified general norms (public order, equity, and decency) and administrative rulings and practices. Second, the institutional arrangements of any actual polity cannot be deduced from universal liberal and demo-

cratic principles but are deeply (and to a certain degree also morally legitimately) embedded in the history of that nation. Third, the political culture
and civic/political virtues of liberal democracy do not exist in the abstract
either. Last, dominant ethnicity and religion and ruling versions of the history of a polity are inevitably inscribed in its national political identity. Due
to the influx of migrants, this also became visible and dramatized again
inside polities, not only in countries with a predominant ethno-religious
self-conception of national identity but also in countries with a predominant civic or political self-conception. This explains why more or less purely
symbolic issues such as wearing hijabs, turbans, and crosses and the archi-
tectural styles of mosques are so hotly contested and why resistance to
symbolic accommodation is so fierce.[20] In principle, accommodation of
dress codes and pluralization of public cultures and symbols should be
fairly easy because no conflict with liberal-democratic morality is involved
and no costly redistribution is required.

In matters of institutions, political culture, and political identity, then,
the borderlines between legitimate and illegitimate majority particularism
are difficult to draw, and there is no prima facie evidence of what fair or
evenhanded accommodation requires in each case. The cultural needs both
of majorities and of minorities, immigrant minorities among them, are
morally legitimate, and in most cases they clearly conflict with each other.[21]
In my recent book I have tried to show what liberal-democratic morality
(freedom of religion, relational neutrality, evenhandedness) minimally requires in dealing with these public recognition claims: with regard to the
content of education (curricular pluralization and religious education and
instruction in governmental schools), claims to public recognition and financing of nongovernmental religious schools, and pedagogical and educational cultures;[22] with regard to claims of exemption from rules and
practices in private organizations and public organizations and spaces;[23]
with regard to some of the highly dramatized symbolic issues, such as holidays and headscarves;[24] and with regard to representation claims in the
political process.[25] This is not the place to repeat or summarize the results.
Nor is it possible to give even the briefest overview of how different governments actually respond to these claims with changing policies. Instead, I
will confine myself here to a discussion of fairly general prevailing institutional and policy models of accommodating or not accommodating the
cultural needs and claims of immigrant minorities, taking the Netherlands
as an interesting case.

Institutional and Policy Models in Europe: Exclusion, Marginalization, Liberal and Republican Assimilation, Corporatist Multiculturalism, Diversity

Empirically, we are confronted, on the one hand, with a huge variety of actual regimes of government of ethno-religious diversity and related policies and their changes, more rapid or less so.[26] On the other hand, we have to take into account a huge variety of immigrant minorities and their more or less rapidly changing cultural claims both in Europe and by comparison with Canada, the United States, and Australia.[27] We should beware of easy generalizations. Still, it makes sense to construct fairly simple and highly aggregated models of cultural integration policies not only for the purposes of political theory but also because such models are actually constructed and used by state authorities and policy makers in their design and/or legitimation of institutions and policies as well as by judges, administrators, political parties, journalists, NGOs, organization theorists, and management advisers (as in increasingly fashionable "diversity management"). These models are explicitly normative, though some are loosely related to existing institutional patterns and predominant policy traditions. In spite of the variety of policies across fields and levels, state policies are guided, or at least legitimized, by very general and rough models of desirable end states and by acceptable ways to achieve these aims. Public debate and European—national as well as local—policy statements and measures are, implicitly or explicitly, guided by predominant institutional models and policy paradigms. Institutional models of incorporation of ethno-religious minorities can be distinguished by cross-tabulating two options on an axis of cultural incorporation (assimilation or pluralism) and of institutional incorporation (institutional monism or institutional pluralism). A first group of such models includes (1) cultural assimilation combined with inclusion in unchanged monist institutions of the dominant majority (France, "melting" into white Anglo-Saxon Protestant America); (2) institutional and cultural pluralism combined with intragroup assimilation (corporatist multiculturalism, such as the Dutch policy of *integratie met behoud van eigen identiteit* [integration with retention of own identity], the Canadian mosaic, Switzerland, Belgium); (3) inclusion in transformed monist institutions combined with (individual, nonpolitical) cultural diversity (the promise of a postethnic or postnational America); and (4) institutional and cultural pluralism (the promise of flexible, democratic institutional pluralism: "going double Dutch," or associative democracy). Different from these models of long-term incorporation into or inclusion in democratic polities are: (5) models of differential exclusion (short-term incorporation combined with institutional separation and cultural separation and marginalization (guest worker regimes) and (6) nondemocratic and illiberal models of cultural and institutional pluralism (such as indirect colonial rule, postcolonial plural and racist apartheid regimes). There are several closely related policy paradigms. (1) Old and new versions of liberal and/or republican assimilationism: incorporation is a one-way street; minorities have to assimilate by all means; inclusion of minorities as individuals not as collectivities; minorities should not (be allowed to) organize on an ethno-religious basis or be allowed to do so only in "private" or in "civil society," not in "public" or in "political society"; no need to change existing institutions that are presented as culturally neutral. (2) Traditional, inflexible, corporatist multiculturalism policies (MCPs): incorporation is a two-way process; minorities are allowed to retain their cultures and organize as groups both in civil and in political society; their organizations are publicly recognized and at least partly also financed (even if they exercise considerable internal pressure to assimilate); their elites are included in negotiation and policy making; state institutions should be thinner and culturally more neutral. (3) Diversity policies: incorporation is a two-way process; existing state institutions and policies have to change; minorities and majorities are seen as equal, diverse individuals with overlapping, changing, progressively less collective cultures and identities; collective (economic, cultural, recreational, and, particularly, political) organization on an ethno-religious basis should be actively discouraged (if not forbidden, at least not publicly financed or publicly recognized or included in deliberation, negotiation, and decision making). (4) Associative democracy differs from corporatist MCP because it not only guarantees exit rights for dissenting individuals and minorities within minorities but also creates meaningful exit options. Like corporatist MCP, it allows for a wide use of associational freedoms and organizations and meaningful institutional autonomy, but it requires and also monitors nonviolation of minimal moral standards: it makes public financing of diverse minority organizations dependant on more demanding liberal-democratic standards, and it sees that organized minorities within minorities (e.g., women, second generations, diverse religious traditions, and dissenters) and not only traditionalist, orthodox organizations and leaders are fairly represented in deliberations, negotiations, and policymaking, and are also fairly financed. (5) Exclusion and marginalization: minority cultures are backward, inferior, and a threat to the culture of natives, which is presented as liberal and democratic; those who do not assimilate have to be expelled, whatever their legal status; individuals are fully responsible for and have to pay all the costs of their integration; no specific or general policies to fight *achterstand* (serious socioeconomic, educational, housing inequalities) and *achterstelling* (institutional/structural and direct discrimination); freedoms of association and collective organization have to be curtailed.[28]

Diversity and associative democracy, the two normatively most promising institutional models and policy paradigms, are more or less realist utopias. They differ mainly in two regards. First, diversity policies may help to prevent categorization of minorities by state policies but, in the real world, may not be able to fight structural socioeconomic and cultural inequalities. How come "we" as individuals are so equally diverse or different whereas "we" as minorities continue to be so unequal, and what can we do to rectify this? Second, in the real world of asymmetries of political power, diversity policies, by discouraging collective organization and mobilization of ethno-religious minorities, do nothing to challenge and change the majority bias of existing institutions and policies, presented as neutral or universal.

Some brief explanatory remarks are in order. First, these analytical or ideal-typical models in reality are not neatly separated from but usually overlap each other. Second, polities may be characterized by the predominance of a model (path dependency), but predominant models change in a historical perspective or are even replaced. Third, usually several models exist simultaneously within the same polity (at different levels, in different departments). Fourth, even the predominant models are never uncontested. Competing interpretations of the model are important for critics and opponents (e.g., *laïcité ouverte, plurielle* versus *laïcité de combat*).[29] Hence, using references to countries in order to illustrate ideal models can be highly misleading. Last, we can reasonably assume that the highest degree of aggregation and also the highest degree of consistency and coherence of policies will be found in ex ante legitimations and designs. Consistency will decrease when we analyze more detailed laws, policy documents, and actual policies in different fields and on lower levels, as well as in different organizations in different sectors.[30]

Hence, any proper description of the complexity of cultural incorporation policies would require us to analyze (1) public debate and political discourse (from central to local) in different media, by different political actors (public intellectuals, experts, political parties, and increasingly populist leaders in Parliament); (2) legislative alternatives, debates, and actual legislation (on different levels); (3) policy measures by administrations (in different departments, on different levels, on different issues), their implementation, and their intended and unintended effects; and (4) jurisdiction. Here, as in all other policy domains, integration policies have to be clearly distinguished from incorporation processes, and it may turn out that policies do not matter at all, or have mainly or even only counterproductive but foreseeable effects. All this is clearly way beyond what can be covered in one essay, so here I refrain from a comparative discussion of predominant models and changes in Europe and focus on the Dutch case. Yet even then, I present only an extremely rough sketch of predominant models in policy statements on the central and municipal levels, because studies of implementation and, in particular, of actual policy effects are either not available or too complex to present.[31]

Changes in Rhetoric and Practices of Accommodation in the Netherlands: From Multiculturalism to Diversity?

Since the late 1990s, and accelerated after 9/11, there has to varying degrees been a drastic backlash against multiculturalism policies and institutions in most countries, except Canada.[32] More restrictive immigration goes hand in hand with tough assimilation policies under different labels. Changes in the Netherlands have been seen as quite dramatic from within as well as from abroad, because Dutch MCP, together with Canadian and Australian, served as a model for successful pluralist incorporation policies in the 1970s and 1980s, and because these changes showed all the signs of a moral and political panic. In this section, I sketch these developments with a double aim. On the one hand, I want to highlight the differences between rhetoric or politics of symbolic action and actual policy measures, their implementation, and some of their unintended but expectable consequences. On the other hand, I want to highlight important differences between national rhetoric and policies of integration and local rhetoric and policies of integration. Changes in political rhetoric have been most outspoken on the national level but have also infected political debates and policy statements in cities. Even if they have not been followed by similarly dramatic changes in actual policies, as I will show, they have not been innocent (the "power of words"). The political climate became increasingly inimical toward aliens, asylum seekers, immigrants, and *allochtonen*, the (in)famous Dutch legal, statistical, and political category that lumps together ethno-religious immigrants, permanent residents, and naturalized first- and even second-generation citizens of "non-Western" origin.

Yet beneath the surface, so to say, we can also see in municipal policies a hesitant search for and practical experiments with another policy model that seeks to avoid the pitfalls of traditional models of exclusion and marginalization, of assimilation, of corporatist MCP, or of increasingly fashionable diversity. My aim is to demonstrate that local administration is actually in need of and also searching for an associative democratic policy model that is normatively preferable and should be spelled out more clearly and in detail, though it also has to confront serious policy dilemmas and tradeoffs inherent in all immigration and incorporation polices.

Changes in Rhetoric and Policies at the National Level

Up to the end of the 1970s postcolonial and guest worker regimes and the related policy models of differential exclusion and marginalization predominated in the Netherlands, but eventually scientists and administration officials realized that immigrants are here to stay. A new concept of *minderhedenbeleid* (minority policy) was developed in the WRR reports *Etnische Minderheden* (1979), *Ontwerp-Minderhedennota* (1981), and *Minderhedennota* (1983)) combining integration policies—-such as *doelgroepenbeleid* (direct affirmative action), general policies to fight serious inequalities (*achterstand*, serious inequalities), and discrimination (*achterstelling*)—with policies to facilitate retention of culture and identity (*integratie met behoud van eigen identiteit*).[33] Toward the end of the 1980s this predominant corporatist but partly egalitarian multiculturalism model increasingly came under pressure. The focus gradually shifted from facilitation of culture toward socioeconomic integration (*werken, wonen, weten*: work, housing, knowledge),[34] from policies targeting groups to general policies, from rights of *allochtonen* to duties, from caring to actively stimulating participation (WRR reports *Allochtonenbeleid* [1989]; *Contourennota Integratiebeleid* [1994]; *Wet Inburgering Nieuwkomers* [1998]). In this process, the corporatist multicultural model has been replaced by a liberal assimilation model, combined with strong and increasingly vocal undercurrents of marginalization and exclusion: the liberal Bolkestein made political "incorrectness" in talking about immigrants and minorities fashionable,[35] and "Islam" has been blamed as incompatible with "freedom and democracy." After 9/11, with the right-wing populist campaign of Pim Fortuyn, his assassination, and then the assassination of Theo van Gogh, the undercurrent became more radical, outspoken, visible, and missionary, leading to ever more restrictive immigration policies and to increasingly republican rhetoric of assimilative "integration."[36] Nowadays the government of the Netherlands is a forerunner of restrictive immigration policies in all dimensions:

- applicants for *asylum*: strict implementation of the Dublin agreements, making air carriers responsible for rigged documents, short procedures, abolishing rights of appeal by rejected asylum seekers in the new Aliens Laws that came into force in April 2001, expelling nonexpellable asylum seekers from retention centers (policies that triggered not only organized resistance by social movements and NGOs but also administrative civil disobedience by municipalities), all of which contributed to a significant reduction in asylum requests;
- *family reunification*: higher age requirements for spouses of immigrants (twenty-one) and required income guarantees (120 percent of minimum wage), following the Danish example, together with such outlandish requirements as language and integration courses on CD-ROM in the "Rif" (at their own expense) and multiple-choice tests via the Internet or by long-distance calls;
- getting at and trying to expel long-term "white illegal residents" became sharper and more determined through the *koppelingswet* of 1998 (linking data of diverse authorities) designed to exclude those "sans papiers" from work, social security, health care, and education (even for children, which again provoked fierce resistance by NGOs and municipalities), and through extremely restrictive legalization even of "white illegals," changed only reluctantly by the coalition government of the CDA (Christian Democratic Appeal), PvdA (Socialdemocratic Workers Party), and CU (Christian Union) formed in 2007 and fallen in February 2010;
- policies of *zero labor immigration* from outside the European Union, combined with a selective new guest worker regime for highly skilled professionals (blue cards).

Dutch incorporation policies are increasingly dominated by these restrictive immigration concerns as well as by concerns of security and loyalty:

- making *denizenship and even citizenship status more insecure*, e.g., by requiring long-term non-Western (so-called *allochtoon*) permanent residents and citizens to take obligatory integration courses at their own expense and threatening them with expulsion if they did not pass the tests (as in the case of their committing serious crimes); again, this provoked resistance from their own civil servants in the IND (Integration and Nationalization Service), from legal review bodies, lawyers, NGOs arguing that these proposals and legal initiatives violate basic legal norms of equal treatment and will not survive legal scrutiny by the ECJ (European Court of Justice);
- sharpening *naturalization requirements*, restricting dual nationality, and threatening to withdraw Dutch nationality in cases of presumed "crimes against the state."

This all is accompanied by changing fads or hypes in *general "integration" rhetoric and policy proposals* in all dimensions. These proposals entail a lot of paper and hot air without any determined policy efforts; more or less legally enforced "spreading" to prevent ghettos and "black schools"; curtailing or ending public funding for Islamic schools or even all religious schools, or even abandoning article 23 (freedom of education) of the Dutch constitution in order to fight religious fundamentalism, educational "segregation," high drop-out rates for *allochtonen*, and lower educational achievements; prohibiting all subsidies for organizations of *allochtonen*; seriously discussing the introduction of language codes prohibiting the speaking of languages other than Dutch in public; restricting all "external" freedoms of religious expression; prohibiting burkas and chadors and restricting the long-established practice of accommodating headscarves; making a lot of fuss about imams refusing to shake hands with women (e.g., the former minister for immigration and integration Rita Verdonk) or female Muslim teachers in schools;[37] propagating a fairly absolute interpretation of freedom of speech as a "right to insult"; increasing shifts from thin "liberal" interpretations of "integration" (respecting the law of the land and the basic principles of the rule of law and liberal democracy) to thick republican nationalist interpretations: assimilation to "Dutch norms and values," culture, manners, Dutch history (a new history canon has been adopted),[38] and Dutch national identity (in a recent integration film, homosexuality and a very permissive culture of sexual behavior in public are presented as one of the cornerstones of Dutch norms and values) or "European, Judeo-Christian values and culture," all in clear-cut opposition to "Islam."[39]

Restrictive rhetoric and immigration policies and assimilationist (or even exclusivist) rhetoric and policies of "integration" are explicitly meant to reinforce each other in a malign spiral. This package of mobilization issues has been the trade mark of right-wing populist leaders such as Pim Fortuyn and his followers within and outside right-wing parties (including Rita Verdonk and Hirsi Ali in the "liberal" VVD, or Verdonk's new TON movement and Geert Wilders's autocratic PVV [Peoples' Freedom Party]) but it also infected the Christian Democrats (CDA), the social democratic party (PvdA), and—even more—the "socialists" of the SP (Socialist Party).[40] The package is also aggressively promoted elsewhere in the European Union, turning the Dutch government from a pioneer of fairly decent integration policies into a coalition partner of Austria, Denmark, and other countries in what threatens to be a race to the bottom.

"Integration" Policies in Big Cities

While national integration policy shifted from a predominant corporatist multicultural model toward an explosive mixture of predominant republican assimilation with strong exclusivist aspects, we find different mixes of policy models at work at the municipal level.[41] Municipalities have to address the actual claims to accommodation by immigrants and usually do so in a more pragmatic and solution-oriented way than occurs at the national level. They and their umbrella organization (VNG) have often actively or passively resisted ruthless central policy measures to expel illegals, as we have seen. I focus on "Islam and integration" and on policies regarding Muslim organizations in particular because immigrants in the Netherlands are increasingly categorized in religious terms. On the one hand, local policy declarations and measures follow the national trends from corporatist MCP to liberal and increasingly republican assimilation, and to diversity with a varying admixture of marginalization.[42] But on the other hand, they show remarkable differences and greater sensitivity regarding the inherent problems of corporatist MCP as well as assimilation and diversity.

Amsterdam, Rotterdam, and Zaanstad shared a predominantly pluralist or corporatist multiculturalism model in the 1980s and early 1990s, aiming to fight inequalities (*achterstand*), discrimination, and exclusion of minorities, to guarantee adequate provision for Muslim practices and autonomy for Muslim institutions, and to recognize self-created ethnic and religious organizations as important partners of local authorities in negotiations, deliberations, and even decision making (*inspraak*, participation). In addition, the city authorities appealed to these organizations to be intermediaries in helping to promote emancipation in *eigen kring* (within their own circle).[43] Utrecht did the same for ethnic minorities[44] but excluded Islamic organizations from advisory councils and working groups in the *Rompnota Minderhedenbeleid* (1981). Utrecht was also one of the first Dutch cities to shift from *minderhedenbeleid* (minority policy) toward *diversiteitsbeleid* (diversity policy) in 1997[45] with a strong focus on:

- *inburgering*: (*toerusting voor de inburgering van oud- en nieuwkomers, die de Nederlandse taal verwerven en maatschappelijk wegwijs worden*): integration (to help old- and newcomers to learn Dutch and find their way in society), the national policy since 1994;
- individual responsibility of immigrants;
- socioeconomic participation (*toegankelijkheid*): private, semipublic, and public organizations have to treat immigrants as equal citizens and also change the provision of goods and services accordingly.

Such participation is also part of the proclaimed policy in Amsterdam (*De kracht van de diverse stad*, 1999): increase the diversity of municipal organizations by employing more women and *allochtonen*. Zaanstad has also been committed to an even-handed representation of the ethno-religious diversity of its residents in its personnel, and in 2000 it introduced a two-yearly evaluative *Regenboogoverleg* (rainbow negotiations/deliberations) between representatives of migrant organizations, civil servants, and local authorities. It is hoped that this will lead to *toenadering* (contact and dialogue) between cultures. This diversity or dialogical paradigm has three main distinctive characteristics.

First, culture and religion are treated as individuals' preferences relevant only to their private life, as a kind of lifestyle. Collective cultural practices, the outward freedoms of religion, and the role of ethno-religious organizations are neglected. Local authorities do not want to categorize individuals and try to avoid such concepts as "ethnic minorities" and "groups" because, as the title of a Utrecht report in 1999 declares, *in de minderheid, dat zijn we allemaal* (We are all minorities). Amsterdam has melted its policies for *allochtonen* and newcomers with *homo- en vrouwenemancipatie-beleid* (gay and women's emancipation policies). The new slogan of its diversity policy became *Allemaal verschillend. Allemaal Amsterdammers* (All different. All Amsterdamers, 1999). Amsterdamers are seen as an aggregation of unique individual citizens, who should develop a *mix-culture*. Zaanstad introduced a different accent by stressing the city's long history of migration: *Zaankanters bestaan niet! Migratie vroeger en nu* (Zaanstaders don't exist! Migration then and now) and, since 2003, a yearly *Wereldreis door de Zaanstreek* (Global journey through the Zaan region).

Second, the role of independent organizations is not *emancipatie in eigen kring* (emancipation within their own circle) but *het leveren van een bijdrage aan het interculturalisatieproces* (to contribute to the process of interculturalization), making measurable contributions to *ontmoeting van allochtonen en autochtonen* (encounters between allochtones and natives).[46] Consequently, local subsidies shifted to result-oriented subsidies for projects instead of subsidies for independent migrant organizations, and the representatives of ethnic minorities in various advisory councils have been replaced by experts (*deskundigheidsmodel, Stedelijk Adviesorgaan Interculturalisatie* [Saluti, 2002]). In 1994, Amsterdam also began replacing structural subsidies for independent organizations with subsidies for projects and activities. The role of advisory councils was reduced, and the councils were disbanded in 2002. New subsidy regulations declared: "Integration and participation are no longer the task of ethnic minorities alone. This means that no longer will initiatives of independent allochtone organizations exclusively be subsidized but also initiatives by other Amsterdamers . . . targeted at the integration and participation of ethnic minorities." These may be "secular as well as religious and also mixed as well as ethnic organizations as long as they enhance integration."[47]

Third, Utrecht local authorities, in a view not shared by independent migrant organizations, see a huge role for themselves in organizing "dialogue" among "diverse" citizens, and this paternalist approach from above has had a considerable impact on the forms and levels of *opinievormende debatten en discussies* (public opinion making and debates). This is in marked contrast to the approach of the Zaanstad authorities, who restricted themselves to advice and cooperation while leaving the initiative for projects and activities to immigrant organizations. In addition, they stimulated the voices of second-generation immigrants and women through established migrant organizations as well as through subsidized projects. This trust in "civil-society initiatives and organizations"[48] has also had an impact on the forms and content of the dialogue that has been focused on broad societal issues, mutual respect, and inclusion instead of polarizing "them" ("Muslims") versus "us." In reaction to the assassination of Theo van Gogh in November 2004, Amsterdam developed a program of action (*Wij Amsterdammers* [January 2005] and *Voortgangsrapportage "Wij Amsterdammers"* [April 2005]) to fight terrorism, radicalization, and polarization. Part of this program has been an attempt to stimulate a "we" feeling focused on Amsterdam, not the Netherlands, and divergent forms of intercultural and interreligious dialogue and interaction among citizens and with local authorities ("city dinners," "day of dialogue," the campaign entitled *Wat doe jij voor de stad?* ("What are you doing for the city?"), a stronger focus on neighborhoods, and "dialogue tables" with mosque associations). The program is guided by a dialogue model promoting individual diversity and also assimilation, but there is a clear tension between these declarations and measures by the majority of the community council and the more pluralist or multicultural view of the mayor, Job Cohen, who has criticized the neglect of collective aspects of religions and of the important role of independent ethnic and religious organizations.[49]

Beginning in 2002, the majority members of the city council (Leefbaar Rotterdam of Pim Fortuyn, CDA, VVD) and the authorities in Rotterdam, while paying lip service to diversity and dialogue, shifted to strong versions of republican assimilation with heavy exclusionist accents (*Het Nieuwe Elan* [The New Elan, 2002] and *Kadernotitie Sociale Integratie in de moderne Rotterdamse samenleving* [Social integration into modern Rotterdam society/community, 2003]) under the spell of securitization. "Integration" now meant outright assimilation into a stylized version of Dutch norms, values, and manners in clear-cut opposition to "Islam," culminating in 2006 in the Rotterdam Code (unilaterally replacing the project of a *samenlevingscharter*, charter of living together). The *beleidsnotitie moskeebeleid* by Pastoors combines a general prohibition on building mosques in a "deviant style" with policies to fight radicalization, announcing that those who *niet wilden meedoen zouden moeten achterblijven* ("those who do not want to integrate have to stay behind") and face exclusion from all social services and benefits.[50]

Within the frame of the action program *Rotterdam Zet Door* (2003),[51] a new plan has been developed under the title *Islam in Discussie*, containing a series of debates: meetings of experts, so-called internal debates within the Muslim community, an information round, and a series of public discussions.

Four themes emerged from the internal debates, characterized by "astonishing nuance and openness": a feeling of being excluded and marginalized; Muslims are not a homogeneous group isolated from the rest; making a difference between religious and ethnocultural issues; take inclusion into a common democratic citizenship as a necessary starting point instead of continuing *allochtonen* talk. The tone changed dramatically with three essays prepared by aldermen in order to stimulate *openbare meningsvorming* (public opinion making) and the round of public discussions in February and March 2005, bluntly stating that "our Jewish-Christian-Humanist main culture" is "the most attractive on Earth," and criticizing "de pacificerende, vredelievende en gematigde weg . . . van het niet-beledigen, het niet-shockeren en het niet-in-hokjes-willen-plaatsen van mensen" ("the pacifying, peaceful, and moderate way . . . of not insulting, not shocking, and not categorizing people"). The predictable result has been a considerable polarization and a public climate increasingly hostile toward *allochtonen* understood as Muslims, a climate that the Rotterdam city government has actively promoted ("dit college een voortrekkersrol gespeeld"). The city of Rotterdam has been a pioneer of "tough" integration policies (mixes of assimilation and marginalization) in the Netherlands, serving as a model for policy makers in The Hague.

All three defining aspects of the diversity paradigm have been criticized by the municipalities. I will briefly summarize their main points before I try to show why associative democracy provides a better model for overcoming these shortcomings without falling back into corporatist multiculturalism or pluralism.

Declaring that "we are all minorities now" or that we are "all different but equal individuals now" still raises questions as to how it comes about that some minorities are clearly "more equal" than others and that some remain more clearly "minorities" than others. Defining away sensitive issues such as structural and cultural inequalities in order to avoid nasty consequences of "categorization" does not resolve the problems at hand, does not end the fact that "they" are categorized by others. Quite the contrary, it makes a clear policy to fight structural inequalities (*duidelijk achterstandsbeleid*) theoretically and practically impossible.[52] Moreover, municipalities could learn from experiences with fashionable "management of diversity" in corporations that the intent to have more women or *allochtonen* as employees, particularly in higher positions, is difficult to realize— and that it may be even more difficult to change organizational cultures from above without adequate representation and voice for the respective "cultural" minorities. Amsterdam's mayor Cohen, among others, has rightly criticized the privatization of cultures and religions.

The changed policies regarding the role of independent organizations in Utrecht were critically evaluated in a recent report (by G. U. Saluti in 2006, accepted by the municipality in *Evaluatie Herijking Migrantenzelforganisaties*), because the policies produced some paradoxical results: (i) Independent organizations thriving on *vrijwilligers* (volunteers) and small-scale activities are increasingly saddled with demanding aims and tasks. They eventually, and predictably, lose out to professional organizations, advice bureaus, project bureaus, intercultural management bureaus.[53] (ii) The core functions of independent organizations (meeting newcomers, providing mutual aid, undertaking the first steps for forming other organizations and for participation) are neglected to the detriment of municipal policy aims (e.g., as intermediaries, *om de boel bij elkaar te houden*, "in order to fight radicalization and terror," the famous phrase coined by Mayor Cohen). (iii) The role of independent organizations in the formation of networks and elites, as "greenhouses for administrative and organizational talent" (*kweekvijver voor bestuurlijk en organisatorisch talent*), and in the organization and mobilization of immigrant minorities (in short: the role of a robust civil society) is neglected or willfully rejected: pacification through individualization that leaves the dominant majority views and practices as "the norm" and tries to deprive minorities of resources (and their organizations and elites) and chances of mobilizing to change this status quo.[54]

Experiences with organizing dialogue demonstrated that there is a huge difference between dialogue in an open atmosphere, aimed at mutual understanding, and polarizing "public debate" or "discussion." Dialogue is easier at neighborhood levels, focused on finding solutions to specific problems that cut across the *allochtonen/autochtonen* divide, involving all relevant stakeholders or voices (including both established minority organizations and youngsters, dissenters, women, and their organizations) as (co-)organizers. These are the lessons from Zaanstad as well as from local dialogues in Amsterdam and Rotterdam.[55] Public debate at the municipal level, under conditions of a predominant national paradigm of republican assimilation with strong overtones of marginalization and exclusion, is easily hijacked by right-wing populists and media hype. It tends to polarize "them" and "us" and is surely counterproductive to achieving its proclaimed aims of fighting radicalization and terrorism.

Associational Governance of Ethno-religious Diversity: A Realist Utopia?

In sum, experiences with local policy making show that the diversity paradigm has important inherent weaknesses. Its aggressive, often secularist individualism is at odds with constitutionally guaranteed associational freedoms of religion. It is a paradigm that defines away rather than addresses problems of structural inequalities and political power asymmetries. It promotes debate but often produces polarization. All this, however, does not mean that the only decent alternative would be to fall back on old-style pluralism or corporatist multiculturalism, rightly criticized by defenders of diversity for state-imposed or facilitated categorization, for internal oppression of minorities within minorities, for conservationism, for the exclusion of dissenting voices from negotiation and deliberation with public authorities. Such an exclusive alternative is for instance reproduced in Amsterdam in the opposition between the majority of the City Council and leading civil servants (promoting diversity) and Mayor Cohen (promoting multiculturalism). Civil servants and policy makers at the municipal level, most outspokenly in Zaanstad and Utrecht (Saluti report), are actually searching for an in-between, and the institutional design and policy proposals of associative democracy, in my view, exactly provide for such a third way that may productively guide their practical experiments.

As already indicated, associative democracy allows us to balance the tensions between individual and associational or collective freedoms of religion in a more sensible and context-specific way.[56] It provides better opportunities for vulnerable minorities within minorities, particularly for children, in two ways. First, it explicitly penalizes violations of their basic interests and rights without overriding the meaningful autonomy of parents or communal organizations in defining and caring for their best interests.

Second, it provides meaningful exit options instead of merely stating their exit rights. It clearly acknowledges the many dilemmas of affirmative action policies, particularly problems of state-imposed categorization, but does not use these dilemmas as an excuse for not engaging in powerful policies to fight structural inequalities. It criticizes the strategies of individualization and privatization, which in combination only protect the privileges of the entrenched ethno-religious majorities presented as "universal" or "neutral." The role of social networks, organizations, leadership, and mobilization of minorities in the political process is not only protected by constitutional freedoms of political communication, it is also needed to correct asymmetries of political power. Different from political pluralism, associative democracy provides opportunities not only for public dialogue and for lobbying but also for some formalized roles in deliberations (e.g., advisory councils), some say (e.g., *inspraak*), and, most important, roles in policy implementation. Associative democracy favors public funding of minority organizations offering services such as education (e.g., Islamic schools) and all kinds of care, provided they live up to agreed-upon standards and are subject to public control, but it also allows for selective funding of representative and political organizations of minorities provided that they accept the basic rules of law and of thin liberal democracy. Accepting public money also means accepting public scrutiny: relevant criteria are representativeness of organizations/leaders (giving voice to dissenters, youngsters, and women within established organizations) and funding new initiatives and organizations (but not "creating" them from the outside or above).[57]

Like all other paradigms, associative democracy also has to address the inherent problems of such institutionalization and funding. This already indicates that none of the existing or new, highly aggregated institutional models or policy paradigms is a panacea able to solve all problems in all contexts and situations. Instead of continuing these fairly abstract and ideological fights, instead of engaging in fashionably rapid changing of models and paradigms, we should focus on policy dilemmas that plague all incorporation policies, take them really seriously, and look for workable answers in order to prevent the conclusions that politics does not matter at all or even makes things worse than they would be without any official "integration" politics.[58]

Conclusion: Some Policy Dilemmas

Recognizing serious dilemmas, tradeoffs, and unintended consequences may help to find ways to deal with them that are morally and prudentially superior. In particular, recognizing them may contribute to the design of more balanced, flexible, context-sensitive policies. In order to achieve this, an institutional turn in political theory is required.

If policies of initial admission are fairly open and nonrestrictive, this puts pressure on the creation of fair incorporation processes in all dimensions, particularly welfare arrangements. If the admission policies are strongly restrictive they may be morally indefensible and create intended or unintended stereotypes about "foreigners" that backfire on the integration of resident immigrants.

If policies of legal incorporation are fair and inclusive (safe and secure denizenship status and easy naturalization) they may serve as important "pull" factors for immigration (in all forms). If they are restrictive and exclusionary they may be morally indefensible and seriously hinder integration processes in all other dimensions.

If policies of socioeconomic integration are weak (neoliberal) or absent, they contribute to the development of ethnic underclasses, ghettoization, structural educational underachievement, crime, and so on, thereby reinforcing ethnic stigmatization. If they are strong—either general "republican" or "socialist" policies of equalizing socioeconomic opportunities or affirmative action policies—they tend to reinforce restrictive immigration policies or dramatize the dilemmas of affirmative action: as morally unjust or legally suspect (undermining equality before and in the law); as "essentialist" categorization and stigmatization; as bureaucratization; as undermining social cohesion; as stimulating ethnic conflicts; and so on.[59]

If policies of cultural integration are strongly assimilatory, they are morally illegitimate and create or stimulate much resistance. In addition, they reinforce stereotypes of immigrants as unwelcome and unadaptable. If they are pluralist they may be conceived as obstacles to "integration," as a threat to "our common culture," "our shared values," and the like.

If integration policies have a strongly monist institutional bias, they may be in conflict with important freedoms (of education, of association, of organization) and may add to the overload of state-run public services. If they allow for a fair amount of institutional separation, they may be perceived as a threat to minimally required political unity, social cohesion, and stability, and they may stimulate the unchecked strategic particularism of ethnopolitics.

If policies regarding the predominant public or political culture are open and accommodationist, stressing its civil or political character, they may reinforce ethnocentric or nationalist reactions (the recent constructions of German, Dutch, or Australian "Leitkultur"). If they are outright ethnonationalist and assimilationist, they create fundamentalisms on both sides.

Policies of not recognizing and not funding minority organizations and leaders have serious downsides, such as huge administrative discretion and unequal legal treatment (because administrations—even in France—cannot avoid dealing with minorities) and, intentionally or not, reproducing cultural and political inequalities. Yet, policies of public recognition and funding (or official institutionalization) also have to address serious dilemmas. How to avoid illegitimate interference in the lawful autonomy of associations? Given the fact that recognition and funding are inevitably selective, how does one avoid seriously unequal treatment and majority bias favoring the already established, large minority organizations? And so forth.

Whatever (mixes of) institutional models and policy options one chooses, one has to deal with serious dilemmas and hard tradeoffs that have to be clearly recognized and explicitly addressed, though in different ways, by moral and political philosophers, by political theorists, by social scientists, and by politicians and civil servants. This essay is not the place to elaborate these dilemmas or to indicate difficult new ways out;[60] it only highlights the practical urgency of this task. Political philosophers and theorists, in critical cooperation with policy makers and representatives of minorities, may contribute to such a process of democratic-experimentalist democratic learning in a modest but meaningful way.

PART IV

Toward Normative Principles

Chapter 14

When and Why Should Liberal Democracies Restrict Immigration?

Stephen Macedo

Immigration Versus Social Justice?

Have patterns of immigration to the United States in recent decades helped to undermine social justice? The increases in immigration that followed the 1965 immigration reforms roughly coincide with the waning of the liberal reformist energies associated with the New Deal and the Great Society. Many factors contributed to this ebbing of progressivism, and it seems very doubtful that immigration was foremost among them, but was it a significant contributor? Immigration—legal and illegal—shapes the labor market, the incentives faced by voters, and divisions and cleavages in society. Immigration helps determine which parties and policies will prevail in politics. Patterns of immigration to the United States in recent decades may have made social justice harder to attain. But can we justifiably seek to shore up social justice at home by excluding from our shores very poor people from abroad in search of a better life?

High immigration is part of the much-discussed phenomenon of globalization: the increased movement of goods, capital, ideas, and people. Who benefits from globalization is a crucial question, and the immigration part of the puzzle deserves greater attention. The logic that drives globalization is often that of economic markets, and the extension of markets has many good consequences, including for many of the poorest people in the world.[1] But how will social justice fare?

Many have argued that "global integration" undermines "economic security and distributive justice," but academics are skeptical. Recent evidence suggests that, in general, it does not seem to be the case that various features of globalization are undermining national-level redistributive institutions. While "globalization in general and capital mobility in particular" may undermine "the bargaining power of low-skilled workers in developed countries," globalization "does not constrain . . . redistributive policies that raise efficiency," such as investments in education and other public goods. And yet, the impact of *immigration* specifically on redistributive policies has not been much studied. One of the few studies available suggests that "immigration undermines support for social insurance programs, perhaps by undercutting feelings of identification and solidarity with benefit recipients."[2]

I want here to take seriously the possibility that immigration to the United States undermines social justice, and to state this worry as sharply as I can, based on the available evidence. Such concerns deserve more attention from scholars even if (as I also believe) it is important not to allow such anxieties to be exaggerated and exploited.[3]

I will begin by describing three paths—economic, cultural, and political—by which immigration to the United States may undermine social justice. I then defend the view that citizens have special obligations to one another with respect to distributive justice: those who are related as coparticipants in a political society have special reasons to be concerned about disparities of wealth and opportunity. A political community's special and urgent obligations to its least well-off members may take priority over the claims of some even poorer people abroad. If particular patterns of immigration worsen domestic economic disparities and undermine commitments to social justice, these are weighty (but not necessarily conclusive) reasons for revising immigration policies. In the end, however, I bring these abstract reflections back to the specific context of American immigration politics and policy. In light of the uncertain magnitude of immigration's deleterious effects on social justice and the high costs of immigration restriction on poor noncitizens, I suggest (with misgivings) the virtues of mainstream and moderate proposals for immigration reform.

My enduring worry is that we are not adequately weighing the costs of immigration to the worst-off Americans. One attractive vision of the future is to go with the flow suggested by the logic of liberal (or neoliberal) cosmopolitanism, embracing more open borders and a wider social diversity. But would we then be undermining those forms of solidarity—already comparatively weak in the American case—on which social justice depends? In response it could be observed that we are the United States of America, not Finland; we are an immigrant society, and that has long been a great strength. There is much truth in this, but we need to know if not all the consequences are good—or if the consequences are not good for all of us.

Immigration Versus Social Justice? Three Paths

Immigration's Impact on Wages at the Bottom

Over the past half century, American immigration policies and practices have become in some respects more accommodating to the less well off abroad.[4] The question is whether this "generosity" has exacted a significant cost in terms of social justice at home.

The basic facts are striking. Whereas in 1970, 5 percent of the general population was composed of immigrants, that percentage is now 12 percent, the highest in eighty years. By 2000, there were fifty-six million immigrants and first-generation Americans (children of immigrants), making up 20 percent of the U.S. population.[5]

The sheer volume of increased labor may have a downward effect on wages overall. However, the composition of the growing immigrant pool has changed markedly as well. Immigrants coming to the United States through the 1950s tended to bring considerable labor market skills with them. Since the 1960s, the skills levels and earnings of immigrants have declined considerably relative to those of the native U.S. population. Most of the growth in immigration since 1960 has been among people entering at the bottom 20 percent of the income scale. This is partly because, as George Borjas observes, "Since the immigration reforms of 1965, U.S. immigration law has encouraged family reunification and discouraged the arrival of skilled immigrants."[6] Whereas in 1960 the average immigrant man living in the United States earned 4 percent more than the average native-born American, by 1998 the average immigrant earned 23 percent less. At the same time, the ethnic makeup of immigration has also changed, with the percentage arriving from Europe and Canada falling sharply and the percentage from Latin America and Asia rising.

On Borjas's influential if controversial analysis, recent decades of immigration have lowered wages and worsened income disparities in the United

States. Borjas argues that by increasing the supply of labor, immigration between 1980 and 2000 lowered the wages of native workers overall by 4 percent. However, because of the low level of education among immigrants, the impact on less well-educated Americans—those with only a high school degree or high school dropouts—has been greater. Immigration from 1980 to 1995 increased the pool of high school dropouts in the United States by 21 percent, while increasing the pool of college graduates by only 4 percent, and this, argues Borjas, contributed to a substantial decline in the wages of high school dropouts (roughly the bottom 9 percent of the workforce), which he estimates at 7.4 percent. It is widely agreed that in the United States in the 1980s and 1990s there was a substantial widening of the wage gap between the more and the less well-educated workers. Borjas has argued that a significant portion—perhaps as much as half—of this widening wage gap between high school dropouts and others was due to the increase in the low-skill labor pool caused by immigration.[7]

Questions about the magnitude—if not the direction[8]—of these effects abound. Economist David Card argues that cities in the United States with a high proportion of immigrants seem to experience a modest widening of the wage gap, but an overall rise in average native wages. He argues that "immigration exerts a modestly positive effect on the labor market outcomes of most natives," but not all.[9] It is certainly possible that some of Borjas's estimates are on the high side, but even Card does not argue that recent immigration has been especially good for natives at the bottom of the income scale. More than a quarter of the high school dropouts now seeking work in the United States are Mexican born, so it is hard to imagine that immigration does not have a downward impact on wages among the bottom tenth.[10] I will not here try to resolve this controversy, but it is certainly plausible to think that increasing immigration over the past three or four decades has worsened the relative standing of the poorest native-born Americans.

Of course, all Americans have benefited from cheaper fruits and vegetables and other products and services that immigrants (including undocumented workers) help produce.[11] Wealthier Americans have benefited from increased access to cheap labor to perform service work—as nannies, gardeners, and so on. Firms have also benefited from cheap labor. However, Borjas and others argue that native-born African American workers suffer disproportionately because they are more likely than others to be low skilled and poorly educated and often compete directly with low-skilled immigrants.[12]

When advocates of large-scale immigration argue that Americans don't want to do the jobs that immigrants do, especially illegal immigrants, one appropriate response is: poorer Americans do not want these jobs, given the prevailing wages and work conditions. Tighten the labor market a lot, and wages will rise. Also, capital will be introduced to provide partial substitutes for labor, eliminating some of the worst jobs and making those that remain pleasanter, with better tools and work conditions.[13]

Let me add one other element to this admittedly controversial labor market story before moving on. As Borjas again observes, nations with notably more progressive domestic policies often have immigration laws that are quite different from those of the United States. U.S. policy since 1965 has emphasized family reunification (including children, spouses, parents, and adult siblings) with a very small percentage of immigrants—around 5 percent in recent decades—receiving visas based on the possession of desirable skills. Canada, by contrast, has a quota system that gives greater weight in admissions to educational background, occupational skills, and English-language proficiency. Canada's policy favors better-educated and high-skilled workers, and this seems likely to have distributive effects that are the opposite of those from U.S. policy. By increasing the pool of skilled workers relative to the unskilled, Canadian policy tends to lower the wages of the better off and to raise the relative level of the worse off.[14]

U.S. policy, by admitting predominantly low-skilled and poorly educated immigrants and their extended families looks generous to some poor persons abroad, but may worsen the relative standing of the American poor. Were the United States to follow Canada and impose an education test on immigration, this would substantially and disproportionately reduce immigration from Mexico and the rest of Latin America.

The discussion so far illustrates one path—via labor market economics —by which recent patterns of immigration may worsen distributive justice in the United States. But there are two other paths—one political and one cultural—by which recent immigration may harm the relative standing of the poorest Americans.

Immigration and the Median Voter

One response to the foregoing argument is that if immigration increases our collective wealth while worsening income disparities across rich and poor, why not welcome immigration and redistribute the surplus via tax and spending policies? Because redistributive policies could compensate for the malign distributive effects of immigration, we need to ask whether immigration has an impact on the likelihood that redistributive policies will be enacted. In fact, there are two ways in which immigration may undermine political support for social welfare and redistributive programs.

Economic inequality in the United States has increased sharply since 1970, but this has not led to increased pressure for redistribution. If anything, the reverse would seem to be the case: the real value of the minimum wage has fallen, and taxes paid by the better off have been cut, including the top marginal income tax rates and the estate and capital gains taxes.

Nolan McCarty, Keith T. Poole, and Howard Rosenthal argue that recent patterns of immigration help explain why increasing inequality has come about without an increase in political pressure for redistribution. Since 1972, the percentage of noncitizens has risen, and their income relative to other Americans has fallen. "From 1972 to 2000, the median family income of non-citizens fell from 82 percent of the median income of voters to 65 percent while the fraction of the population that is non-citizen rose from 2.6 percent to 7.7 percent."[15] This decline in the income of noncitizens has contributed to the falling income of the median family living in the United States (including voters and nonvoters). Meanwhile, however, the income of the median voter—the voter likely to be the "swing voter" who decides close elections—has not fallen. Immigration to the United States has made the median *voter* better off relative to the median *resident*, and this decreases the median voter's likelihood of supporting redistribution. Immigration may have, thus, both worsened the relative standing of the least well-off Americans and made it less likely that crucial swing voters would support redistributive programs.[16]

Excluding immigrants from social welfare services is one way to counteract these effects, but immigrants—including illegal immigrants in many places—will still be provided with a variety of social services, including education.[17]

Recent patterns of immigration to the United States may, thus, worsen the relative lot of the least well-off Americans while also making redistributive policies less politically popular. There is one more way in which recent immigration may worsen the lot of the least well off.

Racial and Ethnic Diversity and the Decline of Civic Solidarity?

There is some evidence that the feelings of solidarity and mutual identification that help support social justice can be undermined by the increased racial and ethnic heterogeneity associated with immigration.[18] Robert Putnam's recent work furnishes evidence that "in ethnically diverse neighborhoods residents of all races tend to 'hunker down'. Trust (even of one's own race) is lower, altruism and community cooperation rarer, friends fewer."[19] The fact that immigrant groups typically have higher fertility rates than natives amplifies the effect. Putnam and others thus argue that increasing ethnic diversity can, in the short-to-medium term, reduce social solidarity and undermine support for the provision of public goods, including programs aimed at helping the poor.[20]

The impact of immigration on a society's capacity to sustain redistributive programs is bound to be complex. In a recent study, Stuart Soroka, Keith Banting, and Richard Johnston argue that "international migration does seem to matter for the size of the welfare state. Although no welfare state has actually shrunk in the face of accelerating international movement of people, its rate of growth is smaller the more open a society is to immigration." They further argue that "the typical industrial society might spend 16 or 17 percent more than it does now on social services if it kept its foreign-born percentage where it was in 1970."[21] Once again, these empirical claims are controversial. Just how immigration and increased ethnic and racial diversity inhibits social spending is unclear: the rise of New Right political parties in Europe is associated with controversies over immigration, and mainstream parties may need to shift to the right in response.[22]

American immigration policy may have made the distribution of income within the United States more unequal while also lessening political support for social provision. Admitting large numbers of relatively poorly educated and low-skilled workers may increase competition for low-skilled jobs, lowering the wages of the poor and increasing the gap between rich and poor Americans. New immigrants' ineligibility to vote may make it less likely that swing voters will support generous social provision, including redistributive measures to offset low wages at the bottom. And immigration's contribution to increased ethnic and racial heterogeneity may also weaken social solidarity and undermine support for the provision of public goods, including those to help the poor. The magnitude of these effects is, as I have emphasized, contested.

The public and political elites seem less committed to public provision of social services than in the days of FDR's New Deal or Lyndon Johnson's Great Society. Have changes in immigration policy contributed significantly to the decline of the American welfare state? The period from the Great Depression through the mid-1960s was one of relatively low inequality, compared with before and after,[23] and also relatively low immigration. Immigration between 1924 and 1965 was defined by the "national origins" quotas that allocated legal immigration on an ethnic group basis in proportion to the ethnic composition of the American population in 1890 (prior to the large-scale migration of Southern and Eastern Europeans). A lot happened between 1924 and 1965 that may have contributed to greater social solidarity; the federal response to the Great Depression and the experience of collective sacrifice and purpose during World War II may well have contributed to what has so often been called "the greatest generation," including with respect to civic life.[24] Public policy may also have contributed to the construction of civic solidarity, as with the G.I. Bill.[25] A great deal also happened after the mid-1960s to help explain the growing skepticism about government-funded social programs, including the decline of organized labor and growing distrust of government in general. Especially important was the increasing tendency of the media and ordinary Americans to associate welfare benefits with racial minorities.[26] Many factors contributed to the decline of progressive energies in American politics after the late 1960s. However, higher immigration and a more ethnically and racially diverse immigration pool may also have played a role.[27]

Social Justice and Membership

Who Counts and How?

U.S. immigration policy confronts us with apparently conflicting claims from our less well-off fellow citizens and from poor persons abroad. Some of our deepest values may also be in conflict, including freedom of movement and openness to diversity, on the one side, and the sort of solidarity and mutual identification on which social justice may depend, on the other. What does justice require of us when it comes to these conflicts?

The promise of American life remains even now in large measure an egalitarian promise that includes fair equality of opportunity. There is widespread support in principle for the propositions that children should not be held back from competing for good jobs and positions of leadership in society by virtue of the accidents of their birth and that the political community should support educational arrangements that promote equal opportunity.

But why should we understand the promise of American life as extending to members only and not to all of humanity?[28] Why are the borders of the political community—the state—morally significant when it comes to the positive obligations we have to one another under the banner of social justice?

Political theorists and ethicists argue for open borders from a great variety of points of view. In a now classic statement, Joseph H. Carens argues that three leading ethical standpoints—utilitarianism, free market libertarianism, and liberal egalitarianism of the sort associated with John Rawls—all argue for largely open borders.[29]

The utilitarian case depends on showing which combination of policies maximizes human happiness overall. Respecting special concern among compatriots might maximize mutual concern among human beings.[30] On the other hand, the great discrepancies in wealth and income across national borders suggest that efficiency and aggregate well-being would increase enormously if free—or at least much freer—movement of people was allowed. Lant Pritchett is among those economists who argue that the free movement of labor might be a far more successful "Plan B" for promoting development among the global poor.[31]

Many free market libertarians argue for largely open borders. It is no business of the minimal "night watchman state" to decide who can be a member, so long as private property rights are respected and everyone pulls his own weight.[32] Milton Friedman argued that "it's just obvious you can't have free immigration and a welfare state," and libertarians tend to oppose welfare state transfers.[33] One might think that freedom of movement is especially well justified in an era in which global commerce is increasing.

Neither the utilitarian nor the classical liberal or libertarian point of view accords a fundamental role to special obligations among compatriots, though utilitarianism might endorse such obligations as the best way of maximizing overall utility.

The sort of liberal egalitarianism associated with John Rawls might also seem to be unfertile ground for according special moral significance to national borders. Rawls's famous thought experiment, after all, asks us to consider what principles of social justice we would adopt if we imagined ourselves in an "original position" behind a "veil of ignorance."[34] We imagine ourselves occupying all relevant social positions—especially the least favored—and ask: What principles to guide the design of society's major institutions would be acceptable to all, and especially those occupying the *least favored points of view*? This famous thought experiment highlights the unfairness of social institutions that reward those who are already advantaged by accidents of fate. If social class, race, religion, and gender are to be regarded as arbitrary contingencies from the standpoint of social justice, surely the same would seem to apply to place of birth. If we are to regard it as arbitrary whether one is born a son of Rockefellers or a woman descended from slaves, is it not just as morally arbitrary whether one is born in Mexico or New Mexico? Open borders would, as Carens argued, seem an obvious extension of Rawls's domestic liberalism. A *cosmopolitan egalitarian* says that nationality or place of birth should not determine what we owe to one another with respect to basic justice.

I am going here to leave aside the utilitarian and libertarian frameworks; both are flawed in a great variety of ways.[35] The free market framework, in particular, gives far too little weight to the demands of social justice: it is an excessively thin account of the claims that citizens of a political community can make on one another. Both views also fail to recognize the moral weight of the special relations of citizens to one another. The Rawlsian view, properly interpreted, furnishes a much more promising framework for thinking about what we owe to others.

The fullest moral demands associated with social justice are expressed in principles designed to regulate the institutions and public rules that help generate inequalities of wealth and opportunity among members of self-governing political communities. On the membership view the fullest ideals of distributive justice hold among members of political communities who are jointly responsible for shared social and political institutions.[36]

Those who do not share the relationship of fellow citizens with us make different—but nevertheless important—moral demands on us.[37] These include duties of assistance to the poor, and also fairness, nonexploitation, and nondomination in our relations with others, and reparation and redress in response to past exploitation or domination. Further, we have powerful reasons to reform the global institutional environment in order to coordinate aid, curb unfair and exploitive relations among states, and foster cooperation to solve common problems. On the membership view of distributive justice, it is wrong to think that when we reach the border we fall off a moral cliff. The special relationship among citizens matters, but it is far from being all that matters. The membership view that I wish to defend takes account of the claims of all persons and accords them equal standing as human beings, but it accepts that various particular relations are morally weighty and generative of additional reasons for mutual concern.

The membership view is regarded by some as morally arbitrary in its treatment of nonmembers, needlessly complex, and at odds with the spirit of democratic liberalism. Some argue that freedom of movement around the globe is a basic human right, subject only to reasonable regulations. Others deny moral significance to the specific relations of citizens and adopt "nonrelational" cosmopolitan principles. I am going to focus here on defending the membership view, both because I think it is correct and because it puts in clear relief some important concerns about immigration's domestic distributive impact.[38]

The Membership-Based View of Distributive Justice

The borders of political societies are morally significant with respect to social justice because principles of social justice are designed to help regulate and justify the relations of participants in systems of collective self-governance. As members of a political community we are joined in a collective enterprise across generations through which we coercively impose an all-pervasive system of law on ourselves.[39] We are born into such associations, and our lives are formed by them: the law and principles of our political regime shape every aspect of our lives. From cradle to grave (and beyond) our interests, identities, relationships, and opportunities are pervasively shaped by the political system which we collectively create and within which we live.

Citizens owe one another a robust justification for the design of those basic social institutions and public policies that shape our life prospects deeply and pervasively. Rawls expresses this thought in terms of his "liberal principle of legitimacy": "Our exercise of political power is fully proper only when it is exercised in accordance with a constitution the essentials of which all citizens as free and equal may reasonably be expected to endorse in the light of principles and ideals acceptable to their common human reason."[40]

Liberal egalitarian accounts of social justice seek to articulate principles for the design of social institutions that are acceptable to all the reasonable members of the society, especially to those who do least well by the terms of our shared institutions. The basic institutions and laws of society—the "basic structure," in Rawls's parlance—which include the constitutional and political systems, the laws governing family life, inheritance, property, commerce, and taxation, pervasively shape people's relations and life chances. We must either justify or work to reform the institutions within which we live. The moral hope is that insofar as we can articulate mutually acceptable principles and approximate their realization in practice we can then sincerely say to one another that the institutions under which we live, and which shape our prospects and plans so deeply and pervasively, are not the results of blind social forces or mere power but rather are regulated by us with a view to our equal moral standing, and they should be freely acceptable to all.[41]

The basic structure is fully legitimate when regulated by principles of justice that everyone (or all reasonable people) should be able to endorse on reflection. Distributive justice plays a crucial role. The principle of "fair equality of opportunity" requires that society take affirmative measures—via public subsidies to education and other means—to ensure that every child has a fair chance to compete for the best jobs and positions of leadership in society, given natural talent.[42] The "difference principle" requires further that inequalities tend to be to the greatest advantage of the least well off in society. These principles expresses to the least well off that they matter as moral equals; they are designed to make the social order freely acceptable to those who do least well by its terms.

What generates and sustains powerful obligations of mutual justification and justice? The best answer seems to me to be the complex relations shared by members of political communities. The directly coercive nature of the political relations associated with states is one important consideration—a fact emphasized by Michael I. Blake, Thomas Nagel, and others—but so is the comprehensive nature of governance relations: the fact that political regulation extends across the whole of life.[43]

The governments of self-governing political communities are recognized by members to be capable of authoritatively resolving conflicts, and of taking decisions that bind us: our government acts as our agent, entering into treaties, making alliances, declaring war, and conducting various undertakings in our collective name. We acquire collective responsibilities through the actions of our government.

And so, Americans take responsibility for what happens in North Dakota and Mississippi in a way they do not for what happens in Chihuahua and Ontario. Citizens look to one another to jointly establish collective programs concerning health and welfare: they view themselves as jointly responsible for the wellbeing, the culture, and the territory of their political society, in perpetuity. As citizens of a political community we jointly create a shared jurisdiction with extensive powers and responsibilities, and we recognize that it is sustained by reciprocal duties and obligations in support of which we can reasonably expect all to do their part.

It is, moreover, hard to understand the reasonableness of making people responsible for the welfare of others without also making them responsible for their governance. It would be unreasonable to assign ongoing responsibility for the provision of health and welfare without also according the authority to regulate medicine, nutrition, parenting, safety, and education. Transplanting domestic principles of justice and the responsibilities they entail to the global level makes little sense without a commensurate transfer of governing authority, that is, absent a cosmopolitan state and a cosmopolitan political community that hardly anyone seriously argues for.

Citizens have powerful obligations of mutual concern and respect, and mutual justification, to one another because the political institutions for which they are co-responsible determine patterns of opportunities and rewards for all.[44] This could not simultaneously be true of the international society, and it is not. Membership in international bodies is mediated by membership in primary political units, namely, the member states of the United Nations or their peoples.[45] International bodies are important, and I support their further development, but they do not have anything like the broad responsibilities of states.[46] And so, as Blake has argued, borders may be morally arbitrary in one sense—they may be the product of considerable historical accident, negotiations, and pressures of all sorts—but they come to acquire moral significance on account of what takes place within them.[47]

The ground of the particular moral demands associated with distributive justice, on this view, is not our common humanity but rather the fact that with some other persons we are joined in a political community: a highly complex, largely involuntary, and morally consequential set of relations. As citizens in a legitimate political community we participate in shaping the awesome coercive powers of the state and expect our fellows to do their part in supporting these institutions, and this gives rise to powerful reciprocal obligations of mutual justification. As liberal contractualists and deliberative democrats emphasize, citizens should seek to assure themselves that the power they collectively exercise over one another is justifiable, and it should be publicly known that the political community and the arrangement of its institutions is shaped by principles that answer to the claims of all members considered as citizens with equal standing. These strong reciprocal obligations of justification are owed to those with whom we participate in a system of joint governance. "Reasonable" persons are prepared to affirm principles of fair governance given the assurance that others will likewise do so.[48]

But, cosmopolitans will retort, is not the well-being of everyone on the globe increasingly dependent on an international "basic structure" of commercial, political, and military relations? Is not the institutional basis for the membership view breaking down in light of the increasing global movement of goods, money, people, and ideas, all coordinated and regulated by international laws and organizations such as the World Trade Organization, the North American Free Trade Agreement, and rules governing property rights? Globalization, on this view, is collapsing the differences between domestic and international society, giving rise to moral relations and demands transnationally that are the same as those that exist domestically.

These are among the most interesting and vexing questions in political theory today. We want, it seems to me, to avoid two extreme positions. So-called statists often seem to minimize duties beyond borders and the moral significance of transnational relations. Cosmopolitans, on the other hand, often assimilate the moral character of international relations to domestic relations among citizens. The membership view argues that relations among citizens are special but not all-important. We can maintain that the full demands of justice are associated with membership in a political community, without taking the extreme view that outside the state there is no justice, only minimal humanitarian concern. Confusion has been created by running together the idea that *full obligations of distributive justice apply only domestically* with the very different idea that *beyond the state our moral relations, duties, and obligations to others are minimal.*

Trade relations, even as shaped and coordinated by a variety of international institutions and agreements, need not have the same moral implications as the wide array of directly and pervasively coercive institutions associated with domestic governance. Of course, fairness is relevant to trade relations and the wide array of governance regimes that do exist transnationally. Our trade agreements and international rules of property should be mutually acceptable and not generative of oppression, exploitation, and well-founded resentment. But it is at least far from obvious that repairing these serious flaws in global governance requires that we replicate domestic political institutions and relations at the global level.

Even on the membership view, we have considerable external duties and obligations, which fall into several categories. First, we have general humanitarian duties to relieve those in distress, and to intervene in the event of gross and systematic violations of human rights, insofar as we can effectively do so. As Rawls says, we should aid "burdened" societies that are incapable of decent self-rule. Such aid has a target: it aims to get societies on their feet so they can run their own affairs decently and legitimately according to their own collective choices. Surely at some point—given an appropriate target of aid—this is unobjectionable?[49]

Whatever the threshold or target is, there are countries that are considerably poorer than the United States that would seem to have passed this threshold some time ago (Portugal, for example, until recently the poorest country in Europe, still has a GDP per capita that is about half that in the United States). It is significant that India, where something like 30 percent of the population still lives on a dollar a day or less according to the World Bank, refused international aid after the tsunami disaster several years ago.

In addition, societies have general duties of fair dealing with one another, requiring nonintervention (except in cases of human rights abuse or aggressive war), nonexploitation, and nondomination, including curbing the capacity of one's citizens or corporations to exploit or dominate persons abroad. The general duty of fair dealing would include doing our fair share along with others to address common problems, including environmental issues such as global warming, disaster relief, and humanitarian assistance. We ought not to free-ride on the efforts of others to deal with common problems.

A third set of obligations concerns rectification, redress, and reform in the face of past particular histories of exploitation or domination. If our government has engaged in abusive relations with other states to their detriment, or if we have allowed our corporations to exploit or oppress poorer and weaker societies, then we acquire debts to these other societies. An account of rectification for past injustices across societies depends on the nature and extent of the injustices, so there is no general story to be told. Moreover, these last two categories argue for an additional and important derivative duty: if current institutional arrangements in the international realm facilitate or permit the domination of weak states by powerful states, then we ought to reform those institutions to curb their characteristic abuses so that their operations and effects are nonoppressive, and to facilitate the development of the poorest regions so that these common trade and political arrangements at the global level are reciprocally justifiable to participants.[50]

On the membership view, which we associate with Rawls, principles of political morality that apply domestically and internationally are different in content. We have at least some special reasons to be concerned about relative shares of wealth among citizens domestically: special reasons to want all children born in our own country to be able to compete for the best jobs and positions of leadership, special reasons to worry about some of the ways in which inequalities of wealth translate into inequalities of power and status (global power is related not only, or even mainly, to per capita wealth but also to size).[51] The idea of a "target of assistance" seems far more appropriate in the international realm. We might also apply the term "distributive justice" at the international level, so long as we recognize that the content and range of application of the appropriate principles will be different.

My sense is that a big part of what worries critics of the Rawlsian view (the membership view) is that differentiating what we owe to members and outsiders sometimes seems to be accomplished by minimizing external moral demands. There are remarks in Rawls's *Law of Peoples* that give this impression.[52] But quietism in the face of global poverty is in no way entailed by the general argument.[53] I understand Rawls to be saying that we don't have the *same* obligations of distributive justice to outsiders as we have to insiders, without (himself) saying a great deal about what we *do* owe to outsiders. I have tried to sketch some additional particulars. The membership view can take account of universal human interests and universal ethical demands, while also attributing proper significance to the demands of citizenship and the political community. This reflects a moral cosmopolitanism that is compatible with the *moral primacy for certain purposes* of nation-states, including the *special obligations* of distributive justice that we have to fellow citizens.[54]

Immigration and Domestic Justice in Context

Domestic justice demands that we craft policies that are justifiable not simply from the standpoint of aggregate welfare—or the greatest good of the greatest number. We must consider the justifiability of shared institutions from the various particular standpoints in our society, especially the standpoint of the least well off among our fellow citizens. The liberal theory of justice is egalitarian: major social institutions and policy choices ought to be judged in important part by their impact on citizens' relative standing. The political equality of citizens requires this sort of "distributive" justification: it is not reasonable to expect poorer fellow citizens to accept policy choices on the ground that they make those with the luck of superior endowment by nature and birth even better off.

Immigration is an especially complex policy arena. We have urgent reasons to shape major public policies and institutions with an eye to the distributive impact. Insofar as immigration policy helps determine our society's capacity to sustain a commitment to the principles of justice, then immigration policy should be designed with an eye toward basic justice. If immigration laws and practices foster large scale movements of people that systematically worsen the conditions of the poorest among us, then we must consider whether there are sufficiently weighty reasons to justify or excuse this.

We also have urgent reasons to assist those who are in need (in absolute terms), including very poor persons abroad. There is, of course, a variety of possible ways of fulfilling our obligations to very poor people abroad. There are also intense debates about which foreign aid programs are efficacious. Candidates for immigration are typically not the poorest of the poor, but many economic migrants do live in conditions of absolute poverty. Recent estimates suggest that Mexican high school graduates can, by leaving Mexico and finding a job in the United States, increase their income sevenfold; Mexican college graduates can increase their income ninefold.[55] Many poor Mexicans greatly improve their families' lots by working in the United States, and the same is true for Turkish workers in Europe and many others. Remittances are a substantial source of income for many developing countries.

As a matter of abstract principle, there need not be a conflict between domestic distributive justice and efforts to make good on what we owe to poor persons abroad. If we think of three distinct sets of claimants—better-off Americans, worse-off Americans, and very poor people abroad—it is clear that we could fashion our distributive and foreign policies so as to promote both domestic fairness, as understood by liberal egalitarians, and a foreign policy characterized by generous aid to the poorest of the globe and reform of the institutions for global governance. There are countries in the world—including Scandinavian countries—that do better than the United States when it comes to both social justice and foreign assistance. The question remains: Do high levels of immigration tend to undermine domestic justice?

Fundamental considerations of domestic distributive justice may seem to favor movement by the United States toward a far more restrictive immigration policy, or perhaps a policy more like the Canadian immigration policy, favoring skills and education-based priorities and curtailing those associated with family reunification, specifically as concerns adult siblings. Some economists argue, however, that skills-based immigration may not help the relative standing of the poor, especially African Americans, on account of the fact that skilled immigration raises the returns to capital, and poorer African Americans own very little capital.[56] Such reforms might or might not have the collateral effect of addressing the labor market argument, described above, and also, at least indirectly, the concerns about ethnic diversity and the median voter.

It has been remarked that of all the imaginable egalitarian policies, the attempt to foster greater social justice via immigration restrictions is the one that imposes the greatest collateral costs on the most vulnerable people.[57] Some argue that the United States cannot at acceptable cost impose far more restrictive immigration policies on account of the fact that it shares a long border with Mexico, income differentials across that long border are extremely high, and there is a long history of movement back and forth. This huge income gradient and the proximity of millions of Mexican peasants creates, it is argued, an economic pull that could only be resisted by cruel border control measures: fences and barbed wire, watch towers and guns, aided perhaps by armed vigilantes.

We must also consider the formidable collateral costs of efforts to restrict immigrants from Mexico and Latin America. The history of recent efforts to control immigration at the border is far from encouraging. Efforts to tighten border security in the late 1980s and 1990s made the immigration problem worse. As Massey, Durand, and Malone explain, tighter border security served mainly to deter migrant return more than entry, leading

Mexican workers to remain longer in the United States and to bring their families with them in many instances. Immigration and Naturalization Service enforcement measures in areas where illegal workers were highly concentrated led them to disperse across the country, making control harder and helping to nationalize the phenomenon of nonlegal migrant workers. While enforcement policies have made illegal border crossing more expensive and often cruelly dangerous, people keep coming.[58]

Creating the apparatus of a police state at the border may be too high a price to pay, even for social justice at home. But there are policy options that could curtail illegal immigration without militarizing the border and imposing the burdens of compliance on poor immigrants seeking a better life. Vigorously enforced employer sanctions, perhaps coupled with a national identity card, would impose the burdens of compliance and law enforcement on American employers. If employer sanctions succeeded in reducing the demand for illegal workers, then potential nonlegal migrants would not be tempted to risk all for the sake of a better life. This is surely the least inhumane way to curtail the hiring of nonlegal workers.

On the positive side, immigration controls that created a very tight labor market at the bottom of the wage scale could help raise wages and work conditions among the working poor. On the negative side, such changes would be a shock to millions of migrant workers and their families from Mexico and elsewhere. It could also be a shock to the American economy—indeed, to American politics and society.

Immigration and Global Development

Rich countries such as the United States also have external duties and obligations to the world's poor, as I have emphasized. So we must also consider the impact of immigration policy on sending countries. As noted above, remittances are a huge part of many sending countries' economies. Poor workers from Mexico can increase their real wages by sevenfold to ninefold by moving to the United States. But what about those who remain behind? Migrants are sometimes relatively highly skilled and enterprising: they and their relatives will benefit considerably from remittances, but the poorest in sending countries are likely to benefit less.[59] And in some cases, poor countries as a whole may suffer from a "brain drain."

The migration of *skilled labor* out of very poor countries may have negative effects at home. The loss of human capital and investment in education—the brain drain—is quite substantial in some of the poorest countries, including some in the Caribbean and West Africa, where the extent of outmigration of persons with college degrees is truly startling. In the Caribbean region in 2000, among those twenty-five years old or older, it is estimated that 41 percent of those with college degrees were living in a country belonging to the Organisation of Economic Co-operation and Development. The corresponding percentage for West Africa is 27 percent, 18 percent for East Africa, 16 percent for Central America, and 13 percent for Central Africa.[60] These figures provide reasons to worry that developing countries are losing not only important economic resources but also a sizable portion of those with the skills and education needed to sustain effective political and social institutions, and to press for political and economic reform. The loss of educated talent could inhibit both the supply and the demand for more effective institutions.[61]

Thus, if domestic distributive justice might call for Canada-style policies that favor high-skilled immigration, justice to poor sending countries may argue for low-skilled immigration, facilitation of remittances, and the encouragement of migrant return after a period of time with enhanced skills and resources.

Conclusion: In Search of the Morally Best in a Complex World

Given the various competing moral demands that I have surveyed above, it is clear enough that it will be a complex matter to discern the ethically best overall immigration policy. It will be more difficult still to enact such a set of policies.

I have argued that we ought to take seriously the proposition that recent patterns of immigration to the United States have been bad for distributive justice. Members of political communities have special obligations of distributive justice to one another. There is a prima facie case in light of these considerations for the United States to move toward a more restrictive immigration policy, perhaps especially with respect to those low-skilled immigrants who compete with the poorest Americans for jobs. John Rawls, meet Lou Dobbs.

It would be morally incumbent upon the architects of this new regime to focus enforcement on U.S. employers and not to visit harsh police-state tactics on poor workers struggling to find a better life. We might also say that in light of the costs of this shift in policy in Mexico, the United States ought to seek ways to increase bilateral aid to Mexico's poorest. Indeed, the United States does not currently do nearly enough to fulfill its duties to aid the world's poorest, and it should act as a much better world citizen in other respects as well.

However, I have also emphasized that the magnitudes of the three negative effects of immigration on social justice are uncertain and contested. While immigration policy is consequential enough to require scrutiny from the standpoint of social justice, we can also now see why many progressives regard immigration restrictions as at best a roundabout and speculative strategy for helping the least well-off Americans. Unlike progressive taxation and inheritance laws, the costs of the proposed immigration restriction fall directly on poor people. There is certainly moral paradox in a policy that is domestically progressive but globally regressive. Some argue that the exclusion of masses of poor and often dark people from our shores in the name of domestic "progressivism" smacks too strongly of a new form of apartheid.[62]

I sympathize with a package of humane and moderate proposals for immigration reform that appear at least plausibly politically feasible. But while this package of reforms addresses some major shortcomings within the current system, it does not directly speak to concerns with domestic distributive justice. The package of reforms that I have in mind is proposed by scholars Douglas Massey, Jorge Durand, and Nolan J. Malone, and it is similar to the bipartisan compromise that gained considerable support in Washington in the spring of 2007. Massey, Durand, and Malone propose increasing the annual quota of legal entry visas from Mexico from 20,000 (the current level, which is the same as for the Dominican Republic) to 60,000. The second element would be a guest worker program to regularize the temporary migration of workers and to encourage their return to their home country. Massey and his colleagues propose making 300,000 two-year work visas available per year for workers from Mexico; these would be renewable once. The bipartisan compromise in Washington would have made between 400,000 and 600,000 two-year temporary work visas available per year. Eligibility would extend to six years, but with a requirement to return home for a year between each renewal. Either of these proposals—if coupled with tough enforcement measures on U.S. employers—

would regularize the flow of migrant workers and rechannel the flow of illegal migrants into a legal flow.[63]

Finally, both Massey and his colleagues and the bipartisan bill would curtail the priorities that are now provided to family members of those who become naturalized Americans: they would eliminate the priority given to adult siblings of naturalized citizens. The scholars recommend making it easier for Mexican relatives of U.S. citizens to get tourist visas, so they can visit and return home more easily. The bipartisan bill would establish a point system giving priority in immigration to those who possess special skills that would help the U.S. economy.

This package of reforms addresses some major problems with our current system. There are currently twelve million illegal workers in the United States, and their nonlegal status makes them vulnerable to exploitation; guest worker status can be portrayed as "second-class status," but it is better than third- or fourth-class status, and it could be quite advantageous to many future migrants. The package of reforms is at least plausibly politically feasible (the proposals give something to a variety of constituencies—to business and pro-immigration groups—and there could be tougher enforcement measures).

Of course, these proposals also have a number of problems. Most seriously, the legislative compromise in Washington, in contrast with the scholars' proposals, gave a central place—and temporal priority—to border security measures. The legislative compromise called for 370 miles of border fencing, high-tech radar and surveillance towers, unmanned aerial spy planes, and 18,000 new border patrol agents. The legislative compromise foundered partly on the claim that it would have conferred "amnesty" on the millions here illegally.[64]

The package of reforms proposed by Massey, Durand, and Malone is far superior. A well-designed guest worker program would markedly improve the situations of many working people who would otherwise seek to enter the United States illegally. In addition, we should hope that guest worker programs and immigration preferences more broadly are designed so as to address the brain drain problems that seem to plague some poorer countries.

An additional reservation about the scholars' package of reforms is that the guest worker provisions would preserve some important benefits for American employers, American consumers, and better-off Americans, while regularizing a system that seems to impose downward pressure on low-wage jobs in the United States.[65] The distributive justice problem should be addressed by explicitly coupling these reforms with measures designed to improve the condition of the poorest Americans; that is, we should treat the collective surplus of these reforms as owed to the least well-off. In practice, unfortunately, it seems unlikely that more generous redistributive policies would be packaged with immigration reform, given the difficulty of securing adequate political support for either sort of reform.

Immigration policy presents conflicting demands among some of our deepest values. A vast and complicated array of policy options lie before us, and the consequences of reforms are hard to predict. Given the intensely fraught politics of immigration, it may be that the best we can do in the near future is to adjust immigration policy in reasonable ways to improve the conditions of temporary workers and to make it easier for them to work and return home.

Policies governing membership can have a significant impact on political communities' capacity to sustain a commitment to domestic social justice. It is morally incumbent on us to treat immigration policy in relation to domestic justice and to weigh the domestic distributive impact of reforms along with the impact on the global poor.

Chapter 15

Expatriatism: The Theory
and Practice of Open Borders

Chandran Kukathas

Every day, large numbers of people cross borders that separate one political jurisdiction from another. Most do so legally, though many break the law in changing jurisdictions. Many more do not cross borders, because they dare not break the law or cannot cross undetected—sometimes because they are denied permission to leave one jurisdiction, and other times because they are prohibited from entering another. Some cross borders fully aware that they are leaving one defined space and entering another, while others have no idea that anything has changed or that the imaginary lines that define distinct regions exist even in the imagination. Borders—political boundaries—are such variable things that encounters with them can be very different experiences. Entering Luxemburg from Belgium is almost always a nonevent. Entering the United States from Mexico can be very eventful. The purpose of this essay to ask why this is so, and whether it must be so. Why must some borders be so difficult to cross? Why can't the move from Mexico to the United States always be as easy as moving from Belgium to Luxemburg? Why should some people be able to move so freely and others not?

Another way to put this is to ask: Why can't all borders be open? The point of this essay is to address this question, both as a conceptual question and as a theoretical—normative—question. Its concern is the movement of people—not of goods or money—across political boundaries. In the end, it tries to offer a defense of open borders. But any such defense must rest on some account of what "open borders" means, and how such a thing is possible. Thus the aim of the essay is to offer an account of the theory and practice of open borders.[1]

Defining Borders

Any defense of open borders must begin by explaining what borders are. Borders are geographic boundaries demarcating or defining political entities or legal jurisdictions. They can be used to distinguish countries or states but can also distinguish a variety of other entities, including subnational administrative units, such as provinces, counties, boroughs, townships, municipalities, Indian reservations (United States), Indian reserves (Canada), cantons, territories, and parishes; and supranational entities (such as empires) or superstates (such as the European Union). Borders today are clearly defined boundaries that are no more than imaginary lines that do not themselves occupy any space. They thus differ from the marchlands of earlier times, when political entities were separated by border regions or borderlands—spaces that were beyond the authority of the rulers on either side. There are remnants of this past practice in the modern world in the shape of demilitarized zones—such as that between North and South Korea—but these are rarities. Borders are notional rather than physical, and can run not only across lands but also across waters, along rivers, through streets, and even through buildings.

Although borders can be delineated using physical objects or structures, this is uncommon. The Great Wall of China, the Maginot Line, the Berlin Wall, the Ceuta Border Fence between Spain and Morocco, and the physical barriers Churchill dubbed the "iron curtain" are examples of structures used to draw the boundaries between different regions. But nowadays political boundaries are established by rules or laws rather than by fences and gates. This point is a significant one because it means that opening or closing borders is not a matter of adding or removing physical objects but of changing rules. Indeed, it could even be a matter of changing legal arrangements that have nothing to do—at least not directly—with movement across borders. Barriers, when they exist at all, come in the form of controls exercised at checkpoints when borders are crossed—controls that might involve the presentation of identity papers, such as a passport, or visas, or other entry permits.

The presence of a border signifies the existence of some authority that operates within the boundaries of a demarcated territory. One of the rights this authority may have is to exclude persons from its territory, but whether or not it does will depend on the kind of entity the authority represents. In international law, states have the right to determine whether, and under what conditions, persons may enter their territories. Provinces, parishes, and towns do not typically have such rights. Nonetheless, it is worth remarking that practice varies considerably. Although in international law countries can exclude persons from their territories, this is not always a straightforward matter. For example, under the Schengen Agreement concluded among European countries in 1985 and 1990, the twenty-five countries of the European Union along with Iceland, Norway, Liechtenstein, and Switzerland adopted measures that have more or less done away with border controls. With the exception of Ireland and the United Kingdom, there are no border controls of any significance within this region of four hundred million people. The Schengen Agreement also provides for a common policy on the movement of temporary visitors, who may travel freely within the region for up to three months. At the other extreme, Sabah and Sarawak, the states of Malaysia on the island of Borneo, require even Malaysian citizens to obtain permission to enter their territories, and they impose limits on the duration of visits and on what activities visitors can engage in. Within states, other entities may also have rights to exclude: U.S. Indian reservations, for example, may restrict entry onto their territories.

More often than not, however, the authorities within borders are responsible for attending to the interests of those within their jurisdiction rather than keeping others out. Provinces, towns, and counties may determine what rights and obligations residents have without having any power to determine who may become a resident. Even nation-states might find their capacity to restrict entry to their territories limited by international and domestic law. For example, the United States, one of the nations that have adopted the norm of *jus soli*, is obliged to admit anyone who was born in its territory as a citizen. Germany, one of the nations that have adopted the norm of *jus sanguinis*, cannot easily deny German residence or citizenship to someone with German ancestry. Countries that are signatories to the 1951 Refugee Convention cannot turn away those who have landed on their territory and asked for asylum—at least, not until such a claim is legally determined to be unfounded. Sometimes, simply crossing a border can give a person rights that the authorities have no power to ignore.

A border, in sum, is a complex notion. It does not merely impose a physical or even a notional barrier to forbid or permit entry from one region to another but specifies, and in some cases works to determine, the rights and obligations individuals and authorities have. Opening and closing borders is a matter not of opening or shutting gates but of changing the working of a complex system of machinery. We should consider this machinery in more detail to try to understand what open borders could mean.

What Are Open Borders?

The openness of borders is clearly a matter of degree. How do we determine whether a border is open or closed—or at least, how open a border might be? To answer this question we need to consider the variety of ways, and the different dimensions along which, borders operate to control the movement of persons. Indeed, we need to recognize that borders can be open in some respects and closed in others. Policy can therefore easily make borders more open and yet, at the same time, more closed. This is because policy can change the terms of entry in a number of different respects. It can vary the terms by specifying (i) what kinds of people may enter and what status they may hold on entering; (ii) how long they may stay; (iii) what qualifications or characteristics they must possess to enter; and (iv) what procedures they must follow to remain within a territory. Policy can also specify (v) the number of people admitted in various categories. Nation-states typically impose strict terms in all five of these respects while other kinds of jurisdictions do not, so most of the following discussion will focus on crossing national boundaries.

Entry Status

Nation-states admit people onto their territories in a variety of categories. It is easier to enter in some categories than in others. People move as tourists, students, diplomats, military personnel, journalists, pilgrims, seasonal workers, guest workers, resident scholars, sportsmen, performers, artists, and immigrants. Most countries make it easy to enter as a tourist, more difficult to enter as a would-be resident or worker, and even more difficult to enter as an immigrant.

In each of these categories entry may be more difficult or less difficult.

Entering as a tourist is easier in some countries than in others. Consider these examples. For most people in North and South America, Australasia, and limited parts of Asia (Japan, South Korea, Malaysia, and Singapore) entering Europe requires nothing more than turning up at a European port or airport. (Everyone else must obtain a visa.) Australia is one of a number of countries that requires everyone to obtain a visa, though it has loosened this requirement by allowing citizens of some countries to obtain their visas online or through travel agents. Brazil requires Australians, Americans, and Canadians—but not British and most E.U. citizens—to obtain visas to enter the country, and charges between $50 and $200 for one. Brazil, like many countries, also requires most visitors (including Britons and E.U. nationals) to have a return ticket and to show evidence of having sufficient funds for the duration of their stay. The United States exempts members of twenty-seven countries from the requirement to obtain a visa to enter as a tourist, though only three from Asia (Brunei, Japan, and Singapore) and none from Africa or South America. It is possible to obtain a visa to travel in North Korea, but only as a part of a state-run tour—no independent travel is permitted.

Entering a country to take up employment is usually more difficult than entering it as a tourist, though the regulations governing this vary widely. Most countries, and all developed countries, require visitors to obtain permission to work, and whether or not permission is granted will depend a range of factors, from seasonal demand for particular workers, to the worker's country of origin, to status of the visitor (who might be eligible for a temporary work visa for holidaying youths). Work visas for professionals may be easy to obtain in some countries in some professions, but it is not always possible for accompanying spouses to secure work permits. In the United States, Australia, and Canada it is necessary for employers applying to hire overseas professionals to demonstrate that no appointment could be made from the ranks of the domestic workforce—though the extent to which such claims are demonstrable is doubtful, and for the most part it is the assurance of the applying employer that settles the matter.

Entering a country as an immigrant is invariably more difficult than entering it as a tourist, though here it has to be noted that there are many kinds of immigrants and many kinds of admission. Immigrants might enter the country with a view to staying temporarily but eventually returning to their homelands; or enter with a view to reuniting with family members who migrated earlier but with no intention of working; or enter with a view to establishing a second home for a part of the year; or enter with a view to settling more permanently but never becoming a citizen; or enter with an intention of becoming a full citizen. Equally, immigration policy may encourage people to enter but discourage them from coming if they would only be dependants rather than workers (and taxpayers); it might encourage them to become residents but make it difficult to become citizens; and it might welcome new citizens but require that they repudiate their former citizenship.

Entry Duration

Most states control border crossing by limiting the duration of any visit. Tourists may usually enter a country only for a limited time, even in cases when they may reenter it without difficulty within hours of leaving it. Work permits and visas also expire. Even those who enter with long-term or permanent employment secured often find that their visas expire and have to be renewed regularly. Many people have lived in countries for decades by renewing their visas every year. In particular cases, however, work visas can only be used for a fixed period before the entrant has to either change status or leave the country permanently.

Entry Qualification

States also control border crossing by restricting entry to those with the right characteristics or qualifications. Restrictions can be based on any number of factors, including ethnicity, nationality, religion, political affiliation, wealth, income, age, health, profession, and criminality. So, for example, Australia restricted entry by ethnicity in the many years while the White Australia Policy was in operation. Malaysia will not admit Israeli nationals except in special circumstances (and forbids its citizens to visit Israel). Every non-U.S. citizen entering the United States or applying for a visa is asked: "Are you or have you ever been a member of the Communist party or any organization dedicated to the violent overthrow of the United States government?" Although it is not the case that membership of a communist party automatically disqualifies one from entry, it is something that has to be satisfactorily explained. A lack of substantial wealth or high income are not in themselves going to prevent anyone from gaining permission to enter a country, but many countries, including Canada and

Singapore, will admit wealthy immigrants who can demonstrate an intention and capacity to invest in the country. People of advanced age can have their applications to immigrate to Australia turned down on the grounds that they will not live long enough to contribute enough in taxes to cover the costs they will impose on existing taxpayers. Australia has also turned away disabled would-be immigrants on the grounds that the costs of their care would outweigh the financial contribution they are likely to make over a lifetime. (There is no provision for those who wish to waive their right to public welfare in exchange for a right of entry.) Would-be visitors can be denied entry, or legal residents deported, if they are found guilty of criminal actions of varying degrees of seriousness. For example, a twenty-year-old man who had been in the United States since he was a baby was deported to Laos, his country of birth, in spite of having no family there and no knowledge of its language or culture—as a result of being found guilty of the illegal possession of a firearm.

Entrant Rights and Obligations

Finally, states can shape the pattern of border crossing by restricting or limiting the rights of outsiders, or by imposing particular duties upon them. For example, those who have entered as residents may be forbidden to work in paid employment. Those with work permits may be restricted to work with the sponsoring employer and prohibited from changing jobs. Spouses of workers may be forbidden to work. Those free to work may find it impossible to work in their fields because their qualifications are not recognized. Those with or without qualifications may find it difficult to compete with the local labor force because labor laws, including minimum-wage laws, do not allow them to offer their services at a lower price. In some countries noncitizens may not own certain forms of property—for example, Thailand and Singapore restrict the rights of foreigners to buy land or residential homes that are not apartments in multiapartment buildings. Foreigners can also find they are limited by being ineligible for certain forms of employment (notably in government), ineligible for social security benefits, and ineligible to participate in the political process (for example, by voting in some or all elections). In some countries foreign residents are prohibited from commenting on local politics, on pain of deportation. Foreign nationals may also face reporting requirements, having to present themselves regularly to immigration officers, to inform authorities of changes of address, and to register their arrivals and departures. Penalties for compliance failures can include deportation and loss of any right of reentry.

Entry Quotas

Most states employ some measures to restrict the numbers of people entering and leaving the country. Though tourist numbers are not typically limited, tourism is controlled by states for various reasons. For example, Nepal tries to limit the number of people trying to climb Mount Everest by imposing high fees on mountaineers. Countries where the volume of tourist traffic puts pressure on important sites have considered trying to limit entry. And Western countries generally make it more difficult for people from poor countries to enter even as tourists because of the risk of overstaying. But by and large, tourism is too lucrative to be limited. Entry in other categories, however, is often substantially limited. The United States admits foreign workers in a variety of visa categories but has firm limits in most of them. It also admits many people as permanent residents through the green card lottery, though no more than 55,000 are awarded each year. Australia has varied its intake of immigrants each year but has tried to keep the numbers within firm limits. It also has special places for humanitarian cases and refugees, though again these are limited in number, and each year many are turned away because the quota has been filled.

Open Borders

In the light of these observations about the way in which border crossings and border crossers are dealt with, what can we say about what open borders are? The answer is that, if the openness of borders is a matter of degree, borders can be more or less open in a variety of ways. People can enter countries with a view to visit, to visit and work, to study, to study and work, to reside, to reside and work, to perform, preach, or conduct research, or to join the host society as a new citizen. State policy can open borders in one or more respects while closing it in others. It might make entry easier by granting more visas or removing visa requirements, by lowering visa costs, by widening the scope of visa waiver programs, and even by ceasing negative advertising.[2] Yet at the same time it might make it more difficult

Table 15.1 Countries/States

	1	2	3	4	5	6	7	8
Entry	Yes	Yes	Yes	No	*No*	*No*	Yes	*No*
Participation	Yes	Yes	No	No	***No***	***(Yes)***	***No***	***(Yes)***
Membership	Yes	No	No	No	*(Yes)*	*(Yes)*	*(Yes)*	*No*

to get work permits or permission to open businesses. It might increase the number of student visas but impose stronger requirements that students must return to their home countries, or make it harder for students to work to support themselves. It might make it easier to enter the country to work but make it harder to renew a work permit. It might make it easier to become a resident but harder to become a citizen, or easier to become a citizen but harder to enter in the first place.

If the openness of borders is such a variable thing, one important problem then is the question of what really matters if one advocates open borders. For the sake of simplifying the problem let us say that there are three dimensions along which the issue can be considered: entry, participation, and membership. The first dimension, entry, covers the freedom of foreigners to enter and reside in a society. Participation covers foreigners' right to take up employment or to trade or open up a business. Membership covers the right of foreigners to become more closely involved in the society—perhaps acquiring the right to take government employment, or participate in elections, or even stand for public office.

A society with fully open borders would be one in which entry, participation, and membership were all possible. A less open society would be one in which entry and participation were possible but membership not. A much less open society would make entry possible but not participation and membership. A society with completely closed borders would not permit entry, participation, or membership. Table 15.1 presents the options that are conceivable. Along the three dimensions there are eight possible kinds of country, distinguished by degree of openness of borders. Country 1 has the most open borders and country 4 the least. Countries 5, 6, 7, and 8 are not feasible possibilities. Country 5 cannot offer membership to foreigners if it will not allow them to enter or participate. Country 6 cannot offer participation, let alone membership, if it will not allow entry. Country 7 cannot really offer membership if it will not allow participation, even if it will allow entry—and is therefore no different from country 3.

Table 15.2

	A	B	C
Entry	Easy	Hard	Very hard
Participation	Hard	Very hard	Easy
Membership	Very hard	Easy	Hard

Table 15.3

	A	B	C
Entry	5	2	8
Participation	5	7	2
Membership	5	9	2

Note: 1 = Easy, 10 = Very hard

This presentation of the possibilities obviously simplifies matters considerably. After all, as has already been noted, entry, participation, and membership are all a matter of degree. Nonetheless, it is worth noting that permitting entry is the first requirement for open borders, since participation is not possible without it; and the right to participate is the second requirement if we assume that membership, by its very nature, means having full rights to enter and participate. To lose the right to participate is to lose one's rights of membership.[3]

To put the case for open borders, then, is really to put the case for lowering or ending restrictions on foreign entry into, participation in, and membership of a state or polity. Borders are more open as it becomes easier to enter, participate, and join. However, what is more difficult to determine is how to interpret an easing of restrictions in some respects but a tightening of restrictions in others. Consider, for example, the three countries A, B, and C, in Table 15.2. It's not clear which of the three has the most open borders. Country A is easy to enter but very hard to join as a citizen; B makes it easy to acquire citizenship but very hard to win the right to work; C is hard to enter but easy to gain working rights in (if you can get in, you can work), yet still difficult to join as a citizen.

Or consider another presentation of the same problem, in Table 15.3, with a numerical weighting given to indicate the degree of difficulty of earning rights to enter, participate in, or become a member of a polity.

Would a move from A to B amount to a move to a regime with more open or less open borders? Is C more open or less open than B or A? To the extent that it is difficult to say, the notion of open borders is unclear or indeterminate. To say which regime has more open or less open borders we need a theory of open borders. This means a theory that explains which restrictions or limitations are more important than others. To the extent that such a theory is a normative theory, it must offer an account of what kinds of restrictions are more defensible or less defensible morally.

Toward a Theory of Open Borders

I want to argue that the most important dimensions along which borders should be open are those of entry and participation. Membership is not a trivial matter, but morally speaking it does not matter nearly as much as the freedom or the opportunity to enter and participate in a society. It is restrictions on entry and participation that are of most concern from the perspective of an advocate of open borders. Before presenting the case for this view, however, I want to look briefly at the question of the purpose (and justification) of closing borders, and then at the prima facie case for opening them.

Arguments for Closed Borders

The very important point to note at the outset is that very few people (or states) advocate completely closed borders. We have already established that the openness or closedness of a border is a matter of degree. The debate is really about how open or closed borders should be. So my analysis of the case for closed borders is of the case for substantial limitations on entry into, participation in, or membership of a society—with the term "substantial limitations" serving to specify only loosely the extent of restriction of the movement of people.

Numerous arguments are advanced for closing borders, but most of them are variations or versions of the following.

1. *Homogeneity arguments.* The existing society has a form or character that would be eroded or corrupted if any or too many people of a different kind were admitted, so entry has to be limited. The White Australia Policy rested in part on such an argument. American resistance to Irish immigra-

tion in the nineteenth century drew on it as well. Japan's reluctance to admit its Korean members to citizenship provides yet another example of this thinking. Nowadays, many countries are concerned about admitting "too many" people from particular groups, or people who are not members of the dominant group in the country, in case the change in the composition of the society proves problematic. This might mean concerns about admitting some nationalities, members of some religions (such as Islam), or people who speak other languages. Sometimes the argument is that it is important to preserve the existing culture or tradition embodied in the nation, so that it might endure over generations to come. The loss of Japaneseness or French Canadian society would be a loss in itself, and measures taken to prevent the dilution and erosion of these societies are therefore justified. A different argument is that a society that admits too many people who are very different will find it lacks the harmony and cohesion it once had. This is bad in itself, for it means social conflict. It is also unfair on existing members of society who might find their surrounds and their lives changing rapidly around them till they find themselves living in a land that is alien to them. The admission of foreigners should be restricted to ensure that a homogeneous society does not become diverse in unfamiliar or uncomfortable ways—even if diversity is not to be repudiated entirely.

2. *Protection arguments.* Closing borders protects some locals from foreigners in a number of ways. Economically, it gives locals a better chance of employment if the extent of the labor market is limited. It also raises domestic wages for the same reason. This clearly protects low-wage employees, but it can also benefit those higher up on the salary scale, depending on what kinds of entry restrictions are in place. Whatever the case may be, the argument is the need to provide locals with economic protection against competition from foreigners. It is important to note, however, that a choice has to be made here to protect some locals at the expense of others, since those who might benefit from competitive foreign labor would be disadvantaged. Protection arguments are therefore always arguments not for protecting locals in general but for protecting some (possibly a majority of) locals. Favored candidates for protection might include particular industries, particular professions, and particular cultural traditions.

3. *Ecological arguments.* Too large or too rapid an increase in the size of the domestic population may be harmful to the local ecology. Some Australian environmentalists argue that the continent is overpopulated and that its delicate natural ecology will be destroyed by population growth (or,

some argue, unless the population is not substantially reduced). It is also argued that population increase might leave domestic society unable to cope with the resulting pressure on society's infrastructure, since it will lead to more congestion, more pollution, and a strain on public services, including transport, sewerage, water, and power.

4. *Social control arguments.* Any stable society, the argument goes, needs to be able to keep control of its population to guard against criminality, political subversion, and terror. This requires close monitoring of the population, and to that extent there must be restrictions on movement in and out of the country as well as a close watch on movements within it by local and national authorities.

5. *Rent preserving arguments.* Members of any country have benefits that accrue to them in virtue of their having access to opportunities outsiders do not. They enjoy the rents that come to those who are advantageously placed. Norwegian and Kuwaiti citizens are the beneficiaries of the wealth that comes to them from the oil that lies within the national boundaries of their states. But such rents may exist not just in the form of access to natural resources but in the shape of the society itself. Someone lucky enough to move to the United States from Haiti will be able to enjoy the gains he can make by working or trading in a stable and prosperous economy with secure property rights and a good measure of personal safety provided by the rule of law. Someone unable to leave Haiti may have limited opportunities to make any gains if everyone around her is poor, her environment is unsafe, and the polity is unstable. Those who live in societies in which they enjoy the rents that go with residence or membership can argue that they need to preserve their past and future gains by limiting access to those rents.

6. *Golden goose arguments.* A related argument is that foreign entry to a society should be restricted if too great an influx of outsiders might change or erode the traditions or practices that made the society prosperous in the first place. People from poor countries are poor often not because their countries lack resources but because their economic and political systems are ramshackle. But if they move to prosperous countries with attitudes or convictions that lead to the breakdown of the economic and political systems of their new societies, everyone loses. Democracies with generous welfare systems might be particularly vulnerable if large numbers of poor immigrants become voters and vote themselves more benefits. The golden goose is killed by foreigners pressuring it for more eggs.

7. *Social justice arguments.* In order to promote social justice within a country, this argument goes, it may be necessary to restrict entry. This is partly because the institutions of social justice can only function if they are recognized as legitimate by the population, and an influx of foreigners might lead to people questioning their obligation to contribute to sustaining those institutions. This may mean that the welfare of outsiders will have to be sacrificed to some degree as they are denied admission, but if social justice matters, then borders will have to be closed at least to some degree— perhaps to a considerable degree.

Arguments for Open Borders

To put the case for opening borders it is necessary to address the arguments for closing them. But before going on to do this it would be useful to note what general reasons there might be for not restricting the movement of people from one country to another. There are several arguments worth considering.

1. *Arguments from freedom.* Closing borders means restricting individual freedom. It means preventing people from moving from one place to another and denying people the opportunity to trade, or sell their labor, or enjoy friendships that are important to them. While this is not a consideration that is necessarily decisive, it is significant nonetheless. Any justification for closed borders has to offer reasons strong enough to warrant the interference with individual freedom—both of those who wish to move and of those who are unable to welcome outsiders as partners, neighbors, colleagues, or employees.

2. *Arguments from global prosperity.* The free movement of people, it can be argued, can contribute enormously to global prosperity. In the barest economic terms, the mobility of factors of production is a good thing, for it allows resources to be deployed where they are most productive. This holds not only for money or physical forms of capital but also for labor or for human capital more generally.

3. *Arguments from justice.* Though it might be argued that social justice requires closed borders, it can also be argued that it is unjust to deny many people, especially the world's poor, access to the benefits of moving to places where they can take a greater share of the wealth the world can provide. Even if wealthy countries begin to contribute much more in foreign aid to poor countries, it is unlikely that this will do nearly as much to

make the poor more prosperous as would allowing them to move, enrich themselves, and enrich others by remitting a portion of their newfound wealth to their distant friends and relatives.

4. *Arguments from humanity.* Even if justice does not mandate sharing national wealth with people from other societies, a principle of humanity suggests that that it is difficult to justify turning the poorest people away from the doors of the richest societies. It bears noting that, on the whole, the well off and the rich have little trouble crossing most borders. The purpose of closed borders is usually to keep out the poor. Given that refugee camps around the world are homes to millions of people, unable to return whence they came but with nowhere decent to go, a policy of closed borders looks difficult to justify.

5. *Arguments from sectional advantage.* Particular groups stand to gain from open borders. Typically, some business enterprises stand to benefit from an influx of immigrants who increase the size of the labor pool and thus push wages downward.

How to Open Borders

What should be evident from the two sets of arguments above is that it would be difficult to make a decisive case for open borders. The problem is that the kinds of arguments in favor of open borders do not, in themselves, supply indefeasible reasons for not closing them. Nor do they, in themselves, undermine (let alone refute) the arguments for restrictions on the movement of people. How can a case for open borders be made?

The most important thing to recognize is that any argument for open or closed borders (remembering that openness is a matter of degree) must involve trading off some considerations against others. The defenders of closed borders do have a point (or a number of points). Opening borders can lead to a loss of homogeneity, may disadvantage some groups, will mean sharing some of the rents currently enjoyed exclusively by a country's residents, and could make it more difficult to sustain institutions of social justice. But equally, there is no denying that border controls limit freedom, impose inefficiencies on the working of the global labor market, amount to unjust treatment of at least some of those who are excluded from particular societies they wish to enter, and require neglecting the needs of some people in desperate need. The question is really not so much one of whether borders should be open or closed *simpliciter* but of how the tradeoff should be made. A theory of open borders, therefore, must be a theory of how to trade off the values that mandate openness against the ones that suggest closure. In the remainder of this essay I want to offer the outline of how such a tradeoff should be made, and to draw out the implications of such a view.

A defensible theory of open borders, I suggest, is one that gives little weight to homogeneity arguments, even less weight to protection arguments, and zero weight to rent-preserving arguments. Greater weight is given to golden goose arguments and also to social justice arguments. The reason for giving little weight to homogeneity considerations is that, in the end, what matters is how the lives of individuals go; the color of a society (literally as well as figuratively) does not matter. It may matter to individuals if a society is transformed so rapidly that their lives become disrupted and even intolerable, but it does not matter whether the next generation is different from this if the next generation is content with its character. The preservation of homogeneity is of little importance in itself.

The reason for giving little weight to protection arguments is that using border controls to protect some groups within a society usually means disadvantaging other groups within the same society. It may be that some groups that are particularly poorly off have some claim to being protected, but even protecting them may be at the expense of others who are just as poorly off and who would gain by the contributions of outsiders. It is hard to see why this would be justified. Protecting groups who are well off to the disadvantage of other members who are well off also seems to be no especially good reason to prevent outsiders from entering a society. It is not a good reason to open borders, either, because lifting restrictions gives advantages to particular groups.

The reason for giving no weight to rent-preserving arguments is that it is difficult to see why the fact that one already enjoys certain advantages is any reason why one should keep it. There may not be any reason to confiscate someone's wealth even if that wealth is just the result of good fortune. But it is hard to see why such a person would be justified in denying others the opportunity to enrich themselves also.

A good measure of importance should be attached to golden goose arguments, since the possibility that an influx of people would undermine or destroy the institutions that made the society attractive to foreigners may be a serious one. In practice, it may be that the number of foreign entrants needed to make this a real concern may be much higher than the number likely to try to visit or immigrate. Nonetheless, the fact that an influx in such numbers is in principle possible may serve to set an outer limit on the openness of borders.

Some importance should also be attached to social justice arguments. Though these may be criticized on a variety of grounds, the salient point is that if the question of justice is going to be raised it is at least an open question what is the relevant context within which justice in distribution is to be considered. While many universalists argue that justice must be global in scope, there is also a substantial case for viewing justice as requiring the existence of an ethical community. Conceding the significance of social justice arguments is a way of recognizing that there is a tradeoff to be made between doing justice within societies and doing justice across societies. It might be tempting to deny that there is a tradeoff involved, and that justice only applies in one of these contexts. But such a conclusion seems to fly in the face of a dilemma that is both significant and real.

Finally, some weight should be given to social control arguments. If the existence of states or polities is taken as a given, then there has to be some recognition of their need to do what is necessary to preserve their integrity. For this they may need to monitor population movements to some degree and have some power to keep out criminals and political subversives.[4] Once again, this supplies a criterion for closing borders to some degree but not for limiting movement in any substantial way.

The tradeoffs among these considerations is only one side of the story. The other side is the matter of whether borders are to be open or closed with respect to entry, participation, and membership. If any significant weight is given to social justice and social control arguments in favor of closing borders, then it becomes important that existing members of states must retain the capacity not only to govern but also to limit the extent to which outsiders can acquire the capacity to do so. Moreover, they will need the capacity to limit the ability of outsiders to enter society and take advantage of the benefits of participation and membership without making any reciprocal contribution. This means that there may be a case for closing borders in the sense of limiting access to citizenship and welfare entitlements, but less justification for limiting entry into the society or restricting rights of participation in economic and civil life. This does not mean it would be justified to limit indefinitely a newcomer's access to full membership and all the political and welfare rights this might involve. Here again there is a tradeoff: if borders are to be as open as possible but complete openness in all respects is not feasible, then membership should be forgone in return for greater opportunity for entry and participation.

The Price of Open Borders

This way of defending open borders will not be congenial to some of its advocates. One of the most prominent political theorists defending open borders, Joseph Carens, has indeed suggested that the case for open borders is best presented as resting on a theory of democratic justice.[5] A just society, in his view, can offer no good reasons for excluding some people from full membership—and considerations of feasibility are, in the end, considerations that take us away from answers to the question of what is morally justified in some deeper sense. The argument offered here, I think Carens would say, yields to concerns of political strategy and so, ultimately, does not offer the best moral argument for open borders.

Nonetheless, I suggest that this is the best way of thinking about open borders and how they can be justified. This is because the morality of political life is the morality of tradeoffs, not the morality of perfect justice. There is politics because people hold different values and also rank or weight differently the values they share. The existence of states, and therefore of borders, is a reflection of this very fact. In a perfectly just world, if such a thing could be imagined, there would be no open borders because there would be no borders and no states. If we begin our inquiry into the matter of open borders with the assumption that states and borders are fixed points in the moral and political universe, then any answer we give the question of how open borders can be must be an answer that is consistent with the continued existence of states and borders. And it must be consistent with an understanding of human motives and human behavior that gives the existence of the state its point. The state in the end is not simply an administrative unit dedicated to the task of administering to technical matters of social organization; it is a political entity that reflects that fact of human disagreement and conflict.

That said, however, this account of open borders will also be greeted skeptically from the perspective of those who would see it as much too sanguine about the feasibility of open borders. Can borders really be open such that entry and participation are fairly permitted (even as rights of membership are difficult to acquire), without great pressure being put on the institution of the state as more people enter its domain? If it is the business of the state to bring about social justice within the polity, how will it attend to the concerns of full citizens and also address the demands of foreign participants in the life of the society? The answer, I think, is that in reality states will always struggle with this problem and will respond by keeping borders more tightly closed. To open borders, from the state's point of view, is always to invite trouble.

This essay began with the question of how open borders could be. It has tried to answer that question primarily through a conceptual analysis of the idea of a border. The ethical conviction underlying the essay is that open borders—a world in which people could move about freely without being hindered from residing or working where they pleased—are highly desirable. The conclusion it reaches, however, is that there is a limit to how open borders can be if they are to remain borders at all.

Chapter 16

Citizenship and Free Movement

Rainer Bauböck

As a set of institutional norms and political beliefs liberal democracy has no serious contemporary rivals.[1] But, as many have noted, there are tensions between the two elements of this compound. One of these tensions concerns freedom of movement. For liberalism, this is a very important value, and political authorities that restrict free movement must have strong reasons to do so. From a democratic perspective, the strongest one is that states must have the power to control immigration in order to maintain the conditions for self-government and equal citizenship.

Immigration controls are often defended by other reasons that aim at maximizing economic utility for the destination country or at preserving its cultural homogeneity. From a liberal perspective these arguments are suspicious because of their obvious partiality or their incompatibility with a commitment to pluralism. For those who value freedom and equality and who believe that democracy is the best way to promote these values, the argument from citizenship is the most powerful one. But democratic polities that are liberal must at the same time strive toward expanding freedom of movement whenever the reasons for restricting it are attenuated. In this essay I explore how the tension could be made productive for this liberal goal by considering citizenship as an argument not only for closing borders but also for opening them.

I regard the citizenship argument for controlling immigration as indeed quite strong and I will endorse it against the two main arguments for global freedom of movement, which refer to positive duties of global social justice and to negative duties of states to refrain from restricting basic liberties, respectively. This controversy has been going on for quite some time,[2] and it is hard to say anything new and original. Several protagonists have recently suggested sophisticated approaches that attempt to reconcile some of the conflicting values.[3] I will comment on these only briefly. My main goal is to explore whether both normative defenses and critiques of immigration controls may have misconstrued the citizenship argument.

Many theorists accept that a democratic conception of citizenship provides reasons for legitimate immigration control as well as for more generous admissions compared with current state practices.[4] I want to take this approach a step further by showing that citizenship not only supports admission priorities within regimes of general immigration control but may also become a reason for expanding general rights and spaces of free movement beyond state borders. If my argument succeeds, then liberal and democratic norms concerning free movement can be reconciled, at least under favorable conditions and in the long run.

The second section provides some empirical groundwork by demonstrating that free movement rights across international borders are currently attached to multiple citizenship in a broad sense, which exists both in a vertically nested constellation in the European Union and in horizontally overlapping constellations between states linked through migration. In the following section I suggest a typology of territorial and personal scopes of free movement rights. The fourth section considers the two arguments for global freedom of movement. The following section discusses citizenship-based defenses of immigration control, while the sixth section shows how the same perspective supports territorial admission of specific categories of persons and general freedom of movement within regional unions of independent states. The final section discusses how these partial regimes of free movement could be expanded.

Nested and Overlapping Citizenships

Most defenders and critics of immigration control share a crucial background assumption about the present world that they build into their normative arguments.[5] They consider the conditions for free movement within a world where: (a) all land is divided into separate state territories in such a way that for each human being who is physically present in a particular place there is one and only one political authority whose laws apply to him or her, and (b) where these political authorities have legal powers to control immigration into such territories.

These are factual assumptions, not normative ones. Proponents of free movement may think that states do not have moral rights to control immigration, but they rarely question that in the current international system they do have positive legal rights to control it. States' de facto powers may not fully match their de jure powers, but irregular immigration is exactly that: it is irregular rather than an exercise of regular free movement rights.

What is problematic about these apparently self-evident assumptions? In a first step, we may question them from a historical perspective. States have not always attempted to control immigration. The large empires of the past had moving frontiers rather than stable territorial borders, and they were generally much more concerned about military control of their territory to prevent incursions by rival political powers or armed "barbarians" than about traders or craftsmen who entered their territories for purposes of peaceful commerce. While free movement across external borders or within the large areas of wilderness or agricultural land was hardly politically constrained, immigration and emigration were tightly controlled in urban centers that were separated from their hinterlands through city walls and border guards. In the sixteenth and seventeenth centuries governments that adhered to economic doctrines of mercantilism regarded the domestic workforce as one of their most important economic resources that needed to be protected by restricting emigration rather than immigration.[6] While the 1648 Treaty of Westphalia is commonly regarded as the birth of the modern international system, in which separate territories and distinct populations are allocated to sovereign states, the idea that states not only have a general right to control immigration but need actual powers to do so gained acceptance only much later, during World War I, when international passports were introduced for reasons of military security.[7] In Europe and America, the second half of the nineteenth century was a period when free movement across state borders was still much more frequently constrained by emigration restrictions than by immigration controls.

The long time gap between the emergence of norms of state sovereignty and the introduction of generalized immigration control highlights an important theoretical distinction between two quite separate functions of political borders: the demarcation of territorial jurisdiction, on the one hand, and the political control of flows, on the other hand. The first and defining function of a political border is to determine the geographical space within

which a political power or authority attempts to enforce collectively binding decisions. In a second sense a border is a site where political powers
attempt to regulate flows of goods and services, money and capital, information and ideas, and people across distinct territorial jurisdictions.[8] Governments' claims to territorial jurisdiction do not necessarily imply or
require any specific powers of control over flows. The power to enforce
laws in a territory and the legitimacy to do so are prior to, and in principle
independent from, the regulation of flows. Open borders must not be confused with the absence of borders.

A political authority may decide not to exercise its control powers because it regards a certain free flow as beneficial for the public good (as
liberal governments generally do with regard to trade of goods and services), or because restricting a flow would violate a basic liberty that liberal
governments are committed to protect (e.g., the freedom of information
and exchange of ideas). In other cases, a territorial authority may not have
any legitimate powers to control a flow in the first place, because these
powers belong to another authority. In occupied territories, such as Germany, Austria, and Japan after World War II or the Palestinian Territories
since 1967, the control over flows, specifically those of people, is largely
exercised by foreign governments, while domestic authorities enjoy only
limited powers of territorial self-administration.

More interesting for my argument is the case of political authorities
governing a territory that is nested within a larger jurisdiction. Local governments of towns and regional governments of provinces or federal states
generally lack legal and political powers to regulate free movement at their
borders. Member states of the European Union have waived their powers
to control immigration by citizens of the other member states. The members of the Schengen agreement have moreover agreed to dismantle border
controls inside the Schengen area. The European free movement regime
still has many exceptions. E.U. citizens' right to settle in other member
states depends on their being employed or self-employed or having health
insurance.[9] Third-country nationals must first gain long-term residence
status in one member state before they can move freely to another one.[10]
Since 2004, several governments have restricted free access to employment
in their countries for the citizens of new member states during an extended
transition period of up to seven years. Finally, internal border controls in
the Schengen area can be temporarily reintroduced if a government claims
that there is a significant risk to its national security. The E.U. regime of

free movement across the borders of independent states is still exceptional in the present world, but it is not without contemporary precedents. Already before joining the European Union, the United Kingdom and Ireland as well as the Union of Nordic Countries had similar agreements, with even more extensive sets of mobility rights.

There is a much less noticed but rapidly expanding regime of free movement across international borders between states that are not bound together in an economic or political union but are connected through migration flows. Multiple nationality entails a right to unconditional admission and immediate access to full citizenship rights in several independent states. The proliferation of multiple nationality since the mid-twentieth century is partly an unintended outcome of states acting independently of each other in determining their respective citizens, and partly the result of changing international norms. Dual citizenship used to be regarded as an evil of the same kind as statelessness, since it could lead to conflicts between states and to cumulative rights and obligations for individuals. These concerns have been much weakened.[11]

Dual citizenship is mainly generated through three mechanisms.[12] First, the diffusion of international human rights norms of gender equality has led most states to modify their nationality laws so that citizenship can be transmitted jure sanguinis by descent from the father's side as well as from the mother's. Today children from binational marriages are therefore in most cases dual citizens. Second, a smaller but growing number of countries also grant some entitlements to citizenship derived from birth in the territory (jus soli). In these countries, children born of two foreign parents will in addition acquire the nationality of their country of birth. Third, a growing number of states also tolerate—de jure or de facto—dual citizenship acquired through naturalization for both immigrants, who no longer have to renounce a previous nationality, as well as for emigrants, who are not deprived of their external citizenship when becoming full citizens of their country of settlement.

In this essay I want to explore whether current provisions for free movement within unions of states and across international borders for multiple citizens could be seen as steps toward global freedom of movement. One could make this argument on pragmatic grounds of feasibility by claiming that states are plainly unwilling to enter into global agreements on free movement but may be more inclined to join or expand the more particularistic arrangements of union citizenship and multiple citizenship. I am, however, not primarily interested in making a "realistic" proposal for political progress.[13] Instead, I will consider migration rights derived from citizenship in a world where political communities are no longer as clearly separate as current political theories presuppose. My claim is that even if we grant normative objections against global freedom of movement that refer to the importance of protecting spaces for democratic citizenship, these same reasons may generate quite extensive rights to free movement where political jurisdictions are vertically nested within each other and where citizenship affiliations to distinct polities overlap horizontally.

This shift in the background assumptions about the world to which theories of free movement apply is partly based on facts and partly inspired by norms. We need to study how present institutions of territorial sovereignty and democratic citizenship have changed in order to better understand the context in which our normative arguments about free movement apply. But I want to suggest also normative reasons why democratic states should be willing to form regional unions and to accept multiple citizenships and the free movement rights that come with these. In this sense I regard the transformation of the Westphalian model not only as a matter of fact but also as supported by normative arguments.

For some, promoting nested and overlapping citizenships conjures up the nightmare of a neomedieval world with blurred and shifting political boundaries and multiple allegiances to competing political authorities.[14] In such a world there might be more freedom of movement, but there would also be much less individual security and fewer spaces for stable democracy. Democracy does indeed require stable territorial borders and determinate political authority.[15] However, it is a conceptual error to believe that these two conditions require independent territorial jurisdictions and exclusive individual memberships.

The first condition says that territorial borders must be stable over time. If states could still freely trade territories with each other, or if citizens could periodically vote whether the region where they live ought to join a neighboring state or become independent, then the negative effects of indeterminate territorial authority would be produced diachronically. Stable territorial borders are a precondition for holding together regional majorities and minorities by providing both with incentives for power sharing as an alternative to majority tyranny and minority exit. Stable borders are also a prerequisite for regional social justice that secures common minimum standards for all citizens across regions with unequal economic resources. More broadly, in order to be willing to accept temporary political defeat and to sacrifice personal preferences for some public good, citizens must be able to imagine a democratic polity as an intergenerational community associated with the same political territory for a long-term future.[16] This requirement becomes stronger the more politically integrated a federation or union is. For example, the British government has accepted a unilateral right of self-determination for Northern Ireland, whereas successive Spanish governments of different political colors have consistently rejected similar claims by the government of the autonomous Basque community. The Treaty of Lisbon (signed on December 13, 2007 and in force since December 1, 2009) includes an exit clause that introduces a procedure under which member states could leave the European Union. There is no need to rehearse here the extensive political theory debates on secession. My point is simply that nested citizenship does not imply that each polity nested within a larger one can freely determine to change its border from an internal to an external one.[17]

The second condition suggests that democracy cannot be stable when several independent governments claim territorial authority within the same territory. Such overlapping territorial jurisdictions are the defining feature of condominiums, in which territorial power is shared horizontally between independent governments. Today condominiums are rare and, indeed, inherently unstable.[18] However, this objection does not apply to vertically nested territorial authorities. In such federal arrangements, governments at different levels are not independent of each other, since their powers are regulated within a shared constitutional framework. Federalism simply adds a territorial division of powers to the functional one between legislature, executive, and judiciary. Under federal arrangements, a plurality of authorities within the same territory is therefore compatible with democratic stability. Independently of whether we want to use the contested label "federal" for the European Union, a politically integrated union of independent states can meet the second condition for the same reasons federal states can.

In a similar way, a plurality of citizenships for migrants is compatible with democracy under transnational arrangements that determine which rights will be protected and which duties can be enforced by which state. Suppose for the sake of argument that citizens of a union and multiple citizens with a third-country nationality are in all respects treated as all other citizens of the state in which they currently reside and have only the one additional right of being able to move freely into another member state of the union or a third country that recognizes them as citizens. There would be no external challenge whatsoever to the full territorial jurisdiction of any of the states involved.

The idea that internal territorial sovereignty must be absolute in this way is, however, itself problematic. It is at odds with present realities in the European Union, which is clearly more than merely an association of states for the purpose of free movement, and it is also indefensible in a world where many people have ongoing social, cultural, economic, and political ties to external countries from which they have come and to which they may want to return. Both union citizenship for sedentary populations and multiple citizenship for migrants generate additional rights that individuals enjoy as citizens of the union or of a third country, such as the franchise in elections for the European Parliament or in migrants' countries of origin. Nested and overlapping democratic communities of this kind may undermine traditional notions of territorial sovereignty, but should be embraced as an extension of democratic principles to political constellations that transcend the nation-state.

A Typology of Free Movement Rights

After this outline of the newly emerging constellations of regional union and multiple citizenship between independent states, let me now consider more closely what kind of rights are involved in freedom of movement. Individuals enjoy freedom of movement in the general sense when there are no laws or administrative controls that prevent them from leaving a current place of residence and from taking up residence elsewhere. As I am concerned here with rights rather than opportunities for free movements, I will not consider other obstacles such as natural barriers (mountains, deserts, water) and social constraints (social and cultural norms or a lack of economic resources and opportunities).

Where there is a political or administrative border between places of departure and destination, freedom of movement is composed of three distinct elements: a right of exit, a right of entry, and a right to settlement at the destination.[19] Depending on which of these elements are included, we find in the literature three different conceptions of free movement. The weakest one associates it only with the right of free exit.[20] In his essay on

Table 16.1 Territorial Scope and Personal Scope of Free Movement Rights

Territorial Scope/Personal Scope	Global	Interstate	Intrastate
Human beings	A	B	C
All citizens or residents	D	E	F
Groups or individuals	G	H	I

"perpetual peace" Kant defends a somewhat stronger right to visit other places, which combines exit and entry rights.[21] In a broader sense, however, I am not free in my choice of destination if I have no right to remain there and can be expelled on the sole ground that my time is up.

Free movement rights can be restricted in two basic ways: by limiting them to a specific territory or to specific categories of persons.[22] Taking independent states as the basic units of the global political system, we can distinguish three territorial scopes of free movement. The narrowest scope is confined to the territories of a single state, a broader one covers the territories of several states, and the largest scope extends to the whole globe. In an analogous manner, free movement can be enjoyed by wider or narrower categories of persons. The most inclusive scope conceives freedom of movement as a universal human right. In narrower arrangements only citizens or residents of a state enjoy this right. And in the most restrictive versions free movement becomes a privilege of certain groups or individuals that is not granted to other citizens. Combining the dimensions of territorial scope and personal scope generates nine theoretical types of free movement, as indicated in Table 16.1.

If one assumes, as I do, that free movement is a very important liberty that has both instrumental and intrinsic value, one can then decide *a priori* how liberals should rank these various categories (e.g., according to their distance from the utopian ideal A). I do not think, however, that any such *a priori* judgment is helpful. Instead, we have to take the nine categories one by one and consider how they might apply in specific contexts and which norms and institutions could support them. I will, however, not go into any detail here, because it is not my aim to match this theoretical typology with empirical cases. The point of this exercise is instead to highlight some particularistic arrangements that are rarely considered in normative debates, to discuss their legitimacy, and to situate them within the wider spectrum of free movement rights in order to find ways toward universal freedom of movement.

Cell A in Table 16.1 represents universal freedom of movement, which entails both unlimited territorial and unlimited personal scope. This is a liberal ideal but clearly a utopian, or at least a very long-term, goal. The only universal human right to free movement that is currently recognized in international law is represented by cell C. This is the right of "everyone lawfully within the territory of a State" to "liberty of movement and freedom to choose his residence" within that territory,[23] which presupposes the power of states to determine through immigration control who is lawfully present. Since C represents a universal human right, restricting free movement within a state territory to long-term residents and citizens (cell F) or to specific groups or individuals (cell I) is hard to defend. The latter can be illustrated by the privileges of political elite members in illiberal states, such as the People's Republic of China and the Soviet Union until 1990, whose ordinary citizens are severely constrained in their rights of internal free movement. Under the broad conception of free movement that includes a right to settlement, one can, however, construct a justification for type F by introducing the further dimension of temporal scope. Short-term sojourners, who can be asked to leave the country after their visa or permit has expired, by implication enjoy only a temporary right to internal free movement and settlement, whereas this right is unlimited for citizens and for foreign nationals who are permanent residents.

Moving back to human rights of free movement in the top row one of the table, we can imagine a constellation represented by cell B where all countries grant exit rights but only a group of states open their borders to the citizens and residents of all other states. This is the ideal captured in Emma Lazarus's poem inscribed on the pedestal of the Statue of Liberty in New York City. It may be defended on grounds of collective self-interest if a country desperately needs immigrants for demographic or economic reasons, but such particularistic reasons for unilateral openness will be undermined by changing conditions, as they were in the United States after World War I. The moral language of freedom invoked by Lazarus will hardly be translated into the language of laws when most other potential destinations of the world's "poor" and "huddled masses yearning to breathe free" keep their doors closed. If other countries are unwilling to share the burdens of open immigration, then states may still be under moral obligations to admit refugees or family members of already settled immigrants, but they cannot be morally required to unilaterally dismantle their immigration controls altogether.[24]

In the middle row of Table 16.1 we find first the converse constellation of the one we have just considered. Cell D represents a country or group of countries whose citizens have not only the right to leave but also a right to enter and settle in all other countries that is withheld from migrants of other origins. There is no strictly corresponding legal arrangement, but citizens of Western democracies not only have more resources for moving to other destinations, they also find more doors open for legal admission. They can travel to a large number of countries without visa restrictions and are often also granted privileged access to residence permits. If B represents a potentially admirable but not morally required policy choice, then D stands for a morally dubious privilege that is nevertheless hard to avoid as an outcome of self-interested decisions by many destination countries that open their doors for economic or political reasons to citizens of particular countries. Cell G further narrows the category of persons who enjoy free movement privileges. We could think of diplomats whose special status in international law gives them much wider access to other countries and stronger protection against expulsion. This is a special case, since they do not migrate in search of economic opportunities, political protection, or family reunification but are sent on missions by governments or international organizations. Diplomatic privileges are granted by states to each other rather than to a group of individuals who use opportunities of free movement to promote their own interests. We could, however, also interpret category G as illustrating global immigration privileges of individuals whose wealth or special talents make them highly welcome in many destinations. Their case is then hardly different from that of migrants facing lower barriers for admission nearly everywhere because of their citizenship of origin.

This leaves us with the two cells in the table that are the ones most relevant to my argument. In constellation E citizens or residents of a particular group of countries enjoy free movement across state borders (presumably of those same countries). Into this category fall the agreements on free movement discussed in the previous section between the United Kingdom and the Irish Republic, between the Nordic countries of Europe, and between the member states of the European Union.

Multiple citizenship between states that are otherwise not linked through similar agreements belongs instead to category H, since it creates special rights of free movement for a subset of citizens who are simultaneously citizens of another country. Is this an unjustifiable privilege that is incompatible with equality among citizens? This depends on the prior question of how citizenship should be allocated among sedentary and migrant populations. Instead of asking why some citizens but not others should have immigration rights in another country, we should ask why migrants with genuine links to two separate countries should waive their right to return to their country of origin before they can become full citizens of their country of residence.

I will have more to say about the legitimacy of free movement rights derived from union and multiple citizenships, but before we explore their potential for approximating the ideal of universal freedom of movement, we need first to consider alternative arguments for this ideal and objections raised from a citizenship perspective.

Global Social Justice and Universal
Liberty Arguments for Open Borders

Open borders can be defended on grounds either of moral principle or economic advantage. The latter argument extends well-known theories about the benefits of free trade to the free movement of workers, and it assumes that unrestricted mobility of both capital and labor leads to the most cost-efficient production and therefore the greatest aggregate economic gains overall. I will leave such economic arguments for free movement aside and focus in this section on the advocacy for open borders on moral grounds.

Many proponents combine two arguments that should actually be considered separately because they refer to different moral values and lead to contrasting policy implications. The first is an argument about global social justice, and the second is about universal liberty.

The moral force of the global justice argument is best captured by Joseph Carens, who has suggested that "citizenship in the modern world is a lot like feudal status in the medieval world. It is assigned at birth; for the most part it is not subject to change by the individual's will and efforts; and it has a major impact upon that person's life chances."[25] Through immigration control the citizens of rich and secure states keep out those unfortunates who have been born as citizens of poverty-stricken, authoritarian, or violence-ridden states.

This is a morally troubling analogy. Yet it is not obvious what it implies. Should liberal states open their doors to free immigration? Or do they instead have a responsibility to improve the lives of those residing in the worst-off countries? Robert Goodin has suggested that the former strategy may be more feasible: "If we cannot move enough money to where the needy people are, then we will have to count on moving as many of the needy people as possible to where the money is."[26] Others have come to the opposite conclusion that assisting domestic development in the worst-off societies may be far more effective as a response to global inequality than moving poor people to rich countries.[27]

Political theorists who propose immigration as a response to global poverty often seem to make several flawed assumptions. First, they assume that the worst off are the ones most likely to make use of free movement rights to improve their lot. But, as we know from empirical studies, it is usually not the worst off who seize emigration opportunities, since using these requires some financial means as well as human and social capital. Second, the outmigration of large groups of the worst off from poor countries is not likely to make those who remain there better off. Positive development effects of emigration through remittances or return can be achieved if migrants are economically successful in their destination countries, which is not likely to be the case when the worst off form the largest migration streams. Third, Goodin's slogan assumes that migrants who move to rich countries will get access to money by moving. Yet in order to earn money they have to be employed, which in turn presupposes that there is sufficient demand for their skills. The idea that moving poor people to rich countries will automatically result in global redistribution of wealth is therefore not obvious. The most likely effect is a reduction in wage differentials between sending and receiving countries, but this is an average effect, and the side effects of deregulating labor markets may well lead to even greater inequality and no net reduction of poverty worldwide.

A more plausible response to worldwide social inequality would be a special regime for refugees from poverty. Such a regime would organize the transfer of the most destitute populations to wealthy countries where they would live on public welfare until they can either fend for themselves in the competitive labor markets of the host country or return to their countries of origin. This idea has been spelled out in detail in recent contributions by Eric Cavallero and by Michael Blake and Mathias Risse.[28] Blake and Risse focus, however, on the moral reasons for accepting such duties of admission and on mechanisms for allocating duties of admission across destination states rather than on the effectiveness of taking in poverty immigrants for reducing global inequalities. They build on a Lockean argument from humanity's original common ownership of the earth, which requires countries to let in immigrants in response to undeserved advantages and relative underuse of natural resources and land. This approach ignores the driving forces of human migration in our time, which are no longer, as in Locke's era, hunger for land and natural resources but rather search for work opportunities in urban centers and labor markets. Demographic and geographic factors such as population density and availability of land either are irrelevant for migration streams from the global South to the North or work in exactly the opposite way by pulling migrants into urban service economies.[29] A theory that builds a moral argument for the admission of immigrants on the unequal distribution and use of natural resources will generate counterintuitive prescriptions.

Cavallero's approach is more closely modeled on actual migration patterns. It assigns admission duties to countries in proportion to the number of immigrants who would apply for immigration given a chance to do so and it allows countries to buy themselves out of such duties through equivalent contributions to the development of sending countries. Cavallero's proposal is also sensitive to the question of whether emigration contributes to development by suggesting that there is an optimum number of admissions in this regard that should determine the global contingent of those to be resettled.[30]

No matter how one evaluates these specific proposals they represent progress in the debate insofar as they acknowledge that the answer to the injustice of global inequality is not open borders but rather some combination of development assistance and controlled immigration that selects immigrants with a view to optimizing development goals.

This perspective is quite different from an alternative argument about global justice, by Chandran Kukathas, that does not rely on the prediction that open borders will improve the situation overall but claims instead that for a significant number of citizens of poor countries "the most promising way of improving their condition is to move," and that it is morally wrong "to deny them the opportunity to help themselves" by searching for income opportunities in other countries.[31] Kukathas refers here to a principle of "humanity," but his case for open borders does not rely on consequentialist considerations about redistributive justice. Even if most citizens of poor countries were not to benefit from freedom of movement, denying this liberty to those who seek it in order to improve their individual fortunes is morally unjustifiable. Kukathas's principle of "humanity" appears therefore to be an extension of his other principle for justifying open borders, which is freedom itself.[32]

The case for open borders is indeed much more straightforward and plausible when made on grounds of universal liberty rather than global social justice. Free movement is a liberty that individuals need instrumentally in order to satisfy basic needs and achieve important goals, such as searching for work where their skills are valued most, or looking for partners with whom they want to live together, or escaping from environmental, economic, social, and political conditions under which they cannot flourish. The freedom to choose one's place of residence, just like the freedoms of speech and association, may also be intrinsically valuable for many people who enjoy geographic movement as an expression of individual liberty or as a collective way of life. From a liberal perspective, the reasons for restricting such an important freedom must be very weighty.[33] Instead of assuming that sovereign states have a self-evident right to control immigration, liberal political theory shifts the burden of justification toward political authorities who have to give reasons for constraining not only free emigration but also free immigration.

In his defense of immigration control, David Miller accepts such a burden but weakens it at the same time by asserting that "liberal societies in general offer their members sufficient freedom of movement to protect the interests that the human right to free movement is intended to protect."[34] For Miller, there is thus no right to free movement between liberal states. Freedom of movement is no longer a right when the interests that this liberty is meant to protect can be satisfied without moving. This purely instrumental interpretation is frequently shared by authors whose primary concern is social justice and equality of opportunities.[35] But this is unacceptable from a liberal perspective. It is just like saying that the freedoms of speech and association become less important once other rights are secure and we no longer need to claim or defend them through public speech and mobilization. If we take seriously freedom of movement as a basic liberty, then the burden of justification for restrictions must remain the same no matter how urgently people need to move in order to satisfy other

basic interests. A purely instrumental view of liberties such as free movement is therefore problematic because it provides political authorities with
wholesale justifications for arbitrary restrictions.

In an ideal world where all human beings enjoy sufficient protection of
their interests within sufficiently large territorial jurisdictions where they
reside, there will indeed be less need to move and settle in another jurisdiction, and fewer people are therefore likely to make the effort to do so.
However, reasons for political authorities to control immigration will simultaneously weaken, since free movement is then no longer likely to
threaten any of the public goods that these authorities have been mandated
to protect. From a liberal democratic perspective, the case for freedom of
movement thus becomes stronger, not weaker, as conditions in sending
countries improve and approximate those in liberal destination states.

Although both social justice and universal liberty seem to provide us
with moral reasons for universal freedom of movement, the two arguments
pull in different directions. Taken on its own, the global social justice argument implies that borders should be opened for moral reasons under conditions when they are least likely to be opened for political reasons. It is an
argument for open borders *now* in a nonideal world that could be improved
through more migration. The liberty argument says instead that states must
have strong reasons for restricting freedom of movement not only for their
own citizens but also for outsiders who want to enter their territories, and
that once they no longer have such reasons they ought to lift restrictions.
It is an argument for first creating the conditions under which open borders
will finally become possible. This argument in no way diminishes the cause
for global justice, whose moral force does not at all depend on what value
one attributes to free movement. Reducing present levels of global poverty
and enabling democratic transitions in societies that live under authoritarian regimes are more important goals than freedom of movement, but
achieving these goals would at the same time greatly strengthen the case for
opening borders.

Citizenship Arguments Against Free Movement

I have questioned how effective free movement would be in reducing unequal opportunities for the citizens of wealthy or poor countries. Yet this
objection still does not fully address Carens's concern that immigration

control, which shuts out the unfortunate citizens of poor countries, turns citizenship into the modern equivalent of feudal status.

Blake and Risse respond to this charge that shared citizenship may be morally *arbitrary* in the sense that it "has come about in a manner for which individuals deserve neither credit nor blame", but that it is not morally *irrelevant*, since "a border does mark something of moral importance—an area of shared liability to a community."[36] Indeed, unlike feudal status, citizenship in democratic countries is an institution that supports important moral values of individual liberty, equality, and collective self-government within a territorially bounded society.

Birthright citizenship specifically secures the continuity of democratic polities across multiple generations. Sustainable democracy requires not merely stable institutions but also a stable territorial core population whose members have been raised as citizens and conceive of their own future and that of their children as linked with this particular country.

In order to understand why this is so, imagine two extreme scenarios. In the first, everybody is an individual nomad, moving from country to country, and nobody is a native or permanent resident. In such a society there could be very little trust and no shared citizenship binding people together under a common political authority they could regard as legitimate, and whose laws they would habitually respect. A society composed of individual nomads of different origins will most likely be either anarchic and violent or governed by an unaccountable power whose rule is based on fear rather than trust.

In the second scenario, everybody is a member of a nomadic tribe that moves collectively from country to country without ever settling anywhere for longer than a generation. In contrast to the nomadic individualists, these nomadic collectivists could develop stable and trusted political institutions, since they would simply carry them along as they go. When they encounter another nomadic group, however, fighting it out would be the only way to determine whose laws will prevail for the time being in that territory, and the losers would be more likely to be enslaved, expelled, or killed off than to be invited to join the tribe as new citizens.

Democracy as we know it could not work in nomadic societies of both kinds. In our world, individual migrants enter or leave state territories. They can stretch their affiliations across international borders and remain citizens of their countries of origin while residing abroad, but they cannot challenge the democratic institutions of their host countries by replacing them with their own.

Democratic citizenship makes individuals equal members of stable territorial jurisdictions in which they are provided with protection of their liberties (such as freedom of speech, association, and religious practice), with rights to hold political authorities accountable (through free and representative elections and other forms of participation), and with a range of public goods that are important for their well-being (such as public education and health care). These are, by and large, the conditions under which political authority can be regarded as legitimate. If it turns out that universal freedom of movement undermines the conditions for democratic citizenship, then immigration control may in principle be justified.

It is not enough, however, to make counterfactual assumptions about the effects of free movement by invoking the nomadic anarchy or invasion scenarios sketched above. Since the burden of argument is always on justifying restriction, those who are seriously concerned about the need to protect spaces for democratic citizenship must demonstrate how these spaces would be jeopardized by opening the borders in their particular countries and under present conditions.

I think that such an argument can succeed in various ways. Let me consider the three dimensions of citizenship outlined above, which roughly correspond to T. H. Marshall's well-known typology of civil, political, and social citizenship.[37] These three bundles of rights are differently affected by open borders because they are different kinds of public goods.

Civil liberties are public goods in the strong sense that they cannot be fully upheld while excluding some from enjoying them. A political community that respects the rule of law and individual freedom cannot maintain apartheid or caste systems that deny basic liberties to a class of the population. The rule of law that protects civil liberties is not cost free.[38] But once it has been established in a territory, then including immigrants hardly creates additional costs. In fact, excluding them is likely to be more costly because it requires a repressive machinery. So for civil liberties there cannot be an argument that each additional immigrant raises the costs for the general protection of these liberties for the resident population. The only plausible objection is that there is a threshold beyond which the stability of a liberal political order might be threatened, not because immigrants are overstretching the state's capacity to protect civil liberties, but because of a backlash among the native population that can be politically exploited by antidemocratic and illiberal forces. This argument supports open borders up to the point when they have to be closed to prevent a nativist backlash.[39]

Political citizenship is a different kind of public good. As with civil liberties, the costs for political participation and representation do not rise proportionally with the number of people enjoying it. More voters certainly mean that more ballots must be printed, but the budgetary costs of including immigrants are hardly a major public concern. Yet political rights are fundamentally different from civil liberties in another respect. They are essentially "club goods," available only to members and to all members equally.[40] Immigrants must in some way qualify for membership before they can claim political rights. They could qualify automatically through a certain period of residence. Or, as is standard practice in democratic states, they must apply for membership, and their qualification is examined and subject to approval in a naturalization procedure. If tourists and other temporary sojourners enjoyed not only civil liberties but also political rights, this would open the door for large-scale abuse of political participation rights by people mobilized from abroad who do not share any responsibility for the election outcome. Political citizenship thus provides us with an argument not for control of access to the territory but for a second boundary that demarcates individual membership in the polity.

Can we at least derive from this an indirect argument for immigration control? If borders are open and many immigrants stay long enough to qualify for citizenship, will the state then have to restrict access to naturalization? And would this not be more objectionable than controlling immigration in the first place, since in a liberal democracy long-term immigrants must be set on the path to citizenship so that they will not be ruled by laws in whose making they are not represented?[41] This objection to open borders assumes that liberal states have a fundamental interest in limiting access to their citizenship. But political membership is not necessarily a scarce good that must be rationed in order to maintain its value. Liberal democracies can thrive with high numbers of naturalizations as long as immigrants qualify individually through a sufficient period of residence that indicates they have acquired a stake in the long-term future of the polity.

The most plausible argument why protecting political citizenship may justify immigration control is once again about a threshold, which is crossed when immigrants no longer integrate into a preexisting political community but instead impose their own rule over natives. If the majority of voters consists of newly naturalized citizens who arrived a few years earlier, then native-born citizens may well think that the intergenerational continuity of their democratic community has been broken and they are now governed by newcomers instead of participating in collective self-government.[42] Yet this is a very high threshold. In a dynamic society of immigration, even a majority of foreign-born citizens need not undermine the sense of continuity of territorial self-government as long as all these immigrants are seen to have joined the existing polity as individuals instead of taking it over as a collectivity.

Social citizenship, in the broad Marshallian sense that includes not only poverty relief and mandatory social insurance but also public education and health care, is again a different kind of public good. Its basic justification is that citizens cannot make responsible use of their liberties and political participation rights unless they receive some minimum education and are protected against various common social and economic risks. Since these are ability-based and needs-based reasons, social citizenship is not linked to membership status in the same way as political participation; it is instead derived from residence and employment. Immigrants are therefore included much earlier in social citizenship than in political citizenship. And for social citizenship the costs of extending full coverage to newcomers may rise in proportion to their numbers. This is not necessarily so, since economically productive immigrants also contribute to maintaining social citizenship through their tax and social security contributions and, more generally, by fostering economic growth. But open doors for immigration mean that states have no control over the composition of inflows. With sudden and huge inflows of poverty-driven migrants it is unlikely that general levels of provision of social citizenship could be maintained. Either everybody would receive lower benefits or immigrants would have to be excluded from some of these, turning them into second-class social citizens. More important, even if migrants are overall net contributors to the welfare state, large uncontrolled inflows can still undermine state efforts to enforce regulatory standards concerning wages and working conditions, housing, or education.

Negative consequences of open borders for maintaining comprehensive social citizenship are not yet a sufficient normative argument for immigration control. Why should potential immigrants who do not enjoy similar levels of social protection in their countries of origin accept this justification? To respond to them we would need to refer to a broader theory of social justice, and liberal theorists disagree profoundly on what social justice requires at the domestic and global levels.

Nonetheless, the social citizenship argument for immigration control can be broadly supported in two ways. First, substantive conceptions of social justice such as John Rawls's or David Miller's presuppose the idea of society as a cooperative scheme in which the benefits of cooperation are to be shared among members. Equal opportunity standards and the difference principle can only be upheld by political institutions within communities of equal citizens. Since there are no equivalent institutions and memberships at the global level, standards of social justice will be different within and across political borders, with the latter referring to basic needs rather than to sharing the benefits of cooperation.[43]

Second, liberal republican approaches may provide an alternative procedural justification for immigration control. Instead of defining in substantive terms what domestic social justice requires, they argue that self-governing political communities must have the power to determine internal standards of this kind based on their particular traditions and the political will of their citizens. If the obligations of a democratic polity toward outsiders were so strong that the polity could not even decide on levels of provision in public education, health care, and welfare benefits for those within their jurisdiction, then such a polity would not really be self-governing (or would be self-governing only as a subpolity nested within an encompassing one that has the power to determine standards of social citizenship).

Only a libertarian position that regards comprehensive social citizenship as an unjust interference with individual property rights could therefore consistently maintain that freedom of movement takes priority over preserving the conditions for social citizenship. Those who think that social justice will be better promoted by dismantling the welfare state may well advocate open borders hoping for just this effect.

I have argued in this section that all three aspects of citizenship provide reasons for political powers to limit immigration. Yet civil and political citizenship arguments refer to immigration emergencies that may justify thresholds but seem perfectly compatible with free movement below these thresholds. Only social citizenship provides reasons for continuous immigration control. The crucial question is then under which conditions the social citizenship objection can become so weak that it no longer counts as an obstacle to open borders. The answer is simple. The argument for immigration control becomes weaker the more standards of social citizenship converge across political borders. This can be achieved through a convergence toward a lowest common denominator, and open borders would contribute to bringing about this result. Alternatively, several polities could develop similar high standards of social citizenship, and restricting free movement between these polities would then become harder to justify.

Liberal Citizenship as a Reason for Admission and Free Movement

Even those who defend immigration control as necessary for the protection of social citizenship will have to accept a series of countervailing citizenship-based arguments for admission on specific grounds.

Liberal citizenship is not an alternative or supplementary set of rights that individuals enjoy instead of, or in addition to, their universal human rights. It includes the latter. As we have seen in the discussion above of civil and social rights, a liberal conception also does not make provision of citizenship rights conditional on membership status, but confers equal rights on all those within the jurisdiction while differentiating the bundle of rights enjoyed by noncitizen sojourners and residents according to the duration of their stay or by other proxies for the strength of their ties to the polity. Of course a democratic polity can decide to add many items to a list of universal human rights, but the crucial difference that citizenship makes is neither in the list of rights nor in the exclusion of nonmembers, but in the assignment of responsibility for the comprehensive protection of rights within a jurisdiction to political authorities who are accountable to the permanent members of the political community. Liberal citizenship thus includes a set of rights to geographical movement, and these, too, are not all reserved for those who have citizen status. We can start to build a citizenship case for open borders by examining these rights one by one.

The first is most narrowly tied to citizenship status. This is the right to return. It is the only unconditional right to immigration recognized under international law. Combined with the universal human right of emigration, it provides citizens living abroad with a one-way option of free movement from any external origin to their country of citizenship. As a long-term option the right to return is generally granted only to those who possess formal citizenship status. Foreign residents who are temporarily outside the country can, however, also claim a temporary right to return. Some states, among them Israel, Germany, and Japan, have expanded the right to return to external populations of noncitizens whom they regard as ethnic kin.[44] And many other states facilitate the transmission of external citizenship across multiple generations or offer descendants of former citizens easy naturalization while they still live abroad.[45]

The second immigration right is for family members of citizens or resident foreign nationals. This right has broader personal scope by giving access to the territory to individuals who do not themselves have prior attachments to the polity through citizenship or residence, but it remains indirectly tied to these selection criteria because it combines a right of the anchor person inside the polity to be reunited with her or his family with a right of outside family members to be admitted. While providing wider access than the right to return, the right to family reunification does not open the borders unconditionally. Individuals who are admitted under such schemes are exposed to various mechanisms of immigration control, ranging from tests of income and adequate housing for those who invite them to language tests for those who want to be admitted. If family reunification is a human right, these criteria are of questionable legitimacy. More generally, however, any policy of family reunification has to come up with some criteria that define the kinship relation to the anchor persons. Kinship may be defined widely (as it is in the European Union for reunification of third-country nationals with EU citizens) or narrowly (spouses and minor children up to a certain age only), but some individuals (e.g., uncles and aunts) will remain excluded under any family reunification right.[46]

The third right of admission grounded in citizenship is asylum for refugees. In their case, there is generally no previous affiliation to the particular polity through citizenship, former residence, ancestry, or family ties. This makes it much more difficult to resolve the question of which state should be responsible for taking in which refugee. In the absence of an international authority that can allocate refugees to states, other criteria must be taken into account. Among these may be absorption capacity, cultural links, and family ties where they exist, economic and political involvement of destination states in the refugee-generating countries, and geographic proximity. States engage in refugee resettlement by organizing direct transfers from the region of origin or admitting asylum seekers who turn up at, or within, their territorial borders. In both cases, the duty of examining refugee claims is fairly clearly allocated to specific states, but the problem remains that many genuine refugees will not be provided with protection through either channel of admission. I cannot explore here the multiple moral and political dilemmas of refugee policy.[47] What I want to point out is that the moral claims of refugees are grounded in their loss of citizenship. Even if they are not stateless in the legal sense, they can no longer avail themselves of the protection of those basic rights that citizenship is supposed to provide. Countries whose political system derives its legitimacy from turning subjects into citizens have a moral obligation to help those who have effectively been deprived of their citizenship. Asylum is a substitute for citizenship, and it must include an offer of future citizenship in the host country if a refugee has no return option or has become a long-term resident.[48]

Taken together, the rights to return, family reunification, and asylum clearly do not add up to a universal right to free movement. All three are instead citizenship-related special entitlements to admission. And the wider the personal scope stretches beyond present citizens and residents, the weaker are the corresponding immigration rights. Family reunification and refugee admission are subject to immigration control and conditions for residence. Even if we regard many of the present conditions as illegitimate, it is not plausible to remove all of them so that any human being could claim a right of entry everywhere on grounds of family ties or asylum. A wish to look for a marriage partner abroad or preferences for the constitution of a destination country over that of one's country of origin do not give rise to admission claims.

Let me now consider two other currently recognized migration rights that seem more promising candidates for broadening the territorial scope and the personal scope of free movement. The first of these is the right of free exit. Some authors have argued that emigration is not free until it is combined with a right to enter other countries. The obvious problem is, however, that emigration rights have a clear addressee—the state of present residence—while the corresponding entry rights that must be guaranteed to make emigration possible are addressed to all, and therefore to no particular, other states. It is in any case not plausible to claim that I cannot exit freely unless all other states are willing to admit me.[49]

Phil Cole makes a consequentialist case for the symmetry between exit and entry rights by arguing that both immigration and emigration may have negative effects that could justify restrictions. If states are permitted to constrain immigration because of its potentially adverse impact on the economy or political stability, then they could invoke similar reasons to restrict emigration when it leads to a loss of human capital or deprives a country of its most active and committed citizens.[50]

This is an unacceptable view if we regard states as voluntary associations of their citizens. An association is inherently illiberal if it prevents its members from leaving but is not similarly required to admit all potential new members.[51] However, the analogy between states and voluntary associations is limited. If liberal citizenship provides protection for basic rights, then liberal states have special obligations to admit immigrants covered by the rights of return, family reunification, and asylum. As we have just seen, special obligations cannot be stretched too far. A liberal democracy is responsible for the protection of the rights for all inside its territory and for some persons outside that territory as well. The former responsibility entails duties to let them leave even if emigration has detrimental effects for the economy or the polity. The duty to let noncitizens immigrate, on the other hand, is circumscribed not merely by potential negative effects but also by the limited perimeter of special obligations. Under a regime of universal freedom of movement, the number of people outside a particular state who would enjoy a right to enter is multiple times larger than that of people inside who can claim a right to leave. If we accept that states may have legitimate interests in controlling flows of people across their borders, then the case for limiting immigration, not just through general admission control but also by determining groups with special admission claims, is much stronger than a consequentialist argument for restricting emigration. Emigration and immigration are thus morally asymmetric because of the associational features of liberal polities and because of the asymmetric nature of corresponding state duties.

Free internal movement is the second universal right that we need to consider to see whether it can serve as a springboard for the liberal goal of universal freedom of movement. As discussed in the third section above, liberal states guarantee free internal movement not just for their citizens but for everybody inside their territorial jurisdiction. Thinking about the interests this right is meant to protect and the conditions under which it can be guaranteed is indeed the most promising starting point for extending free movement beyond the borders of states. Joseph Carens puts the argument from similarity of interests most strongly: "Every reason why one might want to move within a state may also be a reason for moving between states."[52] "The radical disjuncture that treats freedom of movement within the state as a moral imperative and freedom of movement across state borders as merely a matter of political discretion makes no sense from a per-spective that takes seriously the freedom and equality of all individuals."[53]

Michael Blake objects: "We value internal mobility and voting rights as part of the package of justifications for political coercion. We have no equivalent reason to extend these rights to individuals who are not part of the political community in question, but who merely seek to become so subject."[54] This analogy is clearly flawed, since free internal movement, un-like the franchise, is a right of everybody inside the territory. It is also wrong when we consider substate polities, such as provinces or towns, where only members (citizens or residents) can vote but whose borders remain open to protect mobility rights of everyone in the larger state territory.

Yet Blake's general point is worth considering. First, before being admit-ted, and unless they fall into one of the three special categories discussed above, immigrants are not yet in a political relation with the government of their destination.[55] Even if we assume that they have strong interests to enter, it is not obvious that the government of their desired destination is responsible for protecting these interests. Second, the comparison between independent states and provinces or towns suggests that there needs to be some encompassing entity with political institutions that have not only the authority to keep the borders of territorial subunits open but also the re-sources for compensating units burdened by stronger immigration or emi-gration.

Political coordination between the polities whose borders stay open is therefore the crucial condition for freedom of movement. Yet it is not at all obvious that this condition can be achieved only within independent states. The examples of the Nordic Passport Union, the agreements between the Irish Republic and the United Kingdom, and the European Union illustrate that it is possible to create larger areas of free movement under conditions of general political cooperation, shared constitutional traditions and politi-cal values, and comparable levels of social citizenship. These cases show also that coordination does not require strong supranational government. Legal traditions can be as diverse as they are between British common law and Roman civil law in continental Europe. Finally, levels of social citizen-ship vary quite strongly between Scandinavian universalistic welfare re-gimes, British and Irish liberal market regimes, Central European corporatist regimes, and incomplete or incipient welfare regimes in Medi-terranean and Central Eastern European countries.

These empirical observations support again some general conclusions.

Emigration and immigration are morally asymmetric in liberal polities because these have special obligations to protect the rights of their current citizens and residents. Symmetry can, however, be approximated under two contrasting conditions: either if the set of rights that are protected within such polities shrinks to a libertarian minimum that no longer conflicts with open borders for immigration, or if the scope of free movement rights that such polities have to protect includes a growing set of external populations. The conclusions from the previous two sections can be combined as follows. The case for freedom of movement can be made either on libertarian grounds or on liberal egalitarian ones. For the latter approach the two main conditions for free movement across international borders are converging standards of internal social citizenship and external coordination between states that mutually guarantee each other's citizens free admission.

Expanding the Scope of Free Movement

Theories that emphasize the normative contrast between free movement within and across political borders beg the question of how to determine which border is external and which is internal. Instead of presupposing this dichotomy as given, we should consider the possibilities for creating larger spaces of free movement in which external borders are transformed into internal ones.

Free movement has been the core of citizenship of the European Union from its very beginning, long before the terms "union" and "citizenship" were introduced by the 1992 Maastricht Treaty.[56] The European Union need not remain a historically unique experiment. Conditions for free movement across international borders could be further expanded beyond the current member states or could be replicated in other regions of the world. This is the first of three strategies for expanding free movement on a transnational citizenship basis, the potential and limits of which I discuss in this section.

One idea might be to conceive of the present European Union as an ever-expanding union of states in roughly the same way that Kant imagined an ever-expanding association of free republics as the best guarantee for perpetual peace. Yet the European Union is clearly not a Kantian confederation of this kind.[57] It is rooted in Europe and aims at preserving geographic contiguity. Although Canada or New Zealand would qualify under the 1993

Copenhagen criteria for accession,[58] they would not be seriously considered as candidates. On the one hand, the European Union's external borders have expanded in several waves and may eventually reach their geographic limits at the Russian border and the southern shores of the Mediterranean. On the other hand, as the current inclusion of nonmember states (Norway, Iceland, and Switzerland) in the Schengen area indicates, the European Union could well extend its internal regime of free movement to include the territories and citizens of neighboring states who qualify for accession but decide not to join. Yet overall it is clear that EU enlargement and association agreements with neighboring states will remain limited and cannot cover many other regions of the world.

This is why the alternative of creating new regional unions elsewhere is attractive, even if current prospects for such projects are not promising at all. The North American Free Trade Agreement is the most likely candidate, but free movement of workers was explicitly excluded from this treaty. Apart from the development gap between Mexico and the United States, the hegemonic position of the United States makes it difficult to imagine that its government would be willing to compromise national interests for the sake of free movement across international borders. From a normative liberal perspective, however, states that are willing to engage in regional economic integration should also be willing to agree on free movement of workers, and eventually of persons more generally, as an explicit goal of their cooperation. Regional unions may eventually also emerge in Oceania, South America, Asia, and Africa (listed here in descending degrees of probability for this outcome), and these unions could create geographically contiguous and expanding areas of free movement on each continent. Much of today's international migration would then be transformed into *internal* movement within such regional unions.

Once immigration control has been shifted to supranational levels it would become much easier to take the next step toward agreements on free movement between unions rather than between individual states. One could object that unions would be politically integrated to different degrees and that external immigration control of third-country nationals may remain within the competence of member states. If this is the case, then movement between unions would still be controlled by member states separately and according to their own criteria. However, in a supranational area of free movement, prudential reasons for joint immigration control policies will over time become quite strong. The goal of harmonizing external border control has pushed the European Union toward a common list of countries for visa-free entry and has led to the adoption of common minimum standards for asylum and family reunification. Harmonization of immigration of third-country nationals for economic activities is still lagging but has repeatedly been put on the E.U. agenda.

The liberal utopia of a universal right to free movement could then be fully achieved short of creating a world state once every country belongs to a regional union and all such unions have concluded agreements on free movement with each other. Promoting, instead of merely tolerating, multiple citizenship could offer an alternative second strategy for expanding free movement. Imagine a world with universal dual citizenship, in which every human being enjoys rights of free movement between two states and all states recognize dual citizens inside as well as outside their territories. In Table 16.1 we would then register dual citizenship in cell B rather than cell H. Free movement would no longer be a privilege of certain individuals and would become a universal right. Instead of one single country opening its borders to immigration from all possible origins, admission duties would be more evenly distributed across states, each of which would be responsible for opening its borders for a larger set of external citizens.

The limitations of this model are obvious. The territorial scope of free movement would still remain restricted to two countries for every person. And the crucial question remains of how to determine for every human being an external state that has to grant him or her a second citizenship. Assigning second citizenships in a random way or auctioning them off to the top bidder would result in a much more arbitrary allocation than through birthright citizenship and naturalization and would undermine the value and integrity of democratic citizenship as long-term membership in a self-governing political community.

And once we imagine universal dual citizenship, why not take a further step toward multiple citizenship of every human being in all countries, which would again take us toward cell A and a universal right of free movement. This thought experiment is a *reductio ad absurdum* that shows the inherent limitations of the multiple citizenship strategy. In contrast with the first path of interunion agreements, this second path would render citizenship meaningless unless there is a federal world state whose constituent members are nothing more than provinces. In most federal democracies, citizens of the federation are indeed potentially citizens of all federal provinces, too, since they can at any time take up residence there and vote in

provincial elections. However, for reasons spelled out by liberal philosophers from Kant to Rawls, a centralized world state of this kind is hardly
an attractive utopia.

Claims to citizenship must therefore remain based on individuals'
stakes in the future of particular countries.[59] Being born in the territory of
a country, having parents who are first-generation emigrants, and being a
long-term resident immigrant are strong indicators for such ties. Those
who combine several ties of this kind have a claim to multiple citizenship,
and their mobility rights are derived from these multiple affiliations rather
than the other way round. Even a general recognition of multiple citizenship claims will thus not lead to universal freedom of movement, since
large majorities of sedentary populations never acquire stakes in other
countries that would justify offering them a second citizenship. But in a
world where there is no universal freedom of movement, granting multiple
citizenship to multiple stakeholders would at least secure free movement
within transnational spaces for those whose life histories and future prospects are strongly connected with several countries.

Although multiple citizenships cannot be universalized in the absence
of a world state, promoting their broader recognition can do much to expand the personal scope of free movement beyond the fortunate citizens of
stable and wealthy democracies. The category of multiple citizens who
enjoy free movement would be limited to those who already have strong
ties to several societies through past migrations or future return options.
Under present conditions there is of course no guarantee that all states will
tolerate dual citizenship, and the allocation of free movement rights
through this status will thus in many ways remain arbitrary. However, as
comparative studies have shown, there is no clear pattern as to which states
reject or accept dual citizenship. The latter group of countries includes
states on all continents and democratic as well as authoritarian regimes.[60]
Dual citizenship that involves authoritarian states generates problems concerning diplomatic protection and may not entail the guarantee of free exit
that is a necessary condition for free movement. But in many cases holding
two passports does provide even migrants from such countries with additional options to move back and forth, to take care of family in their countries of origin, and to exercise some political voice there.

The strategy of enlarging or replicating regional unions aims at expanding the geographic scope of free movement by creating supranational spaces
within which mobility rights can be internalized in a way similar to how

they operate inside the borders of independent states. The multiple citizenship strategy aims instead at expanding the personal scope of free movement through transnational rights that individuals enjoy in relation to several polities. I will conclude by considering a third option that combines both these aspects and at the same time bypasses some of the obstacles on the path toward universal freedom of movement that we have encountered when following the other two strategies.

The idea is to promote international agreements on free movement between individual states that have developed sufficiently stable forms of liberal citizenship. Whereas sharing internal borders remains an important prerequisite for regional unions that aim at deeper political integration, such agreements would require neither geographic contiguity nor strong supranational governance. In times when a large and increasing share of international travel is by airplane, contiguity is no longer a condition for free movement. States separated by large stretches of land or sea may nevertheless grant to each other's citizens and long-term residents mutual immigration privileges. Instead of putting our hopes on regional unions for whom free movement is a side effect of economic and political integration, we could thus promote international agreements between states whose only purpose is to remove obstacles to free movement among member countries. Such free movement regimes would be more weakly integrated than supranational unions, but they could expand areas of free movement widely beyond the limited geographic range of such unions.

In these respects, the multilateral agreement strategy would be similar in effect to granting multiple citizenship to all the citizens of the countries involved. However, instead of deriving immigration rights from prior claims to citizenship, admission rights would remain attached to the citizenship of origin rather than of destination, as they are in the European Union. Those who enter and settle in another state covered by the multilateral agreement would not already be citizens of that country. Like all other immigrants, they would have to naturalize in order to fully join the political community of their country of settlement. The multilateral agreement strategy for promoting free movement would therefore not give rise to concerns about a devaluation of citizenship in destination countries.

One limitation of this strategy is that it could not provide any guarantee for continuous expansion. Consider a worst-case scenario in which states A and B have had open borders for their respective citizens over an extended period. Then suddenly the democratic regime in state B is overthrown by a military coup, or state B is hit by an environmental disaster. In both cases, there will be strong humanitarian reasons for state A not to close its borders with state B now that B's citizens have basic needs-based reasons to move to A. But these humanitarian reasons may conflict with citizenship-based reasons. If A is really overwhelmed by an inflow from B and cannot arrange some burden sharing with third countries, then it would have to reintroduce immigration control. Even if we accept this decision as legitimate, it would not remove all of A's duties toward its former partner country, since A would still have to give priority to refugees from B over opportunity-seeking immigrants from C or D. The dilemma between citizenship-based reasons for admission and for control will then become sharper, and A's government will have to find a defensible point on the tradeoff curve.

In less pessimistic scenarios, A and B are both stable democracies, and freedom of movement between them strengthens democracy by generating positive competition for citizens' loyalty and voice through improving their opportunities in each territory. Interstate regimes of free movement may thus be self-supportive by diminishing emigration push factors and thereby reducing the threat that mass emigration would pose to the other states in the association.

Conclusions

The three strategies for expanding free movement that I have sketched in the last section are mutually compatible and can be pursued simultaneously. They are certainly not "realistic" under present conditions, but they seem politically feasible in the sense that governments pursuing these strategies would not thereby undermine the conditions for stable democratic citizenship. Instead of sacrificing their citizens' interests for the sake of creating immigration rights for outsiders, they would promote their own citizens' liberties and opportunities by engaging in reciprocal agreements with other states.

Many readers will certainly object that this reconciliation between citizenship and freedom of movement mainly promotes the interests of citizens of wealthy liberal democracies, who are anyway immensely privileged compared to the vast majority of human beings who live in economically deprived and politically unstable or authoritarian regimes.

There is an uncomfortable truth in this objection. But to see what it is, we have to set aside some misinterpretations. First, as I pointed out above, the charge does not apply to the multiple citizenship strategy, which replaces the condition of stable citizenship at the collective level with individual stakeholdership as a criterion for the allocation of free movement rights. Second, criticizing the other two strategies because they create free movement privileges for the citizens of liberal democracies is a bit like saying that we should not care about improving democratic accountability or social justice within Western democracies as long as there are so many countries in which the most basic conditions for these are absent. We expect democratic governments to promote their citizens' interests and to protect their liberties, and free movement within and across political borders has to be counted prominently among these. Third, implicit in this critique is the idea that opening borders for immigration from poor and unstable countries would lead to greater global equality and justice. But, as I have argued, this expectation may be unwarranted. Under present circumstances, global freedom of movement could worsen conditions for creating stable democracies with comprehensive citizenship rights both in countries of destination and of origin. If this is correct, then we have independent reasons for improving economic and political conditions in the worst-off countries and for promoting free movement between states.

There is still a nagging doubt. Free movement for the citizens of stable democracies but immigration control for those who are worse off turns political borders into instruments of discrimination on grounds that liberals have trouble accepting as legitimate. Immigration control involves coercive acts through which political authorities directly structure the opportunities and interfere with the choices of those who want to cross a border. Coercive use of political power is always in need of justification. I have suggested that maintaining the conditions for democratic citizenship may provide justification for immigration control. However, I have simultaneously advocated a gradual expansion of spaces and entitlements for free movement. The combined regime of exemptions for one group and controls for another appears to be discriminatory. When migrants of different origins compete with each other for admission, how can we justify giving free access to those whose need to be admitted is weakest, while submitting others to a needs test or excluding them altogether if their numbers become too large?

This remains a troubling question. The only answer I can offer is that asserting the liberal ideal of universal freedom of movement commits us both to improving conditions under which the ideal becomes feasible and to immediately implementing it where conditions are already in place. The discriminatory features of the best possible immigration regimes under present circumstances seem, then, an unavoidable consequence of aiming for these two goals simultaneously. The long-term hope is that pursing them will allow reduction in discrimination by expanding free movement toward a global scale. This answer offers little consolation to those who are excluded now. The moral dilemmas of immigration control will therefore remain a thorn in the flesh of liberal democracies. It is a painful reminder that the ideals of liberal citizenship cannot be fully realized in a world where most people are deprived of fundamental liberties and means to satisfy their basic needs.

Notes

Introduction

1. For discussions of these developments, see, e.g., Daniel J. Tichenor, *Dividing Lines: The Politics of Immigration Control in America* (Princeton: Princeton University Press, 2002), 203–18, 252–85; Aristide R. Zolberg, *A Nation by Design: Immigration Policy in the Fashioning of America* (New York: Russell Sage Foundation, 2006), 324–418.

2. For a balanced overview of recent immigration-related civil liberties debates, see, e.g., Michael C. LeMay, *Guarding the Gates: Immigration and National Security* (New York: Praeger, 2006), 239–68.

3. E.g., Spencer S. Hsu, "Little New in Obama's Immigration Policy," *Washington Post*, May 20, 2009, at http://www.washingtonpost.com.

Chapter 1. International Migration

1. The Uruguay Round of global trade negotiations and the various regional trade accords (particularly the North American trade agreements)—both starting in the late 1980s—are somewhat arbitrarily chosen as the beginning points of the newest and most intense phase of globalization.

2. World Bank, "Remittance Data: Monthly Remittance Flows to Selected Countries," July 2009, http://siteresources.worldbank.org/intprospects/Resources/334934-1110315015165/RemittancesData_July09(Public).xls.

3. United Nations, Department of Economic and Social Affairs, Population Division (2009), *Trends in International Migrant Stock: The 2008 Revision* (United Nations database, POP/DB/MIG/Stock/Rev.2008).

4. The terms "advanced industrial countries/democracies/societies/economies," "industrial countries," "first world," "developed world," "advanced West," "North," "wealthy nations" and OECD countries all referr to the twenty-four states that were members of the Organization of Economic Cooperation and Development in the early 1990s, before Mexico and some other developing states also became members.

5. Organisation for Economic Co-operation and Development, "International Migration Outlook Annual Report 2008 Edition" (Paris: Organisation for Economic Co-operation and Development, 2008).

6. An entry (or admission) is a problematic measure in that a person will be counted as a separate admission every time he or she enters a country. Business persons, for instance, may enter a country multiple times. Furthermore, most land border traffic is typically not included in data systems. U.S. Department of Homeland Security, "Nonimmigrant Admissions by Class of Admission: Fiscal Years 1999 to 2008," *Yearbook of Immigration Statistics 2008*, http://www.dhs.gov/xlibrary/assets/statistics/yearbook/2008/table25d.xls.

7. Intra-E.U. entries are excluded in this estimate.

8. United Nations High Commissioner for Refugees, *Asylum Levels and Trends in Industrialized Countries First Half 2009: Statistical Overview of Asylum Applications Lodged in Europe and Selected Non-European Countries*, http://www.unhcr.org/cgi-bin/texis/vtx/search?page = search&docid = 4adebca49&query = number%20of%20asylum%20seekers.

9. United Nations High Commissioner for Refugees. *2008 Global Trends: Refugees, Asylum-Seekers, Returnees, Internally Displaced and Stateless Persons*, www.unhcr.org/4a375c426.html.

10. U.S. Department of Homeland Security, *Persons Obtaining Legal Permanent Resident Status by Type and Major Class of Admission: Fiscal Years 1999 to 2008*, in the *Yearbook of Immigration Statistics 2008*, http://www.dhs.gov/xlibrary/assets/statistics/yearbook/2008/table06d.xls

11. Pew Hispanic Center, "Modes of Entry for the Unauthorized Migrant Population," May 22, 2006, http://pewhispanic.org/files/factsheets/19.pdf

12. Ibid.

13. U.S. Census Bureau, "U.S. and World Population Clocks," October 29, 2009, http://www.census.gov/main/www/popclock.html. Central Intelligence Agency, "Mexico," *The World Factbook*, https://www.cia.gov/library/publications/the-world-fact book/geos/mx.html; Central Intelligence Agency, "Canada," *The World Factbook*, https://www.cia.gov/library/publications/the-world-factbook/geos/ca.html; Monica Marcu, "The EU-27 Population Continues to Grow," *Eurostat* (July 24, 2009), http://epp.eurostat.ec.europa.eu/cache/ity_offpub/ks-qa-09-031/en/ks-qa-09-031-en.pdf.

14. United Nations, Department of Economic and Social Affairs, Population Division (2009), *Trends: 2008 Revision*.

15. Ibid.; Australian Bureau of Statistics, *2006 Census Tables: Country of Birth (Region) of Person by Age by Sex*, June 27, 2007, in Commonwealth of Australia, http://www.censusdata.abs.gov.au/ABSNavigation/prenav/ViewData?action = 404&document productno = 0&documenttype = Details&order = 1&tabname = Details&areacode = 0&issue = 2006&producttype = Census%20Tables&javascript = true&textversion = false&navmapdisplayed = true&breadcrumb = TLPD&&collection = Census&period = 2006&productlabel = Country%20of%20Birth%20(region)%20of%20Person%20by%20Age%20by%20Sex&producttype = Census%20Tables&method = Place%20of%20Usual%20Residence&topic = Birthplace&; Statistics New Zealand, *Birthplace (Detailed) by Age Group and Sex, for the Census Usually Resident Population Count, 1996, 2001 and 2006,*

http://wdmzpub01.stats.govt.nz / wds / TableViewer / tableView.aspx?ReportName =
Census2006/Culture%20and%20identity/Birthplace%20(Detailed)%20by%20Age%
20Group%20and%20Sex,%20for%20the%20Census%20Usually%20Resident%20
Population%20Count,%201996,%202001%20and%202006; Statistics Canada, *Immigration in Canada: A Portrait of the Foreign-Born Population, 2006 Census: Immigration: Driver of Population Growth,* http://www.census2006.ca/census-recensement/2006/as-sa/97-557/p2-eng.cfm (modified May 1, 2009).

16. United Nations Population Division, various estimates over the years, including United Nations, Department of Economic and Social Affairs. *Trends and Characteristics of International Migration Since 1950* (New York: United Nations, 1979); United Nations, Department of Economic and Social Information and Policy Analysis, Population Division, *International Migration Policies, 1995* (New York: United Nations, 1996).

17. Cyprus and Malta are the exceptions to this movement and serve to reinforce the "reduction in differentials" point.

Chapter 2. Rural Migration and Economic Development with Reference to Mexico and the United States

I am grateful for the valuable comments made by Professor Michael Katz on a previous version, presented at the conference "Citizenship, Borders, and Human Needs" (University of Pennsylvania, 12 May 2008). I wish to thank Peri Fletcher for her editorial revision of the chapter and Graciela Salazar for revising the first draft. I also wish to acknowledge financial support from the William and Flora Hewlett Foundation.

1. J. Edward Taylor, "International Migration and Economic Development: Puzzles and Policies for LDCs" (paper prepared for the United Nations, New York, 21 March 2006).

2. International Monetary Fund, *Balance of Payments Statistics Yearbook, 2005, Part 2* (Washington, D.C.: International Monetary Fund, 2005).

3. Ibid.

4. J. Edward Taylor and Philip L. Martin, "Human Capital: Migration and Rural Population Change," in *Handbook of Agricultural Economics, Volume I* (New York: Elsevier Science, 2001), 457–511.

5. Taylor, "International Migration," 4.

6. There are other relevant phenomena affecting migration determinants and effects: anthropological, historical, institutional, and sociopolitical, but I will center on the economic aspects. See Gordon H. Hanson, "International Migration and Development," Commission on Growth and Development, Working Paper No. 42, December 2008, for a summary of findings in the literature on worldwide migration and development.

7. In the United States an estimated 69 percent of the 1996 seasonal agricultural service (SAS) workforce was foreign born, and in California, the nation's largest ag-

ricultural producer, more than 90 percent of the SAS workforce was foreign born. The majority (65 percent) of these migrant farmworkers originated from households in rural Mexico (Taylor and Martin, "Human Capital"). See also Consejo Nacional de Poblacian (CONAPO), "Los mexicanos en el mercado laboral estadounidense," *Boletín No. 21*, 2007. Recent data on Mexican rural households reveal that people are leaving Mexico's villages at an unprecedented rate. The percentage of Mexico's village population working in both internal and international migrant destinations increased sharply at the end of the twentieth century. More than half of all migrants leaving Mexican villages migrate to destinations within Mexico. However, villagers' propensity to migrate to U.S. jobs more than doubled from 1990 to 2002 (J. J. Mora Rivera, "Essays on Migration and Development in Rural Mexico," Ph.D. diss., El Colegio de Mexico, 2007).

8. M. P. Todaro, "A Model of Migration and Urban Unemployment in Less-Developed Countries," *American Economic Review* 59 (1969): 138–48.

9. Oded Stark, *Economic-Demographic Interactions in Agricultural Development: The Case of Rural-to-Urban Migration* (Rome: United Nations Food and Agricultural Organization, 1978).

10. David Bloom and Oded Stark, "The New Economics of Labor Migration," *American Economic Review* 75 (1985): 173–78.

11. Details in Taylor and Martin, "Human Capital."

12. David Levhari and Oded Stark, "On Migration and Risk in LDCs," *Economic Development and Cultural Change* 31, no. 1 (1982): 191–96.

13. Rita M. Maldonado, "Why Puerto Ricans Migrated to the United States in 1947–73," *Monthly Labor Review* 99 (1976): 7–18.

14. Douglas S. Massey et al., "Theories of International Migration: An Integration and Appraisal," *Population and Development Review* 19, no. 3 (1993): 431–66.

15. A detailed review of empirical evidence of Todaro and the neoclassical model is in Taylor and Martin, "Human Capital."

16. J. Edward Taylor, "Undocumented Mexico-U.S. Migration and the Returns to Households in Rural Mexico," *American Journal of Agricultural Economics* 69 (1987): 626–38.

17. For the case of rural Mexico-to-United States migration, see Douglas S. Massey, "Understanding Mexican Migration to the United States," *American Journal of Sociology* 92 (1987): 1372–1403; J. Edward Taylor, "Differential Migration, Networks, Information and Risk," in *Migration Theory, Human Capital and Development*, ed. Oded Stark (Greenwich, Conn.: JAI Press, 1986), 147–71.

18. ENHRUM provides detailed sociodemographic and economic information for a nationally representative sample of rural households in Mexico. Current and retrospective migration data from 1980 to 2002, including migrants' sector of employment, were gathered for all household members as well as for children of household heads or spouses who were living outside the household at the time of the survey (http://precesam.colmex.mx). See J. J. Mora Rivera and J. Edward Taylor, "Determinants of

Migration, Destination, and Sector Choice: Disentangling Individual, Household, and Community Effects," in *International Migration, Remittances, and the Brain Drain*, ed. Çaglar Özden and Maurice Schiff (New York: Palgrave Macmillan, 2005).

19. A contribution is this study is that it considers an interrelation between migration and labor sector choice, so the econometric model brings both migration destinations and sectors of migrant employment into an integrated modeling framework.

20. Based on this last result, in ongoing research the effects of climate change in Mexico's rural out-migration are being estimated.

21. Kaivan Munshi, "Networks in the Modern Economy: Mexican Migrants in the U.S. Labor Market," *Quarterly Journal of Economics* 18, no. 2 (2003): 549–99. J. Edward Taylor, "Undocumented Mexico-U.S. Migration and the Returns to Households in Rural Mexico," *American Journal of Agricultural Economics* 69 (1987): 626–38.

22. Policy-related determinants of migration are discussed below.

23. S. Richter, J. Edward Taylor, and A. Yúnez-Naude, "Impacts of Policy Reforms on Labor Migration from Rural Mexico to the United States," in *Mexican Migration to the Untied States*, ed. G. J. Borjas, 269–88 (Chicago: University of Chicago Press and National Bureau of Economic Research, 2007).

24. See M. Katz et al., "The Mexican Immigration Debate," *Social Science History* 31, no. 2 (2007): 1157–89, for differences in job experiences between Mexican men and women migrants to the United States.

25. For example, in the Mexico-to-United States migration context, Hinojosa argues that attempts to eliminate large-scale Mexican undocumented migration through restrictive immigration laws and Proposition 187 in California would have disastrous effects on the U.S. and Californian economies. Raul Hinojosa-Ojeda, "Transnational Migration, Remittances and Development in North America: Globalization Lessons from Oaxacalifornia Transnational Village/Community Modeling Project" (paper presented at the conference "Remittances, as a Development Tool in Mexico," for the Inter-American Development Bank, Mexico City, Mexico, October 2007). For a comprehensive synthesis of research on demographic, economic, and fiscal impacts of immigration in the United States, see James P. Smith and Barry Edmonston, eds., *The New Americans: Economic, Demographic and Fiscal Effects of Immigration* (Washington, D.C.: National Academy Press, 1997).

26. Studies that focus on immigration's impact on local economies may mask the macro effect of immigration on wages and employment (G. J. Borjas, "The Economics of Immigration," *Journal of Economic Literature* 33 [1994]: 1667–1717). Another theme treated in the literature on the labor market in migrant-receiving countries is related to the question of why the payoff to schooling is smaller for migrants in these countries (Barry R. Chiswick and Paul W. Miller, "Why Is the Payoff to Schooling Smaller for Immigrants?" IZA Discussion Papers 1731, Institute for the Study of Labor, 2005; "Educational Mismatch: Are High-Skilled Immigrants Really Working at High-Skilled Jobs and the Price They Pay if They Aren't?" IZA Discussion Papers 4289, Institute for the Study of Labor [2009]).

27. This later situation is documented for the service sector by Chiswick, quoted in Don J. DeVoretz, "Immigration Policy: Methods of Economic Assessment," Working Paper Series No. 04–13, Vancouver Centre of Excellence, June 2004.

28. Taylor and Martin, "Human Capital."

29. Hinojosa, "Transnational Migration."

30. DeVoretz, "Immigration Policy."

31. Ibid.

32. Smith and Edmonston, *The New Americans*. See also F. D. Bean and G. Stevens, *America's Newcomers and the Dynamics of Diversity* (New York: Russell Sage Foundation, 2003), 204–206.

33. DeVoretz, "Immigration Policy," quoting Sergiy Pivnenko and Don J. DeVoretz, "The Recent Economic Performance of Ukrainian Immigrants in Canada and the U.S.," IZA Discussion Papers 913, Institute for the Study of Labor, 2003.

34. M. Katz et al., "The Mexican Immigration Debate," presents a study of the catch-up process of immigrants from a historical, twentieth-century perspective for Southern and Western European immigrantion to the United States as compared with more recent migration from Mexico.

35. J. Edward Taylor, Philip L. Martin, and Martin Fix, *Poverty amid Prosperity: Immigration and the Changing Face of Rural California* (Washington, D.C.: Urban Institute Press, 1997).

36. Taylor and Martin, "Human Capital."

37. Research must include a wider perspective in order to study whether the United States as a whole and/or the state of California are major beneficiaries of large-scale Mexican undocumented migration, as Hinojosa ("Transnational Migration") argues.

38. References in Taylor, "International Migration and Economic Development."

39. Ibid.

40. J. J. Mora, J. Edward Taylor, and Antonio Yúnez-Naude, "Migración rural y desarrollo: El caso de México" (paper presented at the seminar "Globalisation, reconnexion Nord-Sud et recomposition des économies, des sociétés et des territoires" at the RINOS, Aix-en-Provence, July 2007).

41. This result does not support the generally accepted view held in the literature for Mexico that households with international migrants disproportionately spend their income on consumption (ibid.). It is consistent with the results reported by Adams based on a different modeling approach and for rural Guatemala (R. H. Adams, "Remittances, Household Expenditure and Investment in Guatemala," World Bank Policy Research Working Paper No. 3532, March 2005).

42. J. Edward Taylor, Antonio Yúnez-Naude, and S. Hampton, "Agricultural Policy Reforms and Village Economies: A Computable General Equilibrium Analysis from Mexico," *Journal of Policy Modeling* 21 no. 4 (1999): 453–480.

43. This is the case of the sharp devaluation of the Mexican peso with respect to the U.S. dollar in 1994–95. This exogenous shock meant that the value in pesos of

remittances from the United States increased. Another way for the amount of remittances received by migrant-sending countries to exogenously increase is when transaction costs of money transfers from migrants to their places of origin decrease (see below). Based on a multisector model for the whole of Mexico, Zarate-Hoyos reports the multiplier effects of an increase in remittances (G. Zarate-Hoyos, "The Development Impact of Remittances in Mexico," in *Beyond Small Change. Making Remittances Count*, ed. D. F. Terry and S. R. Wilson, [Inter-American Development Bank, 2005], 159–91).

44. Antonio Yúnez-Naude and J. Edward Taylor, "Effects of External Shocks on Small Farmers: A Village General Equilibrium Approach Applied to Mexico," paper presented at the XXVIth International Congress of the International Association of Agricultural Economists, Berlin, August 2000, and Hinojosa, "Transnational Migration."

45. See Mora, Taylor, and Yúnez-Naude, "Migración rural y desarrollo," for a detailed discussion of the general equilibrium effects of an exogenous increase in rural households' income.

46. S. Boucher, J. Edward Taylor, and A. Yúnez-Naude, "Impacts of Policy Reforms on the Supply of Mexican Labor to U.S. Farms: New Evidence from Mexico," *Review of Agricultural Economics* 27, no. 1 (2007): 4–16. The findings of these authors reinforce the conclusion of past research that IRCA did not reduce the supply of immigrant labor to U.S. farms (e.g., see Philip L. Martin, "Trade and Migration; NAFTA and Agriculture," Institute for International Economics, Washington D.C., 1993).

47. In addition, policies attempting to influence the characteristics of migrants have less influence over the characteristics of undocumented migrants.

48. G. J. Borjas, "Welfare Reform and Immigrant Participation in Welfare Programs," *International Migration Review* 36 no. 4 (2002): 1093–1123.

49. Taylor, Martin, and Fix, *Poverty amid Prosperity*.

50. Hinojosa, "Transnational Migration."

51. This is exemplified by the failure of the "New Migration Accord" discussed between the Bush and the Fox governments, which would have legalized current and future migration flows of Mexicans to the United States.

52. Since the market-oriented reforms of the 1990s, government interventions in the rural sector of Mexico have been characterized by exclusion, inequity, and contradictions. In their summary of results from a project to evaluate agricultural policies for the Felipe Calderon administration, Taylor, Yúnez, and Gonzalez conclude that current policy interventions have to be reformed in order to promote development (J. Edward Taylor, Antonio Yúnez-Naude, and A. Gonzalez, "Infrome consolidado," Report for the Project Políticas y Gasto Público Federal en el Sector Rural en México, Inter-American Development Bank and Mexico's Ministry of Finance, September 2007; see also Organization for Economic Co-operation and Development, *Agricul-*

tural and Fisheries Policies in Mexico: Recent Achievements Continuing the Reform Agenda, OECD, 2006).

53. Taylor, "International Migration."

54. A discussion of policies for rural development in Mexico is in Taylor, Yúnez-Naude, and Gonzalez, "Infrome consolidado."

55. This is also reflected in discrepancies in public opinion about the same question, especially in the receiving, developed countries. An example of debates on immigration policies in the United States is Daniel C. Vock, "States think Smaller, Slower on Immigration," at http://www.stateline.org/live/details/story?contentID = 297325.

Chapter 3. Global Migrations and Economic Need

1. For a variety of epochs, geographic foci for analysis, and interpretations see, among others, Immanuel Wallerstein, *The Modern World System I* (New York: Academic Press, 1974); "Globalization and the Financial Crisis," Special Issue of *Globalizations* 7 (1–2) (2010); Sylvia Chant (ed), *International Handbook on Gender and Poverty* (Cheltenham: Edward Elgar, 2010); Folker Froebel, Jürgen Heinrichs, and Otto Kreye, *The New International Division of Labor* (London: Cambridge University Press, 1980); Lydia Potts, *The World Labor Market* (London: Zed Books, 1990); Beverly J. Silver, *Forces of Labor* (Cambridge: Cambridge University Press, 2003); Hagen Koo, *Korean Workers* (Ithaca, N.Y.: Cornell University Press, 2001); A. Aneesh, *Virtual Migration* (Durham: Duke University Press, 2006); Hélène Hirata, Jules Falquet, and Bruno Lautier, eds., *Travail et Mondialisation* special issue of *Cahiers du Genre* 40 (2006); Uma Khotari, *A Radical History of Development Studies* (London: Zed Books, 2006); Michael Peter Smith and Adrian Favell, eds., *The Human Face of Global Mobility*, Comparative Urban and Community Research 8 (New Brunswick, N.J.: Transaction, 2006).

2. Aneesh, *Virtual Migration*.

3. Khotari, *A Radical History*.

4. Saskia Sassen, *The Mobility of Labor and Capital* (New York: Cambridge University Press, 1988); *Cities in a World Economy*, updated 4th. ed., (Thousand Islands,CA: Sage/PineForge 2010), chs. 5–7; Smith and Favell, *Human Face*.

5. Saskia Sassen, *Territory, Authority, Rights*, updated 2nd ed. (Princeton: Princeton University Press, 2008), ch. 5; Heather Hindman, "Outsourcing Difference," in Saskia Sassen, ed., *Deciphering the Global* (New York: Routledge, 2007).

6. Rhacel Salazar Parreñas, ed., *Servants of Globalization* (Stanford, Calif.: Stanford University Press, 2001); Barbara Ehrenreich and Arlie Hochschild, *Global Woman* (New York: Metropolitan Books, 2003); Hirata, Falquet, and Lautier, *Travail et Mondialisation*. Gisela Fosado and Janet R. Jakobsen (guest editors) "Valuing Domestic Work," special issue of *Feminist and Scholar Online*, 8(1) (2009), at http://www.barnard.edu/sfonline/work/index.htm

7. World Bank, *Global Economic Prospects 2005* (Washington, D.C.: World Bank, 2005).

8. United Nations Development Programme (UNDP), *A Time for Bold Ambition*

(UNDP Annual Report 2005); Saskia Sassen, *The Global City*, 2nd ed. (Princeton: Princeton University Press), table 4.5.

9. Kathryn Ward and Jean Pyle, "Gender, Industrialization and Development," in Chris E. Bose and Edna Acosta-Belen, eds., *Women in the Latin American Development Process* (Philadelphia: Temple University Press, 1995), 37–64; C. M. Reinhardt and G. Kaminsky, "The Twin Crisis: The Causes of Banking and Balance of Payments Problems," *American Economic Review* 89 (3) (1999): 473–500; "Globalization and the Financial Crisis," Special Issue of *Globalizations* 7(1–2) (2010); see also Jeffrey Henderson, "Governing Growth and Inequality," in Richard P. Appelbaum and William I. Robinson, eds., *Critical Globalization Studies* (New York: Routledge, 2005).

10. This is a vast literature coming at the questions from multiple angles and diverse places: among others, see Kathryn Ward, *Women Workers and Global Restructuring* (Ithaca, N.Y.: Cornell University Press, 1991); Jean L. Pyle and Kathryn Ward, "Recasting Our Understanding of Gender and Work During Global Restructuring," *International Sociology* 18 (3) (2003): 461–89; Nilufer Cagatay and Sule Ozler, "Feminization of the Labor Force: The Effects of Long-Term Development and Structural Adjustment," *World Development* 23 (11) (1995): 1883–94; Diana Alarcon-Gonzalez and Terry McKinley, "The Adverse Effects of Structural Adjustment on Working Women in Mexico," *Latin American Perspectives* 26 (3): 103–17; Ehrenreich and Hochschild, *Global Woman*; Central Intelligence Agency, "International Trafficking in Women to the United States," prepared by Amy O'Neill Richard (Washington, D.C.: Center for the Study of Intelligence, 2000); International Migration Office, "Trafficking in Migrants," *Quarterly Bulletin* (Geneva: IOM, 2006); Simone Buechler, "Deciphering the Local in a Global Neoliberal Age," in Sassen, ed., *Deciphering the Global*, 95–112; Max Kirsch, ed., *Inclusion and Exclusion in the Global Arena* (New York: Routledge 2006); Giselle Datz, "Global-National Interactions and Sovereign Debt-Restructuring Outcomes," in Sassen, ed., *Deciphering the Global*, 321–50.

11. For critical accounts see, e.g., Ester Boserup, *Woman's Role in Economic Development* (New York: St. Martin's Press, 1970); Carmen D. Deere, "Rural Women's Subsistence Production in the Capitalist Periphery," *Review of Radical Political Economy* 8 (1) (1976): 9–17; Diane Elson, *Male Bias in Development*, 2d ed. (Manchester: Manchester University Press, 1995); Bose and Acosta-Belen, *Women in the Latin American Development Process*; Pyle and Ward, "Recasting"; Sylvia Chant and Nikki Kraske, *Gender in Latin America* (New Brunswick, N.J.: Rutgers University Press, 2002).

12. For a variety of perspectives on this issue see, e.g., Frank Munger, ed., *Laboring Under the Line* (New York: Russell Sage Foundation, 2002); Laurence Roulleau-Berger, ed., *Youth and Work in the Postindustrial Cities of North America and Europe* (Leiden: Brill, 2003); Patricia Fernandez-Kelly, M.P., and Jon Shefner, eds., *Out of the Shadows* (College Station: Penn State University Press, 2005); John Hagedorn, ed., *Gangs in the Global City* (Urbana: University of Illinois Press, 2006); Eleonore Kofman, Annie Phizacklea, Parvati Raghuram, and Rosemary Sales, *Gender and International Migration Europe* (London: Routledge, 2000); Natalia Ribas Mateos, *Una Invitacion a la*

Sociologia de las Migraciones (Barcelona: Ediciones Bellaterra, 2004); Ida Susser, "Losing Ground: Advancing Capitalism and the Relocation of Working Class Communities," in David Nugent, ed., *Locating Capitalism in Time and Space* (Stanford: Stanford University Press, 2002), 247–90; Peter Taylor-Gooby, "Open Markets and Welfare Values," *European Societies* 6 (1): 29–48 (2004); William Julius Wilson, *When Work Disappears* (New York: Alfred A. Knopf, 1997); Kirsch, *Inclusion and Exclusion*.

13. For a range of issues and geographies see "Globalization and the Financial Crisis." Special Issue of *Globalizations* 7 (1–2) (2010); Mahmood Mamdani, *Citizen and Subject* (Princeton: Princeton University Press, 1996); Eduardo Bonilla-Silva, *Racism Without Racists* (Lanham, Md.: Rowman and Littlefield, 2003); Xochitl Bada, Jonathan Fox, and Andrew Selee, *Invisible No More* (Washington, D.C.: Woodrow Wilson International Center for Scholars, 2006); Christopher Chase-Dunn and Barry Gills, "Waves of Globalization and Resistance in the Capitalist World System," in Appelbaum and Robinson, *Critical Globalization Studies*, 45–54; Richard Sennett, *Respect in an Age of Inequality* (New York: Norton, 2003); Nick Pearce, "Diversity Versus Solidarity: A New Progressive Dilemma?" *Renewal* 12 (3), at http://www.renewal.org.uk/vol12 no32004diversityversussolidarity.htm; Revista Internacional de Filosofia, "Inmigracion, Estado y Ciudadania. Simpósio," *Revista Internacional de Filosofia* 27 (July 2006).

14. Boserup, *Woman's Role*; Deere, "Rural Women's Subsistence"; see also more generally Joan Smith and Immanuel Wallerstein, eds., *Creating and Transforming Households* (Cambridge and Paris: Cambridge University Press and Maison des Sciences de l'Homme, 1992).

15. Among others, see Patricia Fernandez-Kelly, *For We Are Sold, Me and My Sisters* (Albany: State University of New York Press, 1982); Mirjana Morokvasic, "Birds of Passage Are Also Women . . ." *International Migration Review* 18 (4): 886–907 (1984); Irene Tinker, ed., *Persistent Inequalities* (New York: Oxford University Press, 1990); Ward, *Women Workers*; Sassen, *Mobility of Labor and Capital*; June C. Nash and María Patricia Fernández-Kelly, *Women, Men, and the International Division of Labor* (Albany: State University of New York Press, 1983); Potts, *World Labor*.

16. Lourdes Beneria and Shelley Feldman, eds., *Unequal Burden* (Boulder, Colo.: Westview, 1992); Ruth Milkman, *Gender at Work* (Urbana: University of Illinois Press, 1987); see generally Silver, *Forces of Labor*.

17. *Feminism and Globalization*, special issue of *Indiana Journal of Global Legal Studies* 4 (1), 1996. On these issues see also, e.g., June C. Nash, *Social Movements* (Malden, Mass.: Blackwell, 2005); Toshio Iyotani, Naoki Sakai, and Brett de Bary, eds., *Deconstructing Nationality* (Ithaca, N.Y.: Cornell University East Asia Program, 2005); Mia Consalvo and Susanna Paasonen, eds., *Women and Everyday Uses of the Internet* (New York: Peter Lang, 2002); Khotari, *A Radical History of Development Studies*; Aihwa Ong, *Flexible Citizenship* (Durham: Duke University Press, 1999); Andrew L. Barlow, *Between Fear and Hope: Globalization and Race in the United States* (Lanham, Md.: Rowman and Littlefield, 2003); Linda Lucas, ed., *Unpacking Globalisation* (Kam-

pala, Uganda: Makerere University Press, 2005); Valentine M. Moghadam, *Globalizing Women* (Baltimore: Johns Hopkins University Press, 2005).

18. See, among others, Elsa Chaney and Mary Garcia Castro, eds., *Muchachas No More* (Philadelphia: Temple University Press, 1988); Sherri Grasmuck and Patricia R. Pessar, *Between Two Islands* (Berkeley: University of California Press, 1991); Parreñas, *Servants* ; Patricia R. Pessar and Sarah J. Mahler, "Transnational Migration: Bringing Gender In," *International Migration Review* 37 (3) (2003): 812–46; Pierrette Hondagneu-Sotelo, *Gendered Transitions* (Berkeley: University of California Press, 1994); Hondagneu-Sotelo, ed, *Gender and U.S. Immigration* (Berkeley: University of California Press, 2003); Ribas Mateos, *Una Invitacion*; Vanessa Tait, *Poor Workers' Unions* (Cambridge, Mass.: South End Press, 2005). There is also an important scholarship on new forms of cross-border solidarity, including organizations that fight the abuses to which women are subjected. Elsewhere I have examined the import of this, including the extent to which these organizations can operate globally by using the existing infrastructures of economic globalization (Sassen, *Territory, Authority, Rights*, chs. 6 and 7; on these infrastructures see also Peter J. Taylor, *Cities in Globalization* (London: Routledge, 2006); Neil Brenner and Roger Keil, *The Global Cities Reader* (New York: Routledge, 2005).

19. Texts where one can find analyses that get at these issues of strategic gendering even though they do not use this term are, among others, Chant, *International Handbook on Gender and Poverty*; Bose and Acosta-Belen, *Women in the Latin American Development Process* ; Saskia Sassen, *Losing Control* (New York: Columbia University Press, 1996); Ward, *Women Workers*; Pyle and Ward, "Recasting"; Chant and Kraske, *Gender in Latin America*; Parreñas, *Servants*; Ehrenreich and Hochschild, *Global Woman*; Cagatay and Ozler, "Feminization of the Labor Force"; Leslie Salzinger, *Genders in Production* (Berkeley: University of California Press, 2003); Christian Zlolniski, *Janitors, Street Vendors, and Activists* (Berkeley: University of California Press, 2006).

20. Sassen, *The Global City*, chs. 8 and 9.

21. E.g., Melissa Fisher, "Wall Street Women," in Melissa Fisher and Greg Downey, eds., *Frontiers of Capital* (Durham: Duke University Press, 2006); see also Hindman, "Outsourcing Difference," for a view from the "expatriate" side of professionals.

22. E.g., Parreñas, *Servants*; Grace Chang, "Undocumented Latinas," in Margaret L. Andersen and Patricia Hill Collins, eds., *Race, Class, and Gender*, 3rd ed. (Belmont, Calif.: Wadsworth, 1998), 311–19; see generally Ehrenreich and Hochschild, *Global Woman*.

23. Sassen, *The Global City*, ch. 9.

24. For overviews of the data see UNDP, *Time for Bold Ambition*; World Bank, "Increasing Aid and Its Effectiveness, in *Global Monitoring Report: Millennium Development Goals* (Washington, D.C.: World Bank), 151–87, at http://siteresources.worldbank.org/intglobalmonitoring/Resources/ch5_GMR2005.pdf; Sassen, *The Global City*, table 4.5,

25. Structural adjustment programs became a new norm for the World Bank and

the IMF on grounds that they were a promising way to secure long-term growth and sound government policy. Yet all of these countries have remained deeply indebted, with forty-one of them now considered highly indebted poor countries. The purpose of such programs is to make states more "competitive," which typically means sharp cuts in various social programs. By 1990 there were almost two hundred such loans in place. In the 1990s the IMF got an additional number of indebted countries to implement adjustment programs. Most of this debt is held by multilateral institutions (the IMF, World Bank, and regional development banks), bilateral institutions, individual countries, and the Paris group. There is a large literature that has sought to document and analyze these costs for women and children; see, among others, Beneria and Feldman, *Unequal Burden*; Bose and Acosta-Belen, *Women in the Latin American Development Process;* York Bradshaw, Rita Noonan, Laura Gash, and Claudia Buchmann, "Borrowing Against the Future," *Social Forces* 71 (3) (1993): 629–56; Carolyn Moser, "The Impact of Recession and Structural Adjustment Policies at the Micro-Level," in *Invisible Adjustment,* vol. 2, 2nd rev. ed. (Santiago: UNICEF, 1989), 137–66; Irene Tinker, ed., *Persistent Inequalities* (New York: Oxford University Press, 1990); Ward, *Women Workers*; Ward and Pyle, "Gender, Industrialization and Development."

26. Michel Chossudovsky, *The Globalization of Poverty* (London: Zed/TWN, 1997); Elson, *Male Bias*; Aminur Rahman, "Micro-Credit Initiatives for Equitable and Sustainable Development: Who Pays?" *World Development* 27 (1) (1999): 67–82; Guy Standing, "Global Feminization Through Flexible Labor," *World Development* 27 (3) (1999): 583–602; Lucas, *Unpacking Globalisation.*

27. For detailed examinations of these options see, Alarcon-Gonzalez and McKinley, "Adverse Effects"; Claudia Buchmann, "The Debt Crisis, Structural Adjustment and Women's Education," *International Journal of Comparative Studies* 37 (1–2) (1996): 5–30; Cagatay and Ozler, "Feminization of the Labor Force"; Erika Jones, "The Gendered Toll of Global Debt Crisis," *Sojourner* 25 (3) (1999): 20–38; Helen Safa, *The Myth of the Male Breadwinner* (Boulder, Colo.: Westview Press, 1995); Pyle and Ward, "Recasting"; Lucas, *Unpacking Globalisation.*

28. The actual structure of these debts, their servicing, and how they fit into debtor countries economies suggest that under current conditions most of these countries will not be able to pay their debt in full. SAPs seem to have made this even more likely by demanding economic reforms that have added to unemployment and the bankruptcy of many smaller, national-market-oriented firms. One indicator of the failure of these adjustment programs to do what they were meant to do is the fact that in early 2006 the leading economies voted formally to cancel the debt of the poorest eighteen countries, and proposed to extend debt cancellation to several more poor countries. See generally Jubilee Debt Campaign UK, *How big is the debt of poor countries?* (2009) at: http://www.jubileedebtcampaign.org.uk/2%20How%20big%20is%20 the%20debt%20of%20poor%20countries%3F + 2647.twl; International Monetary Fund, *Factsheet: Poverty Reduction Strategy Papers (PRSP)* (2009) at: https://www.imf .org/external/np/exr/facts/prsp.htm; International Monetary Fund *Factsheets Debt Re-*

lief Under the Heavily Indebted Poor Country (HIPC) Initiative (2009) at: http://www .imf.org/external/np/exr/facts/hipc.htm.

29. Eric Toussaint, "Poor Countries Pay More Under Debt Reconstruction Scheme?" at www.twnside.org.sg/souths/twn/title/1921-cn.htm.

30. Thomas Ambrogi, "Jubilee 2000 and the Campaign for Debt Cancellation," *National Catholic Reporter*, July 1999.

31. Jubilee Debt Campaign, *How Big is the Debt of Poor Countries?*

32. Asad Ismi, "Plunder with a Human Face," *Z Magazine*, February 1998, at http://www.thirdworldtraveler.com/IMF_WB/PlunderHumanFace.html.

33. OXFAM, "International Submission to the HIPC Debt Review," April 1999, at www.caa.org/au/Oxfam/advocacy/debt/hipcreview.html.

34. Ibid.; UNDP, *Time for Bold Ambition*; Ismi, "Plunder with a Human Face"; Pyle and Ward, "Recasting"; Ambrogi, "Jubilee 2000 and the Campaign for Debt Cancellation."

35. The $120 billion rescue package brought with it the introduction of SAP provisions, which reduce the autonomy of the governments. On top of that, most of the funds went to compensate the losses of foreign institutional investors, rather than to help address the poverty and unemployment resulting from the crisis. In short, several high-growth developed countries in the region saw a global financial crisis destroy healthy economic sectors. IMF structural adjustment programs did not fully recognize the need to delink these sectors, and implemented solutions to a financial crisis at the cost of economic criteria. For a good account of the region, see Kris Olds, Peter Dicken, Philip F. Kelly, Lily Kong, and Henry Wai-Chung Yeung, eds., *Globalization and the Asian Pacific* (London: Routledge, 1999).

36. World Bank, *Global Economic Prospects: Economic Implications of Remittances and Migration* (Washington, D.C.: World Bank, 2006).

37. See also Scott S. Robinson, "Towards a Neoapartheid System of Governance with IT Tools." SSRC IT and Governance Study Group (New York: SSRC, 2001), at http://www.ssrc.org/programs/itic/publications/knowledge_report/memos/ robinsonmemo4.pdf.

38. See generally Manuel Orozco, B. Lindsay Lowell, Micah Bump, and Rachel Fedewa, *Transnational Engagement, Remittances and Their Relationship to Development in Latin America and the Caribbean* (Washington, D.C.: Institute for the Study of International Migration, Georgetown University, 2005).

39. World Bank, "Economic Implications of Remittances"; see also the money generated through illegal trafficking in U.S. Department of State, *Trafficking in Persons Report*, released by the Office to Monitor and Combat Trafficking in Persons (Washington, D.C.: U.S. Department of State, 2004); David Kyle and Rey Koslowski, *Global Human Smuggling* (Baltimore: Johns Hopkins University Press, 2001); Moises Naim, *Illicit* (New York: Anchor Books, 2006).

40. Sassen, *The Mobility of Labor and Capital*.

41. Natacha David, "Migrants Made the Scapegoats of the Crisis." ICFTU Online.

International Confederation of Free Trade Unions: www.hartford-hwp.com/archives/ 50/012.html, 1999.

42. For one of the best accounts of the evolution of this state program see Robyn Magalit Rodriguez, *Migrants for Export: How the Philippine State Brokers Labor to the World* (Minneapolis: University of Minnesota Press, 2010)

43. Satomi Yamamoto, "The Incorporation of Female Workers into a Global City," M.A. thesis, University of Chicago, 2000.

44. There is growing evidence of significant violence against mail-order brides in several countries, regardless of nationality of origin. In the United States the INS has recently reported that domestic violence toward mail-order wives has become acute (ibid.). Again, the law operates against these women seeking recourse, as they are liable to be detained if they do so before two years of marriage. In Japan, foreign mail-order wives are not granted full equal legal status, and there is considerable evidence that many are subject to abuse not only by the husband but by the extended family as well.

45. The Philippine government approved most mail-order bride organizations until 1989, but under the government of Corazon Aquino, the stories of abuse by foreign husbands led to the banning of the mail-order bride business. However, it is almost impossible to eliminate these organizations, and they continue to operate in violation of the law.

46. Yamamoto, "The Incorporation of Female Workers"; Christine Chin, "Walls of Silence and Late 20th Century Representations of Foreign Female Domestic Workers," *International Migration Review* 31 (1) (1997): 353–85; Brenda Yeoh, Shirlena Huang, and Joaquin Gonzalez III, "Migrant Female Domestic Workers," *International Migration Review* 33 (1) (1999): 114–36; Parreñas, *Servants*.

47. Yamamoto, "The Incorporation of Female Workers"; Sassen, *The Global City*, ch. 9.

48. This is a whole subject in itself, with a rapidly growing research literature (see, for instance, John R. Bryson and Peter W. Daniels, eds., *The Handbook of Service Industries* (Cheltenham, U.K.: Edward Elgar, 2006); "World City Networks and Global Commodity Chains" Special Issue of *Global Networks* 10(1): 24–37 (2010). It is impossible to develop the subject here beyond a few summary statements (for a detailed discussion and extensive list of sources see Sassen, *The Global City*, chs. 5 and 6; *Cities in a World Economy*). In my reading, the growth in the demand for service inputs, and especially bought service inputs, in all industries is perhaps the most fundamental condition making for change in advanced economies. One measure can be found in the value of bought service inputs in all industries. For this purpose I analyzed the national accounts data over different periods beginning with 1960 for several industries in manufacturing and services. For instance, the results showed clearly that this value increased markedly over time. It has had pronounced impacts on the earnings distribution, on industrial organization, and on the patterns along which economic growth has spatialized. It has contributed to a massive growth in the demand for

services by firms in all industries, from mining and manufacturing to finance and consumer services, and by households, both rich and poor.

49. For instance, data analyzed by Timothy Smeeding, "Globalization, Inequality, and the Rich Countries of the G-20: Evidence from the Luxembourg Income Study (LIS)," Luxembourg Income Study Working Paper No. 320, prepared for the G-20 meeting "Globalization, Living Standards and Inequality: Recent Progress and Continuing Challenges," Sydney, Australia (May 26–28, 2002), showed that, for twenty-five developed and developing countries, since 1973 the incomes of the top fifth percentile have risen by nearly 50 percent, while those of the bottom fifth have declined by approximately 4 percent. According to the U.S. Bureau of the Census, from 1970 to 2003 the aggregate national income share of the top 5 percent in the United States went from 16 percent to 21 percent, and for the top 20 percent from 41 percent to 48 percent. All these figures will tend to underestimate inequality insofar as the top earners also have nonsalary based gains in wealth, and the bottom fifth measure will tend to exclude many of the poor who lack any source of income and are dependent on friends and family, or become homeless and dependent on charities.

50. Sassen, *The Global City* ch 5; Saskia Sassen, "Global inter-city networks and commodity chains: any intersections?" *Global Networks* 10(1): 150–63 (2010).

51. Sassen, *Territory, Authority, Rights,* ch. 6; Katherine S. Newman, *Falling from Grace* (Berkeley: University of California Press, 1999); James Lardner and David A. Smith, *Iequality Matters* (New York: New Press, in collaboration with Demos Institute, 2005); Lewis Mumford Center for Comparative Urban and Regional Research, *Segregation and Income in U.S. Cities*, at http://mumford.albany.edu/census/index.html, 2000.

52. For details see Bureau of Economic Analysis, "Improved Annual Industry Accounts for 1998–2003: Integrated Annual Input-Output Accounts and Gross-Domestic-Product-by-Industry Accounts," ed. Brian C. Moyer, Mark A. Planting, Paul V. Kern, and Abigail M. Kish, 2004, and especially table 12A. For the most comprehensive source on these services globally see Bryson and Daniels, *The Handbook of Service Industries.*

53. E.g., Christof Parnreiter, "Mexico: The Making of a Global City," in Sassen, ed., *Global Networks/Linked Cities,* 145–82; Sueli Ramos Schiffer, "Sao Paulo: Articulating a Cross-Border Regional Economy," in Sassen, ed., *Global Networks/Linked Cities,* 209–36; Joseph Gugler, *World Cities Beyond the West* (Cambridge: Cambridge University Press, 2004); John P. Koval, Larry Bennett, Michael I. J. Bennett, Fassil Demissie, Roberta Garner, and Kiljoong Kim, *The New Chicago* (Philadelphia: Temple University Press 2006); Sudhir A. Venkatesh, *Off the Books* (Cambridge, Mass.: Harvard University Press, 2006).

54. Sassen, *The Global City,*, chs. 8 and 9, especially tables 8.13 and 8.14.

55. E.g., Parnreiter, "Mexico"; Schiffer, "Sao Paulo"; Gugler, *World Cities Beyond the West*; Buechler, "Deciphering the Local;"; Sassen "Global inter-city networks and commodity chains."

56. As for the consumption needs of the growing low-income population in large cities, these are also increasingly met through labor intensive rather than standardized and unionized forms of producing goods and services: manufacturing and retail establishments that are small, rely on family labor, and often fall below minimum safety and health standards. Cheap, locally produced sweatshop garments and bedding, for example, can compete with low-cost Asian imports. A growing range of products and services, from low-cost furniture made in basements to "gypsy cabs" and family day care, are available to meet the demand for the growing low-income population. There are numerous instances of how the increased inequality in earnings reshapes the consumption structure and how this in turn has feedback effects on the organization of work, both in the formal and in the informal economy.

57. Some of these issues are well illustrated in the emergent research literature on domestic service (see, among others, Fosado and Jakobsen *Valuing Domestic Work*; Arlie Hochschild, "Global Care Chains and Emotional Surplus Value," in Tony Giddens and Will Hutton, eds., *On the Edge* (London: Sage, 2000), 130–46; Parreñas, *Servants*; Ribas Mateos, *Una Invitacion*) and in the rapid growth of international organizations catering to various household tasks discussed later. See also Hindman, "Outsourcing Difference," for the case of expatriates.

58. Home care services include assistance with bathing and dressing, food preparation, walking, and getting in and out of bed, medication reminders, transportation, housekeeping, conversation, and companionship (Fosado and Jakobsen *Valuing Domestic Work*). While less directly related to the needs of high-income professional households, it is the case that many of these tasks used to be in the care of the typical housewife of the global North.

59. Very prominent in this market are the International Nanny and Au Pair Agency, headquartered in Britain, Nannies Incorporated, based in London and Paris, and the international Au Pair Association (IAPA), based in Canada.

60. Sassen, *The Global City*, ch. 7.

61. For detailed analyses see Sassen, *Cities in a World Economy*, chs. 5 and 8.

62. It should be noted that while the supply of government staff is not getting internationalized, there are two emergent trends that constitute a kind of internationalization. One is the recruitment into high government office of distinguished foreigners who have served at high levels of their government. A well-known example is London's recruitment of a former top-ranked public transport government official in New York City to handle the public system in London. The other is the intensifying global networks of specialized government officials, whether competition policy, antiterrorism, or immigration government officials (Sassen, *Territory, Authority, Rights*, chs. 5 and 6); these networks can be quite informal or go beyond the formal institutional arrangements.

63. For empirical specification of this distinction see Sassen, *The Global City*, chs. 8 and 9; *Cities in a World Economy*.

64. To spatialize these interconnections I developed the notion of circuits for the

distribution and installation of economic operations as an analytic device that allows me to track the full array of jobs, firms, and spaces that compose a "sector" or industry. It allows me to capture the variety of economic activities, work cultures, and urban residential areas that are part of, for instance, the financial industry in New York City but are not typically associated with that industry: truckers who deliver the software and cleaners have work cultures, engage in activities, and reside in neighborhoods that diverge drastically from those of financial experts, yet they are part of the industry. These circuits are also methodological instruments to resist the analytic confinement of the low-wage immigrant workforce to "backward" industries just because the jobs appear as such. And they allow us to move into terrains that escape the increasingly narrow borders of mainstream representations of "the" economy and to negotiate the crossing of discontinuous spaces (Sassen, *Territory, Authority, Rights*, ch. 8).

65. There is an interesting parallel here with the earlier analysis in Jonathan Gershuny and Ian Miles, *The New Service Economy* (New York: Praeger, 1983), showing that one of the components of the service economy is the shift of tasks traditionally performed by the firm onto the household: e.g., furniture and even appliances sold unassembled to be put together by the buyer.

66. Sassen, *The Global City*, chs. 8 and 9; *Cities in a World Economy,* chs. 6 and 7.

67. These developments raise several questions regarding the employment of immigrants, which require more empirical research. Most generally, what is the impact of casualization in specific labor markets on employment outcomes for immigrants and, conversely, what is the impact of the availability of a casualized labor force on labor market characteristics? More specifically, does the casualization of the labor market interact with, reflect, or respond to the availability of a large supply of immigrant workers, and if so, in what ways does this happen? Second, to what extent are immigrant workers an effective supply for many of these casualized jobs? And third, how does immigration policy affect the characteristics of the immigrant labor supply, specifically, in what ways does it contribute to casualize or decasualize this labor supply?

68. While this is a controversial subject because there are no definitive data, a growing number of detailed field studies are providing important insights into the scale and dynamics of the informal economy. For a longer perspective, see the studies by Frank Tabak and Michaeline A. Chrichlow, eds., *Informalization* (Baltimore: Johns Hopkins University Press, 2000); Philip Martin, "Economic Integration and Migration: The Case of NAFTA," in *Proceedings of the Conference on International Migration at Century's End: Trends and Issues*, Barcelona, Spain, May 7–10, 1997 (Liège, Belgium: International Union for the Scientific Study of Population, 1997); A. Portes, L. Benton and M. Castells, *The Informal Economy* (Baltimore: Johns Hopkins University Press 1988); Laurence Roulleau-Berger, *Youth and Work;* Fernandez-Kelly and Shefner, *Out of the Shadows;* Venkatesh, *Off the Books;* Zlolniski, *Janitors, Street Vendors, and Activists*, to name but a few field studies on the informal economy in advanced economies.

69. Sassen, *Global City*, ch. 9; *Cities in a World Economy.*

70. Rick Fantasia and Kim Voss, *Hard Work* (Berkeley: University of California

Press, 2004); Tait, *Poor Workers' Unions*. There are numerous instances of how the increased inequality in earnings reshapes the consumption structure in a city like New York and how this in turn has feedback effects on the organization of work, both in the formal and in the informal economy: the creation of a special taxi line that services only the financial district and the increase of gypsy cabs in low-income neighborhoods not serviced by regular cabs; the increase in highly customized woodwork in gentrified areas and low-cost rehabilitation in poor neighborhoods; the increase of homeworkers and sweatshops making either very expensive designer items for boutiques or very cheap products.

71. Robert C. Smith, *Mexican New York* (Berkeley: University of California Press, 2005); Cecilia Menjivar, *Fragmented Ties* (Berkeley: University of California Press, 2000); Mary Waters, *Black Identities* (New York: Russell Sage Foundation, 1999); Marcelo M. Suarez-Orozco and Mariela Paez, *Latinos* (Berkeley: University of California Press, 2002).

Chapter 4. The Immigration Paradox

This chapter draws extensively from two prior publications, Howard F. Chang, "The Economics of International Labor Migration and the Case for Global Distributive Justice in Liberal Political Theory," 41 *Cornell International Law Journal* 1 (2008), and Howard F. Chang, "The Immigration Paradox: Poverty, Distributive Justice, and Liberal Egalitarianism," 52 *DePaul Law Review* 759 (2003). In those articles, a reader may find a more extended defense of some of the claims presented here. I would like to thank workshop participants at the University of Pennsylvania and at DePaul University and seminar participants at the University of Scranton for helpful comments.

1. *See* Jeffrey S. Passel, Pew Hispanic Center, *The Size and Characteristics of the Unauthorized Migrants Population in the U.S.: Estimates Based on the March 2005 Current Population Survey* 2 (2006).

2. *See* National Research Council, *The New Americans: Economic, Demographic, and Fiscal Effects of Immigration,* ed. James P. Smith and Barry Edmonston, 135–53 (1997) [hereinafter NRC].

3. See ibid., 334.

4. 8 U.S.C. § 1611(a) (2000).

5. Ibid. § 1427(a).

6. See, e.g., George J. Borjas, *Heaven's Door: Immigration Policy and the American Economy* 99 (1999).

7. *See* George J. Borjas, "*The Economics of Immigration,*" 32 *Journal of Economic Literature* 1667, 1697–98 (1994); Rachel M. Friedberg and Jennifer Hunt, "*The Impact of Immigrants on Host Country Wages, Employment and Growth,*" *Journal of Economic Perspectives*, Spring 1995, 23, 42; NRC, *The New Americans,* 223. For a survey of some of the recent empirical evidence on this question, see Howard F. Chang, "The Eco-

nomic Impact of International Labor Migration: Recent Estimates and Policy Implications," 16 *Temple Political and Civil Rights Law Review* 321 (2007).

8. Nolan McCarty, Keith T. Poole, and Howard Rosenthal argue that the immigration of relatively unskilled aliens into the United States in recent decades may help explain the failure of the United States to adopt policies to curtail the growth in income inequality during this period. *See* Nolan McCarty, Keith T. Poole, and Howard Rosenthal, *Polarized America: The Dance of Ideology and Unequal Riches* 117–38 (2006). This immigration would have such an effect, they suggest, not only by moving citizens (and thus the median voter) up the income distribution but also because voters are "less eager to redistribute if that redistribution has to be shared with the noncitizen poor." Ibid., 138. Both Rainer Bauböck (in this volume) and Stephen Macedo (in this volume) cite such effects as reasons to restrict the immigration of relatively unskilled aliens. I argue instead that these political considerations militate in favor of the admission of these aliens as guest workers rather than as immigrants.

9. Empirical evidence indicates that immigrant access to public assistance generates significant political opposition to immigration. See Gordon H. Hanson, *Why Does Immigration Divide America? Public Finance and Political Opposition to Open Borders* (2005); Gordon H. Hanson, Kenneth Scheve, and Matthew J. Slaughter, "Public Finance and Individual Preferences over Globalization Strategies," 19 *Economics and Politics* 1 (2007).

10. Michael Walzer, *Spheres of Justice* 60 (1983).

11. Ibid., 61.

12. Ibid., 52.

13. Ibid., 58.

14. John Rawls, *A Theory of Justice* 136–42 (1971).

15. Ibid., 136–37.

16. Ibid., 141.

17. Ibid., 4.

18. Ibid., 75–80.

19. Ibid., 457.

20. See John Rawls, *The Law of Peoples* 39 (1999); Walzer, *Spheres of Justice,* 35–48.

21. Bauböck (in this volume) adopts such a position.

22. J. J. C. Smart, "An Outline of a System of Utilitarian Ethics," in J. J. C. Smart and Bernard Williams, *Utilitarianism: For and Against* 3, 6 (1973).

23. *See* Charles R. Beitz, *Political Theory and International Relations* 143–53 (1979); Thomas Pogge, *Realizing Rawls* 257 (1989); Thomas M. Scanlon, Jr., "Rawls' Theory of Justice," 121 *University of Pennsylvania Law Review* 1020, 1066–67 (1973).

24. Beitz, *Political Theory and International Relations,* 151.

25. See, e.g., Macedo (in this volume); Thomas Nagel, "The Problem of Global Justice," 33 *Philosophy and Public Affairs* 113, 137–40 (2005).

26. A. J. Julius, "Nagel's Atlas," 34 *Philosophy and Public Affairs* 176, 187 (2006);

see Joshua Cohen and Charles Sabel, "Extra Rempublicam Nulla Justitia?" 34 *Philosophy and Public Affairs* 147, 164–75 (2006).

27. Andrea Sangiovanni, "Global Justice, Reciprocity, and the State," 35 *Philosophy and Public Affairs* 3, 7 (2007).

28. Ibid.

29. Rawls, *A Theory of Justice*, 72; see Sangiovanni, "Global Justice, Reciprocity, and the State," 6 (describing theories of "distributive justice that are grounded on the basic intuition that no one should be worse off than anyone else through no fault of their own, whether or not they share in any practices or institutions" as "nonrelational").

30. Pogge, *Realizing Rawls*, 247.

31. Ibid.; see Peter Singer, *One World* 177 (2002).

32. *See* Pogge, *Realizing Rawls*, 240–80; Martha C. Nussbaum, *Frontiers of Justice: Disability, Nationality, Species Membership* 264 (2006).

33. Joseph H. Carens, "Aliens and Citizens: The Case for Open Borders," 49 *Review of Politics* 251, 255, 272 n.8 (1987).

34. Ibid., 256.

35. Carens, "Aliens and Citizens," 256.

36. *See* U.S. Constitution, amendment XIV, § 1; 8 U.S.C. § 1401 (2000).

37. Carens, "Aliens and Citizens," 261.

38. Ibid., 263.

39. Ibid., 270.

40. Ibid. Others have reached similar conclusions regarding immigration restrictions in liberal political theory. See, e.g., Bruce A. Ackerman, *Social Justice in the Liberal State* 93 (1980); Phillip Cole, *Philosophies of Exclusion: Liberal Political Theory and Immigration* 202 (2000).

41. The Declaration of Independence, para. 2 (U.S. 1776).

42. Michael Blake, "Distributive Justice, State Coercion, and Autonomy," 30 *Philosophy and Public Affairs* 257, 257 (2002).

43. Ibid., 258.

44. Ibid., 265.

45. Ibid., 264.

46. Ibid., 265. Walzer also stresses that the threat of state coercion gives rise to claims of justice, declaring: "Men and women are either subject to the state's authority, or they are not; and if they are subject, they must be given a say, and ultimately an equal say, in what that authority does." Walzer, *Spheres of Justice*, 61.

47. Blake, "Distributive Justice, State Coercion, and Autonomy," 280 n.30.

48. Ibid.

49. Ibid., 271 (emphasis added).

50. Blake, "Distributive Justice, State Coercion, and Autonomy," 276.

51. Nagel, "The Problem of Global Justice," 128.

52. Ibid., 127.

53. Stephen Macedo, "What Self-Governing Peoples Owe to One Another: Universalism, Diversity and *The Law of Peoples*," 72 *Fordham Law Review* 1721, 1731 (2004).

54. Nagel, "The Problem of Global Justice," 129.

55. Ibid., 128.

56. Ibid., 130.

57. See 8 U.S.C. §§ 1325, 1326 (2000). In the United States, criminal prosecutions of such aliens under these provisions have increased dramatically in recent years. See Spencer S. Hsu, "Immigration Prosecutions Hit New High: Critics Say Increased Use of Criminal Charges Strains System," *Washington Post*, June 2, 2008, A1.

58. This assumption requires us to reject a principle of global equality of opportunity, for example, but Nagel offers no reason to reject such a principle. As Simon Caney observes, even if "the ideal of citizenship" provides "a reason *for* domestic equality of opportunity, . . . it does not give us an argument *against* global equality of opportunity." Simon Caney, "Cosmopolitan Justice and Equalizing Opportunities," 32 *Metaphilosophy* 113, 126 (2001). That is, even if "the ideal of citizenship" provides "*one* grounding for equality of opportunity," it does not follow that "the ideal of citizenship" is "the *only* grounding for equality of opportunity." Ibid.

59. Sangiovanni, "Global Justice, Reciprocity, and the State," 16.

60. Ibid., 19–20.

61. Ibid., 20.

62. Ibid., 4.

63. Ibid., 26–27.

64. Ibid., 28 n.45 (emphasis added).

65. Ibid., 26.

66. Ibid., 29.

67. Nagel, "The Problem of Global Justice," 133.

68. Joseph Heath, "Immigration, Multiculturalism, and the Social Contract," 10 *Canadian Journal of Law and Jurisprudence* 343, 350 (1997).

69. Ibid., 351.

70. Ibid., 355.

71. Nagel, "The Problem of Global Justice," 128.

72. Heath, "Immigration, Multiculturalism, and the Social Contract," 351 n.25.

73. Macedo, "What Self-Governing Peoples Owe to One Another," 1731.

74. Ibid.; see Macedo (in this volume).

75. Sangiovanni appears to adopt such a position. He argues that "we have special obligations of egalitarian justice to fellow citizens and residents," Sangiovanni, "Global Justice, Reciprocity, and the State," 4, yet also "agrees that immigrants have a prima facie claim to open borders," ibid., 38. Sangiovanni claims that his theory "offers no reason to grant states and their citizens an unrestricted right to close their borders." Ibid., 37. Instead, his theory is "compatible with a prima facie claim in favor of open borders, subject to the proviso that an open immigration policy not undermine the

capability of both the receiving and the sending state to provide those basic goods and services necessary to develop and act on a plan of life." Ibid.

76. Heath, "Immigration, Multiculturalism, and the Social Contract," 347.

77. Ibid., 348.

78. Ibid.

79. Rawls, *A Theory of Justice*, 39.

80. Gordon Hanson finds empirical evidence that recent restrictions on immigrant access to public benefits have softened political support for immigration restrictions. *See* Hanson, *Why Does Immigration Divide America?*, 54–57.

81. James Woodward, "Commentary: Liberalism and Migration," in *Free Movement: Ethical Issues in the Transnational Migration of People and of Money*, ed. Brian Barry and Robert E. Goodin, 78 (1992).

82. Ibid., 77.

83. Ibid., 79.

84. See World Bank, *Global Economic Prospects 2006: Economic Implications of Remittances and Migration* 25–35 (2006); Bob Hamilton and John Whalley, "Efficiency and Distributional Implications of Global Restrictions on Labour Mobility," 14 *Journal of Development Economics* 61, 70–74 (1984).

85. Thus, like Chandran Kukathas (in this volume), I would tolerate restrictions on immigrant access to welfare and to citizenship if those restrictions prove necessary to liberalize access for aliens to our labor market.

86. The United States can grant these and other rights, for example, the right to bring the worker's immediate family to live in the host country or even to naturalize as a citizen after a sufficiently long period of alienage has passed, even to relatively unskilled alien workers without generating a net fiscal burden. See Howard F. Chang, "Guest Workers and Justice in a Second-Best World," 34 *University of Dayton Law Review* 3, 7–8, 12–14 (2008); Howard F. Chang, "Liberal Ideals and Political Feasibility: Guest-Worker Programs as Second-Best Policies," 27 *North Carolina Journal of International Law and Commercial Regulation* 465, 470–73 (2002).

Chapter 5. What Is an Economic Migrant?

1. For a useful, if not entirely up-to-date, comparison of the two border regions see Peter Andreas, *Border Games: Policing the U.S.-Mexico Divide* (Ithaca, N.Y.: Cornell University Press, 2000).

2. Cris Shore, *Building Europe: The Cultural Politics of European Integration* (London: Routledge, 2000).

3. International Organization for Migration, *Migration Trends in Selected Applicant Countries*, Volume III: *Poland. Dilemmas of a Sending and Receiving Country* (Vienna: IOM, 2004); Fundacja Inicjatyw Spoleczno Ekonomicznych (Foundation for Socioeconomic Initiatives), *Cudzoziemcy w Polsce* [Foreigners in Poland] (Warsaw: FISE, 2008).

4. Saskia Sassen, *Guests and Aliens* (New York: New Press, 1999).

5. Among the legal instruments that restrict and impede access to international protection are Council Regulation (EC) No. 343/2003 of February 18, 2003, establishing the criteria and mechanisms for determining the member state responsible for examining an asylum application lodged in one of the member states by a third-country national (commonly known as the Dublin Regulation); Council Directive 2004/83/EC of April 29, 2004, on minimum standards for the qualification and status of third-country nationals or stateless persons as refugees or as persons who otherwise need international protection and the content of the protection granted; Council Directive 2005/85/EC of December 1, 2005, on minimum standards on procedures in member states for granting and withdrawing refugee status.

6. Sandra Lavenex, *Safe Third Countries: Extending the EU Asylum and Immigration Policies to Central and Eastern Europe* (Budapest: Central European University Press, 1999), 163.

7. Didier Bigo, "Security and Immigration: Toward a Critique of the Governmentality of Unease," *Alternatives* 27 (2002): 63.

8. For a general overview of the state of the right to seek asylum in the European Union see Sylvie Da Lomba, *The Right to Seek Refugee Status in the European Union* (Antwerp: Intersentia, 2004). For a detailed discussion of the new politics of compassion towards refugees in France see Didier Fassin, "Compassion and Repression: The Moral Economy of Immigration Policies in France," *Cultural Anthropology* 20, 3 (2005), and Miriam Ticktin, "Where Ethics and Politics Meet: The Violence of Humanitarianism in France," *American Ethnologist* 23, 1 (2006).

9. This thought was expressed by Janusz Grzyb; full quote reads: "We don't want to repeat the mistakes that the French committed with the Arabs and the Germans committed with the Turks. These immigrants do not adapt well to life in their new countries." Dziennik, July 25, 2007. I encountered similar sentiments in the course of my fieldwork, expressed by high-ranking officials of the Border Guard and the Aliens Bureau.

10. Zygmunt Bauman, *Wasted Lives: Modernity and Its Outcasts* (Cambridge: Polity. 2004), 28.

11. To protect the anonymity of informants, all names of persons and institutions have been altered or omitted.

12. This leaves no room for the kind of ambiguity that usually characterizes migrations precipitated by war or political instability. Indeed, it may be the case that not all persons fleeing Chechnya and other post-Soviet republics are victims of *direct, individual* persecution. Many are escaping generalized hardship, destruction, and insecurity created by the two Chechen wars. Some of them, especially those who take advantage of legal assistance provided by human rights organizations based on generally unsafe conditions in their country of origin, are able to obtain "tolerated status" and thus avoid deportation.

13. This is an innovation stipulated in Council Directive 2005/85/EC of December

1, 2005, on minimum standards on procedures in member states for granting and withdrawing refugee status.

14. The original Schengen Agreement was signed by France, Germany, Luxembourg, Belgium, and the Netherlands in 1985. It established common rules regarding visas, asylum rights, and checks at external borders to allow the free movement of persons within the signatory states. Under the Treaty of Amsterdam (1997) the Schengen legislation was incorporated into the European *acquis communautaire*. Today most E.U. states and some non-E.U. ones (Norway, Iceland, and Switzerland) are parties to the convention. The United Kingdom and Ireland are not.

15. Peter Andreas, "Introduction: The Wall After the Wall," in *The Wall Around the West: State Borders and Immigration Controls in North America and Europe*, ed. Peter Andreas and Timothy Snyder (Lanham, Md.: Rowman and Littlefield 2000), 5.

16. See, for example, Heather Grabbe, "The Sharp Edges of Europe: Extending Schengen Eastwards," *International Affairs* 76, 3 (2000); William Walters, "Mapping Schengenland: Denaturalizing the Border," *Environment and Planning D: Society and Space* 20 (2002); Sandra Lavenex, *Safe Third Countries: Extending the EU Asylum and Immigration Policies to Central and Eastern Europe* (Budapest: Central European University Press, 1999).

17. Especially in the years preceding accession, the eastern border issue was receiving a lot of attention, notably in Germany. On March 1, 2000, the Deutsche Presse Agentur ran a headline "Hundreds of thousands of foreigners are poised outside Poland's eastern border waiting to enter illegally on their way to the western Europe." These fears resurfaced in 2007, as the final border checks on the new members' western borders were being abolished.

18. On the explosion of East-West traffic see Krystyna Iglicka, "Shuttling from the Former Soviet Union to Poland: From 'Primitive Mobility' to Migration," *Journal of Ethnic and Migration Studies* 27, 3 (2001). In the years prior to accession, close to five thousand illicit crossers were being apprehended annually on the Polish-German border. This number dropped to under two thousand after the reinforcement of the eastern border (data made available by the Polish Border Guard, on file with author).

19. These were discussed at length in Krystyna Iglicka and Robert Rybicki, *Schengen—Consequences for National Migration Policy* (Warsaw: Institute for Public Affairs, 2002).

20. John Borneman, *Belonging in the Two Berlins: Kin, State, Nation* (New York: Cambridge University Press, 1992); John Borneman, *Subversions of International Order: Studies in the Political Anthropology of Culture* (Albany: State University of New York Press, 1998).

21. The opening of internal borders between the old E.U. member states and the newly admitted ones was gradual. This means that between 2004 and 2007 checks were retained on the Polish-German border and Polish consulates abroad were not authorized to issue Schengen visas. However, from the beginning the newly minted E.U. citizens had the privilege of free travel within Europe (though they did face re-

strictions on employment). Poland (as well as the other postsocialist states admitted to the European Union in 2004) became a full Schengen participant in December 2007, and this is when border checks with Germany, the Czech Republic, and Slovakia were ultimately abolished.

22. Chandran Kukathas, "The Theory and Practice of Open Borders" (Chapter 15, this volume).

23. The European Union's shared approach to asylum is a work in progress, but some essential elements are already in place. Those include the Dublin Regulation of 2003, which stipulates that every asylum seeker can lodge a claim only in the first E.U. country that she or he enters. Should she or he engage in so-called "asylum shopping," that is, file multiple petitions in more than one country, the EURODAC fingerprint database that records biometric information of asylum seekers entering all E.U. countries, and is available to immigration authorities in all member states, will facilitate determining which country is responsible for conducting that applicant's procedure. See also note 5.

24. United Nations High Commissioner for Refugees, *1951 Convention and Protocol Relating to the Status of Refugees* (Article 1, p. 2), at http://www.unhcr.org.

25. Data provided by the Aliens Bureau, on file with author. In 2009, however, the numbers appeared to be increasing. The bureau received 8,138 applications in the period between January 1 and October 1, 2009, in comparison to 8,517 over the course of all of 2008.

26. This changed markedly in 2009 when in the first ten months of the year nearly 45 percent of the applicants were Georgian citizens (in comparison to 0.8 percent in 2008).

27. The sources of these highly specific data on which the office relies to perform its tasks include information sent by embassies, databases with access restricted to state personnel, publications of the governmental Center for Eastern Studies, news from press agencies, local libraries, and E.U.-sponsored conferences and trainings on situation in countries of origin.

28. I am grateful to Professor Michael Katz, who commented on the initial version of this essay, for his observation that drawing distinctions between those entitled and those not entitled to a benefit is a fundamental act of public policy that has a long history of relying on "scientific" methods, only to ultimately produce discriminatory results. See Michael B. Katz, *In the Shadow of the Poorhouse: A Social History of Welfare in America* (New York: Basic Books, 1996 [1986]), 60–88.

29. As Fassin observed in his analysis of the values and norms by which immigration and asylum are thought and acted on in France, the political treatment of aliens "oscillates between sentiments of sympathy on the one hand and concern for order on the other hand, between a politics of pity and policies of control." Didier Fassin, "Compassion and Repression," 366.

30. Karolina Szmagalska-Follis, "Seeing Like a Border Guard: Migration, Policing

and Strategic Subversion in Europe" (paper presented at the annual American Anthropological Association meeting, Washington, D.C., November 28 to December 2, 2007).

31. Saskia Sassen, "Global Migration and Economic Need," Chapter 5 in this volume. Sassen argues that globalization brings the proliferation of what she calls "the professional household without a 'wife.'" She writes that "the absent 'wife' is a factor precisely at a time when professional households are crucial to the infrastructure for globalized sectors and need to function like clockwork. The demands placed on the top-level professional and managerial workforce in global cities are such that the usual modes of handling household tasks and lifestyle are inadequate. As a consequence we are seeing the return of the so-called serving classes in all the global cities around the world, made up largely of immigrant and migrant women." Though Sassen's argument pertains mostly to global cities such as London, New York, and Tokyo, on a smaller scale this phenomenon affects also less prominent urban locations, such as the postsocialist cities of Eastern Europe, where the rapid onset of capitalism upset the traditional household division of labor and also created structural conditions for the emergence of the immigrant "serving class."

32. Inaction vis-à-vis immigration persisted through the period of the nominally left-wing (but actually neoliberal) government that ushered Poland into the European Union and the subsequent conservative rule of the Kaczynski twins. Immigration was not a polarizing factor between the two governments. Rather, both governments worried that an open welcoming of immigrants would have been unpopular due to the fact that Poland's economic growth did not translate into improved economic conditions for vast sectors of the population. The perception of the Polish society as generally impoverished and thus in need of protectionist policies made inaction the safe way to go.

33. In December 2007, when Poland became a full member of Schengen, the practice of almost indiscriminate granting of tourist visas was curtailed. The hitherto free visas became a scarce and costly item (the application fee of 35 euros is nonrefundable and comes on top of the often lengthy and expensive trip to the nearest consulate). This forced many Ukrainians who already worked in Poland to stay on an expired visa and risk deportation rather than return home and apply for a new one, as most had done in the past. Others used the services of intermediaries who procure visas through illicit means at a steep price. It also halted the flow of new workers into Poland, finally forcing the Polish government to introduce a solution (see Epilogue).

34. Sassen, "Global Migration and Economic Need," Chapter 5 in this volume.

35. Until 2007 legalizing an employee for low-skilled work was obstructed by bureaucratic constraints and prohibitive cost. As of mid-2008, Ukrainians can be legally hired in Poland for vacancies which have failed to attract Polish employees. The period of employment cannot exceed six months in any calendar year, taken in two nonconsecutive intervals (in the sequence of three months at work, three at home, three months at work, three at home). Given these restrictions, few employees and few migrants go through the effort of obtaining a permit.

36. Andreas, *Border Games*, 106–12.

37. Even though the Border Guard boasts—in the words of one unit commander—"nearly 100 percent efficiency in catching illegals," there are of course ways to successfully sneak in. Smuggling immigrants is a developing business, and every now and again the press reveals cases of collusion of corrupt guards with the smugglers. A recent report focusing on the Vietnamese in Poland prepared at Warsaw University estimates that there are anywhere between fifteen thousand to twenty-five thousand illegal immigrants from Vietnam living in the country. The majority of them are thought to have entered with the help of smugglers as documented in Miedzykulturowe Centrum Adaptacji Zawodowej (Intercultural Center for Vocational Adaptation), *Raport. Wietnamczycy w Polsce. Perspektywy Adaptacji Spoleczno-Zawodowej* (Report. Vietnamese in Poland. Perspectives on Social and Vocational Adaptation) (Warsaw: Warsaw University, 2008).

38. Verena Stolcke, "Talking Culture," *Current Anthropology* 36, 1 (1995): 1.

39. Ibid.

40. Cited in Dziennik, July 25, 2007.

41. There is vast body of ethnographic work examining the experiential dimension of migrant illegality in the United States. A notable example is the work of Susan Bibler Coutin, who provided a prescient analysis of the condition of legal absence in Susan Bibler Coutin, "Being En Route," *American Anthropologist* 107, 2 (2005): 195; see also Nicholas De Genova, "Migrant 'Illegality' and Deportability in Everyday Life," *Annual Review of Anthropology* 31, 1 (2002).

42. For example, in 2005 forty-three traffickers were prosecuted, compared to thirty-nine in 2004. Department of State, *Trafficking in Persons Report* (Washington, D.C.: Department of State, 2005), and Department of State, *Trafficking in Persons Report* (Washington, D.C.: Department of State, 2006).

Chapter 6. Brokering Inclusion

1. This essay is based from material from my biography of the Tape family, *The Lucky Ones: One Family and the Extraordinary Invention of Chinese America* (Boston: Houghton Mifflin Harcourt, 2010).

Michael Walzer, *Spheres of Justice* (New York: Basic Books, 1983); Bruce Ackerman, *Social Justice in the Liberal State* (New Haven: Yale University Press, 1980); Linda Bosniak, *The Citizen and the Alien: Dilemmas of Contemporary Membership* (Princeton: Princeton University Press, 2006).

2. *Perez v. Brownell*, 356 U.S. 44, 64 (1958) (C.J. Warren, dissenting).

3. Bosniak, *The Citizen and the Alien*; Mae Ngai, *Impossible Subjects: Illegal Aliens and the Making of Modern America* (Princeton: Princeton University Press, 2004).

4. David Cole, *Enemy Aliens: Double Standards and Constitutional Freedoms in the War on Terrorism* (New York: New Press, 2005).

5. Rogers Brubaker, "Citizenship and Naturalization: Politics and Policies," in

Immigration and the Politics of Citizenship in Liberal Democratic Societies, ed. R. Brubaker (Lanham, Md.: Rowman and Littlefield, 1989), 121.

6. One may naturalize after five years of legal residence if one has no criminal record, is not a member of the Communist Party or totalitarian organization, and shows good moral character and attachment to the Constitution, 8 CFR 316 (amended 2003); U.S. Constitution, Art II, sec. 1; U.S. Constitution, Amendment XIV, sec. 1; *Afroyim v. Rusk*, 387 U.S. 254 (1967).

7. Ngai, *Impossible Subjects*, 6, 238.

8. Mae Ngai, "Birthright Citizenship and the Alien Citizen," in *Fordham Law Review* 75, no. 5 (April 2007), 2521.

9. Richard Alba and Victor Nee, *Remaking the American Mainstream: Assimilation and Contemporary Immigration* (Cambridge, Mass.: Harvard University Press, 2003).

10. For example, Linda Basch, Nina Glick-Schiller, and Cristina Szanton Blanc, *Nations Unbound: Transnational Projects, Postcolonial Predicaments, and Deterritorialized Nation States* (Langhorne, Pa.: Gordon and Breach Science Publishers, 1994); Aihwa Ong, *Flexible Citizenship: Cultural Logics of Transnationality* (Durham: Duke University Press, 1997).

11. Alba and Nee, *Remaking the American Mainstream*; on second generation and beyond, Robert C. Smith, *Mexican New York: Transnational Lives of New Immigrants* (Berkeley: University of California Press, 2006); Philip Kasinitz et al., *Inheriting the City: The Children of Immigrants Come of Age* (Cambridge, Mass.: Harvard University Press, 2008); Edward Telles and Vilma Ortiz, *Generations of Exclusion: Mexican Americans, Assimilation, and Race* (New York: Russell Sage Foundation, 2008). See also Danielle Allen et al., "Political Exclusion and Domination," *Nomos* 46 (New York: New York University Press, 2001). For historical perspectives see, for example, Kathleen Conzen et al., "The Invention of Ethnicity: A Perspective from the USA," *Journal of American Ethnic History* 12 (1992): 3–41; Russell Kazal, "Revisiting Assimilation: The Rise, Fall, and Reappraisal of a Concept in American Immigration History," *American Historical Review* 100 (1995): 437–471.

12. Prominent Chinese culture brokers in the late nineteenth and early twentieth centuries include Yung Wing (Rong Hong), Wong Chin Foo (Huang Qinfu), and Ng Poon Chew (Wu Panzhao).

13. *Tape v. Hurley*, 66 Cal. 473 (1885).

14. *Chae Chan Ping v. United States*, 130 U.S. 581 (1889); *United States v. Fong Yue Ting*, 149 U.S. 698 (1893); *Yick Wo v. Hopkins*, 118 U.S. 356 (1886).

15. *Brown v. Board of Education*, 347 U.S. 483 (1954); *Plessy v. Ferguson*, 163 U.S. 537 (1896).

16. *Plessy v. Ferguson*, at 561 (emphasis added).

17. Victor Low, *The Unimpressible Race: A Century of Educational Struggle by the Chinese in San Francisco* (San Francisco: East/West, 1982), 17. Low's work, which relies largely on a reading of the *San Francisco Evening Bulletin*, was an important starting point for my research.

18. "School for the Chinese," *Daily Alta*, June 9, 1853.

19. Ira M. Condit, *The Chinaman as We See Him: And Fifty Years of Work for Him* (Chicago: Revell, 1900), 91; T. Tseng, "Ministry at Arms' Length: Asian Americans in the Racial Ideology of Mainline Protestants, 1882–1952" (Ph.D. diss., Union Theological Seminary, 1994), 52; "Claims of the Chinese on Our Common Schools, Card from the Rev. Mr. Speer," *Evening Bulletin*, June 20, 1857.

20. In San Francisco, the Baptist Mission, Methodist Chinese Church, and Women's Occidental Board of the Presbyterian Church each sponsored day schools. "Statistics of Chinese Churches," 2–3; "Claims of the Chinese on Our Common Schools."

21. Low, *Unimpressible Race*, 7.

22. Wollenberg, *All Deliberate Speed*, 32.

23. Low, *Unimpressible Race*, 23.

24. Ibid., 16, 27.

25. Frederick A. Bee, *Memorial, The Other Side of the Chinese Question: To the People of the United States and the Honorable the Senate and House of Representatives, Testimony of Leading Citizens, Read and Judge* (San Francisco: Woodward and Co., Printers, 1886), 30, 38–39, 47–48.

26. Alexander Saxton, *The Indispensable Enemy: Labor and the Anti-Chinese Movement in California* (Berkeley: University of California Press, 1971); Yong Chen, *Chinese San Francisco, 1850–1943: A Trans-Pacific Community* (Stanford, Calif.: Stanford University Press, 2000).

27. *Daily Morning Call*, March 7, 1878

28. Wollenberg, *All Deliberate Speed*, 33. Wollenberg also points out that regardless of the change in state law, the Chinese were still entitled to public education according to the 1868 Burlingame Treaty with China. From another angle, permanent settlement—especially if it entailed birthright citizenship—undermined exclusion by creating a legal method of entry for those Chinese claiming U.S. citizenship. More than a decade before *Wong Kim Ark*, the San Francisco press fretted that a Ninth Circuit ruling recognizing the citizenship of Chinese born in the United States "still leave[s] open the door for admission on proof of 'citizenship,'" anticipating, of course, the paper-son strategy, by which immigrants gained admission by claiming they were sons of native-born Chinese, that would sustain Chinese immigration throughout the exclusion era. *U.S. v. Wong Kim Ark*, 149 U.S. 649 (1898); *In re Look Tin Sing*, 21 F. 905 (1884); "Citizenship and the Interpreter," *Evening Call*, November 10, 1884, 2.

29. Census of Chinese children in "San Francisco Items," *Union* (Sacramento), February 4, 1885; data on Chinese attending nonpublic schools in Low, *Unimpressible Race*, 54. Yong Chen's sampling of the U.S. census in San Francisco indicated a marked increase in the number of U.S.-born children after 1870. Chen, *Chinese San Francisco*, 56.

30. Petition "To the Honorable the Senate and the Assembly of the State of Cali-

fornia, Signed by 1300 Chinese, Including the Principal Chinese Merchants of San Francisco, Sacramento, etc.," 1877, J. G. Kerr, trans. (Bancroft Library).

31. The U.S. Census of Population, 1880, lists Joseph Tape's residence at 1771 Green Street.

32. U.S. Census of Population, 1870, 1880.

33. Otis Gibson, *The Chinese in America* (Cincinnati: Hitchcock and Walden, 1877). He ran the Methodist mission in Chinatown and testified before many official commissions on behalf of the Chinese during the 1870s. He was despised by nativists, who burned him twice in effigy and attacked his mission on Washington Street.

34. Frederick Bee, quoted in *Evening Bulletin*, October 4, 1884.

35. General School Law of California, Sec. 1662 (1880).

36. Wollenberg, *All Deliberate Speed*, 25–27.

37. *Evening Bulletin*, January 15, 1885; Wollenberg, *All Deliberate Speed*, 40.

38. San Francisco Board of Supervisors, *Report of the Special Committee on the Condition of the Chinese Quarter and the Chinese in San Francisco* (San Francisco, 1885), 59–62.

39. *Union* (Sacramento), January 10, 1885, 8. Assembly Bill 268 added the following to Section 1662: "and also to establish separate schools for children of Mongolian or Chinese descent. When such separate schools are established Chinese or Mongolian children must not be admitted into any other schools." The provision was repealed in 1947.

40. The doctrine of plenary power in immigration was set in the *Chinese Exclusion Case* and *Fong Yue Ting*.

41. *Wong Kim Ark*, at 731 (J. Fuller, dissenting).

42. Ibid., at 694.

43. *Slaughterhouse Cases*, 83 U.S. 36 (1873).

44. In the *Santa Clara* case, handed down on the same day as *Yick Wo*, the Supreme Court recognized the right of corporations to equal protection under the Fourteenth Amendment. *County of Santa Clara v. Southern Pac. RR*, 18 F. 385 (C.C.D. Cal. 1883), affirmed 118 U.S. 394 (1886). Morton Horowitz has persuasively argued that the theory of corporate personality did not emerge until the turn of the century and was then read back onto *Santa Clara*; the "real significance" of the case, according to Horowitz, was that it expanded the scope of the Fourteenth Amendment. See Morton Horowitz, *The Transformation of American Law, 1870–1960* (New York: Oxford University Press, 1992), 69. But see also Thomas Wuil Joo, "New 'Conspiracy Theory' of the Fourteenth Amendment: Nineteenth Century Chinese Civil Rights Cases and the Development of Substantive Due Process Jurisprudence," *University of South Florida Law Review* 29 (Winter 1995), 353, arguing that Justice Stephen Field used Chinese cases during the 1880s to rewrite his *Slaughterhouse* dissent into ninth circuit law, culminating in *Yick Wo*.

45. Linda Bosniak, "Membership, Equality, and the Difference That Alienage Makes," *New York University Law Review* 69 (December 1994), 1947.

46. Congress repealed the Chinese exclusion laws in 1943, as a wartime political measure aimed at combating Japanese propaganda that the United States held racist policies against Asians. Chinese Repeal, Act of 17 Dec. 1943 (57 Stat. 600).

47. *Tape v. Hurley*, 66 Cal. 473 (1885), Affidavit for Writ of Mandate, 3–4.

48. The NAACP and JACL were always careful to choose for test cases plaintiffs who were assimilated and middle class. When deployed in legal cases, however, the claims of the plaintiffs cannot be taken at face value. Affidavits and photographs are carefully scripted briefs, not untrue but often based on selective truths made for the purpose of argument. On racial uplift, see Kevin Gaines, *Uplifting the Race: Black Leadership, Politics, and Culture in the Twentieth Century* (Chapel Hill: University of North Carolina Press, 1996).

49. *Daily Alta*, April 16, 1885, 1.

50. Mrs. Tape's letter is read in Asian American studies courses and can be found on various Asian American civil rights Web sites. The letter began to circulate after it was reprinted in Judy Yung, ed., *Unbound Voices: A Documentary History of Chinese Women in San Francisco* (Berkeley: University of California Press, 1999). It also was featured in the Organization of American Historians' *Magazine of History* (Winter 2001).

51. Census records and published accounts of Tape's life give inconsistent years of birth and arrival in the United States. Tape may have been as young as twelve when he came to the United States.

52. In some documents, "Chew" is written as "Jeu." Joseph Tape's obituary states that he delivered milk for Matthew Sterling's dairy farm on Van Ness Avenue in San Francisco. Sterling is listed in the 1870 census with a fourteen-year-old Chinese male servant in his household. "Joseph Tape, Local Pioneer, Is Dead," *Daily Gazette* (Berkeley), March 11, 1934, 16; U.S. Census of Population, 1870.

53. In 1892 Mary Tape told a newspaper interviewer that she arrived in 1868, spent a few months in Chinatown (about which she said she had no recollection), and then was raised at the home of the Ladies Protection and Relief Society. "What a Chinese Girl Did," *San Francisco Morning Call*, Nov. 23, 1892. The Rev. Otis Gibson wrote that in 1869 he met one or two young Chinese women at the Ladies' Home, who had "escaped their confinement" and received help from the Rev. Augustus Loomis, the Presbyterian missionary in Chinatown. Gibson, *The Chinese in America*, 201.

54. U.S. Census of Population, 1880; Sanborn Fire Insurance Map for San Francisco (vol. 2, 1893); discussion of vegetable men in Him Mark Lai and Philip Choy, interview with Mamie Tape Lowe and Emily Lowe Lum, July 29, 1972, Portland, Oregon (copy in possession of author). I am grateful to Him Mark Lai for sharing this tape recording with me.

55. "What a Chinese Girl Did."

56. On home births, see Interview with Mrs. Herman Lowe, July 7, 1930, file 5017/562, Records of the Immigration and Naturalization Service, RG 85, National

Archives—Pacific Alaska region (Seattle); on Mary Tape's artistic endeavors, see *Art Catalogue of the Twentieth Industrial Exposition of the Mechanics Institute of the City of San Francisco, 1885* (San Francisco: P. J. Thomas, 1886), 51–53, 104; "Our Chinese Edison"; Peter Palmquist, *Shadowcatchers: A Directory of Women in California Photography before 1901* (Acatia, Calif.: n.p., 1990), 215. On domestic isolation of Chinese merchants' wives in America, see Judy Yung, *Unbound Feet: A Social History of Chinese Women in San Francisco* (Berkeley: University of California Press, 1995).

57. Lai and Choy, interview with Mamie Lowe and Emily Lum.

58. Ibid.

59. *Evening Bulletin*, April 14, 1885, cited in Low, *Unimpressible Race*, 71–72.

60. Sanborn Fire Insurance Company map of San Francisco, 1893, vol. 2 (microfilm). On Frank fighting with Irish boys, see oral history interview with Ruby Kim Tape by Jeffrey Chan, December 12, 1974, Combined Asian American Resources Oral History Project, Bancroft Library, University of California, Berkeley.

61. Lai and Choy, interview with Mamie Low and Emily Lum. California and most western states barred blacks, American Indians, and "Mongolians" from marrying whites. On interracial sex and marriage in the northeast, see Thomas LaFargue, *China's First Hundred: Educational Missions in the U.S.* (Pullman: Washington State University Press, 1987); John Tchen, *New York Before Chinatown: Orientalism and the Shaping of American Culture, 1776–1882* (Baltimore: Johns Hopkins University Press, 1999); Mary Lui, *The Chinatown Trunk Mystery: Murder, Miscegenation, and Other Dangerous Encounters in Turn-of-the-Century New York* (Princeton: Princeton University Press, 2003).

62. Lai and Choy, interview with Mamie Lowe and Emily Lum.

63. Low, *Unimpressible Race*, 79–80.

64. Ibid.

65. Palmquist, *Shadowcatchers*, 215.

66. Lai and Choy, interview with Mamie Lowe and Emily Lum; Wollenberg, *All Deliberate Speed*, 44. Joseph Tape purchased the house, a two-bedroom Victorian cottage, from the developer William Bissell, for about $1,000. Berkeley property assessment records, 1895, 1896, Bancroft Library, University of California, Berkeley. I thank Daniella Thompson for this reference.

67. U.S. Census of Population, 1910, 1920; Lai and Choy, interview with Mamie Lowe and Emily Lum; Statement of Robert Park, January 31, 1921, file 12016/1898, San Francisco District 12016 case files, INS-SF; Statement of Wong Fun [mother of Herbert Chan], November 15, 1920, file 24563/9–4, San Francisco District 12016 case files, INS-SF.

68. "Chinese Blood Goes into the Bureau," *Morning Call* April 4, 1905, 7; Statement of Robert Park, January 31, 1921, INS-SF; U.S. Census of Population, 1900, 1910; Lai and Choy, interview with Mamie Lowe and Emily Lum; Yuk Ow et al., *History of the Sam Yup Benevolent Association* (San Francisco: Sam Yup Benevolent Association, 2000), 214.

69. Tape's expressing business for passengers arriving on Pacific Mail ships and Southern Pacific trains is described in advertisements that appeared regularly in *Zhongxi Ribao* during the first two decades of the 1900s. In 1907 Tape was described as a "wealthy expressman . . . [who] is engaged by railroad and steamship companies to look after Chinese immigrants in transit through the U.S." See *Morning Call*, April 4, 1904. The U.S. Census of Population, 1910, lists Joseph Tape as a "transportation clerk" for the Southern Pacific Railroad. On Tape's bonding business, see Edward White to Commissioner General, exhibits A and C, May 10, 1922, file 12019/01, entry 9, Records of the Immigration and Naturalization Service, RG 85, National Archives (Washington) (hereafter "INS"); "Former Policeman and U.S. Investigator Takes up New Role," clipping fragment, ca. 1923, copy in Frank Tape file, Him Mark Lai papers, Ethnic Studies Library, University of California, Berkeley.

70. "Former Policeman and U.S. Investigator Takes Up New Post."

71. Norma Alarcón, "Traddutora, Traditoria: A Paradigmatic Figure of Chicana Feminism," *Cultural Critique* 13 (Fall 1989): 57–87; Neal Salisbury, "Squanto: Last of the Patuxets," in *Struggle and Survival in Colonial America*, ed. David G. Sweet and Gary B. Nash (Berkeley: University of California Press, 1981), 228–46; Gunther Peck, *Reinventing Free Labor: Padrones and Immigrant Workers in the North American West, 1890–1930* (New York: Cambridge University Press, 2000).

72. The most influential theory of immigrant assimilation was developed by Robert E. Park and the Chicago school of sociology in the interwar period. Park argued that a defining social process of modern society, especially urban society, was the "race relations cycle," in which immigrants and racial minorities experienced successive stages of contact, competition, accommodation, and eventual assimilation. Robert E. Park, "Race and Culture," *Collected Works* (New York: Free Press, 1950), 1:149–50.

73. Here Gordon revised Park's view that assimilation was organic and inevitable; Gordon's pessimism derived in large part from the persistent socioeconomic subordination of urban blacks and Puerto Ricans, which vexed social scientists in the 1960s. Milton M. Gordon, *Assimilation and American Life: The Role of Race, Religion, and National Origin* (New York: Oxford University Press, 1964). For a recent appraisal of assimilation theory, see Richard Alba and Victor Nee, *Remaking the American Mainstream: Assimilation and Contemporary Immigration* (Cambridge, Mass.: Harvard University Press, 2002). Alba and Nee argue that assimilation does not mean only integration into the social and economic mainstream but can also include incorporation into subordinated or marginalized social structures.

74. None of the Tapes is listed in extant baptism and membership records of the Presbyterian Chinese Church in San Francisco and the Knox Presbyterian Church in Berkeley. The elder Tapes were married in 1875 by the Reverend Augustus Loomis, head of the San Francisco mission. After Mamie Tape married Herman Lowe, the couple lived across the street from the women's rescue mission on Sacramento Street, and Mamie became a close friend of Tien Fook Wu (Wu Tianfu), the assistant to Donaldina Cameron, matron of the mission, although Mamie herself was not a

churchgoer. Frank Tape and Robert Park are mentioned in mission publications. *Tape v. Hurley*, [Joseph Tape] Affidavit for Writ of Mandate; Lai and Choy, interview with Mamie Lowe and Emily Lum; author interview of Carolyn Lum, August 8, 2005, Portland, Oregon; Ira Condit, "Americanized Chinese," *Woman's Work* 17 (August 1902), 219.

75. On practices of illegal immigration and corruption in the Immigration Bureau, see Erika Lee, *At America's Gates* (Chapel Hill, NC: University of North Carolina Press, 2003) .

76. Richard H. Taylor to Commissioner General, "Escape of Chinese Crewmen," July 2, 1909, file 52114/4A, INS; "Chinese Smuggled in by Mail Ships," July 24, 1908 [San Francisco *Examiner*], file 52114/4, INS; John B. Densmore, Report to Secretary of Labor Wilson, January 11, 1916, INS (microfilm, supplemental reel 4); Statement of Watchman David F. Graham, December 8, 1915, INS (microfilm, supplemental reel 4). See also Robert Barde, "The Scandalous Ship Mongolia," *Steamboat Bill* 250 (August 2004): 112–18.

77. According to Seid Gain, Tape had "a very limited knowledge of the Cantonese dialect, and no knowledge of written Chinese." Frank Larned, memorandum for the Assistant Secretary, 13 March 1908, file 53360/34, entry 9, INS.

78. US Commission on Industrial Relations, *Industrial Relations: Final Report and Testimony* v. VII, "Smuggling of Asiatics," 64th Congress, 1st session, Senate doc. 415 (Washington, D.C., 1916), 6127.

79. Testimony of Henry White, ibid., 6133–35, 6149; testimony of Henry Monroe, ibid., 6187–88, 6192–93.

80. Testimony of Henry Monroe, "Smuggling of Asiatics," 6192–93; R. P. Bonham to Commissioner General, 22 Aug. 1914, file 3864, INS; "Tape Arrested on Smuggling Charge," *Seattle Times*, 16 April 1914, p. 3; "Defendants win in Tape Prosecution," *Seattle Times*, 11 Dec. 1914, p. 13; "Tape Is Acquitted of Second Charge," *Seattle Times*, 18 Dec. 1914, p. 10.

81. On dismissal of Frank Tape, see Ralph Bonham, Memorandum to Commissioner General, August 22, 1914, and Commissioner General, Memorandum for the Secretary, September 2, 1914, file 5300/910B, INS; on jury service, see "First Chinese Called on Jury Here Real American," *Chronicle*, March 20, 1923.

82. "Federal Officials Bribed by Chinese is Charge," *Examiner* (San Francisco), 29 Oct. 1915, p. 1; "Secretary Wilson Orders Sweeping Alien Investigation," *Examiner*, 20 Nov. 1915, p. 1; "Indictments in Mongolia Case," *Examiner*, 4 Feb. 1916, p. 7; "US Secrets Stolen from Angel Island," *Examiner*, 20 Dec. 1916, p. 1; "Two More in Immigration Service Ousted," *Chronicle* (San Francisco), 12 June 1917, p. 11 (referring to Chinese interpreters Edward Park and W. H. Thatcher); "15 Indicted in Angle Isle Graft Plots," *Examiner*, 20 Oct. 1917, p. 10. The indicted included the three attorneys, an inspector, four clerks, two stenographers, an automobile agent, and three local Chinese residents); see also telegram, Densmore to Secretary of Labor, 6 April 1917; Memorandum, SF District Commissioner to Commissioner General, 20 April 1917,

typesheet, "Addresses and telephone numbers of Attorneys and Brokers who Practice in Chinese Cases," and sundry transcripts, depositions, and exhibits from the investigation in file 12016/176–1, box 4, series 232, INS, National Archives (San Bruno).

83. Robert E. Park, *Race and Culture* (Glencoe, Ill.: Free Press, 1964), 111–12, 354–56; Everett V. Stonequist, *The Marginal Man: A Study in Personality and Culture Conflict* (New York: Scribner's, 1937).

Chapter 7. Immigration, Citizenship, and the Need for Integration

1. See Adrian Favell. "Integration Policy and Integration Research in Europe," in *Citizenship Today*, ed. A. Aleinikoff and D. Klusmeyer (Washington, D.C.: Carnegie Endowment for International Peace, 2001).

2. Irene Bloemraad, *Becoming a Citizen* (Berkeley: University of California Press, 2006).

3. Christian Joppke, "Transformation of Citizenship: Status, Rights, Identity," *Citizenship Studies* 11 (1) (2007): 37–48.

4. John Rawls, "Justice as Fairness: Political Not Metaphysical," *Philosophy and Public Affairs* 14 (3) (1985): 227.

5. In some places, "reasonable" is a qualification of the "doctrines" that people hold, in others a qualification of the people themselves (e.g., John Rawls, "The Idea of Public Reason Revisited," *University of Chicago Law Review* 64[3] [1997]: 805).

6. John Rawls, *A Theory of Justice* (Cambridge, Mass.: Harvard University Press, 1971).

7. John Rawls, *Political Liberalism* (New York: Columbia University Press, 1993).

8. See Michael Sandel, "Review of Political Liberalism," *Harvard Law Review* 107 (1994): 1765–1794.

9. Dominique Schnapper, *Providential Democracy* (New Brunswick, N.J.: Transaction, 2006).

10. John Rawls, "The Idea of an Overlapping Consensus," *Oxford Journal of Legal Studies* 7 (1) (1987): 1–23.

11. Jürgen Habermas, "Geschichtsbewusstsein und posttraditionale Identität," in his *Eine Art Schadensabwicklung* (Frankfurt am Main: Suhrkamp, 1987).

12. Habermas quoted in Cécile Laborde, "From Constitutional to Civic Patriotism," *British Journal of Political Science* 32 (2002): 593.

13. Sandel, "Review of Political Liberalism," 1769.

14. Though the price for this, as Arash Abizadeh ("Liberal Nationalist Versus Postnational Social Integration," *Nations and Nationalism* 10[3] [2004]: 231–250) showed, is the civic nationalists' lapse into ethnic reasoning, thus blunting the ethnicity versus culture distinction that is dear to them for normative-political reasons.

15. Will Kymlicka, *Multicultural Citizenship* (Oxford: Clarendon Press, 1995), 173.

16. Ibid., 188.

17. Rogers Smith, *Stories of Peoplehood* (New York: Cambridge University Press, 2003).

18. Shmuel N. Eisenstadt and Bernhard Giesen, "The Construction of Collective Identity," *Archives européennes de sociologie* 36 (1) (1995): 75.

19. Oral statement by Bernhard Giesen, Holberg Workshop in Honor of Shmuel Eisenstadt, June 10–11, 2007, Hebrew University, Jerusalem.

20. Krishan Kumar, "Core Ethnicities and the Problem of Multiculturalism: The European Experience" (unpublished manuscript, 2007, on file with author), 17, 23.

21. House of Commons, *Encouraging Citizenship* (London: H.M. Printing Office, 1990), 8.

22. Katharyne Mitchell, "Educating the National Citizen in Neoliberal Times: From the Multicultural Self to the Strategic Cosmopolitan," *Transactions of the Institute of British Geography* n.s. 28 (2003): 387–403.

23. Ibid., 398.

24. House of Commons, *Encouraging Citizenship*, 3.

25. Crick Commission, *Education for Citizenship and the Teaching of Democracy in Schools: Final Report of the Advisory Group on Citizenship* (London: H.M. Printing Office, 1998), 8.

26. Ibid., 17.

27. Audrey Osler and Hugh Starkey, "Citizenship Education and Cultural Diversity in France and England," in *Citizenship and Political Education Today*, ed. Jack Demaine (Basingstoke: Palgrave Macmillan, 2004), 12.

28. Ibid., 23.

29. Emmanuel Todd, *Le destin des immigrés* (Paris: Seuil, 1994).

30. Christian Joppke, "The Retreat of Multiculturalism in the Liberal State," *British Journal of Sociology* 55 (2) (2004): 237–257.

31. Adrian Favell, *Philosophies of Integration* (London: Macmillan, 1997).

32. Crick Commission, *The New and the Old: Report of the "Life in the United Kingdom" Advisory Group* (London: H.M. Printing Office, 2003), 11.

33. Ibid., 20.

34. Ibid., 13–14.

35. Home Office, *Improving Opportunity, Strengthening Society: The Government's Strategy to Increase Race Equality and Community Cohesion* (2005), available at www.homeoffice.gov.uk.

36. Ibid., 21, 42.

37. Ibid., 42.

38. Ibid., 49.

39. Tony Blair, "Our Nation's Future—Multiculturalism and Integration," available at http://www.number-10.gov.uk/output/Page10563.asp (last accessed June 25, 2007).

40. Commission on Integration and Cohesion, *Our Shared Future* (2007), p. 38, available at www.integrationandcohesion.org.uk.

41. Ibid., 45.

42. Zali Gurevitch, "'Olam': Big Time in Israeli-Jewish Culture" (talk at Holberg Workshop in Honor of Shmuel Eisenstadt, June 10–11, 2007, Hebrew University, Jerusalem).

43. Ines Michalowski, "Bringschuld des Zuwanderers oder Staatsaufgabe? Integrationspolitik in Frankreich, Deutschland und den Niederlanden" (doctoral dissertation, University of Münster and Institut d'Études Politiques de Paris, 2007), 124f.

44. Aristide Zolberg and Long Litt Woon, "Why Islam Is Like Spanish," *Politics and Society* 27 (1) (1999): 5–38.

45. Per Mouritsen, "The Particular Univeralism of a Nordic Civic Nation," in *Multiculturalism, Muslims and Citizenship*, ed. T. Modood et al. (London: Routledge, 2006), 76.

46. Quoted in ibid., 89, n. 3.

47. CDU, "Arbeitsgrundlage für die Zuwanderungs-Kommission der CDU Deutschlands" (2000; manuscript on file with author).

48. Ibid.

49. Christian Joppke, "State Neutrality and Islamic Headscarf Laws in France and Germany," *Theory and Society* 36 (4) (2007): 313–342.

50. Ibid.

51. Mouritsen, "The Particular Univeralism of a Nordic Civic Nation," 84, 77.

52. Ibid., 81.

53. Ibid., 82.

54. Hartmut Esser, "Welche Alternativen zur 'Assimilation' gibt es eigentlich?" in *Migration-Integration-Bildung*, ed. K. Bade and M. Bommes (Osnabrück: IMIS-Beiträge no.23, 2004): 45–66.

55. Rogers Brubaker, "The Return of Assimilation?" in *Toward Assimilation and Citizenship*, ed. Christian Joppke and Ewa Morawska (Basingstoke: Palgrave Macmillan, 2003), 51.

56. Han Entzinger, "Changing the Rules While the Game Is On: From Multiculturalism to Assimilation in the Netherlands," in *Migration, Citizenship, Ethnos*, ed. G. Yurdakul and Y. M. Bodemann (Basingstoke: Palgrave Macmillan, 2006), 141; Anna C. Korteweg, "The Murder of Theo van Gogh," in Yurdakul and Bodemann, *Migration, Citizenship, Ethnos*, 163.

57. J. Duyvendak, T. Pels, and R. Rijkschroeff, "A Multicultural Paradise? The Cultural Factor in Dutch Integration Policy" (unpublished manuscript, 2007, on file with author).

58. Ibid., 29.

59. Ralf Poscher, "Du musst nicht verfassungstreu sein," *Frankfurter Allgemeine Zeitung* 28 June 2007, 7.

60. Interior Ministry of Baden-Württemberg, "Gesprächsleitfaden für die Einbürgerungsbehörden" (Az.: 5–1012.4/12, September 2005, copy on file with author).

61. Rüdiger Wolfrum and Volker Röben, "Gutachten zur Vereinbarkeit des Gesp-

rächsleitfaden für die Einbürgerungsbehörden des Landes Baden-Württemberg mit Völkerrecht" (unpublished manuscript, Heidelberg, 2006, on file with author).

62. Ibid., 15.

63. Ibid., 16.

64. Rogers Brubaker, *Citizenship and Nationhood in France and Germany* (Cambridge, Mass.: Harvard University Press, 1992).

65. Habermas, "Geschichtsbewusstsein und posttraditionale Identität."

66. For an informative overview of history textbook battles around the world, see "Where History Isn't Bunk," *The Economist*, March 17, 2007, 65–66.

67. Habermas, "Geschichtsbewusstsein und posttraditionale Identität," 170.

68. Talcott Parsons, *The System of Modern Societies* (Englewood Cliffs, N.J.: Prentice-Hall, 1971).

69. Ibid, 114.

70. Eric Kaufmann, *The Rise and Fall of Anglo-America* (Cambridge, Mass.: Harvard University Press, 2004).

71. Arash Abizadeh, "Does Collective Identity Presuppose an Other?"*American Political Science Review* 99 (1) (2005): 45–60.

72. Ibid., 46.

73. Wolfgang Schäuble, "Muslime in Deutschland," *Frankfurter Allgemeine Zeitung* (September 27, 2006), 9.

74. William Galston, "Two Concepts of Liberalism," *Ethics* 105 (1995): 516–534; John Gray, *Two Faces of Liberalism* (Cambridge: Polity Press, 2000).

75. Will Kymlicka, "Testing the Bounds of Liberal Multiculturalism?" (unpublished manuscript, 2005; on file with author).

76. Ibid., 8.

77. Bhikhu Parekh, "Superior People: The Narrowness of Liberalism from Mill to Rawls," *Times Literary Supplement* (February 25, 1994), 11–13.

Chapter 8. Engendering Culture

1. For challenges to the way in which this academic debate is framed, see my "Feminism Versus Multiculturalim," *Columbia Law Review* 101 (2001): 1187 (critically responding to Susan Moller Okin's *Is Multiculturalism Bad for Women?* [Princeton: Princeton University Press, 1999]); Sarah Song, *Justice, Gender and the Politics of Multiculturalism* (Cambridge: Cambridge University Press, 2007); and Anne Phillips, *Multiculturalism Without Culture* (Princeton: Princeton University Press, 2007). Song criticizes how political theorists have too narrowly framed the dilemmas of multiculturalism as a tension between multiculturalism versus feminism, group rights versus women's rights, or culture versus gender, and asks that we consider how minority cultures are both internally contested and interactive with majority cultures. Song, *Justice, Gender and the Politics of Multiculturalism,* 4–5. Phillips argues against the presumption of great cultural difference that typically underlies discussions of feminism and multiculturalism; her prescription is to shift away from the belief that multi-

culturalism necessarily involves group rights. See generally Phillips, *Multiculturalism Without Culture.*

2. Karolina Szmagalska-Follis, in her chapter in this volume, "What Is an Economic Migrant?" describes how the presumption of hierarchical cultural difference forbids some migrants entry all together. She reports that the culture of some immigrants is used by Polish immigration officials to rationalize forbidding entry to Poland, as their culture makes it difficult, if not impossible, for them to adapt.

3. Or, "we have principles, you have practices"; see Anne Norton: "Liberalism is presented as a set of ideas and principles, despite the fact that the practices of Western liberal cultures may not accord with these. Other cultures, not of the West . . . are assessed not according to their principles but according to their practices." Anne Norton, "Review Essay on Euben, Okin, and Nussbaum," *Political Theory* 29:5 (October 2001): 736–49 (describing the approach of Susan Moller Okin, Joshua Cohen, Matthew Howard, and Martha Nussbaum in *Is Multiculturalism Bad for Women?*).

4. Frantz Fanon described the shift from biological to cultural explanations for racial subordination as a progression from vulgar to cultural racism. See Frantz Fanon, *Toward the African Revolution,* trans. Haakon Chevalier (New York: Grove Press, 1988), 31–35.

5. For a description of how such selective blaming occurs in cases of adolescent marriage involving immigrants and white Americans see Leti Volpp, "Blaming Culture for Bad Behavior," *Yale Journal of Law and the Humanities* 12 (2000): 89.

6. Alan Pred, *Even in Sweden: Racisms, Racialized Spaces, and the Popular Geographical Imagination* (Berkeley: University of California Press, 2000), 75 (emphasis in original).

7. See Tanya Eisere et al., "Haunted by History," *Dallas News,* January 10, 2008.

8. Joanna Cattanach, "Activist Ayaan Hirsi Ali Tells Dallas Crowd of Islam Honor Killings," *Dallas News,* February 21, 2008.

9. To give another example of a recent case where the motive is unclear but Islam is to blame: In December 2007, sixteen-year-old Aqsa Parvez was murdered in Ontario, Canada, by her father, a Pakistani immigrant. The friend at whose home Aqsa had been living prior to her death asserted that there were many sources of conflict between the girl and her father, that whether Aqsa wore a hijab outside the house was only one of these sources of conflict, and that other women in the Parvez family did not wear the hijab. A number of imams described the murder as the product of family violence, and as against the teachings of Islam. But articles with titles like "Horror Under the Hijab" immediately circulated, claiming that Aqsa was strangled by her father for defying her father's command to wear a hijab and asserting that she was yet another victim of an honor killing. See http://en.wikipedia.org/wiki/Aqsa_Parvez.

10. See these and other comments on Michelle Malkin's blog, at http://michelle malkin.com.

11. I will not focus on honor killings here, other than to say that it is important to note scholarship observing that honor killings in the "East" and crimes of passion

in the "West," though differentiated in their victims (daughters, sisters, and mothers versus wives, ex-wives, girlfriends, and ex-girlfriends), are similar in how they are tolerated in both Arab and the U.S. legal systems. See Lama Abu-Odeh, "Comparatively Speaking: The 'Honor' of the 'East' and the 'Passion' of the 'West,'" *Utah Law Review* 1997 (1997): 287. Lila Abu Lughod has important work forthcoming on honor killings.

12. For a discussion of how "illiberal" Muslim practices are believed to directly threaten a substantive liberalism that is now increasingly the identity of citizenship in European states, see Christian Joppke, "Immigration, Citizenship, and the Need for Integration," in this volume.

13. Pred, *Even in Sweden*, 75–76.

14. See Moira Dustin, *Gender Equality, Cultural Diversity: European Comparisons and Lessons* (London: Nuffield Foundation, 2006).

15. Saba Mahmood, "Retooling Democracy and Feminism in the Service of the New Empire," *Qui parle* 16:1 (2006).

16. See Veit Bader's discussion in "Associational Governance of Ethno-Religious Diversity in Europe: The Dutch Case" in this volume, where he describes the Dutch shift from a corporatist multicultural model to a liberal assimilationist one, with increasingly strong undercurrents of marginalization and exclusion. For a critique that takes history to show the flaws in canonical assumptions about immigrant settlement and then political incorporation, see Mae Ngai's chapter in this volume, "Brokering Inclusion: Education, Language, and the Immigrant Middle Class."

17. See Irene Bloemraad's chapter in this volume, "'We the People' in an Age of Migration: Multiculturalism and Immigrants' Political Integration in Comparative Perspective."

18. Sherene Razack, panel entitled "Multiculturalism Versus Feminism, Round Two: Feminist Responses to Violence Against Muslim Women" at Brown University Pembroke Center Symposium on Gender and the Politics of "Traditional" Muslim Practices, Providence, Rhode Island, March 7, 2008.

19. At the May 2008 Penn Program on Democracy, Citizenship and Constitutionalism symposium on which this volume is based, it was suggested that a better term for this might be the "repoliticization of culture," since culture was so heavily politicized through these events. This is an important point, but my emphasis in this essay is to examine how a focus on the cultural origins of subordination removes the onus from the state, therefore depoliticizing events through an overemphasis on culture.

20. See, e.g., Hemant A. Pradhan, "An Arranged Marriage," *Washington Post*, September 5, 2000, A24. This letter to the editor responds to the heading of an article about the trial of Alpna Patel, who had stabbed her husband to death. See Maureen O'Hagan, "An Untraditional Death: Trial Bares Promise, Pitfalls of Arranged Marriage," *Washington Post*, August 29, 2000, B1. The letter argues that suggesting that arranged marriage was to blame for murder would be analogous to calling the death of Nicole Brown Simpson a "pitfall of dating." Pradhan, "An Arranged Marriage."

21. The lack of clarity as to what constitutes a forced marriage is also an issue. While one might presume that forced marriage should be simply defined as marriage of a person without his or her consent, a Council of Europe study defines forced marriage as: "An umbrella term covering marriage as slavery, arranged marriage, traditional marriage, marriage for reasons of custom, expediency or perceived respectability, child marriage, early marriage, fictitious, bogus or sham marriage, marriage of convenience, unconsummated marriage, putative marriage, marriage to acquire nationality and undesirable marriage—in all of which the concept of consent to marriage is at issue." Cited in Dustin, *Gender Equality, Cultural Diversity*, 9.

Among the many strange things about this definition is its failure to include among the examples the category of marriage against the will of one or both parties. We see instead the complete slippage between arranged and forced marriage, such vague terms as "traditional marriage" and "undesirable marriage" (from whose perspective?) as well as inclusion in this category marriages where the only victim may be the state, assuming both parties are engaged in its sham nature (marriage to acquire nationality, bogus or sham marriage, marriage of convenience).

The efforts of various European governments to target the issue of forced marriage is an important area of inquiry. See Sherene Razack, *Casting Out: The Eviction of Muslims from Western Law and Politics* (Toronto: University of Toronto Press, 2008) (arguing that forced marriage reforms in Norway have more to do with teaching "them" how to behave than having any meaningful antiviolence objective, relying upon the figures of the civilized European, the imperiled Muslim woman, and the dangerous Muslim man); see also Helle Rytkønen, "Europe and Its 'Almost-European' Other: A Textual Analysis of Cultural and Legal Practices of Othering in Contemporary Europe" (Ph.D. diss., Stanford University, 2002) (examining forced marriage reforms in Denmark). Rytkønen documents the historical impetus for these reforms (mayors concerned about overcrowding in cities) and conducts a powerful theoretical analysis that helps explain why Denmark has legislated the strictest reforms, requiring Danes seeking to sponsor non-Danish immigrant spouses to be twenty-four years old, have access to a certain amount of living space, and have with the potential spouse a greater connection to Denmark than any other country.

22. According to one commentator: "The practice of arranged marriages in particular has aroused the ire of many Norwegians as it so clearly conflicts with ideals of individuality and equality that the Norwegians hold so dear. Arranged marriages are not forbidden in Norway although forced marriages are. But obviously the Norwegians are unlikely to understand an ideology which puts the interests of the family before those of the individual in a society where many parents, if not most, breathe a sigh of relief when sons and daughters finally leave the nest at the age of 19–20." Thomas Hylland Eriksen, "Norway a Multiethnic Country," http://odin.dep.no/odin/engelsk/norway/social/032091-990909/index-dok000-b-n-a.html, cited in Razack, *Casting Out*, 124.

23. See http://www.marriedbyamerica.com.

24. I should point out here that the negative characterizations of "arranged marriage" have been made of marriage more generally. There is a long critique of "romantic" marriage as not, in fact, a choice; as a hegemonic institution pressuring individuals into a particular privileged arrangement that is used to police the boundaries of social acceptability; as still retaining vestiges of coverture; and as a failed institution. See generally Martha Albertson Fineman, *The Neutered Mother, the Sexual Family and other Twentieth Century Tragedies* (New York: Routledge, 1995); Nancy D. Polikoff, "We Will Get What We Ask For: Why Legalizing Gay and Lesbian Marriage Will Not 'Dismantle the Legal Structure of Gender in Every Marriage,'" *Virginia Law Review* 79 (1993): 1535; Joan Williams, *Unbending Gender: Why Family and Work Conflict and What to Do About It* (Oxford: Oxford University Press, 2000).

25. Bhikhu Parekh, *Rethinking Multiculturalism: Cultural Diversity and Political Theory* (Cambridge, Mass.: Harvard University Press, 2000), 275.

26. Ayelet Shachar, *Multicultural Jurisdictions: Cultural Differences and Women's Rights* (Cambridge: Cambridge University Press, 2001). In this book, Shachar lays out a developed multicultural prescription for what she calls "nomoi" communities, namely, religious communities, that would allow for joint governance by both state and religious communities. She proposes, with a specific focus on family law, that nomoi communities be allowed to control demarcating functions, for example, who may belong to the group through marriage but not be allowed to control distributive functions, such as property relations on death or divorce.

27. Shachar also mentions matters of virginity and sexual purity that may be significant to a community as possibly creating strong pressures to remain in an arranged marriage. Ibid., 103.

28. In Louisiana, the only grounds on which one can receive a divorce in a covenant marriage are the following: (1) The other spouse has committed adultery. (2) The other spouse has committed a felony and has been sentenced to death or imprisonment at hard labor. (3) The other spouse has abandoned the matrimonial domicile for a period of one year and constantly refuses to return. (4) The other spouse has physically or sexually abused the spouse seeking the divorce or a child of one of the spouses. (5) The spouses have been living separate and apart continuously without reconciliation for a period of two years. (6)(a) The spouses have been living separate and apart continuously without reconciliation for a period of one year from the date the judgment of separation from bed and board was signed. (b) If there is a minor child or children of the marriage, the spouses have been living separate and apart continuously without reconciliation for a period of one year and six months from the date the judgment of separation from bed and board was signed; however, if abuse of a child of the marriage or a child of one of the spouses is the basis for which the judgment of separation from bed and board was obtained, then a judgment of divorce may be obtained if the spouses have been living separate and apart continuously without reconciliation for a period of one year from the date the judgment of separation from bed and board was signed. New Louisiana Covenant Marriage Law. See La. Rev.

Stat. Ann. secs. 9:234, 9:272–75, 9:307–9 (2004). For the Arkansas and Arizona statutes see Ark. Code Ann. Sec. 9–11–801 (2004) and Ariz. Rev. Stat. Sec. 25–901 (2004). For a discussion of covenant marriage, see Chauncey E. Brummer, "The Shackles of Covenant Marriage: Who Holds the Keys to Wedlock," *University of Arkansas at Little Rock Law Review* 25 (2002): 261; Joel A. Nichols, "Louisiana's Covenant Marriage Law: A First Step Toward a More Robust Pluralism in Marriage and Divorce Law?" *Emory Law Journal* 47 (1998): 929.

29. Mae M. Ngai, *Impossible Subjects: Illegal Aliens and the Making of Modern America* (Princeton: Princeton University Press, 2003), 177–79.

30. Eric Yamamoto et al., *Race, Rights and Reparation: Law and the Japanese American Internment* (Gaithersburg, Md.: Aspen Law and Business, 2001), 216. As has been pointed out, answering yes to question 28 made Issei (first generation) Japanese Americans stateless, since they were ineligible to naturalize as U.S. citizens and would be forswearing allegiance to Japan. Ibid.

31. See Chris K. Iijima, "Reparations and the 'Model Minority' Ideology of Acquiescence: The Necessity to Refuse the Return to Original Humiliation," *Boston College Law Review* 40 (1999): 385.

32. See Ngai, *Impossible Subjects*, 201, arguing that the effort by the government to impose a normative cultural citizenship when Japanese Americans were denied citizenship as a matter of explicit legal rights and obligations could only have perverse results, namely, citizenship renunciation requests by 5,500 interned Japanese Americans (5,409 later requested to have their citizenship restored).

33. Michi Weglyn, *Years of Infamy: The Untold Story of America's Concentration Camps* (New York: Morrow, 1976).

34. See Caroline Chung Simpson, *An Absent Presence: Japanese Americans in Postwar American Culture 1945–1960* (Durham: Duke University Press, 2001). As she argues, this not only reflected the American propensity for seeing Japanese Americans as Japanese aliens but also assisted in constructing a particular idea about the culture and character of both Japanese and Japanese Americans. Ibid., 45–47; see also Orin Starn, "Engineering Internment: Anthropologists and the War Relocation Authority," *American Ethnologist* 13 (1986): 700.

35. Thomas James, *Exile Within: The Schooling of Japanese Americans* (Cambridge, Mass.: Harvard University Press, 1987), 87.

36. As Justice Murphy wrote in *Korematsu* in a sharply worded dissent: "In support of this blanket condemnation of all persons of Japanese descent, however, no reliable evidence is cited. . . . Justification for the exclusion is sought, instead, mainly upon questionable racial and sociological grounds. . . . Individuals of Japanese ancestry are condemned because they are said to be a large, unassimilated, tightly knit racial group, bound to an enemy nation by strong ties of race, culture, custom and religion." *Korematsu v. U.S.*, 323, U.S. 214, 234 (1944) (Murphy, J., dissenting).

37. This photograph and caption can be found on pages 178–79 of Ngai, *Impossible Subjects*.

38. See Home Secretary David Blunkett, *Secure Borders, Safe Haven: Integration with Diversity in Modern Britain* (Norwich: Her Majesty's Stationery Office, February 2002), available at http://www.sofn.org.uk/london/articles/Secure%20Borders,%20Safe %20Haven.pdf.

39. The White Paper also proposed extending the British period of conditional residency from one year to two years, to increase the chance of "exposing sham marriages," since, the White Paper states, the concern is for residents "duped" into marriage to bring a spouse from overseas to Britain. The couple are asked to prove the strength of their love during these two years by living "without recourse to public funds." Ibid., 100.

40. See Chapter 7, "Marriage/Family Visits and War Criminals," ibid., 99.

41. Ibid. The government appears to be articulating a position here in favor of intraracial marriages.

42. Colin Blackstock, "Blunkett in Clash Over Marriages," *Guardian*, February 8, 2002, at http://www.guardian.co.uk/uk/2002/feb/08/race.immigrationpolicy.

43. See Ratna Kapur, "Monsoon in a Teacup," *Legal Affairs* (September–October 2002), http://www.legalaffairs.org/issues/September-October-2002/review_kapur_sep oct2002.msp. See also her discussion of the White Paper in Ratna Kapur, "Travel Plans: Border Crossings and the Rights of Transnational Migrants," *Harvard Human Rights Journal* 18 (2005): 107.

44. The age at which one could sponsor a spouse's entry was changed in 2005 from sixteen to eighteen, although sixteen is the age at which individuals can normally marry with parental permission in the United Kingdom.

45. See Home Office, "New Arrangements for Partners," March 13, 2009, at http://www.ukba.homeoffice.gov.uk/sitecontent/newsfragments/ Newarrangementsforpartners.

46. See Uma Narayan, *Dislocating Cultures: Identities, Traditions, and Third World Feminisms* (New York: Routledge, 1997), 178 (describing the subjecting of new brides from India in arranged marriages to virginity tests as the "low point" of British immigration policy); see "Asylum Seekers: The New Enemy Within," *SchNEWS* 54 (December 21, 1995), http://www.schnews.org.uk/archive/news54.htm (stating, "No one should imagine that Labour will oppose racist immigration laws—when they were in government they forced Indian and Pakistani women to undergo virginity tests on arrival in Britain in order to get into the country!"); see R. Warah, "Southall Black Sisters," http://www.ncbi.nlm.nih.gov/entrez/query.fcgi?cmd = Retrieve&db = Pub Med&list_uids = 12287625&dopt = Abstract (mentioning illegal virginity tests as the target of a campaign by Southall Black Sisters).

In contrast, *lack* of virginity today is used by immigration inspectors as a basis for immigration admission. This is in Denmark, where proof of premarital sex in the form of an illegitimate child can be a sign of a voluntary marriage. Rytkønen discovered this through an interview with the Danish Immigration Service. In Denmark, the age for legal sex is fifteen, and the age for marrying is eighteen (sixteen with the permission of the Queen); sex before marriage is therefore legal. See Rytkønen, "Europe and Its 'Almost-European' Other."

47. U.S. immigration law contains a provision that appears designed to discourage the variant of arranged marriage where the couple has not met before marriage. See 8 U.S.C.A. §1184 (stating that a fiancé or fiancée visa shall not be issued unless the couple had previously met in person within two years before the date of filing the petition). See Stephen Legomsky, *Immigration and Refugee Law and Policy* (New York: Foundation Press, 2002), 369, pointing to this requirement and asking to what extent U.S. immigration laws should "respond to cultural norms different from our own." I would add here that, given the difficulty of transnational travel for many individuals, it might not be unusual for couples in a "love marriage" to not meet in person for two years before filing a fiancé or fiancée petition.

48. Obviously there is a long history of using the status of women as a proxy to target communities in general; we could think here of how the status of women was used as an index of civilizational development that justified colonialism and we could also consider how "gender apartheid" under the Taliban functioned to justify U.S. invasion of Afghanistan.

49. See Statement by Jacques Chirac, President of the Republic, January 28, 2004, at http://www.info-france-usa.org/news/statmnts/2004/chirac_secularism012804.asp.

50. Ibid.

51. See, e.g., Moustafa Bayoumi, "How Does It Feel to Be a Problem?" in *Asian Americans on War and Peace*, ed. Russell Leong and Don Nakanishi (Los Angeles: UCLA Asian American Studies Center Press, 2002).

52. See Elaine Sciolino, "France Turns to Tough Policy on Students' Religious Garb," *New York Times*, October 22, 2004, A3. She writes: "Officially the law is aimed at enforcing France's republican ideal of secularism. Unofficially it is aimed at stopping female Muslim public school students from swathing themselves in scarves or even long veils." Ibid.

53. See Elaine Sciolino, "Sikhs in France?" *New York Times*, January 12, 2004, A3.

54. See "Le magazine *Elle* lance un appel contre le voile," *Elle*, December 5, 2003 (describing the veil as a "symbole visible de la soumission de la femme"). Signatories included Isabelle Adjani, Sonia Rykiel, Isabelle Huppert, and Emmanuelle Béart.

55. As Saba Mahmood writes, that the veil is widely assumed to be a symbol of something reflects secular reasoning. In a critique of secular normativity, she notes: "It is widely assumed that the veil is a symbol whose variable meanings inhere either in the woman's intentions or in the context of its adornment. Whether it is those who hail the veil as a symbol of their religious or cultural identity or those who spurn it as a symbol of women's oppression (as to many feminists), the idea that the veil should be understood primarily as a sign (that signifies *something*) reigns supreme. Women who contend that the veil is part of a religious doctrine, a divine edict, or a form of ethical practice and that it therefore has nothing to do with 'Identity' are usually judged to be victims of false consciousness, mired in a traditionalism that leads them

to mistakenly internalize the opinions of misogynist jurists whom they should resist." Saba Mahmood, "Secularism, Hernmeneutics, and Empire: The Politics of Islamic Reformation," *Public Culture* 18 (2006): 323.

56. See T. Jeremy Gunn, "Religious Freedom and *Laïcité*: A Comparison of the United States and France," *Brigham Young University Law Review* 2004 (2004): 469–70 (criticizing the weak evidence on which the Stasi Commission based its finding of coercion as the basis for girls wearing headscarves).

57. At issue seems both the wearer's perspective and how the headscarf is read by others. On how the wearer's identity shapes whether one's wearing a headscarf is perceived as fashion or faith, see Homa Hoodfar, "The Veil in Their Minds and on Our Heads: Veiling Practices and Muslim Women," in *The Politics of Culture in the Shadow of Capital*, ed. Lisa Lowe and David Lloyd (Durham: Duke University Press, 1997), 248, 270 .

58. See "Petition contre une loi d'exclusion: Un voile sur les discriminations," http://www.islamlaicite.org/rubrique13.html, translated as "Veiled Discrimination").

59. For an analysis of another undertheorized aspect of the headscarf debate, see Joan Scott, "Symptomatic Politics: The Banning of Islamic Head Scarves in French Public Schools," *French Culture, Politics and Society* 23 (2005). Scott argues that what is at stake in the prohibition of the veil is protection of French republican notions of sexuality against the "disturbing difference of Islam—an Islam whose difference is phantasmatically cast in terms of a difference of sexual practice." This reflects a contradiction at the heart of the republican vision represented by women: "their difference is both denied and avowed." In republicanism, equality depends on sameness, which is achieved by abstraction, but sex is not considered susceptible to abstraction. To cover this contradiction, French politicians and republican theorists have elevated sexual difference to a distinct cultural character trait with great emphasis on the public display of women's bodies. Scott writes: "Perhaps the most stunning contradiction was the alliance of so many French feminists who in the name of emancipation of Muslim girls, rushed to support a law that offered the status quo in France (women as the *object* of male desire!!) as a universal model of women's liberation. Entirely forgotten in the glorification of the freedom of French sexual relations was the critique of these same feminists, who for years have decried the limits of their own patriarchal system with its objectification of women and overemphasis on their sexual attractiveness. It is the power of their unconscious identification with the republican project that led many of them to unequivocally condemn the head scarf/veil as a denial of women's rights and to talk as if the status of women in France were not a problem at all."

60. "Veiled Discrimination."

61. Ibid.

62. Ibid.

63. Ibid.

64. Ibid.

65. See Jane Kramer, "Taking the Veil," *New Yorker*, November 22, 2004, 59 (describing the accusations of strangers that a young veiled Muslim woman was carrying bombs in her bookbag). Kramer describes how multiple issues are circulating in the debate—September 11, the invasion of Iraq, concern about terror networks in Europe, anti-Semitism, a turn to religious fundamentalism or to a Muslim identity in the face of state racism and social isolation, feminist perspectives on both sides of the ban, and the coercion of girls. Ibid., 59–71.

66. See Commission de Reflexion sur l'Application du Principe de Laïcité dans la République, *Rapport au Président de la République*, December 11, 2003, http://lesrap ports.ladocumentationfrancaise.fr/BRP/034000725/0000.pdf.

67. Stasi apparently became furious that only the "repressive aspects" of his commission's recommendations were implemented. See Dominique Gerbaud, "Reconcentre avec Bernand Stasi," *La Croix*, January 8, 2004 ("Bernard Stasi est encore furieux que les deputés n'en aient garde que les aspects repressifs.")

68. For a rare mention of the affective realm as playing a role, see Rytkønen, "Europe and Its 'Almost-European' Other." She writes: "A survey conducted by the city of Copenhagen on how the local authorities handle problems in the immigrant population points out that culture in too many cases functions as a filter for understanding issues that might be related to age, generational differences, social circumstances, and 'general heart ache' (Helmer Strøvelbæk, coordinator of a group of experts on immigrants from the city of Copenhagen's in Berlingske Tidende 4.11.00)."

69. Another way to phrase this would be to see whatever "cultural practice" is at issue as only one of many interrelated problems. See Rytkønen: "Rather than seeing forced marriages as one of many interrelated problems in a socially isolated family with high unemployment, mental and/or health problems, as some resource centers and ethnic task forces point out, the law focuses exclusively on marriage practices (see Helle Stenum in Information, 2.7.01). . . . The criticism is echoed by Schierup (1993) who argues that all complexities are reduced to absurdity when problems in the Danish immigration debate are framed as cultural differences rather than considered in their political, social and economic contexts" (ibid.).

70. Christian Joppke made this comment at the May 2008 symposium that gave rise to this volume.

71. Katrin Bennhold, "A Veil Closes France's Door to Citizenship," *New York Times*, July 19, 2008.

72. See Joan Scott, "Symptomatic Politics." Or, as stated by a commentator at the May 2008 symposium on which this volume is based, from the virginity tests at Heathrow that restricted entry to the United Kingdom, to the lack of virginity rebutting a forced marriage that therefore allows one entry to Denmark, it's "all about controlling vaginas."

73. See Sarah Song's chapter in this volume, "Three Models of Civic Solidarity."

74. In fact, the phone call for help was not made by an adolescent but seems to have been made by Rozita Swinton, a thirty-three-year-old with a history of imperson-

ating abuse victims. Arian Campo-Flores and Catharine Skipp, "Rozita Swinton's Bad Call," *Newsweek*, August 4, 2008, http://www.newsweek.com/id/148992/page/1.

75. See *Reynolds v. United States*, 98 U.S. 145 (1878) (Supreme Court decision holding that Mormon polygamy was not protected as the free exercise of religion in an opinion that stated: "Polygamy has always been odious among the northern and western nations of Europe, and, until the establishment of the Mormon Church, was almost exclusively a feature of the life of Asiatic and of African people.") See Sarah Barringer Gordon, *The Mormon Question: Polygamy and Constitutional Conflict in Nineteenth-Century America* (Chapel Hill: University of North Carolina Press, 2002); see also Sarah Song, *Justice, Gender and the Politics of Multiculturalism* (Cambridge: Cambridge University Press, 2007).

76. See Adam Nagourney and Laurie Goodstein, "Mormon Candidate Braces for Religion as Issue," *New York Times*, February 8, 2007.

77. For a sign of public perception we could also note here the visit of Oprah Winfrey to the Yearning for Zion Ranch, which appears on her Web site with videos of "A Day in the Life" at the ranch and "Hair How-Tos" ("Wonder how the women on the YFZ Ranch create those hairstyles? Watch them do their 'dos!'") See http://www.oprah.com/dated/oprahshow/oprahshow-20090325-polygamist-ranch. The residents of the Yearning for Zion Ranch are, arguably, presented both as objects of curiosity and with sympathy.

78. See "Ranch Raid Reminds Us of Dangers to Kids," *Herald-Zeitung*, April 12, 2008, Editorial Board.

79. See Lisa Sandberg, "Raid on Polygamous Sect Costing State $25,000 Per Day," *Houston Chronicle*, April 12, 2008.

80. See Michelle Roberts, "Yearning for Zion Ranch Case Gears Up," *San Francisco Chronicle*, October 25, 2009, at A10.

81. See Sherene Razack, *Casting Out* (arguing that Muslims are being expelled from membership in the political community of various Western states).

Chapter 9. Three Models of Civic Solidarity

For comments on earlier versions of this essay, I am grateful to audiences at the Penn Program on Democracy, Citizenship, and Constitutionalism; the Kadish Center Workshop on Law, Philosophy, and Political Theory at Berkeley Law School; the 2008 Western Political Science Association annual meeting; and the UCLA Legal Theory Workshop. I am especially grateful to Irene Bloemraad, Ming Hsu Chen, Michaele Ferguson, Kinch Hoekstra, Chris Kutz, Anne Norton, Eric Rakowski, Andy Sabl, Samuel Scheffler, Seana Shiffrin, Rogers Smith, and Alex Zakaras.

1. David Miller, "Multiculturalism and the Welfare State: Theoretical Reflections," in *Multiculturalism and the Welfare State: Recognition and Redistribution in Contemporary Democracies*, ed. Keith Banting and Will Kymlicka (Oxford: Oxford University Press, 2006), 328, 334.

2. Charles Taylor, "Why Democracy Needs Patriotism," in *For Love of Country?* ed. Joshua Cohen (Boston: Beacon Press, 1996), 121.

3. Robert Putnam, "*E Pluribus Unum:* Diversity and Community in the Twenty-first Century," *Scandinavian Political Studies* 30 (2007): 147, 149. See also Alberto Alesina and Eliana La Ferrara, "Who Trusts Others?" *Journal of Public Economics* 85 (2002): 207–34.

4. Alberto Alesina et al., "Public Goods and Ethnic Divisions," *Quarterly Journal of Economics* 114 (1999): 1243–84; Rodney E. Hero and Caroline J. Tolbert, "A Racial/Ethnic Diversity Interpretation of Politics and Policy in the States of the U.S.," *American Journal of Political Science* 40 (1996): 851–71.

5. Barbara Arneil argues that social capital theory implies that "if one wished to construct the most trusting hypothetical community in America, it would be a culturally homogeneous one, with a reawakened Protestant Church and dominated by a strong, middle-class set of values" (*Diverse Communities: The Problem with Social Capital* [Cambridge University Press, 2006], 140).

6. Charles Taylor, "Democratic Exclusion (and Its Remedies?)," in *Multiculturalism, Liberalism, and Democracy,* ed. Rajeev Bhargava et al. (Oxford: Oxford University Press, 2000), 149.

7. See Habermas, "Citizenship and National Identity," in *Between Facts and Norms: Contributions to a Discourse Theory of Law and Democracy,* trans. William Rehg (Cambridge, Mass.: MIT Press, 1996), 500. See also Habermas, "A Genealogical Analysis of the Cognitive Content of Morality" and "The European Nation-State: On the Past and Future of Sovereignty and Citizenship," in *The Inclusion of the Other: Studies in Political Theory,* ed. Ciaran Cronin and Pablo De Greiff (Cambridge, Mass.: MIT Press, 1998); Jan-Werner Müller, *Constitutional Patriotism* (Princeton: Princeton University Press, 2007).

8. Habermas, "Citizenship and National Identity," 495.

9. Ibid., 498–99.

10. Margaret Canovan, "Patriotism Is Not Enough," *British Journal of Political Science* 30 (2000): 413–32.

11. Habermas, "The European Nation-State," 113, 115–16.

12. Patchen Markell, "Making Affect Safe for Democracy? On 'Constitutional Patriotism,'" *Political Theory* 28 (2000): 51. Markell argues that Habermas's own reflections about the interdependence of facticity and validity suggest that attachment to constitutional norms is only possible via a "supplement of particularity."

13. Habermas, "Citizenship and National Identity," 500.

14. Philip Gleason, "American Identity and Americanization," in *Harvard Encyclopedia of American Ethnic Groups,* ed. Stephan Thernstrom (Cambridge, Mass.: Belknap Press, 1980), 31–32, 56–57.

15. Bernard Yack, "The Myth of the Civic Nation," *Social Research* 10 (1996): 196.

16. Rogers M. Smith, *Stories of Peoplehood: The Politics and Morals of Political*

Membership (New York: Cambridge University Press, 2003), 95. See also *Civic Ideals: Conflicting Visions of Citizenship in U.S. History* (New Haven: Yale University Press, 1997).

17. Immigration and Nationality Act §337(a), 8 U.S.C. §1448(a) (1982).

18. Edward Rothstein, "Connections: Refining the Tests That Confer Citizenship," *New York Times*, January 23, 2006.

19. See http://www.uscis.gov/files/nativedocuments/100q.pdf (accessed November 28, 2008).

20. Habermas, "The European Nation-State," 118.

21. Charles Taylor, "The Politics of Recognition," in *Multiculturalism: Examining the Politics of Recognition*, ed. Amy Gutmann (Princeton: Princeton University Press, 1994); Will Kymlicka, *Multicultural Citizenship: A Liberal Theory of Minority Rights* (Oxford: Oxford University Press, 1995).

22. 8 U.S.C., section 1423 (1988); *In re Katz*, 21 F.2d 867 (E.D. Mich. 1927) (attachment to principles of Constitution implies English literacy requirement).

23. Müller, *Constitutional Patriotism*, 87. Müller argues that constitutional patriotism would require those seeking inclusion to learn the dominant language of the country and acquire some knowledge of the history of the host country. He implies such requirements are free of cultural and ethnic associations.

24. See Joppke's chapter in this volume.

25. Act of Mar. 26, 1790, ch. 3, 1 Stat., 103, and Act of Jan. 29, 1795, ch. 20, section 1, 1 Stat., 414. See James H. Kettner, *The Development of American Citizenship, 1608–1870* (Chapel Hill: University of North Carolina Press, 1984), 239–43. James Madison opposed the second requirement: "It was hard to make a man swear that he preferred the Constitution of the United States, or to give any general opinion, because he may, in his own private judgment, think Monarchy or Aristocracy better, and yet be honestly determined to support his Government as he finds it"; Annals of Cong. 1, 1022–23.

26. 8 U.S.C., section 1427(a)(3). See also *Schneiderman v. United States*, 320 U.S. 118, 133 n.12 (1943), which notes the change from *behaving* as a person attached to constitutional principles to *being* a person attached to constitutional principles.

27. See *In re Saralieff*, 59 F.2d 436 (E.D. Mo. 1932) (attachment requires belief in representative government, federalism, separation of powers, and constitutionally guarantee individual rights); *Schwimmer*, 279 U.S. at 644 (attachment to constitutional principles disqualifies conscientious objectors to military service); *Ex parte Sauer*, 81 F. 355 (Tex. Dist. Ct. 1891) (attachment requirement disqualifies believer in socialism).

28. Internal Security Act of 1950, ch. 1024, sections 22, 25, 64 Stat., 987, 1006–10, 1013–15. The Internal Security Act provisions were included in the Immigration and Nationality Act of 1952 (Act of June 27, 1952, ch. 477, sections 212(a)(28), 241(a)(6), 313, 66 Stat. 163, 184–86, 205–6, 240–41.

29. Gerald L. Neuman, "Justifying U.S. Naturalization Policies," *Virginia Journal of International Law* 35 (1994): 255.

30. On the need to distinguish the variety of "claims of culture" and on the distinctive nature of religious claims in particular, see Sarah Song, "The Subject of Multiculturalism: Culture, Religion, Language, Ethnicity, Nationality, and Race?" in *New Waves in Political Philosophy*, ed. Boudewijn de Bruin and Christopher Zurn (Basingstoke: Palgrave Macmillan, 2008).

31. David Miller, *On Nationality* (Oxford: Oxford University Press, 1995), 25.

32. Ibid., 25–26.

33. On the civic-ethnic distinction, see W. Rogers Brubaker, *Citizenship and Nationhood in France and Germany* (Cambridge, Mass.: Harvard University Press, 1992); David Hollinger, *Post-Ethnic America: Beyond Multiculturalism* (New York: Basic Books, 1995); Michael Ignatieff, *Blood and Belonging: Journeys into the New Nationalism* (New York: Farrar, Straus and Giroux, 1995); Yael Tamir, *Liberal Nationalism* (Princeton: Princeton University Press, 1993).

34. Anthony D. Smith, *The Ethnic Origins of Nations* (Oxford: Blackwell, 1986), 216.

35. Miller, *On Nationality*, 122–23, 153–54.

36. Miller states, "But the principle of nationality is resistant to special rights for groups, over and above what equal treatment requires, because of the fear that this will ossify group differences, and destroy the common nationality on which democratic politics depends" (*On Nationality*, 153–54). For defense of group-differentiated rights from liberal and democratic perspectives, see Will Kymlicka, *Multicultural Citizenship: A Liberal Theory of Minority Rights* (Oxford University Press, 1995), chs. 5–6, and Sarah Song, *Justice, Gender, and the Politics of Multiculturalism* (Cambridge: Cambridge University Press, 2007), ch. 3.

37. Aristide R. Zolberg and Long Litt Woon, "Why Islam Is Like Spanish: Cultural Incorporation in Europe and the United States," *Politics and Society* 27 (1999): 5–38.

38. See Stephen May, "Misconceiving Minority Language Rights: Implications for Liberal Political Theory," in *Language Rights and Political Theory*, ed. Will Kymlicka and Alan Patten (Oxford: Oxford University Press, 2003), 123–52; James Tully, *Strange Multiplicity: Constitutionalism in an Age of Diversity* (Cambridge: Cambridge University Press, 1995).

39. Samuel P. Huntington, *Who Are We? The Challenges to America's National Identity* (New York: Simon and Schuster, 2004),12. In his earlier book, *American Politics: The Promise of Disharmony* (Cambridge, Mass.: Belknap Press, 1981), Huntington defended a "civic" view of American identity based on the "political ideas of the American creed," which include liberty, equality, democracy, individualism, and private property (46). His change in view seems to have been motivated in part by his belief that principles and ideology are too weak to unite a political community, and also by his fear about immigrants maintaining transnational identities and loyalties—in particular, Mexican immigrants, whom he sees as creating bilingual, bicultural, and potentially separatist regions (*Who Are We?* 205).

40. Huntington, *Who Are We?* 31, 20.

41. Christian Joppke, "The Evolution of Alien Rights in the United States, Germany, and the European Union," in *Citizenship Today: Global Perspectives and Practices*, ed. T. Alexander Aleinikoff and Douglas Klusmeyer (Washington, D.C.: Carnegie Endowment for International Peace, 2001), 44. In 2000, the German government moved from a strictly *jus sanguinis* rule toward one that combines *jus sanguinis* and *jus soli*, which opens up access to citizenship to nonethnically German migrants, including Turkish migrant workers and their descendants. A minimum length of residency of eight (down from ten) years is also required, and dual citizenship is not formally recognized. While more inclusive than before, German citizenship laws remain the least inclusive among Western European and North American countries, with inclusiveness measured by the following criteria: whether citizenship is granted by *jus soli* (whether children of noncitizens who are born in a country's territory can acquire citizenship), the length of the residency required for naturalization, and whether naturalized immigrants are permitted to hold dual citizenship. See Marc Morjé Howard, "Comparative Citizenship: An Agenda for Cross-National Research," *Perspectives on Politics* 4 (2006): 443–55.

42. Charles Taylor, "Shared and Divergent Values," in *Reconciling the Solitudes: Essays on Canadian Federalism and Nationalism*, ed. Guy Laforest (Montreal: McGill-Queen's University Press, 1993), 183.

43. Ibid., 183, 130.

44. Horace M. Kallen, *Culture and Democracy in the United States* (New York: Boni and Liveright, 1924), 114–15.

45. Michael Walzer, "What Does It Mean to Be an 'American'?" (1974); reprinted in *What It Means to Be an American: Essays on the American Experience* (New York: Marsilio, 1990), 46.

46. Kymlicka, *Multicultural Citizenship*, 191.

47. Taylor, "Democratic Exclusion (and Its Remedies?)," 163.

48. The differences in naturalization policy are a slightly longer residency requirement in the United States (five years in contrast to Canada's three) and Canada's official acceptance of dual citizenship.

49. See Irene Bloemraad, *Becoming a Citizen: Incorporating Immigrants and Refugees in the United States and Canada* (Berkeley: University of California Press, 2006). It is important to note that Canada's multiculturalism policies are not a perfect example of deep diversity, since they originated in part as a way to counter rising Québécois nationalism, suggesting not only a lack of deep diversity with respect to other groups but also the ways in which recognition of some groups might be used against the recognition of others. But the idea of deep diversity can be extended beyond immigrant groups to include national minorities in Canada, in precisely the way Taylor has suggested, which would acknowledge a variety of ways of being Canadian.

Chapter 10. Immigration and Security in the United States

1. National Commission on Terrorist Attacks, *The 9/11 Report: The National Commission on Terrorist Attacks upon the United States* (New York: St. Martin's, 2004);

Stephen Flynn, *America the Vulnerable: How Our Government Is Failing to Protect Us from Terrorism* (New York: HarperCollins, 2004).

2. Steven A. Camarota, "The Open Door: How Militant Islamic Terrorists Entered and Remained in the United States, 1993–2001," CIS Paper No. 21 (Washington, D.C.: Center for Immigration Studies, 2002); Janice L. Kephart, "Immigration and Terrorism: Moving Beyond the 9/11 Staff Report on Terrorist Travel," CIS Paper No. 24 (Washington, D.C.: Center for Immigration Studies, 2005).

3. Ariane Chebel d'Appollonia and Simon Reich, eds., *Immigration, Integration, and Security: America and Europe in Comparative Perspective* (Pittsburgh: University of Pittsburgh Press, 2008); Nazli Choucri, "Migration and Security: Some Key Linkages," *Journal of International Affairs* 56:1 (2002) 97–122; Jef Huysmans, *The Politics of Insecurity: Security, Migration, and Asylum in the EU* (London: Routledge, 2006); Michael C. LeMay, *Guarding the Gates: Immigration and National Security* (Westport, Conn.: Praeger Security International, 2006); Christopher Rudolph, "Security and the Political Economy of International Migration," *American Political Science Review* 97:4 (November 2003): 603–20; Christopher Rudolph, "Globalization and Security: Migration and Evolving Conceptions of Security in Statecraft and Scholarship," *Security Studies* 13:1 (Autumn 2003): 1–32; Christopher Rudolph, *National Security and Immigration: Explaining Policy Development in the United States and Western Europe Since 1945* (Stanford: Stanford University Press, 2006); Myron Weiner, ed., *International Migration and Security* (Boulder, Colo.: Westview Press, 1993).

4. See Rudolph, *National Security and Immigration.*

5. The theoretical argument follows (ibid.).

6. Ibid.

7. Barry Buzan, *People, States and Fear* (New York: Longman, 1991); Barry Buzan, Ole Wæver, and Jaap de Wilde, *Security: A New Framework for Analysis* (Boulder, Colo.: Lynne Rienner, 1997); Rudolph, *National Security and Immigration.*

8. Rudolph, *National Security and Immigration.*

9. Hans J. Morgenthau, *Politics Among Nations*, 7th ed. (New York: McGraw-Hill, 2005).

10. Richard N. Rosecrance, *Rise of the Trading State* (New York: Basic Books, 1986).

11. I have referred to this elsewhere as the Threat Hypothesis (Rudolph, *National Security and Immigration*).

12. Stephen D. Krasner, *Sovereignty: Organized Hypocrisy* (Princeton: Princeton University Press, 1999).

13. Ole Waever, "Societal Security: The Concept," in *Identity, Migration, and the New Security Agenda in Europe*, ed. Ole Wæver et al. (New York: St. Martin's Press, 1003).

14. Ole Wæver, "Societal Security: The Concept," 23.

15. Christopher Rudolph, "Sovereignty and Territorial Borders in a Global Age," *International Studies Review* 7:1 (Spring 2005): 1–20.

16. Lewis Coser, *The Functions of Social Conflict* (Glencoe, Ill.: Free Press, 1956).

17. Samuel Huntington, *Who Are We? The Challenges to America's National Identity* (New York: Simon and Schuster, 2004).

18. I have referred to this elsewhere as the Rally Hypothesis (Rudolph, "Security and the Political Economy of International Migration" and *National Security and Immigration*). Clearly, there is a notable exception to this "rally effect"—those who by nationality, ethnicity, or ideology are directly associated with the external enemy threatening the state. The internment of Japanese Americans during World War II is but one example. I have referred to this exception to the rally hypothesis elsewhere as the "adversary corollary" (Rudolph, "Security and the Political Economy of International Migration").

19. Myron Weiner and Sharon Stanton Russell, eds., *Demography and National Security* (New York: Berghahn Books, 2001).

20. Aristide R. Zolberg, "From Invitation to Interdiction: U.S. Foreign Policy and Immigraton Since 1945," in *Threatened Peoples, Threatened Borders,* ed. Michael S. Teitelbaum and Myron Weiner (New York: W. W. Norton, 1995).

21. In fact, Truman was so upset with the low quota levels that he vetoed the bill. Congress, however, later passed it over his veto.

22. Thomas Borstelmann, *The Cold War and the Color Line: American Race Relations in the Global Arena* (Cambridge, Mass.: Harvard University Press, 2002); Desmond King, *Making Americans* (Oxford: Oxford University Press, 2000).

23. Daniel J. Tichenor, *Dividing Lines: The Politics of Immigration Control in the United States* (Princeton: Princeton University Press, 2002).

24. Kitty Calavita, *Inside the State: The Bracero Program, Immigration, and the INS* (New York: Routledge, 1992).

25. Rudolph, *National Security and Immigration.*

26. Rudolph, "Security and the Political Economy of International Migration."

27. James J. F. Forrest, *Protecting America's Targets* (Westport, Conn.: Praeger, 2006).

28. Congressional Research Service, "The USA Patriot Act: A Legal Analysis," for *CRS Report RL31377* (Washington, D.C.: Congressional Research Service, 2002).

29. Dan Eggen and Robert O'Harrow, Jr., "U.S. Steps Up Secret Surveillance," *Washington Post,* March 24, 2003.

30. These are referred to as "T7" countries: Cuba, Iran, Iraq, Libya, North Korea, Sudan, and Syria.

31. The "List of Twenty-six" countries is composed of Afghanistan, Algeria, Bahrain, Djibouti, Egypt, Eritrea, Indonesia, Iran, Iraq, Jordan, Kuwait, Lebanon, Libya, Malaysia, Morocco, Oman, Pakistan, Qatar, Saudi Arabia, Somalia, Sudan, Syria, Tunisia, Turkey, the United Arab Emirates, and Yemen.

32. *Migration News* (various editions), available online at http://migration.uc davis.edu.

33. Daniella E. Bove-LaMonica, "Visa Security for a Post-9/11 Era," in *Homeland Security: Protecting America's Targets,* ed. James J. F. Forest, 202–19 (Westport, Conn.: Praeger, 2006).

34. *Migration News,* April 2004.

35. Ibid., January 2005.

36. Ibid., January 2004.

37. Margaret Stock, "Immigration and National Security: Post-9/11 Challenges for the United States," in *Homeland Security: Protecting America's Targets,* ed. James J. F. Forest, 117–43 (Westport, Conn.: Prager, 2006).

38. Rey Koslowski, "Real Challenges for Virtual Borders: The Implementation of US-VISIT," *Migration Policy Institute Report* (Washington, D.C.: Migration Policy Institute, June 2005); Jason Ackleson, "Migration and the 'Smart Border' Security Environment," in *Homeland Security: Protecting America's Targets,* ed. James J. F. Forest (Westport, Conn.: Praeger, 2006).

39. Camarota, "The Open Door"; Kephart, "Immigration and Terrorism."

40. Koslowski, "Real Challenges for Virtual Borders"; Rudolph, *National Security and Immigration.*

41. *Migration News,* October 2005.

42. Sylvia Moreno, "Detention Facility for Immigrants Criticized," *Washington Post* (February 22, 2007), A3.

43. *Migration News,* April 2004.

44. I have argued elsewhere that such "finessing" of contrasting interests marked U.S. policy prior to 9/11. However, rather than making policy more "closed" via added screening mechanisms, the state used largely symbolic border enforcement policies and programs to appease political pressures to respond to societal insecurities. See Rudolph, *National Security and Immigration;* also Andreas, *Border Games;* Cornelius, "Appearances and Realities."

45. *Migration News,* January 2004.

46. Michael Fix and Paul T. Hill, *Enforcing Employer Sanctions: Challenges and Strategies* (Santa Monica: RAND, 1990).

47. Anna Gorman, "Employers of Illegal Immigrants Face Little Risk of Penalty," *Los Angeles Times,* May 29, 2005.

48. *Migration News,* July 2005.

49. Sixty-three percent of respondents reported it to be a "very serious" problem, while another 28 percent said it was "somewhat serious." Poll available online at: http://www.foxnews.com/projects/pdf/050305_poll.pdf.

50. Available online at: http://www.field.com/fieldpollonline/. See also *Migration News,* April 2006.

51. Camarota, "The Open Door"; Kephart, "Immigration and Terrorism."

52. Douglas Jehl, "U.S. Aides Cite Worry on al Qaeda Infiltration from Mexico," *New York Times,* February 17, 2005.

Chapter 11. Citizenship's New Subject

A special thank-you to Rogers Smith for his encouragement. To fellow participants whose commentary led to a spirited debate, my sincere gratitude. Elspeth Wilson's hospitality ensured a wonderful stay at Penn. Finally, my thanks to Kevin Olson who continues to push me in fruitful directions.

1. Rogers M. Smith, "Modern Citizenship," in Engin Isin and Bryan Turner, eds., *Handbook of Citizenship Studies* (London: Sage, 2002).

2. Tomas Hammar, *Democracy and the Nation State: Aliens, Denizens and Citizens in a World of International Migration* (Aldershot: Avebury, 1990).

3. Thomas Faist, "Transnationalization in International Migration: Implications for the Study of Citizenship and Culture," *Ethnic and Racial Studies* 23:2 (2000): 202.

4. Ibid.; Christian Joppke, *Selecting by Origin: Ethnic Migration in the Liberal State* (Cambridge, Mass.: Harvard University Press, 2005).

5. Joppke, *Selecting by Origin*; Aristide R. Zolberg and Long Litt Woon , "Why Islam Is Like Spanish: Cultural Incorporation in Europe and the United States," *Politics and Society* 27:1 (March 1999): 5–38.

6. Kamal Sadiq, *Paper Citizens: How Illegal Immigrants Acquire Citizenship in Developing Countries* (New York: Oxford University Press, 2009).

7. In some advanced European states, such as France and Germany, members are required to carry national ID cards, but even this does not match the absolute monitoring of individuals in totalitarian states.

8. In contrast, status was bundled with rights, even when in practice groups such as women and blacks were excluded from the equal practice of citizenship rights. Acquiring citizenship rights that accompanied status only became possible after prolonged social and political struggles (Smith, "Modern Citizenship").

9. "In most circumstances, the radical divergence between these two answers is hardly noticed, because each answer is viewed as relevant to a different domain" (Linda Bosniak, *The Citizen and the Alien* [Princeton: Princeton University Press, 2006], 34).

10. Jean-Jacques Rousseau, *The Basic Political Writings* (Indianapolis: Hackett, 1987).

11. Faist, "Transnationalization in International Migration," 206.

12. Ibid., 191.

13. Ibid.

14. Rainer Bauböck, "Stakeholder Citizenship and Transnational Political Participation: A Normative Evaluation of External Voting," *Fordham Law Review* 75 (2007): 2395.

15. Ibid.

16. Hammar, *Democracy and the Nation State*.

17. Bauböck, "Stakeholder Citizenship and Transnational Political Participation," 2395–96.

18. Ibid.

19. Ibid.

20. Hannah Arendt, *The Origins of Totalitarianism* (San Diego: Harvest Books, 1968).

21. Bosniak, *The Citizen and the Alien*, 34.

22. *The Citizenship Act, 1955* (Delhi: Universal Law Publishing Co., 2004): 1. The principal legislation is the Citizenship Act of 1955, amended in 1986, 1992, 2003, and 2005.

23. "A Guide for the Voters," Election Commission of India (2006), pp. 1–2, available at www.eci.gov.in/ECI_voters_guideline_2006.pdf.

24. National Election Commission of India No.3/4/ID/2006/J.S.II/(WB), General Elections to the Legislative Assembly of West Bengal—Commission's Order Regarding Use of Electoral Photo Identity Cards.

25. Bauböck, "Stakeholder Citizenship and Transnational Political Participation," 2406–09.

26. Tribune News Service, "2 cr Bangladeshis in India: Fernandes Says Proxy War by Pak Main Challenge," September 28, 2003, available at http://www.tribuneindia.com/2003/20030928/main1.htm.

27. *Telegraph* (Calcutta), "AASU Targets Gogoi over Illegal Migrants," July 19, 2004.

28. For more on illegal immigrant voters, see Sadiq, *Paper Citizens*.

29. *Telegraph* (Calcutta), "Nadia Scanner on Intruders—Survey to Identify Bangladeshis Begins," February 13, 2006.

30. *Telegraph* (Calcutta), "Voter ID? Rs. 1000 for a Fake," February 12, 2007.

31. Rajeev Bhattacharyya, "Assam 'D' Voters in Vanishing Act," *Telegraph* (Calcutta), July 16, 2005.

32. *Telegraph* (Calcutta), "Enter the Election Boss," January 9, 2006.

33. Ibid.

34. *Telegraph* (Calcutta), "Nadia Scanner on Intruders."

35. Ibid.

36. *Telegraph* (Calcutta), "MLA on Poll Roll Twice Over," January 18, 2006.

37. *Assam Tribune*, "B'deshis Figure in Tripura Rolls," January 19, 2008.

38. *Times of India* (subsection Economic Times), "BJP Smells a Rat in Revision of Electoral Rolls," December 8, 2007.

39. *Hindu*, "35,000 Fake Voters Names Deleted from Delhi Rolls," April 25, 2005.

40. The BJP opposes Muslim immigrants while welcoming Hindu immigrants from Bangladesh as "refugees." *Telegraph* (Calcutta), "20 Indians Asked to Prove Citizenship," June 16, 2007.

41. Ibid.

42. *Telegraph* (Calcutta), "Anil Breathe Fire on Bangladeshi Purge," February 27, 2006.

43. Ibid.

44. Anindya Sengupta, "Terror on the Tree Top, Midnight Knock for Intruders," *Telegraph* (Calcutta), April 21, 2006.

45. Bauböck, "Stakeholder Citizenship and Transnational Political Participation," 2421.

46. Ibid., 2406.

47. For more on stakeholders and democratic political participation see Rainer Bauböck, "Expansive Citizenship—Voting Beyond Territory and Membership," *Political Science and Politics* 38:4 (2005): 683–87 and "Stakeholder Citizenship and Transnational Political Participation.".

48. Bauböck, "Stakeholder Citizenship and Transnational Political Participation"; Bauböck, "Expansive Citizenship."

49. Seyla Benhabib, "Twilight of Sovereignty or the Emergence of Cosmopolitan Norms? Rethinking Citizenship in Volatile Times," *Citizenship Studies* 11:1 (2007): 19–36.

50. The foremost of these being: Universal Declaration of Human Rights 1948; the Convention on a Rights of a Child; the International Covenant on Economic, Social and Cultural Rights; Declaration on the Human Rights of Individuals who are not Nationals of the Country in which they live; International Convention on the Protection of the Rights of All Migrant Workers and Members of their Families; Convention on the Elimination of All Forms of Discrimination Against Women.

Chapter 12. "We the People" in an Age of Migration

1. Incorporating some new data, this chapter extends arguments introduced in Irene Bloemraad, *Becoming a Citizen: Incorporating Immigrants and Refugees in the United States and Canada* (Berkeley: University of California Press, 2006) and "Unity in Diversity? Bridging Models of Multiculturalism and Immigrant Integration," *Du Bois Review* 4 (2) (2007): 317–36.

2. A notable disjuncture exists between multiculturalism as political theory and as immigrant public policy. Much early theorizing on multiculturalism came from Canadian scholars who balanced three sets of minority claims: those of aboriginal peoples, those of long-standing incorporated nations such as the Québécois, and those of migrant-origin populations. Writers such as Will Kymlicka and Charles Taylor give greater moral weight to aboriginals' and national minorities' claims than to those of immigrants, but as Christian Joppke notes, the public discourse on multiculturalism, in Canada and in Europe, has almost exclusively focused on immigrants (Joppke, "The Retreat of Multiculturalism in the Liberal State: Theory and Policy," *British Journal of Sociology* 55 [2] [2004]: 237–57).

3. William Rogers Brubaker, "The Return of Assimilation? Changing Perspectives on Immigration and Its Sequels in France, Germany, and the United States," *Ethnic and Racial Studies* 24 (4) (2001): 531–48; Han Entzinger, "The Rise and Fall of Multiculturalism: The Case of the Netherlands," in *Toward Assimilation and Citizenship:*

Immigrants in Liberal Nation-States, ed. Christian Joppke and Ewa Morawska, 59–86 (New York: Palgrave Macmillan, 2003); Joppke, "Retreat of Multiculturalism."

4. Samuel Huntington, "The Hispanic Challenge," *Foreign Policy* (March/April 2004): 30–45; Arthur M. Schlesinger Jr., *The Disuniting of America: Reflections on a Multicultural* Society (New York: W. W. Norton, 1998).

5. For example, two well-regarded overviews of immigrant assimilation in the United States, by Richard Alba and Victor Nee, *Remaking the American Mainstream* (Cambridge, Mass.: Harvard University Press, 2003), and by Frank D. Bean and Gillian Stevens, *America's Newcomers and the Dynamics of Diversity* (New York: Russell Sage Foundation, 2003), do not address political or civic incorporation, nor does the review of the assimilation literature undertaken by Mary C. Waters and Tomás R. Jiménez, "Assessing Immigrant Assimilation: New Empirical and Theoretical Challenges," *Annual Review of Sociology*, 31 (2005): 105–25.

6. There is some evidence that this is changing with a new wave of political scientists, often of immigrant backgrounds. See, for example, Lisa García-Bedolla, *Fluid Borders* (Berkeley: University of California Press, 2005); S. Karthick Ramakrishnan, *Democracy in Immigrant America* (Stanford: Stanford University Press, 2005); Janelle S. Wong, *Democracy's Promise* (Ann Arbor: University of Michigan Press, 2006); and S. Karthick Ramakrishnan and Irene Bloemraad, *Civic Hopes and Political Realities* (New York: Russell Sage Foundation, 2008).

7. Robert E. Park and Ernest W. Burgess, *Introduction to the Science of Sociology* (Chicago: University of Chicago Press, 1969 [1921]); Robert E. Park, "Assimilation, Social," in *Encyclopedia of the Social Sciences*, ed. E. R. A. Seligman and A. Johnson (New York: Macmillan, 1930), 281–83; William Lloyd Warner and Leo Srole, *The Social Systems of American Ethnic Groups* (New Haven: Yale University Press, 1945); Milton M. Gordon, *Assimilation in American Life: The Role of Race, Religion and National Origins* (New York: Oxford University Press, 1964).

8. Gordon, *Assimilation in American Life.*

9. Nathan Glazer and Daniel P. Moynihan, introduction to *Ethnicity: Theory and Experience*, ed. Nathan Glazer and Daniel P. Moynihan, 1–28 (Cambridge, Mass.: Harvard University Press, 1975); Alejandro Portes and Min Zhou, "The New Second Generation: Segmented Assimilation and Its Variants," *Annals of the American Academy of Political and Social Science* 530 (1993): 74–96; Min Zhou, "Segmented Assimilation: Issues, Controversies, and Recent Research on the New Second Generation," in *The Handbook of International Migration: The American Experience*, ed. Charles Hirschman, Philip Kasinitz, and Josh DeWind, 196–211 (New York: Russell Sage, 1999); Alejandro Portes and Rubén G. Rumbaut, *Immigrant America: A Portrait*, 2nd ed. (Berkeley: University of California Press, 2006).

10. Portes and Zhou, "The New Second Generation"; Zhou, "Segmented Assimilation."

11. Alba and Nee, *Remaking the American Mainstream*

12. Portes and Zhou, "The New Second Generation."

13. Mary C. Waters, *Black Identities* (Cambridge, Mass.: Harvard University Press, 1999).

14. Portes and Rumbaut, *Immigrant America*; Portes and Zhou, "The New Second Generation."

15. Min Zhou and Carl L. Bankston III, *Growing Up American: How Vietnamese Children Adapt to Life in the United States* (New York: Russell Sage Foundation, 1998).

16. Portes and Rumbaut, *Immigrant America*, 162.

17. Alejandro Portes and Rubén Rumbaut (*Immigrant America*, 117–67) adopt the view that economic marginality and nativist attacks spur reactive ethnicity, but the general portrayal of political integration is one of immigrants' "passive endurance."

18. Alba and Nee, *Remaking the American Mainstream*.

19. Robert A. Dahl, *Who Governs?* (New Haven: Yale University Press, 1961).

20. Ibid., 32–36.

21. The political incorporation approach has roots in both American sociology (e.g., Nathan Glazer and Daniel P. Moynihan, *Beyond the Melting Pot* [Cambridge, Mass.: MIT Press, 1963]; Glazer and Moynihan, "Introduction") and political science (e.g., Michael Parenti, "Ethnic Politics and the Persistence of Ethnic Identification," *American Political Science Review* 61 [3] [1967]: 717–26). More recent work in this area is split between European social scientists working within the social movements literature (e.g., Ruud Koopmans, Paul Statham, Marco Giugni, and Florence Passy, *Contested Citizenship* [Minneapolis: University of Minnesota Press, 2005], and American political scientists working within a tradition of behavioral and racial minority politics. These two research streams largely evolved in isolation from each other.

22. Gordon, *Assimilation in American Life*.

23. Interestingly, economic integration—probably the primary interest of contemporary sociologists—does not figure among the seven.

24. Gordon, *Assimilation in American Life*, 71.

25. Based on Gordon's examples, ibid., I use the term political assimilation for what he labels 'civic assimilation," the "absence of value and power conflicts."

26. Ibid., 77.

27. Charles Taylor, "The Politics of Recognition," in *Multiculturalism*, ed. Amy Gutmann, 25–73 (Princeton: Princeton University Press, 1994); Will Kymlicka, *Multicultural Citizenship* (Oxford: Clarendon Press, 1995); Bhikhu Parekh, *Rethinking Multiculturalism*, 2nd ed. (New York: Palgrave Macmillan, 2006).

28. Taylor, " "The Politics of Recognition"; Joseph Raz, "Multiculturalism: A Liberal Perspective," *Dissent* (Winter 1994): 67–79.

29. Huntington, "The Hispanic Challenge."

30. Todd Gitlin, *The Twilight of Common Dreams* (New York: Metropolitan Books, 1995); Richard Gwyn, *Nationalism Without Walls* (Toronto: McClelland and Steward, 1995); David A. Hollinger, *Postethnic America* (New York: Basic Books, 2000); Brian Barry, *Culture and Equality* (Cambridge, Mass.: Harvard University Press, 2001).

31. Neil Bissoondath, "A Question of Belonging: Multiculturalism and Citizenship," in *Belonging,* ed. William Kaplan, 368–87 (Montreal: McGill-Queen's University Press, 1993); Gywn, *Nationalism Without Walls*; Hollinger, *Postethnic America*; Barry, *Culture and Equality.*

32. Patrick Weil, "Why the French Laïcité Is Liberal," *Cardozo Law Review* 30 (6) (2009): 2699–2714.

33. See, for example, Simon's discussion of the policy uses of statistics in Australia, Canada, the Netherlands, and the United States: Patrick Simon, "The Measurement of Racial Discrimination: The Policy Use of Statistics," *International Journal of Social Science* 183 (2005): 9–25.

34. Robert R. Alvarez, "A Profile of the Citizenship Process Among Hispanics in the United States," *International Migration Review* 21 (2) (1987): 327–51; Philip Kasinitz, *Caribbean New York* (Ithaca, N.Y.: Cornell University Press, 1992); Michael Jones-Correa, *Between Two Nations* (Ithaca, N.Y.: Cornell University Press, 1998); Irene Bloemraad, "The Limits of de Tocqueville: How Government Facilitates Organisational Capacity in Newcomer Communities," *Journal of Ethnic and Migration Studies* 31 (5) (2005): 865–87; Bloemraad, *Becoming a Citizen*; Wong, *Democracy's Promise.*

35. Karthick S. Ramakrishnan and Celia Viramontes, *Civic Inequalities* (San Francisco: Public Policy Institute of California, 2006); Ramakrishnan and Bloemraad, *Civic Hopes.*

36. Bernhard Ebbinghaus and Jelle Visser, "When Institutions Matter: Union Growth and Decline in Western Europe, 1950–1995," *European Sociological Review* 15 (1999): 135–58.

37. Jones-Correa, *Between Two Nations*; Louis DeSipio, "Building America, One Person at a Time," in *E Pluribus Unum?* ed. Gary Gerstle and John Mollenkopf, 67–106 (New York: Russell Sage Foundation, 2001); Wong, *Democracy's Promise.*

38. Anthony M. Messina, *The Logics and Politics of Post-WWII Migration to Western Europe* (New York: Cambridge University Press, 2007); Karen Schönwälder, "Trendsetter Obama? The Ascent of Immigrant Voters and Politicians in European States," MMG 09–03 Working Paper, Göttingen, Germany, Max Planck Institute for the Study of Religious and Ethnic Diversity, 2009.

39. For those who agree that group organizing based on religion, ethnicity, race, or national origin is a legitimate and possibly fruitful basis for democratic engagement, the subsequent question becomes the extent to which government should support cultural minorities. For example, in his recent call for a new civic nationalism to integrate immigrants in the United States, Noah Pickus, *True Faith and Allegiance* (Princeton: Princeton University Press, 2005), acknowledges the legitimacy of ethnic associationalism and advocates greater government involvement in immigrant integration to foster what he calls a "Madisonian nationalism." There are thus overlaps between Pinkus and the position outlined here, but the multicultural approach is more supportive of immigrants' cultural identity and collective organizing, viewing them as a path to national attachment. Pinkus is wary of dual attachments and loyalties.

40. Ibid., 12–13.

41. Keith Banting, Richard Johnston, Will Kymlicka, and Stuart Soroka, "Do Multiculturalism Policies Erode the Welfare State? An Empirical Analysis," in *Multiculturalism and the Welfare State: Recognition and Redistribution in Contemporary Democracies*, ed. Keith Banting and Will Kymlicka, 49–90 (Oxford: Oxford University Press, 2006).

42. I thus move from considering multiculturalism as political theory to examining it as public policy. As noted by other observers (Augie Fleras and Jean Leonard Elliot, *Multiculturalism in Canada* [Scarborough, Ont.: Nelson Canada, 1992]; Lance W. Roberts and Rodney A. Clifton, "Multiculturalism in Canada," in Peter S. Li, ed., *Race and Ethnic Relations in Canada*, ed. Peter S. Li, 120–47 [Toronto: Oxford University Press, 1990]), the term "multiculturalism" can be used as an objective description of a country's demographic composition, a normative statement reflecting a society's views of diversity, a specific political theory, or a set of government policies.

43. Banting et al., in "Do Multiculturalism Policies Erode the Welfare State?", summarize the multicultural policy domain around the early to mid-1990s. An alternative measure by Koopmans et al., *Contested Citizenship*, spanning 1980 to 2002, examines five indicators: cultural requirements for naturalization; religious rights outside public institutions, especially for Islam; cultural rights within institutions; institutions for political representation; and affirmative action. Of the five countries they consider, the Netherlands ranks as the most multicultural, Great Britain and possibly post-2000 Germany rank in the middle, and France and Switzerland are the least multicultural. The two approaches provide relatively similar categorizations.

44. Ron Hayduk, *Democracy for All* (New York: Routledge, 2006).

45. Bloemraad, *Becoming a Citizen;* Schönwälder, "Trendsetter Obama?"

46. An alternative measure of immigrants' citizenship points to the same conclusion. Naturalization rates—calculated as the annual number of naturalizations over the noncitizen foreign "stock"—are higher in countries that embrace multiculturalism than in those more ambivalent about or antagonistic to recognizing pluralism. Weak multicultural states such as Germany, Italy, and Switzerland recorded an annual naturalization rate—the number of immigrants' acquiring citizenship over the total stock of noncitizens—of less than 1 percent in the early 1990s (James Clarke, Elsbeth van Dam, and Liz Gooster, "New Europeans: Naturalization and Citizenship in Europe," *Citizenship Studies* 2 [1]: 43–67 [1998]; Koopmans et al., *Contested Citizenship*). In stronger multicultural states, the naturalization rate was about 6.5 percent in the Netherlands and Sweden in 1994 and 10 percent in Canada for the same period. The United States had an intermediate naturalization rate of about 3 percent (Bloemraad, *Becoming a Citizen*).

47. Those wishing to collect data on representation face two challenges: countries do not collect immigrant and ethnoracial population statistics the same way (making it hard to identify the relevant population of electors), and information on the immigrant or ethnoracial background of legislators is not readily available. The birthplace

of a legislator is often one of the few comparable pieces of information, but as I explain below, this can be problematic, since a simple foreign-born count will include the children of expatriates born in a foreign country or colony. Anthony Messina's comparison of electoral representation in 2002 across five European countries examines ethnic minorities, rather than foreign-born. He finds, similar to the pattern I report, high representation in the Netherlands, and no representation in France. Among his other countries, Belgium scores second best in representation, though quite a bit lower than the Dutch, followed by Great Britain and Germany. Richard Alba and Nancy Foner compare representation of specific minority groups at the level of sub-national governments. They are unable to standardize their representation figures by the ethnic group's share of the general population, so comparison is difficult, but the general pattern is consistent: high representation in the Netherlands, intermediate representation in the United States and Great Britain, and low representation in Germany and France. Anthony Messina, *The Logic and Politics of Post-World War II Migration to Western Europe* (New York: Cambridge University Press, 2007); Richard Alba and Nancy Foner, "Entering the Precincts of Power: Do National Differences Matter for Immigrant Minority Political Representation?" in Jennifer L. Hochschild and John H. Mollenkopf, eds., *Bringing Outsiders In: Transatlantic Perspectives on Immigrant Political Incorporation* (Ithaca, N.Y.: Cornell University Press, 2009).

48. In January 2006, with the election of a minority Conservative government to replace the previous Liberal majority, forty-one foreign-born MPs were elected out of a total of 308 seats.

49. Bloemraad, *Becoming a Citizen.*

50. Michael Adams, *Unlikely Utopia* (Toronto: Viking Canada, 2007), 74–75.

51. Bloemraad, *Becoming a Citizen.*

52. Adams, *Unlikely Utopia,* 75.

53. Michèle Tribalat, "Une estimation des populations d'origine étrangère en France en 1999," *Population* 59 (1) (2004): 65.

54. Eric Keslassy, "Ouvrir la politique à la diversité" (Paris: L'Institute Montaigne, 2009), 19.

55. Underrepresentation is likely driven, in part, by the American primary system and the significant financial resources needed to make a credible run for office in the United States (Bloemraad, *Becoming a Citizen*).

56. Koopmans, et al., *Contested Citizenship.*

57. Bloemraad, *Becoming a Citizen;* Irene Bloemraad, "Becoming a Citizen in the United States and Canada: Structured Mobilization and Immigrant Political Incorporation," *Social Forces* 85 (2) (2006): 667–69.

58. F. H. Leacy, ed., *Historical Statistics of Canada,* 2nd ed. (Ottawa: Statistics Canada, 1983); Campbell Gibson and Emily Lennon, *Historical Census Statistics on the Foreign-Born Population of the United States: 1850–1990,* U.S. Census Bureau Working Paper 29 (Washington, D.C.: U.S. Government Printing Office, 1999).

59. U.S. Census Bureau, "Profile of Selected Demographic and Social Characteris-

tics for the Foreign-born Population: 2000," (March 2005), at http://www.census.gov/population/cen2000/stp-159/foreignborn.pdf / (accessed April 13, 2010); author's calculation, based on Statistics Canada, "Selected Demographic and Cultural Characteristics, 2001 Census," at http://www12.statcan.ca/english/census01/products/standard/themes/RetrieveProductTable.cfm?Temporal = 2001&pid = 68533&apath = 3&gid = 517770&meth = 1&ptype = 55496&theme = 43&focus = 0&aid = 0&placename = 0&province = 0&search = 0&gc = 0&gk = 0&vid = 0&vnamee = &vnamef = &fl = 0&rl = 0&free = 0 /.

60. Michael Fix, Jeffrey Passel, and Kenneth Sucher, "Trends in Naturalization," in *Immigrant Families and Workers: Facts and Perspectives Series*, brief No. 3 (September 17, 2003), at http://www.urban.org/url.cfm?ID = 310847 Washington, DC / (accessed September 16, 2005).

61. Bloemraad, *Becoming a Citizen*.

62. Ibid.; Bloemraad, "Limits of de Tocqueville," 865–87.

63. Leslie Pal, *Interests of State* (Montreal: McGill-Queen's University Press, 1993); Heritage Canada, "Canadian Heritage Performance Report for the Period Ending March 31, 1997," at http://www.pch.gc.ca/pc-ch/mindep/perf/96-97/english/contents.htm.

64. Citizenship and Immigration Canada, *Audit of Settlement Contributions Programs* (produced by Corporate Review, Strategic Policy, Planning and Research, Ottawa, Ont.: Citizenship and Immigration Canada, 1995).

65. House of Commons, *Settlement and Integration: A Sense of Belonging, "Feeling at Home"* (for the report of the Standing Committee on Citizenship and Immigration, Ottawa, Ont.: Communication Canada, 2003), 2.

66. Nicole Marwell, "Privatizing the Welfare State: Nonprofit Community Organizations," *American Sociological Journal* 69 (2) (2004): 265–91; Héctor R. Cordero-Guzmán, "Community-Based Organisations and Migration in New York City," *Journal of Ethnic and Migration Studies* 31 (5) (2005): 889–909; Els de Graauw, "Nonprofit Organizations: Agents of Immigrant Political Incorporation in Urban America," in Ramakrishnan and Bloemraad, eds., *Civic Hopes and Political Realities*.

67. Silvia Pedraza-Bailey, *Political and Economic Migrants in America* (Austin: University of Texas Press, 1985); Jeremy Hein, *States and International Migrants* (Boulder, Colo.: Westview, 1993); Portes and Rumbaut, *Immigrant America*.

68. Jeremy Hein, "Ethnic Organizations and the Welfare State: The Impact of Social Welfare Programs on the Formation of Indochinese Refugee Associations," *Sociological Forum* 12 (2) (1997): 279–95; Irene Bloemraad, "Limit of de Tocqueville" and *Becoming a Citizen*.

69. Sarah Horton, "Different Subjects: The Health Care System's Participation in the Different Construction of Cultural Citizenship of Cuban Refugees and Mexican Immigrants," *Medical Anthropology Quarterly* 18 (4) (2004): 472–89.

70. Fix, Passel, and Sucher, "Trends in Naturalization." This model of structured mobilization—where state settlement policy facilitates immigrants' political integra-

tion—applies not only to refugees in the United States, but also to immigrants in the Netherlands. Maria Berger and Floris Vermeulen's research on Turkish immigrants suggests that local multicultural policies generate more interconnected ethnic organizations in Amsterdam than in Berlin, facilitated Turks' penetration into elected politics. Maria Berger and Floris Vermeulen, "Civic Networks and Political Behavior: Turks in Amsterdam and Berlin," in Ramakrishnan and Bloemraad, eds., *Civic Hopes and Political Realities*.

71. According to Jan Willem Duyvendak and colleagues, these attacks are misplaced, given solid evidence of socio-economic mobility among second generation immigrants in the Netherlands. Jan Willem Duyvendak, Trees Pels, and Rally Rijkschroeff, "A Multicultural Paradise? The Cultural Factor in Dutch Integration Policy," in Hochschild and Mollenkopf, *Bringing Outsiders In*. See also Entzinger, "The Rise and Fall of Multiculturalism"; Koopmans et al., *Contested Citizenship*; Ellie Vasta, "From Ethnic Minorities to Ethnic Majority Policy: Multiculturalism and the Shift to Assimilationism in the Netherlands," *Ethnic and Racial Studies* 30 (5) (2007): 713–40.

72. Kymlicka, *Multicultural Citizenship*, 179–81; Parekh, *Rethinking Multiculturalism*, 365–67.

73. Lincoln Quillian, "Group Threat and Regional Change in Attitudes Toward African Americans," *American Journal of Sociology* 102 (3) (1996): 816–60; Lawrence D. Bobo and Mia Tuan, *Prejudice in Politics* (Cambridge, Mass.: Harvard University Press, 2006).

74. Alberto Alesina, Edward Glaeser and Bruce Sacerdote, "Why Doesn't the United States Have a European-Style Welfare State?" Brookings Papers on Economic Activity (2001): 187–254.

75. Robert D. Putnam, "E Pluribus Unum: Diversity and Community in the Twenty-first Century," *Scandinavian Political Studies* 30 (2) (2007): 137–74.

76. Banting et al., "Do Multiculturalism Policies Erode the Welfare State?" 49–90.

77. Christel Kesler and Irene Bloemraad, "Does Immigration Erode Social Capital? The Conditional Effects of Immigration-Generated Diversity on Trust, Membership, and Participation across 19 Countries, 1981–2000," *Canadian Journal of Political Science* 43 (2) (2010).

78. Jan Delhe and Kenneth Newton, "Predicting Cross-National Levels of Social Trust: Global Pattern or Nordic Exceptionalism?" *European Sociological Review* 21 (2005): 311–27; Eric M. Uslaner and Mitchell Brown, "Inequality, Trust, and Civic Engagement," *American Politics Research* 33 (6) (2005): 868–94.

Chapter 13. Associational Governance of Ethno-Religious Diversity in Europe

1. This point is completely neglected in the misleading criticism of my 2007 book by Christian Joppke, "Is Religion the Problem?" in "Review Symposium on Secularism or Democracy? Associational Governance of Religious Diversity," *Ethnicities* 9 (4): 560–66 (2009).

2. See Veit Bader, *Rassismus, Ethnizität, Bürgerschaft* (Münster: Westfälisches

Dampfboot, 1995), 94–113, and "Freedom-Fighter Versus Stubborn Collectivist? A Rejoinder to Baumann," in *Ethnicities* 1 (2): 282–85 (2001).

3. Veit Bader, "Ethnicity and Class: A Proto-Theoretical Mapping Exercise," in Wsevolod W. Isajiw, ed., *Comparative Perspectives on Interethnic Relations and Social Incorporation* (Toronto: Canadian Scholars Press, 1997), 106–8.

4. Bader, *Rassismus, Ethnizität, Bürgerschaft*, 14–62.

5. See Ralph Grillo, "Islam and Transnationalism," in Ralph Grillo and Benjamin F. Soares, eds, *"Islam, Transnationalism and the Public Sphere in Western Europe"*, Special Issue of *Journal of Ethnic and Migration Studies* 30 (5): 861–78 (2004); John Bowen, "Beyond Migration: Islam as a Transnational Public Space," *Journal of Ethnic and Migration Studies* 30 (5): 379–94 (2004); Peter Mandaville, *Transnational Muslim Politics* (London: Routledge, 2001); Armando Salvatore, "Authority in Question," *Theory, Culture, and Society* 24 (2): 135–60 (2007).

6. See extensively Bader, *Rassismus, Ethnizität, Bürgerschaft*, chs. 1 and 3.

7. Raymond Breton, *Ethnic Identity and Equality* (Toronto: University of Toronto Press, 1990); Dirk Hoerder, "Segmented Microsystems, Networking Individuals, Cultural Change," in Veit Bader, ed., *Citizenship and Exclusion* (London: Macmillan, 1997), 81–95; Tariq Modood et al., *Ethnic Minorities in Britain* (London: Policy Studies Institute, 1997), 9.

8. Veit Bader, "Culture and Identity: Contesting Constructivism," *Ethnicities* 1 (2): 287ff. (2001).

9. Or more broadly the "fourth generation of human rights" in international and European treaties and covenants.

10. For a discussion of individual and associational/collective religious freedoms (as part and parcel of "classical" civic rights) and the inherent tensions, see Bader, *Secularism or Democracy*, ch. 4.

11. Veit Bader, *Kollektives Handeln: Pro-Theorie sozialer Ungleichheit und kollektiven Handelns*, vol. 2 (Opladen: Leske & Budrich, 1991), ch. 5.

12. Bader, *Secularism or Democracy*, 189ff.

13. Matthias Koenig, "Staatsbürgerschaft und religiöse Pluralität in post-nationalen Konstellationen," Ph.D. thesis, Philipps-Universität Marburg, 2003, 159–62, and "Öffentliche Konflikte um die Inkorporation muslimischer Miderheiten in Westeuropa," *Journal für Konflikt und Gewaltforschung* 6 (6): 92ff. (2004).

14. Rainer Bauböck, *Paradoxes of Self-Determination and the Right to Self-Government* (Vienna: IWE, 2002); Felice Dassetto, *Paroles d'islam* (Paris: Maisonneuve et Larose, 2000); Rogers M. Smith, *Stories of Peoplehood* (New York: Cambridge University Press, 2003).

15. Ruud Koopmans, Paul Statham, Marco Giugni, and Florence Passy, *Contested Citizenship* (Minneapolis: University of Minnesota Press, 2005), and contributions to the "Review Symposium on Contested Citizenship" in *Ethnicities* 8: 128–143 (2008); Joel S. Fetzer and J. Christopher Soper, *Muslims and the State in Britain, France, and Germany* (New York: Cambridge University Press, 2005); J. Christopher Soper and

Joel Fetzer, "Religious Institutions, Church-State History and Muslim Mobilization in Britain, France, and Germany," *Journal of Ethnic and Migration Studies* 33 (6): 933–44; Veit Bader, "Regimes of Governance of Religious Diversity in Europe," *Journal of Ethnic and Migration Studies* 33 (6): 871–87.

16. Joseph H. Carens, "Two Conceptions of Fairness," *Political Theory* 25 (6): 814–20 (1997), and *Culture, Citizenship, and Community* (Oxford: Oxford University Press, 2000).

17. Cultural inequalities in this sense are generally neglected by Brian Barry and many other liberal and republican political philosophers; see Veit Bader, "Defending Differentiated Policies of Multiculturalism," in John Biles and Paul Spoonley, eds., "National Identities," Special Issue of *Canadian Ethnic Studies* 9 (3): 197–215 (2007).

18. Veit Bader, "The Cultural Conditions of Trans-National Citizenship," *Political Theory* 25 (6): 793–96 (1997); Bader, *Secularism or Democracy*, 85f.; Bhikhu Parekh, *Rethinking Multiculturalism* (Cambridge, Mass.: Harvard University Press, 2000).

19. Actually they differ widely with regard to the degree of "relational neutrality." For the different degrees of actual secularization of the state in a comparative perspective see John Madeley, "Religious Establishment and the Dilemmas of Civil Religion," unpublished paper (2008); Jonathan Fox, *Religion and the State* (Cambridge: Cambridge University Press, 2008).

20. Bader, *Secularism or Democracy*, 166–71. Public recognition claims generally, particularly claims for representation in the political process, are highly visible issues of "neutrality" that cannot be avoided; they are highly dramatized and politicized. These are the main reasons why pragmatic accommodation is so difficult in practice.

21. Accommodation involves high symbolic costs (Dassetto, *Paroles d'islam*, 39), as can easily be seen in the cases of recent waves of neonationalism in many states in Europe (but also in Australia, less so in Canada)—its different forms (civic nationalists, republicans, and aggressive secularists among them), intensities, and particularly its impact on politics. See Veit Bader, ed., "Multicultural Futures? Institutional Approaches to Pluralism," Special Issue *Canadian Diversity/Diversité* 4 (1) (2005); Per Mouritsen and Knud Erik Jurgensen, eds., *Constituting Communities* (London: Palgrave, 2008). Contrary to the explicit intentions and rhetorics of politicians, we see a remarkable shift from "thick" to "thin" nationalism (see Veit Bader, "The Cultural Conditions of Trans-National Citizenship," *Political Theory* 25 (6): 798f. [1997], for a provisional typology), from old-style ethnic nationalism to "liberal nationalism" to recently fashionable "civic nationalism," even if there is so much talk of "Leitkultur" in the actual attempts to define the hard core of the Danish, Dutch, German, and so on, "nation" and its particularist "norms and values," which in fact produce the most ridiculous redefinitions of national culture and identities (even right-wing populists style themselves as the world champions of sexual and gender equality in Denmark and the Netherlands, and libertarian, permissive sexuality in public spaces figures prominently, e.g., in Dutch *inburgeringscursussen*).

22. Bader, *Secularism and Democracy*, 155–63 and ch. 10.

23. Ibid., 164–66.

24. Ibid., 166–71.

25. Ibid., 171ff.

26. The following sections are based on Veit Bader, "Changements Récents dans les discours et les politiques d'immigration et d'incorporation aux Pays-Bas," *Revue Ethique Publique* 9 (2): 51–69 (2007). See Bader, *Secularism or Democracy,* for a brief indication of the diversity of regimes of governance of religious diversity (and for further literature). See for regimes of governance of Muslims in Europe, Bader, "Regimes of Governance."

27. Veit Bader, "Dutch Nightmare? The End of Multiculturalism?" *Canadian Diversity/Diversité* 4 (1): 9–11 (2005); see also Bloemraad in this volume.

28. See in a similar way Marcel Maussen, *Ruimte voor de Islam?* (Apeldoorn: Het Spinhuis, 2006), 54ff.: marginalization model (predominant in colonial and guest worker regimes), a liberal assimilation model, a republican assimilation model, a corporatist pluralist or multiculturalism model, a diversity or dialogical, interculturalist model.

29. Bader, *Secularism or Democracy,* 315f. n. 10.

30. The task of social sciences is to describe and explain these predominant and oppositional models, their actual impact on policies, and their effects. It includes the analysis of the actual power relations between the different (coalitions of) actors constructing and using such models or discursive frames, politicians, judges, philosophers, and social scientists as public intellectuals, journalists, and so on, and their impact on public discourse. In policy evaluation studies, the sharp line between descriptive and prescriptive analysis is already blurred, though they are usually guided by the stated aims of policy makers (Veit Bader and Ewald R. Engelen, "Taking Pluralism Seriously," *Philosophy and Social Criticism* 29 [4]: 382–88 [2003]). All those (most prominently: political philosophers and theorists) who design alternative institutions and policies of incorporation or want to defend or modify existing ones, have to spell out their own normative principles and also discuss issues of empirical feasibility.

31. The diagnosis and explanation of the perceived disaster (see note 36 below for some authors and critics of the said "multicultural drama") of Dutch integration policies as caused by MCP is at first sight really astonishing because it is so obviously wrong. It neglects (i) common integration problems in European countries that result from postcolonial and guest worker regimes, and (ii) differences in the socioeconomic contexts of these countries. (iii) It dramatically overestimates the impact of all possible varieties of incorporation policies, and (iv) neglects the unintended negative side effects of (old and new) republican and liberal assimilationist policies that are presented as the optimal alternatives. (v) It does not compare the actual processes and results of incorporation in different fields and countries in a fair and detached way. This is no place to discuss whether Dutch incorporation policies performed better or worse in terms of labor market participation and/or self-employment, housing, education, political participation, social integration (e.g., friendships, rates of intermarriage), legal

incorporation, cultural toleration, transformation of public culture, and so forth, according to (contested) standards, compared with (which) other countries and their respective mixes of integration policies, policies that, by the way, are nowhere consistent, neither in a temporal perspective nor regarding the different levels and agencies of government. At the zenith of the moral and political "integration panic" in the Netherlands, a parliamentary commission was set up. When this commission (named after its chairperson, the VVD member of Parliament Stef Blok) presented its report in summer 2005, showing, as could be expected by any social scientist, a mixed picture of incorporation processes and policies clearly at odds with the now politically correct MCP bashing, the report was derided in predominant parliamentary political circles and media, and the integrity and independence of scientific institutions and advisers has been challenged (see interview with Duyvendak in *Eurosphere, Dutch Country Report*, IMES, Amsterdam 2010).

32. Bader, ed., "Multicultural Futures?"; see also Bloemraad in this volume.

33. See Hans Vermeulen and Rinus Penninx, eds., *Immigrant Integration: The Dutch Case* (Amsterdam: Het Spinhuis, 2000); Han Entzinger, "The Rise and Fall of Multiculturalism," in Christian Joppke and Ewa Morawska, eds., *Toward Assimilation and Citizenship* (New York: Palgrave Macmillan 2003); Peter Scholten, "Arbeidsdeling en Immigrantenbeleid (Work Sharing and Immigration Policy)" *Ethiek & Maatschappij (Ethics and Society)* 9 (2): 73–91 (2006).

34. Before the end of the 1980s, MCP in the Netherlands was predominantly cultural policy, but it took quite some time before, fairly tame and modest, socioeconomic integration policies really took shape in the mid-1990s (WBEAA (*Wet Bevordering Evenredige Arbeidsdeelname Allochthonen)* and law SAMEN, later the SME (*Small and Medium Enterprises)* convenants). See Ewald Engelen, "The Economic Incorporation of Immigrants: The Netherlands," in Jochen Blaschke and Bastian Vollmer, eds., *Employment Strategies for Immigrants in the European Union* (Berlin: Parabolis, 2004), 445–96.

35. Baukje Prins, *Voorbij de Onschuld* (Amsterdam: Gennep, 2004).

36. "Incorrect" politicians, political journalists (Paul Scheffer), philosophers (Herman Philipse). and even social scientists (Ruud Koopmans) make multicultural policies in all varieties, not only the rigid, "corporatist polder" version, responsible for the declared "multicultural drama" (recently even for the assassination of Theo van Gogh) (see the polemical criticism by Jan Willem Duyvendak, Ewald Engelen, and Ido de Hahn, *Het Bange Nederland (The Frightened Netherlands)* (Amsterdam: Bert Bakker, 2008). They, eventually, have the "courage" to "dare" to tell us the "truth" that MCP has caused a serious lack of "integration." They are joined from abroad by French republican assimilationists like Kepel and Joppke and English liberal assimilationists like Trevor Phillips selling their preferred, biased models of incorporation informed by an idealized picture of their countries' policies. Ole Waever discusses these changes as consequences of "securitization" (Waever, "World Conflict over Religion," in Mouritsen and Jurgensen, *Constituting Communities*, 208–35).

37. The balanced judgment of the Commissie Gelijke Behandeling produced a public outcry and the recommendation by the secretary of state Verdonk to dissolve the commission.

38. "Canoncommissie" (2006, 2007), http://www.entoen.nu, www.entoen.nu; see Maria Grever, Ed Jonker, Kees Ribbens, and Siep Stuurman, *Controverses rond de canon* (Assen: van Garcum, 2006), The Swedish debates on a literary canon in 2006 were remarkably different.

39. Many proposals are still in the making. Laws have not yet passed Parliament or the Senate. Increasingly also courts, legal advisory bodies and legal experts oppose and try to block these developments because they are incompatible with Dutch law, consitutional law, and European and international covenants that are binding law in the Netherlands and the European Union.

40. In this regard, the electoral losses of explicit right-wing parties in the elections of November 22 (from twenty-six seats in 2002 to nine) and also the losses of the "liberal" VVD, using Iron Rita rhetoric and policies (from twenty-eight seats in 2003 to twenty-two), is less encouraging than one might think at first sight because CDA, PvdA (loss of nineteen seats), and also the big winner SP (from nine to twenty-five seats) have adopted the essential parts of these "integration" discourses and measures. Still, the new government has started to replace the rhetoric of confrontation with one of moderation (Ella Vogelaar as new state secretary of IND in the spring of 2009 replaced by Eberhard van der Laan mainly for this reason).

41. I draw extensively on Maussen's study (*Ruimte voor de Islam?*) of policy declarations and measures in Amsterdam, Rotterdam, Utrecht, and Zaanstad, which focuses on four domains: (i) Islam and integration; (ii) provisions for religious practices; (iii) Islamic organizations; (iv) antiradicalization. All English translations of policy documents are mine.

42. Ibid., 224ff.

43. For Amsterdam: ibid., 67ff. (even strengthened in Maussen's *Raamnota Gemeentelijk Minderhedenbeleid* in 1989). Rotterdam's policy declarations and measures have been characterized, from 1984 on, by a mix of a pluralist and a dialogical model known as "critical dialogue": subsidies only for activities focused on integration in the socioeconomic sphere that are not at odds with municipal policies ("op integratie gerichte activiteiten in de sociaal-culturele sfeer," "die niet op gespannen voet met gemeentebeleid staan") (*Minderhedenbeleid in een gewijzigde situatie* [1985]). The main aim has been *aanpassen* (assimilate) (*De nieuwe Rotterdammer* [1992]): language, norms and values, manners. From 1995 onward, local authorities, supported by some scholars, promoted a version of Islam "made in Holland," completely individualized and decoupled from ethnicity and culture (*notitie De Veelkleurige Stad* [1998]). For Zaanstad: *Adviescommissie Buitenlandse Werknemers* (1972–1988). In 1994 categorical minority policies were replaced by general policies to fight *achterstand* (negative privileges), but after 1997, minority organizations may again receive subsidies on the condition that they contribute to the "social infrastructure."

44. *Migrantenraad* (1972–1978) and *Ambtelijke Coördinatiegroep* (1979 onward).

45. Report *Burgers als ieder ander* (Citizens Like All Others, 1996) versus paternalizing "traditional minority thinking" and targeting *doelgroepen* (specific groups); in 1997 *Van Minderhedenbeleid naar interculturalisatie.*

46. Utrecht, 2004.

47. "Integratie en participatie zijn niet langer een zaak van de ethnische minderheden alleen. Dit betekent dat niet langer alleen intitiatieven van allochtone zelforganisaties voor financiële ondersteuning in aanmerking komen maar ook initiatieven van andere Amsterdammers . . . gericht op de inburgering en participatie van etnische minderheden." Het "kunnen zowel seculiere als religieuze en zowel gemengde als etnische organisaties zijn als ze maar de integratie bevorderen." *Subsidieverordening Integratie en Participatie*, 2004, 8. Zaanstad is a bit different because since 1998 there has been more space for subsidies for independent ethnic organizations (Maussen, *Ruimte voor de Islam?* 178f.).

48. Maussen, *Ruimte voor de Islam?* 179ff.

49. Ibid., 76–78. In the Netherlands, mayors are appointed by the crown, not chosen by or responsible to the municipal council. Mayor Cohen has explained his vision in many lectures and public statements. Diversity talk is particularly strong in policy statements drafted by civil servants.

50. As with national measures, these local measures of marginalization and exclusion or expulsion are at odds with existing Dutch and European law.

51. SPIOR (Stichting Platform Islamitische Organisaties Rijnmond) was established in 1988 as an organization to represent Muslim interests, to participate in formal *overleg* (discussion) with authorities, and to help mosque associations. SPIOR defended a pluralist dialogical vision and was praised in a report by the COS (Centrum voor Onderzoek en Statistiek) in 2003 and also by neighborhood councils, but B&W (mayor and aldermen) declared that this "does not live up to the society of today" ("voldoet niet aan de samenleving van nu").

52. See also Bloemraad in this volume.

53. Mayor Cohen has also forcefully criticized this (Maussen, *Ruimte voor de Islam?* 77f.). In addition, they tend to see themselves as providers of services and short-term projects, not as interest organizations and cores of social movements. This may be an intended side effect (see Justus Uitermark and Frank van Steenbergen, "Postmulticulturalisme en Stedelijk Burgerschap," *Sociologie* 2 (3): 265–87 [2006]).

54. Local authorities don't like to see immigrants organizing as ethnic groups, because this is said to breed segregation and isolation; see for criticism Bader, *Secularism or Democracy*, ch. 9, and Steve Vertovec, "New Complexities of Cohesion in Britain," the recent report of the U.K. Commission on Integration and Cohesion (Wetherby, U.K.: Communities and Local Government Publications, 2007). Cf. also Jean N. Tillie, "Social Capital of Organizations and Their Members," *Journal of Ethnic and Migration Studies* 30 (3): 529–41 (2004), and Bloemraad in this volume, but this is clearly at odds with the statement (Amsterdam 2003, 10) "de overheid gaat er niet

over de vraag langs welke weg een burger tot emancipatie komt" ("government should not intervene or decide issues of how citizens achieve emancipation"). Amsterdam even requires a "diverse samenstelling van hun eigen bestuur en personeel" ("a diverse composition of its own administration and personnel"). Yet, at the same time there is "behoefte aan woordvoerders van bepaalde groepen burgers en aan vertegenwoordigers van de 'Marokkaanse gemenschap' of van moslims" ("a need for spokespersons of different groups of citizens and for representatives of the 'Moroccan community' or of 'Muslims'"). Dismantling advisory councils for minorities damages the networks between organizations and leads to more isolated organization less able to represent interests and to contribute to the development of social and political trust among their constituencies (see Floris Vermeulen, *The Immigrant Organizing Process* [Amsterdam: Amsterdam University Press, 2006]; Uitermark and Steenbergen, "Postmulticulturalisme en Stedelijk Burgerschap").

55. Maussen, *Ruimte voor de Islam?* 73.

56. Bader, *Secularism or Democracy*, chs. 4, 7.

57. Ibid., chs. 8, 10.

58. E.g., by declaring integration to be a nonissue now, as was tried without much success in the early stages of the 2005 election campaigns by most parties except right-wing parties and Verdonk—a strategy that only helps to further delegitimize political parties and representative democracy.

59. See my six rules of thumb for flexible and wise policies of affirmative action (Veit Bader, "Dilemmas of Ethnic Affirmative Action," *Citizenship Studies* 2 [3]: 462ff. [1998]). The recommended general policies to fight structural disadvantages of minorities in an indirect way depend on well-functioning welfare arrangements that, paradoxically, are now under attack, under "reconstruction," or in serious decline in all European states, without viable powerful alternatives. Without such safe institutional backings it is incredibly difficult to prevent strategies of *divide et impera,* particularly under conditions of negative sum games.

60. See Veit Bader, "Dilemmas of Multiculturalism: Finding or Losing Our Way?" *Canadian Diversity/Diversité* 4 (1): 87 (2005) for the immigration/welfare dilemma; *Secularism or Democracy*, ch. 8, for the dilemmas of institutionalization.

Chapter 14. When and Why Should Liberal Democracies Restrict Immigration?

1. On the spread of markets and the impact on the world's poor see, for example, Jeffrey Sachs's work (see http://www.earthinstitute.columbia.edu/). The opening of China and India to world markets has caused enormous domestic disruption, and their development has been uneven, but it has also led to an astonishing decline in the numbers of people living in desperate poverty.

2. These quotations are all from the editors' introduction to *Globalization and Egalitarian Redistribution*, ed. Pranab Bardhan, Samuel Bowles, and Michael Wallerstein (Princeton: Princeton University Press, 2007), 2, 7, describing the contribution

to that volume by Stuart Soroka, Keith Banting, and Richard Johnston, "Immigration and Redistribution in a Global Era," in *Globalization*, 261–317, which I discuss below.

3. Patterns of immigration differ across countries, and the impact of immigration likewise varies, so I limit myself largely to the United States.

4. The pages that follow draw on Stephen Macedo, "The Moral Dilemma of U.S. Immigration Policy: Open Borders vs. Social Justice?" in *Debating Immigration*, ed. Carol Swain (Cambridge: Cambridge University Press, 2007).

5. See George J. Borjas, *Heaven's Door: Immigration Policy and the American Economy* (Princeton: Princeton University Press, 1999), 8–11. The final statistic, on foreign stock, is from Dianne A. Schmidley, "Profile of the Foreign-Born Population in the United States: 2000," *U.S. Census Bureau, Current Population Reports, Series P23–206* (Washington, D.C.: U.S. Government Printing Office, December 2001), available at http://www.census.gov/prod/2002pubs/p23-206.pdf

6. George J. Borjas, "The U.S. Takes the Wrong Immigrants," *Wall Street Journal* (April 5, 1990); the quote continues, "75 percent of legal immigrants in 1987 were granted entry because they were related to an American citizen or resident, while only 4 percent were admitted because they possessed useful skills."

7. Borjas, *Heaven's Door*, 11, 22–38, 82–86, 103–4; and Borjas, "Increasing the Supply of Labor Through Immigration: Measuring the Impact on Native-Born Workers," Backgrounder, *Center for Immigration Studies* (May 2004): The impact on blacks and Hispanics is especially great because they form a disproportionately large share of high school dropouts; the effect holds regardless of whether immigration is legal or illegal. See also Borjas, "The Labor Demand Curve Is Downward Sloping: Reexamining the Impact of Immigration on the Labor Market," *Quarterly Journal of Economics* 118, no. 4 (November 2003): 1335–74.

8. "It is now generally accepted that immigration has negative economic consequences for low-wage workers in general and for African Americans in particular," Hannes Johannssons and Steven Shulman, "Immigration and the Employment of African American Workers," *Review of Black Political Economy* 31, nos. 1–2 (2003): 95–110, here 95.

9. See David Card, "How Immigration Affects U.S. Cities," Center for Research and Analysis of Migration, Discussion Paper, 11/07, Department of Economics, University College, London, available at http://www.econ.ucl.ac.uk/cream/pages/CDP/CDP_11_07.pdf.

10. George Borjas and Lawrence Katz point out that immigration from Mexico to the United States is a fairly recent phenomenon: "In 1940, 0.5 percent of all male high school dropouts were Mexican immigrants. Even as recently as 1980, only 4.1 percent of male high school dropouts were Mexican immigrants." By 2000, however, the figure was 26.2 percent. Borjas and Katz, "The Evolution of the Mexican-Born Workforce in the United States," Working Paper 11281, National Bureau of Economic Research, 9; available at http://www.nber.org/papers/w11281.

11. Douglas S. Massey, Jorge Durand, and Nolan J. Malone, *Beyond Smoke and*

Mirrors: Mexican Immigration in an Era of Economic Integration (New York: Russell Sage, 2003), 150–51; conceding the wage effects discussed earlier, see 154.

12. Borjas, "Increasing the Supply of Labor." For more fine-grained analyses that, nevertheless, confirm the proposition that immigration has worsened the relative standing of many native-born Americans, see the essays in Daniel S. Hamermesh and Frank D. Bean, eds., *Help or Hindrance? The Economic Implications of Immigration for African Americans* (New York: Russell Sage, 1998). In that volume see Borjas, "Do Blacks Gain or Lose from Immigration?" which argues that neither skilled nor unskilled immigration is likely to help blacks relative to others but, paradoxically, the "deficit" that blacks suffer from immigration may be highest when immigration is exclusively skilled as opposed to unskilled immigration, because although skilled immigrants are less likely to compete with black workers, skilled immigration's greatest positive impact is nevertheless as a complementary factor in production to capital, and native blacks own very little capital; see pp. 67–68. See also the interesting essays by, among others, Cordelia Reimers, Kristin F. Butcher, and Peter Shuck, suggesting (among other things) that while recent immigration likely has a negative impact on the wages of white and black high school dropouts (especially those in this group with relatively high wages), it may increase the wages of native Hispanic high school dropouts, perhaps due to the fact that they can serve as intermediaries and interpreters between employers and immigrants. Shuck also points out that recent immigrants were a major target of political dissatisfaction during debates over the 1996 welfare reform act.

13. Of course, a more fine-grained analysis would break the labor market argument down by employment sector.

14. Borjas, *Heaven's Door*, 176–77. Australia and Ireland have introduced similar education- and skills-based quota systems, see Steven Malanga, "The Right Immigration Policy: Not amnesty or guest workers, but newcomers who would strengthen us," *City Journal*, Autumn 2006.

15. Nolan McCarty, Keith T. Poole, and Howard Rosenthal, *Polarized America: The Dance of Ideology and Unequal Riches*, Walras-Pareto Lectures (Cambridge, Mass.: MIT Press, 2006), Chapter 4.

16. Congress restricted alien access to many federally funded welfare benefits in 1996. This would seem one way to help dampen the downward effects argued for by McCarty et al. Nevertheless, immigrants to the United States receive various forms of public assistance at a higher rate than native Americans. Howard F. Chang, "Public Benefits and Federal Authorization for Alienage Discrimination by the States," *New York University Annual Survey of American Law* 58 (2002): 357–570. See also Gordon H. Hanson, Kenneth F. Scheve, and Matthew J. Slaughter, "Public Finance and Individual Preferences over Globalization Strategies" (January 2005), NBER Working Paper W11028, available at SSRN: http://ssrn.com/abstract = 645270, arguing that "exposure to immigrant fiscal pressures reduces support for freer immigration among natives, especially the more-skilled" (online abstract).

17. Malanga argues that "though the federal government bans illegal aliens from receiving many benefits, several states and cities have made themselves immigrant havens by providing government services through a don't-ask, don't-tell policy. New York City, for instance, offers immigrants, regardless of their status, such benefits as government-sponsored health insurance, preventive medical care, and counseling programs. Some states have moved to ensure that illegals receive in-state tuition discounts to state colleges, even though out-of-state American citizens don't qualify for those discounts." See Malanga, "The Right Immigration Policy."

18. As David Miller puts it, "A shared identity carries with it a shared loyalty, and this increases confidence that others will reciprocate one's own cooperative behavior," *On Nationality* (Oxford: Oxford University Press, 1995), 92. Michael Walzer argues that the provision of social goods depends on shared social meanings, which in turn depend upon the enforcement of political boundaries, *Spheres of Justice*, chapter 2, "On Membership."

19. Robert D. Putnam, "E Pluribus Unum: Diversity and Community in the Twenty-First Century: The 2006 Johan Skytte Prize Lecture," *Scandinavian Political Studies* 30, no. 2 (June 2007): 137–74, 137.

20. A. Alesina and E. La Ferrara, "Who Trusts Others?" *Journal of Public Economics* 85 (2002): 207–34, finding that homogeneous places tend to be more trusting; Alberto Alesina, Reza Baquir, and William Easterley, "Public Goods and Ethnic Divisions," *Quarterly Journal of Economics* 114, no. 4 (November 1999): 1243–84; William Easterly and Ross Levine, "Africa's Growth Tragedy: Policies and Ethnic Divisions," *Quarterly Journal of Economics* 112 (1997): 1203–50.

21. Stuart Soroka, Keith Banting, and Richard Johnston, "Immigration and Redistribution in a Global Era," in Pranab Bardhan, Samuel Bowles, and Michael Wallerstein, eds., *Globalization and Egalitarian Redistribution* (Princeton: Princeton University Press, 2007), 278.

22. Soroka, Banting, and Johnston argue that the "effect seems wholly political and wholly through its direct impact on mainstream governing parties," and reflects the influence of "perceived cultural threat and economic cost," ibid., 278–79. The challenge is to devise ways to "combine openness at the global level with social integration at the domestic level," ibid., 279. There is a burgeoning literature on ethnic diversity and public good provision; see James Habyarimana, Macartan Humphryes, Daniel N. Posner, and Jeremy M. Weinstein, "Why Does Ethnic Diversity Undermine Public Goods Provision?" *American Political Science Review* 101, no. 4 (November 2007): 709–25, which notes that "the empirical connection between ethnic heterogeneity and the underprovision of public goods is widely accepted," though there is no consensus on "the specific mechanisms through which this relationship operates," 709. See also Alesina and La Ferrara, "Who Trusts Others?"; Easterly and Levine, "Africa's Growth Tragedy." It is worth noting that, so far as the United States is concerned, higher immigration also coincides with the increased racialization of welfare policy in the media, a phenomenon described by Martin Gilens, *Why Americans Hate Welfare: Race,*

Media, and the Politics of Antipoverty Policy (Chicago: University of Chicago Press, 1999).

23. Kevin Philips, *Wealth and Democracy: A Political History of the American Rich* (New York: Broadway Books, 2002). The middle decades of the twentieth century, up to the late 1960s, also coincides with the era of high social capital that Robert Putnam has written about: the "greatest generation" of social connectedness, social trust, and support for improved social justice. Robert D. Putnam, *Bowling Alone: The Collapse and Revival of American Community* (New York: Simon and Schuster, 2000).

24. See Putnam, *Bowling Alone.*

25. See Suzanne Mettler's account, *Soldiers to Citizens: The G.I. Bill and the Making of the Greatest Generation* (New York: Oxford University Press, 2006).

26. A phenomenon described by Gilens, *Why Americans Hate Welfare.*

27. Again, the evidence seems far from conclusive. See Cybelle Fox, "The Changing Color of Welfare: How Whites Attitudes Towards Latinos Influence Support for Welfare," *American Journal of Sociology* 110, no. 3 (2004), 580–625, which argues that in areas with high concentrations of Latinos, negative stereotypes among whites toward Latinos' work ethic are undermined, but whites also want to spend less on welfare.

28. I draw on Eamonn Callan's excellent unpublished paper, "Integrating Immigrants," presented at the Program on Ethics and Public Affairs, University Center for Human Values, Princeton University, October 4, 2007. The majority of Americans continue to believe in the idea of equality of opportunity; see Jennifer Hochschild and Nathan Scovronick, *The American Dream and the Public Schools* (New York: Oxford University Press, 2003). Some who are here illegally but for a long period of time may also have earned the promise.

29. Joseph H. Carens, "Aliens and Citizens: The Case for Open Borders," *Review of Politics* 49, no. 2 (Spring 1987): 251–73.

30. See Robert E. Goodin, "What Is So Special About Our Fellow Countrymen?" *Ethics* 98, no. 4 (1988): 663–86.

31. For the impact of labor migration on development, see, for example, Lant Pritchett, *Let Their People Come* (Washington, D.C.: Center for Global Development, 2006), and see the interview with *Reason Magazine*, "Ending Global Apartheid; Economist Lant Pritchett defends immigration, the least-popular—and most-proven—idea for helping the world's poor," *Reasononline*, February 2008, at http://www.reason.com/news/show/123912.html.

32. See Robert Nozick, *Anarchy State and Utopia* (New York: Basic, 1975). For a recent statement, see Chandran Kukathas's essay in this volume.

33. Interview with Milton Friedman, *Forbes* (December 29, 1997). Also, see his interview with Tunku Varadarajan, "The Romance of Economics, Milton and Rose Friedman: Dinner with Keynes? Yes. War with Iraq? They disagree." *Opinion Journal from the Wall Street Journal Editorial Page* (July 22, 2006), available at http://www.opinionjournal.com/editorial/feature.html?id = 110008690: "Is immigration, I asked,—

especially illegal immigration—good for the economy, or bad? 'It's neither one nor the other,' Mr. Friedman replied. 'But it's good for freedom. In principle, you ought to have completely open immigration. But with the welfare state it's really not possible to do that. . . . *She's* an immigrant,' he added, pointing to his wife. 'She came in just before World War I.' *(Rose—smiling gently:* 'I was two years old.') 'If there were no welfare state,' he continued, 'you could have open immigration, because everybody would be responsible for himself.' Was he suggesting that one can't have immigration reform without welfare reform? 'No, you *can* have immigration reform, but you can't have *open* immigration without largely the elimination of welfare.' "

34. See John Rawls, *A Theory of Justice* (Cambridge, Mass.: Harvard University Press, 1971).

35. For those interested in the flaws, the literature is vast. A good place to begin is Will Kymlicka, *Contemporary Political Philosophy* (New York: Oxford University Press, 2002).

36. I have explored this argument at length elsewhere: "What Self-Governing Peoples Owe to One Another: Universalism, Diversity, and *The Law of Peoples*," *Fordham Law Review*, Special Symposium Issue on Rawls and the Law, 72 (2004): 1721–38.

37. I leave aside Robert Goodin's instrumental defense of special duties to compatriots; Goodin argues that, for a variety of reasons, including proximity and administrative convenience, it makes sense to assign compatriots special responsibility for each other's well-being as a way to best approximate ethically universal duties; see "What Is So Special About Our Fellow Countrymen?" And see the useful discussion in Kok Chor Tan, *Toleration, Diversity, and Global Justice* (University Park: Pennsylvania State University Press, 2000), 180–91. My defense is not instrumental or part of a maximizing strategy. The position I defend would be closer to that defended by Samuel Scheffler, who argues that special relationships often generate special reasons for action; see his *Boundaries and Allegiances: Problems of Justice and Responsibility in Liberal Thought* (Oxford: Oxford University Press, 2001).

38. For a useful development of relational versus nonrelational versions of cosmopolitan morality, see Andrea Sangiovanni, "Global Justice, Reciprocity, and the State," *Philosophy and Public Affairs* 35, no. 1 (2007): 3–39.

39. The discussion that follows draws on a more extended explication and defense of the Rawlsian position in Macedo, "What Self-Governing Peoples Owe to One Another." Others have developed versions of this approach, including David Miller, Michael I. Blake, Donald Moon, Joshua Cohen, Leif Wenar, and Andrea Sangiovanni. Sangiovanni's recent intervention seems to me very helpful, and I draw on it below; see "Global Justice." I agree with Sangiovanni that the content, scope, and justification of principles of social justice make most sense when conceived of as principles for regulating the mutual relations of citizens in a political community. While it is important to distinguish domestic and global political relations, and the regulative principles appropriate to each, that effort at distinction should not be confused with a minimization of the principles that apply to relations of states and peoples across borders.

40. John Rawls, *Political Liberalism* (New York: Columbia University Press, 1993), 137.

41. I explore the centrality of mutual justification to liberal democratic constitutionalism and its place in defining the virtues of liberal citizens and public officials in *Liberal Virtues: Citizenship, Justice, and Community in Liberal Constitutionalism* (New York: Oxford University Press, 1990).

42. The upshot of Rawls's famous thought experiment is his argument that two basic principles of justice would be chosen by citizens of modern pluralistic democracies: "1. Each person has an equal claim to a fully adequate scheme of equal basic rights and liberties, which scheme is compatible with the same scheme for all; and in this scheme the equal political liberties, and only those liberties, are to be guaranteed their fair value. 2. Social and economic inequalities are to satisfy two conditions: (a) They are to be attached to positions and offices open to all under conditions of fair equality of opportunity; and (b), they are to be to the greatest benefit of the least advantaged members of society." Principle 2 (b) is also known as the "difference principle." Rawls, *Political Liberalism*, 5–6. See also his *Theory of Justice* (Cambridge, Mass.: Harvard University Press, 1999).

43. See Michael I. Blake, "Distributive Justice, State Coercion, and Autonomy," *Philosophy and Public Affairs* 30, no. 3 (Summer 2001): 257–96; and Thomas Nagel, "The Problem of Global Justice," *Philosophy and Public Affairs* 33, no. 2 (April 2005): 113–47. Sangiovanni seems to me to get closer to capturing the "complex fact" of collective governance. We should not, in this regard, be misled by the idea that a liberal constitutional democracy is a system of "limited government" and that principles of liberal justice are limited in their content, and perhaps even "neutral" with respect to conceptions of the good life. The political arrangements of liberal democracies regulate our lives as a whole, in their every aspect, even if the content of some political principles is limited.

44. For a related account, see Ronald Dworkin, *Sovereign Virtue: The Theory and Practice of Equality* (Cambridge, Mass.: Harvard University Press, 2000), 1–2.

45. The U.N. Charter and the Universal Declaration of Human Rights are instruments created by "the peoples of the United Nations" or "member states." Contrast the phrasing "We the peoples of the United Nations" and "We the people of the United States," which open the preambles to the U.N. Charter and the U.S. Constitution. The U.N. Charter closes, "IN FAITH WHEREOF the representatives of the Governments of the United Nations have signed the present Charter." These matters cannot of course be resolved by these textual or historical facts alone. Provinces and states within nations, autonomous territories, and plural or consociational regimes raise additional issues not covered here.

46. The civil service of the European Union is tiny—roughly equivalent to that of a medium-sized European city—and its taxing capacity and competences are likewise highly circumscribed; see Sangiovanni, "Global Justice," and Andrew Moravcsik, "In

Defense of the Democratic Deficit," *Journal of Common Market Studies,* 40, no. 4 (2002): 603–24.

47. Blake, "Distributive Justice, State Coercion, and Autonomy."

48. It is worth noting that deliberative democrats such as Amy Gutmann and Dennis Thompson also emphasize, as much as John Rawls, the central importance of practices of reciprocal reason-giving and reason-demanding; see *Democracy and Disagreement* (Cambridge, Mass.: Harvard University Press, 1996); and *Why Deliberative Democracy?* (Princeton: Princeton University Press, 2004). Deliberative practices answer to the need to justify coercive laws with shared moral reasons, and also promise to improve the quality of decisions.

49. I should emphasize that on the Rawlsian view, "decent" societies that are fully respectable members of international society not only have a sufficient level of material resources but also respect their members human rights and sustain governing practices that, if not fully democratic, really do represent and take seriously the interests and views of all groups in society; I explore these issues at greater length in "What Self-Governing Peoples Owe to One Another."

50. What constitutes fair arrangements for the support of global institutions is an open question to be taken up in the context of those institutions. The Irish have a GDP per capita ($43,000) about 60 percent greater than New Zealanders' ($26,000); I am doubtful that this matters in itself, though it may be relevant in assessing relative contributions to multilateral institutions, where the principle of "ability to pay" would seem relevant both internationally and domestically.

51. China and India wield considerable global power, in spite of their per capita poverty. My brief observations on this score run counter to some of what Charles R. Beitz says in "Does Global Inequality Matter?" *Metaphilosophy* 32, nos. 1–2 (January 2001): 95–112.

52. Such as Rawls's remark, citing David Landis, that poverty is often attributable to faulty culture, see Rawls, *Law of Peoples,* 117, note 51.

53. I understand Cohen and Sable to be operating within a broadly Rawlsian paradigm, but at a finer-grained level of institutional and policy detail, which is what is needed; see Joshua Cohen and Charles Sabel, "Extra Rempublicam Nulla Justitia?" *Philosophy and Public Affairs* 34, no. 2 (March 2006): 147–75, and their response to Thomas Nagel, "The Problem of Global Justice," *Philosophy and Public Affairs* 33, no. 2 (April 2005): 113–47; see also A. J. Julius, "Nagel's Atlas," *Philosophy and Public Affairs* 34, no. 2 (March 2006): 176–92.

54. It confuses matters when critics of the membership view (with respect to distributive justice) raise examples such as starvation in Bangladesh or the unfairness of international agreements on intellectual property and patent protection. It is common ground that there is a duty of assistance, and that global institutions need to be reformed.

55. Mark Rosenzweig, "Global Wage Differences and International Student Flows," *Brookings Trade Forum* (Washington, D.C.: Brookings Institution), figure 4;

and see Devesh Kapur and John McHale, "What Is Wrong with Plan B? International Migration as an Alternative to Development Assistance," *Brookings Trade Forum* 2006 (2006) 137–72.

56. See Borjas, "Do Blacks Gain?"

57. Economist Brad DeLong said something to this effect on his blog, "Morning Coffee Videocast: Immigration Is a Good Thing" (May 4, 2006), available at http://delong.typepad.com/sdj/2006/05/morning_coffee__2.html

58. See Massey, Durand, and Malone, *Beyond Smoke and Mirrors.*

59. See Kapur and McHale, "What Is Wrong with Plan B?" 137–72, 167–68.

60. Ibid., 163.

61. Ibid., 164–66.

62. See the interviewers' comments in the *Reason* magazine interview with Lant Pritchett, above.

63. Massey, Durand, and Malone, *Beyond Smoke and Mirrors,* 157–63.

64. The bipartisan compromise is described by John Hughes, "Merits of the Bipartisan Immigration Reform Deal: It's a Welcome Sign That Statecraft Can Rise Above Partisan Politics," *Christian Science Monitor,* May 23, 2007, available at http://www.csmonitor.com/2007/0523/p09s02-cojh.html.

65. Is it possible to combine elements of both approaches? We might limit the sectors in which guest workers may be employed to minimize competition with the native poor. But labor restrictions on migrant workers risk promoting exploitation; see Michael I. Blake, "Discretionary Immigration," *Philosophical Topics* 30, no. 2 (Fall 2002): 273–89.

Chapter 15. Expatriatism

1. I have offered a defense of open borders elsewhere. See Kukathas, "The Case for Open Immigration," in Andrew I. Cohen and Christopher Wellman (eds.), *Contemporary Debates in Applied Ethics* (Oxford: Blackwell, 2005), 207–19. For a contrary view in the same volume see David Miller, "Immigration: The Case for Limits," 193–206. For other works on open borders see Alan Dowty, *Closed Borders: The Contemporary Assault on Freedom of Movement (Twentieth Century Fund Report)* (New Haven: Yale University Press, 1987); Phillip Cole, *Philosophies of Exclusion* (Edinburgh: Edinburgh University Press, 2001); Teresa Hayter, *Open Borders: The Case Against Immigration Controls,* 2nd ed. (London: Pluto Press, 2004); Antoine Pécoud and Paul de Guchteneire (eds.), *Migration Without Borders: Essays on the Free Movement of People* (New York: Berghahn Books, and Paris: UNESCO, 2007); Linda Bosniak, *The Citizen and the Alien: Dilemmas of Contemporary Membership* (Princeton, N.J.: Princeton University Press, 2006). For a defense of limits to immigration see Peter C. Meilander, *Toward a Theory of Immigration* (London: Palgrave Macmillan, 2001). The most important advocate of open borders in liberal political theory is Joseph Carens. See in particular his "Aliens and Citizens: The Case for Open Borders," *Review of Politics* 49 (1987), 251–73. For a survey of ethical issues in immigration see Kukathas, "Immigra-

tion," in Hugh Lafollette (ed.), *The Oxford Handbook of Practical Ethics* (Oxford: Oxford University Press, 2003).

2. Australia in the late 1990s, when it was worried about the small increase of refugees, began a campaign in selected countries warning of how dangerous Australia was with its many snakes and crocodiles, and how difficult it would be for people to adapt to its permissive moral standards. Nick Squires, "Australia Uses Its Wildlife to Scare Away Refugees Snakes and Crocodiles Are a Deterrent, but Possums Are Owner-Friendly," *Sunday Telegraph*, June 18, 2000.

3. I note that criminal punishment involving detention or imprisonment supplies a possible exception. However, imprisoned citizens do not lose all rights of participation, even though deprived of liberty; and the deprivation of some rights is temporary.

4. I have not discussed further the ecological arguments, mainly because they seem to me not as substantial as some advocates of border controls think. I mention them only for the sake of completeness.

5. See, among his extensive writings, Joseph Carens, "A Reply to Meilander: Reconsidering Open Borders," *International Migration Review* 33:4 (1999), 1082–1097; "Live-in Domestics, Seasonal Workers, and Others Hard to Locate in the Map of Democracy," *Journal of Political Philosophy* 16:4 (2008), 419–445; "The Rights of Irregular Migrants," *Ethics and International Affairs* 22:2 (2008), 163–186; "The Integration of Immigrants," *Journal of Moral Philosophy* 2:1 (2005); "Who Should Get In? The Ethics of Immigration Admissions," *Ethics and International Affairs* 17:1 (2003), 95–110.

Chapter 16. Citizenship and Free Movement

Special thanks to Linda Bosniak, Oliviero Angeli, and Lea Ipy for detailed comments on an earlier draft.

1. For a critical view that regards dual citizenship as an obstacle to immigrant integration see Stanley A. Renshow, *The 50% American: Immigration and National Identity in an Age of Terror* (Washington, D.C.: Georgetown University Press, 2005).

2. One can find a few side remarks on freedom of movement throughout the history of political philosophy, but the contemporary debate really starts with the two contrasting statements by Michael Walzer, *Spheres of Justice: A Defense of Pluralism and Equality* (Basic Books, New York, 1983), chapter 2; and Joseph Carens, "Aliens and Citizens: The Case for Open Borders," *Review of Politics* 49, no. 2 (1987): 251–73. For a comprehensive overview see Veit M. Bader, "The Ethics of Immigration," *Constellations* 12, no. 3 (2005): 331–61.

3. Eric Cavallero, "An Immigration-Pressure Model of Global Distributive Justice," *Politics, Philosophy and Economics* 5, no. 1 (2006): 97–127; Michael Blake and Mathias Risse, "Is There a Human Right to Free Movement?" (Immigration and Original Ownership of the Earth Faculty Research Working Paper Series RWP06–012, John F. Kennedy School of Government, Harvard University, Cambridge, Mass., April 2006); Michael Blake and Mathias Risse, "Migration, Territoriality, and Culture" (Fac-

ulty Research Working Paper Series RWP07–009, John F. Kennedy School of Government, Harvard University, Cambridge, Mass., February 2007).

4. Walzer, *Spheres of Justice*; David Miller, "Immigration: The Case for Limits," in *Contemporary Debates in Applied Ethics*, ed. Andrew Cohen and Christopher Heath Wellman (Malden, Mass.: Blackwell, 2005), 193–206; David Miller, *National Responsibility and Global Justice* (Oxford: Oxford University Press, 2007).

5. Blake and Risse ("Migration, Territoriality, and Culture," 3, n. 4) do acknowledge in a long footnote the historical and moral contingency of the modern state and the international state system, but then assume that alternative models with overlapping sovereignties or an emerging world state can be set aside for a normative discussion of immigration rights.

6. Julius Isaac, *Economics of Migration* (New York: Oxford University Press, 1947), 13–19; Rey Koslowski, *Migrants and Citizens. Demographic Change in the European State System* (Ithaca, N.Y.: Cornell University Press, 2000), 58; Aristide Zolberg, "The Exit Revolution," in *Citizenship and Those Who Leave: The Politics of Emigration and Expatriation*, ed. N. L. Green and F. Weil (Urbana: University of Illinois Press, 2007), 33–66.

7. John Torpey, *The Invention of the Passport: Surveillance, Citizenship, and the State* (Cambridge: Cambridge University Press, 2000).

8. The sites of control over flows need not physically coincide with the borders that demarcate jurisdictions but can be also located inside the territory, as in the case of work site controls for employment of irregular immigrants, or outside, as are passport and visa controls at departure from international airports. These examples illustrate an internalization or externalization of control enforcement that still refers to the crossing of a well-demarcated political border (Zolberg, "The Exit Revolution"). Such "displacement" of the control sites may be criticized in various ways, but it does not signal that states attempt to restrict internal freedom of movement or to exercise political authority in a foreign territory.

9. European Parliament and Council Directive 2004/38/EC of April 29, 2004 on the right of citizens of the Union and their family members to move and reside freely within the territory of the Member States.

10. Council Directive 2003/109/EC of November 25, 2003 concerning the status of third-country nationals nationals who are long-term residents.

11. Randall Hansen and Patrick Weil, eds., *Dual Nationality, Social Rights and Federal Citizenship in the U.S. and Europe* (Oxford: Berghahn, 2001); David Martin and Kay Hailbronner, *Rights and Duties of Dual Nationals—Evolution and Prospects* (The Hague: Kluwer Law International, 2003); Thomas Faist and Peter Kivisto, eds., *Dual Citizenship in Global Perspective* (London: Palgrave Macmillan, 2007).

12. Tomas Hammar, *Democracy and the Nation State: Aliens, Denizens and Citizens in a World of International Migration* (Aldershot: Avebury, 1990), 106–14.

13. I agree in this respect with Chandran Kukathas that political theory should be sensitive to conditions for realizing normative proposals under current conditions but

"needs also to be suspicious of feasibility considerations, particularly when they lead us to morally troubling conclusions" (Chandran Kukathas, "The Case for Open Immigration," in *Contemporary Debates in Applied Ethics,* ed. Andrew Cohen and Christopher Heath Wellman (Malden, Mass.: Blackwell, 2005), 207). For a general discussion of the tension between idealist and realist approaches in normative theories applied to migration rights see Joseph H. Carens, "Realistic and Idealistic Approaches to the Ethics of Migration," *International Migration Review* 30, no. 1 (1996): 156–70.

14. Hedley Bull, *The Anarchical Society* (New York: Columbia University Press, 1977).

15. Miller, *National Responsibility and Global Justice.*

16. Allen Buchanan, *Justice, Legitimacy, and Self-Determination: Moral Foundations for International Law* (Oxford: Oxford University Press, 2004); Rainer Bauböck, "Paradoxes of Self-Determination and the Right to Self-Government," in *Global Justice and the Bulwarks of Localism: Human Rights in Context,* ed. Chris Eisgruber and Andras Sajo (Leiden: Martinus Nijhoff, 2005), 101–28.

17. The right of free movement within a federation or union may even help to stabilize territorial borders by mixing local populations and reducing thereby the likelihood of secessionist challenges. In certain cases, free movement can, however, also be experienced as a threat to the intergenerational continuity of a smaller nested polity that wants to preserve its distinct cultural identity and cannot do so through assimilating newcomers. Indigenous peoples have therefore often claimed rights to restrict access or settlement of nonindigenous citizens in their autonomous territories.

18. Stefan Wolff, *Disputed Territories: The Transnational Dynamics of Ethnic Conflict Settlement* (Oxford: Berghahn Books, 2004); Rainer Bauböck, "The Trade-Off Between Transnational Citizenship and Political Autonomy," in *Dual Citizenship in Global Perspective,* ed. Thomas Faist and Peter Kivisto (London: Palgrave Macmillan, 2007), 69–91.

19. Chandran Kukathas, "Immigration," in *The Oxford Handbook of Practical Ethics,* ed. Hugh LaFolette (Oxford: Oxford University Press, 2002), 107–22.

20. Alan Dowty, *Closed Borders: The Contemporary Assault on Freedom of Movement* (New Haven: Yale University Press, 1987).

21. Immanuel Kant, "Zum Ewigen Frieden," in *Werke in sechs Bänden,* vol. 6 (1795; Cologne: Könemann, 1995).

22. One could add further dimensions that would measure material grounds for limiting free movement rights, such as concerns about public order and national security, or individual requirements, such as skill levels, but then we would be analyzing controlled immigration rather than free movement. I assume therefore that free movement refers to some combination of a territory within which movement is not politically constrained with a category of persons who are not subject to emigration and immigration controls.

23. International Covenant of Civil and Political Rights, Article 12 (1).

24. See Cavallero, "An Immigration-Pressure Model of Global Distributive Jus-

tice," for a proposal of international burden sharing that involves trading immigration quotas.

25. Joseph H. Carens, "Migration and Morality: A Liberal Egalitarian Perspective," in *Free Movement: Ethical Issues in the Transnational Migration of People and of Money*, ed. Brian Barry and Robert E. Goodin (University Park: Pennsylvania State University Press, 1992), 26.

26. Robert E. Goodin, "If People Were Money . . . ," in *Free Movement: Ethical Issues in the Transnational Migration of People and of Money*, ed. Brian Barry and Robert E. Goodin (University Park: Pennsylvania State University Press, 1992), 8.

27. Philippe van Parijs, "Commentary: Citizenship Exploitation, Unequal Exchange and the Breakdown of Popular Sovereignty," in *Free Movement: Ethical Issues in the Transnational Migration of People and of Money*, ed. Brian Barry and Robert E. Goodin (University Park: Pennsylvania State University Press, 1992); Thomas Pogge, "Migration and Poverty," in *Citizenship and Exclusion*, ed. Veit Bader (Basingstoke: Macmillan, 1997), 12–27.

28. Cavallero, "An Immigration-Pressure Model of Global Distributive Justice"; Michael Blake and Mathias Risse, "Is There a Human Right to Free Movement?" and "Migration, Territoriality, and Culture."

29. See Saskia Sassen, *The Global City: New York, London, Tokyo* (Princeton, N.J.: Princeton Universtiy Press, 1991). David Miller makes the same mistaken assumption that population density is an argument against admitting further immigrants: "Countries that are already crowded and congested . . . will have an interest in keeping them out" (*National Responsibility and Global Justice,* 223). The reason why Australia and Canada are among the countries with the highest per capita intake of immigrants is, however, not that they have a lot of empty land but, on the contrary, that they are among the societies with the highest rates of urbanization worldwide.

30. One inconsistency in Cavallero's proposal is between his goal of preserving full autonomy of political communities, including with regard to their immigration policy, on the one hand, and the obvious need for global government institutions that could impose and enforce the duties that immigration destination states would incur under his scheme, on the other hand.

31. Kukathas, "The Case for Open Immigration," 211.

32. Ibid., 210.

33. Ibid., 210.

34. Miller, "Immigration: The Case for Limits," 206.

35. Carens, "Migration and Morality"; Bader, "The Ethics of Immigration."

36. Blake and Risse, "Is There a Human Right to Free Movement?" 16.

37. T. H. Marshall, "Citizenship and Social Class," in *Class, Citizenship, and Social Development: Essays by T. H. Marshall* (1949; New York: Anchor Books, 1965).

38. See Stephen Holmes and Cass Sunstein, *The Cost of Rights: Why Liberty Depends on Taxes* (New York: Norton, 1999).

39. Bruce A. Ackerman, *Social Justice in the Liberal State* (New Haven: Yale Universiy Press, 1980), 88, 95.

40. Charles Tiebout, "A Pure Theory of Local Expenditures," *Journal of Political Economy* 64 (1954): 416–24; James Buchanan, "An Economic Theory of Clubs," *Economica* 32 (1965): 1–14.

41. Walzer, *Spheres of Justice*; Joseph H. Carens, "Membership and Morality," in *Immigration and the Politics of Citizenship in Europe and North America*, ed. Rogers W. Brubaker (Lanham, Md.: University Press of America, 1989).

42. See Michael Dummett for a lucid discussion of "submergence" as a threshold for legitimate immigration control. Drummett, *On Immigration and Refugees* (New York: Routledge, 2001), 50–53.

43. Thomas Nagel defends a radical version of this argument that regards redistribution across international borders as a matter of humanitarian duties rather than of justice. Moderate cosmopolitans argue instead that states do have duties of social justice toward noncitizens outside their borders but these are different from their duties towards citizens and residents. Nagel, "The Problem of Global Justice," *Philosophy and Public Affairs* 33, no. 2 (2005): 113–47.

44. Christian Joppke, *Selecting by Origin: Ethnic Migration in the Liberal State* (Cambridge, Mass.: Harvard University Press, 2005).

45. See Bauböck, "Free Movement and the Asymmetry Between Exit and Entry," *Ethics and Economics* 4, no. 1 (2006), at http://ethique-economique.net/, for state practices among the fifteen "old" member states of the European Union and Andre Liebich, "Altneuländer or the Vicissitudes of Citizenship in the New EU States," in *Citizenship Policies in the New Europe*, ed. Rainer Bauböck, B. Perchinig, and W. Sievers (Amsterdam: Amsterdam University Press, 2009), 21–42, for a comparison of policies in Central Eastern Europe.

46. See Iseult Honohan, "Reconsidering the Claim to Family Reunification in Migration," *Political Studies* 57, no. 4 (2009): 768–87 for a discussion of normative standards for family reunification.

47. For discussions of these issues see, e.g., Andrew Shacknove, "Who Is a Refugee?" *Ethics* 95, no. 2 (1985): 274–84; Matthew Gibney, *The Ethics and Politics of Asylum: Liberal Democracy and the Response to Refugees* (Cambridge: Cambridge University Press, 2004).

48. See Art. 34 of the 1956 Geneva Refugee Convention, which asks signatory states to facilitate the naturalization of refugees.

49. Miller, *National Responsibility and Global Justice*.

50. Phillip Cole, *Philosophies of Exclusion: Liberal Political Theory and Immigration* (Edinburgh: Edinburgh University Press, 2000), 43–59; Lea Ypi, "Justice in Migration: A Closed Borders Utopia?" *Journal of Political Philosophy* 16, no. 4 (2008): 391–418.

51. Bauböck, "Free Movement and the Asymmetry Between Exit and Entry"; Miller, *National Responsibility and Global Justice*.

52. Carens, "Aliens and Citizens," 27.

53. Ibid., 28.

54. Michael Blake, "Universal and Qualified Rights to Immigration," *Ethics and Economics* 4, no. 1 (2006): 5, at http://ethique-economique.net.

55. Michael Blake, "Immigration," in R.G. Frey and Christopher Wellman (eds.), *A Companion to Applied Ethics*, (Oxford: Blackwell, 2005), 224–37.

56. Elisabeth Meehan, *Citizenship and the European Community* (London: Sage, 1993); Jo Shaw, "Citizenship of the Union: Towards Postnational Membership?" (Jean Monnet Working Paper 6/97, Harvard Law School, Cambridge, Mass., 1997); Antje Wiener, *"European" Citizenship Practice: Building Institutions of a Non-State* (Boulder, Colo.: Westview Press, 1998).

57. Rainer Bauböck, "Why European Citizenship? Normative Approaches to Supranational Union," *Theoretical Inquiries in Law* 8, no. 2 (2007): 452–88.

58. These criteria include a functioning market economy, stable democratic institutions, the rule of law, human rights, and the protection of minorities.

59. Rainer Bauböck, "The Rights and Duties of External Citizenship," *Citizenship Studies* 13, no. 5 (2009): 475–99.

60. Thomas Faist, "Dual Citizenship in an Age of Mobility" (conference paper for the Transatlantic Council on Migration, Migration Policy Institute, Washington, D.C., 2008).

Contributors

Veit Bader is Professor Emeritus of Sociology and Professor Emeritus of Social and Political Philosophy at the Institute for Migration and Ethnic Studies, University of Amsterdam. He is the author of seventeen books and edited volumes, including *Secularism or Democracy? Associational Governance of Religious Diversity* (Amsterdam University Press, 2007), and numerous articles.

Rainer Bauböck is Professor of Social and Political Theory at the European University Institute and Vice Chair of the Austrian Academy of Science's Commission for Migration and Integration Research. He is the editor or co-editor of nine books in English and several in German, and author of *Transnational Citizenship* (Edward Elgar, 1995) along with numerous articles.

Irene Bloemraad is Associate Professor of Sociology at the University of California, Berkeley. She is the author of *Becoming a Citizen: Incorporating Immigrants and Refugees in the United States and Canada* (University of California Press, 2006) and numerous articles in journals and edited volumes.

Howard F. Chang is the Earle Hepburn Professor of Law at the University of Pennsylvania. His publications include "A Liberal Theory of Social Welfare: Fairness, Utility, and the Pareto Principle," *Yale Law Journal* 110: 173–235 (2000) and "Liberalized Immigration as Free Trade: Economic Welfare and the Optimal Immigration Policy," *University of Pennsylvania Law Review* 145: 1147–1244 (1997), among many other works.

Christian Joppke is Professor of Political Science at the American University of Paris. His books include *Citizenship and Immigration* (Polity, 2010), *Se-*

lecting by Origin (Harvard University Press, 2005), and *Immigration and the Nation-State* (Oxford University Press, 2000).

Chandran Kukathas holds the Chair in Political Theory in the Department of Government, London School of Economics. He is the author of *Multiculturalism* (Blackwell, 2010) and *The Liberal Archipelago: A Theory of Diversity and Freedom* (Oxford University Press, 2003), among other works.

Stephen Macedo is Professor of Politics and Director of the University Center for Human Values at Princeton University, where he also founded the Princeton Program in Law and Public Affairs. His many writings include *Diversity and Distrust: Civic Education in a Multicultural Democracy* (Harvard University Press, 2000) and *Liberal Virtues* (Oxford University Press, 1990) and the co-authored *Democracy at Risk: How Political Choices Undermine Citizen Participation, and What We Can Do About It* (Brookings, 2005).

Mae Ngai is Lung Family Professor of Asian American Studies and Professor of History at Columbia University. She is the author of *The Lucky Ones: One Family and the Extraordinary Invention of Chinese America* (Houghton Mifflin Harcourt, 2010) and *Impossible Subjects: Illegal Aliens and the Making of Modern America* (Princeton University Press, 2004).

Demetrios Papademetriou is the President and Co-Founder of the Migration Policy Institute and author of numerous works on migration, including *Immigration Policy in the Federal Republic of Germany: Negotiating Membership and Remaking the Nation* (with Douglas B. Klusmeyer, Berghahn Books, 2010) and *Gaining from Migration: Towards a New Mobility System*, (with four co-authors; Organization for Economic Cooperation and Development, 2007).

Christopher Rudolph is Associate Professor in the School of International Service at American University. He is the author of *National Security and Immigration* (Stanford University Press, 2006), as well as articles in the *American Political Science Review, International Organization, Security Studies*, and other journals.

Kamal Sadiq is Associate Professor of Political Science at the University of California, Irvine. His writings include *Paper Citizens* (Oxford University

Press, 2009), "What's Morality Got to Do with It? Benevolent Hegemony in the International System of South Asia," *Comparative Studies of South Asia, Africa and the Middle East* 29:306–32 (2009), and "When States Prefer Non-Citizens over Citizens: Conflict over Illegal Migration into Malaysia," *International Studies Quarterly 49*: 101–22 (2005), among other works.

Saskia Sassen is the Robert S. Lynd Professor of Sociology at Columbia University. She is the author of *Territory, Authority, Rights* (Princeton University Press, 2006), and *A Sociology of Globalization* (Norton, 2007), among numerous other works.

Rogers M. Smith is the Christopher H. Browne Distinguished Professor of Political Science at the University of Pennsylvania and Chair of the Penn Program on Democracy, Citizenship, and Constitutionalism. He is the author of *Stories of Peoplehood: The Politics and Morals of Political Membership* (Cambridge University Press, 2003) and *Civic Ideals: Conflicting Visions of Citizenship in U.S. History* (Yale University Press, 1997), among other works.

Sarah Song is Professor of Law and Associate Professor of Political Science at the University of California, Berkeley. She is the author of *Justice, Gender, and the Politics of Multiculturalism* (Cambridge University Press, 2007) and "Democracy and Noncitizen Voting Rights," *Citizenship Studies* 13: 607–20 (2009), among other works.

Karolina Szmagalska-Follis is Lecturer in the Department of Anthropology, National University of Ireland, Maynooth. Her articles include "Are Europe's New Boundaries Like the Iron Curtain? 1989, Borders and Freedom of Movement in Poland and Ukraine," *International Journal of Culture, Politics and Society* 22: 385–400 (2009) and "Repossession: Notes on Restoration and Redemption in Ukrainian-Polish Borderlands," *Cultural Anthropology* 23: 329–360 (2008).

Leti Volpp is Professor of Law at Boalt Hall, University of California, Berkeley. Her recent publications include *Legal Borderlands* (co-edited with Mary Dudziak) (Johns Hopkins University Press, 2006); "The Culture of Citizenship," *Theoretical Inquiries in Law* 8: 571–602 (2007), and "Disappearing

Acts: On Gendered Violence, Pathological Cultures and Civil Society,"
PMLA 121: 1631–1637 (2006).

Antonio Yúnez-Naude is Director of the Centro de Estudios Económicos at
El Colegio de México. His many publications include *El Agua en Mexico*
(with Hilda R. Guerrero Garcia Rojas and Josué Medellin-Azuara; El Trim-
estre Economico, 2008) and *Education, Migration, and Productivity* (with J.
Edward Taylor; Organization for Economic Cooperation and Development,
1999).

Index